The New Food Garden

Growing beyond the vegetable garden

Frank Tozer

Green Man Publishing
Santa Cruz

ISBN: 978 -0- 9773489 - 4 - 7

Library of Congress Control Number: 2010914989

Green Man Publishing
Santa Cruz
P.O. Box 1546
Felton
CA 95018

Visit us online @ Greenmanpublishing.com

Printed in the USA

The New Food Garden

Contents

Introduction

Throughout most of American history the vegetable garden was an integral part of most rural American homes. It reduced living costs, improved nutrition and provided security it times of uncertainty. It was only after the second world war that increasing affluence caused gardeners to turn away from these productive roots and concern themselves more with making places look attractive. We are now at the point where the pendulum is starting to swing back towards productivity once again. With the evolving economic crisis and growing concern about the environment, it is now becoming more apparent that gardening isn't just an interesting hobby, it can make a real difference to your quality of life.

The most obvious way that gardening can improve your life is as a source of healthy and delicious food. It can also help us to reduce our impact on the earth, as we use less energy and water to grow food, and it enables us to recycle a lot of our wastes. On a more subtle level it can help to soothe frazzled 21st century minds by reconnecting us with nature.

The purpose of this book is to bring food growing into your garden, not only in the vegetable garden, but everywhere else too. I believe growing food should be an integral component of the complete home and a part of everyday life. If you eat food it makes sense that you should know something about producing it. This is not just a book about home food production however, it is also creating a home garden that is efficient, beautiful and produces an abundance of food with a minimum of work and resources.

The main source of inspiration for this book comes from the home gardens of peasants around the world. People who own a small piece of land and use it to produce most of their own food. People in places as diverse as India, Guatemala, Tanzania and Nepal have created quite similar gardens, based on the same principles. These gardens consist of several layers of productive plants, trees, shrubs, perennials and annuals, and are an important source of nutrition, as well as herbs (culinary and medicinal), fuel, craft materials, animal feed, fuel, building materials and more. The sale of some of surplus items often provides a small income. These home gardens are usually maintained by one family for their own use and help to keep the family together. They give elderly people an important purpose close to home and help to educate the young in the art of living from the earth. From a global viewpoint these gardens are important as storehouses of genetic diversity, as they often contain heirloom varieties of crops, as well as more unusual food plants.

Generally there is little formal design in these gardens. Local knowledge and custom determines the most convenient placement of each component. Plants are primarily arranged to maximize productivity in a small area and tend to grow in a jumble of flowers, vines, herbs, fruiting shrubs and vegetables. The vigorous and easily grown plants commonly form their own loose plant communities that are self-sustaining to some degree. Any useful or attractive plant that will grow easily will be planted and given a chance to establish itself.

We no longer have these kinds of home gardens in industrialized countries, but the original European cottage gardens were similar in many ways. These were found around the houses of better off working people (mostly self-employed artisans such as weavers, who owned a small patch of land and worked from home). These gardens were the source of much of their food, medicines, strewing herbs, smoking materials, tea, wine, dyes and more (as well as extra income).

These gardens weren't just productive, they were also very much lived in. Clothes dried on the washing line, children played, chickens foraged, people ate, sat and talked outside. The toilet was in the garden and the 'night soil' was eventually used as fertilizer. Chamber pots of urine were emptied there. Any household wastes were all disposed of there.

Compare these gardens with what we create in developed countries today. The average civilized gardens is little more than a decorative setting for the house, its main purpose being to maintain the value of the property (or at least not draw the ire of neighbors). The resulting gardens are homogenized, unimaginative and unproductive, filled with plants whose main purpose is looking good (like popular culture celebrities).

This situation might be tolerable if these gardens were energy efficient and worked well, but they don't. With their jumble of exotic species they deprive native wildlife of food and replace natural ecosystems. They also require a lot of labor and resources to keep them looking "good". Americans use 800 million gallons of gas and 67 million pounds of pesticides annually just to grow lawns. Devoid of any real purpose or ecological integrity such gardens are above all an eloquent statement about our alienation from nature.

Fortunately all of this is about to change, we are starting to rediscover the garden as a place that helps us to live better. A place we enjoy being in, that provides us with delicious food, beauty, comfort and soothing sanctuary. A garden that will also help us to reduce or recycle a lot of our waste (and maybe even teach us that we are a part of nature too). Since I embarked upon writing this book many people have told me they have been thinking along similar lines, so it is already happening.

I don't pretend to be suggesting a new way of gardening, I'm just proposing we take the best practices from around the world and combine them to reinvent a very old kind of garden. As a culture we have lost the folk wisdom acquired over generations of living in one place, but we do have access to more resources than any people in history have ever had. With a click of the mouse we can tap into the vast amount of knowledge available online (although don't believe everything you read online - or anywhere else for that matter), and can communicate instantly with like-minded individuals anywhere in the world. We also have a much greater range of useful plant species and cultivars available to us, as well as all of the material resources of a consumer culture bursting at the seams with stuff.

There is a lot to learn in this kind of a garden and everyone is a pioneer, out on the cutting edge of human knowledge (without even leaving the comfort of your own home). We need the effort of people in every geographical area to investigate what works for them and communicate it with neighbors (and people in similar situations around the world).

If we are to create a productive garden that doesn't absorb all of our daylight hours, we must avoid the mistake of traditional gardening in attempting to impose human ideas on to nature. We need to learn from nature and start gardening more intelligently, so we can direct her awesome powers of abundance. If we just abide by her rules she will do a lot of the work for us. We can use food producing trees, shrubs, vines, perennials, annuals and fungi to create a unique type of garden that largely functions like an ecosystem.

Gardening with nature doesn't mean you have to be a biologist or ecologist. All we have to do is provide the right plants and nudge nature in the direction we think she should go. Like a CEO of a large corporation we don't need to concern ourselves with the mechanics of how everything works. We can let others (nature in this case) do all the work, while we take the credit and reap all of the benefit. If you try and micro-manage everything down to the number of earthworms you are going to run into trouble.

The new food garden isn't so much a place, as a process, a symbiotic relationship between humans and nature. The gardener, the land, the plants and the rest of the natural world working together to create a place that is more diverse and productive than it would naturally be. My ultimate aim is to create a productive garden that looks as if it evolved without human intervention.

Benefits of the new food garden

Many people are discovering that cooking and eating fine food is one of the greatest pleasures in life and the best way to get the best ingredients available anywhere is to grow them yourself. You can quite literally eat like a queen while spending very little money. Nothing will ever taste as good as the food you grow yourself, because no commercial grower puts as much love into it as you do. Spring Strawberries, summer Nectarines, winter Broccoli and carrots are astonishingly good, as if they have been blessed by some magical taste fairy (this is the first time I have ever used the word fairy in my writing).

Growing your own food is a fascinating learning process, and one of the more surprising things you will learn is that it is more of a pleasure than a chore. There is beauty and joy in raising a Mulberry tree from a cutting or an Artichoke from a seed. Carrying a full basket into the kitchen and making a whole meal from it is wonderfully satisfying. Growing food connects you to the earth quite literally, in that your own body eventually comes to be made up of elements that came from a few square yards of your garden soil (if this doesn't alter your outlook nothing will).

Food gardening promotes better health through superior nutrition. Not only can you get fresh produce, you can also grow uniquely nutritious foods and herbs, enabling you to create your own superior food supplements, green drinks, raw foods and juices. This type of garden can return our diet to the diversity of our hunter gatherer ancestors.

Gardening is a powerful natural antidote to the artificial, everyday world. Gardeners often come home from work after a long day and go out into the garden and do some more work. They get up early in the morning so there is time for a stroll around the garden and spend their precious free time on weekends on their knees, sweating and getting dirty. The garden starkly illustrates how industrialism has degraded human life by strictly separating it into work and leisure (production and consumption). Gardening exists outside these boundaries by being work and play at the same time. This is an alien concept to modern ears, in fact I can't even think of a word for it in the English language.

Researchers in the Netherlands discovered that the incidence of many physical diseases and mental problems are reduced when people simply live near to natural areas. It seems that human bodies are programmed to live near plants and that our health is partly dependent on doing so. Imagine how much more profound this effect is when you live in a beautiful garden.

The garden is a place where we interact with the natural world on a intimate physical level. It is where the forces of nature and human energy combine to create a place of beauty and abundance. Creating a garden is a journey, the creation, maintenance, enhancement and perfection of which will take you the rest of your life. That is what is meant by the saying "the garden cultivates the gardener".

Environmental problems and gardening

No conscious person living today can totally ignore our looming environmental problems. It's becoming ever more obvious that endlessly accelerating economic expansion (coupled with a growing population) on a finite planet will eventually run into some mathematical problems, and even before that into some quality of life issues.

We can try to ignore reality by choosing not believe it, but that won't make it any less real and ultimately our children will pay the price. Many of our looming problems (income disparity, injustice, water depletion, war, pollution, even global warming) actually have fairly simple solutions, if only we would deal with them in a meaningful way. We have been brainwashed into believing that our well being is directly connected to how much fossil fuel we burn, and that using less can only mean deprivation and misery. Anyone who spends an hour or two each day sitting in traffic knows this is not quite true. The truth is that curtailing our obsessive compulsive over-consumption could actually improve our quality of life by giving us more time to enjoy life.

One of the reasons we choose to ignore environmental problems is that with each succeeding generation we are becoming more and more estranged from the earth that sustains us. Our technology has given us the illusion that we are somehow separate from the planet we live on. This distance enables us to ignore habitat loss, species extinction, logging ancient forests, mountaintop removal, oil spills, toxic waste dumps, air pollution and global warming as if they don't really affect us (for as long as the bar is still serving, we can pretend the ship isn't sinking). If our civilization is to survive as a place you would want your children to live in, we have to advance past the industrial age and reconnect with the earth, as a society and as individuals.

One of the simplest ways we can reconnect with the earth is to grow some of our own food. This can also help us to recover a measure of independence from the corporate industrial world that has come to dominate our lives. We need to re-learn how to physically sustain ourselves and regain some measure of independence from a system we have no control over.

The New Food Garden

Growing food can help us to eat and live better, reduce our impact on the earth and bring us back under the benign influence of Mother Nature. If we could produce 25% of the things we need from our own gardens we could dramatically reduce our impact on the earth. Human beings have lived comfortably without consuming the earth in the past (that's what it really means when they call us consumers) and we can learn how to do it again. If the human race wishes to get to the end of the 21st century we may all need to become gardeners.

Using this book

Countless books have been written about creating gardens, mostly written by affluent people who make a living either designing gardens or writing books. I wanted to write a down-to-earth practical book, based on my experiences and ideas obtained while creating my own garden. This has been done while (mostly) holding a full time job and raising 3 children from the wrong side of the poverty line. Often I was short of time as well as money, as weekends are often taken up by kids soccer games and other family activities. These things have given me an acute awareness of the value of economy in the real world (and how it is closely related to being green.

I find most design books to be of limited use, and then mostly as source of ideas and inspiration. I created this book as a collection of idea to inspire you to get growing. I suggest you start by reading it through thoroughly and take notes of anything that particularly interests you, so you will remember them when you get to work on your own garden.

You can use this book in different ways to suit your needs. You might simply refer to the topics that interest you and work on them as time and money allows. You might break your garden up into smaller, more manageable pieces and work on them one at a time, until you have changed your whole garden. You might even attempt to transform your entire garden in one massive blitz (good luck with that).

The strategies you adopt in your garden will depend upon where you live; the limitations of site, climate, pests and more. Every garden has its strengths and weaknesses and it is important to devise the right techniques for each situation, whether sheet mulching, growing field corn or forest gardening.

To help expand the range of possibilities I have suggested some options you might not have thought about. I have included fairly detailed information on most topics, but there is a limit as to what will fit in one book. If you are embarking upon an entirely new project, such as building a pond or growing mushrooms, you should check out some of the more specialized websites and books.

Ultimately the garden is your project of course and you have to do most of the work. Don't too get carried away with the technical stuff; what happens in the garden is the important part. The most important thing is to just get out there and do something. Often people don't make real improvements to their lives because they don't know where to start, or it doesn't seem like enough. Yet a journey of a thousand miles begins with one footstep, so just get started and the direction to go will often become obvious.

If I were starting a new garden I would begin by creating and planting some growing beds outside the kitchen door (assuming it has enough sun of course). I would add other elements and extend out into the garden as time, enthusiasm and money allowed. I would also think ahead to my next moves. Fruit trees and shrubs take a while to grow, so I would start planting them around the garden.

Gardens get better and better for as long as you care for them. You identify problems and find solutions, you try new things, new plants and new ways of growing. You build on your successes, refine existing parts, expand into new areas and add new plants and other components.

I have given you a lot of technical information in this book, but the last thing I want to do is make it sound like a job. I approach gardening not as a designer, landscaper, farmer, artist or environmentalist, but simply as someone who loves plants and tending the earth. I look upon my garden as a living entity and my task is to understand it, work with it and appreciate it. In return it feeds me, teaches me and helps to keep me healthy and sane, Gardening should be something you do because it makes you happy. Ultimately you make the garden a part of yourself, just as you become a part of the garden.

Mapping and evaluation

Getting to know the land

Before you do any serious garden planning you need to learn about the site; its topography, microclimate, native vegetation, wildlife and more, The more you understand the place, the easier it will be to make the plants and other components fit and the better the garden will work as a whole. Each piece of land is unique and you will want to take advantage of its assets (slopes, aspect, trees, water) and minimise any problems (slopes, aspect, trees, water).

To get a feel for a place you need to spend time there, walking, relaxing and working Take a chair and sit in different places just watching (nothing else). Sit in the garden at different times of the day, at different times of the year and in different weather. Some people advise that you don't do any major work until you have studied the land for a whole year, through the full solar cycle. In this way you get to understand the land more fully and will be able to create a garden that suits the spirit of the land.

Mapping the site

If you are going to design your garden on paper, you need an accurate plan of the site. This isn't a problem because drawing up a plan is one of the best ways to get to know the land. It makes you really look closely at every part of the site.

The traditional way of drawing an accurate site plan is by going out with a measuring tape, paper and pencil. Use graph paper on a large clipboard and take measurements with a 100 or 200 feet tape measure (attach an old screwdriver to the end so you can fix it in the ground). If you have the original plot plan this will be a good starting point, as it will give you the size and shape of the lot and the location of the house. It will also help you to locate the original survey markers on the ground. Mark the location of the boundaries and survey markers on your site plan.

Normally you begin your survey by creating and measuring some base lines, which are straight lines that extend out from the walls of the house. Sight down the wall so that you align both corners, or sight down the wall and have someone move a string line and stake until it is directly in line with the wall. Run these base line strings out to the edge of the property. You can then take measurements off of these lines to get accurate positions for other objects.

You can also use triangulation to determine the location of objects. Just measure the distances from two known points to the object. Then set a drawing compass to those distances on the plan and draw arcs from the known points. Where they intersect will be the location of the object.

Draw every important object in the garden in its exact position. Start with the house location and lot lines and then fill in the smaller details (outbuildings, walls, large plants, paths, fences, drains, rock outcrops, paved areas, driveways even the location of windows, overhanging eaves, doors, downspouts and more). The location of these objects needs to be fairly accurate, otherwise when you start transferring your measurements to the base plan they won't fit properly. Check them by adding up all of the individual measurements against your measurement for the entire garden.

If the garden has a slight slope, note this on the plan. If there is a significant slope you may want to measure it. The easiest way to do this is to borrow a laser or surveyors level, though you could also use a water level, or even a long (16 or 20 feet) board and a carpenters level. Note the slope on the map as deviations from a datum point of 100 (this is usually the house level) and further points are either more or less than 100.

Drawing up a site plan is best undertaken in winter when there is less undergrowth and it is easier to get around (and plants are less easily damaged). This also gives you something garden related to do, while the plants are resting.

Google earth, a new way to map

Drawing up an accurate plan of the garden, with everything in its correct place can take a lot of time. However there is now a significant new tool to help in the form of the internet site Googleearth.com.

Google earth contains close-up satellite images of the earth and makes the task of drawing out a plan a lot simpler. If you live in the right area (many rural areas don't have very detailed coverage) you can get a usable (and free) image of your garden site straight off of the internet. The best photographs are very detailed (any more detailed and sunbathers better watch what they wear), and show the location of every large object in the garden (that is visible from the air, not hidden beneath large trees or other objects). You can simply trace the garden plot onto a piece of paper and enlarge it to a suitable size. All you then have to do is determine the exact scale of the photograph by measuring the actual distance between two visible points (such as the roof of your house).

If you live in a rural area that is only covered by the less detailed photographs (as I do) it can still be helpful in showing you the shape of your land and the relative location of the major components. You will just have to take more measurements in the garden to fill in the details.

A potential disadvantage of using Google earth is if it replaces time in the garden with time indoors on a computer. However it saves so much time it is a very useful tool. Just make sure you spend that time saved doing something else in the garden, such as observing and making notes.

Drawing up the base plan

Using all of your field measurements (or Google earth picture) draw up the plan of the garden on grid paper (10 blocks to the inch). Use fairly large sheets of paper (24 x 36, 17 x 22 or 11 x 17) so you can draw the plan in the middle, leaving wide margins for writing notes. In a big garden you might have to use several sheets of paper. In a very large garden you may want a separate large-scale plan (1"= 8 feet) for the areas around the house and a smaller scale plan (1"=20 ft.) for the outer zones, where less detail is required.

The base plan should accurately show the location of every significant object in your land. You use this as a base (hence it's called the base plan) and lay tracing paper over it to do your planning. Don't clutter the plan with non-essential details though, write notes in the margins instead. When designing it's good to have a fairly clean sheet so you aren't influenced by things that aren't important. You will have spent quite a lot of time preparing your map, so its a good idea to make several copies.

Mark the direction of true north (not magnetic north) on the map, so you can mark the path of the sun. If you don't have a compass it's due south at 12:00 in winter, or at 1.00 PM in summer (adjusting for daylight saving). To locate it precisely in the garden, hammer a stake into the ground and wait until noon on a sunny day (or 1.00 during daylight saving). At the stroke of noon (more or less) you hammer another stake into the ground, in the shadow cast by the first. A line through the two stakes will be aligned exactly north and south.

An alternative to drawing out a base plan is to take digital photographs from the highest point you can and simply draw on those for the plan. This isn't as good, but it's a lot easier.

Site analysis

In the process of drawing up the base plan you identified all of the prominent features of the site. You now need to study each of these in turn and identify its advantages and drawbacks. Begin your site analysis by recording your first impressions of the land as you walk around, starting with its obvious strengths and weaknesses. Write down all of your observations in a notebook (or on the corresponding area of the survey plan) as they occur to you.

You can practice your site analysis any time you visit other gardens. Look for their strongest and weakest points and their the most favorable microclimates. Think about where you would put a vegetable garden, where you might plant fruit trees, the best areas for relaxation, which areas would need screening for privacy?

Boundaries

It is important to know the correct location of your lot lines, so refer to your survey map and stakes and mark their location on the ground. You don't want to cut down your neighbors trees or build that greenhouse straddling the property line.

Make a note on the condition of existing fences, walls or hedges. Are they are in the right place and in good shape? Are they effective at providing privacy and security? Will they keep the dog in?

Soil

The soil affects the garden in many ways and you need to know what type of soil you have. Your local county extension agent has detailed soil survey maps that can help in this (these are usually available at your local library too). If you can't find these, it isn't too difficult to work out the type of soil by its feel (see below).

A chemical soil test isn't absolutely necessary, but it can help you learn more about your soil and will point out any serious deficiencies.

Soil doesn't usually vary much in a small garden (unless it is from human disturbance), but you should watch out for any unusual soil conditions (rich, poor, sandy, clay, rocky, acid, wet, dry) and mark them on the plan. New house lots often have only subsoil or fill, covered with a few inches of imported topsoil.

Determining soil type

You can get a good idea of the type of soil you have by performing this simple procedure.

Moisten a small handful of soil (traditionally spit is used for this) and knead it between your fingers to break down its structure. Roll the moistened soil into a ball and then squeeze it into a ribbon between thumb and forefingers. The longer the ribbon the more clay it contains.

Sand: The large individual grains are visible in a sandy soil. It has a gritty feel and makes a grating sound when squeezed between the fingers. These soils don't hold together in a ball very well and don't stick to the fingers.

Sandy loam: This resembles a sandy soil in that it feels gritty and the particles are visible. However it is more cohesive and can be rolled into a ball or shaped into a cube. If you try and roll the ball into a cylinder it will break apart. It doesn't stick to the fingers.

Silt: These particles have a smooth, silky, feel and you can't distinguish the individual particles. Silt soil can be rolled into a cylinder quite easily and sticks to the fingers.

Silt clay: These soils have a silky feel, but are also somewhat sticky. They can be rolled into a thin thread and then shaped into a rather delicate ring. They stick to the fingers and make them dirty.

Clay: Wet clay is sticky and almost as malleable as putty when moist. A thread of clay soil can be shaped into a fairly strong ring. It doesn't stick to the fingers.

One of our goals is to grow plants in their own preferred habitat. Therefore it follows that to increase diversity in the garden we should preserve any variation in soil type. Don't try and turn the whole garden into moisture retentive, well drained, neutral, fertile soil. Once you are aware of variations in soil type, you can find suitable plants to put there. Special niches might include highly acid soil, hot dry soil, wet soil and high nitrogen soil. The existing vegetation can be a big help in deciding what to plant (see below).

Soil isn't the first consideration when choosing the site for a vegetable garden because your gardening activities will drastically change the soil over time. It's nice to start with a deep fertile soil, but it is less important than sunlight and aspect. The plants that really benefit from fertile soil are the fruit trees. Give them the best soil in the garden and they will grow faster and be more productive.

Areas of particularly poor soil might be used for non growing areas, such as driveways, patios, building sites, ponds and more.

The type of soil might also be significant in other ways. For example a patch of pure clay soil might be used for making bricks or tiles or even sealing ponds.

Weed indicators

Existing weeds can tell you something about the soil they are growing in.

Acid soil: Bracken Fern, Buttercup, Coltsfoot, Corn Spurrey, Dock, Horsetail, Plantain, Sheeps Sorrel, Wild Strawberry.

Alkaline soil: Campion, Ox Eye Daisy, Poppy, Salad Burnet, Tansy, Yarrow.

Rich garden soil (high nitrogen): Look for vigorous growth of garden weeds such as Amaranth, Chickweed, Chicory, Cleavers, Ground Elder, Groundsel, Lambs Quarters, Orach, Sow Thistle, Speedwell, Stinging Nettles and Yarrow.

Wet soil: Cattails, Green Algae, Horsetail (especially poor soil), Loosestrife, Mints, Mosses, Sedges, Wiregrass.

Dry soil: Broad Leaf Dock, Dandelion, Groundsel, Fireweed, Shepherds Purse.

Poor soil: Clover, Mullein, Wild Carrot, Wild Radish, Fireweed.

Compacted soil: Pineapple Weed, Great Plantain, Silverweed.

Soil pH

Most crop plants prefer to grow in a neutral or slightly acid (pH 6.0 to 7.0) soil, because this is the range where the most nutrients are most available. You can determine the pH with a simple soil test kit. If done carefully it will be accurate enough for most purposes (most errors come from an inability to compare the colors accurately). If a test indicates that your soil is very acidic, or alkaline, you will have to correct it in the places you want to grow most conventional crops.

Existing vegetation

Plant growth is one of the most reliable indicators of soil fertility. Are the plants deep-rooted, healthy and vigorous, or shallow rooted, stunted and quick to bolt? If a soil has an abundance of vigorous healthy weeds, it will probably grow good crops too.

Take note of the kinds of plants that already grow on the site: trees, shrubs, wild flowers (and any ornamentals if the site was once a garden). Are these an asset (are they beautiful or productive, do they prevent erosion, fix nitrogen or feed wildlife?) Or a liability (are they ugly, unstable, diseased, do they take too much water?) Are they native or introduced? How big are they likely to get and do you have enough room for them?

Generally if existing plants are healthy and not interfering with anything else you should keep them (especially if they are native). They are already established and growing without your input and help to make the garden look more mature. Of course you shouldn't let them get in the way of bigger plans though.

It is good to learn how to identify any wild plants you come across. Many are useful and might be incorporated into the garden rather than eliminated. There may even be rare plants that should not be disturbed.

You may find invasive or otherwise unwanted species (Scotch Broom, Japanese Rose, Kudzu, Blackberry, Periwinkle, Ivy) that will have to be dealt with (sooner is better than later). My garden has a huge swath of Poison Oak that probably covers a quarter of my property. I plan to remove at some point, but only when I run out of space elsewhere. You might consider saving a fast growing vigorous nitrogen fixing species such as Broom, for use as a source of biomass for mulch or compost. The frequent cutting would keep it under control.

Trees and shrubs

The most significant existing plants are the trees and large shrubs. Which species are on the site and are they an asset or a problem? Are they beautiful, do they shelter the garden, do any produce food or other useful materials? Are they species that stand firm in wind, or that frequently blow over? Are any growing too close to the house or other buildings? Are there dead trees or dead branches that could fall and damage the house, fences or something else? Do they have invasive roots that penetrate water pipes or heave paving surfaces? Are they to the north of the garden where they help to shelter it, or to the south where they cast shade? Are they healthy or ailing in some way? (Signs of disease include flaking bark, bracket fungi, thin canopy, dead branches and cavities).

Trees affect all of the plants growing around them. The most obvious way they do this is by casting shade, which varies according to species (Chestnuts cast deep shade, Black Locust light shade). They also develop a spreading root network that can take most of the available nutrients and water from the soil. It's commonly said that tree roots only come out as far as the drip line. This may be true of a tree growing in rich moist soil, but it isn't always the case. If a tree growing in poor dry soil detects a good source of water or nutrients in one direction it may send out roots several times further than the drip line.

Trees sometimes affect neighboring plants in beneficial ways. They temper the climate underneath them, which can protect nearby plants from frost. They may provide light shade and increase humidity which can be beneficial in hot climates.

Large trees shouldn't grow within 15 feet of buildings for several reasons. They drop leaf litter which clogs rain gutters and can become a fire hazard in dry weather. In high winds they may drop limbs on the house. In a drought some trees may take so much water out of a clay soil that it shrinks and causes foundations to crack.

Lawns

If you already have an existing conventional garden it probably includes extensive lawns. If the climate is suitable for growing grass (cool and moist) you may want to keep some of these until you find a better use for the space. If the climate is totally unsuited to lawns then you should remove them all (just stop watering and they will disappear).

Think of any turf you remove as a resource. In a dry climate use it to make turf-loam. In a wet climate you might use some of it to create a turf wall or living roof (or even a sod hut).

Existing hardscape

Are existing elements an asset or a problem? Are they still useful or should they be removed, reused, renovated or rebuilt? Buildings affect the garden around them with rain shadows, shade and more.

Privacy

How private or public is the garden? Obviously this is a more important question in the city than it would be in the country. Are there places you will need to screen from public view, or neighbor's decks and windows?

Growing Sites

Identify the best sites for growing annual vegetable crops. The most important criteria is that they get as much sunlight as possible, though of course the soil is also important. They should also be away from low-lying frost pockets (some way up a slight slope is good). In cool climates a slight southern or western slope is usually considered the best location because it is warmer, though it may need shelter from cool westerly winds.

You should also identify any unusual conditions that may require specific types of plants (standing water, hot and dry, frost pockets).

Views

Does your garden have any views worth emphasizing? If there are then note the best viewing points (mark with arrows), as the garden will tend to look outward towards them. Is anything interfering with these views? If you opened up existing vegetation or altered fences would you get an attractive view.

Are there any unattractive areas you will want to screen from view (if you can't eliminate them from your neighborhood?). A simple way to identify eyesores is to take a digital photograph; anything that spoils the picture is a problem. Think about how you might hide or disguise these things.

Water

What sources of water does the property have (well, creek, springs, pond, lake, rainfall, city?) How much water is available on site? Too little or too much can be a problem, or an opportunity to try something different. In the ideal garden you would have an unlimited supply of free, year round, gravity fed water.

Are any water sources likely to present a problem with flooding, waterlogged soil or mosquito's? Is there any possibility of it containing harmful salts or biological or chemical pollutants?

The right topography might make it possible to create a dam or pond. This would not only be an important garden feature, but also a possible source of irrigation water and fire protection. Identify potential dam/pond sites by slope, soil type and water flow (also find out whether they would be legally allowed). In suitable situations you might even look into possible power generation from water.

Topography

This affects the garden in several ways and can make working in the garden easier or harder. Slopes are more difficult to work with than flat areas, but give you the opportunity of using terraces to get interesting changes in level. Slope also makes it possible to use gravity for irrigation and water features (if the water is stored high up) They also shed cold air and so can have less frost.

Flat

Flat land is easy to work on and design for, though it can be monotonous and you may have to work to give it some height. Beware of flat areas at the base of hills, as cold air may drain down and collect there at night, creating frost pockets.

Gentle slope

A slight south-facing slope is an excellent garden site. It gets some additional solar gain but isn't steep enough to interfere with walking or working.

Moderate slope

As a slope gets steeper it becomes harder to walk and work on unless terraced. Water tends to run off without soaking in, so the beds must be sited carefully to avoid erosion in heavy rain.

These slopes are not steep enough to present potential soil problems, so they can be good places to put buildings. This leaves the flatter land for growing crops. They also give you a view, are above potential flooding and lend themselves to earth sheltering.

Steep slope

As a rule these are not good garden sites because they require a lot of extra work to make them attractive and productive. However if that is all you have and you are willing to work at it, they can sometimes be terraced to make exceptionally attractive gardens.

Slopes of more than 1:3 are potentially unstable and must be treated carefully to avoid erosion. The best idea is to plant trees and shrubs, as their deep permanent roots will bind and hold the soil in place. Even then the soil may tends to want to creep slowly downhill.

Steep slopes are also unstable visually and need tall components and flat areas to balance them out.

Drainage, rainfall and runoff

How rain enters the soil and how long it stays there is determined by topography and soil type. Rain falling on a steep slope may run off before it has a chance to soak in, potentially causing erosion. Rain will percolate into a sandy soil quickly and may drain away equally rapidly. Water enters a heavy clay soil slowly and may puddle on the surface in heavy rain. However once in the soil is will stay there for a long time.

To get an idea of how rainfall behaves in your garden you should go outside during heavy rain and watch how it moves. Note where the highest and lowest points of your land are and whether water drains on to your land from elsewhere. Does all of the water soak into the soil or does some run off elsewhere. Also watch what happens to rainfall that lands on impervious surfaces. Does it run off down storm drains, or is there somewhere it can soak into the soil and recharge the groundwater?

If you can see water running over the surface, rather than soaking in, you have a problem. Water picks up speed as slope increases and starts to carry soil particles with it. Look for places where water is piling up soil or surface duff in small ridges alternating with small areas of bare soil.

Serious erosion often occurs when water from a large area drains down through a narrow gap. The moving water finds the fastest way to drain away downhill and in the process it erodes the soil and kills any plants that grow there. The resulting loss of plant cover then increases the erosion and small gullies form on the slopes. This causes the water to move even faster, creating more erosion. Where the ground flattens out below the slope the water slows down and drops any soil it is carrying, causing soil to build up.

Dealing with erosion is simple in theory, you just have to slow the water down, so it has time to soak in to the soil.

You can get an idea of the soils ability to absorb water by going out into the garden towards the end of a heavy rain (maybe take a digital photograph). Dig a hole and see if you can hit water. If you do then go out again the next day and note how much water remains.

Wet soil

The growth of moisture loving plants indicate areas that are wet year round. Wet areas can occur for a variety of reasons. Sometimes water drains onto the land from elsewhere and accumulates. It may also occur because the water table is very high (dig drains to channel the water away downhill and use raised beds). It may also be caused by poor drainage due to an impervious layer of compacted soil, or simply because the soil is a heavy clay that doesn't drain well (add organic matter and cultivate deeply).

Underground water can have a big effect on plant growth. In arid areas it is beneficial where water loving plants may be found tapping into underground sources. In wet areas it can be a problem if the soil becomes waterlogged. This means less oxygen in the soil, which reduces biological activity and plant growth.

Too much water in the soil will prevent you from growing most conventional crops, but this doesn't mean you can't grow anything. Instead you have to turn to specially adapted plants such as Watercress, Willow or Cattail. Don't look upon wet areas as a problem, they can be an opportunity to create another kind of habitat (pond, wetland, bog) which increases diversity. Wetlands can be extremely productive, so take advantage of them if they exist, or if they can be created easily.

Dry soil

Shallow soil, sandy soil, the tops of slopes and south and west facing slopes tend to dry out fairly quickly. If rainfall is limited these areas should be planted with drought tolerant plants that are adapted to your climate. In extreme situations these may even be xerophytes such as Cacti, Agaves or Yuccas.

Fire

In areas with hot dry summers you should be aware of the potential for wildfires, a natural, if rare occurrence that is potentially devastating for your garden. Steep slopes, strong winds, hot sunny weather, long periods without rain and tinder dry vegetation all spell potential trouble. Heat rises, so fire travels uphill much more rapidly than it moves downhill. This means that the tops of steep slopes are the most at-risk areas (especially when downwind of prevailing winds). You can't eliminate fire risk entirely, but you can reduce it considerably with a few simple steps. See Fire for more on this.

Flooding

Low-lying areas near rivers are prone to flooding in very wet weather (that's why they are called flood plains). If you live in a low-lying area you should find out about past floods, their frequency and how high the water came. If a major flood occurs all you can do is make sure that you, and your most valuable possessions are out of the way (and be prepared for some major garden damage).

History of the site

In Feng Shui they also consider the previous occupants of the land, what they did and whether this had negative or positive effects. As with much of Feng Shui this might seem a little out there, but it has a very practical aspect. Was the land a sacred burial site or a place for fixing cars? (At one time it was common to dispose of used motor oil by dumping it in a hole in the ground). Did they have a corral for horses that compacted the soil to a hardpan? Did they secretly manufacture methamphetamine and dump the waste?

Pollution

It is important to be aware of any possible sources of contamination. A leaking septic tank is usually fairly obvious (especially in wet weather) by its characteristic sulphurous smell. Keep your food garden areas far from well-traveled roads (ideally at least 100 feet away), as they are the sources of various pollutants. The lead may be gone from the gasoline, but all that we burned for years went somewhere. (Where did it go?) The site of old buildings are also suspect, as paint was once commonly made with lead and soils around such sites commonly contain high levels of this toxic metal. Ground water pollutants in well water are another possible hazard. Commercial soil amendments such as composted sewage sludge may contain high levels of heavy metals.

Though there is only a small possibility of these kinds of problems in most places, you should be aware of them, because once such substances are in your soil they are hard (or impossible) to get rid of.

If your garden is happily free of pollution you should do your best to keep it that way. Avoid treated wood, toxic paints, pesticides, chemical fertilizer, petroleum based chain saw oil (use vegetable based oil), household and other chemicals and leaky old cars.

Utility lines

Note the location of any electric, water, gas or sewer lines, both above ground and below ground. Also mark the location of the septic tank and leach field. With luck most of these should be marked on your house plan. If they aren't marked anywhere you may be able to work it out by deduction. If the pipe from the propane tank goes into the ground here and comes out of the ground by the house there, then the line probably goes fairly directly between the two. You can get a locator service to detect the lines, but that costs money.

Other problems Make note of any other problems, old cars, utility poles, logging debris, unpleasant smells and more. Less obvious problems might include sources of unwanted noise (roads, electric sub stations, neighbors), proximity to street, lights (from streets, cars or neighbors), or high voltage power lines.

Neighbors may be good or bad (or worse). If good you may want a gate to their property, if really bad you may want a fence and a hedge and trees.

Sometimes there are covenants and restrictions on your title that limit certain activities. These might prohibit drying your laundry outside, allowing your lawn to get overgrown or putting up a fence around the front garden.

Once you have identified potential problems you can start thinking of ways to solve them. These might be big problems (lack of summer water, too much sun, too little sun) or small problems (lack of privacy, ugly view).

Wildlife

What kind of animals live on the site and how might they might affect the garden? From a gardening viewpoint some animals are a problem (deer, rabbits, raccoons, gophers, groundhogs, quail) and some are an asset (earthworms, bees, lizards, toads, bats, snakes, insectivorous birds).

You may want to encourage beneficial wildlife by creating places for them to live (bird houses, bat boxes, piles of rocks for lizards, places for mason bees and more. You should at least refrain from doing anything that would adversely affect them.

Climate and microclimate

Climate

Macroclimate is the climate of a large geographical area and is determined by latitude, altitude, the water cycle, wind and proximity to large bodies of water and land masses. It is the most significant factor determining what kind of plants you can grow successfully and what kind of garden you can have. You can use various techniques to slightly alter the climate, but this is one of the main factors limiting what you can grow (unless you build a heated greenhouse or a bioshelter).

Every climate has its advantages and disadvantages. In my garden we have a long 220+ day frost-free growing season, but for much of that time there is no appreciable rainfall. We are limited in what we can grow by the amount of water we have available during that time. We also have mild winters, which can bring problems with lack of winter chill (some cold weather plants need a minimum amount of cold weather before they will happily flower). When I lived in Western Washington there was insufficient heat for my Tomatoes and Peppers. In my garden in Connecticut everything grew fantastically well in the warm humid summer months, but there were lots of insect pests and everything came to an abrupt standstill in winter.

Some climates are more predictable than others, but often the weather varies considerably from one year to the next. In my garden we have had winters with no significant frost at all and others with snow on the ground for several weeks. Rainfall has been as little as 30" or as much as 100". Every region also has its extreme weather hazards, drought, hurricane, tornado, wildfire and flooding.

Most gardeners are familiar with the USDA climate zone maps, based on annual minimum temperature. These are useful as a relative comparison as to what plants are likely to die in each area, though many other factors may affect this. They are limited in that they only tell you how cold it gets and not for how long, or how humid or dry or hot it gets. A garden in zone 8 in Washington state will have quite different plants from one in zone 8 in Georgia. Sunset magazine has produced some useful maps that take into account other factors that affect plant growth. Go to Sunset.com to find these.

Many factors affect climate on the local level. The tops of hills are commonly colder than lowlands in the daytime because of the elevation. At the same time they are sometimes warmer at night (and may have less frost) because cold air is heavier than warm air and sinks and accumulates in low spots. Cities tend to be warmer than the countryside around them because of the extensive areas of thermal mass (dark colored buildings, roads and other paved areas). The leeward side a mountain (the rain shadow) tends to be significantly drier and sunnier than the windward side. Forests affect the climate by transpiring huge amounts of water into the atmosphere (a single tree may release hundreds of gallons of water daily).

The seasons

The seasons are caused by the tilting of the earth making the days shorter or longer. The earth receives solar heat in the daytime and loses solar heat at night, so the proportion of day and night determines whether the earth gains heat or loses heat day by day. During the long days and short nights of summer the land gradually gets warmer. In the winter the long nights and short days mean the land gradually gets cooler. This is why the warmest days are after the summer solstice and the coldest ones are after the winter solstice.

The tilting of the earth also causes the winter sun to strike the earth at a more oblique angle, so its energy is spread over a larger area. This means that winter sun is much weaker than in summer, when the sun strikes the earth at a more direct angle and the energy is concentrated on a smaller area (and I thought it was because we were further from the sun!) We see this effect every day as the suns angle changes in the sky. The sun is much weaker in the morning and evening than it is at midday.

When the day length drops below 10 hours a day plants grow very slowly, even if temperatures are warm enough for growth.

Learn about your climate

Try and learn as much as you can about the climate in your neighborhood, as it will help you in planning the garden. You can often get useful information from local weather websites (there is probably some weather buff in your area who posts their own weather data online). You might also contact your local fire station, airport, newspaper, TV station or cooperative extension service office. The more local the data, the better, as weather can differ considerably in a few miles I live only about 10 miles away from Santa Cruz, but I'm 2300 ft. higher up and a whole zone colder in climate. A rain gauge and maximum/minimum thermometer will allow you to keep your own records (record unusual weather in your garden journal).

Latitude

This is important because it determines day length; the further north you go, the longer the days in summer, and the shorter the days in winter. Day length is significant because it affects flowering, bulbing and fruiting.
Find out the length of the day on the summer and winter solstices (June 21st and December 21st). More sunlight means more growth and in the far north the very long days of summer can produce extraordinarily large vegetables. Conversely when the day length drops below 10 hours in winter there is very little plant growth, even if the weather is warm enough. You need to know when the day length drops below 10 hours in fall (usually in November) and when it goes above 10 hours in spring (usually in February)

Altitude

For every 1000 feet of elevation gain, the temperature drops by roughly 4° F. (this may be offset by other factors however).

Wind

Direction of prevailing winds
Direction of coldest winds
Maximum wind speeds and frequency

Temperature

This is important because plants grow better in warm weather and slow down when it gets cold. This happens because the speed of a chemical reaction increases with temperature, so photosynthesis is more efficient in warmer weather.
Hottest temperature of the summer.
Coldest temperature of the winter
Hottest months
Coldest months

Frost

Average date of last spring frost
Average date of first fall frost
The dates of these frosts can vary as much as 6 weeks from year to year.

Length of growing season - This is usually considered to be from the last killing frost of spring to the first killing frost of autumn. This isn't always very meaningful however. In some places the ground may be frozen for months and all plant growth comes to a halt. My garden gets occasional frosts and snow, but much of the time between these is so mild that many hardy crops never really stop growing.

Precipitation

Rain can be a mixed blessing. It is vital of course and in the scheme of things more rain is generally better. However it isn't always beneficial. Too much rainfall can cause waterlogging, erode the soil and leach out nutrients. Rainfall at the wrong time can contribute to a variety of plant diseases and pests.

Rainfall can vary enormously from year to year, one year may endless rain and flooding, while another year may bring sunny skies and drought.

Rain falls unevenly in the garden according to the topography and vegetation. Tall objects such as trees and buildings interfere with rainfall patterns, causing more to fall in some places and less in others. Trees with dense foliage shed rain mostly out at the drip line, whereas trees with light foliage drip evenly underneath, There will also be more rainfall on the windward side of the tree, as it is blown under the canopy. The leeward side may have a rain shadow extending out well beyond the drip line.

For planning irrigation, rainwater harvesting and erosion control it is helpful to know:
Maximum annual rainfall
Average annual rainfall
How much rain has fallen in 24 hours, a single storm?
The wettest and driest months
How much snow do you get, and in what months?
Where does it accumulate?

Microclimate

Microclimate is the climate on the ground in your particular garden and can be quite different from the macroclimate around about. Two gardens in the same area may have quite different growing conditions. In winter the bottom of a hill may remain shady and frozen, while only a few hundred yards away at the top it may be sunny and mild.

You may have noticed how the growing conditions in your garden vary in different areas. Often there will be a noticeable difference in temperatures in the space of only a few feet. Some places may be hard hit by frost while nearby spots may be completely untouched. Probably the best-known example of a useful beneficial microclimate is a south facing stone wall. This traps the sun and stores heat, while sheltering the area from cooling winds. This creates a microclimate that is considerably warmer than the surrounding area.

The value of a particular microclimate depends upon the climate and season. In a cool climates a south facing wall will be prized for being warm and sunny, whereas in a very hot climate it could be too hot and dry for most plants. Conversely a cool shady moist spot may be a problem area in a cold climate, but just what you need in hotter areas.

Identifying suitable microclimates and using them to best advantage is an important aspect of successful gardening (particularly in cooler climates). Mark any microclimates (hotter, drier, shadier, windier, colder) you identify on your plot plan, so you can use them to best advantage.

Microclimate isn't set in stone, it can often be altered to better suit your needs. In fact any time you add something to the garden you alter the microclimate around it. By careful placement of these elements you can make sure they have a beneficial effect, rather than a negative one.

Sunlight and shade

The amount of sun hitting the garden varies enormously from summer when the sun is high in the sky, to winter when it is at its lowest. You won't get a complete picture of the sun and shade potential of a site until you have lived there for a whole year.

Exactly how much sun or shade is desirable in the garden depends upon the climate and time of year. What would be a pleasant warm sunny spot in early spring, might be unbearably hot in midsummer. Alternatively what might be cold and gloomy in November might be cool and delightful in August. Note areas of bright sun and deep shade (these vary from summer to winter of course) and mark them on the map.

Sun

In temperate climates the main area of activity is to the south side of the house because that is the sunniest place. In such areas you need to be aware of anything to the south that might block the sun, especially when it is low in the sky in winter.

Though gardeners might prefer a mix of sun and shade, most crop plants need as much sun as they can get if they are to produce to their full potential. This means vegetable growing areas need a minimum of 6 hours of direct sun daily and preferably a lot more. The time of day your garden receives sun is also significant, as the sun is most intense from about 10.00 am to 3.00 PM. If your garden gets most of its sun earlier or later than this it will need more.

In mild climates winter sun is important because it enables you to grow crops right through the winter. This is much lower in the sky of course, so make sure it isn't obscured by anything you create. You might even have a separate area for winter vegetables. The greenhouse needs winter sun more than summer sun, as that is when it really gets used. In winter you need to remember that those places that are open and sunny during the day, are the places that are open and frosty on winter nights.

Shade

Shade isn't all the same, it varies according to what causes it. The shade cast by a building is different from that cast by a tree. Shade also moves with the sun of course, so even the north side of a house gets sun in the morning and evening. Shade can be an asset or a problem, depending upon your climate and the time of year.

Beneficial shade:

In very hot climates shade is an ally rather than an enemy. Without shade the garden will be unbearably hot for most of the day in summer. In such places many temperate zone plants actually grow better with light shade. It reduces water loss from evaporation and transpiration and cools plants enough that they can keep growing. Many desert plants can only become established under the protective shade of nurse trees and shrubs.

In hot climates your activity areas will vary according to where shade can be found. In such cases you may want to create shade over a large part of the garden, using trees, arbors and trellises with vines or even shade cloth or sunshades.

In desert areas the outdoor living area may actually be to the north of the house, where shade is most dependable. You can take advantage of this shade to create a refuge from summer heat. Add some water (a fountain or waterfall) and an overhead trellis of vines to create a cooling shade garden.

An overlooked aspect of shade is its effect at night. Shade reduces radiation heat loss from the ground and so makes shaded areas warmer than those in the open. This can enable frost tender plants to survive in areas where they otherwise couldn't. It is also one reason for the beneficial edge effect that occurs at the edge of woods. There is enough sun for good growth, but also sufficient shade to keep the area warmer and protect plants from frost.

Problem shade:

In cool northern climates shade is often a problem because it keeps the soil colder and wetter and means less light for photosynthesis. This is particularly problematic in spring, when the sun is still fairly weak and you want the soil to warm up as quickly as possible.

North facing shady spots (especially the north side of a house) are notorious as some of the most difficult areas in the garden. They are of little value for most food plants (though they might be used for growing fungi), so are often used for paths, compost piles, parking, firewood, storage, covered porches and storage buildings.

Sun angle

The altitude of the sun affects the amount of shade you have to contend with and varies according to the time of year. In summer the sun may be almost overhead and cast little shade, while in winter it might be down near the southern horizon and cast long dark shadows.

Vegetable gardening in the shade

In a small garden you may have little choice about where to put your intensive vegetable crops and may have to make do with a partly shady spot. You can still have a vegetable garden with some shade, it just won't be as productive. Your edible crops will grow more slowly and probably won't yield up to their full potential. However any harvest at all can be looked upon as a gain. In such cases you will want to concentrate on the more shade tolerant crops. These include most leaf crops, as well as carrot, pea, onion, radish, cauliflower and cucumber. You could also try some of the more unconventional, but very shade tolerant, crops such as Stinging Nettle and Ostrich Fern.

There are ways to (slightly) increase the amount of sunlight your vegetable garden receives. You might be able to judiciously trim the lower branches of trees (see Crown lifting), or even coppice them. Some gardeners have increased the amount of light on their vegetables by painting surrounding surfaces white, or by using white gravel for pathways.

Air movement

Air is affected by friction just like anything else, so the air close to an object (the ground, buildings, walls, trees) moves more slowly than air in the open. This slower moving air mixes less with the faster moving ambient air and so may slowly become colder or warmer. Warm air is also less dense than cold air (and so lighter) and so rises above it, while cold air sinks. The air movement created by the continuous warming and cooling, creates distinct air currents in the garden. Of particular significance is the downward movement of cold air at night. This settles in the lowest spots, creating a colder microclimate known as a frost pocket (see below for more on this).

Wind

Watch how the wind moves through your garden, following the path of least resistance just like water. Note which areas are exposed to its full force and which are sheltered from it (snow will generally be deepest in the least windy places). Identify the direction of prevailing winds and note it on the plot plan. Also look for potential wind funnels and other areas of turbulence. If your garden is exposed to frequent strong winds then dealing with them will be a high priority, especially if you live in a cool climate.

Wind has a significant effect on microclimate and may be good or bad, depending upon its intensity and the time of year.

Light summer winds can be beneficial in that they improve air circulation, which can reduce the incidence of mildew and other fungus diseases in humid areas. They can also protect against frost pockets by preventing cold air from settling in one place. In hot weather a light wind has a cooling effect on plants as well as humans, and can sometimes reduce water loss. In very hot areas cooling breezes make outdoor living areas more comfortable, and you might even attempt to funnel a breeze to them. Wind is also essential for wind pollinated plants of course. Less obviously it can help to strengthen the trunks of trees (this is why staking trees is now frowned upon).

Strong winds are detrimental in that they can cause physical damage, stunt growth, pile up snow in drifts, bring salt (on coasts), prevent bees from pollinating crops and blow heat out of buildings. They can also increase water loss (by increasing soil evaporation and plant transpiration) to the point where plants have to stop growing. Cold dry winter winds can be particularly devastating and are a common cause of plant mortality.

Wind chill effectively lowers actual temperature, so that exposed areas may be several degrees colder than sheltered ones. In cold climates this can be a big obstacle to early and late season plant growth and may cut total yields by as much as a half.

Frost

Frost occurs in two distinct forms, radiation frost and advective frost. Radiation frost occurs when the ground gradually radiates heat through the night until it drops to freezing point. This effect occurs everywhere but is most severe in places that are wide open to the sky. Advective frost is more localized and occurs when sinking cold air accumulates in low-lying valleys and hollows (these are known as frost pockets - see below).

The effects of frost are rarely uniform and they can assist you in locating the warmest and coldest areas of the garden. The areas where frost is thickest are the coldest, while areas with the lightest frost (or none at all) are the warmest. To find out if a low spot is a frost pocket just go outside after a very mild frost. The areas with frost on them will be the frost pockets. Wooded areas are less affected by frost because the trees slow down cold air movement, and limit heat loss through radiation.

Cold doesn't kill plants uniformly. A sudden early cold spell in November might kill plants overnight, whereby a colder spell in January (when plants are more hardened) might not affect them at all. Wet soil exacerbates freezing by conducting heat more effectively. Deep snow acts as insulation and protects plants from severe cold. Cold air is heavy, so the higher parts of a tree may be unaffected by frost, even though lower branches are hard hit.

Frost isn't always bad, it may even be helpful in that it can kill insect pests and gives fruit trees their needed chill hours.

Frost pockets

These occur when heavy cold air moves slowly downhill (like honey) and collects in the lowest hollows. On cold winter nights frost occurs in these places even though higher spots nearby may be untouched. Any low-lying area surrounded by higher land is potentially a frost pocket, so mark it on your plan.

Frost pockets can also occur higher up on a slope, if a barrier such as a fence blocks the free downward flow of cold air. Such a barrier is known as a frost dam and causes cold air to accumulate above it. Avoid creating frost dams by using open fences, raising them up off the ground slightly, or angling them downhill. All of these ploys allow cold air to keep moving.

To avoid frost damage put only fully hardy plants in a frost pocket (tender plants should be placed further up the slope). In very mild winter areas fruit trees may be planted in frost pockets to maximize the number of winter chill hours they receive.

Heat Sinks

Any large mass (buildings, walls, rock outcrops, paved areas, standing water) absorbs heat from the sun and air during the day and slowly releases it at night. This heat storage effect can make adjacent areas warmer at night so they suffer less from frost. In the cooler parts of Europe gardeners have long planted tender, heat loving fruit trees against south facing stone walls so they can benefit from this additional warmth. When these walls are also under the eaves of a roof they create one of the warmest microclimates in the garden (they may be a whole zone warmer).

Paved areas such as pathways, patios and driveways may get very hot on summer days (too hot for bare feet) and radiate this heat out at night, thus creating a warmer area adjacent to the path.

Large bodies of water act as heat sinks and can significantly alter the climate around them. The water absorbs heat over the course of the summer and slowly releases it through the winter. The bigger the volume of water the greater the effect of course, with the ocean having the greatest effect. In winter the land near a large area of water may be as much as 10° Fahrenheit warmer. Conversely in summer a large body of water can absorb so much heat they make the whole area cooler. This tempering effect also occurs on a smaller scale and even a modest size pond can raise the temperature around it by enough to enable tender plants nearby to scrape through the winter.

Soil

Soil also holds a lot of heat and uncovered soil may give off enough heat at night to protect plants from mild frost. Mulch can sometimes increase frost damage by insulating the soil so it releases less heat. Of course bare soil will get colder and freeze more deeply than covered soil, which can also damage plants. Moist soils can retain more heat than dry soils, so plants growing in them sometimes suffer less from frost.

Humidity

Humid air holds more moisture than dry air and so can retain more heat, which may also help to reduce frost damage. This is another reason woodland tends to be warmer than open areas and why land near large bodies of water is warmer.

Rain shadow

A rain shadow is created when tall objects shelter the ground from falling rain. The ground close to tall walls and underneath house eaves is often much drier than nearby soil.

Trees

Trees have a significant moderating effect on growing conditions. In winter the area underneath them is usually warmer because they slow down cold winds, increase humidity and block heat radiation. In summer they keep the area cooler by shading the soil, providing evaporative cooling, increasing humidity and precipitating fog. An opening in a forest (and the edge to some extent) has the best of both worlds. It is sunnier than the forest, but still gets the benefit of the tempering effect of woodland.

Slope

The orientation of the land has a major effect on microclimate. Maximum solar gain is received when the sun is at right angles to the ground and in northern latitudes the sun is always south of overhead. If level land receives 100 units of sunshine, a south-facing slope may get 105, while a north facing one may only get 85 units.

Eastern slopes

Eastern facing slopes are exposed to early morning sun and so warm up quickly, which is an asset in spring and fall, but may increase frost damage in winter. However there is less plant growth because they get their sun while temperatures are lower and photosynthesis is slower. They don't get much hot afternoon sun, so are cooler and moister than south or west facing slopes. They also get less cold westerly winds.

Eastern slopes have the most moderate temperatures in the garden, which is useful in hot climates and for plants that can't tolerate extreme heat, cold or drought.

Southern slopes

These are usually the warmest areas of the garden and actually have a slightly longer growing season (it's as if they are further south). They are the best sites for vegetable gardens in all but the hottest climates and are particularly useful for winter, early and late vegetable crops and heat loving plants.

Plants on south facing slopes start growing earlier in spring because the soil warms up faster. This can make them vulnerable to late frosts (don't plant early blooming fruit trees there).

Another problem is that additional heat gain causes the soil to dry out faster and plants to transpire more. This means that plants will require more irrigation water (or you could plant more drought tolerant species). Because these slopes get drier they are also more likely to burn in a fire. Snow and ice melts quickly on south facing paths and driveways because of the additional solar heat.

Western slopes

These slopes have cooler mornings but hotter afternoons because they get direct sun at the hottest time of day. This means they dry out quickly and are also more likely to burn in a wildfire. They also have wider daily temperature fluctuations as they warm up considerably during the day and then cool down dramatically at night. This can result in more frost damage to plants in winter.

These slopes are commonly exposed to prevailing winds, which can further dry the soil and increase plant transpiration. These winds can also chill plants and cause physical damage.

West facing living areas get a lot of direct sun through their windows. This is nice in winter, but tends to overheat the rooms in summer (you may have to provide some kind of shade to prevent this). West facing woodwork deteriorates significantly faster than that facing any other direction.

Northern slopes

These get sun in the morning and evening in summer, when it is weakest and hits the ground at an oblique angle. In winter they may be in more or less permanent shade. Because they get the least solar gain of any slopes, they have the coolest growing climate and the shortest growing season.

A northern exposure isn't always a disadvantage however. Exposed to cold winter winds and with less direct sun, there are smaller temperature swings, which can actually mean less frost damage. This is because plants stay dormant longer and don't start flowering and growing until later in the season. If plants do get frozen they only thaw out slowly, which results in less damage.

In hot dry climates north-facing slopes always have the most vegetation because they hold on to moisture for longer. In very hot climates this might be a place for the patio or even the vegetable garden. When growing temperate zone fruit in mild winter areas you may be faced with the problem of a lack of winter chill. In such cases a north-facing slope may give your trees the extra cold they need.

Shady north facing areas are commonly used for non-living area buildings and other components (such as wood storage). In cold winter areas they are not good places for driveways and parking areas because they tend to stay covered in ice and snow for long periods.

Plants that grow naturally in the forest understory often do well on these slopes, as they are accustomed to lower light levels. These slopes can also be good places to grow fungi.

Position on slope

The position on a slope also affects the growing conditions.

At night the bottom of a slope is often cooler than the top because cold air is heavier than warm air and drains downhill to collect in valleys (causing the aforementioned frost pockets). In winter the temperature is generally more stable and there is less frequent freezing and thawing.

When water drains downhill it often takes soil and nutrients with it, so soil at the bottom of a slope tends to be moister, more fertile and deeper. There is also less evaporation from the soil, because these areas are less exposed to drying winds and direct sun.

The top of a slope tends to be drier, windier, sunnier, warmer and less prone to early frosts. In dry areas these places should be planted with more drought tolerant plants.

Planning the garden

Design is basically about coming up with the best solution to a particular set of problems presented by your site (you identified these in your evaluation). It is about arranging the garden logically, so it works on a practical level with a minimum of expense and labor. To do this you need to know what components you need (rest areas, activity areas, storage areas, growing areas) and then work out the best arrangement for them.

Before you can start planning your garden you have to clearly define what you are trying to accomplish and what you would like your perfect garden to look like. The first purpose of this type of garden is to provide food and you might want to grow as much of your own food as possible. Alternatively you might want a low-maintenance garden that produces some food, or you might want a garden that provides you with an income. You could also be into collecting unusual varieties of fruit trees or perennial edibles.

The garden isn't just a place to grow food however, it is also a part of your home. A place to be lived in and used, which means it should be as comfortable and functional as any other part of your home. It should also be beautiful (a work of art even), though I don't advocate spending much time on this aspect initially, it comes later.

The garden should also be a part of the larger regional landscape, so it is immediately obvious which part of the country you are in. It gets this from using local materials, building styles and plants that fit the local climate (especially natives).

My ideal garden

I first imagined my ultimate garden many years ago after reading Edgar Andersons description of the home gardens of Central America. These gardens were a productive multi-layered mix of trees, shrubs, vines, perennial vegetables, annual crops, self-seeding annual vegetables and flowers.

My primary goal is to create an efficient garden that produces as much food as possible with the minimum of work and resources. A place where you could go out at any time of the year and harvest food for a meal. In my ideal garden the areas around the house consists of intensively cultivated food producing plants. There is a lot of space devoted to the vegetable garden and its raised beds, a cut and come again salad garden and areas for other highly productive plants. There are also protected areas for tender fruit trees and other prized plants, as well as a food pond and arbors of fruiting vines to provide screening and summer shade as well as food.

Further away from the house there would be a larger area for staple row crops such as Corn (maybe in a three sisters garden) potatoes, dry beans and more. There would also be a forest of food producing trees, shrubs and vines. Interspersed between these would be patches of perennial vegetables, as well as independent annual vegetables and wild food plants. Forest gardens such as this are especially well suited to larger areas as they are fairly low-maintenance.

In a large garden the land at the outer edges of the property could be left in its natural state as a wildlife refuge and would require no attention at all (this could also be a source of useful wild plants).

A good way to visualize your perfect garden is to draw it out on a large sheet of paper. This is so useful that you might want to try it several times to draw out your thoughts. The drawing doesn't have to be perfect, it just has to get you to thinking about what you want.

Things the garden should do for us

It should produce as much food as possible: vegetables, salad, fruits, herbs, and even staples like potatoes, beans and corn. It should also produce herbal teas, medicines, super nutritious foods, smoking materials, craft materials and more.

It should produce many of the materials used in its construction and maintenance (fencing, posts, mulch materials, stakes and more).

It should use no more water than that which falls upon it naturally. This means absorbing all rainwater, with no runoff going down storm drains.

It should be as comfortable and practical as anywhere else in the home, so it gets used and not just looked at.

It should be a beautiful and efficient place to relax, talk, sleep, play, entertain, work, meditate and create.

It should give us ways to reuse or recycle our waste products (kitchen scraps, human waste, gray water).

Creating and tending the garden should challenge us intellectually, physically and creatively.

It should generate its own fertility and improve the land it sits on.

No fossil fuels or toxic chemicals should be used in its creation and upkeep.

It should provide refuge and habitat for wildlife, from microbes to insects, birds, reptiles, mammals and more.

Once established it should be low-maintenance, so we spend our time enjoying it, not working on it.

The existing garden

Your garden already exists in some form (even if it's just wild land) you are merely modifying it to better suit your needs. Whatever hopes and aspirations you have for your garden, they must be based on the reality of the existing site (no faith based gardening here). You must design the garden to take advantage of the assets of the site topography and microclimate.

Look at what you have and decide what parts you like and what you don't. What you want to keep and what you want to change. The more existing components and plants you can incorporate into the new design, the easier your task will be and the quicker you will have the garden you want.

The most important existing element in the garden is the house (if you change the house to improve the garden, you can consider yourself a real gardener). This is such a dominant element that you usually tailor everything else to work with it. The shape, style and the materials used in its construction should all be reflected in the garden.

You also need to think about the existing plants and which ones you wish to keep. Established trees and shrubs have a major visual impact in the garden and you should cherish them. You can't buy the time it took to grow such plants, so don't eliminate them just to get "a clean slate" It makes sense to use the existing plants to form the framework of the garden where possible. You just fill in the missing pieces with useful plants of your choice. These plants don't require any work from you because they are already there. Try and find uses for them, so you can justify having them.

If you already have good size useful trees growing in the right places you are very lucky. When I started to work on my land I found several small Chestnut trees already growing there. Many people would have cut them down without thinking, just to clear the site (they would probably have re-sprouted anyway, but that's another story). They are one of my favorite trees so I just cleared out the ailing Monterey Pines that surrounded them. Given full sun these trees responded vigorously and five years later I am already getting a significant crop of nuts every year (90 pounds from one tree). I also found some Persian Walnut trees (I can't imagine how they got there) and these are also growing rapidly and starting to bear. Now I just have to figure out how to get the nuts before the squirrels.

Even if you think you will have to remove existing trees eventually, you might want to retain them for a few years, to add height to the garden while other plants are growing. You might also coppice them, so they continue to grow as shrubs rather than trees. Their vigorous new shoots help to give height to the garden and can later be used for fences, trellis, firewood , etc.

Site constraints

Every site has its drawbacks and problem areas. Good design means coming up with creative solutions to minimize any possible problems.

I have had 3 gardens where tall trees to the south cast a band of deep shade across the site (in fact I have never had perfect southern exposure). In these situations you might plant shade tolerant understory trees (such as Pawpaw or Silverbell), with a row of shade tolerant shrubs (Blackcurrant or Salal) in front of them. This steps down the vegetation down without blocking any more light.

In very hot climates you need to incorporate a lot of shade into the design if it is to be comfortable in summer. This could be trees, arbors, shaded walkways and more.

Steep slopes aren't very conducive to human activity and can be prone to erosion if their soil is disturbed. In most cases they are best left alone with their existing vegetation. If space is very short they might be used for permanent plantings of fruit bearing trees and shrubs. Moderate slopes can be made productive by terracing (which sound easy if you say it quickly).

Sometimes the soil is less than ideal. New construction often leaves the land with a few inches of nice topsoil spread over a compacted mix of subsoil, building debris and/topsoil. One area of my land was once a horse corral and has a 3" thick layer hardpan (it resembles soft concrete) a few inches down. Compacted soil is a lot easier to deal with before you plant anything, while you can deep cultivate. If it already exists you can try deep rooted plants (especially spike rooted plants like Daikon). Mulching can also help by encouraging soil life.

Garden size

Experienced gardeners sometimes say that a large garden is more of a liability than an asset. It takes a lot of work, plants, materials and time to get it established and keep it looking good (in my garden I always seem to be fetching something from somewhere else). A small garden is much easier to live with. You can take care of it well and take pride in your productivity per square foot. You can increase the growing space available by fully utilizing all of the garden layers from the soil up to the shrubs and trees and vines. You can even grow things on arbors, walls and roofs.

If you have a small area of land you will be limited by the physical size of the space you have to work with. However having a large piece of land doesn't necessarily mean you should create a large garden. There are other limits on how big a garden you should create, such as how much work and money you want to expend. In dry areas you may be limited by the amount of water you have available.

In most situations you don't really have to make any final decision on the size of the garden. You simply start working on creating a small garden in the area around your house. You then expand as space, enthusiasm, time and money allows. In twenty years time you may be half way to the next county.

Low-maintenance

Garden size is intimately related to how much maintenance it requires. You can only do so much work, so unless your garden is very small you have to really concentrate on making everything as low-maintenance as possible (especially once you get out past the house zone). If you don't then either the garden will take over your life and make you a serf, or it will get neglected and become a mess. The garden is supposed be satisfying and pleasurable, so don't bite off more than you are prepared to chew.

The more you alter the natural vegetation, the more nature works against you. If you want to minimize your workload, the garden will be a compromise between what nature wants to grow and what you want to grow. In most temperate areas the natural vegetation is some form of woodland, so it follows that an ecologically based productive garden should largely consist of trees and shrubs. On the other hand most familiar human foods are derived from annual crops, which need full sun for maximum productivity. Hence the ideal food producing garden should be a mix of sunny areas for annual crops and forested areas of woody perennial crops. Such a configuration will also have lots of highly desirable and productive forest edge.

I find abandoned gardens that have been left in the care of nature for a few years to be particularly appealing and a good model for the new food garden. The pampered weaklings have disappeared and only the well adapted and strong plants remain. We should start out with the plants that can grow without any attention from us. It's very rewarding when plants start acting like they belong there and if you can achieve this then you will have only minimal maintenance to do. Ultimately I'm aiming for a garden that looks as if it evolved out of the earth without human intervention.

Water use

Gardeners in dry climates need to think about water use throughout the design process. We have to start looking beyond simply turning on the tap whenever the soil gets dry and start to garden more intelligently. We need to organize our gardens to make our water resources stretch as far as possible. This means using water conserving plants, mulch, soil improvement, rainwater harvesting, gray water and drip irrigation, It can also involve a network of low paths and swales to direct runoff to retention basins where it can soak in to the ground.

One way to minimize water use is to use native plants, but in most cases these aren't very productive. A more fruitful approach is to emphasize crop plants from arid areas of the world.

In wet climates you may have the opposite problem, and have to work out where to put drains or ditches to get rid of water effectively, or direct it to somewhere it won't cause problems. In this case you might use it to create ponds, marshes and other life enhancing features.

Do it yourself

We live in a time where everything has been commercialized, commodified, specialized and compartmentalized, to the point where many people feel incapable of doing things for themselves. If people want a garden (and have the money) they call in a professional and have it designed for them. I have never approved of delegating garden design to anyone else (which is good because I couldn't afford it anyway). It takes the garden out of your hands and makes it someone else's creation. Even when I have been doing the designing and installing for others I still disapprove. I have found that if people aren't motivated enough to create the garden themselves, they usually aren't motivated enough to give it the tender loving care necessary to perfect it. An alternative to doing it all yourself is to do it with a group (see Cooperative gardening).

For the garden to work its full magic it should be designed by you, built by you and maintained by you. Few things in life are as satisfying as creating and refining a beautiful and highly productive garden, so don't let anyone deprive you of the experience. I am a great believer in equal parts physical, mental and creative work and gardening is an invigorating combination of all three. In fact this is one of the reasons it is such a satisfying activity. Another problem with paying someone to create your garden is that it creates dependency, they know how it works better than you do. If you create it and something goes wrong, you know how to fix it.

Even though everyone doesn't have an aptitude for design, anyone with sufficient motivation and interest can produce a great garden. Natural landscapes are beautiful without humans obsessing about proportion, texture, shape or color wheels, which suggests that we place rather too much emphasis on "design". Nature will do most of the hard work if you let her. You don't even have to understand it all, just assemble the pieces, sow the seeds and let her get on with it.

Cost

This is a significant aspect of any kind of design because there is no point in designing something you can't afford. The biggest single cost in a conventional landscaping job is usually labor, but this isn't an issue if you are doing your own work. Plants are my biggest expense because I keep buying interesting new ones. You can reduce this cost by propagating plants yourself, but it takes a while to grow trees and shrubs to a useful size. Alternatively you could just buy the plants you want and then offset their cost by propagating them, and selling the resulting plants to others who are just starting out.

If you are poor console yourself with the thought that necessity is the mother of invention. These types of food garden were originally created by poor people to improve their lives, not as a way to spend money. Let your poverty stimulate you to be more creative.

Idea folder

Create a folder to hold all of the plans and notes you make pertaining to your garden (activities, components and more), as well as pictures and magazine clippings. It also serves as a reminder of things to include.

You might also have a folder on your computer, where you keep digital notes as well as pdf's from useful websites. It could also include a digital picture gallery of things that inspire you, and one of your garden in its various stages.

Inventory of resources

Your site analysis identified the resources (stone, logs, brushwood, wild plants, water sources, sun, soil, views and more) that are available on the site. These are the cheapest (their only cost is your labor) and most natural resources you have and you should make maximum use of them. You should also think about what is available locally at low cost: wood, stone, straw, wood chips, horse manure, seaweed, recycled lumber, used bricks, salvaged concrete, scrap metal as well as anything you have managed to acquire. Their availability can help you to keep costs down and may affect your design decisions.

There are also community resources to consider. These includes people, community gardens, colleges, garden centers and more. These can help with advice, plants (buy, swap, give away), mutual admiration, work trade or even having an experienced person to water while you are on vacation. On a larger scale there are also the fantastic global resources of the internet, if you are prepared to go out and find them.

You should also consider your personal resources and abilities. Building a garden involves a lot of different skills, planting, carpentry, plumbing, masonry, moving soil Most aren't difficult and you could certainly accomplish them all if you are motivated.

There is also the question of how much time and money you can afford to spend on the garden. Are you a nuclear family with only one gardener, an extended family with several interested people, or a commune of fanatical gardeners. If you only have an afternoon every other weekend it's going to take a long time to recreate the Garden of Eden. I don't really count my time in this equation because working in the garden is as much a part of my life as eating.

If you don't have much time or money you should concentrate on the most labor saving, low-maintenance and low cost components and plants. If this isn't feasible there is always the old trick of teaching a workshop on the subject and get people to pay you for the experience of working on your project.

Activities

Start your planning by identifying the various activities you and your family will want to do in the garden. These might include: growing food, cooking, eating, talking, reading, propagating plants, collecting plants, cutting flowers, swimming, yoga, praying, carpentry, repairing cars, disposing of garbage, recycling waste, drying wet clothes, storing things, baking pizza, playing with children, sitting by a fire, barbecuing, writing, showering, making love, exercising the dog, sunbathing, throwing parties (black tie cocktail parties or all night raves?) soaking in a hot tub, sleeping, making music, painting, listening to music, meditating, massage, playing games, solitary meditation and more.

If your activity list gets too long you will have to prioritize it in order of importance. Separate what you can't live without from what you think would be nice to have.

Essential components

Once you have your list of important activities, you should go through it and write down what components each will require. These might include: growing beds, a nursery bed, patio, deck, barbecue, sand pit, play area, bed, fire pit, wood shed, pond, shower, bathtub, gray water treatment marsh, hammock, sitting area, tool shed, a stage for performing, greenhouse, sauna, garbage/recycle area, beehives, hedgerow, sweat lodge, eating area, trampoline, sleeping area, parking areas, mulch storage, water storage, tea garden, pizza oven, compost area, worm bin, rainwater collection, playhouse, clothes drying line, composting toilet, pergola and more.

In some cases only one component will work (sitting by a fire requires a fire), but many activities can be done in more than one way, using a number of different components. For example kitchen scraps might be put in a compost pile, fed to worms, buried in holes, fed to chickens or spread out under sheet compost. Keeping plants supplied with water might mean using drip irrigation, mulch, gray water, rainwater harvesting and adding organic matter to the soil (you could also concentrate on drought tolerant plants).

In some cases several different components may be used to perform one thing. Growing vegetables may require water, compost, a greenhouse, fertile growing beds, shelter and more. Supplying water for irrigation may require a well, a holding tank, a rainwater harvesting system and / or irrigation equipment.

When you start working on this you will find that most components have more than one use. Shrubs may be planted as a barrier hedge, but they can simultaneously screen unwanted views and produce fruit, firewood, mulch and compost material. Some also fix nitrogen. An outdoor bed can be used for sleeping at night, massage, making love and relaxing during the day. Often these additional functions depend upon their location, so they need to be considered carefully.

Make notes on components

After you have made a list of necessary components you should read about them in the relevant sections of this book (and elsewhere) and make notes on anything that is particularly relevant to your situation. What does each component require to function properly (water, sun, shade, privacy, shelter from wind, access to road, a slope?) What else can it do and what additional things does it produce (food, shade, ornament, support, beauty?)

Also think about how each component might interact with other elements? Will it work more effectively if it is grouped with something else (fire, sweat lodge and pond, or the greenhouse, garden beds and compost pile.) Sometimes a component must be physically separated other components. The children's play area should be well away from the greenhouse. The sleeping area should be well away from the public road.

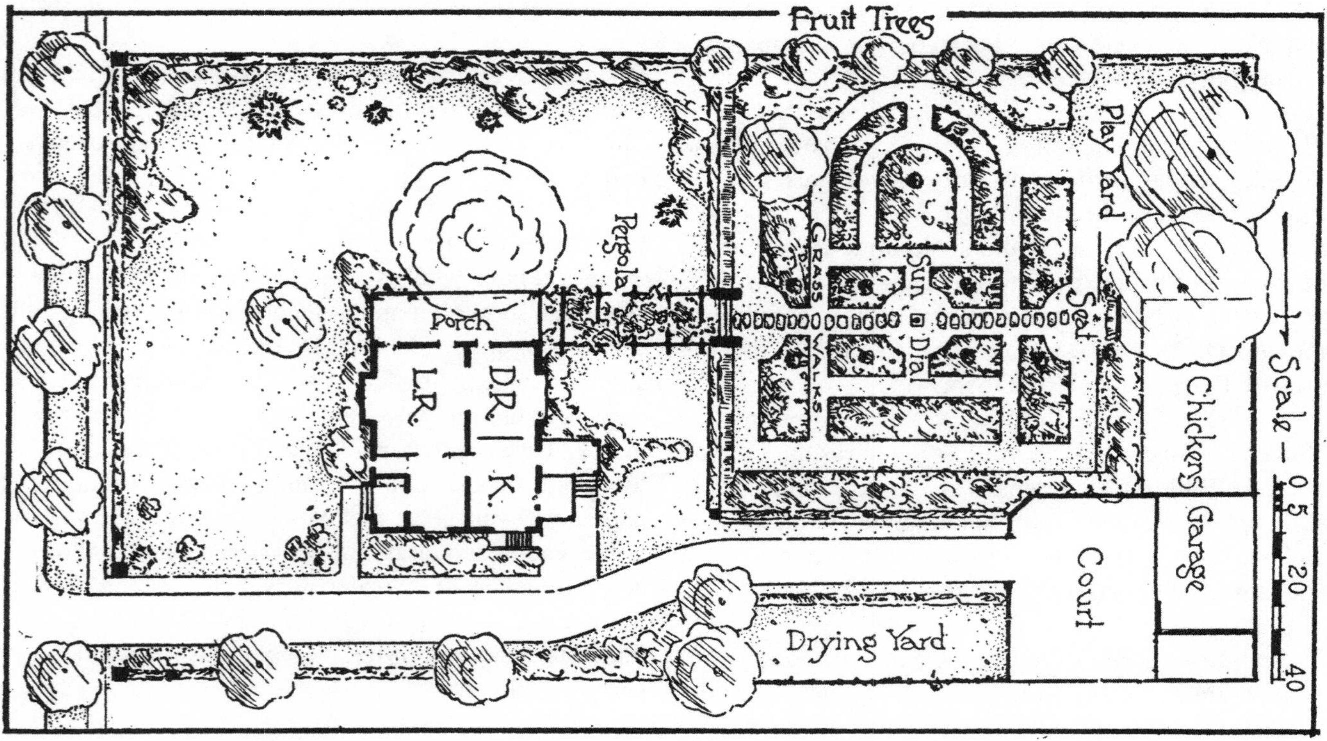

Designing the garden

Designing an entire garden from scratch is commonly discussed in books, on television and with those who can afford to hire a landscape architect. However in the real world most of us are modifying an already existing garden and do it a little bit at a time. We add new stuff, or renovate what already exists, as time and money allows. In these situations the design work is so straightforward you usually make your decisions in the garden as you work. This is known as field design and works well for small projects, but you could also do a large garden in this way. You just have to break it up into a series of separate areas and work on one at a time.

Most professional designers frown upon working directly in the garden (they would), yet gardening is an organic activity and it is perfectly natural to just go out and start doing things. For the non-designer the advantage of working directly in the garden is that you have that immediate feedback. I find that many of my most insightful ideas and observations come while doing repetitive physical work and my mind is wandering. The end result may not be as efficient as it could have been (and you may have to re-do or move things occasionally), but it gets things growing. Nature is very forgiving and will usually hide any mistakes (especially in the small garden).

The problem with designing the more complex garden in the field, is that it is harder to see the bigger picture, or introduce more abstract concept like hydrozones. There is also a tendency to build on what already exists, which can prevent you from seeing alternatives that might work better. Another problem is that you have so many choices things often get placed arbitrarily. If you don't have much experience it can be hard to visualize something that isn't there. Only later (usually just after you put your tools away) do you realize that an element would have been better placed somewhere else.

Traditional home gardens weren't designed on paper, they were laid out logically and grew organically over time. However their creators had the benefit of generations of intimate knowledge of growing plants and what works best in the immediate area. In trying to create our garden we are much more on our own. We can compensate for our deficiencies in practical knowledge by using paper, pencil, eraser and logic to translate our abundance of written knowledge into a real garden. With the internet we can share ideas with like minded gardeners around the world.

I find it best to create the basic framework of the garden on paper, as it's easier to place the various components to best advantage. I then like to do the rest out in the garden, to create the organic garden organically. As I said previously gardening is a process, rather than a goal and you should enjoy it rather than obsess about it.

Planning on paper

The next few pages describe how to create a garden on paper. This is helpful because it gets you thinking about the best ways to arrange the various components so they work together efficiently. It is especially useful for dealing with more abstract concepts such as zoning (watering zones, activity zones or fire zones), that aren't always obvious when you are out in the garden. It's always easier to move stuff around on paper than it is in the garden, so try and make your mistakes there, before you start working outside.

Having an accurate scale plan also helps in the building stage. We can calculate runoff for water storage, planting distances, numbers of plants, quantities of materials and more. It can also help with organizing the work, so you do everything in the right order.

Your first design task is to break up the garden into separate areas, according to what you want to do with each part. You probably already have some plans for certain areas, while others will be determined by the site itself. For example the area between the house and driveway is usually the front entrance garden. The sunniest part of the property will usually be used for the vegetable garden. The south facing side of the house (off of the kitchen) is the best place for the outdoor living area.

Activity zones

One of the most useful tools for design is the concept of zones, whereby we separate the garden into a series of concentric zones centered around the house. This is central to the whole process of designing and building the garden, because it helps you decide where to put things, the order in which you create them and how much maintenance each area requires.

Zoning helps to define the best areas to put things, according to how often we need to attend to them. It organizes the garden into a series of concentric zones of activity around the house. The innermost area (zone 1) is centered around the house because that is where we naturally spend the most time, This is where we put the components that need the most attention, you use the most, or simply like the most. The outermost circle (zone 5) is at the edge of the property where we go the least often. Here we put the elements you use the least and require no attention. Zoning is most valuable in the large garden where you have to maximize efficiency to get anything done. It is much less useful in the small garden, where everything is conveniently nearby anyway,

The elements in the inner zones are more formal, costly and closely packed together. The materials used are harder, less natural and need to be more durable because they get more wear. As you move further away from the house, the materials become softer, more informal, rustic, natural and further apart. This logical gradation helps to give the garden cohesion.

Zoning also helps when you are organizing the construction of the garden. You start by working on the house zone and when that is done you work your way out through the zones in turn. As you move out the areas become lower maintenance, which means using locally adapted plants, mulch and maybe drip irrigation (it depends upon how much productivity you want). If the garden suddenly requires too much work then you have gone too far.

The zones described in permaculture books are most relevant on a larger homestead or farm scale and often emphasize livestock. I have adapted the concept to make them more relevant to the garden situation.

Zone 1 (The house zone)

The area adjacent to the house is the most important part of the garden because it is where you spend the most time. The plants and components in this area are those that need the greatest amount of attention; at least daily and sometimes several times a day.

Components:

This area tends to have a lot of paving in the form of paths, patio or decking. Any area that isn't paved should be used for growing something, usually in defined beds (in gopher country these will be protected with wire). It usually has quite a few other important components too, perhaps an attached greenhouse, root cellar, tool shed, worm compost bin (ideally near the kitchen door for convenience) and a recycling area.

Plants:

Space is limited in this area, so it is intensively planted with plants that provide a high yield per square foot. This is also the place for those plants that are used the most (herbs, salad mix) or need the greatest amount of attention (watering, feeding, pruning, weeding, protection from frost).

Herbs, salad mix and tea plants are planted close to the kitchen door, where they are conveniently available during food preparation. If you have room you could also include raised beds for intensively grown annual crops (in a small garden the main vegetable garden will be located here), as well as trellised vines, espaliers, edible ornamentals and flowers.

This is a good place to put those bush fruits that are particularly attractive to birds, such as raspberries and blueberries. People and pets hang out here a lot of the time, so the fruit will be somewhat less accessible (beware of berry colored bird droppings though).

This is also the place to put tender plants that are not well adapted to your climate, but you really want to grow anyway. South or west facing walls are particularly useful for this because they provide a warmer microclimate. It is easier to give them the extra attention and resources they require (such as protecting them from frost on cold winter nights).

The plants are closely spaced in beds and heavily mulched to improve the soil, reduce maintenance and give a neater appearance (use your best mulch).

There should be no bare soil anywhere. Plants are protected from herbivores with fences and sheltered by windbreaks. The soil in the intensive growing areas will be routinely amended to maximise productivity.

Water

In dry climates the plants that require frequent watering are placed in this zone. In fact the size of this zone is sometimes determined by how far a hose can reach. Not only can the plants be conveniently watered easily here, but it's nice to have their more luxuriant growth where you can see it. Well watered succulent green plants are more fire resistant, which can be significant in some areas.

Water for irrigation will usually be supplied via a drip irrigation system with a timer. The water would ideally be supplied from a rainwater catchment system and supplemented with gray water from the house. If this isn't practical then you will use the tap water from the house of course.

This is also a good place for the food pond because you spend a lot of your time here and can really appreciate it.

Zone 2 (The vegetable garden zone)

The plants and components in zone 2 generally need attention only every day or two. If enough resources exist, or the garden is small enough then much of what I wrote about zone 1 might also apply here.

Components:

The most important elements in this area are the intensive kitchen garden beds and their associated elements: as well as a free standing greenhouse, shed, compost area and nursery bed. It might also include a root cellar, tool shed, chicken shed and more.

Plants

The plants in this zone only need attention (such as feeding, watering) every 2 or 3 days. The most important plants are in the intensive vegetable garden, though this is also a good place for fruiting vines, bush fruit, perennial vegetables, mushrooms (in intensive beds) and small trees in polycultures.

This is a good place to put those fruit trees that are attractive to birds, such as Cherries and Mulberries (watch out for berry colored droppings). Vacant areas may be planted with living mulch/green manures

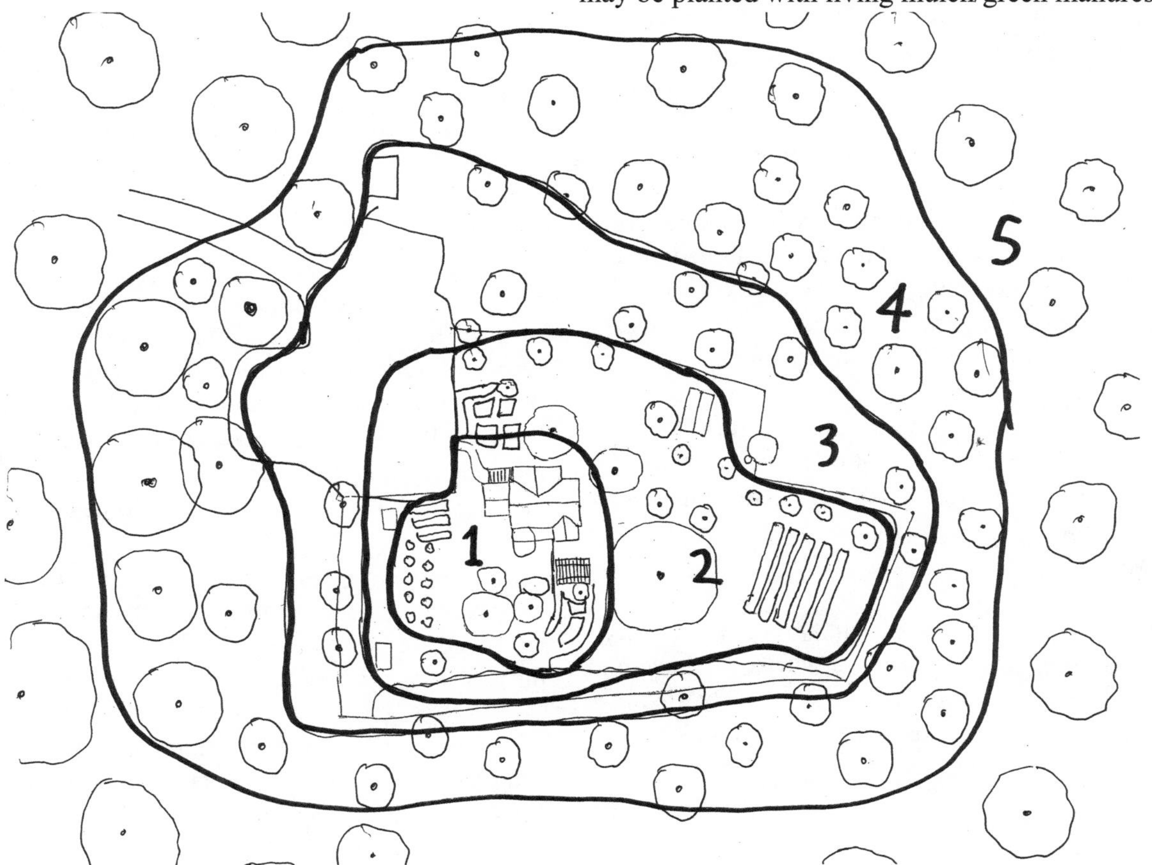

or patches of herbs for tea. The soil is amended and mulched around all significant plants (though all soil will be mulched if enough is available). This whole area should be securely fenced to keep out deer.

Water

In dry climates this area will have a drip irrigation system with a timer. There is often a pond for growing food and water storage, and perhaps a water tank for storage of rainwater from the roof or elsewhere.

Zone 3 (middle zone)

The plants and components in this area should be able to go up to a week without needing attention.

Components:

Sheds, beehives, windbreaks, ponds,

Plants

This area contains plants that only need water perhaps once a week. They might be grown in a large staple crop row garden, a three sisters garden, a dry farmed planting or a forest garden. Especially productive larger plants (Bamboo, dwarf fruit trees, bigger bush fruit) belong out here, along with beds of the more independent perennial vegetables. There could also be large patches of vigorous independent herbs for drying for tea. You might also have areas of living mulch and biomass crops (for use as mulch or for composting).

Woody non-food bearing plants may be coppiced to produce mulch and poles and to keep their size under control. This is a good way to deal with existing natives without killing them, though you might also plant species from a similar climate zone.

This could be a good place for outdoor mushroom cultivation, taking advantage of existing irrigated wood chip mulched beds. You could also coppice logs for growing wood loving species.

Water

In dry climates you can expand the range of crops by putting this area on a drip irrigation system (this could be on a timer or manually operated). It might also contain large water storage areas such as ponds,

Zone 4 (Semi-wild zone)

The plants and components in this section only need occasional attention (often just when harvesting or pruning).

Components

There aren't many components out here, perhaps beehives, a shed, camping shelter, sweat lodge or a fire pit.

Plants

This is the best place for a forest garden of independent, vigorous, long-lived, locally adapted useful plants (wild foods wild herbs, bee forage plants, edible fungi). You might also have improved varieties of wild plants.

This is a good place for potentially invasive useful plants such as Mint, Jerusalem Artichoke and Bamboo. There is less chance of them becoming a problem out here because there is plenty of space.

You will have to help these plants to get established (feeding, watering and weeding) and perhaps also to maximize harvest, otherwise they should pretty much look after themselves.

Water

Large water storage projects such as ponds or dams are usually placed out here.

Zone 5 (The wild zone)

If you have enough room this is the place for large nut trees such as Chestnut and Walnut, as well as coppiced firewood trees. It will mostly consist of native plants that grow wild around about, with perhaps a few locally adapted useful plants from further afield. The plants here should be totally independent and ask nothing from you (except perhaps to get established).

You might also selectively cut existing trees (maybe coppice them) to improve conditions for the rest. Use the wood for building, fencing, firewood or other purposes (brush, poles, mulch).

You might also try to grow edible mycorrhizal fungi by inoculating tree roots with spore soup (see Mushrooms and fungi for more on this).

Sectors

Your evaluation highlighted the exterior elements that affect the garden, such as wind, sun, rain and fire, as well as views, sources of noise and more. Sector planning is a permaculture tool that makes us aware of which direction these exterior elements come. We can then place our components to offset any negative effects and enhance any positive ones. These elements usually have to be placed in specific locations to work properly.

Offsetting negatives might mean placing a windbreak to slow wind, a wall to slow wildfire, or screens to hide a neighbors floodlights. Emphasizing positives would be removing objects that cast shade, creating swales to catch rainwater, trapping the sun with a stone wall.

Activity areas

You have made a list of the activities you wish to do in the garden, you now have to decide where to do them (zoning helps here too). Start by determining how much space these activities (and their associated components) require. Each area needs to be the right size for its function and properly oriented to the sun, wind and topography. Many of activities can take place in the same area, but a few need their own exclusive space.

Identifying growing areas

All of the areas not required for specific activities will be used as growing areas. These don't have to be showpieces, as their purpose is to grow food and other useful plants. See Where to plant for more on this.

Bubble diagrams

A bubble diagram is a rough sketch in which you draw out the important activity areas as bubbles over the plan (use tracing paper). It can help you to decide on the best places for the various activity and growing areas in relation to the site and each another, without too much detail to get in the way of thinking. The bubbles overlap where different areas merge, or are divided by a line where they need to be separate. Arrows are used to show you how to move around.

The garden zone and sector concept (see below) can help you to organise the bubbles for greatest efficiency.

Keep the garden compact where possible. Fill in the empty inner zones rather than spreading things out all over the place. Any time you involve distance you increase the amount of walking (and moving things), which takes time away from more productive tasks.

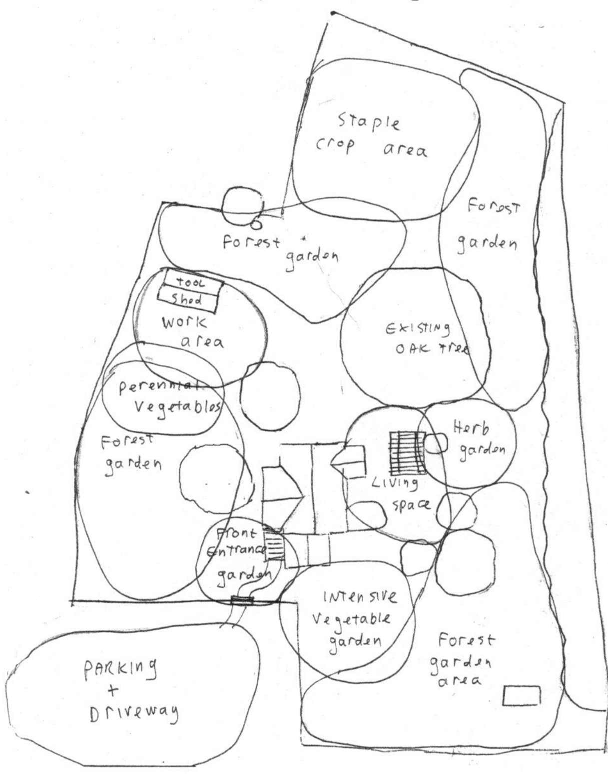

Play around with you bubble diagrams to see how you can best take advantage of the site (sun, shade, views, slope, proximity to house). Also go outside and see how your ideas work in reality. This is the foundation of the garden plan so it is important to get it right. When you finally get the diagram you really like, you transfer it on to the base plan.

Assembling the garden plan

By now you should have a pretty good idea of what kind of garden you are aiming for. What elements you need to include, what you want to grow, what you want to do there and what it should look like. You now have to gather all of the various parts and arrange them so they work together.

The next step is to transfer your bubble diagram on to a sheet of tracing paper laid over a copy of the base plan (don't draw on the plan itself until you have the final design worked out. You can then start to create your garden plan by roughly outlining the shape of the activity and growing areas, existing components, zone circles and relevant sector information. This will help you to find the best places to put all of the various elements. This is important because it reduces the amount of work you have to do, and makes the garden more efficient, productive and attractive.

You might find it helpful to make scale cardboard cutouts for each component (greenhouse, shed, firewood shed, windbreaks, compost pile, pond, patio, chicken run, water storage, gray water system, mulch store, worm bin and more) and move them around on the plan.

Designing a garden doesn't have to be very complicated. Like building a jigsaw puzzle, you can start with the corners, edges and other easily identified parts and go from there. It's up to you how much you do on paper and how much you do in the garden. Whatever you do, the aesthetic arrangement of individual features is much less important than getting everything to work with the site, the microclimate and the other components.

Don't get too obsessed with details at this stage. It just makes things more complicated than they have to be. You only need to get the basic elements down on paper; a lot of the other stuff is more easily done in the garden itself. More important than detailed drawing is to keep notes of what is important to you. Whenever you start work on a section of the garden you can then consult your garden folder for notes and ideas. You will be incorporating a lot of new things into the garden and don't want to overlook anything.

I don't really like the idea of coming in with a preconceived garden in a box and completely replacing what already exists. I prefer to let nature take the lead, keeping established plants and building the garden around them as a symbiotic partnership, A new design gives you the opportunity to improve the worst areas of the site and this is where you should initially concentrate most of your attention. Any especially attractive areas don't need improvement and should be treated very carefully or even left alone completely (maybe fence them off on your plan).

Separate areas

If you are going to do all the work of creating the garden yourself, there is no way you can do it all at one time, so there is no need to design it all at once. It is better to break it up into more manageable sized chunk so there is less to think about at one time. You could actually design your whole garden as a series of small sheets of paper, one for each area, with a master sheet showing how they all fit together.

In conventional gardening they divide the garden into separate areas (rooms), each a garden unto itself. This makes each part seem larger and more important, which can be particularly useful in a small garden. It also means that you have to walk around and explore because you can only see a small part of the garden at one time. Like rooms in a house, each area has it's own focus, features, atmosphere and viewpoints.

Breaking up the garden into separate enclosed areas also reduces the risk of deer devastating your garden. If a falling tree crushes your fence while you are on vacation and deer get through, they will still be confined to one area of the garden, and won't have free run of the whole place.

Dividing up the space

Your basic plan shows the organization of the whole garden, with the activity and planting areas, existing components, zone circles and relevant sector information. The next step is to work out how you will physically divide the garden into these separate areas. To do this you need to get out into the garden with a tape measure and some tall stakes and see what works.

The most obvious way to divide the garden is to create demarcation lines using already existing elements: the house, other buildings, paths, slopes and more. You could use existing trees and shrubs as a guide to breaking up the space (I have used completely random wild plants). You might cut them to the ground and allow them to regrow as healthy new coppice growth, You can also extend imaginary lines out from existing buildings, driveways and walls, and build fences, paths, screens, trellises and more to separate them.

When dividing an area you should think about the shape of the spaces you create, because this affects how you perceive them. As with any room it is the space in between that is important, not the walls. They should have a shape and character of their own and not just be empty space. Perspective changes the size and shape of an area, so it can look significantly different in real life than you imagined on paper.

It is generally best to avoid perfectly straight lines and right angles, unless you have a formal areas. Go for graceful natural curves, or naturally occurring forms (branches, meanders). Any open areas should usually have curved edges. Broad open areas invite you to linger, so are better for living areas. Long narrow spaces encourage you to move through them, especially if they are curved and the end is hidden (inviting you to investigate). Height further emphasizes narrowness.

Enclosing an area alters it dramatically. Before it is built there is open space and sun, once it is in place there is a mix of sun and shade, privacy, shelter, security and a sense of inside and outside.

Dividing elements
When separating and enclosing the various spaces you have lots of options as to materials, height and design. They could be transparent or opaque, low or tall, hard or soft, living or dead. Your choice of materials will determine how much shade is created and may alter the microclimate in other ways too. They will also determine how the space feels. Tall solid walls in a small space make it feel smaller and create a lot of shade (in such situations it's generally better to use low or open dividing elements, such as a picket fence).

When choosing a dividing element you aren't just limited to fences, walls and hedges. Other alternatives include: buildings, berms, growing beds, screens, windbreaks, ponds, trellises, terraces, steps, decks, patios, rills, arbors, wetlands, paths, different levels, ditches, pergolas, retaining walls, trees and shrubs.

Turning spaces into rooms
When an area has a purpose and a distinctive character of its own it becomes a garden room. It might become a kids play area, a sitting area, a tea garden, a bedroom, an entryway, or a dining place. The room becomes a setting for a particular activity that helps to define its character. This is further enhanced with furniture, ornament, unique materials and special plants.

An ornamental space generally benefits from a focal point to act as a visual center and unify the whole. This could be almost anything from a borrowed view, a pond, a statue or even a particularly attractive plant. More functional areas don't need this because the function becomes the focus.

Flooring is one of the easiest ways to define a room, because it immediately distinguishes it from the rest of the garden.

A garden room might also have a ceiling, especially in hot climates where shade is so important for comfort. Arbors and pergolas are a favorite ceiling component, as they not only provide shade, but also cast interesting patterns of light on the ground. They also make an area feel more intimate and secure. Careful pruning of trees can create an overhead canopy (a green ceiling), while leaving useful open space below.

Main components

You will need to decide where to put these important components and areas.

House area
Living area
Vegetable garden
Fruit trees
Pond
Forest garden
Herb garden
Storage shed
Irrigation
Rainwater collection
Gray water

Placing the main components

After deciding on the size, shape and placement of the various areas you are done with the first design phase. You can now turn your attention to placing components in each of the separate garden areas in turn, starting with the front door and back door and related living areas. After designing these, you can move on to other areas and their components.

The approximate location of many components was determined when you marked out the various activity areas. Now you have to decide exactly where they will best perform their own functions and any additional ones. Once you have these in place, you can go on to the minor components, add seating at appropriate spots and connect everything with paths,

Before deciding on how to arrange an area it is a good idea to go and sit there for a while (take a comfortable chair and relax). This will help you to get a feel for the place.

Factors that determine placement

Determining the best place for most components is basically common sense. Their location should be determined by your needs (where you want them), their needs (what they require to function best) and their relationship to other components. Whenever you place anything, you should have a reason for putting it there, Place the component where:

- It can best perform its primary function.
- Its requirements (sun, water, shelter from wind, access to road) can be easily met.
- It can perform other useful functions. For example a building could also act as a screen, provide shade, support plants, block wind and divide the garden.
- It can help other elements to work more effectively (or at least not interfere with them).
- It can best take advantage of the site: the sun, slope, shade, water flow, wind and more.
- It's products (food, seedlings, compost, shade, clean water) can be most conveniently used.

Suggestions on placing components

Topography will sometimes determine the location of a component. A south or west facing slope creates a warmer microclimate and is ideal for intensive vegetable beds and fruit trees. A pond or water tank is most useful for irrigation if it is high enough to allow for gravity flow. It's easier to move heavy loads downhill, so put compost and mulch piles above the garden. Fire runs uphill, so your defensible space should mostly be concentrated below the house and garden. A gray water irrigation system works best in a sunny place downhill from the house.

Some activities and components must be oriented to the sun to get the best from them. The most obvious examples of this are the main intensive vegetable growing beds. These need as much sunlight as you can give them and should get the sunniest spot in the garden. This is particularly important for winter growing beds, when the sun is a lot lower and there is more shade. A greenhouse needs winter sun too (summer sun isn't so important), so put it where the low angle sun won't be blocked. If you want to maximize solar gain in any new building orient it east to west and make sure it isn't shaded.

Hiding an unwanted view or blocking noise may require that an element goes in a certain place.

Sometimes you must modify an area to make it suitable for a component. For example erecting a windbreak for your vegetable garden, draining a wet area or cutting trees to reduce shade. Don't create unnecessary work for yourself by putting things in the wrong places.

You can make a neglected area more useful by placing a high traffic component (outhouse, tool shed) there. I neglected the far end of my garden until I moved the greenhouse there. This actually wasn't the best place for the greenhouse, but it really worked to make that area more important. It now gets visited several times a day. Of course don't put an important component too out of the way, or it may end up getting neglected as well.

If a component really can go anywhere, then you should put it in the worst place that will work. In this way it will enhance that place and leave better areas for other uses.

Cluster the components

Some components have associated elements that naturally go with them, so the output of one can be the input of another. For example the greenhouse, vegetable garden, nursery beds, propagation area, tool shed, compost area and sitting area usually go close together. A sweat lodge needs a source of water for cooling off, such as a shower, pond or stream, as well as a fire pit and a source of fuel. The worm bin and your AACT maker should be together.

A few components are very much antagonistic and should be kept far apart. A children's play area should be far from the greenhouse or sleeping area. The outdoor bed should be away from the street.

Clustering components helps to simplify the design process, because once you have a definite location for the most important element, then the associated components will simply go in the best places close by.

Buildings

Buildings must always be placed where they can best fulfil their intended purpose, though if you have several options then you should consider any additional roles they may play. They can provide shade, collect rainwater, act as a windbreak, screen unwanted views and be used as boundaries.

All buildings should be regarded as potential growing space. They might have living roofs, trellises on their walls covered in plants, or they might be used to support arbors or ropes covered with climbing vines.

Buildings are also important visual elements and should be attractive and consistent with other buildings. Those close to the main house should complement it, or at least share certain elements such as color and materials. Those further away can be more individualistic. Really ugly buildings can be disguised with climbing plants, living walls, green roofs and more.

Usually it's better to cluster buildings together, rather than scattering them all around the garden. You might even have them sharing walls (a greenhouse could be attached to the south facing wall of a shed).

Access and circulation (paths)

Paths are first and foremost practical elements and should generally be placed where they will work best. This may be where people want to walk, or where you want them to walk (not always the same thing). They should take a fairly direct and efficient route from the house to each of the major components and between them. Don't have them wandering all over the place, or make them any longer than necessary. This not only causes unnecessary walking (and frustration), but also requires more paving material.

The main access routes (house to driveway, kitchen to vegetable garden) will be determined fairly early in the design, but may be modified after the location of the major components is decided. Often you will have already physically created the most obvious paths simply by walking around the garden. See Access for a lot more on planning your pathways.

Paths aren't just for getting from A to B, they are also important garden building blocks and visual element. Like fences they help to define the shape of the garden and break it up into smaller unit's. In summer they are the first line of defense in preventing the whole garden from turning into an amorphous mass of vegetation. In winter, when plants die back, they take on even greater visual importance because they may be one of the few things left to look at.

Organizing the planting areas

The planting areas are primarily functional and need to be arranged for efficiency and productivity (all of the food plants should be easily accessible). It is very important to reduce the maintenance of these areas to a minimum by using low/no-work plants, such as natives and locally adapted crops. All of the soil should be covered with something (plants, mulch or paving) to reduce weed growth and water loss.

A large growing area (such as a vegetable garden) could be given its own mini zones, radiating out from the paths according to the need for accessibility and maintenance. Frequently used areas would be near the center (or paths), the less used ones would be further away and accessible by stepping stones.

Normally you will decide on the location of the major trees and shrubs and special planting beds on paper and do the rest while working in the garden.

Growing beds

For efficiency the intensive growing areas are usually arranged in beds. These are an important visual element, and you might want to vary their shape for ornamental reasons. Beware of getting too carried away with visual effect however, otherwise you may end up doing a lot of unproductive work just to keep it looking good (boxwood hedges come to mind).

Rectangular beds aren't as interesting as other shapes, but they are efficient, easy to work with, compact (you can get a lot of beds in a small area) and lend themselves to drip systems and easy calculation of square footages. They are also easier to wire for protection from gophers. If you want a more interesting design you can arrange them in a geometrical potager type garden.

Curved or free form beds are more interesting to look at, but also more complex and labor intensive to create. Gentle curves following the drip line of a tree work great in less formal settings. If you like the idea of a more free form garden, just make sure it is a fairly strong design, so it will hold up under the weight of all that vegetation.

Permaculturists sing the praises of circular keyhole beds and while they certainly make the garden more attractive, I'm not convinced by the arguments for their greater efficiency. It's claimed that a keyhole bed has only a small area of path relative to the size of the bed, but that's only if you don't count the path on the outside of the circular bed. I once built a garden of keyhole beds and really liked the way it looked, but I never felt it created more growing area. I may be missing something but it seems to me a square foot of ground can only fit a certain number of plants, no matter which way you arrange it. Nor am I impressed by the fact that one sprinkler waters all, as I much prefer drip systems. That said I would have used them in my present garden on purely visual grounds if it weren't for gopher problems.

The garden perimeter

The area where tame garden meets wild area needs careful planning, otherwise unruly wild plants will be continually encroaching upon the cultivated areas. A solid fence will work (though plants may come underneath or through any chink. To prevent seriously invasive plants you could bury a root barrier of concrete, plastic or metal (aluminum works well because it doesn't deteriorate) along the perimeter. You might also use vigorous perennials (Comfrey, Day Lily, Horseradish) that form a solid underground barrier of roots, tough enough to keep invaders at bay.

Other factors to consider

Height / the third dimension

Drawing a two dimensional plan can make it hard to visualize the garden in all it's full surround sound, technicolor 3-D glory. This is unfortunate because the vertical elements are important visual components. As the eye moves around the garden it tends to pause on the tall vertical features, such as buildings, trees, posts, walls and trellis.

A flat site can be made more interesting by adding height. The easiest way to do this is with tall trees, shrubs, bamboos and climbing plants. You might also create berms to add height (and create a beneficial microclimate) or use solid dividers such as fences, walls, hedges, trellis and screens. Buildings can also help. Of course using tall plants also increases the growing area of the garden, which can increase its productivity.

Any time you add a tall element to the garden you need to consider how it will affect the things around it. The most obvious effect is the shade it creates. Most food producing plants don't like shade, so keep tall objects to the north side of important growing areas. Tall walls and fences may also dry the soil around them (by creating a rain shadow) and block or funnel the wind (causing turbulence). They can also store heat and create a sheltered microclimate. Psychologically they add atmosphere and an increased sense of security. Of course trees, shrubs and other living elements also compete for nutrients and water in the soil. This can be significant in some situations, especially in small gardens.

The impact of the shade cast by a tall object depends upon its orientation to the sun and the time of day it occurs. Objects to the north can be as tall as you like because they won't cast shade on the garden (you want them tall so they help to shelter the garden from strong wind). Shade from the east isn't very significant either, because the sun is weaker when low in the sky and air temperatures are lower in the morning (so photosynthesis is slower anyway). A southern exposure should be fairly clear for maximum photosynthesis, though the sun is higher in the sky when to the south, so moderate height objects are tolerable (though they may be a problem in winter). The western side is actually the most critical for shade, as we can get a lot of photosynthesis in the warm afternoon and evening hours. The sun gets lower as it goes to the west, so objects to the west should be low.

Earthworks

In some situations you might want to reshape the earth to create berms, ponds, swales and terraces to increase rainwater infiltration, or just to create different growing conditions. These can make a big difference to the comfort and practicality of the garden, They can also help to separate and define the different areas and make them more interesting.

Creating diverse growing conditions

A diversity of plants and habitat makes the garden more able to tolerate disturbance. You can increase the diversity of your garden by creating different growing conditions: dry, sunny, shady, wetland, pond, arbors, living roofs, living walls and more. You will often do this incidentally as you add components, but you can also do it intentionally to increase wildlife habitat.

Terraces

Slopes are sometimes terraced to create flat ground that is more convenient for human activity, This can also improve rainwater infiltration and prevent erosion. South facing slopes are most useful as their southern exposure creates a warm microclimate (especially when stone retaining walls are used). In cool climates these are highly prized for growing heat loving tender plants.

Shallow slopes (up to an 18° angle) can be terraced without building retaining walls. Just create a sloped earth bank between the flat terraces and plant with vegetation to prevent erosion. This can be any useful permanent plants: vines, low shrubs, groundcover, herbs or other perennials (maybe even a polyculture or various species).

Steeper slopes (up to 26°) can be terraced using low retaining walls. These should be a maximum of 36" high, which is generally the tallest you can legally go without a building permit. They should also lean inwards slightly (2" in 12"). Several low retaining walls are easier to build than one tall one, as there is less earth moving with a low wall.

On very steep slopes (over 26°) the retaining walls have to be higher and so get harder and more expensive to build. A series of large terraces is a big project, with possible serious consequences if they collapse (building codes require that they be designed by an engineer). This becomes a major project that is hard to justify in terms of cost and effort (unless all of your land is steep hillside). Steep slopes may even require steps so you can get around.

Terraces are usually built along the contour, starting at the lowest point. The first retaining wall is built and soil is pulled down from above to make a flat terrace. Ideally you should keep the topsoil on top and the subsoil on the bottom, but this isn't always easy.

Retaining walls for terraces can be made from reinforced concrete, stone, broken concrete, logs, heavy 3 x 10 timbers or railroad ties Dry stone walls are good because they don't need drainage. Old tires have been used for retaining walls and work great if you don't mind having hundreds of old tires in your garden, perhaps leaching who knows what into your soil (where I live you would probably need a permit for this as well).

A retaining wall must be strong enough to hold back all of that soil. Any posts should go into the ground deeper than the height they have to retain. If the wall isn't porous it will need a drain behind it to allow water to get out. This becomes critical as walls get taller, as water pressure can push them over. Put in a drain and backfill it with gravel (this is a good place to use up any concrete rubble). Any wall built without concrete should incorporate vegetation to help stabilize it.

Privacy

American gardens have traditionally been quite open to public view, particularly at the front (some local ordinances forbid enclosing the front yard). In these more crowded times privacy is becoming more appreciated and many gardens are now enclosed. You may want to delineate private activity areas near the house and screen them accordingly. The degree of privacy you require will depend upon the area. In some places you may be looked upon as hostile if you fence your yard, in others you will be looked upon as some kind of exhibitionist if you don't.

There are a lot more ways to create privacy than just a standard solid wood fence. You can use any combination of trees, shrubs, hedges, bamboo panels, screens, trellises, walls and various structures. You can add vines to make fences and walls more interesting and productive.

The height of a privacy screen can vary according to where it is located. A six feet tall screen is considered standard for privacy, but if you are only screening a sitting area then 4 feet might be enough. Normally you don't want to make it any higher than necessary, because you may add unwanted shade too.

Windbreaks

The placement of these is usually determined by the site; they go where they will most effectively block the wind. Usually they can also perform additional functions such as screening out ugly views, blocking noise, giving privacy and acting as a fence. See Windbreaks for more on these.

When siting buildings and fences you need to take care that you don't actually increase wind speed by funneling it through a narrow gap (the Venturi effect). If you already have such a spot, don't plant wind vulnerable plants there. Also keep greenhouses, seating areas and swimming pools away from it. Maybe you could put a wind generator there.

Storage

A shed is pretty much essential for keeping tools and materials safe, dry and in one place (where they can be easily located). In many places it is also necessary that they can be securely locked up.

It is also nice to have somewhere to store garden materials, lumber, wire fencing and all that stuff you bought on sale but don't yet have a use for. I have what can only be described as a small lumberyard out in a corner of my garden. This isn't very attractive so is screened from view.

Compost, mulch and manure should ideally be kept in a convenient central location, close to the main vegetable garden. You don't want to have to move them any more than necessary. They should also be well away from any sitting areas, as you don't want to smell them while you are relaxing (though they shouldn't really smell bad).

You might also need a storage place for larger items, motorcycles, cars, RV's boats.

Utilities

Once you have determined where you need electrical outlets, water faucets, irrigation risers and lighting, you can decide where to lay underground plumbing or electrical lines. To save work these should go in the same trench.

Aids to visualization

To get a better idea of how your plan will look in reality, you can physically mark things out directly on the ground. Use hoses or lines of ground limestone or wood ashes for curved lines. Use poles and stakes and string to get an idea of the height of components. Use cardboard and stakes for fences or walls. Set up furniture where you want to sit. Keep these things in place for several days, so you get a feel for how it would be, while you think of ways to improve them.

Legal niceties

There are often legal restrictions as to what you can and can't do on your property. Your title may include restrictions banning washing lines or tall front fences, or it might dictate compulsory lawn mowing every third Sunday. There are also building codes and planning laws to think about.

It goes without saying that you should always be considerate and respectful of your neighbors and not do anything that might adversely affect their gardens. Don't plant invasive plants near the property line, don't direct runoff water on to their land and don't block their sunlight. This is not only the right thing to do, it is commonly required by law.

You should also make sure your property is safe, so you don't get sued because of your pond, slippery paving or falling trees.

Efficiency and ecology

Efficiency means working with nature, rather than against her. Whenever you try to perpetuate something nature doesn't like (bare soil, a lawn in a dry climate) the result will be unstable and you will have to work (watering, weeding, mowing, fertilizing, trimming, thinning, fighting pests and disease) to maintain it.

Looking through conventional gardening books it is striking how much work you can create for yourself when you try to make nature conform to your ideal. Gardening can become an endless round of planting, deadheading, weeding, mowing, trimming, pruning, weeding, shearing, edging, raking and more weeding. No doubt this is a throwback to when people of importance had gardeners, so the more manicured your garden the more status you had.

In our nature-alienated and over-civilized society we have been indoctrinated to associate order and neatness with productivity and efficiency (the ultimate is straight clean, weed free rows of a single type of plant in a field of bare soil). Visual disorder and untidiness have become associated with inefficiency, poor planning and general slovenliness. In reality neatness may be a symptom of an overly simplistic view of things. That weed free crop surrounded by bare soil can only be maintained with large inputs of energy and is detrimental to the soil anyway.

Having an efficient garden means maximizing your returns for the effort expended. Decide how much time you can afford to devote to your garden and how you want to spend it. Do you want a small garden that will be meticulously cared for (with the rest in a natural state) or do you want a large area that is in a semi-wild state? If your time is limited you should think about this carefully, especially if you have a big garden. It is important because it affects how good your garden will look, how well it will function and ultimately how good you feel about it (is it a joy or a burden?)

If you plan carefully and use the right techniques (no-dig, mulch, drip irrigation), you can greatly increase the efficiency of your work time and eliminate a lot of the most tedious and repetitive work. Gardening often involves hard work, but this should have a meaningful goal and shouldn't need repeating every three weeks.

Labor saving suggestions

There are lots of ways to reduce work through design and a little thought now can save a lot of time in the future.

Use species (and varieties) that are adapted to your climate and situation (natives are particularly trouble free). Don't use plants that need more water than you can easily provide.

Avoid plants that won't grow well without frequent attention. Tender plants may be hit hard by frost every year (and require protection any time the temperature nears freezing),

Also avoid plants that are too vigorous for the site and so require constant pruning. Don't put vigorous plants where they may encroach on paths or other areas that people use a lot.

In a dry climate you should install a drip irrigation system. The initial work and expense of installation is nothing compared to the saving in water, frustration and time, as well as improved growth.

To simplify watering you should group plants with similar water requirements together.

In hot dry climates you should avoid lawns. They are the most wasteful component of modern gardens, taking more time, work, chemicals and water than anything else. You feed your lawn with expensive fertilizer and water to make it grow longer and then mow it every couple of weeks with a noisy, smelly, polluting machine to make it shorter. Instead of lawns you can cover large areas with groundcovers, locally adapted shrubs, native plants or a forest garden.

Bare soil grows weeds, erodes, gets muddy when wet, dries out rapidly, oxidizes organic matter, loses nutrients and can bake rock hard in summer. Keep it covered with plants or mulch and your life will be a lot easier.

Renounce your bourgeois neatness fetish and learn to love weeds, leaf litter and decaying vegetation. Cleanliness may be next to godliness somewhere, but not in the garden. In the garden it is an unhealthy obsession, as well as a losing proposition. There is absolutely no virtue in having row after row after row of completely weed free vegetable beds. It reduces biological diversity and leaves insects with no choice but to eat your crops. It is also a lot of work and deprives you of some good edible plants (weeds).

Any time you create a suitable niche (intentionally or not) something will try to grow there and won't stop trying, ever. You need to fill that niche before nature does. When making a flagstone path you can butt the stones as close together as possible, or you can leave a couple of inches between the flagstones and plant compact perennials such as Corsican Mint, Creeping Thyme or Chamomile. If you choose the first course you will have created an ideal niche for certain plants between the stones (they like the stone mulch, clear root run and the water that drains from the stones). As a result weeds will always try to grow there and you will be weeding indefinitely.

If people take short cuts and wear away vegetation don't repair the damage, just make that the path.

Keep your cultivated areas small and don't try to tame the world. If your garden is bigger than you need, let most of it revert back to native vegetation.

Of course if your garden is to produce much food it will require some maintenance. This leads us to the question of when extra work is worthwhile and when it isn't. If the work is justified by the reward then you will do it happily.

Fire

In hot dry wooded areas the threat of forest fire is an ever present danger every summer. Having experienced a wildfire in each of the last two summers this has become much more real to me than it once was. In the right conditions a fire moves very quickly and can destroy your garden in minutes (not to mention your house). By the time friends realized there was a fire on its way, they just had time to jump into their car and drive away, taking only the clothes on their backs. Fortunately there are lots of steps you can take to reduce the danger to your property and person. A little forethought now could save a lot of problems later.

Any dry vegetation can turn into a wildfire when conditions are right, but grassland, leaf litter and small shrubs can act like tinder and instantly turn a spark into a flame. When the fire inspector came to my house the only thing that concerned her was a patch of dry grass close to the house. Evergreen shrubs (such as chaparral) and trees don't ignite quite as easily as grass, but they burn much more fiercely. Moist deciduous woodland is much less inflammable, though it sometimes burns in spring before leafing out.

Fire varies in intensity according to how much fuel is available. When there is little ground fuel a fire burns slowly and doesn't harm tall, fire resistant trees. When there is a lot of ground fuel a fire burns everything before it, from the soil to the treetops.

The buzzword with fire protection is defensible space, which means creating a buffer zone around your house that fire can't easily cross. This is a non-inflammable area at least 30 feet wide and can incorporate driveways, patios, paths and non-inflammable plants. By incorporating a buffer zone into your master plan you can reduce the danger of fire considerably.
In high fire risk areas think about what the garden elements are made of, and use non-inflammable stone, brick, concrete and metal where possible. Patios are much better than decks in these situations, because they generally quite fireproof.

It is also important to keep the area around the house free of inflammable leaf litter, weeds and other dry debris. Pay particular attention to the roof and gutters. Dry leaves can sit there like tinder and are easily ignited by the flying embers coming off a fire. Also remove overhanging branches of inflammable trees.

Fences can cause wind turbulence which makes embers fall behind them. This can be a problem if there are dry plants growing on either side; the whole thing can quickly ignite and burn along the fence. For this reason it is important to keep fences free of inflammable material.

Heat rises, which means fire travels uphill much more rapidly than it descends (especially in conditions of high wind and low humidity). It is said that the speed of a fire doubles for every 10° increase in slope angle. You should take this into account when planning the garden layout.

Any water (pond, swimming pool, gray water field, even irrigated crops) should ideally be on the fire prone side.

Earthen berms are very effective at deflecting heat and can slow the progress of a fire. Bare soil areas also slow a fire; as if there is nothing to burn it won't.

Stone or brick walls can stop a ground fire in its tracks. If you live up-slope of lots of dry vegetation such a wall might be worth thinking about. Perhaps have a clear firebreak downhill from the house, then a wall with a patio and succulent green plants above it.

Sheds, wood piles, mulch piles and anything inflammable should ideally be up slope from the house.

Plants and fire

Planting is significant because it determines how readily an area will burn. Think about the kinds of plants, how much vegetation there is and its proximity to the house.

In areas subject to regular wildfires the native trees and shrubs are often so flammable they are known as pyrophytes (fire plants). They burn so quickly that the tops are gone before the heat builds up enough to damage the roots. Pyrophytes are considered to be fire tolerant because their tops can be burned to the ground and they will re-sprout from the root, reinvigorated. Obviously you don't want these kind of plants close to your house. Instead you should use plants that are not only non-inflammable, but are actually fire retardant. Most common crop plants are high water use and have succulent green leaves that smolder rather than burn (deciduous fruit trees are also good).

Avoid hedges of dry plants, as fire can move along them quickly (like a fuse). Hedges of moist succulent vegetation (Prickly Pear is good) are a different matter and may actually slow a fire for a while (though they may eventually be consumed). A windbreak of fire resistant trees can intercept flying embers and slow the spread of fire.

In hot dry areas you want to use drought tolerant plants to conserve water, but these often tend to be highly inflammable. Moisture loving plants are fire retardant, but of course demand irrigation. One solution to this is to use plants that store water for long periods, the succulents such as *Sedum* and *Mesembryanthemum*. These can be used as fire retardant groundcover for vacant spaces (they also prevent dry grass from growing there). If they contain a lot of dry dead plant matter even these will burn however. Another solution is to grow irrigated food crops and kill two birds with one stone.

Keep all of the plants near the house well watered. In an emergency sprinklers can be used to wet the area around the house so it won't burn easily. Some homeowners even install a sprinkler system on the house (this would need its own power source).

Beware of shrubs creating a ladder effect and allowing flames to climb up into the treetops or on to your house.

Grazing animals and chickens can keep vegetation low (this works even better if the area is irrigated to grow feed for them).

Aesthetic factors

There are plenty of things to think about when first creating your garden, so keep the initial design phase simple and don't torment yourself too much with aesthetics. However at some point in the future you might want to make your garden a little more aesthetically pleasing. Below are a few concepts from conventional landscaping that may be of use.

Balance

Balance just means keeping things in the right proportions. Don't have one area packed with interesting stuff and another area almost empty. Balance areas with a lot of hardscaping, with others filled mostly with plants. Strong shapes should be balanced by other strong shapes, without too much repetition. Tall objects could be balanced by lower ones (tall trees often have lower ones around them). Large open areas could be balanced by small enclosed ones. Orderly areas might be balanced by wild areas.

Color

Color affects the way we perceive an area, hot colors feel warmer and closer, cold colors feel cooler and further away. This effect is sometimes used in small gardens to make them seem larger (plant warm colored flowers are placed close by and cool colored ones further away).

The commonest color in the garden is green of course, which can get monotonous if not broken up with other colors. The easiest way to bring color into the garden is with low-maintenance perennials and self-seeding annual flowers. These require very little work on your part. Many fruits (and some leaves) are also colorful.

Color in the garden doesn't only mean flowers, it also means painted fences, walls, doors, tiles, fabric, stained glass, furniture and buildings. An effective strategy is to echo the color of plants with paintwork. Paint can also help to unify scattered elements such as buildings, fences and furniture. A problem with paint is that when you paint anything it will eventually need repainting, which can be difficult if plants have grown up around it in the meantime (use stain instead). Also painted wood can't usually be recycled.

Concealment

You can hide unattractive elements with screens,

hedges, fences, buildings, arbors, bamboo, shrubs, trees and vines (native plants are particularly good for this because they don't stand out).

It is important that your attempt to hide or disguise things is subtle, otherwise you may just draw attention to it. A long linear screen is often less effective than a single large plant strategically placed to simply break up the outline. Usually the best screen has another purpose as well.

The eye can also be distracted from eyesores by placing a particularly interesting focal point (pond, artwork) nearby.

A simple way to hide objects such as propane tanks is to cover them with netting and let plants grow over them (don't use too fine a mesh or birds, snakes and other wildlife may get entangled in it).

Depth
Traditionally a garden is given depth by putting low plants, paths and groundcovers in the foreground, furniture, mid size plants and planted beds in the middle ground and tall shrubs, trees, walls and buildings in the background.

Destinations
These are places of interest that motivate us to walk through the garden to visit them. They may be sitting places, artworks, ponds, fruit trees, views or buildings.

Focal Points
As our eyes wander around the garden we tend to follow horizontal lines, and pause on verticals and anything else of interest. You can encourage the eye to pause where you want by providing something interesting to look at. Humans are narcissistic creatures and find our own works more interesting than large undifferentiated masses of vegetation (no doubt because masses of vegetation are so commonplace). These human elements act as focal points to attract the eye and give it somewhere to pause. They also act as signposts indicating the comforting presence of human activity.

Each area of the garden should have something of interest as a focal point. This could be an arch, ornament, pond, fence, unusual plant, statue, sculpture, seat, gate, furniture, sundial, pergola and more. Don't have more than one focal point in each area though, or you risk making the garden look like a miniature golf course.

When placing any garden component you should consider how it will affect the view. Everything that is visible is potentially ornamental, so make it all look good. You already have an advantage in that useful elements are more authentic and relevant than those that are purely ornamental. Think of your garden as a movie set in which everything must look authentic. Compost bins, tool shed, greenhouse, tools (don't leave them laying around), wheelbarrow, even you should dress appropriately (what you find appropriate is a personal decision of course).

Movement
In Feng Shui some movement in the garden is considered desirable. You can introduce this with wind chimes, birdbaths, kinetic sculptures, smoke, windmills and flags (these could be the stars and stripes, a rainbow, the jolly roger or Tibetan prayer flags, depending upon your affiliation). Some plants (Aspens, Bamboo) move all the time and work well. Water is always moving too and could include rain chains, waterfalls, fountains and more.

The opposite of movement is stillness which is also desirable in certain situations. This can be emphasized with large boulders, statues or still water pools.

Proportion
All elements should be scaled according to the size of the garden and the things around them. Small objects have a tendency to look even smaller when placed outside and can almost disappear. Human created elements tend to shrink as plants grow larger around them, so make them too big rather than too small. A tree that is too big can make everything around it look small.

Sound
The garden should sound good as well as look good and in urban areas this often means eliminating unwanted noise. You can't close down a freeway (not for long anyway) so your next best option is to reduce the noise with berms, walls, hedges or trees, or a combination of these (ideally at least 25 feet deep).

Even simpler is to mask unwanted noise with pleasant sounds, such as falling water (dripping, trickling, splashing), wind sculptures and chimes or rustling leaves (Aspen, Bamboo and Eucalyptus are good).

Some animals are renowned for the soothing sounds they make. These include bees (attract them with Rosemary, Lavender and other nectar laden flowers), cicadas and birds (attract with food, water and shelter). Water will attract frogs, who get very noisy during mating season. Even if you don't need to mask any unpleasant noise, it may be worthwhile to add these pleasant sounds.

A garden-wide stereo system could also be used to mask noise, but it is definitely a last resort (and choose your music carefully, Puccini blends fairly easily, Nine Inch Nails not so easily.

Style
The style of the garden should be compatible with the house, location and climate. An English cottage garden out in the Mojave desert won't fit in very well.

Surprise
A sense of surprise (or even mystery) helps to make the garden more interesting and is one of the reasons gardens are commonly divided up into separate sections. This prevents you from seeing too much from any one place, so you have to keep moving.

Surprise is surprisingly lacking in many gardens, but isn't hard to create. It can be anything unusual or unexpected: hidden sculpture, a cave, spirit houses, mandalas, mazes and more.

Texture
The sense of touch can be satisfied by having a variety of garden surfaces with different textures. Slate, boulders, pebbles, sand, glass, water, wood, marble, copper, gravel, earth, wood chips, weathered wood, painted wood, hypertufa. Of course plants have a huge range of textures on their surfaces.

Unity/consistency
The garden may be divided into separate rooms, but they are all parts of the same whole and should work together to create a complete picture. The major components should relate to each other, the landscape and the house, whether by design, materials, color, planting or something else. Linear elements such as paths, streams, fences and walls all help to unify the garden.

Unify separate parts of the garden by using clusters of the same plants, fencing, path materials, shapes, colors mulch, groundcover or other elements. At the same time you should limit the number of objects, textures, colors and single plants. Too many different elements can make the garden look chaotic and disorganized.

Views
When deciding on the location of windows, seating areas, tables, work bench, paths, greenhouse and gateways, you should think about the view from them. You may be lucky and have spectacular distant views, or you might have to create an interesting focal point nearby.

You can't really create a spectacular view, but you can affect one. You might cut down plants to create a new viewpoint (be careful you don't expose things best left hidden), or you might plant a screen to direct your view.

Decorating the garden

Art
In an ideal world art would be in everything you do in life, but it's hard to make art out of sitting in traffic, grocery shopping or paying bills. The garden is your ideal world and your chance to liberate your "inner artist". Quite literally anything goes, so use paint, plywood cutouts, painted rocks, scarecrows, cast concrete, wire (draw 3 dimensionally with it), broken tile and anything else you can come up with. If you have any natural local clay you could use it to make sculptures and fire it in a pit. Almost anything you create will look good out in the garden, no matter how primitive or crudely made.

Art works especially well in the garden because it adds a human touch to nature and makes it into something special. It is important that they be mostly your art however (or friends art), not simply stuff you buy. In this way they help to personalize your garden.

Paint is another easy way to make the garden more artsy (remember that most painted wood isn't recyclable though). Have your children (or grandchildren) paint some rocks for you (with waterproof paint). They could also cast some concrete pavers.

Every object you put in the garden should be beautiful, whether a sculpture, a path or a shed. For garden use it should also be fairly weather resistant (unless you want it to slowly decay).

Ornamentation

Ornamentation also helps to personalize the garden and make it unique to you and your family. Any kind of ornament will work, so long as it is relevant to your life in some way, or to the history of the garden. Those you create yourself, out of things that you like, are especially good because they really mean something (unlike most of the commercial stuff). To me it seems against the spirit of gardening, even a bit pathetic, to go out and buy a pre-rusted garden ornament in an antique shop.

Ornamentation can be almost anything depending on your taste and situation. Statues, sculpture, lanterns, fountains, earthenware, old wheelbarrows, scarecrows, mirrors, buckets, rusted watering cans, even an old car could work (drain out the fluids and cover it with vines as a playhouse). You can also salvage things for the garden. I have seen old tires made into urns and rocking horses. Upturned clay plant pots look good and provide refuge for small creatures. Often the best ornaments also have a purpose, such as seats, birdbaths, sundials and containers for plants.

Some ornaments can add sound, such as gongs, bells and wind chimes. Others might be used to confine rampant growing plants such as the Mints, or as support for climbing plants.

Concrete carving

This technique enables you to easily make authentic looking "stone" sculptures, using a special mix of concrete and other additives. You can make any kind of stone carving you like, from Neolithic stone carvings to cubist statues. These are great personalized garden ornaments and (most importantly) are sure to impress your friends.

This is very much simpler than real stone carving, as the "stone" is carved before it is fully cured. It is still relatively soft at this stage and can be carved with simple tools.

The concrete mix can vary, depending upon what look you are after, but a basic mix might consist of:

1 part cement (this can be regular gray Portland cement, but the more expensive white gives you a mix that is easier to color)
2 parts sand (this can be anything except beach sand)
3 parts gravel (very fine gravel works best)
Color
Vermiculite or other material for texture

The whole procedure is pretty straightforward, you just mix up the concrete and put it into a mold. You may need to use a releasing agent (or line it with plastic) so it comes free easily. The concrete is removed from the mold from 6 to 24 hours later, depending upon the temperature. If you do it too soon the whole thing may just crumble, if you leave it too long it will be harder to carve. Carving is easy if you do it at the right time. Use any old tools: scrapers, saws, files, etc. The best way to learn this is to do it and experiment.

As a last resort you might also buy stuff of course (take no notice of me sundials, urns, statuary, balls on posts, birdbaths, dovecotes can all add a touch of elegance.

If you really have no artistic ability whatsoever don't despair. You can get inspiration from books, or by looking in other peoples gardens. Once you see what they have done in similar situations, it is sure to get your imagination fired up. If even that doesn't work, just copy them (not close friends of course, that could be embarrassing when they come to visit) .

Placing artwork and ornaments

Use artwork and ornamentation as a focal point to make an area more interesting. It could be immediately obvious as a focal point, or it might be half hidden to be discovered as you explore the garden.

Large art objects bring a suggestion of drama, while small ones suggest intimacy. However any ornament should be proportional to the space it occupies, not too big or small (except when used for dramatic effect).

Container plants

These are useful as focal points and to mark a special stairway or path, though they can be moved around the garden as necessary. Containers for planting might include plant pots, troughs, plumbing fixtures, galvanized containers, sections of clay pipe, chimney pots, sinks, corroded brass buckets, even old toilets have been used. The only criteria is that it must have holes for drainage (though pots could be placed inside it). See Planting in containers for more on this.

Birdhouses

Birdhouses (or dovecotes if you prefer) are a vernacular art form that adds to the garden even if no birds actually live in them (it's better if they do though). They can be anything from hollowed out gourds or logs to elaborate multi turreted dovecotes. They are not only ornamental in themselves, but with luck may also attract interesting birds.

Renta-hermit

In Victorian Britain it was once fashionable for a large estate to have a resident hermit, who lived in a specially made rustic retreat. A few people actually made a living as professional hermits for while. If you are interested in reviving this you could no doubt find someone pretty easily. If your garden and retreat are really nice (and have fast wi-fi) you might shoot me an e-mail.

Animals

There are many books on how to attract wildlife to your garden, but as this type of garden matures and diversifies, animals will come whether you want them or not. Some people like to have domesticated animals in their garden, claiming they bring it to life and make it more whole. In a few cases they can also increase your self-sufficiency with minimal extra work.

Bees – These are one of the easiest creatures to deal with, after the initial investment and effort of getting them established. Bees are so independent you can just forget about them while they work for you, making honey and pollinating your fruit trees and other plants. A good hive can produce 100 lb. of honey in a year, so bees were very important for peasant families before the introduction of sugar. They were so highly prized they were treated as special members of the family and were even told of important family events such as births and marriages.

Put a beehive well away from frequently used areas, but fairly close to large areas of flowering plants. They will also go and forage in neighbors gardens.

If you don't want to deal with bees you might allow a beekeeper to put hives in your garden in exchange for a share of the honey.

Chickens and ducks - If you are aiming for a greater degree of self-reliance then chickens or ducks can be useful. They have long been prized as a way to convert things we can't eat into high protein food, and it is possible to pretty much feed them from the garden. Of course if you are going out and buying bags of chicken food you aren't really producing food, you are just converting it from one form to another.

Chickens can be used to clear and manure small areas of vegetation by confining them in a moveable pen known as a chicken tractor. They can also be housed under the staging in the greenhouse, where they will provide carbon dioxide and body heat (they benefit from the warmth and shelter of the greenhouse).

If given the chance they will eat slugs, snails and many insect pests (Guinea Fowl can help to keep an area free of ticks). In areas with a lot of garden insect problems, chickens have been used to protect the vegetable garden by creating a chicken moat. This consists of two fence that completely surround the intensive garden, with the chickens running between them. The fences keep larger pests out of the garden and keep the chickens confined. The chickens prevent any pests moving into the garden from elsewhere.

Fish - A fishpond could work well if you eat fish, but it is quite an involved process and well beyond the scope of this book.

Koi bring beauty, movement and life into the garden and are quite fascinating. They are too expensive to eat, but you might be able to raise them for sale.

Feeding chickens from the garden

The most obvious way to feed chickens is to allow them to free range around your garden, so they can eat wild greens, seeds, insects and anything else they can find. You can also give them your kitchen scraps (anything they don't eat can go into your worm bin). Of course you can't let them go just anywhere as they will then eat many of your crop plants too.

You can grow your own chicken feed in the form of seed bearing plants, such as Quinoa, Amaranth, Millet, Giant Lambs Quarters, Buckwheat, Cleavers, Sorghum and Sunflower. Just throw the plants to the chickens and let them do the harvesting. You can also feed them whole pumpkins, just smash them up.

Chickens also like fresh greens like Wheat and Barley grass, Kale, Lettuce, Spinach, Orach, Cleavers and Giant Lambs Quarters. You don't even have to harvest this stuff; the birds will do it themselves. Chickens will also eat perennial Comfrey and Stinging Nettles, to the point where you may have to protect the plants so they can recover. Their greens can be dried for winter feed.

The birds will also eat any windfall fruit, in fact some species (Mulberries, Persimmons) have been planted specifically to feed chickens. Chestnuts, Oaks and other nuts are also good, though you will have to smash the shells (the birds will pick out the kernels).

Corn and beans are also good, but require grinding. Very small potatoes or sweet potatoes can be cooked and fed to chickens.

You could also feed them excess worms from a worm bin or even breed maggots.

Dogs - An active dog can be a big help in keeping raccoons, deer and other mammals out of the garden. If it is active enough you won't even need a fence. It has to be out in the garden at night though and it has to be big and aggressive enough, otherwise raccoons will just intimidate it. Of course an untrained dog can also make a big mess as it jumps about, runs over beds, dig holes and scratches up plants.

The dog that guards the garden should have a kennel for comfort. Give the dog it's own covered spot near the area to be guarded and have a source of water and both sunny and shady areas. Unfortunately there isn't a canine equivalent of Catnip to keep dogs interested.

In a large garden you might have a dog run where you could exercise your dog with frisbee, balls and sticks, in the comfort of your own home. Put it out in the wild area where it won't damage important plants.

Cats - A skilled and motivated cat can be a very effective rodent catcher, but they also catch a lot of innocent wildlife too. There's nothing like having a half dead gopher dropped on your bed at 3.00 a.m.

Rabbits are often said to be the best backyard meat producer, though being cute and fuzzy many people have problems killing them (it's too much like killing and eating your cat). Permaculturists are fond of describing how well these and other animals can fit into the scheme of things. As a vegetarian I'm the wrong person to talk about this though (I feel guilty about killing Alfalfa sprouts).

Wildlife

You can increase the diversity of wildlife by planting their preferred food plants, supplying water (birdbath, pond) and by creating a diversity of habitat (all of which you will be doing anyway). This might include ponds, wooded areas, open areas, moist soil, standing dead wood, pits and mounds and piles of rocks or logs. You might also provide refuges and nesting sites, such as upturned plant pots or bundles of hollow stem plants such as Bamboo or Tithonia.

The final plan

In as much as there is a final plan, you almost have it. You now transfer all of your final ideas on to the paper plan, so they are all in one place. Of course you will be learning an adjusting this plan as you go, and will slowly refine the garden. Before you actually start building any new section of garden you should re-evaluate your paper plans in the light of what you have learned in the meantime. As you gain experience and confidence you will be better able to judge how well things will work.

The evolving garden

Gardening is an evolutionary activity and commonly the garden will grow over time. You aren't finished with design just because it is planted, mulched and growing. In fact the end of the design phase is rather like the end of a pregnancy; it is more of a beginning than an end. Nature is never static and your garden will always be growing and changing; day to day, through the seasons and over the years. Things change especially rapidly in this kind of garden because you are constantly cutting plants for food, building materials, mulch and more. If traditional gardens resembled painting, then this kind of garden is more like performance art.

The changing proportions of growing plants will radically alter the garden over time. Some plants grow so well they threaten to take over, some will just stay as they are and some may start to fade and die (or be killed). As the garden matures plants sometimes start self-sowing that never did before. Flowers may bloom for longer and be more productive and may even suffer less from frost. Trees get bigger and may start to affect the plants around them (or require paths to be rerouted). The amount of shade will also increase. Coppiced plants change even more rapidly as they go through their cutting and growth cycles.

There are also be human changes. It's hard to imagine, but before you know it that childrens play area will be empty and silent (enjoy it while you can). As you get older you become less able to do hard physical work, and may want to make the garden lower maintenance.

You can plan for some of the changes that will take place in the garden in the future, but you must always live with the now. As you live with your garden you will continually think of ways to improve it and to correct earlier mistakes. No garden is ever totally perfect, there are always improvements to be made, new elements to be added and adjustments to be made in response to unforeseen situations.

The great thing about gardening is that no matter how poor the initial design, it will get better as nature gets involved. With enough flowers, herbs, shrubs, trees and vines, even a wrecking yard could look like the garden of Eden.

Choosing plants

For convenience sake I've separated planting the garden from designing the garden, but they are both parts of the garden design process and are created simultaneously. The hardscaping is important for human convenience and comfort, but gardening is really about plants. A garden is a place where you can really get to know your plants intimately. You get to watch them up close through every stage of their life cycle and learn their likes and dislikes. Plants physically make up most of the garden and provide most of its interest. They also produce food of course, which is a what this kind of garden is really about.

Which plants?

Grow what you eat, eat what you grow

The first rule of food gardening is to grow the things you enjoy eating. If it doesn't get used, then it is a waste of space. This may seem like stating the obvious, but it's easy to get sidetracked into growing stuff because it grows well and is interesting. Then you end up with a garden full of fascinating stuff that no one uses. If you see this happening you must be ruthless and purge some of the plants you don't use. Of course in a big garden (and if you have enough water) you can grow everything that can survive.

Some food plants aren't as useful as others. Some don't taste very good. Some require a significant amount of processing, which can reduce their appeal (especially if they are inexpensive to buy). Be cautious about those multi-use plants that sound great on paper, but aren't very good for any one thing and so don't actually get used for anything.

Useful plants

Most of the plants in the garden should earn their keep in some way. This is most often as food, but it could also be for medicine, cosmetics, crafts, drinks, perfume, cut flowers, or as raw materials for specific crafts (basket making, dyeing, woodworking, wine or beer making). A very important, though not very glamorous) use is as a source of biomass for mulch and making compost. Some plants have multiple uses; they might produce fruit, have edible flowers, fix nitrogen, look good, smell good and give shade. A few might simply have interesting historical uses and be grown as a topic of conversation.

Whereas the ornamental gardener strives to have something in flower all the year round, I aim to have a succession of foods available year round. Plants that produce in winter and early spring are particularly useful in this regard. In my garden these include Lemons, Mandarins, Kiwi Vines, Jerusalem Artichoke, Oca, Lettuce, Kale, Brussels Sprouts, Cabbage, Broccoli, Leeks, Hamburg Parsley, Carrot, Parsnip, Spinach, Cornsalad, Cilantro, Radicchio, Welsh Onions, Bay, Parsley and more.

There is a lot of room for experimentation with unusual wild plants to produce low-maintenance and perennial crops. I'm always looking for low work edibles, which is one of the reasons I wrote The Uses of Wild Plants.

I have found the Plants for a future database (pfaf.org) to be helpful. It lists plant uses, propagation requirements, size of plants, habitat and more.

Uses of plants

Productive gardening isn't just about planting the right things in the right places and taking care of them. It is also about making the fullest use of the plants as they grow. Using each species for multiple purposes, using cut and come again techniques to maximize yields, using flowers, saving seed. You can use woody prunings for fences, stakes, supports for plants, dead hedges and of course mulch. Use green leaves and shoots for green manure, compost, liquid fertilizer, mulch and more.

Low-maintenance plants

Wild plants are able to grow without our help because they are perfectly adapted to their location. We run into trouble with domesticated plants when we ignore their needs and put them where we want them to grow. This only works for as long as we are prepared to care for them and they disappear as soon as we stop. The key to an easy gardening life is to identify the natural conditions of the site (soil type, microclimate, moisture) and use plants that are adapted to grow there. Any plant that is well suited to the growing conditions can be low-maintenance. Several times I have discovered plants I thought had died, still surviving years after I forgot about them.

Most common vegetable crops are adapted to growing in the rich, moist, neutral soil of the vegetable garden, and need a considerable amount of care if they are to be productive. However you have a lot more options for the rest of the garden. You can use suitably adapted low-maintenance trees, shrubs, perennial food crops, herbs for most of the growing areas. Anywhere that isn't needed to produce food should be planted with no-maintenance native plants (these are also used to create the garden framework).

If you don't have a lot of time to spend in your garden (or if you have a lot of space) you will want to concentrate mostly on lower maintenance plants. Traditionally this meant tough plants like Ivy, Periwinkle and Juniper that can survive anywhere, but these plants don't produce anything worthwhile (except for some biomass).

Though low-maintenance is a desirable goal, it has to be balanced against productivity. If you want a highly productive garden you will have to use highly productive plants, which usually require some maintenance. I love fruit trees (and their fruit) and can't have enough of them. To me their beauty and fruitfulness are the essence of the garden, but I read one book that solemnly warned the reader to never plant fruit trees because the mess and work involved in growing them. You have to find a balance between how much work you are prepared to do and how much you want your garden to produce. I'm happy to do extra work (especially interesting work like pruning) if I get a good return for my effort.

Another aspect of low-maintenance is choosing plants that are the right size for the location. As soon as you start squeezing plants into spaces that are too small, you are creating work for yourself because you will eventually have to start dealing with competition.

For an easy life avoid plants that are too aggressive, tender, weak or fussy. All of these extremes mean additional work.

Climate adapted plants

Plants that are adapted to your local growing conditions require less resources and care and so are easier to grow. The food crops that are adapted to your climate (and you like to eat) will be important elements in your planting scheme.

There is also considerable variation in climate adaptation within most common crops and you can find varieties suited to almost any climate (there are apples for North Dakota plains and Apples for Beverly Hills). Choosing the right variety for your area can make a big difference in your success.

The more difficult the climate, the more important it is to use well adapted plants. I have tried just about every useful plant I have been able to find and the ones that have really thrived are – predictably – those from a similar Mediterranean climate.

The best way to find out which plants will produce reliably in your garden is to talk to an experienced local gardener about what they grow. As a bonus they will often give you divisions, cuttings and seeds of suitable plants. You should also look at what is already growing around you, in nearby, parks, waste places, woods and botanical gardens. Local nurseries can also be helpful and generally carry plants that do well in the area.

You should also take a look at the naturalized plants that grow around about. Suburban areas are often full of interesting useful escapees from garden. These are good plants to use because they are already growing by themselves (and can often be obtained for free). In my area Centranthus, Nasturtium, New Zealand Spinach Watercress, Alyssum and Pampas Grass are just a few of the useful escapes I've seen growing wild.

Just because a plant isn't commonly grown doesn't necessarily mean it won't do well in your climate. If you do your research you will find many unusual plants that are fairly easy to grow. It's just that people don't grow them because they aren't very familiar (or because they are hard to find).

Native plants

The ultimate low-maintenance, climate adapted, plants are the natives of your area; the plants that would be growing there if it weren't a garden. These are ideally adapted to local conditions of course and thrive with minimal care and attention. They also help to give the garden a sense of place in the larger landscape

Of course local conditions vary enormously, so just because a plant is native to your area, this doesn't mean it is adapted to the conditions in your garden, When we talk about using native plants we mean using those that would naturally grow in your conditions.

If you grow useful native plants you can have productivity as well as low-maintenance (you can have your fruit and eat it too). A surprising number of wild plants produce food or other useful products, such as teas, fruits, greens, nuts, medicines, compost material, wildlife food and more. It is a good idea to use these to create the framework of the garden (hedges, shade trees, windbreaks, groundcovers and more) and to fill in any vacant areas. Even if you don't find a use for a native plant, some wild animal no doubt will.

In dry areas, where the availability of water is a major factor, native plants become even more important.

Insectory and Bee Plants

These provide food for the adult forms of many predatory insects and can increase the population of these beneficials in the garden. The small nectar rich flowers of members of the Carrot (*Apiaceae*), Daisy (*Asteraceae*) and Mint (*Lamiaceae*) families are particularly valuable in this regard.

If you keep bees you may want to grow some plants to supply nectar early and late in the year (many plants produce nectar in summer). Even if you don't have bees you may want to attract them (and other beneficial insects) for pollination, pest control and diversity. The most useful herbaceous bee plants include Borage, Buckwheat, Clover, Thyme, Dead Nettles and Mints. Useful woody species include Almond, Basswood. Tupelo, Lavender and Rosemary.

Insecticidal plants

These plants can be used to control or repel pests in the garden. Some have an effect while growing (*Tagetes* is nematocidal), but most are used as insecticides or repellents after processing in some way. Such plants include Pyrethrum Daisy, Tephrosia, Garlic, Tobacco, Hot pepper and more.

Fungi

If you can get mushrooms such as the King Stropharia or Shaggy Mane established in your garden, they will produce food with little work from you. All you have to do is supply them with a fresh layer of mulch every year.

Commercial crops

If you have the room and resources you might think about possible commercial crops (vegetables, fruit, herbs, seedlings, basket Willows, edible fungi). If you want to try growing something new on a commercial basis, I suggest you start small initially and experiment until you get it right, before making a big investment.

Plants you can depend on

Some plants can be relied upon to produce food almost every year with very little care. As you gain experience you will learn which of these will work in your situation.

In my vegetable garden I have found Russian Kale, Chard, Giant Lambs Quarters, Rhubarb, Welsh Onion and Amaranth (edible seed and leaves) to quite literally grow themselves.

Trees that bear fruit reliably in my garden include: Apples, Cherries, Chestnuts, Plums, Peaches, Mandarins, Nectarines and Walnuts.

Other reliable fruiting plants include Kiwis, Strawberries, Blackberries, Raspberries (sometimes 2 crops in a season), Grapes, Lemons (they produce almost continually year round) Figs (often produce twice in a season), Alpine strawberries (I have harvested fruit for eight months straight), Strawberries and Blueberries (if you keep birds away).

As for flowers I have found Hollyhock, Evening Primrose, Yarrow, Malva and Calendula to be almost indestructible. These are real no maintenance ornamentals and flower for months at a time.

Many herbs are true no-work plants including: Chives, Sage, Marjoram, Mints, Oregano, Rosemary, Bay, Vietnamese Coriander and Cilantro.

Adapting the site to fit the plant

Though it makes sense to choose plants that are adapted to the growing conditions, you also want to grow foods that you will eat. There's no point in growing things that are well adapted to your site, if you ignore them and go out and buy the things you like to eat. If a plant isn't well suited to your garden and you can't find a suitable existing microclimate, you could try permanently altering the growing conditions to suit it. You might use windbreaks, walls or other thermal mass to create a suitable microclimate. You can also give plants additional protection over the winter (even to the point of wrapping deciduous species).

Be warned that growing plants that aren't well adapted to the conditions can be frustrating. They often don't fruit well and are vulnerable to extreme weather that comes along every so often. Tender plants won't survive very cold winters and many cold winter plants won't thrive in mild climates where they don't get a long enough winter rest.

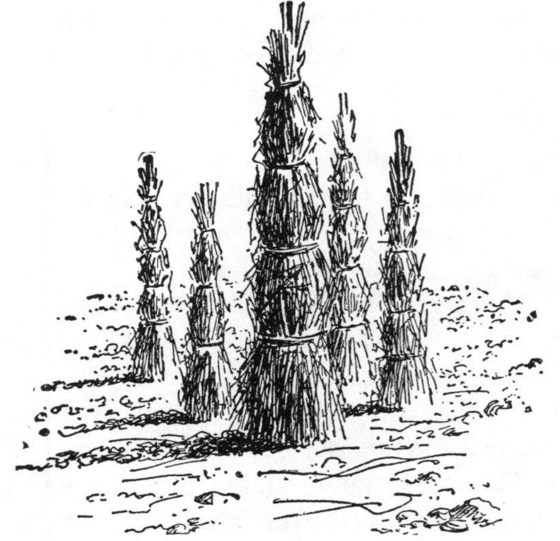

If you really want to experiment with marginal plants then go for it (that's what gardening is all about), just don't become too attached to them and don't get your hopes up too high. Even if you succeed in producing fruit or whatever, it may not taste the same as it would under ideal conditions. Oranges are sour in cool climates because heat is needed to produce the sugar that makes them sweet. Spearmint growing in hot dry soil will be inferior to that growing in cool, moist conditions. There's no point growing something you like to eat, if it doesn't end up tasting as you like it.

Other reasons to grow plants

Of course you don't have to listen to my advice on what to plant; you can grow any plant you choose for any reason at all. Here are a few good reasons.

Beautiful plants

Beauty is everything in conventional gardening, which I think is a bit shortsighted. We all appreciate beauty of course, but most of us don't choose our friends purely on the basis of their appearance, we take other qualities into account too. I don't think we should choose our plant friends in this way either, we should choose them for what they will give us (this isn't the best way to choose human friends though.) It's nice if your plants are beautiful, but beauty really is in the eye of the beholder. All healthy, vigorously growing plants are beautiful, its just that some are more so than others.

Beauty doesn't preclude utility of course and many useful plants are often just as attractive as any ornamental. Peaches, Juneberry, Persimmon and Almonds are all spectacular when in bloom and go on to bear delicious and attractive fruit. As water becomes scarcer and more expensive, it is a lot easier to justify a beautiful garden if it is also producing food.

Favorite plants

Gardening is supposed to be fun and if you particularly love some useless plant then of course you should plant it. I particularly love Sunflowers and would grow them even if they didn't produce edible seeds. I also love Jasmine for its billowing scented flowers (though I probably wouldn't grow it if it didn't grow like a weed). I also grow Mock Orange (*Philadelphus*) simply because this tough plant was a favorite of my dad and was one of only two vigorously living things in out paved city backyard (Spearmint was the other).

Family Trees

You could plant special trees to mark family occasions like births, marriages and deaths. You might also plant a tree for each member of the family (let everyone choose a tree of their own).

Scented plants

Smell is our most under utilized sense but we can help to remedy this by making the garden a feast for the nose. There are tons of wonderfully scented plants to choose from: trees, shrubs, vines perennials and annuals.

Scented flowers work best in protected areas (courtyards, porches and enclosed garden rooms), where the scent can linger without getting blown away. Plants with scented leaves may be used as path edging, or even on the paths if low enough. They release their scent as they get brushed or crushed as you go past.

There are also the powerfully night scented white flowers that only open at dusk. These should be placed around windows and doors and on the patio where you relax in the evening.

Some of my favorite scented plants

Trees – Citrus, Balsam Poplar.

Shrubs – Azalea (some), Rose, Lavender, Angels Trumpet.

Vines – Jasmine, Honeysuckle, Moonflower, Stephanotis.

Perennials – Pelargonium, Mints (especially Orange Mint), Lilies, Violet.

Annuals – Night Scented Stock, Nicotiana, Patchouli

Practical considerations

Where to find plants

The best (or at least the fastest, easiest and cheapest) way to get plants is from friends and neighbors who already grow them. After a few years of gardening most people have a surplus of the plants that grow well in their gardens (which are exactly the ones you want). These can be divided, grafted or grown from cuttings. There is a good and pragmatic reason for gardeners to be generous with their spare plants and cuttings; they are a good insurance policy. If you lose a plant for any reason you can always get it back again from someone you gave it to.

The commonest fruiting trees and shrubs are readily available as bare root plants in garden centers in spring (and to a lesser extent in pots later on). The best place to get more unusual plants is from the various mail order companies. The internet makes this much quicker than it used to be. In many cases you can look through their catalogs on-line, order immediately and have your plants in a few days.

An interesting source of plants I have only recently discovered is craigslist.com, where people list plants they have grown in their own gardens. I recently bought some unusual adaptogenic herbs I hadn't seen anywhere else from there. I also got to meet someone who shared an interest of mine. The potential here is enormous for finding interesting plants that can be grown locally, and for meeting like-minded gardeners.

The cost of Plants

It is said that the cost of plants is only about 15–20% of the cost of a landscaping job. If you are doing the work yourself then you will be saving a lot of money on labor, so can afford to spend a little more on plants. Plants can be a great investment (if they don't die on you) and it really pays to concentrate on acquiring them in the early years. Those $10.00 plants may seem expensive, but next year they will have grown into $40.00 plants and will seem like a bargain.

If you are poor I suggest you avoid the marginally hardy plants that might, or might not, survive in your garden. Concentrate on those you know won't die simply because you forgot to cover them on a cold winter night.

At the end of the summer my local garden center often has a sale on ragged looking perennials that have sat crowded in their pots for months. I find these are often a good deal. I just divide them up and they come up as several rejuvenated plants the following spring.

When you bring any plant into your garden it is important to make sure that it is healthy and not carrying any pest or disease.

Getting plants from the wild

I hesitate to mention this because it is just inviting criticism, but I feel I have to say something. Conventional wisdom says we should never take plants from the wild as it disrupts and degrades native ecosystems. Obviously we need to protect out natural resources, but I don't think you need to completely rule out using local wild plants. In fact if you are going to grow native plants then you should use those that are part of the local gene pool and you can only do this by using plants of local provenance.

This doesn't mean I am advocating that you go out and help yourself to any interesting plants you come across (you should never do this). I am saying you could use your intelligence and propagation skills to take cuttings, remove suckers, layer some branches and collect seed of suitable species (if it is abundant). You might also thin out and transplant overcrowded seedlings, most of which would die anyway. These activities do much less damage than the overpopulation of deer caused by our wiping out their predators. In this way you can get planting stock without harming wild plants.

Invasive plants

The reverse of taking plants from the wild is accidentally introducing them into the wild. When creating a low-maintenance garden we prize plants that thrive with little care, but this independence presents the possibility that they may naturalize in the wild and become a pest. You need to be aware of this and if there is any possibility of a plant becoming a problem you should avoid it.

There is also the issue of plants getting out of control in your garden. Some creeping plants (Bamboo, Mint) will spread inexorably if they aren't confined or restricted in some way. They may be kept within bounds with plastic root barrier, sheet metal, concrete or even the house foundation). In dry climates you can often keep a plant under control by not watering it,

Existing plants

Existing plants can potentially provide you with a ready made garden framework, so make use of them where possible. If in doubt, leave it in - you can always remove a plant later. You could also plant in between the existing plants and then remove them later.

Ease of propagation

Some plants are very easy to propagate vegetatively (*Ficus, Morus, Ribes, Rubus, Eleagnus, Lycium, Vitis, Salix, Populus, Rosa, Robinia*). These species are well represented in my garden because it didn't cost much to build up a stock of plants. All I had to do was buy one (where self-fertile) or two (in the case of cross-pollinated) plants and take cuttings.

Some plants are easy to grow from seed and these will be important, because buying a packet of seed can be much cheaper than buying even a single plant. This not only gives you a lot more plants for your money, it also gives you more genetic diversity than a bunch of cuttings. This isn't necessarily a slow process either, given the right conditions some seedlings can grow amazingly fast.

How many trees do you need

The number of trees you can use depends upon how much room you have A small garden may only have room for a few compact dwarf trees and you will have to plan where to put them carefully. A big garden gives you much more freedom and might even have room for large nut trees such as Walnuts, Pecans or Chestnuts. In some places the limiting factor may be how much water you have available, or how much shade you want to create.

There is also the consideration of how much work you want to do. In a very large garden you could go on planting forever, but of course you have to consider the work involved and what you will do with all of the food (I suppose you could create a uniquely diverse farm).

The more plants you have of each species, the greater the number of varieties you can have, and the longer the harvest period. However a family only needs so many lemons or Bay leaves, so don't grow more than you need. If you are growing ten times more than you can use, just because they grow easily, you aren't being more productive.

The plant list

Your plant list should include all of the plants you want to grow, the quantities needed and their growing preferences. Are they sun lovers, nitrogen fixers, shade tolerant, heavy or light feeders, moisture loving or drought tolerant? Do they need acid or alkaline soil? Compiling this list will involve some research to find out which varieties will work best for you, in terms of climate, flavor, maintenance and more.

After a while you will develop a list of reliable plants that are best suited to your garden (and neighborhood). Plants that produce useful foods; are productive and require little maintenance.

Your plant list should be divided according to how much attention the plants require, as this will simplify placing them in the garden (they will go in the appropriate zones). You could further divide the list according to the type of plant (large trees, small trees, dwarf trees, large shrubs, climbers, small shrubs, vines, perennial herbs, annuals, aquatics), or by their growing preferences (full sun, light shade, deep shade, moist soil, dry soil). You could also organize them by the roles they play (screens, hedges, overhead shade). In arid areas you will probably divide them according to their water requirements (low, medium and high) and perhaps subdivide for sunlight requirements

Maintenance levels

Native plants - (Trees, shrubs and wild plants) These totally independent plants will be mostly concentrated in the outer zones, but may also be used for the permanent garden framework (hedges, shade trees, screens, windbreaks and more).

Weeds – (Amaranth, Lambs Quarters, Purslane, Dandelion) These grow themselves of course, so provide food with no effort from you. Of course they can become a problem if they get out of hand, but if your garden is heavily mulched they shouldn't be an issue. You can also keep them under control by regular harvesting.

Potentially invasive plants – (Mints, Jerusalem Artichoke, Bamboo). These plants will happily grow without your assistance, but you need to keep an eye on them as they can become a problem if they get out of hand. They be kept under control by using them.

Independent, vigorous and long-lived, locally adapted plants – (Hollyhock, Calendula, Evening Primrose, many herbs). I love these species as they are useful , yet are capable of living completely independently.

Plants that need occasional help - These plants may need assistance to get established and perhaps occasional feeding, watering and weeding to maximize harvest.

Plants that need regular help - These plants need intermittent feeding, watering and weeding. They should be in zone 1 or 2.

Plants that need frequent attention - These need attention (feeding, watering, weeding, protection from frost) on a regular basis. They are the most time consuming plants to grow and belong in zone 1. To justify their cultivation they have to provide a good crop.

Where to plant

Planning the growing areas

Your goal is to create a situation whereby your plants have everything they need to grow and function happily, so they will be productive with a minimum of attention. It is especially important to put food-bearing plants in the right place, because it isn't enough for them to just survive, to be productive they need to thrive.

The next step is to decide which plants to put in each area. Many factors will influence where you put them: the growing conditions, the purpose of the area, how much maintenance they require, their water and pollination needs, their final size and the convenience of maintaining and harvesting them. Paper planning is the easiest way to organize all of these separate elements and come up with a workable plan that minimizes maintenance and water use. It's hard to organize your plants properly without it.

The trees (and larger shrubs) are the first priority, because they get so big and need so much time to grow. They will become the framework of the garden in years to come, so it's important to put them in the right places (not too close to each other, to established trees, to buildings or where they will cast unwanted shade). A good way to do this is to plan them on paper, using cut out circles (to the scale of your plan). Move them around on the plan until you come up with an arrangement you like (you could also make cutouts of other components). If you put them in exactly the right places, they can also provide shade, privacy, shelter from the wind and more.

Some people like to work on a small section of the garden at a time, designing and then fully planting it, before moving on to the next section. This can work out okay, except that all of the plants receive an equal amount of light, which isn't good for shade lovers (it also requires a lot of plants). Another way is to plant the trees and large shrubs (the earlier the better) in all of the areas (mulch and lay down irrigation if needed). You can then go back later and plant the rest as plants become available.

Identify the growing conditions

Any area of the garden that isn't used for specific activities can be used for growing plants. These areas don't have to be beautiful, so concentrate all of your effort into making them productive, efficient and low-maintenance.

Intelligent planting starts with identifying the growing conditions in an area, which might include full sun, part shade, deep shade, dry soil, average soil and wet soil. You must also take into account any variations in microclimate due to slope, wind, thermal mass, sun exposure and more. These could be used to give tender plants extra heat (or hardy plants extra chill). Problem areas (frost pockets, shade, unusually wet, dry or acidic soil) will require specialized plants that can tolerate the conditions. Any area with distinct differences will be considered a separate growing area and should be marked down as such on your site plan.

The growing areas will vary in size according to their use, which could include growing intensive vegetable crops, staple crops, fruit trees, bush fruit, edible ornamentals, perennial vegetables, forest gardens, herbs and more.

How many growing areas you need will depend upon how much food you want to grow and how much space the plants require. Don't plant more than you need of each crop (plant a greater variety instead).

In addition to the growing conditions you have to consider other factors, such as the distance of an area from the house (especially for the vegetable garden) and the amount of attention you want to give to each one. Think about zoning when deciding on these. The growing areas for high maintenance plants must be close to the house. Lower maintenance ones are mostly further away (though you should try to make them all as low-maintenance as possible). In dry climates the amount of water you can supply to each area will be also be a factor.

If the whole garden has very uniform growing conditions you can alter some areas to suit your needs. Plant trees for shade, raise a bed area for better drainage, slope the beds to the south for greater solar gain. A wall could block the wind and trap the sun. You could also build a pond and a bog area.

Planting the growing areas

For low maintenance it is essential to give your plants the growing conditions they evolved to grow in. If you do this they will be happy and grow well without needing much attention from you. This is one of the most important things you can do to make the garden function well.

With a few important exceptions, food producing plants are more productive if they get full sun, because they can photosynthesize more food. To successfully grow most common food crops you have to give them the best growing areas in the garden (whether spots for individual plants or areas for growing beds). The vegetable garden area requires sun and more sun if it is to be productive as well as fertile soil (it should also be near the house). Fruit trees need sun and rich deep soil.

You need to decide which growing areas are best suited to each purpose (herb garden, staple food garden, forest garden). If you are lucky you will have lots of good locations, in which case you can concentrate on placing the activity areas first. In a small garden you have to use the best areas for plants, so don't put other components there. In those situations you may even have to adapt the location to fit the plants.

Planting

Planting for maintenance

If your planting list was arranged according to the amount of attention the plants require, then you will plant according to the zones. The high maintenance plants are placed in the intensively managed areas close to the house, and lower maintenance ones go further out. The latter can be planted anywhere of course, but it makes sense to put them in areas that may be neglected (and save the limited space in the intensive areas for weaker plants).

Planting to build the garden

Some plants have special functions as windbreaks, screens, hedges and sources of shade. Their placement is pretty straightforward as you put them where they will best do the job. Of course you also have to choose the right species for the existing growing conditions (see below for more on this).

Planting for water requirements

In a dry climate you have to balance the number, species and arrangement of plants, to the amount of water that is available. Divide your plants up into categories according to how often they require water (water loving, semi-drought tolerant and drought tolerant). You then separate the growing areas into hydrozones, according to how often you will water them.

Hydrozones

3 days - Plants that need a lot of water should be grown in the inner zone, where you use multiple drip lines to keep the soil in the beds fully moist.

1 week - The second zone could have plants spread out along a single drip line.

3 weeks - The third zone could have individual drippers wherever necessary.

Never - Plants in this zone depend on nature for their water (either from rainfall or moisture held in the soil, Some crop plants may be grown if widely spaced, so each plant can get enough water. This area mostly consists of native (or locally adapted) plants that fend for themselves.

If you live in a climate with frequent rainfall you can just let nature take care of the irrigation. If you live in a dry climate you can use a variety of strategies to make your precious water go further. The common water loving vegetable crops must get all of the water they need for good growth. There are plenty of drought resistant plants for use in drier areas (these are often more productive if irrigated, but can do well without it.

It is important to segregate the plants according to how much water they require. It is much easier to give them the right amount of water if you put all of your water loving plants in one place and all of your drought tolerant plants in another. If you mix them up you can never quite get the watering right.

The right place for each plant

There are plants suited to every location in your garden, from moist fertile soil to gravel, baking sun, deep shade, permanently wet areas and cracks in the driveway. You have to not only match the plants to the growing conditions, but also take into account other factors, such as their size, shape and compatibility with neighbors.

Placing the conventional annual food plants is pretty straightforward, they mostly go in the intensive kitchen garden, with its relatively small area of rich pampered soil (rich, moist, neutral loam and lots of sun), though they may also go in the row crop garden, or anywhere else that has suitable conditions.

Fruit trees need full sun, as well as the most fertile soil available (it’s harder to improve the soil once trees are in the ground).

Any plants that require intensive care, rich soil and lots of water should be placed close to the house, where you can lavish attention on them.

The more independent plants can be used to fill in any vacant areas of unimproved soil (an empty spot requires more work than a filled one.)

Locally adapted species, able to survive on what nature provides, are planted in the lower maintenance areas

Finally out at the edges of the garden we have native vegetation that can look after itself.

Sometimes a plant decides for itself where it wants to grow. Self-sown seedlings may spring up, fragments of plant may produce buds and start growing, or they may send out runners or creeping roots. It is always gratifying when a plant makes itself at home in this way and I try and give plants every opportunity to do it.

Whenever you plant, don’t put all of your plant eggs in one basket. Take out insurance and plant everything in more than one place.

Arranging the plants in the growing area

Your garden is three dimensional and you can get a lot more growing area if you think of it in this way. Each growing area can have several layers: ground layer, herb layer, shrub layer and a tree layer. You can plant it with a range of important species (trees, shrubs, vines, groundcovers, vegetables, soil improvers, insectory plants and more.

Small plants are usually placed in beds, short rows, or singly, anywhere the conditions are suitable and space allows. Normally you will just mark out areas for these when planning, and decide on their exact location when out in the garden.

Many of the plants in my garden are natives and have been left to grow where nature intended. Most of the shrubs (and quite a few trees) were cut down to the ground at some point in the last few years and they have come back with beautiful vigorous new growth. I like these new plants so much I decided to work around them.

You can enhance the productivity of the garden by planting independent useful edibles (Chinese Yam, Chinese Artichoke, Jerusalem Artichoke, Grapes, Blackberries) in any vacant spot that suits them.

Height

When placing tall plants in the garden you need to pay particular attention to their orientation to the sun and how their shade affects neighboring plants. Some plants benefit from the shade of taller plants, some don’t mind it and some can’t tolerate it at all. See Height/three dimensions for more on this.

In the traditional herbaceous border the taller plants go at the back and the shorter ones at the front, so all are equally visible and all get lots of light. This higher to lower planting plan is commonly echoed in the whole garden, with the tallest densest plantings at the edges and the lighter, lower plantings in the middle, for a bowl-like arrangement. You can vary this in some places, putting taller plants almost to the front. If a bed can be viewed from two sides, the taller plants might be in the middle, to create a kind of mounded planting.

The right spacing

Correct spacing means putting plants close enough together to maximize productivity at maturity, but not so close that there is serious competition for light, water and nutrients. Climate affects spacing, so that in dry climates (where water is limited) or northern areas (where the sun is weaker) plants need to be spaced further apart.

For minimal maintenance you need to get the planting density right. Too far apart and there are opportunities for weeds to come in. Too close together and they will eventually start to compete for light, water and nutrients and will require thinning and pruning and more.

In dry areas plants should be spaced further apart, so they have a greater volume of soil to forage for water and nutrients.

When deciding on a spacing for your plants remember that plants grow bigger. In 5 years that 5 foot sapling may be 20 feet tall and 10 feet wide. That tiny little Blackberry shoot may become a dense thicket of vegetation 12 feet in diameter.

Frost tender plants

If you want a frost tender plant to survive in a marginal climate you must choose a protected warm microclimate. An example of this is growing tender fruits against a south facing stone wall, where the heat absorbed by the wall helps to ripen the fruit and protects the plant from frost.

All frost tender plants are not created equal. Some keel over and die if you whisper that frost is in the forecast, others can tolerate repeated mild frosts (Stevia, Gotu Kola and Vietnamese Coriander all usually survive the winter in my garden). Plants can often be kept alive by seemingly insignificant protection, such as a few inches of mulch, some plant debris or simply being overshadowed by a taller plant or overhanging branch.

One way to find the warmest spots in your garden is to plant a marginally hardy plant in various places. The places where it survives will be the warmer ones. You can also go outside after a light frost and see where it sits and where it doesn't.

Using plants to build the garden

Plants create much of the fabric of the garden, as screens, shade, hedges, background plants, accent plants, focal points, barriers, groundcovers and more. These are the easiest plants to plan for because their location is determined by their purpose. You just have to decide which useful plants will work best with the existing growing conditions.

Framework plants

The tall permanent plants (trees, shrubs, Bamboos) define the shape of the garden by separating different areas, filling in space and adding height. They also obscure parts of the garden, making large spaces more intimate, comfortable and private. Vines and smaller plants can be used to clothe and soften the walls, paths and buildings. Of course they all add visual interest.

Hedge plants

A hedge is a row of plants so closely spaced that their branches intermingle and resemble one long linear plant. Hedges are the most ecologically friendly and resource efficient way of enclosing or dividing land, though they do take a while to get established. They also work as windbreaks and screens, direct movement and give privacy. See Hedges for more on this.

Foliage plants

Traditionally foliage plants were grown to provide a neutral backdrop for more important features. Every plant is a foliage plant of course, so concentrate on those with other uses as well. The ideal foliage plant will also produce something useful (fruit perhaps) and thrives with little care.

Edging plants

Low-growing useful plants (Alpine Strawberry, Alyssum, Carrot, Basil Garlic Chives, Parsley, Lettuce, Thyme) can be grown along the edge of paths and harvested as needed. See Paths for more on this.

Groundcovers and living mulches

Low-growing groundcovers are used to cover and protect bare soil and to keep out weeds. They can be used wherever there is a need to fill in an expanse of unused open ground. These plants must to be well adapted to the conditions if they are to be successful, so select the species carefully. See Groundcovers for more on this.

Nurse plants

These fast growing and vigorous pioneer trees are planted alongside delicate trees (sometimes even in the same planting hole) to nurse them through the first few difficult years. They help by improving the soil, providing shade, giving shelter from the wind (and often fixing nitrogen too). The thorny species may also offer protection from herbivores. When the crop plant is finally growing vigorously they can be removed.

By definition nurse plants can thrive without any help from you. Of course the kind of plants that will work as nurse plants varies according to the climate and growing conditions. A few may also offer other products too (food, fertilizer and more).

Important nitrogen-fixing nurse plants include *Acacia. Alnus, Robinia, Cystus, Celtis, Eleagnus, Hippophae, Ceanothus, Prosopis, Spartium* and *Albizia* species.

Non-nitrogen fixing nurse plants include *Crataegus, Rubus, Lycium, Morus, Quince, Sambucus, Salix, Cistus* and *Lavatera* species.

Barrier plants

These vigorous plants are used as buffers between wild areas and cultivated ones. Plants like Comfrey, Day Lily and Jerusalem Artichoke create such a dense network of roots they can prevent invasive creeping plants (such as the mints) from spreading. Some may also help with pests.

Soil improving plants

These plants enhance the soil in a variety of ways. The leaf litter they produce feeds earthworms and a myriad of other soil organisms and enriches the soil with organic matter. Their roots stimulate soil life, draw nutrients from the subsoil, improve soil structure and add organic matter when they decay. Some species host nitrogen fixing bacteria and fungi and so enrich the soil with nitrogen. See Soil improving plants for more on these.

Specimen plants

These particularly beautiful or striking plants are commonly used singly as focal points. They are much loved by ornamental gardeners who obsess about them no end. Tall edible plants that are attractive enough to be used in this way include Globe Artichoke, Asparagus, Angelica and Lovage.

Traffic control

You can control the way people move around the garden by using plants as physical barriers (such as hedges).

They can also define special areas that are not to be walked upon (such as an area of groundcover).

Climate control plants

Plants have an important role in altering the microclimate to make the garden more comfortable in extreme weather.

In hot climates it isn't pleasant to sit out in the open garden during the heat of the day. The only way to make it comfortable is by providing shade (it may be 20° cooler under a leafy canopy than it is in the full sun). Trees and trellised vines can be used to shade as much of the garden as you need for comfort. Shade isn't only beneficial to people, light shade can also helps plants by reducing water loss from evaporation and transpiration. You may have noticed that large leaved species don't wilt nearly as much when growing in the shade.

A windbreak of trees or tall shrubs can protect the garden and house from cold winter winds. These plants must be tall, strongly anchored and tolerant of wind. Use a mix of fast growing species for quick effect and slower growing ones to fill in and eventually take over. See Windbreaks for more on these.

In cool climates a hedge of evergreens can be used to create a sun trap/windbreak to make sitting outside much more pleasant. It could also be used to funnel cooling summer breezes to where you want them.

A large deciduous tree on the southwestern side of the house can prevent it getting overheated by the summer sun. It should be deciduous so it doesn't block the more welcome winter sun. A vine growing up the western wall could also help to keep the interior cooler.

Native plants

Vigorously growing native shrubs and trees can be used as windbreaks, hedges, screens and other parts of the garden framework. Coppiced native shrubs have helped to shape parts of my garden.

Shade plants

Some plants have evolved to grow in the shade of forests and often have large, dark green leaves (for greater photosynthesis). They also often have a creeping habit, so they can move towards areas of higher light.

Placing the major plants

Trees

Big, long lived and beautiful, trees are one of the main visual and structural elements in the garden. Trees get bigger and bigger over time and dramatically alter the space around them. They also take a long time to grow, so you need to think carefully about where to put them before you plant. It's hard to imagine that 6 feet sapling as 30 feet tall and 20 feet in diameter, but it will happen, so be sure you give it enough room.

Benefits of trees

Trees create hospitable microclimates for plants (and animals) by slowing wind, stabilizing air temperature, reducing frost, increasing humidity, precipitating fog and more. Forests are warmer in winter and cooler in summer than open areas. The temperature in a forest in summer may be as much as 30° cooler than in the open nearby. The ground under trees warms up more slowly than in the open, so stays cooler during the day. At night it cools more slowly and so stays warmer.

Trees have other virtues too. They are some of the best windbreak plants. They provides food and habitat for wildlife. They reduce noise by physically blocking sound, as well as by making their own soothing sound (the wind in the trees). They also absorb air pollution. When trees drop their leaves they enrich the earth with humus and form the basis of the forest food chain. Rain dripping from trees can contain more nutrients than that which falls directly to earth.

Fruit trees bring a regular series of changes to the garden year and really help to connect you to the seasons. There is always something to look forward to. In late winter their flower buds swell and become flowers. These are followed by leaves and swelling fruit, which ripens and is harvested. This is followed by leaf fall and then the whole cycle begins again.

Problems with Trees

There are also problems associated with trees growing in gardens.

Shade

The biggest problem with trees (and the most common reason they are removed) is the shade they create. A single large tree can shade a considerable area of ground and make it impossible to grow a conventional productive garden.

When planting trees you must think about their final size, not the size when planting. A newly planted tree doesn't produce much shade to speak of, but every year it creates an ever-expanding circle of shade. In a few year a group of trees will transform a sunny area into a shady one. Don't create large areas of unwanted shade slap in the middle of important garden areas, unless you plan on eventually replacing the sun loving plants with shade loving ones.

In a small garden you have to get creative when placing trees, because you need to minimize the amount of shade. A common ploy is to plant them on the north side of the garden (obviously you shouldn't shade important parts of your neighbors garden though). You might also place trees where they will cast shade on non-growing areas, such as buildings or driveways (though watch out for this preventing ice from melting in winter).

Competition for water and nutrients

Trees don't only inhibit neighboring plants by casting shade. As they get bigger their root system spreads out further and further, filling the soil with roots and taking most of the available water and nutrients. This makes life very difficult for any shallow rooted plant growing nearby, so it is important to keep trees well away from vegetable growing areas. If you want to grow shallow rooted plants around trees, you have to give them additional water and nutrients.

Slow growth

Another problem is that trees grow so slowly. You plant a tree and it is merely a stick for the first couple of years and doesn't start to act much like a tree for at least 5 years. You need to think long term with trees, plant them and look after them, but then go on to other things. On the other hand they do give you something to look forward to, as every year they get bigger. Be patient and they will grow and become beautiful and fruitful. Incidentally don't be tempted to let them produce a couple of fruit the first year, just to see what it tastes like, as this will set them back a lot.

Buildings

Trees planted close to buildings can cause problems. Falling branches may damage the roof, while leaf litter falling on the roof can clog gutters and downspouts. In hot dry weather it becomes a potential fire hazard. In certain circumstances (mostly in dry clay soil) the roots of trees have been known to damage house foundations.

Water pipes

Keep water loving species such as Willows and Poplars away from leach fields and drain pipes. Their roots can penetrate even the tiniest crack and enter the pipe. Once inside they grow rapidly to take advantage of all that water and in time they can block it completely.

Mess

Some trees drop a lot of mess when fruiting (Mulberries, American Persimmon, Plums). Mulberries are notorious for coloring bird droppings purple. Succulent fruit can leave paving slippery and could be hazardous to your health.

Nitrogen fixing trees

These enrich the soil with their annual leaf fall and are an important source of fertility in the permanent plantings. They also increase the diversity of the garden. Some nitrogen fixing trees produce excellent firewood and could be coppiced as a dual fertility/fuel source.

Using trees in the landscape

Fruit and nut trees form the backbone of the productive garden, helping to separate and define the different areas.

Trees act as screens to block out unwanted views and give privacy.

Trees can be used as focal points, especially the more interesting looking species such as the Persimmon and Pawpaw.

In hot climates you could plant trees around your patio, or put your patio under existing trees. These can be shaped by cutting out lower branches and encouraging them to go in the direction you need shade. By doing this you can create a green ceiling for an open air room.

Planting shade trees is a long term investment because it may be at least 10 years before they start to create much useful shade. Use the larger edible or useful ones, such as Avocado, Cherry, Chestnut, Persimmon or Walnut.

Small trees can be used in hedgerows and windbreaks.

Placing Trees

Where you put trees will depend upon what you want them to do and what growing conditions they prefer. With something so big you also have to take into consideration how they will affect other plants and elements around them. Make sure that the shade they cast won't become a problem in a few years and that the roots won't spread where they aren't wanted (and rob neighbors of water and nutrients).

As trees get taller they start to act as screens. This is useful if you want to divide an area, hide something ugly or simply create a sense of mystery. It is bad if it obscures a special view, or makes part of the garden feel too enclosed or small.

Position the larger trees first and then the smaller ones. Very small dwarf trees can be used like shrubs and planted almost anywhere. The smaller trees often work better when planted in clusters, rather than by themselves (not too close they crowd each other though). You could use several different varieties of a tree crop for a staggered harvest, or perhaps closely related species. Grouping trees can also help with pollination.

Of course you need to plant trees where they will grow well. For fruit trees this means a fertile soil and at least 6-8 hours of full sun (more is even better). Trees really respond to their location, so a tree in a good spot may put on 6 feet of growth in a season, whereas one in a poor location may only grow a few inches.

Don't plant a sapling close to an established tree and expect it to do well. It just won't be able to compete with the well established roots and encroaching shade (trees seem to sense when the situation is hopeless and don't even try) You will have a lot more success if you plant your trees at least 10 feet away from the drip line of established trees.

If you plant fruit trees close to public roads you will probably lose fruit to passers-by. You might be perfectly happy with this, but also be aware that slippery fallen fruit may cause some litigious person to fall and blame you.

Don't plant trees in any area that may have to be excavated at some point in the future (such as over underground utilities). Avoid planting under overhead power lines as the utility company may butcher your trees at some point. Also keep them away from septic leach lines. Don't put trees that need to be sprayed regularly near the house (especially windows and doors), or you will be spraying the house too.

It's best to separate similar species of trees with another species (maybe a nitrogen fixer). They will still close enough for pollination. If you plant them side by side it makes life easier for pests and diseases.

Making use of favorable microclimate

It is possible to grow trees that are somewhat too tender for your climate by planting them in the warm microclimate against a south facing wall. Avoid putting early blooming plants (Apricot and Almond) in low-lying frost pockets, where a severe frost might kill the flowers. Early bloomers are sometimes put on north facing slopes to deliberately delay their flowering. If you live in a mild climate, trees that require a long chilling period should be placed in colder areas, or even in frost pockets.

Spacing

If you are to give your plants enough space, you need to know how big they will get and how far they might spread. We are now fortunate in being able to choose the ultimate size of our plants by using dwarfing rootstocks (see Rootstocks), These allow us to tailor the size of the tree to fit into almost any size space.

The actual spacing you will use depends upon the final size of the tree and what you trying to achieve. Usually you will allow for the full diameter of each tree canopy at maturity, so the branches of neighboring trees just barely touch. Sometimes you may plant slightly closer than this so they merge together to become one visual unit. Of course you can also plant further apart for a park-like arrangement, or even plant trees by themselves.

Newly purchased trees are so small there is a tendency to plant them too close together. This is the biggest mistake because they will eventually start to compete with each other and all will suffer. The only remedy for this is to remove some trees, just when they should be starting to bear well (wasting a lot of time and effort). Give your plants enough room!

Intercropping
Newly planted trees will have a lot of empty, sunny space around them for some time. This can be used to grow bush fruits, perennial vegetables or even annual crops. It is important that such plants don't compete with your trees though, so keep them a reasonable distance apart (and keep everything well fed and watered).

Groundcover under fruit trees
Grass and fruit trees don't mix because they compete for water and nutrients in the same part of the soil (in arid areas grass has been known to reduce the growth of young trees by up to 90%). The easiest way to keep grass from growing underneath your fruit trees is to use a mulch out to the dripline.

In humid climates the best way to keep grass away is by planting groundcover underneath the trees. This could be almost any herbaceous plants, but deep rooted species like Dandelion, Red Dock, Radish, Carrot, Parsnip, Caraway, Artichoke and Burdock are all good choices. See Planting the ground layer for more on this.

Shrubs
Shrubs are some of the most important plants in conventional landscaping. Along with the trees they form the framework of the garden, either individually, in clusters on in rows (as hedges). They are also among the most productive plants in the garden, producing a variety of useful products,

The bush fruits are very reliable and independent food plants, producing abundantly every year while asking very little from you. They are amongst the tastiest treats in the garden and almost everyone likes them. They are also uniquely nutritious, containing vitamins, minerals and some unique antioxidants and other phytonutrients (several species have been called superfoods),

Shrubs tend to work better than trees in a small garden because they are more compact and cast less shade. They are also smaller, so you need more of them for visual effect. In fact you don't usually think of individual shrubs at all, but rather as clusters or rows of plants. These can be repeated around the garden for unity. Also like trees they take several years to really get going, so be patient in the meantime.

Shrubs are generally pretty tough and are particularly useful in problem areas, where most other plants don't do well (dry, shady or very weedy places) They tend to be more drought tolerant than trees and in many arid areas they are the dominant plants.

Where to plant shrubs
If you are serious about growing bush fruit you could put them in their own section of the kitchen garden, in their own garden room, or use them as a hedge. If you are growing fruit that is attractive to birds, you should arrange them so they can be covered with netting when necessary. In some areas they have to be planted in cages to prevent birds from eating them all.

Some shrubs can get quite tall and should be placed where they won't cast unwanted shade on the rest of the garden. You might plant them on the northern edge of the garden (where they will act as a windbreak), along a path, or against a fence, They can also be grown in their own permanent areas, or simply planted as a productive understory layer in the forest garden.

You don't need to get to these plants very often (sometimes just to harvest), so they are often placed in the middle of a bed to reduce maintenance (use stepping stones for access).

Using shrubs in the landscape

Hedges
One of the best known use for shrubs is for making hedges. These work as windbreaks, garden dividers, barriers and screens and are often better than trees because they have more foliage close to the ground (trees lose their lower branches as they get taller). Hedges have great visual impact in the garden and also increase biological diversity by attracting animals, birds and insects (see Hedges for more on these)

You could use a single species to create a fairly formal hedge (the drawback to formal hedges is the maintenance they require). You could also use several species to create a productive multi-purpose hedgerow. This should be looked upon as a type of forest garden and planted with other useful plants (fruiting vines, perennial vegetables, herbs) to make it more productive. It can then produce fruit, edible leaves, tea, poles, shoots, biomass (for mulch), livestock feed and more,

Groundcover
Low-growing shrubs are some of the best groundcover plants for problem areas, because they are so tough.

Specimen plant
A particularly striking shrub might be used alone as a specimen plant.

Erosion control
Some deep rooted, creeping shrubs are well suited to preventing soil erosion on steep slopes. See Plants for erosion control.

Shrubs for compost or mulch material
Any fast growing shrub can be useful as a source of biomass for mulch or compost material. The best species are those that regenerate quickly after cutting, especially the nitrogen fixing members of the *Fabaceae*. Any time I prune shrubs I now chop up any unwanted prunings for mulch (larger prunings are good plant supports). If I have a lot of prunings I chip them with my small electric shredder (it can handle shoots an inch or so in diameter).

I already discussed coppicing in the section on trees, but many shrubs (either existing or planted) can be coppiced to produce mulch material. See Coppicing for more on this useful technique.

Edible shrubberies
Open bush land can be very productive and low-maintenance. You could try emulating the techniques of forest gardening and create a food shrubbery or edible scrub garden.

Vines and climbers
Fruiting vines give you a relatively fast way of adding height to the garden and of increasing photosynthetic area (the more leaves the more productivity). The annual growth rate of established vines can be quite awesome and may reach 30 feet in one season. A few can eventually grow as big as modest size trees with trunks 9" or more in diameter. This vigorous helps to create a feeling of luxuriance and abundance, especially when laden with fruit.

Using vines in the landscape
The most useful climbing species are those that produce edible fruit (Grape, Kiwi, Passion Vine), though the versatile vines do much more than just produce food, they also have important landscape uses.

One of the most important uses of vines is to create overhead shade. This is done by training them over arbors, pergolas, arches and other structures. The dappled shade they cast on the ground can be very attractive.

Vines can also be used to create living walls on your house and other buildings. This doesn't just make the house look nicer, it can also reduce energy usage by providing shade from the sun and shelter from the wind. For best effect the trellis should be a few inches away from the wall.

Herbaceous perennial vines die back to the ground and disappear completely in winter (Groundnut, Hop, Maypop). These are the best plants to use for shading buildings in summer (they grow vigorously enough to completely block the sun - sometimes to 20 feet or more). In winter they vanish completely, allowing the sun to shine through unobstructed.

Climbers can be trained over fences and buildings to soften their outline, reduce their visual impact and tie them in to the garden. The same plants on different buildings (and other components) help to unify the picture by covering them in the same green mantle.

Many climbers are very ornamental (Passion Vine, Mashua and Morning Glory are some of the most architecturally spectacular plants to be found anywhere) and you might let a few plants climb through more mundane plants to jazz them up and add color.

Vines can be used as screens to hide expanses of bare wall and other uninteresting things. Just train them on a trellis or wire fence. The annuals can be used as fast growing temporary screens or sun shades, and to add seasonal interest to dull areas.

Vines can be used to create a fedge by training them along a wire fence. This can be used as a boundary fence, privacy screen or windbreak and only take a couple of years to become effective. See Fedges for more on this.

Thorny plants such as the climbing Roses can be trained on walls or fences to deter people from climbing on them. Don't put any of these plants in well traveled areas (trellis or patio) where they might injure passers by. I personally know two people who have had their eyeballs punctured by spiny plants.

Vines can be grown on trellis over windows to block out intense summer sun. Use a deciduous perennial or an annual, so they won't interfere with winter sunlight.

Evergreen vines can provide shade and privacy year round.

Vines on supports have many of the same visual effects as shrubs, but are quicker to grow, more sculptural and you can more easily control their underlying shape.

Scented climbers like Honeysuckle, Jasmine and Climbing Roses are traditionally used to give form, color and scent to the area around the doorway.

Some vines can even be grown indoors if it is light enough. Tender plants might be wintered indoors and allowed to climb out through an open window. In chilly England Grapes were often grown in this way and used to provide summer shade for the greenhouse.

There are quite a few useful nitrogen fixing vines in the bean family These fast growing plants can be used to produce nitrogen rich biomass.

Practical considerations

As with any other plant it is important to match the plant to the growing conditions. Life 20 feet up a concrete wall can be tough, so choose a plant that can do the job.

Climbers grow tall and should be placed where they won't shade or smother other important plants.

Many vines are adapted to start out growing in the shade of a supporting plant, but eventually overreach it and then flower in the full sun. This is why many vines tolerate shade, but fruit better in full sun.

When planting a new arbor you could plant annual vines along with the desired permanent vines. These will give you foliage and shade for the summer, while the permanent plants are growing (of course they mustn't inhibit the permanent plants though.

Placing the minor plants

The smaller plants are fairly easy to move around, so you don't need to worry too much about where to put them in the planning stage. Just specify areas for the growing beds and decide what goes where, as you are actually working in the garden.

Herbaceous perennials

Perennials may take several growth forms: clumpers, runners, mat formers. They store food for the winter in various tubers, tap roots, rhizomes or bulbs, so are able to have a rapid burst of growth in the spring. Many die back in winter if it gets too cold. A few may do the same thing in summer if it gets too hot and dry.

Edible perennials may be scattered around the garden anywhere suitable openings can be found. Most do better when planted in single species groups, rather than as individuals, in fact it might help to look upon the whole colony as the plant, rather than the individual. There really is strength in numbers, so that even though the plants at the edge of a colony might get nibbled, the ones in the middle will be secure. A colony also has enough plants that you can harvest some without affecting the rest. You can thin out crowded colonies by moving some plants (these can be replanted or potted up and sold). In the case of plant-replant perennials you can move them as you harvest.

You could also plant a mixed species colony, but this usually doesn't work so well, because there is a tendency for the most vigorous species to take over.

Annuals and biennials

In the wild the annuals naturally move around as suitable open, disturbed soil becomes available. In the garden they can likewise be used to fill any vacant disturbed soil (many are happy in fairly poor soil).

Some fast growing annuals thrive in dry climates, by the simple expedient of growing when there is available moisture. When the soil becomes too dry in early summer they simply set seed and die. When the rains start again the next fall the seeds germinate and a new generation starts over.

Annuals are usually direct sown, though the more difficult species might have to be grown from transplants initially. If you plant them in a place they really like, they will often self-sow.

The annual vegetables are mostly planted in a specially designated kitchen garden area, where they can be given everything they need for maximum productivity.

Grasses

These are common everywhere, but become the dominant species in meadows and prairies, where pressures from herbivores, fire, mowing or lack of rainfall keeps larger plants in check. They are very important in conventional gardening because they make up the precious lawn. You could try creating a food producing prairie type lawn, using perennial grasses, bulbs and wildflowers (edible ones of course). You might also try growing grasses for their edible seed (a wheat lawn), as a source of nutritious grass juice, or simply for cutting for mulch or compost material. See Groundcovers for more on this.

Flowers

Flowers can make even the most mundanely arranged garden look spectacular and give it a feeling of being loved. Use them as part of the larger picture, rather than as isolated fragments. They are mostly placed where people can see and enjoy them the most. In the front entrance garden, near other doorways, around sitting and eating areas and anywhere else we spend a lot of time.

If you put them in the right place many flowers will grow without any effort on your part. Some of these are well behaved and settle into the garden to do just what you ask of them. Others (Creeping Bellflower, Calendula, Hollyhock, Soapwort) are more unruly and act more like weeds than delicate flowers (which is not necessarily a criticism).

You should plant plenty of flowers of different kinds, with early, mid and late blooming varieties and species so there is always color in each area. If you think this is a bit frivolous then use flowers with edible parts and tell yourself you are adding to the productivity of the garden. See Edible flowers for a list of these.

Climbing flowers and window boxes can help to blur the distinction between house and garden.

Herbs

These were a significant component of the traditional cottage garden and should be in yours. Most herbs are little changed from wild plants and grow with a wild vigor and independence that fits the new food garden perfectly. I have herbs scattered throughout my garden and they are some of the most trouble free plants I have.

Herbs can be planted anywhere in the garden where the growing conditions suit them (intensive garden, ornamental garden, forest garden, wild garden). Many herbs are attractive enough to be grown as ornamentals in the front entrance garden.

A sampling of important culinary herbs should be close to the kitchen door (you might have them elsewhere also), as they will get used a lot more often if you don't have to spend 5 minutes going out to get them. You will probably want to grow herbs that are used in quantity (Basil. Garlic) in the vegetable garden as well. Tea herbs could be grown out in their own garden, complete with an area to make and enjoy the tea.

Perennial herbs will grow wherever conditions are right. I once went around planting pieces of plants (obtained by dividing older plants) in various spots and many have become a permanent feature.

Annual herbs are often grown in the vegetable beds, but can also be planted in any suitable spot. Many will self-sow if you give them the opportunity (which means giving them bare soil and allowing them to set seed). Parsley and Cilantro appear as volunteers all over my vegetable garden beds (and paths). If you recognize these while they are young you can move them to a suitable spot (or pot them up.

Herb are generally beneficial in the garden as their flowers provide nectar for bees and predatory insects.

Some aromatic plants (Chamomile, Thyme, Corsican Mint) may be planted alongside paths (or in herbal lawns) where the trampling of feet will release their scent. Some of the more drought tolerant species do well in containers.

Care after planting

You aren't finished with the plants once they are in the ground and growing independently, you still have to keep an eye on them. It doesn't take long before it is obvious whether a plant likes the growing conditions or not (is it 6" tall and turning brown or 6 ft. tall and a lush green). If it isn't thriving you might think about moving it before it succumbs (especially if it is unusual, or you had to buy it).

Determining the ideal location for plants and finding combinations of plants that grow by themselves is an ongoing process. You can incorporate what you have learned from one area into the next section of garden.

Most plants need some attention when they are first planted: watering, pruning, mulching and protection from being eaten. Once they are established most should pretty much look after themselves (if you put them in the right place). Then all you have to do is keep them under control so they don't inhibit their neighbors. Spreading perennials benefit from thinning every year or two, which is a good opportunity to move them and expand your stock of plants.

Natural selection

If a plant dies this is a pretty good indicator that something is wrong (i.e. the plant can't survive where you put it). Likewise if a plant simply sits there and doesn't get any bigger (it may keep putting out new leaves and they repeatedly die off). This can happen for a variety of reasons: it could be too wet, too dry, too shady, too sunny or lacking in a particular nutrient, The plant may have been damaged before planting, infected by a disease, or its roots might have been eaten by a pest. I had a thriving Mulberry tree suddenly stop dead, when most of its roots were eaten by gophers (you can usually tell whether a tree is securely rooted or not, by rocking it back and forth). If a plant is obviously struggling then you should attempt to remedy the situation before it dies.

Plant succession

When a natural wooded area is disturbed by fire, flood or hurricane, nature responds with a succession of different kinds of vegetation that eventually return it to a pre-disturbance state.

In the typical succession the newly disturbed soil is first colonized by annual weeds, such as Amaranth, Lambs Quarter, Purslane and Chickweed. These cover the soil and protect it from erosion, oxidation and nutrient leaching. The annuals are followed by perennial weeds such as Dandelion, Dock, Fireweed, Plantain and Stinging Nettle. These enrich the soil and set the stage for woody shrubs (Blackberries, Roses, Hazel, Broom) to come in. As these grow up they further enrich the soil with leaf fall and protect the first tree seedlings (Birch, Alder, Poplar, Juniper) from deer and other herbivores. These pioneer species need light to germinate and grow rapidly in the open habitat above the shrub layer (many also associate with nitrogen fixing organisms).

As the trees get bigger the increasing shade of the canopy starts to affect the shrubs beneath them and they decline in vigor. Finally climax forest trees take over (their seeds are able to germinate and grow in shade). During all of this time there are equally significant changes underground. Organic matter slowly accumulates in the soil from all of the plant growth, so the soil becomes more fertile. This also causes fungi to become the dominant soil organisms.

Mature trees aren't the end of the story though, because nature is never static. When any disturbance brings light back to the forest floor, the pioneers return. In any forest all of the different stages of succession will be occurring simultaneously.

Succession is a fundamental part of the way nature manages the land and we should follow her lead, rather than resisting it. Most conventional gardens are deliberately (if unconsciously) kept in an unstable early stage of succession, because that is what we have come to understand as gardening. However nature will never stop trying to move on. The resulting conflict is what we have come to call maintenance and is the source of a lot of the drudgery many people associate with gardening (really hardcore gardeners like it of course).

Whenever you plant trees and shrubs in an open site, you are setting in motion a series of changes that will transform the area. If you work with this natural tendency to succession, your life will be a lot easier. I never consciously intended my garden to become a forest garden, but parts of it are gradually turning into one. I started out growing annual crops , but over time I have introduced perennials, shrubs and trees. These have grown so enthusiastically they are starting to take over, so I am slowly moving my annual crops to other areas (eventually I may run out of these and have to move).

Nothing in the garden is really permanent and the cultivated and semi-wild areas can shift according to your needs. Plants are very dynamic and may change an area in ways you did not envisage. If you don't like what is happening at any time you can change it, You might need more space for annual crops and so open up a wild area to cultivation by planting a sheet mulch garden or three sisters garden. Conversely you might plant an intensively cultivated area with trees and gradually convert it into a forest garden.

Materials

Once you have an area planned out, you can start thinking about what materials and surfaces to use. For the most part these should be fairly simple and inexpensive (ostentatiousness doesn't work in the garden). The zoning concept is helpful here, in that it places the hardest wearing, most manufactured and attractive materials near to the house (where they get the most wear and are most visible). These are also the most expensive materials (both financially and ecologically) and are only needed in fairly small quantities in this limited area. Softer, more natural (and cheaper) materials are used further away from the house. This gives a nice gradation which helps the house blend into the garden.

The hardscaping (built) elements are the most energy and resource intensive and expensive part of a landscaping job. It's up to you to decide how much hardscaping you have and of what kinds, but many gardens have far more than they really need. Generally softer materials such as mulch, earth, plants or stone (all from the garden) work well enough for most places. Less is greener.

Financial impact

Even though most landscaping materials come out of the ground, they aren't cheap because they are heavy and cost a lot to transport. If you just go down to a landscape supply store and buy all of your materials you can spend a lot of money. There are ways to avoid doing this but you do have to work at it. If you have a large garden you will soon realize one of its main disadvantages, you need a lot more of every material.

Environmental impact

When deciding upon the materials to use, you should consider the environmental impact of obtaining them. There are plenty of ways to spend money to help destroy the planet we depend upon (donate to your local congressman, buy an SUV or stock in BP), but gardening should not be one of them. There is no virtue in being tasteful and artistic in your own space if you are leaving a legacy of ugliness and destruction elsewhere (like those beautiful New Age shops selling crystals mined who knows where).

I would avoid all lumber cut from old growth trees (though most of these are just about gone anyway) as well as tropical hardwoods. I also try and avoid new brick and concrete because they require a lot of energy to make. Rock is often obtained in less than sensitive ways and leaves the landscape looking a lot less attractive than it was. A lot of stone is now shipped from China, which doesn't seem like the most efficient use of fuel.

Sadly we can't always afford the luxury of being totally pure, we have to do what we can afford. A lot of "green building" materials are so expensive their relevance is debatable. Hopefully they will get more affordable as they become more popular. Also the fact that you can afford to use "renewable" oak posts for your timber framed gazebo isn't altogether being honest with yourself (we won't save the earth by cutting down trees). Being green means making do with what you already have, scavenging, recycling and using your imagination rather than your credit card. Of course sometimes you have to buy stuff that will help you save in other ways (water pipe for a drip irrigation system will ultimately save you a lot of time and water).

A lot of the landscapes you see in books and magazines just flaunt their profligacy and almost seem designed to use a maximum quantity of natural resources. It seems the rarer and more costly the materials, the more exclusive (and hence better) it is thought to be. The average family doesn't need 3000 square feet of Redwood deck or granite patio. I have a particular aversion to conspicuous consumption. It offends my sense of justice that some people have a complete second kitchen outdoors, with marble counter tops, stainless steel fridge, sink and grill, while others don't have enough to eat.

A nice (though often overlooked) fact is that conserving resources can often mean conserving money. Using salvaged material is cheaper than buying new stuff and of course the resources from your own land don't cost anything (if you count your labor in such an equation you need to spend more time in your garden).

Simple materials

Use the simplest and most inexpensive material that accomplishes the task you have set for it. For the most part this means using materials that can be found on the site, or are available locally. Most simple materials are also repairable, which means if they break they don't have to be thrown away.

The best garden materials are not only simple, they are also weatherproof and age gracefully so they actually look better as they get older. Japanese gardeners particularly prize materials that are humble in origin but bear this patina of age and wear. They even have an expression for it: wabi sabi. This is one of the reasons Japanese gardens have so much character.

If you want the garden to be your personal refuge from the world, you might also want to avoid the materials and plants commonly seen in everyday life. These include asphalt, poured concrete, gravel, diamond trellis, shaped concrete pavers, bark chips, Junipers, Japanese maples, Petunias, Impatiens and the like.

Local materials

Your choice of garden materials should largely be decided by what is available locally. Look at what materials are commonly used in gardens in your area. Go around local garden centers and builders supply stores and check out what is available and how much it costs. This will also give you a better idea of the economics of your plans.

Using local materials not only saves on transportation, but it also connects the garden to the region around it. Every part of the country has some naturally available resources and you should use them for most of your needs. Around here we have a lot of Redwood in the form of boards, logs and poles, as well as various types of cordwood, shoots, brush, wood chips and sawdust. Other areas may have lots of stone, hardwoods, dry leaves, leaf mold, gravel, seaweed and more. Urban areas have unlimited possibilities for salvaging.

Extreme local materials

The first place you should look for materials is in your own garden. These might include poles, rocks (in rocky soils you will always be looking for ways to get rid of those you remove from the ground), logs, brushwood, sand and even earth (soil can be used for soilcrete or rammed earth, clay can be used for adobe brick, tiles, sealing ponds) and more. You should also think about growing materials (Willow, Chestnut, Bamboo) for use in the garden. See below For more on this.

Old and salvaged materials

If you can't get something from your own garden, you will have to look further afield. The United States has an almost unlimited supply of used building materials of all kinds: lumber, windows, stone, brick, broken concrete and much more. This is where urban gardeners have a decided advantage over their rural sisters. You can find salvaged material for almost any use, the only requirement is a little imagination on how to use it (and a truck to transport it). Using salvaged materials is a cottage garden tradition and is almost essential if you are to build a garden without spending a lot of money.

Used materials also meet our criteria of being inexpensive and having little environmental impact. They also tend to have more character than bland new stuff. They come with a history and are pre-aged with a patina that helps to make the garden more unique.

The problem with the really nice old materials is finding them. If you just want to go and buy them you will pay "collectible" prices, because they will be sold as chic or antique. To get them at a reasonable cost you have to hunt for them. I find country and suburban yard sales to be one of the most fruitful sources of garden related stuff (also flea markets and thrift stores). Scrap metal yards can be a gold mine for metal objects. Dumpsters are good for construction materials. The town landfill is the ultimate place for salvaging if it's allowed. Unfortunately Santa Cruz is very possessive of its garbage, preferring to bury a lot of it rather than allow people to recycle it (the town isn't very friendly to dogs either). I have to mention craigslist.com separately as a fantastic resource for finding anything used. If it still has any value, it will be listed for sale there multiple times.

The key to getting salvaged materials is to pick up anything that might potentially have a use, when you see it. Don't wait until you need something before starting to look. Many times I have passed something up and then I had a great idea of how I could have used it. This means you need somewhere to store all of this stuff of course.

Reusable materials
Some materials are relatively expensive to buy initially, but have a long useful lifespan and can easily be reused (Redwood, bricks, stone, metal). Just make sure you use them in a way that makes it easy to reuse them at a later date (set bricks on sand, not in concrete). Even better is to get them after their first use, when they are a lot cheaper.

Low-maintenance
The best materials are those that don't require any maintenance after installation, Whenever you start having to regularly, clean, paint or bring things inside for the winter, you are looking at more work.

Buying materials
If you can't use what you already have and can't beg, steal or borrow it, then you will have to buy it. Try and get stuff when it is on sale, which means taking advantage of deals when they come along (often at the end of summer when shops are already thinking about Halloween). If you wait until the job grinds to a halt from lack of materials you will pay top dollar.

I always look out for stuff I can get at a reduced price. Broken flagstone, slightly twisted fenceposts, warped boards, bags of fertilizer with holes in them. The bigger stores will often give you a discount if you order a lot at one time

Growing materials
Gardening is an activity where we think in the long-term, so it's not unreasonable to take this a step further and grow your own garden materials. Obviously these won't be available when you first start your garden, but as time passes you will be glad you did (and most can be harvested over and over again). If such a plant is low-maintenance, ornamental and useful too, it can be a very worthwhile crop.

Suitable sized poles from any trees or shrubs can be used for plant stakes and supports. The long flexible stems of woody vines can be used for making baskets and as a base for wreaths.

Bamboo is a versatile garden building material and depending upon its size it can be used for fence panels, poles, plant supports and more. It is easily grown in most areas (the problem is keeping it under control).

Willow is less well known than Bamboo, but has quite a few potential uses in the garden and deserves to be more widely utilized. Their long flexible shoots can be used to make arches and arbors to support climbing plants and as fences and screens. Thinner shoots can be woven to create wattle fence panels and as edging for beds. Willow is very easily propagated from cuttings and is so fast growing it can be used as a source of biomass for composting. It rots quickly if it stays wet, so keep it from contact with the ground .

Chestnut is a fast growing tree that can be coppiced to produce firewood, fenceposts, stout poles for arbors and palings for fencing.

Black Locust: This fast growing nitrogen fixer can be coppiced to produce rot resistant fenceposts and good firewood.

Some plants can be useful as twine for tying up plants. New Zealand Flax (*Phormium*) is the probably best for this, but there are many others. The stems of Honeysuckle and Morning Glory can be used directly. The leaves of Iris, Cattail, Stinging Nettle, Hemp, Flax, Kniphofia and Yucca can all be twisted and used.

Common local materials

Wood

Wood is one of the most basic and versatile garden materials and is used for fences, arbors, plant supports, furniture, ornamentation and much more. In some areas wood is abundant and fairly cheap, in others it is scarce and expensive. It's best to use local wood where possible, especially that which has grown in your garden.

Dimension lumber

When I use sawn wood outdoors it is usually recycled, as it is cheaper, has less environmental cost and frequently comes with an aged look that I like. It helps that I have been a building contractor for a long time and often get free old wood (it's the only fringe benefit of such a job). I also happen to live where Redwood is commonly used. This is so durable it is often re-usable, even after many years outside.

When I use new wood, I try to stick to the rule that whatever I build should last longer than the wood took to grow. This usually means using rot resistant wood outdoors, as anything else just doesn't last. I also try to avoid direct contact between wood and the ground, as this drastically shortens the life of any wood.

I like to avoid pressure treated wood for the most part, though with the removal of the arsenic and chromium it has become significantly less toxic in recent years. If you do use pressure treated wood you should be aware that the preservative only penetrates about a half inch into the wood. If you cut the wood you will expose the untreated wood inside. Never put the sawn end of a pressure treated fence post into the ground, as it will rot within a few years.

When most softwoods go outside they are painted or stained to make them last longer. Unfortunately painted wood can't be recycled easily. It may also be hard to re-paint if covered in plants. Stain often works better and it just fades away (I'm not sure about burning it though).

The recycled plastic "wood" such as Trex is rapidly gaining in popularity for use in decks and landscaping, as it doesn't rot.

Wooden Poles

If you have coniferous trees on your property you may be able to obtain useful round poles from small overcrowded trees. You might also get hardwood poles by coppicing (these are usually more durable than softwood poles).

Poles can be used for all manner of garden structures: arbors, pergolas and the like. They will last longer if peeled and kept from contact with the ground (put them on concrete piers).

When I'm cutting trees I save any long poles with a fork at the end, as they make good supports for heavily laden fruit tree branches. Thicker poles can be used as fenceposts (see Boundaries for more on this).

Brushwood

This has a surprising number of uses in the garden and shouldn't simply be burned as waste material. It can be used for plant supports (see Temporary plant supports), woven into fences or dead hedges (see Boundaries), or simple piled up as a windbreak or refuge for small animals.

Brushwood can also be used to enrich the soil. You can combine it with soil to make a berm, bury it in trenches on the contour, or use in hugelkultur beds. You can also leave it piles to slowly break down. If nothing else it can be used for mulch. I have a small electric shredder that works well for chipping small shrubs up to an inch in diameter. It gives me an easy way to produce small quantities of mulch and get rid of woody brush at the same time (it's time consuming though).

Wood Chips

These are the all purpose material for paths and as mulch for permanent plantings. You can use as many wood chips as you can get, so be on the lookout. Around here tree trimmers are happy to dump a truckload on your property.

Stumps

If you can't face the task of digging stumps out of the ground, they can be carved into pedestals or seats (this is only worthwhile if they are a durable type of wood). If they are already out of the ground they can be used for fences.

Shoots and suckers
Longer shoots, such as fruit tree prunings can be woven like those of willow.

Bark
This can be used as a long lasting mulch. Shredded bark is even better than chipped bark.

Stone

Stone is attractive, durable and comes in a wide variety of colors and textures. Local stone always looks great and helps to gives the garden a regional character. If you have stone in your garden it will be one of your most basic resources. If you don't, but have a truck, you can often pick it up elsewhere (I mean this literally). Stone is almost prohibitively expensive to buy where I live.

Many areas are blessed (or cursed depending on your viewpoint) with an abundance of stones of all sizes. I used to moan about the rocky New England soil where every time you poke a fork into the ground you hit a rock. Now that I garden in almost completely rock free soil (and have stood in the landscapers yard goggling at the price of stone), I have developed a new appreciation of stone as a free resource. If you have enough stone it can be used for everything from edging beds and paving to building walls.

Stone looks and feels hard (because it is) and it should be used sparingly. It is most useful in small amounts, such as for stepping stones, paving, low walls. Too much stone may make your garden feel too hard.

Types or rock
Rock comes in every size from sand to gravel to pebbles to cobbles to boulders. All of these have their uses in the landscape, particularly as paving for paths and patios (See Paths for more on these).

Sand, decomposed granite
These are most often used as a base for paths and patios, but they can also be used as a surface material. Decomposed granite packs down firmly to form a fairly hard surface, especially if a little Portland cement is added.

Gravel
This inexpensive and versatile material makes a quick and easy path, though it may need edging to stop it spreading. It is also good for flat driveways.

Cobbles
These small 3-4" diameter rocks are commonly set in concrete for use as paving.

Block pavers
These rectangular stone blocks are one of my favorite paving materials, but are usually prohibitively expensive.

Boulders
These are commonly used for ornamentation, especially around ponds. They can also be used for low retaining walls.

Fieldstone
This is sedimentary rock that can be split along one plane to make randomly shaped flat sheets. These are used for paving patios and paths and must be fitted together like a jigsaw puzzle.

Flagstone
This is fieldstone that has been cut into regular squares or rectangles. It is the ultimate paving material, but prohibitively expensive where I live.

Adobe and cob – I haven't had any experience with these, but apparently they have been used for garden walls.

Brick

Brick is not stone but is used like it for walls, paths, patios, pedestals, columns, path edging and more. Traditionally bricks were made of fired clay, but today they may also be made of concrete. Either way they are very energy intensive to produce, so I try to find used brick.

Salvaged brick is widely available but (because of the labor of cleaning it) may well cost more than new brick. If you live in the right area, you can probably salvage your own brick. Unfortunately in earthquake prone California we don't have a lot of brick buildings left to demolish.

The big advantage of buying brick is that it is delivered to your site on nice neat pallets. Salvaging brick means going out and getting it yourself. Because of its weight (a single brick may weigh 5 ½ pounds) this becomes an act of ecological virtue (or poverty)). My little Toyota pickup struggles to carry much more than 200 bricks, which cover about 40 square feet of path. This means quite a few trips to get any quantity, so the closer the source the better. When you factor in your time, gas, considerable wear and tear on your hands, back and vehicle, and the time it takes to clean the bricks of mortar, those free bricks aren't necessarily that cheap (or even ecologically virtuous).

Brick should be set in a bed of sand for good drainage. This also makes them easy to move and re-use. You can make a firmer bed from concrete, but this makes them harder to reuse in the future.

Concrete

This is so versatile that it gets a reluctant nod of approval even though it is energy intensive to produce and not always good Feng Shui. It is relatively cheap and can be used to replace some things that were once done by skilled hands (and are now prohibitively expensive), such as masonry columns for pergolas and retaining walls. Poured concrete is a very useful and versatile material. It can be colored, stamped, imprinted, carved, cut, embedded and more. Any time you do anything unusual you should experiment with a small area first, as it may not turn out as you expect.

Large areas of poured concrete should be avoided where possible. They are not good because they smother the earth, prevent rain percolation and are generally bad for chi. If you must use it (maybe for rainwater collection), then make expansion joints to stop it cracking. These can be simple saw cuts or they might be a row of bricks or other decorative features.

If you must use concrete for paving it is better to use it in smaller modules such as block pavers. These have become popular in recent years. Depending upon the type, they can look just like stone, or they can look very factory made and institutional.

It is possible to cast a few special personalized concrete pavers yourself to add interest to a path. This gives you a good opportunity to get creative with color and by embedding various items. Making them is a lot of work though and I wouldn't want to cover much area with them.

Salvaged broken concrete can be pretty versatile and has the added virtue of being a waste material. Again the big drawback is its weight. It is extremely heavy to transport and you won't get many slabs in the back of a Prius. However if you are breaking up an old concrete driveway or patio then you should reuse it rather than dumping it.

Hypertufa is a concrete material made with peat moss to make it lighter and more porous. It can be used to create 'stone' containers for planting and as a coating for stucco walls. Concrete has also been made using soil instead of sand.

Metal
Feng Shui advises that you should have some metal in the garden. This might be fences, gates, furniture, sculpture or trellis. Metal goes particularly well with plants and can provide a variety of ornamental effects.

Copper water pipe and plumbing fittings were once commonly used for trellises and arches, but they have become a lot more expensive recently. Steel reinforcing rods are cheaper and can be used to make large, strong and airy structures such as arbors (how about a large domed sitting area covered in vines?). You could wire them together (this makes them easy to re-use), though welding is stronger and more permanent.

Galvanized or copper pipe can also be used to make fountains.

Corrugated sheet metal is a too often overlooked garden material. A very versatile material, it can be used for much more than simply roofing. Use it for fences, walls, edging and retaining walls (paint the back of it with tar to prolong its life). You can often get this inexpensively at scrap yards and it comes with a nice patina of age (also known as rust).

Glass
This isn't much used in gardens but it can be very ornamental in the form of sculpture, mirrors and old bottles. Old glass doors can make transparent panels for fences.

Plastic
Plastic would be entirely on my list of materials to avoid, except that it has several unique uses, that we can't easily do without. It is the most practical material for lightweight greenhouse glazing, re-usable pond liners, garden plumbing and drip irrigation.

Materials to avoid

The green consumer is a contradiction in terms. I don't garden to give me a reason to buy more stuff and I try not to buy anything new (I know, this doesn't help the GDP). However some products are particularly bad and I try to avoid using them when possible. Of course sometimes we end up using these things because they are all we can afford.

Hardwoods
Many landscaping books casually recommend hardwoods for outdoor use, with the qualifier that they are obtained from sustainable sources. This sounds "green" but what does that really mean? Cutting down a 100 year old Oak tree and planting an acorn could be called sustainable forestry (in fact it often is), but is your need for an arbor a good enough reason for it? Especially if you already have softwood poles growing on your land.

Tropical hardwoods
Some companies promote their "sustainably harvested Teak', but of course these plantations are growing where natural forests once stood. The wood is then transported 1000's of miles to your garden.

Old growth trees
Redwood and Cedar may not travel as far as Teak, but if you have ever seen the freshly cut stump of an ancient tree it might dampen your pride in that clear heart Redwood deck. On the other hand recycled Redwood is a fantastic material. Second growth Redwood can also be good.

Pressure treated wood
I appreciate the fact that pressure treated wood lasts much longer than untreated wood, but it is too toxic to use safely in many situations. Manufacturers claim the toxins are bonded to the wood and don't leach out, but that is nonsense. The wood does eventually rot and the toxins go into the soil. Some people warn against using pressure treated wood near food crops, I prefer not to use it near anything.

Pressure treated wood has become considerably less toxic in recent years with the removal of the chromium and arsenic. Be aware of this if you salvage old pressure treated wood, as it may well still contain these metals.

Concrete
I already discussed the virtues and uses of concrete. The big problem with concrete is that it usually means strip mining to obtain the limestone and a lot of energy and CO2 emissions to make the cement that holds it together. According to one industry website, producing a yard of concrete creates 400 pounds of CO2, which is the equivalent of burning 16 gallons of gasoline. I try to avoid concrete if there is any alternative.

Peat Moss
In England there has been a long campaign to get gardeners to stop using peat moss in the garden, because it's use has resulted in the destruction of many peat bogs. I have already talked about considering the environmental impact of our materials and I commend these efforts. However you have to look at the bigger picture of where it comes from. In Ireland 10% of electricity is produced from peat burning power stations. It's use for starting seeds pales in comparison to this. I would never use it in quantity as a soil amendment though (leaf mold is much better anyway).

Paint
I don't really recommend paint, It isn't particularly durable outside (which means work repainting) and eventually breaks down into the soil. The soil around old buildings is often contaminated with lead from old paint (fortunately this is now banned). If you must use paint then try and use the newer eco paints. Another problem is that painted wood can't be recycled.

VOC's.
When possible you should avoid wood stains, glues and anything else containing volatile organic compounds.

Plastic
Plastic is toxic to produce, commonly breaks down in sunlight, is often hard to recycle and sometimes has hidden health effects. Unless specially treated for outdoor use (with toxic additives) it weakens and breaks down when exposed to the ultraviolet rays in sunlight (plastic tarps barely last through one season). There are some unique garden uses for plastics, but they are used a lot more than they need to be, simply because they are cheap and easy to manufacture. Plastic furniture, plastic cushions, plastic sheds, plastic fences, plastic tools, plastic trellis. All are ugly and not very strong (and when they break they are almost impossible to repair).

How toxic is that plastic?
When using plastic we should consider hidden costs, such as the pollution produced in its manufacture and disposal. The most commonly used plastics (from least toxic to most toxic) include:

High density polyethylene HDPE – The least toxic plastic for tanks and irrigation pipe. Polyethylenes are fairly simple polymers though they often contain additives for UV and heat stabilization. They are fairly easy to recycle and are a good substitute for PVC.

Polyethylene-Terephthalate (PET) is made from ethylene glycol and dimethyl terephthalate. It often incorporates UV stabilizers and flame retardants. It is also fairly easy to recycle.

Ethylene propylene diene monomer EPDM – The least toxic plastic for pond liners and living roofs.

Cross linked polyethylene pipe (XLPE or PEX) is a good alternative to PVC if you can afford it. Like PVC it can't be exposed to sunlight.

Polycarbonate – Used for greenhouse glazing and very durable. Manufacturing may involve using phosgene (of poison gas infamy), as well as methylene chloride, chloroform, 1,2-dichloroethylene, tetrachloroethane and chlorobenzene. It is possible to recycle polycarbonate, but it commonly isn't.

Acrylonitrile-butadiene-styrene (ABS) Manufacture involves butadiene, styrene, acrylonitrile all probable human carcinogens.

Polystyrene (PS) manufacture involves (benzene) (styrene and 1,3-butadiene). It can be recycled, but commonly isn't.

Poly vinyl chloride PVC – Used for pond liners and irrigation pipe. During manufacture dioxin and other dangerous pollutants are created. It commonly contains additives that aren't chemically bound to the plastic and so leach out. It can't be recycled because of its chlorine and additive content. I used it for my irrigation system without thinking about all of this, but now wish I hadn't.

The house area

I have spent a while discussing the process of designing a garden on paper, but many people prefer to just go outside and start working. I will now discuss most of the major components you might want in your garden, in their approximate position from nearest to the house to the furthest away.

The house

Siting the house

Not many of us have the luxury of choosing where to put our house, but it should ideally be ⅓ of the way back on the lot (to give a larger private space at the back) and there should be more space to the south and west, where the warmest and sunniest areas are located. The ideal in Feng Shui is to have the back of the garden slightly higher than the front and the eastern side slightly higher than the western side.

In and out

The house and garden are not separate entities; they are parts of the same whole. One is the inside living area and one is the outside living area. In most homes the inside is more comfortable than the outside, so this is where we spend most of our time. To encourage us to go outdoors more, we need to make it as welcoming and comfortable as the inside.

The garden should be inviting, with a gradual transition from the house to the garden. We can reduce the boundaries between inside and outside, and lure people outside, by creating intermediate areas that are not quite indoors or outdoors. Depending upon the climate these areas might include any of the following: a patio, a deck, a covered porch, a courtyard, a partly enclosed outdoor room (with both open and enclosed walls), a screened porch, an attached greenhouse, or a shady arbor.

You can also reduce the distinction between house and garden by training espaliered trees and climbing plants on the walls and by planting things in containers and window boxes. There should also be comfortable chairs, a table, and perhaps an outdoor fireplace.

From the reverse perspective you can put the things normally found in the garden in the house, such as ponds, rocks, poles, dried flowers, twigs and garden furniture.

House related elements

Some of the following elements are more building projects than gardening ones, but they can make such a big difference to the house and garden (and the way you use them) that you might want to consider them.

Balcony

A balcony connects the upstairs rooms to the garden. Vines can climb up from the ground , while other plants can be grown in containers. If a balcony is big enough (at least 6 feet deep) it is a wonderful place to sleep on hot summer nights. It can also be a place to grow a considerable amount of food in containers, though this is only usually worthwhile if growing space is limited elsewhere.

Courtyard

Courtyards, created by having rooms on three sides were common in hot climates in the past. They provide a natural outdoor living area and a secure comfortable transition from the house to the garden. You can't easily reshape your home to create a courtyard, but if you are planning an addition for your house, you might consider it.

Covered Porch

The covered porch is traditional in hot climates and provides an intermediate protected area that is more comfortable than the outside. It provides a shady refuge from the heat of the day and shelter from the rain. It is the perfect place to sit on warm evenings, and makes a great place to sleep when the nights get too hot.

You can use indoor furniture on a covered porch because it is protected from the elements. It also gives you a good place to put things you can't leave outside, but don't want in the house (be careful this doesn't result in it becoming a storage area though).

A covered porch is basically a deck with a roof over it and isn't hard to build. In very hot climates it usually goes on the south or west side of the house (or both), where it can help to keep the interior of the house cool. A southern location doesn't work too well in cooler climates, as it can make the interior of the house too dark. In such cases it probably makes the most sense to put it on the west side. It is sometimes placed on the north side, as this is already shaded (and it is often used after the sun is down anyway).

Entrance areas

This is the most public part of the garden, so if you want to dress to impress this is the place to do it. The doorways are particularly important transition spaces and should be treated as special areas with their own planting and purpose.

Front doorway

The front entrance is usually the most important in the house and its primary importance should be obvious to anyone first viewing the house. The front door doesn't have to be visible from the driveway (or garden gate), but the way to get to it should be obvious.

This area is more formal than other entrances and has more ornamental features. It is common to have artwork, or some other ornamental object by the main doorway, where it can be easily seen and admired by visitors. There could also be a matching potted plant at either side of the pathway (or steps) and perfumed vines nearby to scent the area.

The walkway to the front door should be broad, smooth, impressive and flat (any changes in level should be through steps with handrails). It should ideally approach from below, looking up at the house. There may also be an overhand to protect the door from the rain and a light to help you find your keys.

Other doorways

These are more relaxed and should have a comfortable seating area adjacent to them. Outside the kitchen door there could be salad beds, herbs and some vegetables (or even the whole kitchen garden).

The front garden

This is the part of the garden that is most visible to the outside world and creates a setting for viewing the house. For this reason it is traditionally the most ornamental and well maintained section of the whole garden. This doesn't necessarily require a great deal of effort though, as there are plenty of beautiful low-maintenance useful perennials and self-sowing annuals and biennials (see Flowers). It can also include ornamental edibles, such as Kale, Asparagus, Artichoke, as well as herbs, fruiting shrub and small trees. Use your most attractive mulch to conserve moisture and keep down weeds and nice paving to provide a firm footing.

Attached greenhouse

An attached greenhouse gives you a comfortable place to relax when it's too cold to be outside. In cool temperate climates this is the ultimate transition between indoors and out and should be as big as possible because it will become an important living area.

This kind of greenhouse should be attached to the sunny south facing wall of the living room, where it can symbiotically exchange heat with the house. It gives heat to the house during the day, but may require some from the house at night to prevent it getting too cold (open the vents when you go to bed). There should be doors to both the inside and the outside (opening onto the outdoor living areas).

The attached greenhouse is not just a living area, it is also be used for raising seedlings and growing a range of tender plants (Pineapple, Banana, Papaya). It is also warm enough to overwinter tender plants that can't survive outside. This can be a very important use and can save you money every year.

An attached greenhouse may get very hot in summer, so must be well ventilated (you might even have removable windows you can take out for the summer). You could also use shade cloth.

A greenhouse doesn't have to be expensive. I have built some very effective ones out of scrap 2 X 4's and sheet plastic. I couldn't honestly say these were attractive, but they worked really well.

You could put a shower or tub in the greenhouse so it can benefit from the waste heat (maybe run it into a tank in the floor). You might also run the bathtub gray water out into the greenhouse, where it can release its stored heat, before going elsewhere (don't store it for too long or it will start to smell).

For growing food through the winter an attached greenhouse is the ultimate convenience. It allows you to produce salads, leafy greens, microgreens, wheatgrass and herbs, all in the comfort of your own home.

Greenhouse window

In cold climates a south facing window greenhouse can be very useful for overwintering tender cuttings, starting seeds, raising micro-greens and more (you might want one in your bathroom too).

Roof greenhouse

If you wanted to get adventurous you could replace your whole roof with a greenhouse. Suppose you have an old house that needs a new roof. What if, instead of replacing the roof, you remove it completely and replace it with a greenhouse? Reinforce and insulate the existing upper floor and there are all kinds of possibilities for a new kind of food producing green roof. Bananas, Papayas, Avocados. Maybe the sky really is the limit.

Home office / workshop

If you work from home, whether fixing cars, cabinetmaking, or simply in an office, you can often bring your work out into the garden. Build a workplace there and make a garden setting for work. This should be attractive because you spend a lot of time there.

A workshop shares many of the same needs as the potting shed, so they could go together. It should have water and a sink (this could be from a hose pipe). It helps to have a covered area for storage and as a sheltered place to work in bad weather. If you make things it's helpful to have access for a vehicle to bring in materials and take finished stuff out.

A yurt works well as a semi-permanent garden office. It is arguably a temporary structure, so you may get away without getting a building permit (if all else fails you can always plead ignorance).

The roof of a suitably oriented workshop, shed or carport could be the place to locate a solar water heater or photovoltaics.

Mudroom

In cold climates there is often an unheated room attached to the kitchen, where people can take off or put on outdoor clothing in comfort. It is also a good place to keep shoes, outdoor clothing, worm bins, recycling area, some firewood, even a freezer and other food storage. It also acts as an air lock to keep heat in the house.

Roof

Wide roof eaves are an important climate control element, as they block the high summer sun from entering the house and overheating it. At the same time they allow the lower angle winter sun to enter the house and warm it.

Flat roofs that can be used as living space or living roofs are perhaps the most functional, if not the most visually interesting. However they have to be carefully built if they are to remain waterproof. If you are going to spend much time on them there should be a parapet wall for safety and privacy. In a small garden you might have a deck built up over the roof to provide additional living space. A flat roof also provides easy access to any solar electric or hot water panels on the roof.

In Greece flat roofs are commonly used as living space and often have a grape arbor on them to make them usable during the heat of the day. These vines are planted in the ground and trained up on to the roof.

Roof gutters are commonly the collector part of a rainwater collection system. Any type of roof will work for collecting irrigation water, though if you want to be able to drink it, metal roofs are probably the best (asphalt shingles aren't good).

If your house doesn't have gutters you may have to protect the soil beneath eaves from erosion by roof runoff (use tough vigorous plants, paving or gravel).

Screened porch

In many areas biting insects make the outdoors unbearable at certain times of the year, especially in the evenings. In such places the covered porch often becomes the screened porch. Some screened porches have interchangeable windows and screens for ultimate versatility.

Cooling the house

The cheapest and simplest way to keep the interior of a house cool is to prevent heat from entering it in the first place. Good wall and roof insulation is the most obvious and cost effective way to do this, but landscaping can also help too.

I already mentioned that broad roof eaves can help, by shading the walls and windows in summer when the sun is high.

An arbor (sometimes called a loggia) can be attached to the south of the house to provide summer shade (and grow fruiting deciduous vines).

A solar pergola can screen the south side of the house. It has louvers that allow low angled winter sun to penetrate but keep out high summer sun. The angle of the louvers is set to the angle of the sun at the winter solstice.

A tall deciduous tree to the southwest of the house can shade it in summer (keeping it cooler), but lets light through (if somewhat reduced) in winter. Don't put tall evergreens directly to the south of the house as they will cast shade all of the time.

South and west facing windows can overheat the house on summer afternoons as the sun descends and shines directly in. Awnings, shades or curtains can reduce the heat gain.

Living roofs were originally devised as a way of insulating houses; to keep them cooler in summer and warmer in winter.

Shade house

In hot tropical and desert climates a shade house is often attached to the cooler northern side of the house. It is screened to keep out insects and has water to increase humidity. It may have vines growing over the roof for additional shade in summer, when the sun is almost directly overhead.

House services and utilities

Solar hot water and photovoltaics

These aren't really garden components, though they are sometimes placed in the garden. The cost of a solar hot water heater is easy to justify, it just doesn't make sense to use fossil fuels to heat water when the sun heats up your roof every day. Photovoltaics are still a bit pricey for the average homeowner, but it would be nice to at least be able to run your indispensable items off the grid. We badly need some kind of solar loan program, whereby we can borrow money to install solar hot water and electric systems. We could then pay back the loan using the savings on our utility bills. It seems likely that in the not too distant future we will all be able to be independent of centralized power.

Photovoltaic panels are most often installed on the house roof because it gets the most sun and the space isn't generally used for anything else. Ground mounted panels are easier to install and maintain, but take up ground that could grow plants. They work best if you have a south facing hillside and lots of space (you can grow plants around them of course, so long as they don't shade the panels). You could also put them on a car port, shed or even an pergola, where they could provide summer shade as well as electricity.

Compost bins

For composting kitchen scraps I prefer a worm bin as it doesn't attract rodents and raccoons like a compost bin. It also works better with the small but steady stream of scraps that emanates from the kitchen.

Clothes drying line (solar clothes dryer)

The clothesline is the simplest and most cost effective way to utilize solar energy. The ultimate energy efficient clothes dryer, it replaces the biggest energy hog in the house, the electric or gas clothes dryer. It's been estimated that the electric clothes dryers of America use 10% of all residential electricity and require the burning of 30 million tons of coal a year. If you use this simple piece of cord regularly it could save you several hundred dollars a year. Amazingly clothes lines are actually forbidden for the 60 million Americans who live where this simple solar device is banned as a threat to property values.

In hot sunny weather with a light wind blowing, a clothesline will dry your laundry almost as quickly as a mechanical dryer. The only problem with drying your clothes outside is that direct sunlight will bleach anything that is left out for too long. The solution to this is to turn colored clothes inside out, or put the line in light shade.

It is undoubtedly more work to hang clothes out to dry, than it is to simply transfer them into the dryer, but most people could probably benefit from a little extra exercise.

Wet laundry can be heavy so the washing line should be as close to the house and washing machine as possible. Ideally it should be invisible from the street or inconspicuous, so as not to offend the sensibilities of sensitive neighbors, or invite the theft of your lingerie. It should also be away from children's play areas to prevent mishaps.

A big aid in using a washing line is to have a prop, which is simply a length of wood with a notch in one end. This is placed under the middle of the line to keep it from sagging under a heavy load of laundry. It is held in place by the line and the weight of laundry.

Outside toilet

If you thought the washing line gets bad press, wait until you start using your own solid waste (the stigma is so great I can't even call it by its proper name) Doing this is a perfectly logical and reasonable idea, but it presents a major social problem (there are also potential health problems, but these are easier to deal with). We have become so removed from our own bodies and waste products that we try to avoid them at all costs. This deep rooted and pervasive attitude will have to change at some point. There is a looming permanent water shortage in many areas and flushing up to 8 billion gallons of purified water down the toilet every day (not to mention vast quantities of valuable plant nutrients) just isn't sustainable. There are several ways you can deal with this "waste that can not be named". Building departments have an inspector who makes sure you have a flush toilet in your house, but they don't have an inspector to make sure you use it (not yet anyway).

The old fashioned privy
This was simply a hole in the ground covered by a shed with a built in seat (with a hole in it). In these days of superior hygiene, greater population density and concern about groundwater contamination, the pit toilet is less than satisfactory. It concentrates the waste in one spot, which makes it harder to decompose and means there is a greater potential for groundwater contamination. It is also hard to recover it for re-use when it is down in a hole in the ground.

Composting toilets
There are also modern composting toilets, with various methods of ensuring the waste is safe for re-use. These can make sense if you need another toilet, but don't want to mess with all that plumbing. They are a good way to reduce your water use, or to ease the pressure on an ailing septic system (a gray water system may help with this as well). The biggest problem with commercial composting toilets is that they are expensive (though you will be saving on plumbing and water.

Humanure toilet
The simplest way to get your shit together is the simple system devised and described by Phillip Jenkins in The Humanure Handbook. His inexpensive method is not only less polluting than the traditional earthen pit outhouse, but it also produces usable fertilizer. Obviously it does entail some commitment and care to keep up on the work though. If you are interested in pursuing this I recommend the book, but I will describe it briefly.

The toilet
This is basically a 5 gallon bucket inside a plywood box with a toilet seat on top. The box doesn't even have to be airtight because the covering material (usually sawdust) prevents any odor seeping out. Jenkins suggests having 4 or 5 buckets and lids so you can collect enough waste to build a hot compost pile.

The humanure toilet works perfectly in the old-fashioned country outhouse. It is nicer to use any toilet in a well-ventilated outdoor space and it is no hardship to walk out into the garden to use it. In times past the outhouse was one of the most frequently visited parts of the garden and had a well-beaten path to it. Traditionally it was sited near the woodpile, so you could collect firewood on the way back from the toilet. Obviously it should be away from the living areas of the garden (not too far) and it should be private.

The cover material
This prevents odor, absorbs moisture and provides carbonaceous material for the composting process. Jenkins choice of material is fresh hardwood sawdust from a sawmill, but peat moss, rice hulls, leaf mold or even straw have also been used.

Using the toilet
Put a couple of inches of cover material in the bottom of the bucket and start depositing both solids and liquids (don't you just love the euphemisms). After each use you throw on another layer of cover material. When the bucket is full put the plastic lid on and start another bucket.

Hot composting the waste
When all of the buckets are full they are composted in the middle of a hot compost pile. The hot composting (up to 160° F.) will kill any pathogens in the manure, which is important for health and safety.

Urine

Using your own urine isn't quite as socially unacceptable as using your solid waste, but it is still frowned upon. This is another area where social stigma commonly prevents people from doing what is sensible. We need to get over it and grow up, because urine is a useful high nitrogen fertilizer and too valuable to be flushed away. I read somewhere that one person produces enough nitrogen annually to fertilize 1000 square feet of garden (which is a nice round number). Someone came up with the idea of calling it liquid gold, to make it sound nicer and give use more appreciation of its value

There is less reason to be afraid of urine than solid waste as it is normally sterile so there aren't many health risks (except hepatitis). As a liquid it is also much easier to deal with. Day urination can be directly onto the compost pile or the roots of trees. If you must have a fixed pissing place a straw bale makes a good garden urinal. After you get used to going outside to relieve yourself, the idea of peeing into a bowl full of drinking water starts to seem a bit weird, which it is.

Traditionally night urination was done into a chamber pot, though as a man I prefer an enclosed container, as it is less odorous and there is less danger of spillage. It is important that urine be used immediately; if it sits for any length of time it will begin to smell and become very unpleasant.

Collected liquid gold can be diluted with four parts water and used immediately as a liquid fertilizer, or added to the compost pile as an activator. It is also effective as a mildewcide.

Gray water

Gray water is any water that has been used in the house, but doesn't contain sewage. Apparently the average indoor daily water use in the USA is somewhere around 70 gallons per person. In dry climates it is absurd to use this water once and then flush it away. See Gray water for ways to use it.

Outdoor shower

A nicely built and planted outdoor shower can become a popular garden feature. In warm weather it is a much more sensual and pleasant experience than an indoor shower. The water can easily be solar heated to reduce energy consumption and simplify installation.

A shower area requires full sun and complete privacy and should be fairly close to the house for easy access. Plant sweet smelling vines or bushes around it as a screen. The waste water can go directly into the ground, or to specially designated plants. If you live in a very cold climate you could put your shower in the greenhouse where it is warmer.

Wood shed

If you use wood for heating or cooking, a covered wood shed will ensure that it stays dry. The simplest form of woodshed is a freestanding structure with four posts and a roof (some kind of sides are also good to stop wind blown rain from soaking the wood).

The woodshed should be close to the house for easy access, ideally somewhere you pass daily. Traditionally it was located between the outside toilet and the house so you could pick up some wood on your way back to the house. Nowadays you would probably want it between the house and car, or by the recycling area. If you buy wood the shed should be close to the driveway for ease of unloading wood. A lightweight wood shed could be moved to where you split wood (it could be anchored by the weight of firewood). A translucent shed could heat up in the sun and dry the wood faster.

If you rely on firewood for your heat it makes sense to have a place to store a modest quantity of wood inside. Then you never have to go outside on cold nights. Just refill it periodically with a wheelbarrow, ideally through a special small door directly to the outside.

Storage

This is important if your garden isn't going to be full of stuff. A shed keeps it all in one place, ensures it stays dry and makes it easier to find things (at least you know it in the shed somewhere). In many areas it needs to be lockable to prevent theft.

Service area

You might want a flat area for garbage cans; recycle bins, storage, propane tank or whatever. These are usually near the driveway for easy pickup or delivery. This isn't a very attractive area, so is commonly screened in some way. You might also put it close to the woodshed, so you can pick up wood after dropping off recycle stuff and garbage.

Worm bin

A worm bin allows you to recycle kitchen scraps without feeding rats and other pests. It should be located somewhere convenient for the kitchen and should ideally be shaded and sheltered from rain and temperature extremes. It doesn't produce a big volume of material, so doesn't have to be near the vegetable garden. See Worm composting for more on this.

Parking spaces

Traditional cottage gardens didn't have these, but like it or not they are now necessary (and often legally required). I favor some kind of separation between garden and car (with a fence and gate), but you might want to make it part of the garden.

If space is at a premium you could build a carport and have a living roof, or grow vines over it. This disguises it and provides extra growing space at the same time. You could also put solar panels up there. See Driveways for more on parking spaces.

Planting the house area

The area immediately adjacent to the house is the most important planting area in the garden, because it is also your living space. You see the plants here every day, so it is where you put the plants that need the most attention.

The plants around the house are conveniently located for any watering that is necessary. This is particularly useful in arid areas, as it will soon be obvious if plants are wilting from lack of water. This area is also convenient for receiving runoff from the roof, as well as household gray water.

From an aesthetic viewpoint it's nice to have the greenest and most succulent plants around the living areas where they can best be appreciated. These are also less flammable of course, which can be an issue in fire prone areas.

When plants are close to the house it's easier to protect them from frost, as you can quickly run outside and cover them, or even run a few incandescent light bulbs outside. Any plants growing close to south facing walls will also get extra heat from the sun.

Because you spend so much time in this area, you are more likely to see pests before they do any serious damage. Birds and other animals are less likely to come up to the house when people are around.

All of the growing areas around the house should be mulched heavily with your most attractive mulch material (it will be very visible).

Growing food in the house

Your house can also produce food, in fact in cold winter weather it may be the only part of your property that is warm enough to do so. Of course to do this you must have an area that gets sufficient light and warmth for good plant growth.

Microgreens, grass juice - These can be grown all winter, so long as you have somewhere that gets enough light, such as a windowsill (or even better a greenhouse window).

Sprouts - If you don't have a warm and sunny enough place indoors, you can always sprout seeds to provide salad material. These really can grow anywhere. Sprouting is very worthwhile and is one of the best reasons to save your own seed (especially from the easily saved Brassicas). If you grow sprouts in volume, they can provide most of the bulk for a salad, just add a few microgreen herbs for flavoring.

Baby greens - You can grow Lettuce for baby greens in plant pots or flats on a shelf. You will need quite a few pots for a significant and sustained harvest.

Mushrooms - These are particularly suitable to indoor growing as they require very little light (some can be grown in a warm dark closet). There are commercially available mushroom growing kits for a variety of species These make mushroom growing much easier, so are a good way to start. They are quite expensive however, so after you gain a little experience you may want to mix the substrate and grow the spawn yourself. See Mushrooms and fungi for more on this.

Types of plants

The plants in the area immediately around the house don't only produce food, they also help to lessen the distinction between house and garden, and make it more beautiful and pleasurable to live in.

Flowers

If you plan on having any purely ornamental flowers, they will be most appreciated on the approach to the front door and around the patio at the back.

Scented plants

Put these around entrances, windows and sitting areas, where their scent can be enjoyed. They are always good Feng Shui.

Entrance plants

A pair of matching plants in pots astride the front path, or at the bottom of the stairs, can add a touch of formality to the entrance.

Container plants

Use these in the most visible areas around the house, to soften hard paved areas (deck, patio, paths, stairs). with vegetation. The biggest thing about containers is remembering to keep them watered and you are less likely to forget if you can see them all the time.

Vegetables can also be grown in containers, though I don't really recommend it if you have any alternative. Containers can dry out rapidly in hot weather and plants don't really like having their roots confined to a small volume of soil. The one advantage of growing crops in containers is that you can move the plants around, to give them more sun or to protect them from frost. In fact using containers you can grow crops almost year round. Nor are you limited to conventional containers, you can also use grow bags, garbage cans, straw bales and more.

Tender fruit trees can be grown in large pots and brought inside for the winter. If you are really on top of this you could grow lemons, papayas, bananas, pineapples.

Fruiting plants

Plant the smaller and more attractive fruiting plants around the house (Citrus, plums, berries). In a small garden you might use multi-grafted family fruit trees with several varieties on the same tree. Put very frost tender plants against the south facing house wall, where they will benefit from the warmer microclimate. It's also convenient if you have to run out and cover them on freezing nights.

Kitchen herb bed

There should be a bed of important culinary herbs growing near the kitchen door, where they are conveniently available for cooking. Different herbs need different growing conditions (moist, average and dry soil, sun and part shade), so be sure to give each species what it needs. A simple way to do this is to build a ziggurat bed, which consists of several progressively smaller wooden frames stacked on top of each other.

Climbing plants

An arbor attached to the house can support fruiting or flowering vines, which in turn provide shade. These are particularly useful in hot climates, as they prevent sunlight entering the house and heating it up (they can keep the interior of the house significantly cooler). Climbing plants can also make the house more attractive by softening its outline and helping to connect it with the garden.

Climbing plants can be allowed to climb directly on the house (downspouts work well), but this can complicate any maintenance work. More often they are attached to trellises or arbors. Whatever support you use, it must be strong to support the weight, but preferably not too massive looking. If you are growing fruiting plants the supports shouldn't be so tall that you can't reach the fruit for harvesting. See Climbing plants for more on this.

In Mediterranean countries its common to see a grape arbor on a balcony or flat roof, providing shade from the intense sun. In most cases these are planted in the ground and trained up on to the roof, sometimes up 2 stories or more.

Grass juice bed

Grass for juicing could be grown in a small intensive bed close to the house, where it can be tended easily. This is the most cost effective way to grow this valuable nutritional supplement. See Juice Lawns for more on this.

Edible landscape garden

In recent years has their been a movement to rehabilitate food plants and bring them back into the garden with 'edible landscaping'. This means planting the more attractive vegetables, shrubs and trees in place of, or mixed with, traditional ornamental flowers and shrubs.

Edible landscaping works best when it concentrates on the fruiting trees, shrubs and perennial herbs and these should form the basis of the ornamental areas of the garden (with perhaps a few exceptional ornamentals thrown in). Quite a few crops are spectacular enough to be grown as ornamentals (Asparagus, Globe Artichoke, Quinoa, Lovage, Okra, Scarlet Runner Beans, Sunflowers) anywhere in the garden. I have also had success with other perennial vegetables (Rhubarb, Mashua, Oca) and long season, repeat harvest crops (Kale, Chard, Parsley).

The edible ornamental garden isn't the place for high productivity, but supplements the kitchen garden with additional interesting foods, while at the same time making your garden look nice. Its a lot easier to justify using scarce water on ornamentals if they are also producing food.

Living roofs

Living roofs have been popular in various parts of the world in the past, most notably Scandinavia and Kurdistan. They were valued for their insulating qualities in keeping the house warm or cool (this was before fiberglass insulation). Living roofs have received renewed attention in recent years, mostly as a way to make urban areas more environmentally friendly. The center of this interest is in eco-friendly Germany and neighboring countries, where many large buildings now have living roofs (they are even mandatory in some places).

Most modern living roofs aren't really intended for human use. They consists of a thin layer of growing medium and plants and are intended to provide a green mantle to reduce cooling needs and provide vegetation to lessen environmental impact. These roofs are most relevant to city areas, where there is a lot of impervious paved surface and land for growing plants is scarce. It's a fairly safe bet that most urban rooftops will eventually be treated in this way (the only doubt is whether urban civilization survives).

The traditional Scandinavian turf roof consisted of roof sheathing boards, covered with a layer of overlapped Birch bark sheets (layered like shingles to shed water). This was then covered in a layer of small twigs for drainage and a layer of turf. This could be an interesting way to use the turf from your lawn (though it may be hard to get the mower up there.) These roofs lasted about 20 years or so, if they didn't catch fire in the interim. Of course with modern building materials we can create living roofs that will last almost indefinitely

Advantages of living roofs

- They enable us to build structures without depriving the earth of surface vegetation (it is just transferred up to the roof).

- They can significantly reduce the energy needed for cooling a building. The surface of a typical exposed roof might reach 150° F. while underneath a living roof it usually doesn't go much above 80° F.

- Living roofs absorb dust and various air pollutants, while giving out oxygen.
- They reduce runoff from the roof.
- They protect the roofing membrane from sunlight and so prolong its life.
- They encourage wildlife

Climate for living roofs

Living roofs work best in cool humid areas where there is enough water from rainfall to keep the roof growing throughout the growing season. In dry climates you would need irrigation to keep plants green through the summer months, which kind of negates the whole principle of green building. You could just allow the roof to dry out in summer, as natural vegetation does, but a roof covered in tinder-dry plant material could be a fire hazard.

Other places for green roofs

Green roofs are not only for houses, in fact it might be easier to use them for sheds, root cellars, pergolas, car ports and other structures. Such structures will have to be more strongly built to accommodate the extra weight, but if you are building from scratch this isn't a big deal.

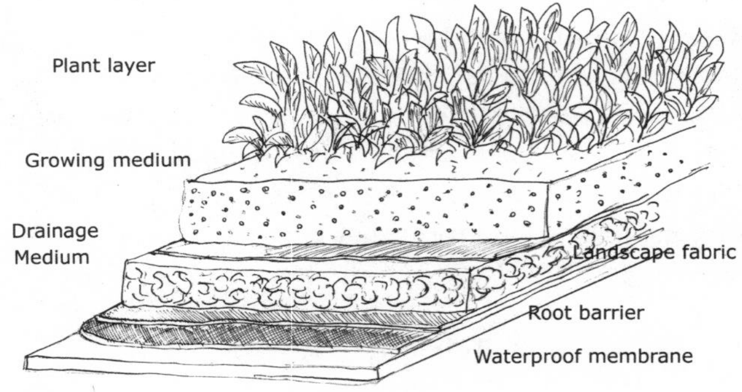

Creating a living roof

You can't just put plant a living roof on an existing house, even if it is flat enough. A living roof weighs a lot more than a conventional roof because it is carrying the weight of the plants, the growing medium and a fluctuating amount of water. You need to be sure the roof structure can take all of the extra weight. Retrofitting an existing roof can be costly, but if you are planning any alterations (and the climate is amenable) you might think about it.

The layers of a living roof

A modern living roof consists of several distinct layers, each performing a separate function. There is:

- A waterproof membrane to keep the roof watertight.
- A root protection barrier to protect the membrane from roots.
- A drainage layer to drain away excess water. This may be gravel, pumice, broken clay pots and tiles.
- A layer of landscape fabric to keep the growing medium out of the drainage layer.
- A growing medium, usually consisting of a mix of gravel, pumice, lava rock, crushed clay or concrete.
- The green roof at the California Academy of Sciences in San Francisco has a layer of plastic trays shaped like egg cartons underneath it. These act as reservoirs to hold water and have holes in the top. If the reservoirs fill with water the excess can drain away.

Depth of growing medium

Obviously the thicker and moister the layer of growing medium, the greater the range of plants that can grow there.

Shallow - Only a few plants (mostly succulents such as the Sedums) can grow successfully in a thin layer of growing medium, especially in a harsh climate (hot dry summers and cold winters are the worst).

Medium - A few edible plants can be grown in a slightly deeper layer of growing medium (a medium medium). Dry land herbs such as Oregano, Marjoram and Sage can all do well (though they aren't very convenient for the cook to dash out and pick).

Deep - If the rooting medium is deep enough (6-12 inches) you can grow a much greater variety of plants, even shrubs such as *Caragana, Cytisus, Genista and Juniperus, Ononis, Rosa and Rubus*. These give a very different look from the flat succulents or grasses.

You can also vary the depth of rooting medium to get a diversity of growing conditions.

Sloping roofs

It is possible to plant a living roof on a low pitched roof, but you have to prevent the growing medium from sliding. This is most easily done by using a homemade grid of rot-resistant 2x lumber, though this isn't very attractive.

Choosing plants for living roofs

A rooftop is a pretty inhospitable place for most plants, with shallow soil, harsh sun and extreme fluctuations in soil moisture and temperature. Only specialised plants can thrive in these condition (they need to be drought, heat and cold tolerant, shallow rooted and able to spread easily).

Some of the most useful living roof plants come from alpine or seashore habitats and are somewhat succulent. This helps them to survive lengthy periods of drought. Shortgrass prairie could be another model for a living roof. It has even been suggested that you could produce a perennial edible seed producing roof, using species such as *Elymus canadensis, Bouteloua curtipendula, Sporobolus heterolepis* and others. I imagine these would need to be pretty pampered to persuade them to actually produce anything edible (and it might be tricky to harvest them).

You can direct sow a roof with seed, or you can plant it with small plants. In a moist climate you could also just leave it to grow whatever shows up and manages to survive.

.

Living roof plants

The following species have been grown on roofs and have other possible uses as well.

Achillea millefolium
Agastache rugosa
rupestris Good bee forage species
Allium acuminatum
cernuum
moly
schoenoprasum
tuberosum
Alyssum montanum
Anthemis tinctoria
Armeria maritima
Artemisia ludoviciana
Calluna vulgaris
Coreopsis lanceolata
Dianthus arenarius
Eriogonum flavum
Eriophyllum lanatum
Fragaria chiloensis
Galium verum
Hieracium lanatum
Lavandula angustifolium
Linum perenne
Lotus corniculatus – nitrogen fixer
Oenothera caespitosa
missouriensis)
incana
Opuntia humifusa(compressa)
Origanum vulgare
Phacelia campanularia
Salvia officinalis
pratensis
Santolina rosmarinifolia
Saponaria ocymoides
Sedum purpureum
telphium
divergens
Sempervivum tectorum This plant was traditionally grown on roofs in parts of Europe, hence the name. The fleshy leaves contain a gel that can be used like that of Aloe for burns, sores and stings.
Tradescantia
Thymus citriodorus
praecox
pulegioides
Triteleia ixioides
Tulbhagia violacea

Living walls

You don't often see plants growing vertically because land is seldom vertical. However many herbaceous plants are just as happy to grow vertically as horizontally, so long as they can get the water, nutrients and light they need. Patrick Blanc, the best known exponent of vertical gardens, was inspired by the way plants grow vertically on trees in tropical rainforests. He has created many plant walls consisting of plants growing in pockets of felt and fed hydroponically. His mature walls resemble green murals and are mostly used to bring plant life to urban areas, where vertical space is much more available than precious horizontal space.

Living walls help to reduce the environmental impact of a building in much the same way as the more familiar living roof; by clothing it in life giving vegetation. I have no doubt both are going to be much more common in the future. Like living roofs they are most relevant to urban areas, but actually more useful because buildings have a lot more wall than roof. They are also more easily seen from the ground, so have more visual impact. In urban areas plants on walls provide significant benefit to wildlife in the form of food and habitat (some plants are more useful than others of course)

One of the main virtues of living walls is their ability to lessen temperature swings. A good living wall cover can reduce daily temperature fluctuations in the interior by as much as 50%. Some species can keep a building cooler in summer, others can keep it warmer in winter. Deciduous plants should be used where there is a need for summer cooling, as they allow the sun to penetrate in winter. Evergreens should be used in very cold areas as they provide better winter insulation.

The value of living walls is pretty limited in a garden situation, where we have plenty of horizontal space and so don't need to plant the much more challenging vertical areas. They could be useful in small gardens or where you have a large wall you want to cover.

A south facing masonry wall with overhanging eaves creates a mild microclimate that is useful for more tender species. Living walls also work very well with balconies, as the plants become more easily accessible.

Plants for living walls

The most obvious plants for living walls are the climbers (see Climbing Plants for more on these), but other types can be used too, you just have to give them a way to hold on to the fairly smooth vertical surface. There are commercially available systems for doing this, whereby you put the plants in pockets of growing medium in a hanging fabric sheet. These are somewhat complex and expensive though, as they require drip irrigation and hydroponic feeding.

You can also put trailing plants such as Nasturtiums in large planters on balconies and allow them to hang down. If they are not planted in the ground then drip irrigation becomes essential (they produce too much foliage and transpire too much to be hand watered. Most vines aren't good for growing downward as they are programmed to grow upwards. If you try and hang them, they will simply reverse direction and grow back up the hanging parts.

Espaliers

These can be used to clothe walls with live growth that looks good and ultimately produces fruit.

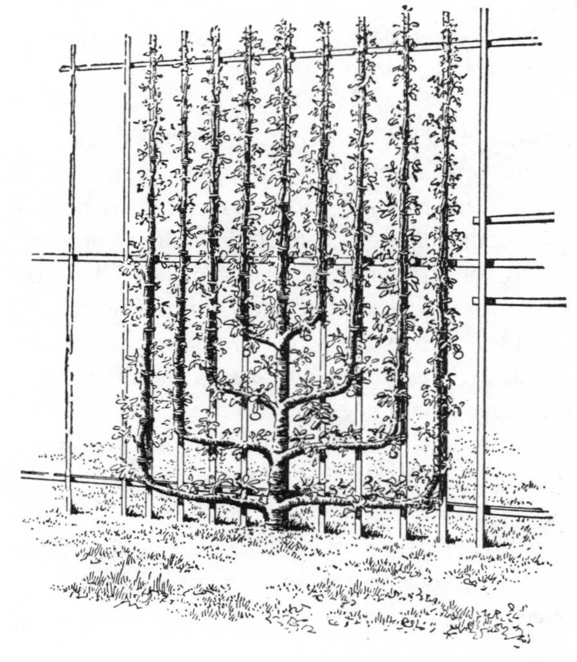

Outdoor living areas

Moving away from the house you enter the outdoor living area of the garden. The priority here is to make a place so comfortable, attractive and pleasant that it becomes the place where everyday life takes place during the warmer months. The more time you spend in the garden, the more you learn and the more productive you can make it.

Climate

Comfort outdoors is mainly determined by the temperature; if it is too hot or too cold you will simply go inside where it is more pleasant. To make the outdoors comfortable you have to mitigate the effects of extreme temperature and take advantage of any hospitable microclimate. Planning for this is complicated by the fact that there are enormous seasonal differences between the hotter months and the colder months. There are also fluctuations on the same day, so that in the cool of morning you may want sun, but in the heat of the afternoon you may need shade. This means that the same area must serve several different purposes

Sun exposure

In most situations the living area is located to the south side of the house, where it gets the most sun. In cool climates the sun is important for its warming effect, but it is also important everywhere for its psychological benefits. People like to be able to see the sun, even if it is too hot to actually sit in it. If a living area isn't bright and sunny it won't get used very much.

Of course the living area gets sun from different directions as the position of the sun changes through the day. This enables you to take advantage of the fact that the western side of the house stays warmer in the evening, and the eastern side warms up faster in the morning.

In very hot climates the living area might be to the northeast of the house, where it can serve as a refuge from the intense afternoon sun. This gets sun in the coolest part of the day, and shade in the hottest part.

Sources of shade

Trees - If you have existing shade trees consider yourself lucky and look after them. You can't buy the time it takes for a tree to grow, so don't cut any down without thinking very seriously. Decks and patios can be built around trees to provide a special naturally shaded place.

Pergola, loggia or Arbor - You can train vigorous, sun loving vines up on to these overhead structures. See Pergolas and Arbors for more on this.

Canopies and awnings - Simply large sheets of canvas or other UV resistant material, these are useful because of their flexibility. They can be pulled out when you need shade and put away when you don't. In winter they can be taken down and stored away. If the fabric is waterproof they can also provide shelter from rain and be used to collect rainwater.

Awnings could be the automated factory made retractable things like you see on the side of RV's. These aren't very attractive but are efficient and easily rolled up or down. They could also be a simple as an old salvaged sail suspended from cords.

Windbreaks

In cool climates the wind often makes sitting outside uncomfortable. The sun may warm up an area nicely, but if a cool wind gets up it will blow all of the warmth away. A windbreak can radically transform a windy spot into a warm sheltered nook, that is even comfortable in winter. See Windbreaks for more on this.

The outdoor living area must have shelter from cold winds, which usually means a windbreak to the west (the house should already block wind from the north). If you use stone or concrete walls to deflect the wind, they will also absorb the sun and can create a sun trap that gets significantly warmer than surrounding areas.

Biting insects

In many areas mosquitoes, blackflies, horseflies, gnats, no-see-ums, deer flies and other insect pests are the biggest reason people leave the garden and go into the house. Even flies that don't bite can become very irritating when you have a cloud of them buzzing around your head. These can be especially troublesome in spring when there is a lot of moisture around.

Unfortunately there aren't many good ways to deal with biting insects. Probably the most effective and permanent solution is the screened porch, but that keeps you out of the garden proper. You could use insect repellents, though I'm very reluctant to put pesticides on my skin). Scented repellents such as citronella candles are only marginally effective. The smoke from a fire pit is more effective, but breathing smoke is probably just as unhealthy as insect repellent. You could (should) encourage insect eating birds and bats with nesting sites. If all else fails you can try psychically communicating with them to tell them they are unwelcome.

Other things that affect comfort

Minor irritations can also affect how comfortable you are in the garden. It's nice to be able to walk around without getting foxtails in your socks, mud on your slippers, ticks on your ankles or Poison Oak on your bum.

Privacy is needed for psychological comfort and in crowded urban areas it may be one of your primary concerns. Creating privacy without blocking too much sun or making the garden feel small and fortress-like can be tricky. Just remember that you don't necessarily have to block a view completely; often a couple of strategically placed bushes will do the trick. See Privacy for more on this.

Make it comfortable in the evening

Many people get the most use out of their garden in the evenings after work, so think about how you can make it comfortable at these times. Heat lamps are sometimes used where evenings are cool, though I find it hard to justify using fossil fuel to heat the night. See Fireplaces below for more on this.

Patios and decks

A patio or deck provides a comfortable area for everyday outdoor activities and is the most important activity area of them all. It acts as an intermediate room that extends the house out into the garden and in good weather it can become your main living area (some people even sleep there on warm summer nights). People have told me that decks I have built have changed their home lives, by getting them outside more.

As the most human centered part of the garden the patio (or deck) should be made into something special. It should have its own focus, perhaps a view of the garden, a fireplace or a water feature. A pond or fountain works especially well here, as you can really appreciate it. In a city the sound of water falling water is often used to mask the ever present noise.

Location

The patio or deck is usually adjacent to the kitchen and living room, because these are the natural centers of household activity. It usually becomes the main access route between the house and garden, so the way into other parts of the garden should be obvious. Generally you don't want the patio attached to a bedroom (that needs privacy), though sometimes a ground floor bedroom might have its own private area.

Relaxation

An area for relaxation should have:

Quiet

Warmth

Enclosure

Comfortable furniture

Freedom from insect pests

A nice view.

Sun or shade (depending upon climate

Attractive scented plants.

Size

The dimensions of the patio or deck are often related to the size of the house. One rule of thumb says its width should be at least 2/3 the height of a two story wall (or as wide as the height of the eaves of a one story house).

Of course the main criteria as to how big to make it will be how many people are to use it (this means regularly, not for that wedding that takes place every 5 years). The rule here is to allow 125 square feet per resident. Of course if you love throwing enormous parties it will have to be bigger than if you are a recluse who shuns all human contact.

You could also determine how big an area you need by setting up your outdoor furniture and measuring how much room it takes. Or you might compare an indoor room to an outdoor one, taking into account that an outdoor area needs to be somewhat bigger (people prefer to be further apart when sitting outside).

There is a school of thought that too big a patio is better than too small. It's true that it's nice to have plenty of room for entertaining, but many people go overboard. There are far too many 3000 square foot, multi-level decks whose main function on to impress visitors (presumably with their high cost). At 125 square feet per resident that would be enough for 24 residents. Small patios can be nice too, as they tend to feel more private and personal.

Patios

A patio is a smooth flat area for relaxation, and is usually paved with hard materials such as brick, tile, flagstone, cobbles, concrete or wooden blocks. These should be compatible with the house, so the patio feels like a natural extension of it.

Designing a patio

A rectangular patio works well when it is connected to the house. Feng Shui advises that you avoid straight edges though and suggests making the patio curved or stepped rather than rectangular or square. This can also help the patio merge more easily into the garden. You could even have a bit of patio completely separated from the rest.

The patio shouldn't be paved right up to the house, There should be a planting bed (at least 36" wide) between the house and patio, to break up the large expanse of paving and introduce plant life

Building the patio

The first step in building a patio is to get the site level and clear of tree roots, perennial weeds, stones and other debris. The finished patio should be at the same level as the interior floor, or one step down and you may need to excavate to accomplish this. You then lay down an inch or so of gravel for drainage, followed by a weed barrier to prevent any weeds coming up between the paving. This is followed by two inches of compacted sand. This needs to be perfectly flat, which is done by laying down leveling boards and screeding to them. You then lay down the flagstone, brick or concrete pavers and fill the gaps between them with sand.

It's not a bad idea to put a piece of 3 or 4" conduit under the patio, in case you have to run electric or water lines at some point. You don't want to have to dig up part of the patio.

Drainage

When building a patio it is very important to give it a slight slope (1 : 50 or 1 : 100) away from the house so that it can drain properly. You may also have to arrange for the dispersal of rainwater from the roof (perhaps run a 3" or 4" drain pipe under the patio).

There are two approaches to dealing with rainwater on the patio. You can make it of permeable materials so rainfall can simply percolate through it (this will still need some slope so water doesn't puddle in heavy rain). If the patio is impervious you must slope it slightly and think about where the water will go. This could collect in a canal or rill and then drain into a pond, rain garden or other water feature.

Patio paving materials

The patio is usually the largest expanse of paving in the garden, and if it is all of one type it can look rather monotonous. It is better to mix up 2 or 3 materials and make a pattern (this is also a good way to make expensive paving go further). Don't use more than 3 paving materials or it can start to look too busy.

In Feng Shui brick or stone patios are recommended, because the small units allow air, water and chi to permeate through to the earth. Large continuous areas of poured concrete are frowned upon because they prevent this from happening. They also suggest breaking up any large expanses of paving with planting beds and containers of plants, as well as arbors to cover the area with living plants.

You can also use softer (and cheaper) material for a patio, such as decomposed granite, gravel, or wood chips. These have some advantages in that they don't absorb heat and get too hot for bare feet. They also feel closer to the earth. You could have a small hard paved area for the sitting and eating areas and a larger soft paved area for other activities. See Paths for more on paving materials.

Decks

Decks are similar to patios in many respects; the main difference is that they don't disturb the soil or affect drainage. It has been said that decks are more ecologically sound than patios, because they don't cover up the earths surface, but I don't really buy this. A well made patio made of local materials, will last almost indefinitely, but a wooden deck has a relatively limited life span (and there are over 30 million of them in the USA, which is a lot of trees). My criteria for using wood is that the object made from it should last longer than the wood took to grow – which doesn't apply in this case.

A deck feels more like a part of the house than a patio does, as it is made of similar materials and is close to the same level as the interior floor. It's almost as if you brought a floor of the house outside.

Decks come into their own on steeply sloping sites, or where you don't want to cover the ground for some reason. They can even be attached to the second story of a house, to provide additional living space, a higher vantage point and a great sleeping area. The space under a tall deck is great for storage. You could even attach a corrugated plastic roof to the underneath of the deck to keep things dry.

Designing a deck

Most of the things I wrote about patios regarding shape, size and screening for privacy, apply equally to decks. However you have greater flexibility in a deck because it can be different heights in different places, with sections at house level and sections at ground level. A deck needs to be at least 6 feet in width to be of use as living space (any less is just a walkway) and 8 or 10 feet is much better. Decks more than 30" off the ground need to have some kind of handrail.

You can use color (paint the handrail or posts) to unify the house and deck. They can also have built in benches and planter boxes to connect them to the garden.

A deck can be made more fire resistant by enclosing the sides to prevent fire getting underneath.

Deck materials

Decks must be made from rot resistant wood if they are to last, and many magnificent 500 year old

Redwoods and Cedars have ended their lives hosting barbecues. Pressure treated wood is commonly used for the framing because it is cheaper and isn't visible from the finished deck.

If you can't get recycled wood there is also the option of the increasingly popular recycled plastic composite decking. This is a better use than the landfill, but it will eventually deteriorate and become plastic waste once again.

If a deck is not to deteriorate it will need regular maintenance. Remove leaves and other debris from between the boards (they trap moisture and hasten rot) and treat it with preservative (more chemicals). Doing this conscientiously can prolong the life of the deck almost indefinitely.

Developing the outdoor living space

Sitting places

Probably the first requirement for an outdoor living area is that is has somewhere comfortable to sit, for resting, talking, drinking tea, reading and thinking. The sitting area should combine all of the elements necessary to make it a nice place to be.

Conventional landscaping says that a seating area should be partly enclosed (a wall, an arbor, a hedge), so one looks out from a place of psychological security (and for privacy). Traditionally such spaces are round or square as these shapes encourage conversation and sitting. It should also have a focal point as a center. A summer sitting area needs shade, greenery and perhaps water. You might also plant scented plants to perfume the air. A winter sitting area would require uninterrupted sun and protection from cold winds.

You may want additional sitting places for different times of the day (morning, midday, sunset, night) and maybe even a covered sitting place for wet weather.

Additional sitting areas can be located anywhere else in the garden you naturally want to sit. There should definitely be a resting place in the vegetable garden and perhaps in other places where you spend a lot of time (the greenhouse, propagation area.). You might want a sitting area in a sheltered spot, by a pond, fountain or other water feature, by the back door, under shade, alongside a path, in a sun trap or by a great view or prized artwork or plant. The sitting place itself can be in a fairly uninteresting location, as it is only a space for a table and chairs. It is placed adjacent to the most attractive views, so you can sit and look at them.

Sitting places are also visual elements in themselves (they suggest relaxation and comfort). With a couple of attractive seats and a small table, a sitting area becomes a focal point as well as a garden destination. The sitting area should actually enhance its location, making it a special place in it's own right.

Take a chair out to where you think a sitting place should be located and sit there for a while. Is it a good place? Are any nearby places better? How could it be improved? (More shade, privacy, a focal point?)

Furniture

Sitting outdoors should be as comfortable as sitting indoors. The seating should be comfortable, attractive, durable and weatherproof. Seats with backs tend to be the most comfortable and are best for lounging and conversation. Benches are most often used for brief rest or thinking.

Chairs are also focal points, so the style of the furniture should work in the garden setting. Especially ornamental or attractive chairs may even be located specifically where they can be admired. For example at the end of a path where they provide a sense of termination.

If you have lots of money you can buy some really beautiful outdoor furniture. If you don't have much money you can make your own and add another level of your being to the garden.

Lounge chairs you can lay down on are pretty much an essential for the living area, as they enable you to really relax (or even go to sleep). You should have at least two, with a small table for drinks.

The most trouble free seating is made of stone, rot resistant wood or metal (cast iron or aluminum work well). These are totally impervious to the weather and can stay outside year round.

The most comfortable seating uses softer materials such as canvas, wicker or cushions. You can't leave these outside year round, so you need somewhere to store them for the winter. Make sure any cushions are the type that don't mind getting wet and dry out easily. A cluster of pillows on a rug under a tree can make a very comfortable relaxation area. Of course any cushions (or furniture) can be used outside if under a covered area.

Simple flat benches can be made from anything that is sufficiently stable. The simplest consists of two log rounds (or concrete blocks) with a plank of wood. A large slab of stone on two flat boulders is even better.

Most indoor furniture doesn't last very long outside, as it isn't made to be exposed to the elements. A metal indoor table might work if treated with preservative and covered in a plastic tablecloth. I don't have a problem with old living room furniture finding a resting place outside. This isn't impractical in the dry California summer, though it will slowly disintegrate. A nice battered old couch helps to set a rural redneck ambience. All you need to complete the picture is a shotgun on the wall, a few lines of beer bottles, a couple of junk pickups and some country music.

You will want a small table for the sitting area. This might be a round café table or a small side table to hold a coffee cup.

I like the wood and fabric chairs that can be hung from a porch roof or a tree.

A retaining wall is an obvious place for a built in bench. If you are ambitious you might also build seats into an arbor.

If you want to color your wooden furniture, stain is better than paint. Dark greens, browns, blues and grays all work well.

If you are handy with tools the traditional Adirondack chair is pretty easy to make. Its design makes it very comfortable (for a wooden chair) and its wide arms double as tables for coffee or a book. Because it is made completely out of wood you don't have to worry about it getting wet. You might also make some footstools for added comfort.

Water features

These are mostly ornamental rather than practical, but open water brings such beauty and interest to the living area that I consider it essential. They also provide a visual focus where none naturally exists. I discuss ponds, tubs, fountains, sculptures, ditches, marshes, bogs and more, in the section on Adding water to the garden.

Fireplace

An outdoor fireplace is the best way to get people out into the garden on cool evenings and nights. In fact I consider it to be one of the essentials for every garden. Sitting around a fire with friends and family and dog (and beer) on a cool night is probably the second oldest form of human social activity. It satisfies on some primitive level that a propane heat lamp just can't touch.

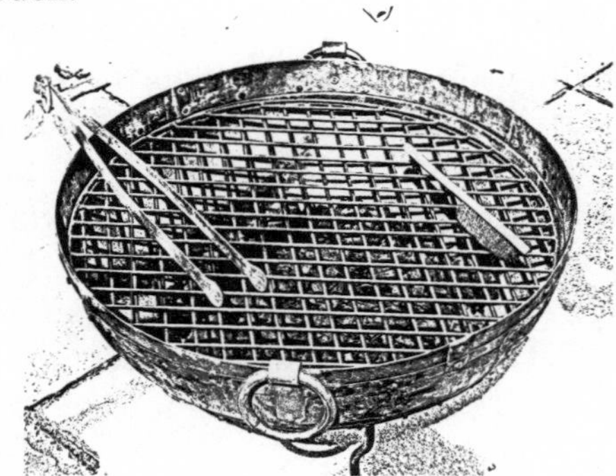

The outdoor fireplace actually does multiple duty. It brings the family together, it entertains you, warms you and gives you a way to get rid of woody garden waste. It even converts that waste into usable wood ash fertilizer (if you don't burn anything toxic in it).

The fireplace should be in the outdoor living area, but not so close to the house that it sends smoke into it. You could also have a fire pit out in the wild garden for a more back to nature experience.

A fire pit doesn't have to be very elaborate (stainless steel, damper, vents, blowers and chimney - over engineering is a curse of modern society). You can just dig down to mineral earth and make a ring of stones. Perhaps have a few log rounds to sit on.

If you don't want to build a permanent fire pit you can buy some very practical metal fireplaces. These have the advantage that you can move them around, even when there is a fire going (admittedly you may not need to do this very often). They usually have a grate too, which means they can be used for cooking (throw some ears of corn on it, straight from the garden).
If you use your fireplace a lot you may want to have a separate set of chairs for it.

Cooking area

For many people the cookout is one of the most important summer garden activities. The simplest outdoor cooking area is just a convenient spot for the portable barbecue, downwind of the house and sitting areas. Built-in barbecues look great on architect's drawings, but I have seen more than one gathering leaves (one had actually been converted into a water feature). The mobile grill is more versatile and convenient, because it can be moved around according to the wind and taken undercover in case of rain.

Of course the extreme consumer (who probably isn't reading this book, but that's beside the point) won't be satisfied with a mere built in barbecue. He (or she) will want a complete built-in outdoor kitchen complete with barbecue, grill, smoker, deep fat fryer, sink, fridge, dishwasher, granite counter tops, teak dining table and chairs, fireplace, floodlights, outdoor propane heaters, wide screen TV and bathroom (and maybe a spare bedroom too, in case people eat too much and feel ill).

Plant culinary herbs around the cooking area (Basil, Bay, Chives, Myrtle, Oregano, Rosemary, Sage, Welsh Onion), as well as scented flowers and perhaps some tea plants. In fact here is a place for edible landscaping to really make sense: Tomatoes, Cucumbers, Peppers, Lettuce and more.

A brick pizza oven is an interesting cooking accessory that lets you invite people over for pizza instead of a barbecue. In medieval England bakers ovens were heated with bundles of dry sticks, which could be a good use for some garden waste.

If you want to get more eco than your neighbor you could use a charcoal hibachi grill instead of propane (going even further you could make your own charcoal out of coppiced wood). You could also build a horno out of clay. Or you could forget about burning altogether and build one of the various kinds of solar ovens. Going one better you could eat everything raw and see who's really macho at the Monday night football game.

Eating Area

Any outdoor meal is a special occasion, so make a special area for it. If you enjoy eating outside then a dining area will be an important part of the patio or deck. It should be close to the kitchen and any outdoor cooking area and needs good access paths, electricity, water, lighting, comfortable seating and a fairly large table. Depending upon the climate it might be partly shaded for protection from the sun, or it might have a solid roof to keep off the rain. A classic accessory for the table is a big umbrella for summer shade. A canvas awning (perhaps an old sail) will also work for this. In some cases insect netting may be needed too.

The size of an eating area will depend upon how many people it is to accommodate. For 6 people it should be at least 14 x 10 feet

A large table for family dining can easily be made from 2 x 6's (when covered with a nice tablecloth it will be perfectly elegant) and can be as big as you want. If you don't have any suitable chairs you could make some benches too.

Sleeping area

The garden should have an area for serious relaxation, to counter the idea that it is just a place for work. This could be sun loungers on the patio, a hammock strung between two shade trees for afternoon naps, or a fully made up bed for sleeping under a summer full moon.

An outdoor bed can be quite practical, as it gives you a great place to sleep on hot summer nights, or to put extra guests (they might wonder whether they are being particularly favored or slighted.) Put it where it will get the best view of the night sky, unobstructed by too many trees. In less than reliable climates you could even have a covered roof over the bed, though this will block out your view of the stars.

In densely populated areas an outdoor sleeping area will need privacy, which usually means keeping it in the back of the garden. It might also need a windbreak or insect netting to hold back the hordes of biting bugs (this could be an elegant hanging mosquito net).

A sleeping area can be a simple raised platform with an old futon and cushions covered in fabric. An old metal bed frame with wooden slats and a futon would work too. Obviously you will have to take the futon indoors after use, so it doesn't mildew and wildlife doesn't take up residence.

The outdoor bedroom should be planted with night-scented flowers such as Angels Trumpet, Moonflower, Night Scented Stocks or Night Scented Phlox.

Lighting

Lights undoubtedly make the garden more useful and comfortable at night, but they should be used judiciously because they can easily spoil the atmosphere. There is nothing more lovely than a garden by summer moonlight and nothing more annoying than having your night vision spoiled by a neighbor switching on the lights (sensor lights are even worse.) Fortunately you should be able to block a lot of distant light with carefully placed fences and plants. We should all learn to love the night and not be afraid of it. Out in the Mojave Desert I was struck by the fact that most houses had floodlights on all night. For some reason people couldn't deal with the magical desert darkness.

Lighting will attract many night flying insects, so don't have it too close to your relaxation areas. Lights are so effective at this they are sometimes placed over a pond to attract insects for fish to eat.

I prefer to only put electric lighting close to the house and only use it when really necessary. Low voltage lighting is most often used because it is safe enough to be installed by anyone. Solar lights are becoming more practical and hence more popular. Candles in lanterns (or paper bags) are nice for atmosphere, but not practical on a larger scale (and also a potential fire risk). The most energy efficient lighting is the LED type, but this is more expensive to buy. Another way to save energy (and light pollution) is to have a timer to turn the lights off at a pre-determined time.

Types of lighting

Task lighting - As the name suggests this is used for illuminating specific tasks, such as putting out the compost or getting firewood.

Up lighting - This is used to illuminate individual features such as statues, plants and buildings. I prefer to keep up lighting to a minimum because it is a major cause of light pollution.

Spot lighting - This is used to light specific objects.

Path lighting - This shines down on to the path to illuminate it without causing glare. They are usually low voltage, or more recently solar.

Sensor lights – We've all seen these lights turn on when they detect movement. They are common in cities and suburbs where people are afraid of crime and everywhere people are afraid of the dark. They can be annoying if they keep getting turned on by moving animals.

Electric outlets

Lay power lines for outlets (and lights) when first laying out the garden (along with water lines). Ideally put high voltage cables in a conduit and bury them 18" deep, so you don't spear them while digging. While you are doing this you could install some outlets for plugging in lights, music, power tools and other stuff. Any outdoor electrical installation should be totally weatherproof of course.

Hot tub

The hot tub/spa has become a popular garden feature in recent years. In cold weather this is a great luxury, but use a lot of energy which makes it notoriously expensive to run. An electrician once told me that he removed three or four electric hot tubs every year, because people couldn't afford to run them (an old hot tub could make a good rainwater catchment tank or food pond).

Hot tubs can be heated with wood if you have a snorkel stove. You might also rig up some old solar hot water panels.

If you really enjoy soaking in hot water, an outdoor bathtub can replace a hot tub (though you can't fit more than two people in it). A friend simply lights a small fire underneath one end of an old cast iron bathtub (he has to lay on a foam mat because the tub gets hot). He adjusts the temperature by adding cold water when it starts to get too hot. The used water is drained out and channeled into the garden.

Swimming pool

A swimming pool gives you a great way to cool down in hot weather and guarantees you will have friends in summer. However it is expensive to heat (you heat up the water and it heats up the air) and only really make sense in areas with long hot summers where it can warm up naturally (a solar pool cover helps a lot, as does a solar water heater). In short summer areas a pool is only useful for a third of the year at best, which makes it hard to justify the expense (no doubt this is why they are looked upon as a luxury in colder areas). Of course most pools use toxic chemicals to keep them clean. See Water features for more on natural swimming pools.

Summerhouse

The summerhouse originated in cool rainy Britain as a place to enjoy the garden in unpredictable weather. It gives you a reliably comfortable place to sit, talk, sleep, read and entertain whatever the weather, and can be used for everything from afternoon tea to illicit trysts. You can also sleep in it at night, or use it as a summer guest bedroom. On a more mundane level it is a good place to leave things overnight, or over the winter (it shouldn't become a storage shed though).

The summerhouse usually has a raised wooden floor to keep it dry. There are also large doors or panels that can be opened in warm weather or closed when it is wet or cold. In insect country it would also need screens. Electricity would make it more useful. It is important that it be large enough for real use (10 feet diameter is probably the minimum), so will only really fit in a large garden.

A summerhouse should be well designed and beautiful because it is a strong visual element and provides a centerpiece and focal point for it's own garden area. There should also be plenty of plants (vines especially) to tie it in to the rest of the garden.

Gazebo A gazebo is a summerhouse specifically designed for viewing (gazing at) the garden. Hence they were placed where they could take advantage of a special view such as a lake, distant mountains or a flower garden.

Overhead structures for plants

Arbors

In hot climates an arbor provides essential summer shade for the sitting or eating area. Without it the garden would be too uncomfortably hot to be useful. By acting as a ceiling it also gives the area beneath it a sense of intimacy and enclosure. The sun shining through the planted arbor casts a interesting mix of light and shade on the ground.

The sense of intimacy is enhanced even further if the arbor is partially enclosed on the sides (trellis is good for this). This can also help to shelter it from the wind.

An arbor also gives us a way to grow another layer of specialized food producing plants. In this case the highly productive and delicious fruiting vines such as Grape or Kiwi. You might also add a few strongly scented vine such as Honeysuckle or Jasmine

The arbor also has other garden uses:

- It is an important visual element that gives immediate height to the garden.
- An eating area is often covered by an arbor to create a special place for summer dining.
- A strongly built arbor might support a swing or a hammock.
- A modern use for an arbor would be to support a solar hot water heater or photovoltaic panels.
- An arbor covered in fruiting vines could be a destination in some corner of the garden.
- In a wet climate you could have an arbor with a solid (but transparent) roof. You can still grow vines over it, but will always have a dry area no matter what the weather (screw it from underneath and you can take it down to clean it if necessary). If the weather is generally cool you could also have transparent sides to windward and make a warm sun trap.

Size

If your arbor is to support the more vigorous fruiting vines it will have to be a large and fairly substantial. One mature fruiting Kiwi plant may sprawl over 20 feet and weigh several hundred pounds. A minimum size for four vines would be 18 feet x 24 feet but even bigger is better. It should also be at least 8 feet tall, as shoots will hang down underneath and reduce the headroom considerably.

Building arbors

The arbor should be attractive even though it will soon be partially obscured by vegetation. The style you choose should complement the house.

Round peeled poles from the woods can be used to make a rustic looking arbor. This is the cheapest (and most ecologically sound) way to get the support structure you need. The round horizontal members also shed rain better than squared ones. The best poles would be rot resistant Chestnut which doesn't have much sapwood, but any straight poles could be used (just build it in such a way that you can replace the individual members if they start to rot).

Formal arbors can be made with large white painted 6 x 6 posts and finials (smaller 4 x 4 posts are strong enough but not very imposing visually) . Masonry columns are also very formal and durable, but potentially expensive to build. If you have salvaged brick and some rebar you could do it yourself (just make sure they are perfectly plumb).

You could also cast concrete columns in place using sections of cardboard form tube. Just make sure you give them a strong foundation, make them plumb and vibrate well to eliminate voids. You could also cast columns in sections using form tubes (make a jig and you can insert sections of rebar to pin them together). The best time to make these is when pouring another concrete job. Just order an extra yard of concrete (remember that's 16 gallons of gasoline) to fill the columns (and be ready with extra help).

You could decorate your arbor with fabric, paint, ornaments and any kind of artwork. If you plan on painting it be aware that it will be hard to re-paint when it is covered in vines. A stain is may be a better choice, as it will just fade away.

The area under an arbor should be fairly easy to clean because of bird droppings, fallen fruit and leaves.

An arbor doesn't provide much shade until the plants get well established. To provide shade in the meantime you can lay poles or wooden lath on top, or use reed or bamboo mats or canvas. These can be removed in winter, or when the plants get big enough to provide the required shade.

Any tall open structure can be vulnerable to the wind, and may require extra bracing in windy areas.

Pergolas

Pergolas were originally used to support fruiting vines and keep the fruit up off the ground. The term is now usually used for an arbor that covers a walkway. A pergola makes a strong vertical element in the garden, and is also useful for separating different areas.

Generally a pergola consists of pairs of upright posts, connected by thick cross members and is at least as wide as it is tall. The distance between each pair of uprights should be at least 1 ⅓ of the width. These are connected with wooden members laid lengthways on top, and then the cross pieces go on these. It is important that the pairs of posts are plumb and that the cross members are level.

A pergola can be built using any of the materials used to build an arbor: rustic poles, sawn lumber, metal or stone columns with wooden beams and cross members. For added refinement the cross members often have decorative ends, though they are soon partially hidden by vegetation. The materials they are made from are less important than the plants that grow on them.

Ideally the paving under the pergola should be smooth, so it is easy to clean away fallen leaves and fruit.

Arches

An arch may be used to frame a view, act as a focal point, mark the location of a path or simply to emphasize a transition. Of course they also support climbing plants. They should be quite tall and wide (a minimum of 8 feet high at the center), as vining plants will hang down, making them quite a bit lower.

A single arch can be used to frame a special view. A double arch gives more space for climbing plants to get a hold. A series of large arches (even if quite widely spaced) can create the impression of a tunnel along a path. These work best in a very sunny spot and might cover a path for some distance. Often they have a focal point at the end. Like the similar pergola a tunnel becomes a strong dividing element in the garden.

Rustic arches can be made from flexible natural materials such as bent wooden poles, Bamboo or Willow shoots (you can weave an arch). These may not last very long, but long enough to give the garden an extra dimension while trees and shrubs are growing. Long Willow shoots stuck in the ground can root to create a living green arch, which should last much longer.

More durable materials include rebar, plastic coated tubular steel, copper pipe or even reinforcing wire mesh. Steel rebar can be used for making large, very strong arches and dome structures.

A traditional idea for an arch is to train trees up temporary flexible poles and twist them together at the top. Eventually the trees grow together and the poles are removed, to leave a living arch.

Ropes

Ropes or steel cables can be strung between buildings or other structures and used for supporting vines. This simple idea has many potential uses. For maximum strength and durability and minimal sagging use wire cables and turnbuckles, securely attached to buildings with screw eyes.

A parallel series of such wires could be used to create a minimalist arbor for supporting vines. Just make sure it is sufficiently well anchored to support the weight.

Children and gardens

If you have children they will be a big factor in your garden design because they spend more time there than most adults (unless you allow them to spend their lives on facebook or playing computer games). Your main goal here is to make sure your children grow up with fond memories of the garden and an appreciation of the real (natural) world. I still remember eating golden raspberries in my grandmas garden 50 years ago. In fact you might say this book is the fruit of those plants.

The needs of children will change over the years, so anything you create for them won't be used for very long, Plan on converting it into something else when they outgrow it.

It is important to consult with your children to find out what they want and make it work for them. What they need will depend upon how old they are. They may want a playhouse, a garden, a tree house or a fort. If they are old enough you might just provide the materials, tools and advice and let them build their own structures. They will learn some skills and appreciate it more (it's also less work for you).

A play area for small children should be visible from the kitchen and living room windows, so you can keep an eye on them. It should be secure (so they can't get away from you), warm, sheltered and have a mix of sun and shade. Young children like areas they can dig up and make a mess in, so it should include a sand box and water.

Older children could be given their own area to do as they please. This could be fairly wild, with places to hide, camp or build a BMX track. For the benefit of everyone this should be well away from the house.

Adults might want a play area for sports such as croquet, volleyball, basketball and badminton. These tend to be noisy and public so keep them near the street (where neighbors can join in) and away from quiet areas.

Stray children can sometimes be a problem, entering the garden to take fruit or vandalize things (glass greenhouses may be particularly vulnerable). There are many options in your arsenal of deterrence. Barbed wire is out, but you might try naturally intimidating barriers of Poison Oak, Stinging Nettles or brambles (though the fruit might be counter productive). Of course it is usually easier to just make friends with them.

Some people imagine that because children are closer to the earth than adults they must be interested in gardening. Children do have an instinctive interest in the natural world (they certainly like to get closer to the earth than adults), but gardening mostly seems like incomprehensible grown up work to them. They are more interested in exploration and doing things rather than goals, so if you want them to enjoy nature you will just let them play in the garden. Don't try to harness them as a free labor force, it won't work.

Kids like action toys, such as slides (I've seen a great one made out of sheet metal running down the side of a hill), rope swings, paddling pools, climbing frames. Of course if you worry about liability you might not want such potentially dangerous things in your garden (I mean the children not the play things). They might also want a playhouse, toy storage and perhaps a small garden plot

Elemental forces
When thinking about a place for younger children, think about the elemental forces, earth and water. These have a primal attraction for children and will keep them occupied for hours. Actually there is also another intriguing element kids love: fire, but everyone knows playing with fire can be trouble.

Water is the ultimate kid magnet and will draw them like moths to as flame (to avoid the same result, make sure any water feature is totally safe). They will spend hours messing about with any kind of water. A small pond is good, but water moving in streams or channels is even better (maybe get a hand pump so they can move water back up hill and then release it).

Playing with the earth is almost as attractive to children as water and can lead to all kinds of creative play. Mix earth and water together and you have mud or child heaven (and laundry hell - let them go naked). Sand is preferable to earth from a parents viewpoint, because it is much cleaner. You can make a sandbox in about 20 minutes by making a frame out of four boards with a piece of landscape fabric underneath. It will probably need a cover to keep out cats (make this from painted plywood and it can also serve as a low table). Portable plastic sand boxes work well enough, but are pretty ugly.

Tunnels
Children like cave-like structures they can crawl into. The easiest (and cheapest) way to achieve this is to grow one. Weave a tunnel or dome of long supple shoots and grow vines (annual or perennial) over it.

Swings
A swing is a great feature for children and adults alike, in fact I would call it an essential. Hang it from a suitably protected tree limb (the higher the limb, the wider the arc of swing). The bottom end of the swing may be a stick, a tire or a comfortable seat. You can also get hanging chairs that are much more comfortable than a simple swing.

To get the rope over a high limb, tie a stone to the rope and throw it over the limb (carefully so it doesn't hit you in the face when it swings down). Then tie the free end to the trunk.

Playhouse
A nicely built playhouse can be a focal point, a house in miniature. This is popular with both boys and girls, though they may have different ideas as to how it should look. Make it big enough that it can be used for something else after the children have grown (or as a spare summer sleeping space). Build it soon though, so they can get their use out of it, because it won't be needed for long.

Tree house

A tree house can be a magical place for kids. It should be high enough to be exciting (and should feel like it's in the trees), but not so high that a fall would be potentially fatal. Obviously where you put it is dependent on finding a suitable tree. Don't put it where shouting children (or falling children) will disturb the atmosphere of the garden.

Of course there is no reason to discriminate against adults here. You might want a tree house for yourself as a refuge, study, or even a spare bedroom.

Trampoline

This is always a big hit with kids because defying gravity appeals instinctively. It is also a low impact way for adults to exercise and have some fun at the same time.

Ball games

If the garden is big enough you might want an area for ball games. Keep in mind that this will need to be relatively flat and smooth. A lawn for soccer or croquet, a basketball hoop, a volleyball net.

Planting for children

You may not have thought about planting things specifically for children, but this is the best way to get them interested in gardening. The garden becomes much more rewarding (and meaningful and memorable) for children when they can forage for tasty treats in it.

Use your imagination when planting the childrens areas and grow plants that will interest them. Any plants with tasty edible parts are good. Favorites in my garden include Alpine Strawberries, Anise Hyssop, Blackberries, Blueberries, Donut Peaches, Fennel, Honeyberries, Raspberries, Rhubarb (warn them about the poisonous leaves), Sage, Spearmint, Strawberries and Stevia (my kids wrap a Stevia leaf in a Spearmint leaf for an all-natural sweet treat).

Avoid thorny plants for the sake of the children and fragile plants for the sake of the plants. Creeping, vigorous, even invasive plants work best

Spot plant favorite vegetables (Cucumbers, Peppers, Carrots, Sugar Snap Peas) around the larger garden as well, so they can go out foraging. At the same time educate them about potentially dangerous plants and about not eating anything they don't know to be edible.

Children have an affinity for tall, luxuriant, jungle-like plants that tower over their heads, such as Sunflowers, Amaranth, Quinoa, Corn (try Popcorn), Scarlet Runner Bean, Gunnera, Chayote. Try making a maze out of your Corn planting, or completely surround their playhouse with Corn or Sunflowers. Allow some Scarlet Runner Beans to climb up and make the growth even thicker. You might, or might not, get a good harvest but the kids will certainly have fun and will remember it for the rest of their lives.

You could also grow a Sunflower (or Corn) house. Plant a circle or rectangle of Sunflowers and when they are a foot or so high plant beans (Scarlet Runner Beans work great) around them.

The sprawling vines and the colorful fruit of Pumpkins make them another natural choice for childrens gardens. Let them write their names or draw on the immature fruit.

Vegetable beds

Some children will want to emulate you and have their own bed for growing flowers and vegetables. It's best if this is close to your intensive vegetable beds, so you can make sure it is looked after (if your children are to look upon gardening as a positive experience they need to have some success).

Start children with the more vigorous and easy to grow crops (Sunflowers, Carrots, Corn, Squash) so they don't get discouraged. Also things they particularly like, such as Strawberries, Melons, Spearmint, Blackberries (ideally thornless).

Lawns

A large lawn is an attractive place for children to play, in fact I would say this is probably the best reason to have a lawn. If you live in a suitable climate it can be a fairly low-maintenance area. Ideally keep it small enough that you can cut it with a push mower (or the older children can).

Planting the outdoor living area

Planting ideas

You will spend a lot of time on the patio or deck, so put your most attractive and prized plants around it. They will help to soften the area and bring the garden closer to the house. Have some intensive beds for growing highly prized crops (salads, tomatoes, melons). This is a place where edible landscaping can really show what it's capable of, so plant attractive vegetables, culinary herbs, fruiting shrubs and small or espaliered fruit trees.

Some of the species around the deck should also be out in the garden, to help to connect the two.

Use lots of scented plants, as well as those that attract butterflies and hummingbirds.

You may need to plant screens for privacy here. Fruiting hedges work well and their berries are less likely to be eaten by birds when humans are hanging about a lot of the time.

Grow a tea garden, so you can grab a few leaves for a cup of fresh tea whenever you want. It would be great to be able to ask someone what kind of tea they would like and then reach out and pick it. See Herbs for a listing of tea plants.

Train climbing vines on an arbor to provide summer shade and fruit.

Herb Garden

Many traditional gardens feature a separate "herb garden". This is often a rather artificial creation, included for aesthetic or vaguely romantic reasons rather than practical purposes. The popular culinary herbs have a variety of differing requirements and don't really grow together very well. Some like it hot and dry (Sage, Rosemary, Thyme, Oregano) while others prefer cool moist places (Mint, Lovage, Watercress).

You should definitely have a small herb patch close to the kitchen door, for the convenience of whoever is cooking.

There is also a place for a bigger herb garden if you want to grow a lot of herbs and other unusual edible plants. This could even be in its own garden room. Its main virtue is in giving you a place where you can conveniently locate and care for a whole range culinary and medicinal herbs, as well as other useful plants. It can contain a variety of habitats from rock garden to pond. This area should be fairly close to the house (perhaps off of the patio), not just for culinary convenience but because it is such a fascinating place from a horticultural viewpoint.

Mushrooms and fungi

A shady north facing wall might be a good place for growing fungi. Stack inoculated logs there, where you can keep an eye on them (they can fruit quite quickly once they start).

Planting in containers

Plants in containers help to bridge the gap between the house and garden, indoors and outdoors. They also help to make dull areas more interesting. For example they are often used to break up and soften large areas of patio or deck. They also look good on wide steps.

One of the main virtues of containers is that they make plants mobile and so more versatile. Plants in containers can be moved around to follow the sun and switched between shady and sunny areas. They also enable you to grow tender plants outside in summer and move them indoors for protection in cold weather. Dwarf Bananas, Citrus, Figs, Bay even Papaya can do well in containers.

Growing in containers is also an effective way to confine rampant growers such as Bamboos and Mints. They also work well where there is little natural soil. Annuals can be direct sown in containers for maximum effect with little work.

Problems with containers

The big drawback of container plantings is that they contain so little soil they dry out quickly, especially in hot climates. There are a number of ways to reduce the amount of watering they need.

Use the largest container you can, and fill it with a good potting soil. You can line the sides of terra-cotta pots with plastic to reduce evaporation. You can also bury the bottoms of containers in the ground (to keep them cooler and connect them to the ground).

Of course the easiest way to keep your container plants moist is by setting up drip irrigation and this is pretty much essential in very dry areas. If this isn't possible you could have a reservoir of water in the bottom of the bowl and stand potted plants in it.

Choosing containers

Almost anything that can hold soil and has drainage holes has been used to grow plants at some point. This includes the traditional terra-cotta plant pots, ceramic pots, old buckets, stone troughs (or fake ones made of hypertufa), sinks, barrels, old watering cans, wheelbarrows, old toilets and much more.

If you are using terra-cotta pots make sure they are intended for outdoor use, as some indoor pots will disintegrate if exposed to repeated frost and moisture.

If a pot is on the ground you tend to just see the plant in it, so if you have particularly attractive pots then raise them up to make them more visible. Big ugly pots can be hidden behind attractive smaller ones. You can cluster small pots together for more impact. Even stacks of empty terra-cotta pots can be ornamental and provide refuge for wildlife.

One rule of thumb says that a plant should be twice the height of its container.

I like the effect of window boxes, as they can make plants visible from inside the house. The box should be firmly attached to the windowsills, but the plants should be in individual containers sitting in the box. This makes it easy to attend to plants in hard to reach boxes. You can also have a water reservoir to reduce the frequency of watering.

Hanging baskets

These can be particularly ornamental as they allow plants to cascade down, rather than growing up.

The vegetable garden

The vegetable or kitchen garden enables us to grow a lot of food in a small space and so receives the most attention and resources of any part of the garden. It is where you will grow the bulk of those familiar foods you eat in quantity every day and all the other areas are just supplemental to this. I have already written two books about growing a vegetable garden (The Organic Gardeners Handbook and The Vegetable Growers Handbook), so I am not going to go into great detail here.

Even ornamental gardeners are often devoted to their vegetable gardens, not just because it produces food, but because it involves us more fully than any other area. I recently read a book by a famous gardener in which he confessed that when he and his partner get too old to maintain their large garden, the kitchen garden would be the last part they would give up. Many other gardeners feel the same way.

Vegetable gardening attracts such devotion because it is rewarding is so many ways. It is the most interesting part of the garden, because so much is going on all the time and things change so quickly. It is challenging to grow food to perfection. There is the psychological satisfaction of producing your own food, which is the most basic and essential of all human activities. Of course the ultimate reward is the unsurpassed quality of the food.

Ornamental or productive

Traditionally the vegetable (or kitchen) garden was quite separate from the ornamental garden. There are several reasons for this, some silly and some perfectly reasonable.

One silly reason was old-fashioned Victorian snobbery. Vegetables were grown by poor people out of necessity and were therefore considered low class. As a purely utilitarian feature they were hidden away where genteel eyes wouldn't be offended. Surprisingly this attitude is still persists in some places, so that some housing developments still attempt to prohibit vegetable gardens.

Even today the vegetable garden is sometimes hidden away because it is thought to be unattractive when compared to the flower garden. I can't understand such an attitude. The primary focus of this area may be on producing food, but the vegetable garden has a beauty that is more than skin deep. We need to broaden our idea of beauty beyond rigidly defined aesthetics, to include diversity, productivity and ecological integrity. In 1845 William Cobbet wrote "It is most miserable taste to seek to poke away the kitchen garden in order to get it out of sight. If well managed nothing is more beautiful than the kitchen garden".

A more sensible reason for isolating the vegetable garden is that there are inherent differences in the culture and uses of ornamentals and annual vegetables. It is easier and more efficient to plant and tend large quantities of crop plants if they are all in one place. It takes quite a lot of space to grow enough vegetables to feed a family, even when they are planted altogether. It takes even more space (and water, labor and time) if they are scattered around the garden.

I prefer to keep most of my vegetables in one place for ease of cultivation, but I certainly don't try to hide them away.

Different kinds of vegetable garden

Different people approach the vegetable garden in different ways. How you grow your vegetables will depend upon what you want the garden to look like, the crops you want to grow and your temperament. No kind of garden is better than any other, it just depends upon what you are trying to achieve.

The intensive vegetable garden

This kind of garden usually consists of a series of permanent raised, wide beds and is used to grow the vegetables needed in quantity for everyday use. The garden is treated like a miniature farm, with orderly beds of crops, designed and planted for efficiency. The plants are there to produce food and anything that helps them do this is encouraged (careful spacing, weeding, thinning, fertilizing, watering).

This kind of garden has a lot going for it, especially when you are starting out. It is generally easier to keep things under control when everything is laid out in linear beds. It simplifies calculating bed areas for fertilizing, crop planning and rotations. It's also easier to lay out drip irrigation, or use an overhead oscillator. Planting in beds also makes it easier to support and protect the plants with netting or row covers.

This type of garden can produce a lot of food in a small space, so is popular with city gardeners. It isn't usually very big, so should be near the kitchen where it can be easily tended and harvested.

The informal cottage vegetable garden

The vegetable garden doesn't have to be a utilitarian place. It can be productive and attractive at the same time, even a fun place to hang out. If designed and maintained properly it can be more than just a food producing area, it can become a living space as well. You may find you spend more time here than you really need to, because it nurtures you spiritually as well as physically.

This kind of garden usually consists of wide beds for the production of a wide variety of vegetable crops. However these may be of diverse shapes and sizes and hold a variety of edibles: salads, potherbs, edible flowers, herbs and even fruiting shrubs. Though this type of garden is fairly informal for the most part, it could include a row of intensive beds for crops that lend themselves to that regime.

You have to keep on top of this type of garden, otherwise it can descend into unproductive chaos. In fact it is generally less productive per square foot than the more regimented intensive vegetable garden.

The potager

What we have come to know as a potager garden consists of a series of beds laid out in a geometric pattern for maximum ornamental effect. These are consciously intended to be ornamental and somewhat formal (they are inspired by the French tradition of large ornamental food gardens). A potager is usually placed close to the living area because it is so ornamental.

In recent years the geometric potager garden has become quite trendy with wealthy Martha Stewart types. If you own a vineyard and need a focal point for your mansion this could work well (so long as you have a couple of gardeners to attend to it). I suspect that many of these gardens (usually part of a larger garden) are intended more as an ornamental talking point (or status symbol), rather than a source of food. A clue is when they have more path than bed area and some of the bed area is taken up with inedible edging plants.

I like this kind of arrangement and think it works well as a dual purpose feature. It is very ornamental while at the same time it can also produce a lot of food. The key is to approach it as a working garden not some kind of art piece.

This type of garden lends itself to using different shaped and colored vegetables (Kale, Chard, Beets, Peppers, Rhubarb all have wonderful colors).

Traditional row crop vegetable garden

If you have lots of room and wish to grow a lot of food with the least effort and resources, you should reconsider the old-fashioned row crop garden. Whereas the intensive vegetable garden is designed for growing a lot of food in a small area, this kind of garden is intended to require minimal work, water and other inputs. Which goes to show there really isn't much that is new in gardening (and that our grandparents were smarter than we give them credit for.

To grow row crops you need a bigger area than you would for an intensive garden because the plants are spaced further apart. However you need worry less about fertility and water, because the plants have a larger volume of soil to obtain nutrients and water. There will also be more weeds because there is a greater area of soil, but that's why we have the expression "your own row to hoe".

Row cropping was devised as a way for farmers to easily grow large areas of crops with the aid of mechanization. Even at the home garden level you can benefit from this aspect, by using a wheel hoe and a seed planter.

Another reason the staple food garden is usually quite big is because you will be growing things in greater quantity, almost like a small farm. Here is the place to grow the nutritious and productive staple foods you eat every day: potatoes, beans, peas, field corn. These are then be stored over the winter in some kind of root cellar.

Intensive/row hybrid garden

Many commercial market gardeners now create beds with a tractor and then plant in rows on the beds. You could garden in this way too, using permanent beds to reduce compaction, but planting in widely spaced rows to reduce the need for water and fertilization. It can also be mulched to feed the soil and conserve moisture.

Three sisters garden

Field corn is the easiest and most space efficient staple grain to grow, but it still requires quite a bit of room to grow in quantity. You can increase its efficiency by interplanting with beans and squash in a polyculture known to Native Americans as the three sisters. In this very efficient system the corn stalks provide support for the beans, while the Squash creates a living mulch that cover the ground. The beans supply nitrogen to the soil.

In a three sisters garden the corn is planted 5 to 6 seeds to a hill and left to grow for several weeks. When the seedlings are about 10″ tall they are earthed up to a height of about 6″, to give them more stability. After this is completed 10 to 12 pole beans are planted in a circle around the growing corn, a few inches away from them. These sprout within 7 to 10 days. A week after they have germinated, 5 squash seeds are planted around them, about a foot further out.

Once everything is growing there is little left to do, except ensure that the plants aren't overtaken by weeds and have enough water. You may want to help the individual Pole Beans find corn stalks to climb and direct the growing Squash vines so they cover the ground more evenly.

Two sisters and their cousin garden

The three sisters concept opens up a whole new avenue for different combinations of crops. If for example you don't much care for squash you might replace it with kale or potatoes. You might replace the corn with Jerusalem Artichokes. You could use Groundnut or another climber instead of beans.

Grain garden

Most people eat a considerable quantity of grain, which needs more space than can easily be spared in the vegetable garden. This doesn't require a lot of attention however, so if you have enough room you could have a separate grain plot out in zone 2.

Dry vegetable gardens

Before electricity and piped water made irrigation the norm, growing vegetables in dry areas meant planting in very widely spaced rows or hills. This type of garden works well in dry weather because there is a larger volume of soil for each plant, so there is less competition for water and nutrients. Yields are lower per square foot when grown in this way, but you simply plant a bigger garden. If you have plenty of space, but a limited amount of water, this is the way to grow most of your crops.

Practical aspects of the kitchen garden

Organization

To get the best productivity out of your vegetable garden it helps to be organized and keep records. If you don't plant an annual crop at the right time it may not perform as well as it might have (in some cases it won't perform at all). Keep records of the dates you planted everything: potatoes, Broccoli, Garlic, Winter Wheat, Mushrooms and which flowers were blooming in the garden at the time. At harvest time you write down what your results were and evaluate whether you planted too early, at the right time or too late. This will be a big help when it comes to planning next years garden.

Location

Sunlight is the single most important factor when siting the vegetable garden. The majority of crop plants need at least 6 to 8 hours of direct sunlight a day to grow well. A fertile soil is also a big help, but is less important than sun, because you can improve it over time. In cool climates you also need protection from strong winds. If any favorable microclimate is available (such as a south facing slope) this is the place for the kitchen garden.

If you have a choice the vegetable garden should be fairly low down on a slope, to avoid high winds and to get better soil with more moisture. However it should not be so low that it is in a frost pocket. In very dry climates you might put the vegetable garden in any area with naturally moist soil. A flat area may not be as warm as a sloping site, but its easier to work with.

If there were a ten commandments of gardening, the second would be "Thy veggie garden shalt be near thy kitchen". This may seem like a trivial matter but it's important because the further the vegetable garden is from your house the less you will take care of it. Someone once estimated (don't ask me how) that the harvest declined by 30% when the garden was over 100 feet away. You might think this doesn't apply to you because you are so enthusiastic and 101 feet isn't really much further than 99 feet. However it will make a difference as to how often you enter your garden, which affects how much you will grow and use. If you can't put the whole vegetable garden close to the kitchen, you should at least have a few beds close by.

When the vegetable garden is close to the house it gets tended more conscientiously, not only because it is more convenient, but because everything is so visible. You have to make more effort to keep it looking good because any mess is so painfully obvious.

If intensive vegetable garden space is limited then use it for compact crops that require more care, such as Onion, Garlic and Carrot. The more independent, ornamental or space hungry crops (Tomato, Cucurbits, Corn, Kale) can go wherever you can fit them.
The vegetable garden is one of the most important destinations in the garden and should ideally be in its own area as a dead end. Don't put it en route to somewhere else, otherwise plants may get damaged by passing children, dogs, wheelbarrows and more.

Protection

After years of depredations from deer, rabbits, raccoons, quail, squirrels, gophers and birds, I finally realized that it's best to design this area for protection right from the start. Erect a full 7 ft. tall bird / gopher / raccoon / deer proof perimeter fence and you will no longer have to worry about these pests beating you to you carefully tended crops. This can make the garden a lot more productive, lower maintenance and less frustrating.

In extreme cases you might also have to add a roof net to keep out birds and squirrels. If you covered this in plastic for the winter, you could even create a greenhouse garden (this would need to be designed to stand up to winter storms though).

Planting

When arranging the vegetables in the garden you need to make sure the taller plants don't cast too much shade on the smaller ones. In the traditional herbaceous border the taller plants go at the back and the shorter ones at the front, so all are equally visible and all get lots of light. This higher to lower planting plan can also be used in the vegetable garden (though of course you have to orient them to the sun too).

Tall crops: Amaranth, Jerusalem Artichoke, Globe Artichoke, Brussels Sprouts, Cardoon, Corn, Giant Lambs Quarters, Quinoa.

Climbing crops: Beans (Pole), Cucumbers, Peas, Summer Squash, Winter Squash.

Medium crops: Asparagus, Broccoli, Eggplant, Fava Beans, Garlic, Kale, Leeks, Mustards, Okra, Peppers, Potato, Summer Squash (Bush), Tomato.

Low crops: Arugala, Beet, Cabbage, Carrot, Lettuce, Mustards, Onion, Shallot, Shungiku.

Creeping crops: Alpine Strawberry, Chive, Parsley, Purslane, Thyme, Violet.

Vegetable garden size

The size of your vegetable garden will depend upon how much you want to grow, how much room is available and what kind of garden you have. If your garden is very small you will probably want to use intensive raised beds to maximise production per square foot. If you have lots of room but little water, you might go for an old fashioned row garden to reduce inputs and maintenance.

To a large extent productivity has more to do with how it is worked than its size. Over-enthusiastic gardeners often create vegetable gardens that are too big and then don't look after them properly. The garden ends up being half empty most of the time and gets messy and overgrown with weeds.

If you have never had a vegetable garden before, you should probably start out with no more than two hundred square feet of intensive beds. This should be fairly manageable, as it can be securely fenced, watered, fertilized and weeded and is easier to maintain (so it looks better too). As your skill and confidence builds you can expand accordingly.

If you wish to grow enough food to actually feed your family, you have to expand your horizons and plant on a larger scale. A couple of pounds of field corn or 20 pounds of potatoes won't feed four people for very long. Even with highly intensive methods it takes a considerable amount of space to be self-sufficient in vegetables. For a family of 4.2 you might need 100 Tomato plants, 300 lettuce, 400 onions, 20 squash, 300 potato, 1000 carrot, 1000 beans, 75 garlic and more. Obviously the exact size of this garden is affected by many variables: number of mouths to feed, the fertility of the soil, your skill and your ambition.

Laying out the growing areas

The shape of the vegetable garden is usually determined by the site, but you might want a particularly decorative shape, such as a square or circle or even a potager. In Feng Shui they recommend a rectangle or square. The classic English vegetable garden was a rectangle 1 ½ to 2 times as long as it was wide. There was an entrance on a short side and it was divided equally into 4 quarters, with water in the middle. Apparently the cross shape dates back to monastic gardens – talk about old habits die hard.

Growing in rows

Row cropping works best for tall vigorous crops, such as Corn, Dry Beans, Quinoa, Amaranth and Potato (it's easier to earth up plants in rows).

If you plant in rows you don't have to create beds, but you do have to dig a bigger area because there is a lot of wasted space between each row. The plants are spaced further apart, so there is more soil for each plant and so less competition for water and nutrients. Labor saving devices such as seed drills and wheel hoes are designed for row planting. This is good because a larger area of disturbed soil means more annual weeds (if you are an optimist you will look upon this as more edible weeds).

This kind of garden is more gopher resistant than a row of intensive beds because the plants are further apart, so the gophers have further to go between each plant (this makes them more obvious and gives you more time to catch them).

Growing Beds

Permanent intensive beds (usually somewhat raised) first became popular in this country about 30 years ago and have changed the way many Americans think about growing vegetables. The permanent beds of deep, rich, moisture retentive soil are never walked upon so are always loose and friable. They are from 3 - 5 feet wide so you can reach to the middle from either side. They are separated by permanent paths, so all of your effort and fertilizers can go into the soil where the plants grow and none is wasted on the paths.

When the beds are raised above the surface of the ground, the soil warms up faster in spring, which can be a significant advantage in cold heavy soils. These beds are especially useful in problem soils, as you can essentially create your own soil. In hot climates raised beds may dry out too quickly, in which case the bed can be flat, or even sunken slightly.

Intensive growing beds provide the most efficient way to grow plants in terms of yield per square foot of land. The high level of fertility means plants can be spaced closer together, and less land is used for paths. They are best used for intensively grown crops such as salad mixes and for growing large numbers of small plants, such as Basil, Carrots. Garlic, Leek, Lettuce and Parsnips.

Gardeners argue about whether the beds should be oriented north/south or east/west, but in general it really isn't that important (both have their advantages). If the garden is on a slope you will probably want to plant across the contour to reduce erosion (though Alan Chadwick's beds went straight up and down quite steep (south facing) hills – presumably to maximize and even out sun exposure.

Beds against walls or fences that are only accessible from one side should be shallow enough that you can easily reach to the other side; a maximum of 30".

Beds and paths

When designing the layout of the beds you should think about access for pedestrians, wheelbarrows, garden carts and hoses. The main paths around the edge of the garden (and the central dividing path) should be wide enough for 2 people to walk side by side or to push a garden cart (3 feet is minimum). The paths between the beds can be narrower (a foot is the minimum comfortable width), so they don't waste space on unproductive areas (some gardens have more path than bed).

If you have very long intensive beds you may want to cut them in half with a wide access path (at least 3 feet wide). This will minimize circuitous walks around the beds (or jumping over them).

You might want one area to be accessible to a truck for bringing in manure, mulch and other bulk materials.

Wooden boxed bed

Gophers and vegetables don't mix and are often kept apart by creating wooden sided beds lined with gopher wire. This must be fastened carefully if it is to be effective and all of the wood should be above the ground (gophers will sometimes chew through buried wood). Wooden beds also work well for people who can't bend easily and anyone who craves neatness.

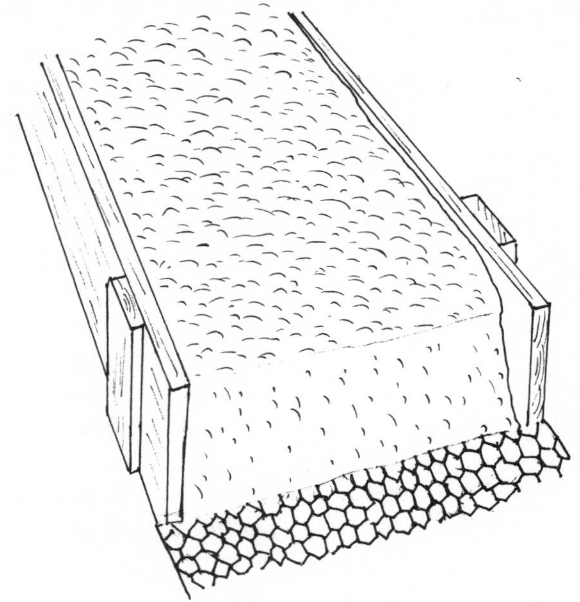

I have never liked wooden beds because they are expensive to build and not permanent (eventually the wood rots and the wire rusts). You could try building more durable beds by laying down plastic coated gopher wire (this would last indefinitely), building a form and pouring durable concrete sides. Make the form re-usable and you could make an unlimited number of identical beds.

Sunken beds

In very dry climates raised beds can lose moisture quickly from evaporation. In these extreme situations flat or sunken beds are a better choice. Make sunken beds by digging out the topsoil and putting it to one side, then remove some of the subsoil to lower the level. Finally replace the topsoil and shape the bed. The excavated subsoil can be used to raise the paths around the bed, or for a wind deflecting berm. Add a drip system to maximize your efficient use of water.

Different uses of beds

To minimize soil compaction most of your plants should be grown in permanent beds. The type of bed you create can be adapted to what you are growing. Some crops are happy to be crowded together and need only a small amount of space, others need lots of space. Some crops are harvested frequently over a long period; others are harvested all at once. Some need lots of attention, others very little.

How many kinds of bed you have in your garden will depend upon how big and diverse it is. In a small garden you might only have a few intensive vegetable beds. In a large garden you might have 5 or 6 different kinds of beds, which might include:

Salad bed

I like to grow salad crops on a cut and come again basis. This gives you a continuous harvest over an extended period, rather than a lot of salad at one time. The best way to do this is to is to plant a small section of bed every couple of weeks. A single bed should be large enough to handle several rotations or you could have several small beds. You might want to have this bed close to the kitchen door for culinary convenience.

These beds could become an attractive feature if carefully shaped and then planted with different colored and textured plants.

In hot weather closely spaced beds of salad mix do best if watered frequently with overhead mini-sprinklers. This not only supplies the abundant water they need, but also keeps them cooler.

Polyculture beds

The polyculture bed is a logical progression from the salad mix bed and give us a way of managing intensive beds that is more natural and less labor intensive. Growing this kind of bed is quite similar to growing a cut and come again salad mix bed. However it functions over a longer period of time and produces a greater variety of crops. It is planted in spring and gives you a succession of crops maturing one after the other.

Planting a polyculture bed

This bed is cropped very intensively so you need to fertilize it generously before you start. Incorporate three inches of compost, along with a fertilizer mix, into the top 6 inches of soil.

Start your bed by direct sowing seeds of your favorite salad crops (lettuce, arugala, radish, chicory, spinach, mizuna) as you would a salad mix bed. The difference is that you choose plants and varieties that mature at different times, rather than all at once. You also plant a variety of other species, onions (sets or seedlings), carrot, parsnip, Hamburg parsley and Amaranth. These exploit different parts of the growing environment (tap roots, fibrous roots, creepers, tall and short plants). The bed should be planted so there is a seed every ½" – 1". At the same time you sow the bed you should start Broccoli, Kale, Chard, Tomato and Peppers in the greenhouse.

The key to a successful polyculture is to harvest thin frequently, as this helps to ensure that the plants have enough space for good growth without any crowding. You can start harvest thinning whole plants as soon as they reach a usable size. This gives the remaining plants more room to grow. Always harvest with a view to improving the stand by thinning overcrowded parts. Water after each harvest thinning to help the remaining plants recover from the disturbance.

As the plants get bigger you remove whole plants to leave more room for those remaining. You can also fill in the bigger gaps with transplants from the greenhouse. As the weather warms up you can put in Tomatoes and Peppers (and perhaps other warm weather crops). After the salad greens are finished you still have Carrots, Parsnips and the later plantings to look forward to. Kale and Chard can produce for the rest of the season.

You can extend the life of the spring planted bed by transplanting warm weather crops into it as the cool weather crops start to fade. You might also allow some plants to flower and set seed so you can replenish your seed stock.

Perennial food bed

Perennial food plants give you another way to grow food with minimal work and many deserve to be more widely grown. I prefer to keep these separate from the annual beds, as mixing them complicates maintenance. They could be grown individually or several species might be grown together as a polyculture. A perennial bed could also form a protective border around the annual garden (beware of harboring snails).

The only limit here is your imagination. A perennial polyculture bed might combine Chinese Artichoke, Chicory, Oca, Good King Henry, Turkish Rocket and more. You could have tall vining perennials such as

Mashua or Groundnut with salad annuals growing in the shade underneath them. A perennial bed might even contain an entire plant community of fruit tree, shrubs, perennial vegetables, annuals and other plants. Going further with this idea you might have a prairie bed, a marsh bed, or a meadow bed.

Fertility bed

These roughly made beds are used to grow non-food plants for periodic cutting for mulch, compost or green manure. These plants are quite independent and could be placed at the edge of the garden, where they can act as a buffer to distract pests (snails, birds) from the main beds and to deter invasive wild plants from creeping into your intensively cultivated areas. Such beds could be any size or shape and could be irrigated with gray water

These beds could be either annual or perennial. An annual bed might include nitrogen fixing Clovers, peas and beans and as well as Sunflowers, Hemp, Sorghum, Buckwheat and more. A perennial bed might include nitrogen fixing Clovers, Alfalfa and Sweet Clover (a biennial) as well as Comfrey, Jerusalem Artichoke and more.

Wild beds

You could have beds for growing useful wild plants with very little effort. In California most herbaceous plants die out in summer because it gets too dry. If you water an area regularly you can persuade many edible wild plants to grow through the summer. These are able to grow larger than they would in natural conditions and can be more easily protected from gophers and other predators. See Useful wild plants for possible new crops.

Nutrition bed

This type of bed is used to grow low-maintenance super nutritious plants for adding to salads and making green drinks. Such plants might include Filaree, Malva, Gotu Kola, Ashwaghanda, Sushni, Gynostema, Bacopa and more.

You could plant a series of small succession plantings of Wheatgrass or Barleygrass for juice extraction. This is the easiest and most cost effective way to grow this valuable nutritional supplement. It is also a way to improve the soil, as all of the organic matter from the root biomass stays in the ground.

Drought tolerant crop bed

These are used for growing crops without regular irrigation. These can be further from the house and larger in size, to make up for their lower yields.

Repeat harvest beds

Leafy plants such as Kale, Mustard, Basil and Chard need to be planted annually, but can then be harvested for an extended period by picking individual leaves. These work well in long narrow beds as a border alongside a path. It's easy to pick from both sides and they get lots of light. Fruiting crops such as Tomatoes, Peppers, Squash and Cucumber could also be grown in these narrow beds.

Special plant bed

You can grow any particularly valuable or useful plant in its own wide bed. You might want a richly fertilized permanent bed for Asparagus or Rhubarb, a moist beds for greens or flowers for cutting, or a raised dry bed for drought tolerant herbs such as Sage and Thyme.

Fruit beds

To maximize fruit production you could grow a hedge of bush fruit in an intensive bed, perhaps with a groundcover of strawberries or other edibles. The whole thing could easily caged to protect it from birds.

Water vegetable bed

This is basically a pond for growing water vegetables such as Watercress or Water Spinach. It consists of a sunken bed lined with an impermeable liner so that it holds water; It is refilled with some soil and then topped up with water. See Food Ponds for more on these.

Vegetable garden components

Vegetable gardening is a simple activity and doesn't require much in the way of tools of equipment, but there are a few things that can make your life easier and more productive.

Compost Area

If you make a lot of compost it's nice to have a specific area set up for it. In a small garden this might simply be a plastic bin to take care of kitchen scraps, or a three bay compost bin. In large gardens it might be a large shaded area for windrow type composting. Even if you prefer to move your compost piles around

the garden (building them in different places benefits the soil), you may still want a place to store leaf mold, manure, wood chips and soil. This area could also hold the worm bins, as these need shade from intense sun and protection from raccoons and rats.
\
The compost area should be close to the main vegetable growing area, so you don't have to move materials or finished compost very far. If you import a lot of bulk materials it should ideally have easy access to the road, so you can unload directly from a truck to the pile. You don't want to have to move manure or other materials any further than necessary. Ideally this area will be downhill of the road, but uphill of the garden, to make it easier to move bulk materials.

This area should be protected from extreme weather. In hot areas it needs shade, while in cold areas it needs sun and protection from wind and rain. It should also have a source of water to keep the piles moist.

It is important that the compost area doesn't become a feeding station for rats, flies and other wildlife. In the city unenclosed bins almost invariably attract rats, though the homeowner is often unaware of them. The popularity of composting has been a great boon to these creatures and they are the main reason composting is illegal in some places. If this is the case a worm bin is a good alternative

Garden shed

A spacious garden shed is almost an essential. It is used for storing tools, amendments, seeds, stakes, hoses, irrigation components and all of the other stuff the garden requires. It is also a good place to store and process seeds and herbs, keep gardening books and relax in wet weather. If you are a high tech gardener you might also have a computer there for quick reference. Ideally it will be well organized inside and comfortable.

It's important that the shed be rodent proof. Not only will rats and mice eat anything even remotely edible (including large seeds, tubers and bulbs), they may also gnaw on anything made of leather, rubber, paper, cardboard or wood.

The shed should be located close to the main vegetable garden for ease of getting tools and putting then away, so they don't get left out in the sun or rain. It should be put where it won't cast shade on the growing beds (such as the north side of the garden). You may also want it to have electricity.

In my perfect garden the tool shed would have a covered area (with a transparent roof) adjacent to it, where you could work in the rain. This would act like an extended open greenhouse and give you an extra place to store tender plants in winter. You might even grow some tender plants under it permanently. This area is a good place for a workbench too.

A shed is a significant visual feature of the garden, so make it ornamental as well as practical. Metal sheds are popular (I suppose they are quite secure unless the thief has a can opener)), but they are ugly, as are most manufactured sheds (the plastic ones are probably the worst). If you are handy I urge you to build your own shed to complement the house.

If your shed isn't very attractive you might train climbing plants up the sides to hide it. You could also use a screen, or just decorate it with paint or other artwork.

Access to the shed should be via a path that is wide enough for a garden cart or wheelbarrow.

Greenhouse

The greenhouse is the foundation of the productive garden and is an essential for the serious gardener. It greatly expands your plant raising capabilities and pays for itself eventually in plants. It also adds a great deal to the pleasure of gardening.

The primary use of the greenhouse is to grow seedlings for transplanting into the garden. From mid winter through late spring it is usually packed with seed trays and plants. It is also useful for vegetative propagation, drying plants, over wintering tender plants from the garden, growing greens in winter and heat loving crops in cool summer climates. It won't stay very warm in winter, unless you get serious about heat storage and insulation. The ultimate for very cold climates is a triple glazed solar greenhouse with insulated shutters.

On a personal level the greenhouse gives you somewhere warm and pleasant to work on cold or wet days. If big enough it can also be a place to sit and relax and in cool temperate climates this can become one of its most important functions. It could even be used for drying wet laundry.

Where

The greenhouse needs full sun in fall, winter and spring so place it accordingly. Summer sun is less important in all but the coolest climates. It should also have shelter from strong winds, as these can cool it down significantly or even blow it apart. It shouldn't be too close to tall trees, as they cast shade, drop leaf litter, sap (which dirties the glazing) and even limbs. You should also keep it away from the children's play area (especially where they play ball games).

Permaculturists say the greenhouse should be in zone 1 so it is convenient to get to. This isn't a bad idea, but I find that once you start planting in spring it becomes a major activity center in itself, and you are out there every day anyway. Perhaps the most logical place to put it would be to the north side of the main vegetable growing area, in the sunniest spot you have. It's nice if the greenhouse has electricity and water, which is easier if it isn't too far from the house.

For cold climates a solar greenhouse is far superior to the traditional gable design. It has several features that make it more efficient.

- There is a solid insulated north wall to reduce heat loss. There is little reduction in light from this wall being opaque, because the sun is always well to the south in winter. The bottom sections of the side and front walls may also be solid and insulated, to further reduce heat loss (again without reducing light levels significantly). These opaque interior walls are usually painted white to increase the reflection of light on to the plants.

- The south facing glass front is angled to ensure maximum light penetration in winter when the sun is low. This reduces light penetration in summer, when the sun is high and so reduces overheating.

- There is some heat storage in the form of plastic barrels of water painted black and set against the solid north wall, where they double as a shelf. This thermal mass absorbs some of the heat entering the greenhouse during the day (making it slightly cooler). At night this heat is released into the greenhouse, keeping it warmer. In very cold climates there may also be thick insulated opaque curtains or shutters. To reduce heat loss these are closed at night and in very cold weather.

A solar greenhouse could be attached to the south facing wall of the garden shed. This supplies a stable and solid back wall for the greenhouse. The greenhouse might even be used to supply surplus heat to the building.

I have built a number of utilitarian greenhouses out of salvaged 2 x 4's and polyethylene sheet. These weren't very attractive but they were almost as effective as commercial greenhouses and cost next to nothing.

A greenhouse doesn't have to be very big if it is just for growing seedlings. If you live in a cool climate and want to grow plants for their whole lives, then it can't ever be big enough. If space is very limited you can buy (or build) a combination tool shed and greenhouse.

Chickens have been housed in the greenhouse for the winter (confined under the staging and with their own entrance). They benefit from a warmer shelter and give the greenhouse carbon dioxide and some body heat.

You could also supply extra carbon dioxide and heat by having a compost pile in the greenhouse. Alternatively you could grow mushrooms or brew beer.

> **A cautionary tale**
>
> Aluminum / plastic / polycarbonate greenhouses are very light and need to be securely anchored to the ground. I bought a used one that didn't come with any instructions or prominent warning. I assembled it and weighed it down with concrete blocks. One stormy night soon after I got it, the whole thing came loose from its moorings and sailed away into the night. Fortunately I was able to salvage the polycarbonate glazing (it is very tough and flexible) and built another greenhouse with a stronger (and heavier) wooden framework.

If you are very ambitious (or live in a harsh climate) you could create a greenhouse dome to cover an area of you garden with a milder climate, complete with fruit trees, pond and more. A dome doesn't have to be hugely expensive; a simple willow, rebar or pipe dome covered with UV resistant plastic doesn't cost that much (it might not stand up to snow though). You could also use a large commercial greenhouse for this.

Cold Frame

A cold frame is essentially a small greenhouse and is used for raising seedlings and protecting plants. In cool climates it can also be very useful for extending the growing season. In chilly Britain the larger kitchen gardens often had row upon row of brick cold frames for producing early lettuce, carrots, potatoes, strawberries, melons and peppers. When the plants grew big enough (and the weather was warmer) the glass lights (lids) were taken off and the plants left to grow.

Table

In a warm climate you won't need a greenhouse for starting summer seedlings, you can just start them outside on a table (to keep them up off the ground). This should be protected with netting, to prevent birds playing havoc with the tender seedlings.

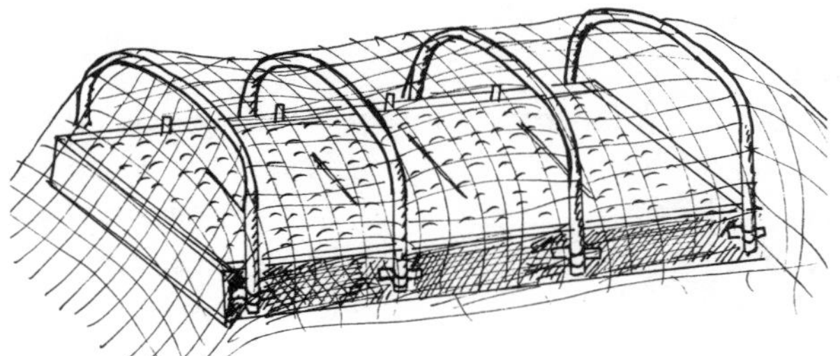

Nursery bed

This is used for growing on seedlings and rooted cuttings and to give expensive or rare small plants additional protection. It can also provide a temporary home for any small plants you don't really have a permanent home for.

In a large garden the nursery bed could be quite extensive as you can use a lot of plants. It could even morph into a nursery garden, with a whole series of beds for raising seedlings or cuttings of trees, shrubs and perennials, There might also be a bed for stooling rootstocks and more. If you really get into this, it could easily become a source of income. If you are going to all the trouble of stratifying and germinating tree seeds then planting a hundred Pawpaw trees isn't much harder than planting ten

As your garden develops you may find that many crops will volunteer. Any interesting volunteer seedlings that appear can be transplanted to the

nursery bed until they are big enough to go out in the larger garden.

The usual place for the nursery bed is near the greenhouse and propagation area/workshop. It needs plenty of sun.

Propagation unit

If you raise a lot of plants from cuttings, it's nice to have a dedicated propagation unit. You can do it with plant pots and plastic bags, but this works much better and will eventually pay for itself. It is usually kept in the greenhouse, where it can easily be kept warm and humid.

Sink

An outdoor sink is very useful for cleaning vegetables, hands and other things. Newly harvested crops can be washed and stripped of unwanted parts before they go inside. The waste stuff goes straight on the compost pile, the water goes straight into the garden. In this way it conserves water and helps to keep the kitchen sink clean.

The sink should be located near the greenhouse, propagation area and potting bench. It doesn't need to be connected to anything permanent, just attach a hose for water and have a bucket underneath for the water to drain into (or a perforated drain pipe).

Vegetable storage

A large productive garden will produce a large volume of food, which must be stored carefully if it is to last long enough for you to eat it. This means you need somewhere to store it.

Small to moderate quantities of vegetables can be stored in the ground. One of the best (if somewhat cumbersome to install) containers for this is a 36″ section of 18″ to 24″ diameter concrete culvert. Dig a hole, put a wire screen in the bottom (to keep out rodents), then install the pipe and some gravel for drainage. Cover the top with another piece of wire screen and a foot of mulch to prevent it from freezing.

The best way to store vegetables and fruit over the winter is in a root cellar. This must stay above freezing in winter and was traditionally dug into the side of a steep bank, where the earth would provide humidity and a cool stable temperature. It could even have a living rood. This kind of root cellar takes a lot of work to build, but if you have the time and energy it will be worthwhile (it can also be quite picturesque).

A root cellar can be also constructed in a basement, where it is more convenient for the cook. It should be built on the cooler northeast side of the house, away from any heat pipes. The floor should be earth or concrete and there should be a window to vent to the outside. You only have to build two walls because the house provides the other two, along with the floor and ceiling. Insulate all of the walls and ceiling and cover with a vapor barrier to keep the humidity up. Cover the windows to keep the room dark. Put in slatted shelves and store the vegetables in open slatted wooden fruit containers.

If your root cellar is not inside the house it's nice to have a pantry for storing enough food for a few days (ideally on a north wall to keep it cooler). You then only have to go to the root cellar occasionally.

Solar dehydrator

If you have lots of fruit bearing plants (Figs, Apricots, Plums, Apples, Mulberries, Cranberries, Grapes, Tomatoes) you will get far more fruit than you can use fresh and a lot may go bad before you can use it. If you live in a hot dry climate you can reduce the amount of waste by investing in (or building) a solar dryer. This enables you to dry some of the surplus for later use. It can also be used for drying herbs and even vegetables. If your climate is too cool or humid for solar, you could use an electric dryer.

Fruit cages

Many birds live to eat small fruit such as blueberries and raspberries and will consume your entire crop if given the opportunity. The most foolproof way to prevent this is to completely enclose your prized fruit in a cage.

You can buy expensive commercially made cages or you can make your own. The simplest, cheapest and least invasive (if not quite foolproof) cage begins with a tall chicken wire fence around the berry plot, supported on strong posts. When the berries are starting to ripen you put netting over the top, supported on steel cables or arched metal supports (attached to the strong posts).

In some areas birds don't only go for fruits, they will also eat leafy vegetables and can devastate newly planted seedlings. Where I live some gardeners get so frustrated by repeated wildlife depredations that they cage the whole vegetable garden. A simpler way to protect seedlings is to make some small cages or frames that fit over a single bed (1 x 3 and chicken wire). This makes it quick and easy to protect young plants until they are well established.

Some people have had to create caged gardens to keep squirrels out of their vegetables. These need to be much stronger and more carefully constructed however, as squirrels are intelligent and will search for weaknesses. A chain link fence with a chicken wire roof could work (though it isn't exactly attractive).

Hose center

The sun is very hard on hoses in hot climates. Not only does the ultraviolet light degrade the hose from the outside, but any water trapped in a closed hose may become hot enough to cause it to burst (always leave a hose open). Hoses will last much longer if you keep them out of the sun when they are not in use, ideally in their own covered hose center (make one for each faucet). If it is it big enough you could also keep plastic buckets there (they degrade in sunlight too), as well as small tools and maybe a notebook and pencil.

Season extension

In mild climates you can grow crops right through the winter if you are on top of things. You can also do this in colder climates too, but you need the help of some more specialized equipment (greenhouses, cloches, cold frames, poly tunnels, hoop houses). I don't have the space to get into this here, but fortunately there is an outstanding book on the topic The Four Seasons Gardener by Elliot Coleman.

Sitting area

It is important to have a comfortable place to sit and relax right next to where the work takes place. This gives you somewhere to rest, drink tea, think about the task in hand, and to contemplate the meaning of life (or if you already know it, to decide whether its safe to tell anyone else). It will need shade in hot weather.

Managing the vegetable garden

To grow an unnaturally large amount of food in a small area requires us to bend some of natures rules somewhat. We have to disturb the soil more, we add more nutrients and we plant large numbers of the same kind of plant close together.

I have already written extensively about growing a vegetable garden in The Organic Gardeners Handbook and am not going to repeat myself here. In fact I want to encourage you to go beyond traditional gardening practices. Most temperate zone gardeners think too linearly, so there is a product and a goal for every crop we plant. We need to start thinking about harvesting food from plants at every stage of their life cycle. Sow a crop extra thickly and then eat the thinnings. Take individual leaves from the same plants for months. Eat the flowers, immature fruits, ripe fruit and then allow plants to ripen seed for planting next year (allowing plants to flower and set seed also provides food for predatory and pollinating insects). Plant a new crop to grow up among an older crop and replace it. Sow the seed of two crops at one time, so that one can benefit from the protection and water given to the other. When both have emerged one crop may be transplanted elsewhere.

Interplanting

A simple way to increase productivity is to plant seedlings of fast maturing green vegetables in between slower maturing crops. In this way you can grow 2 crops at the same time.

Mulching

I keep mentioning that nature doesn't like bare soil, yet the nature of growing annuals means that there is repeated soil disturbance. A couple of inches of straw mulch really helps to protect the soil and conserve moisture

Pests

One of the simplest ways to deal with many pests is to plant extra food crops. If you plant only the number of plants you want to eat and some are eaten by pests you have a problem. If you plant 30% extra and some gets eaten it doesn't matter. Planting extra doesn't take much more time, it just requites a bit more space.

Watering the vegetable garden

This area has the most critical need for water of any part of the garden because vegetables must get all the water they need if they are going to be productive. If you live where summers are very dry you will probably want to install a drip irrigation system. It reduces water consumption, saves time and reduces weed growth.

I find the best way to water vegetable garden beds is with in-line drip emitter tubing, which is ¼" black PVC pipe with drip emitters pre-installed every 6″. This works in much the same way as a soaker hose, but is more durable and versatile. You can cut and configure it any way you want and repair it easily (unlike soaker hose). Lay out three drip emitter lines 16" apart, beginning about 8 inches in from the edge of the bed.

Irrigating the vegetable garden is complicated by the fact that different crops require varying amounts of water. Also their needs vary at different stages of growth, seedbeds may need watering 2 or 3 times a day, whereas mature vegetables may only need water every few days. This means that different areas of a growing bed can require different amounts of water. You can try to arrange the plants according to their water requirements, but it isn't easy unless you plant in large blocks that all require the same amount of water. The simplest solution to this problem is supplemental hand watering: water everything for the same length of time and then give thirsty crops some additional water by hand.

If you turn on your irrigation lines manually, it's a good idea to have a timer to turn the water off after a pre-set time. Then you won't forget and leave it on all night.

See Watering and Irrigation for more on this rather complicated topic.

Volunteers

Many plants have the ability to set seed and self-sow if you give them the opportunity. I really like the idea of getting food without having to grow it. Self sowing greens can be left undisturbed to grow anywhere they aren't in the way. However they commonly fall in a relatively small area near the mother plant and get overcrowded. I often transplant the best seedlings to a suitable site (sometimes back into the intensive garden) where they can grow to maturity .

Volunteers can be unpredictable, sometimes they are very useful, sometimes they need controlling and sometimes they revert to their wild ways fairly quickly. Of course if you intend to eat any volunteers you have to identify them properly (eating Hemlock instead of Parsley could have unintended consequences (you may poison yourself.

Self sowers vary by region, but I have found the following to be very useful: Amaranth, Arugula, Carrot, Chard, Cilantro, Cornsalad, Dill, Kale, Lamb's Quarters, Lettuce, Mustard and. Parsley. Most of the Brassicas don't work very well because they cross-pollinate so easily (you could end up with a Cabbarabi or a Brussccoli).

The semi-wild area

Out past the vegetable garden zone we enter the more natural and informal semi-wild garden zone. With most of our attention taken up with the living areas and vegetable garden, this area has to be designed to function with minimal maintenance. This is the place for those fairly independent useful plants that are adapted to the growing conditions in your garden and don't need much help to grow. You usually have to help them get established by watering, mulching and protecting them from deer, rabbits and gophers. Once they are established they should be able to take care of themselves.

The dominant plants out here are tree and bush fruits along with any potherbs, salad plants, herbs and other plants that can grow independently. Some of these may be traditional cultivars of useful trees, shrubs and perennials, some could be the more independent vegetables and others could be edible wild plants.

The materials and components used out here tend to be more natural in form, lower maintenance and more widely spaced. There aren't many human made components, though you might want a fire pit, sleeping platform or sweat lodge.

The forest garden

In the forest garden we arrange the various kinds of cultivated plants so they behave like a natural plant community and grow without too much assistance from us. Emulating a young forest, there is a canopy layer, an understory shrub layer and a perennial/ groundcover layer. This kind of garden gives you a way to make large areas productive without requiring too much work or resources and is ideally suited to filling up unused space in a larger garden. If you only have a small garden there are better ways to use it to produce food.

The foods produced in the forest garden are quite different from those of the vegetable garden and supplement it perfectly. It may even produce some unusual staple foods such as chestnuts and acorns (you just have to work out how to incorporate them into your diet).

It is important that the forest garden contains foods that you actually use. Don't let it fill up with things you don't eat or use, just because they grow well and thrive there. Blackberries and Blueberries will always get eaten, but Chokeberries and Goumi berries may not. If this area isn't supplying useful materials or helping to feed you it isn't working.

Forest gardening isn't just the process of creating a forest garden, it is different way of growing food and you can apply the same techniques to other situations too. You could have a forest hedgerow garden, a shrub forest garden or even a single tree with associated plants (this could be anywhere in the garden).

Plant communities

Most wild plants don't grow in isolation, they are surrounded by other plants (either the same species or different ones) and they all have to find a happy medium that makes the best use of available sunlight, soil and other resources. When the right combination of plants grow together they don't just coexist, they form predictable and stable communities. There are distinct layers where each species fills a specific ecological niche and has its own role to play. As a community they maintain the conditions suitable for their collective growth and the stability of the community, without any single species becoming dominant (I can't help thinking they might be trying to tell us something).

The key to forest gardening is to put plants with complementary growth habits together, so they can live together harmoniously like a natural plant community. There may be trees, shrubs, creepers, clumpers, climbers, tall sun loving species and low-growing shade tolerant groundcovers. Some plants may occupy the same space at different times (spring flowering bulbs and summer herbs). Some plants occupy different parts of the same area. Plants with similar growing requirements can be planted separately, perhaps on different sides of the tree).

A forest garden community should contain a variety of plants, to increase overall fertility and stability of the community. There should be nitrogen fixers, dynamic accumulators, tap rooters, biomass producers, insectory plants, groundcovers and more.

You could choose the plants for your forest garden by educated guesswork, taking into account all of their growth requirements. Plant a variety of different species (as many as 8 or 10 in total) and see what happens. When choosing plants it helps to look at how wild plants form communities. Observe how the plants arrange themselves, what roles do they play and what species are there. You could even try emulating a local plant community, by substituting similar useful plants for each species.

Shade

Forest gardens are most commonly found in the tropics, where the sun is very intense and the understory plants actually benefit from the reduction in sun intensity to be found underneath the tree canopy. In the temperate forest garden the sun is much weaker and if understory plants are to thrive, the canopy has to be much more open. The term forest garden may be somewhat misleading because these gardens resemble an early succession (young) forest rather than the shady place we usually think of as a forest.

We can employ various strategies to make sure the understory of a forest garden isn't too shady:

- Spacing is the most important factor of course, because the wider the spacing the more light can penetrate (see below for more on this). In fact often the trees may be so widely spaced the area feels more like a park or garden than a forest.

- We can raise the canopy by removing some of the lower branches (see Crown lifting).

- We can use plants with fairly light or open foliage, such as Black Locust and Walnut.

Starting the forest garden

Like any other aspect of gardening, creating a forest garden isn't a very difficult project, Forest is the natural vegetation of most temperate areas and left to itself the land will eventually turn into woodland. If we can align our interests with this natural ecological succession, we can get mother nature to do most of the work. We just have to ensure she does it with the species of plants that we want

The forest garden consists of four loosely defined layers: canopy, shrub layer, herb layer and ground layer. These have to be arranged to ensure that the larger plants have enough room and that all of the plants receive enough light, water and nutrients. Otherwise it isn't much different from any other type of gardening. You don't even need to have all four layers everywhere, in fact the forest garden works best when its height is uneven and irregular.

Quick forest garden

It is possible to create a forest garden in a single day. Using sheet mulch you can plant everything needed to turn a patch of ground into a garden in a few hours (once you have spent a few days getting all of the materials together). See Sheet mulching for more on this.

Creating a quick garden in this way can be very exciting, though of course planting is just the beginning. There will be many more happy days spent playing with it. One drawback of this method is shade loving understory plants may have too much sun initially. However if you plant sun loving understory plants they will eventually become uncomfortable with the increasing shade and may have to be replaced.

Slow forest garden

In most cases creating a forest garden is a long term project. The first step is to get the canopy trees (top layer) established and then you plant the other layers as plants become available (you may even grow them yourself). The slow forest garden then evolves at your own pace in a natural progression.

The tree layer

Trees are the most important part of the forest garden and everything else revolves around them. They must be carefully selected for size, compatibility, pollination, disease control and more. The size of the trees that form the canopy is dependent upon the size of the garden. In a large garden you might use medium sized trees; in a small garden you might use dwarf trees. Taller trees give you more options for spacing, but smaller trees are easier to harvest and create less shade.

The trees that work best in the forest garden have deep roots, an open growth habit and leaves that allow a lot of light to penetrate. They also tend to leaf out late in spring. Most fruit trees have fairly dense foliage, but they work quite well because they don't have very aggressive or hungry roots. This makes it possible to grow other plants fairly close to them.

Most trees in the forest garden tend to be either fruiting species or nitrogen fixers. The most frequently used fruit bearing species include Apple, Apricot, Cherry, Pear, Plum and Peach (these can all be grown on dwarfing rootstocks to keep them at a smaller size). You might also consider naturally small trees, such as *Amelanchier, Asimina, Cercis, Cydonia, Diospyros, Eleagnus, Fuchsia, Morus, Rhus.*

One rule of thumb says the garden should contain ¼ - ⅓ nitrogen fixing trees and shrubs (Black Locust, Alders, Acacia and Mesquite are all good for this).

Evergreens trees (and shrubs) cast a lot of shade, so if you use any they should be placed at the northern edge of the garden. The hardier species can be used to shelter it from cold winds. The tender evergreens (Citrus, Avocado) can't be used in this way of course.

Placing

When deciding where to put the trees you have to think about pollination, disease control, compatibility and keeping competition and shading to a minimum. You also have to ensure that the growing conditions (soil, sun, moisture, microclimate) are appropriate for the individual trees needs.

To minimize the effects of pests and diseases don't plant similar species next to each other, have at least one plant in between.

Spacing

The one immutable law of forest gardening is to give your plants enough room and you transgress it at your plants peril. The biggest (and commonest) mistake you can make is to put the trees too close together as this reduces their productivity through competition for light, water and nutrients. Just when your garden should be coming into full bearing you may have to cut some trees down. Repeat after me "I will not put my trees too close together".

The correct planting distance between the trees will also be affected by the climate, the plant (which species, variety and rootstock) and what kind of garden you are trying to create. The easiest way to think about spacing trees is by the size of their crown when mature. The best way to make sure you don't put your trees too close together is to plan them out on paper. Cut out paper circles (to scale) and move them around on your garden plan until you come up with an arrangement you like.

Spacing options

The minimum safe spacing has the crowns of the trees just barely touching at maturity, which is how they are often planted in orchards. Planting on a grid pattern leaves small openings in the middle of each four trees which allows some light to hit the forest floor. If you plant in offset rows you can get more trees in an area, but will have less light down below. This spacing works best in southern areas where the sun is very intense, as it gives more shade to the understory plants. It can also work where you have trees of different heights, where the crown of lower trees may be underneath the crowns of the taller ones.

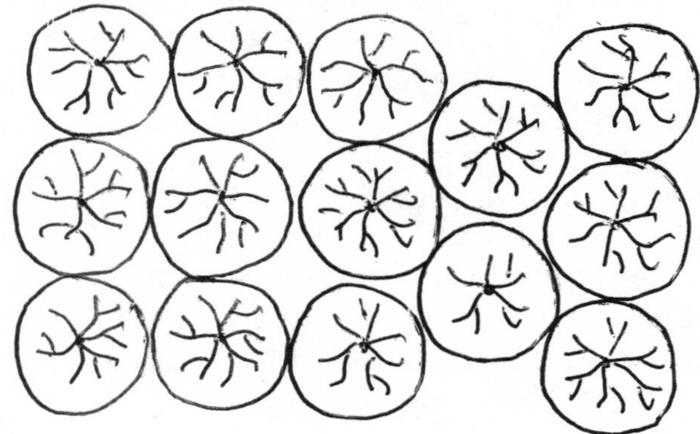

Though the above patterns work well in an orchard setting, the forest garden needs more light on the forest floor. You can achieve this by leaving 25% - 50% of extra space between the mature crowns. This results in a fairly open woodland with plenty of room and light for other plants to grow around them. This gives enough shade to protect plants from temperature extremes, but there is still enough light for most plants to grow well. This spacing works better for trees with dense foliage and in cooler northern areas. It can also work well where low fertility or lack of water might otherwise limit growth.

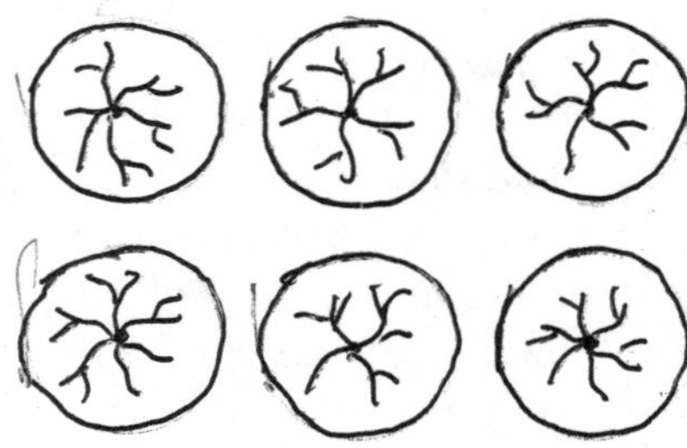

Of course you could space your trees even further apart, with spaces the diameter of the tree crown in between the trees. You might argue that this is no longer a forest, but do we care? We are not attempting to recreate a real forest anyway, we are trying to find the best ways to grow food.

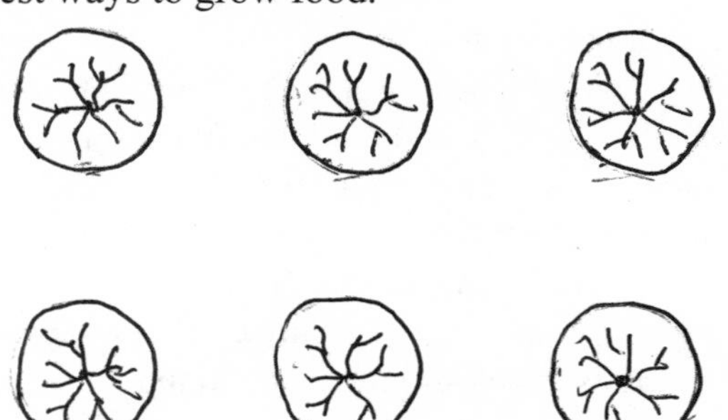

Most forest gardens won't have a single uniform spacing, but rather it will vary throughout the garden. You will probably use all of these different ways of spacing, with clusters of closely grouped trees in some places, along with widely spaced trees and single trees dotted around randomly. This looks more natural and provides a greater diversity of growing conditions.

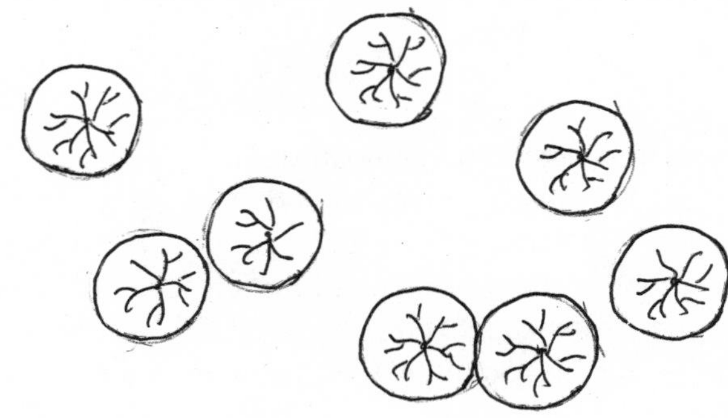

Arranging for height

Basically this means organizing the garden so the trees don't cast too much shade on each other, or on the shrubs below.

In a small garden you have to think carefully about where to put the taller plants. Probably the best idea is to group them on the north side of the garden, as this will minimize shading (don't shade your neighbors garden though). You might even line them up like a hedge close to the northern boundary, with the smaller shrubs and herbaceous plants in tiers to the south, coming down to ground level.

In a larger garden you have many more options. You could have a bowl-like arrangement, with trees at the edges and lower plants towards the middle (perhaps with annual crops in the center). You might also cluster the trees in small groups, and put other plants in the sunny areas in between. They could also be spread out unevenly and interspersed with other plants in the sunny areas. Generally the taller trees should go to the north side of smaller ones to minimize shading.

Any large forest trees should go out at the edges of the garden, where they won't cast unwanted shade. Though rarely considered garden trees, the large nut trees are a fantastic resource, producing huge amounts of food regularly. The large lumber trees might also be grown if you have a really big area (grow Walnuts and you get two for the price of one).

In a very large garden you might even separate your forest garden into two zones. The high maintenance zone could contain cultivated plants that requires some care, while an outer, lower maintenance zone would mainly consist of productive wild plants that are almost completely independent.

The shrub layer

The placement of the bigger shrubs should be planned out along with the trees (there is little functional difference between a large shrub and a small tree). The placement of smaller shrubs is usually decided out in the garden, along with the perennials. Shrubs generally tend to be faster growing and more easily moved than trees, so there is a little bit more margin for error in planting them.

Most of the shrubs you use will bear edible fruits, such as the Currants, Raspberries, Blueberries, Salal and Hazel. The nitrogen fixers are also important as well (*Ceanothus, Cytisus, Eleagnus, Caragana* and more). These can be coppiced periodically by cutting them down to the ground, and the leaves and branches used for mulch.

Placing shrubs

As with any other plants you have to find a site that fulfills their growth requirements (sun, shade, moisture, nutrients and more) and habits (root shape, rooting depth, growth seasons, height). The growing conditions found around a tree vary according to the shade it casts, which is related to its height. The south side being much sunnier than the north side.

The forest dwelling shrubs can tolerate quite a lot of shade, and can go on the north and east side of trees. The pioneer species and nitrogen-fixers need full sun if they are to be productive and should be placed on the south and west sides. Taller shrubs could go to the north also. Of course you will also put shrubs in the open areas between the trees.

Don't make things difficult for yourself by putting plants where they will get in the way of harvesting or maintenance operations.

It's not good a good idea to place shrubs underneath the canopy of the trees, as both plants will suffer from the competition (the low light will cause the shrubs to get taller but they won't be as productive). It's generally best to plant shrubs no closer than the drip line of the full sized tree. An exception to this is when you have a tree with very tall crown, in which case you might be able to plant underneath it (on the sunny side). You may have to give these extra water and nutrients to compensate for the increased competition.

When planting shrubs in the shade around trees, it's better to use young plants, as these seem to adapt better than older ones.

The vine layer

Most vines evolved to climb up on other plants, so they are quite shade tolerant when young. Most need full sun for best fruit production though. They are useful in the forest garden because they provide another productive layer of food plants and don't take up much space on the ground.

The type of vine affects how you use it. The herbaceous vines die back to the ground each year, so don't get enormously tall. The woody vines just keep on getting longer (if not pruned) every year and can reach up into the treetops, where they are hard to reach.

Some vines can be incredibly vigorous (can anyone say Kudzu?) and left to their own devices they can damage trees by depriving them of light or girdling them. These species should be kept off of trees and trained on their own supporting trellis, arbor or fence (preferably something low enough that the fruit remains accessible).

Less imperialistic species can be allowed to climb up into existing trees (this is a good way to make existing native trees or nitrogen fixers more productive). You may have to do some crown lifting of the lower branches to allow enough light through. Of course you also need to be able to get to the fruit. It would be very frustrating having beautiful bunches of grapes you couldn't reach.

Planting the ground layer

The amount of sun and shade on the ground will vary considerably according to how you placed the trees. The shady areas will increase over the years, so most of the ground layer plants should have some degree of shade tolerance. The species will thrive as the canopy develops, whereas those that need sun will start to fade.

When planting underneath the fruit trees you should simply dig individual holes in suitable spots, taking care not to disturb the larger tree roots any more than necessary. Use mulch to prevent annual weeds germinating in the newly disturbed soil around them. Make sure you don't put any plants where they will get in the way of harvesting or maintenance operations.

Herbaceous perennials

These can be sited more casually than the woody plants, as they are smaller, shorter lived and more easily moved.

Perennials are important in the forest garden because they act as groundcover to fill in open areas and prevent weeds and grasses (the enemy of fruit trees) from getting established. They come in all shapes and sizes and you will want a variety of plants with different growth habits.

- Clumpers (Comfrey, Day Lily, Sorrel, Tradescantia), You need lots of these to fill an area, as they don't spread very rapidly.

- Creepers (*Lamium, Polygonum, Nettle, Asarum, Viola*). These create dense colonies that enlarge gradually.

- Spreaders (*Aegopodium, Fragaria, Hemerocalis, Podophyllum*). These species are quite mobile and will move to the places best suited to them. In the conventional garden controlling them can become a problem, but this shouldn't be an issue in the wilder garden.

- Deep rooted species include: Dandelion, Red Dock, Radish, Carrot, Parsnip, Caraway, Artichoke and Burdock.

- Bulbs (*Alliums, Camassia, Erythronium, Lilium*), Some bulbs are adapted to complete their life cycle in spring, before the trees leaf out. These might be grown around the drip line of the trees or out in clearings or meadows.

Perennials don't just provide food, they can also fix nitrogen, accumulate nutrients, attract beneficial insects and suppress weeds. Any of these plants that aren't used for food can be cut periodically for use as compost or mulch materials.

Perennials are usually planted in single species colonies or drifts, as their numbers helps to protect them. See Growing vegetables in small patches for more on this kind of planting.

Perennial vegetables

Food producing perennials vary greatly in their need for sun and their value in the forest garden. Some can work well in the more open parts.

The leafy greens are the most useful as they tend to be quite shade tolerant. These mostly produce food from late winter through early summer, though some can be useful year round. Useful species include Chicory, Dandelion, Red Dock, Good King Henry, Turkish Rocket, Sorrel, Seakale, Rhubarb, Malva, Ox eye Daisy, Miners Lettuce, Dandelion, Chicory and Stinging Nettle.

The perennial root vegetables mostly need full sun to be productive, so can only be grown in the sunniest parts of the forest garden. Generally they are best planted in other areas of the garden, where there needs are more easily met. Species that can tolerate a little shade include Chinese Artichoke, Groundnut, Jerusalem Artichoke, Skirret and Chinese Yam. See Perennial Vegetables for more on these.

Other kinds of plants

Annuals
These aren't very important in the forest garden because there is little of the disturbed sunny soil that most of them prefer. There are plenty of other places in the garden more suited to growing annuals, so it's not worth putting too much effort into them here.

They can be useful for filling in any disturbed vacant areas that do occur, whether sunny, partly shady or fully shady. You can also plant them in the sunny areas around newly planted trees. This can enable these areas to produce a crop while the trees are maturing (just make sure they don't inhibit the trees).

Annuals are best planted in drifts rather than singly, as this is how they tend to grow naturally. They are usually direct sown initially, though you might use transplants in some situations. You might also just scatter any spare seed on any bare soil and see what comes up.

If an annual is growing in the right place it will often self-sow. If this happens you can leave the seedlings where they emerge, or you could transplant some to other locations (even to a conventional growing bed).

Annual vegetables
The partly shaded forest garden is very limited in its ability to grow conventional vegetables (some leafy greens do okay) because they need full sun for best growth. It makes no sense to create a semi-shady area in your garden and then try to grow sun loving plants there. It makes a more sense to grow shade tolerant plants there and put your common crops in the sunnier and more open garden areas.

Some of the more vigorous vining annual vegetables such as beans and squash might be grown in the sunny areas between the trees. Sweet Potatoes or potatoes could also work, though of course you will disturb the soil when you harvest their roots.

Useful wild plants
Many shade tolerant wild edibles do well in the forest garden and can be truly no-work food producers. See Weeds and wild plants for more on these.

Mushrooms
Fungi are one of the most important components of any ecosystem and you shouldn't overlook them here. You will be creating ideal conditions for the natural soil fungi by your soil improvement activities and these species should respond quickly. If the soil is very poor you might want to inoculate your trees with mycorrhizal fungi to improve health and speed growth (normally this shouldn't be necessary though). Some of these also produce edible fungi.

You could also start growing edible saprophytic mushrooms on logs, straw or wood chip mulch and add yet another layer of productivity to the area. See Mushrooms and fungi for more on this.

Fertility plants
The nitrogen fixers, dynamic accumulators and biomass producers are all important for improving soil fertility without disturbing the soil (or any effort on your part). See "Using plants to improve soil fertility" for more on these. Ideally the nitrogen fixers should make up a good proportion (up to one third) of all the trees and shrubs in the garden. These should be interplanted among the productive trees and shrubs.

Caring for the forest garden
Though the forest garden is designed to be low-maintenance, there is still some work to do, particularly in getting the plants established. Wild gardening doesn't mean simply casting the plants out into the wilderness. No matter how hardy the established plants are, most young plants need some nurturing initially. They don't have an extensive root network and can't compete with well-established natives.

When you first plant the garden the trees will be so far apart and cast so little shade, that you can plant almost anything in between them. These open areas gradually diminish as the crowns of the trees fill in. Hopefully you won't plant them too close together and it won't eventually become necessary to control them by pruning. Some pruning may still be needed to encourage fruiting and new growth (and in the case of the nitrogen fixers to produce mulch material).

When creating a forest garden you can adjust the growing conditions, encourage or discourage individual plants and experiment to see what works best. If some plants don't do well, forget about them and try something else. If an individual plant does exceptionally well (and you can use its products), then propagate it, plant it and let it self-sow.

If an area starts to get too shady, you may have to prune to allow more light through to the ground. Don't just randomly cut out individual branches though, as this may just encourage extra vigorous re-growth. A much better idea is to raise up the canopy by systematically removing all of the lower branches (these are less likely to regrow because they are partly shaded). See Crown lifting for more on this.

If you live where gophers are a problem it can be impossible to establish a good herbaceous ground layer. These rodents will eat anything that isn't planted in a basket and can really limit self-propagating plants. Any new plant that appears will be killed eventually, unless you dig it up and replant it in a basket. You can trap gophers, but this will be a never ending job because you will be creating perfect gopher habitat. A better solution is to create an underground barrier of 36" wide gopher wire around the perimeter to keep them out.

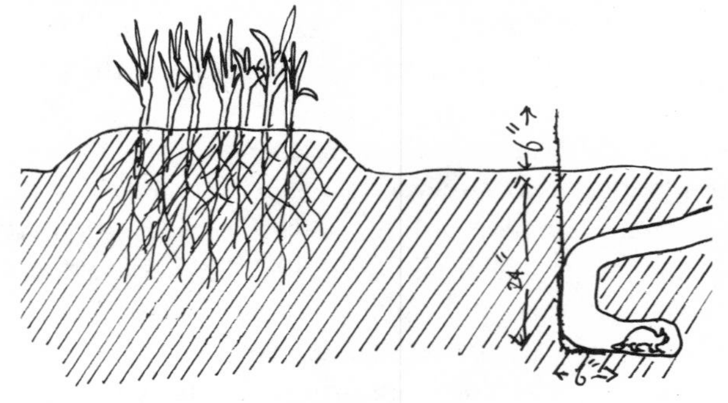

Adaptation for dry climates

If you want to create a forest garden in a dry climate you have to adapt your strategy to take water into account. Some purists frown upon irrigation as unnatural and unsustainable, but you will get a lot greater productivity if you irrigate occasionally.

The best way to organize the dry land forest garden is to divide it up into hydrozones. Maybe have areas you never water, areas you water every 3 -4 weeks and areas you water every week. You then place the appropriate plants in the appropriate places, set up a drip system and watch the garden grow.

In very dry areas it may not be possible to maintain a continuous herb layer to protect the ground because you don't have enough water. As I said previously if nature doesn't want to do something, don't try and force it on her. If she doesn't co-operate in creating the herbaceous layer, then maybe try using a low growing layer of drought tolerant shrubs instead.

Wild ideas for semi-wild gardens

In areas where woodland isn't the natural vegetation you might think about other ways to grow wild food gardens. Here are a few ideas.

Disturbed soil

A semi-wild garden could be simply be an area of disturbed soil (maybe a series of pits and mounds, created by digging a series of holes and piling the soil in mounds beside them). In California most herbaceous plants die out in summer because it gets too dry. If you water an area regularly you can persuade many edible wild plants to grow through the summer. Taking this to its natural conclusion would be a succession garden that changes over the years as natural succession takes place.

Forest edge / hedgerow garden

This is basically a linear forest garden; the forest edge with the rest of the forest left out. A hedge of large shrubs and small trees planted with a diversity of other useful plants. It can be used as a border for the northern edge of the garden, or as a dividing element.

This type of garden is designed and planted in the same way as a forest garden, but has more light because it is only one tree wide. Choose sun loving trees and plant them far enough apart so their canopies just touch at maturity.

Prairie or meadow

If you presently have a very large lawn you could look to the prairie for an entirely different model for a low-maintenance perennial food growing system. You could grow edible bulbs, herbaceous perennials and grasses. Natural prairies form where woody plants are inhibited by low rainfall, grazing or fire. You can inhibit them intentionally by annual mowing. I won't pretend to know very much about this, but it is certainly worth investigating.

Useful meadow plants include: *Achillea, Camassia, Cardamine, Fritillaria, Heracleum, Liatris, Rumex, Sanguisorba, Asclepias, Cichorium, Chrysanthemum, Plantago, Lotus* and *Trifolium* species.

At some point in the future it may be possible to grow a perennial grain field, as some practical perennial grain crops are being developed. Potentially useful species include:

Intermediate Wheatgrass (*Thinopyrum intermedium*)
Eastern gamagrass (*Tripsacum dactyloides*)
Agrotriticum (a hybrid)
Perennial buckwheat (*Fagopyrum dibotrys*)
Sorghum halepense (hybrids with *Sorghum bicolor)*
Illinois bundleflower (*Desmanthus illinoensis*)
Maximilian Sunflower (*Helianthus maximiliani*)
Alfalfa (*Medicago sativa*)

Wetland

If you have an abundance of water then a wetland food garden could be highly productive (see Food Ponds for more on this).

Alley cropping

Alley cropping is a type of agro-forestry utilizing rows of tough and well adapted (often nitrogen fixing) trees, shrubs or large grasses (Bamboo, Elephant Grass, Vetiver) planted anywhere from 6-20 feet apart. Food crops are grown in beds planted in the alleys between the rows, where they benefit from the sheltered microclimate. The trees in the rows can be trimmed to keep them low, so they don't create too much shade. The material cut from rows is used for mulch, animal feed, green manure, firewood or poles.

The alleys don't have to be in straight lines, the rows of trees could be used to create any shaped garden you choose.

Growing vegetables as wild plants

If you have the room you might want to experiment with growing vegetables as wild plants, especially if you have lots of seed as a result of saving your own. Probably the best known exponent of this was Masanobu Fukuoka. He made it look easy because he knew all about timing. Apparently he simply scattered vegetable seed in his orchard in spring, when the winter weeds were starting to die off. He would sow on a day when rain was expected, so the seed would be kept moist while germinating. After sowing he cut back all of the weeds and left them to cover the newly sown seed. He cut back the weeds several times more after this, until the vegetables were big enough to handle the competition.

Wild vegetables can be grown in small patches anywhere in the garden that suitable growing conditions exist. This works particularly well in the partly shady garden, because you can take advantage of any sunny spot, no matter how small.

The crops best able to compete as wild plants are those that germinate and grow quickly (Beans, Kale, Spinach, Mustards and other Brassicas), or are propagated vegetatively (Garlic, Potatoes, Sweet Potatoes, Jerusalem Artichokes). There are also those crops that are little changed from wild plants (Burdock, Cornsalad, Dill, Fennel, Ground Cherry, Parsley, Sorrel and Salsify).

Experimenting to see what works in your situation can be fascinating. The main thing is to plant the crops at the right time and in the right conditions. If you don't really know what these are, you might try scattering seed randomly and see which plants come up where. Allow the most vigorous plants to set seed and let this disperse naturally (or scatter it to spread it around more evenly).

The wild area

In a large garden any areas not directly needed for producing food or other human purposes could be left in their natural state, or allowed to revert back to it. If an area is completely disturbed you could recreate its natural state by planting native plants. Decide which species to plant by looking at what grows in similar natural areas in the neighborhood (or as close by as you can get). You might also want to encourage some of the less common native species of your area. These may be harder to get established though, as they can be picky about where they will grow.

Though this area is for native plants that can grow completely independently, this doesn't mean it can't be productive. Walnuts, blackberries, wild plums, mushrooms and other wild edibles could all be encouraged (especially if the rest of your garden isn't very big).

Though these kind of wild areas are most suitable for large gardens, even the smallest garden could benefit from having a bit of wilderness, even if only a few square feet. It's kind of nice to reintroduce a few real native wild plants to urban areas that they once completely covered (maybe we can help nature to turn back the tide even now!)

Mushrooms

You might also try to encourage edible fungi, perhaps even cultivating local strains. See Mushrooms for more on this.

Semi-wild ideas for wild gardens

This area could have no human created components or intrusion, or it might be a wild play area for wild children.

Buildings

You might want to have a shed out there to sleep in, or keep stuff in. Make it look old and rustic like it has always been there, perhaps by training some wild vines over it, or planting a patch of Stinging Nettles.

Sauna/sweat lodge

This is used to induce sweating for pleasure as well as for its reputed health benefits. You could build an elaborate Finnish style sauna, or perhaps an underground sweat lodge that is the central feature of its own area. Alternatively you can make one in a couple of hours for next to nothing out of Willow shoots and old carpet (cover it with something natural to hide this). Don't use plastic sheeting as it doesn't breathe.

The sweat lodge needs a fire pit, a source of fuel and water for cooling down. Ideally this will be a natural stream, pond, or swimming pool, but a cold hose pipe shower will also work. It should be well away from the house to enhance its primitive aspect and for greater privacy.

You may grow plants with aromatic branches nearby, such as Balsam Poplar, Myrtle, Mugwort or Sage. These can be used to scent the water.

Camping area

In a large garden this is the place for a camp site. This might be simply a space for a tent and a fire pit, or you might want something that is actually semi-permanent, so you can go outside and sleep there any time you feel inspired. The traditional open fronted Adirondack log lean-to could work, or you might go with something a little lighter, made of poles. This could be covered in bark or fir branches (for aesthetics) or a tarp for efficiency.

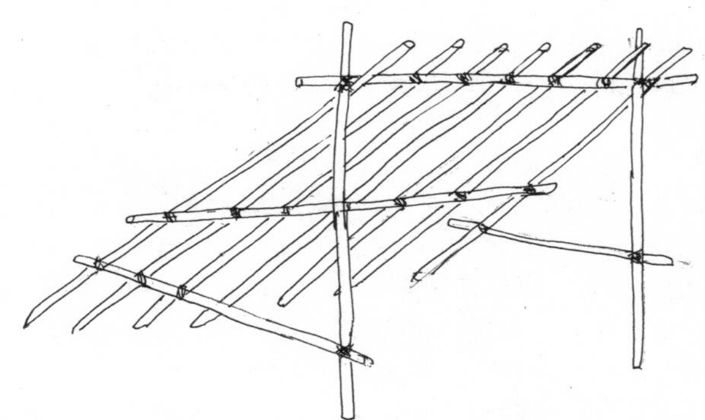

Access and paths

Paths should be efficient, safe, secure, comfortable and attractive. They are one of the most basic building blocks of the garden, in fact you could lay out the whole garden around the paths.

Uses of paths

- The primary purpose of paths is to link the various parts of the garden efficiently, safely and economically. Good paths make the garden easier to move around and easier to work in.

- Paths play an important role in shaping the garden by dividing it into separate areas. At the same time they create a network of access routes around the garden that help to unify otherwise unconnected areas.

- Paths are places where human movement gets etched into the landscape. They direct your movement by making you go in one direction or the other. They take you to where the path builder wants you to go (ideally to places worth seeing and by an interesting route).

- A well designed path should draw you out into the garden and encourage you to explore. It does this by concealing most of the route, so you keep moving to see where it goes.

- Paths are important visual elements as they differentiate the human dominated areas from the plant dominated ones. They lead your eyes around the garden and provide a background for more important elements. They also help to maintain order if the garden gets overgrown

- Paths provide useful edge habitat for plants.

- Impervious paths (and roads) can be used to intercept and channel runoff water into swales or catchment areas such as marshes and ponds. This may be an important feature in arid areas, where all of the precious rain that falls on your land must be absorbed.

- Paths of sharp cinders (and perhaps sawdust) may act as a barrier to slow down the movement of snails and slugs.

- By clearly defining areas to be walked upon, paths help to reduce soil compaction.

- Stone, brick and concrete can create a warmer microclimate by absorbing heat during the day and releasing it at night.

Locating the paths

Paths generally start or end at existing doors, gates or openings and run parallel to fences, planting beds and other linear components. They don't need sun or rich soil, so don't waste good growing land on them if it can be avoided (often it can't). Use shaded areas, the north side of walls and buildings, the area next to fences or hedges (over the root zone).

The main paths are practical elements of course and must be efficient. They should be fairly direct and take the easiest and most logical route between doors, gates and important destinations (the route you would follow even if the path weren't there). These paths almost locate themselves because they run between important components (either existing or planned).

People tend to choose the most practical route instinctively, so paths commonly become worn in the most logical places. The simplest way to decide where to put your paths is to walk around the garden and let your feet decide, Of course you may choose to modify their placement for other reasons.

When deciding where to put the paths, you should also look at the bigger picture and think about traffic circulation around the whole garden (how the paths link together and how you get to each area). The house, driveway, street, greenhouse, deck, patio and sitting areas are all part of the traffic pattern.

Don't divide up the garden with paths too early in the design, as this limits your thought and imagination. Just put arrows on the plan to indicate circulation patterns.

Not all paths are designed for efficiency, some are purely for pleasure. They lead you to other interesting parts of the garden, or to certain viewpoints (ideally you should be able to see something to walk to).

In small gardens there should be no more path than necessary because they take up space that might be used more productively. They also require materials and maintenance.

Beds go naturally alongside paths, so the location of a path will often determine the location of some growing beds. You might also place beds in certain positions to create interest on a path. Beds placed alongside paths are very visible and easily tended, so can be planted with plants that need frequent attention.

Though all intensively cultivated areas should be accessible, paths don't have to reach every part of the garden. If there is an area of the garden that is very inaccessible you could leave it wild.

Be aware that low-lying paths may act as swales. They collect and channel water and may even turn into ponds in very wet weather. You will have to find ways to deal with this.

Most of the wilder areas don't need fixed paths, you just walk where you need to. If you walk in the same places often enough they it will become a beaten earth track. If you don't walk there frequently, there will be no trace you were ever there.

Path Shape

Depending upon the effect you are aiming for, a path might be a straight wide allee set amongst low beds, or it could be a narrow winding track through dense woodland.

Straight paths have a formal effect that isn't very popular in cottage gardens (except sometimes for front garden paths). They enable you to see a long way ahead, which is useful if you want to emphasize a view, but can make spaces seem smaller (people tend to walk faster on straight paths). In Feng Shui they are frowned upon as too fast and direct.

Very winding paths aren't very satisfactory either and are irritating when you want to get from A to B quickly. If a path has arbitrary curves people will often take the more logical shortcut.

Gentle sweeping curved paths are generally considered preferable, as they are more relaxed, interesting and natural. Curved paths disappear out of sight and so urge you forward to see what is around the bend (this should be something of interest). A curve in a path shouldn't be arbitrary however; it should have visual logic, such as when it follows the contour of a slope, or goes around an obstacle such as a pond, a rocky outcrop or a group of trees or shrubs. Sometimes you may even put something there to obscure the way.

Bends in paths should not be too abrupt, a 90° corner should have a turning radius of at least 5 feet.

You might shape your path so rainwater (or a hose) can wash it clean and then the water will flow to where it can soak in to the soil.

Path size

This is determined by relative importance, so the main paths are wider than minor ones. Their size is also related to the size of the garden and how much space you have to spare. In a large garden you can afford more space for paths than you could in a small one where every square inch is precious. In fact a big garden needs wider, more imposing paths as they have to carry more visual weight.

Generally it's best to err in making the paths too wide rather than too narrow. Paths tend to get narrower with time as plants encroach from both sides. A little-used narrow path may eventually almost disappear, so make them wide initially (walking with wet foliage brushing your legs isn't pleasant). Making paths wider doesn't necessarily means wasting growing space. Plants love the open edge habitat along paths and will soon sprawl out into the margins of the path. Of course wide paths also require more paving material, which can be a problem if you are on a tight budget.

Primary paths: These link the most important areas of the garden (door to gate to vegetable garden) and are often relatively straight and direct. They should be at least 36" wide, which is enough for a garden cart. To emphasize its primary importance the path to the front door might be wide enough for 2 people to walk side by side (4 ½ feet).

These paths are made of the most attractive material you have, as they make a bigger visual statement. These tend to be hard and include stone, cobbles, brick, flagstone, concrete. Loose materials like gravel aren't a good idea near the house because they can get tracked inside and play havoc with wood floors.

You might also add lights, containers, planting beds, pergolas and ornamentation to further distinguish the primary paths and emphasize their importance. I have never found it necessary to have a camber on a path, but this may be needed on very wide paths or in slow draining soils.

Secondary paths: These paths take you to the less important parts of the garden and tend to be curved or meandering. They are also used to create a sense of discovery and to take you on adventures. These paths branch off from the primary paths and are usually narrower (24 - 36" wide).

The materials for these paths tend to be softer and more informal than the primary paths, though they may include a little of those for continuity. Commonly used materials include gravel, decomposed granite, wood chips, pine needles and stepping stones.

Minor paths: These provide access to the least used parts of the garden and may get smaller and smaller until eventually there aren't any defined paths at all. Put them in the places where you already walk anyway. They are rarely paved and usually consist of bare earth. All you are really doing is defining the route you want people to take.

These paths only need to be wide enough for one person to walk on (as little as 12" wide),

Access to densely planted growing areas might simply consist of a few stepping stones. Their purpose is to make you step in the same place every time and so reduce compaction.

Permeability and paths

As much as half of the average garden may be impervious to water, and when multiplied by the tens of millions this has significant ecological effects. Impervious paving prevents infiltration and increases storm runoff and so reduces the amount of water entering aquifers. Paved areas also absorb heat, causing urban areas to get hotter (the heat island effect) and disrupt healthy gas exchange between the air and soil.

We should minimize the areas of impermeable paving in our gardens so rainfall can soak in to the ground close to where it lands. We should also find a way to channel runoff from existing impervious surfaces (such as rooftops and driveways) to where it can percolate into the soil. Any water that leaves your property is wasted and in dry areas you just can't afford to lose it.

The most obvious permeable paving materials are gravel and wood chips, however any material will work if it is composed of small enough units, so water can soak in to the ground between them. This includes brick, broken concrete, and stone pavers.

Making paths more interesting

Paths can be made more interesting with a little imagination. You might have different paving materials on different levels, or you might break up long paths with sections of different materials. If you are going to switch to an entirely different paving material, you should do so at a natural transition point, such as an archway, gate or steps.

The width of the path doesn't have to be uniform from beginning to end. They often get wider at curves destinations and intersections (these wider areas can be used as temporary storage areas for materials such as mulch). They may also get narrower as they get further away from the main garden, to give a sense of depth and importance (obviously this is easier to do with loose paving materials than with hard paving).

Break up long stretches of path with stopping places, such as a pergola, a fruit tree, a seat, an unusual plant, a sculpture or a pond. A junction of two paths could have an interesting tree or other object located near it. A path that ends abruptly should have something of interest there, perhaps a half hidden ornament or a seat.

Arches and arbors can be used to make a special path stand out (and give shade too). They also act as a transition point, giving you a way to separate and define two areas.

Ornamentation

The look of any path can be enhanced with a little ornamentation. You can embed colored tiles, pebbles, broken crockery, glass, or anything else you want to immortalize. A good place for this is at intersections, where the path widens.

Slopes

As the angle of a slope increases walking becomes less comfortable and eventually impossible (steep paths are also prone to erosion). You then have the option of making steps or angling the path up the slope (even switchbacks). Both of these involve a considerable amount of extra work. See Steps for more on this.

Paving materials

Paths are an important unifying element and should be made from materials that are appropriate for your house and garden. Local materials are usually preferable as they help to give a regional feel, are often cheaper and often have less environmental costs.

Frequently used paths around the house are usually paved with hard-wearing materials such as flagstone, cobbles, tile or brick. It's nice to be able to go out of the house barefoot and walk around the immediate area in comfort. You don't need hard paving everywhere however, and as you move away from the house the paving materials should become softer and more natural. The paths furthest from the house will be the softest and most natural (they are often simply compacted earth).

The color of the path material may be significant too. In sunny climates light colored paths can cause unpleasant glare, while dark colors can get very hot (this can be beneficial in cold climates because snow and ice will thaw faster). The best colors are generally the earth tones, which is why most common commercial paving materials come in these shades.

Number of materials

Large expanses of the same paving tend to be boring, so its common to mix and match different materials. Two materials generally work best, one dominant and one complementary. The rule of thumb is don't use more than three.

The right material

The ideal paving material is durable (or easily replaced), porous, attractive and provides a good surface to walk on (non-slip, stable and fairly even). Ideally it would also be inexpensive, but that's asking a lot. Depending upon your choice of paving, the paths can cost nothing or they can be the most expensive part of the garden.

Hard materials

Wood rounds: These can be free if you have suitable logs on site and a chainsaw. They are partly buried so their top surface is level with the ground. This must be done carefully and evenly if they are to look good and not be a tripping hazard.

Wood rounds should be made of a rot resistant wood such as Black Locust, Chestnut, Oak or Redwood (be aware that the sapwood is much less resistant and will rot before the heartwood). However you can square up wooden rounds for a tighter fit (they then become wooden squares) and in doing so you trim off a lot of the sapwood.

Wood: Sawn lumber is sometimes used as a path material, but is hard to justify unless the wood is salvaged and rot resistant. I have seen an interesting short path made from scrap redwood 2 x 4's buried on edge. Even then it is not really durable enough for a permanent path, as any time it is in contact with the soil it will eventually rot. Wood is more suited to use as a boardwalk for maintaining a level on very uneven slopes, or over water or marshy areas.

Stone

Stone can be used for paths in a variety of ways, to give many different effects.

Pebbles: These can be used loose like gravel, but they are not the easiest surface to walk on. Sometimes a thin layer is embedded into concrete to provide an ornamental surface. Pebble mosaics are a vernacular art form and can be quite spectacular. They are time consuming to create however.

Cobbles: You might be able to get these larger pebbles from a streambed, or from the soil if very stony. When laid flattest side up they make an attractive path, though some skill is needed to lay them. They are usually set in concrete, packed tightly to minimize the visible concrete (you can pack smaller pebbles between the larger ones). You might also use larger cobbles at the edges of the path and smaller ones in the middle.

Pavers: These were originally blocks of granite or sandstone, but those are now so expensive that they are usually made of imitation stone (aka concrete). They are laid like bricks on a bed of sand or concrete. They look great but there is the drawback that you usually have to buy them.

Stepping stones: These irregular pieces of fieldstone are spaced one pace apart so you step on each in turn (hence stepping stones!) They work well in dense plantings to stop you walking on the established beds and plants and compacting the soil. It is important that they are laid the right walking distance apart; otherwise they won't be comfortable to walk one.

Flagstone: These are the ultimate natural paving material, very attractive, flat, smooth, durable and quite formal. They are particularly useful for sitting areas, as they provide a smooth, hard level surface. Unfortunately flagstones are unrealistically expensive where I live (and rarely available used).

Flagstones are so heavy they stay put under their own weight, so only need to be laid on a bed of sand. This is useful if you may have to move them at some time in the future. They can also be laid on five blobs of concrete over a base of compacted soil. Don't buy flagstones that are less than 2" thick as they crack easily.

Large areas of flagstone sometimes have the occasional stone missing and the space is filled with plants or different paving material.

Very smooth flagstone (such as marble) can get slippery when wet, icy or covered in algae.

In some places you can buy cast concrete flagstones. These work well, but have the disadvantages of being concrete.

Fieldstone

Irregularly shaped fieldstone is cheaper than flagstone, but more complicated to use (laying them is like doing a jigsaw puzzle). If you can't find a piece that fits you can leave out the odd piece and put in low-growing herbs or other plants. Also leave wide gaps between the pieces so creeping plants can grow between them (scatter flower seed there).

Brick: Salvaged brick is a great paving material. It is flat, smooth, durable, porous, easily laid and has an interesting texture and appearance. It can be laid in different patterns to create different effects. They are also small enough units that they can be used for curving pathways.

It is often said that bricks for outdoor use should be special engineering bricks, as ordinary house bricks can eventually disintegrate if exposed to repeated frost. I don't see this as a big problem. If you set your bricks in sand, any that start to fall apart can easily be pulled out and replaced.

Set the bricks on a bed of sand or crushed stone and you will be able to reuse them at a later date (if you set them in concrete this becomes much harder). If they become uneven over time just take them up and add more sand.

Concrete: Poured concrete is one of the cheapest paving materials, though you have to use some imagination if you want it to look good. It is also very versatile and can be finished in a variety of different ways. You can wash and brush the surface to expose the aggregate, carve it to look like tiles or put small stones or pebbles on the surface. It can be stamped, colored (with paint stain or acid stain), brushed, sprayed and otherwise disguised.

A large area of concrete (a patio or driveway) should have metal reinforcing, be 3-4" thick and expansion joints every 8 feet.

An easy way to make a nice looking, but inexpensive path or patio, is to lay down a grid of bricks and fill the squares in between with concrete. You can then disguise the concrete surface as you see fit.

Concrete is also available pre-cast into a wide variety of paving materials, from imitation flagstone to imitation sets. Some of these look quite good, others have too much of a commercial appearance for my taste.

Tile: These can be used for special areas near the house (a courtyard or patio. They give a very refined almost interior feeling, but they usually need a solid base of poured concrete. Some types of tile are totally weatherproof; but others may gradually break up when exposed to frost, so get something suitable for your climate. Tile needs to be non-slip, otherwise it may get dangerous when wet.

Some inventive people have dug clay locally and fired their own clay tiles in a fire pit (if I had a hat it would be off to them). This is a great idea and worth further investigation.

Soft materials

Soft paths feel quite different from hard ones and give the garden a softer and more natural ambience. They are also generally cooler as most don't heat up as much in summer.

Loose materials don't work very well on slopes. Lightweight materials such as shredded bark or wood chips can get washed downhill in very wet weather. Even heavier materials can slowly move downhill with gravity, if not held in place. Most soft materials require edging (see below).

Loose materials can allow weeds to grow right through them, or even in them. The best way to deal with this is to lay down a layer of cardboard as a weed barrier.

A cubic yard of a loose material such as gravel or mulch will cover 160 square feet to a depth of 2".

Earth: The simplest path material is bare earth that has been compacted by frequent use. It works great in dry climates (most of my paths are earth), but can present problems in very wet areas, where it can get muddy and grow weeds (especially if not used frequently).

Shredded bark and wood chips

These materials work well for informal paths, but eventually break down into organic matter, so periodically have to be renewed by adding a fresh layer on top.

These materials can also be used in more formal areas if you use edging to keep them in place.

Straw: This is inexpensive and attractive, but breaks down quickly (perhaps too quickly) and needs renewing annually. It can also be slippery (especially on slippery slopes). In very dry weather it can also become a fire hazard. It's best to avoid hay as it contains too many weed seeds.

Grass turf: This is sometimes used for paths where the climate is amenable to grass growth. Just mow them with a push mower and use the clippings as mulch on the beds at the sides. Of course they will also need edging occasionally as the grass tries to creep out into the bed (which all means more work).

Sawdust: If you can get this in quantity it can be a pretty good path material. It is very low in nitrogen and so is said to deter weed growth (it may also deter slugs). It eventually breaks down and adds organic matter to the soil.

Sand: This is sometimes used for paths, though it will need a weed barrier underneath it and edging to confine it. In Japanese gardens it is commonly raked into patterns.

Decomposed granite: This fine gravel dust packs down to create a fairly firm surface. In many ways it is like packed earth, but cleaner and neater. Be careful about using it near the house, as it can get tracked inside and scratch wooden floors.

Decomposed granite is usually applied in two separate 1 ½" deep layers. The first layer is put down and tamped firmly, then the process is repeated with the second layer. Portland cement powder is sometimes added to the mix to make it even firmer. An edging material is commonly usually used to keep everything in place.

Gravel (round) and chippings (sharp): These easy to use paving materials drain well and lend themselves to fluid random shapes. They are relatively cheap if you pick them up yourself, or even free if you have a suitable source nearby.

Both of these materials make a noisy crunching sound when walked on. Some people like this sound and the fact that it announces that someone is walking on it.

Gravel doesn't work well near the house as it can get tracked inside (where it can scratch wooden floors). It can also be a problem on slopes as it tends to want to move downhill.

Gravel needs a firm base and some kind of edging to keep it in place. A weed barrier of landscape fabric is often used to stop weeds growing up through (which they tend to do otherwise). Even then weeds will sometimes grow in the gravel itself.

Carpet:
Old wool carpet has been cut into strips and laid down in paths. Put it upside down and its woven backing blends in quite well. Put it the right way up for that indoors outside effect.

Path construction

Start building your paths by removing any good topsoil and throwing it to either side to make a growing bed (or use it elsewhere). The materials used and the type of soil dictates how much of a foundation you need for a path. You may only have to excavate 2" for a decomposed granite path, but you may have to go down 8" or more for a brick and concrete path (if you want the top of the path to be level with the ground). If it isn't possible to excavate you could just raise the soil on either side of the path to create raised beds.

Drainage is particularly important with impervious materials, as rain may stand on it, or run off in streams in heavy rain. A base of gravel (or sand over gravel) can be used to improve drainage in wet areas. A camber in the middle will also help. You should also avoid creating low spots where water may accumulate and sit. A downhill path could become a torrent in wet weather if you don't design it carefully and give that water somewhere to go. Also never have any impervious paving sloping towards your house (for obvious reasons).

Before you put down any paving you may want to lay down a layer of cardboard or thick newspaper to suppress weeds. If you are laying down a hard permanent path you might also want to run a few lengths of 3" pipe under it at strategic places, in case you ever need to run a wire or irrigation pipe underneath it.

Edging materials

These are used to define the edges of a path and give it a more structured and formal appearance. Their use may also be necessary to keep loose paving materials (mulch, gravel) in place.

A variety of materials have been used for path edging, the main criteria is that it be compatible with the paving. Common materials include brick, wooden boards, stone or concrete pavers and recycled plastic 'wood' bender board. No-cost options include sections of tree branches set vertically, recycled bottles or pieces of broken tile (set on edge), twig hoops, poles and short logs.

You could also use no materials at all, Instead you just dig out the path to 3" below the surrounding soil and use the soil edging to keep the loose paving in place. Strips of galvanized sheet metal 12" deep have been used to contain creeping plants. Smaller pieces could be used as edging (though beware of sharp edges). Deeper pieces could be used as a gopher barrier.

Stepping-stones

These are a good option if you need to access an area for harvesting, without compacting the soil, These need to be flat, secure and have a rough texture so they don't get slippery when wet.

Bridges

The simplest bridge is a fallen log or wide plank. If it is so long it sags in the middle, put a support under it. If you have the right site a bridge can be very ornamental, as well as being an archetypal element, giving a psychological effect of transition. Don't have a bridge purely as an ornamental feature, it only makes sense if there is a need for one to cross water or a ravine. A bridge to nowhere just looks silly (a long pond is no excuse either).

Ramps

You can't run a wheelbarrow up or down steps, so may have to provide some other way to get it around. The simplest option is to have an alternate route that avoids the steps, but this can be a pain if it goes too far out of the way. You could also have a strategically placed ramp (maximum slope is 1:20 for ease of use), or you might just have a temporary plank to turn the steps into a ramp.

Steps

Steeply sloping gardens require steps to make them easily accessible. These must be practical: wide, strong, easy to walk on and non-slip. They should also be attractive and constructed of materials that match the house and paths. You can often use the same path material for the treads and use bricks or landscape ties for the risers. Split logs (¼ of a whole log) can be used for rustic steps with mulch paths (I have used split pieces of Oak firewood).

Calculating steps

The formula for outdoor steps is twice the riser height plus the tread should equal 26". The path treads should be 11 - 18" deep and the risers should be 4 - 7". Your actual sizes will vary according to the slope, but a 6" riser and 14" tread is the norm. Whatever measurement you use they should be consistent in height and depth. Don't have too many steps in one flight. If this is happening put in a landing (at least 36" long). This can also be used to change the run calculations).

You can change the depth of your treads according to your design, but the height of the risers should be pretty close to this (because it is the dimension that most human legs find most comfortable, most of the time).

Steps don't just enable you to get from one level to another, they are a transition space that gives you a place to pause before moving on to another area of the garden. They are also a focal point and an opportunity to make the garden more interesting. Steps can be curved rather than straight. Wide steps help to unify the areas they connect, whereas narrow ones tend to separate them. Deep steps can be used as informal seats and as shelves for container plants.

Any even remotely hazardous steps need a secure handrail to prevent people falling down them. This should be fairly smooth, so it's comfortable to hold and doesn't give you splinters.

Planting for paths and steps

Plants can be used to make paths more interesting and productive. You might create a border of compact little edibles, such as Alpine Strawberry, Alyssum, Carrot, Basil Garlic Chives, Parsley, Lettuce, Thyme. You might use aromatic plants as edging, and in crevices in pavement, where they will emit fragrance when walked upon. If the paving isn't particularly attractive, you can soften it with Corsican Mint, Chamomile, Pennyroyal, Marjoram, Thyme, Viola or Bugle (*Ajuga*).

For obvious reasons you shouldn't use spiny or very prickly plants alongside paths. You should also avoid very vigorous or tall plants near the path, as they will encroach and so require regular trimming. Low plants on either side of a path make it feel wider, while tall ones make it feel narrower.

Frequently traveled paths can be planted with plants that require frequent attention, as you will be passing them every day. You often see long planting beds at either side of a path.

Don’t put messy fruit trees near paths, driveways or other paved areas. They can create a mess that needs cleaning up and may even be a slipping hazard.

You can recover the planting area lost to paths (as well as provide shade and create screens) by the use of trellises or tunnels. These can by planted with fruiting vines, or climbing annual vegetables such as Cucurbits and Beans.

Driveways

Cars have come to dominate so much of our lives that I prefer to keep them out of the garden as much as possible. I don’t want a driveway running all over my property, I want it as short and as close to the road as possible. This minimizes the amount of wasted land, paving materials, maintenance and snow removal. This is particularly important in small gardens where space is at a premium.

Many town gardens have the garage behind the house by the back fence, with a driveway running the full depth of the property. This makes no sense at all, especially as relatively few people keep their cars in them anyway (in Santa Cruz they usually have to rent them out as living space to pay the property tax). If you have one of these long paved driveways you may want to think about reducing its length to that of a car or two (city planning laws may insist on you having a number of off road parking spaces though).

Paved driveways have other uses as well as parking cars. They are a good place to work on cars or other projects and make a safe play area for children. They can also be used to collect rainwater, if you make sure there is no oil, antifreeze or other chemicals on them.

If you are building a new driveway and would like to reduce the area of impervious paving surface (and the cost), you could create paved wheel tracks. These consist of 2 parallel paved tracks for the car wheels to run on. The area between the tracks can be filled with gravel, grass or whatever else will grow there. I saw one very steep driveway with steps between the tracks.

The size of a driveway

Traditional landscaping says that a driveway should be a minimum of 8 - 10’ wide on the straight and 10 - 12’ on the curves. Some designers say 12 feet wide is better (they probably drive Ford Expeditions or Hummers), but of course that takes more material. A parking area should have at least an 18’ turning radius. A T-shaped driveway saves space over a turnaround or circular driveway.

In cold climates it’s nice if the driveway gets daytime sun, so ice or snow will melt quickly. You should also think about where the snow can go when clearing the driveway. Incidentally don’t use salt to de-ice paths as it is harmful to plant growth. Use calcium chloride, wood ashes or sand instead.

Coping with rainwater runoff

Runoff from rainstorms quite literally moves mountains and can remove a few tons of poorly designed driveway overnight. A porous driveway must be designed to handle large amounts of water without washing away. I found that a lot of the water coming down my driveway originated from above. If this is the case try to divert it before it reaches the driveway.

An impervious driveway should be designed so all of the runoff water has somewhere to go, other than running off down storm drains.

If your driveway already exists, you should try and channel the runoff water to where it can be used. In an arid climate you might actually value this impervious surface as a rainwater catchment area. If possible you might modify the shape of your driveway to collect rainwater and channel it into a storage pond, tank or retention basin. You could also plant fruit trees and other food plants along the driveway where they can use the runoff directly.

In wet climates you might want a covered walkway from the house to the car.

Materials for driveways

If you are building a new driveway it's best to use a permeable material, unless you plan to harvest the runoff water. If your driveway is fairly level, gravel is one of the cheapest paving materials. This requires a good solid base and edging (and maybe a sloping sub-grade to move water), The gravel is simply dropped in a series of piles and raked level (it couldn't be easier to lay). Decomposed granite can also work well (use a 3" layer for a driveway and compact it with a roller).

Sloping driveways are more difficult, because they have to be able to deal with large amounts of water. If you have the money you could use porous paving blocks. These may be made from recycled plastic or concrete and are filled with gravel or soil. These allow water to percolate through and (if you use soil) plants to grow up between them.

Parking spaces

Traditional gardens didn't have these, but like it or not they are now essential in most cases (and even legally required by city planners. I favor a distinct separation between garden and car, with the car on the outside (perhaps an opaque fence or screen and gate). You might have a small parking area near the house for residents and a larger one further away for visitors. You could also park your car on the driveway out close to the street. Maybe create a turnaround at the edge of the road and fence it off. A simple patch of pebbles can give you a cheap and semi-permanent parking space.

A space 9 x 18 is considered the minimum size for a parking space. If space is at a premium you could build a carport or arbor and grow a living roof or vines. This not only disguises it, but also recovers the growing space.

Of course you might totally disagree with me about cars and want to make yours the main focal point of your garden. You might even want to be able to drive your car up onto the patio, so you can sit and enjoy your garden in comfort. You could create the ultimate American garden, a drive-through.

Boundaries and dividers

A garden has always needed to be fenced to keep wild and domesticated animals from eating the plants. In fact the root of the English word garden refers to an enclosed (girded) area; one that was surrounded by a protective barrier. Many religions talk about paradise as a garden and the word paradise is apparently derived from the Persian word for enclosure. Today that fence isn't just for security, it also gives privacy and helps to clearly define the property lines.

Fences, hedges and walls (for convenience sake I'm just going to refer to fences) perform a number of functions in the garden. Depending upon the circumstances you might need them to do any of the following:

- Their primary purpose is to provide a secure boundary, to keep dogs and children in and trespassers (animals and human) out. Depending upon the circumstances this may require an 8 foot high stone wall, or a few strands of wire.

- It takes a lot of fence to surround a property, which makes it one of the most common and unifying visual elements in the garden. For this reason it is important that the fences be attractive (or unobtrusive) and well thought out. In most cases they should be made from local materials.

- Fences help to define the boundaries and give shape to the framework of the garden.

- Fences help to define special places by dividing the garden into separate "rooms" for different activities. . By enclosing a space you can completely change its character and feel.

- By acting as screens they can provide privacy and hide unsightly objects or unwanted views. They can also obscure parts of the garden to create a sense of anticipation. Sometimes a gap may be purposely left in a wall or fence to emphasize a good view.

- They direct traffic and control movement, by giving you an easy way to go and by preventing shortcuts.

- Walls (and fences and hedges to a lesser extent) create their own microclimate, by reducing wind and trapping or blocking sun. The south facing side of a wall absorbs heat during the day and creates a warm sun trap. The north facing side is in shade for most of the time (it can be used as the wall of a lean-to or storage shed).

- Fences act as windbreaks to provide shelter from strong winds. They can also be used to funnel cooling winds to where you want them. As solid barriers they can divert cold air around the garden and prevent frost. They can also slow the movement of fire

- They provide support for climbing plants (and make it easier to put netting over fruit).

- They act as a backdrop for plants and artwork.

- They muffle unwanted noise (walls and hedges are particularly good for this).

- They can give a feeling of enclosure and security, a sense of being home.

Planning the boundary fences

In small gardens the fences are largely pre-determined, in that they go around the edge of the property. On a very large property you have to decide how much area you want to enclose (your garden doesn't have to incorporate every square foot of your property).

Your choice of boundary material will depend upon your needs, your imagination, the style of house, the neighborhood where you live and what you can afford. The most obvious choice is something that is traditional for your location. This helps to give your garden a regional feel and stops it looking like you just bought it at Home Depot.

Your choice of boundary also depends upon what is outside (a great view, nosy neighbors, a psycho pit bull, street traffic, strong winds) and whether you want to see it or pretend it isn't there.

In the city you may want a strong, relatively opaque barrier for privacy or security. The most obvious choice is a solid fence but be careful: a tall solid fence surrounding a small garden can make it feel even smaller and more confined (as well as shadier).

In the country privacy isn't as much of a concern, so fence are often more open. This is especially true if your surroundings are particularly beautiful, in which case you will want to be able to see through it.

In windy areas you may need the fence to act as a windbreak. This should be semi-permeable so it doesn't cause too much turbulence (See Windbreaks).

If you want to fence your vegetable garden or growing beds, an open fence works best as it creates less shade (in hot climates some plants may even appreciate the light shade they do create). In cooler areas the northern wall might be better closed, to provide shelter from cold winds.

Height of boundaries

The height or a fence or wall is commonly related to the height of nearby buildings and the size of the garden it is enclosing.

In traditional American gardens the fence in the front is lower (no higher than the window sills) than that in the back yard. They also tend to be fairly open, because the front garden is often thought of as a display and the fence is used to frame the composition.

Back garden fences tend to be taller than front ones because this area is used like another room of the house, as a private place for family activities. Not surprisingly it gets much more use than the front garden.

In heavily regulated areas 6 feet is often a maximum legal height for a solid fence. An inexpensive way to increase the height above this is by fastening trellis to the top, or adding post extensions and wire. Vines can then be trained up the fence.

Internal fences and room dividers

Fences, walls and hedges can all be used for room dividers. They don't need to be as strong or secure as boundary fences, so are often thinner and less substantial. It doesn't matter if you can see through it, or if they are high enough to obscure the view. All they really have to do is define the space. In some cases the divider may be little more than a change in vegetation, or flooring. These often work best when they are fairly open, as they don't cast as much shade. Plants work really well in these situations as they are relatively inexpensive, look great and are protected from grazing deer.

Dividing fences can be different heights, depending upon what you are trying to achieve.

- Knee high fences (up to 2 feet) give direction and define specific areas without actually being serious physical obstacles.
- A waist height (3 feet) fence acts to direct your movement, but doesn't cast too much shade.
- A 4 feet tall fence (chest height) may be used to separate parts of the garden into rooms.
- A fence you can't see over (5' 6" - 6 feet tall) offers protection and privacy.

Materials

It takes a lot of posts, rails, boards or wire (or stone or bushes) to go around the perimeter of a property, so this is usually one of the most expensive parts of the garden. If you don't have much money you have to get creative and start looking for salvaged stuff. If this doesn't lead anywhere then plastic or wire netting is the cheapest fencing you can buy (it is also the most invisible). Wooden fencing can get quite expensive if you have to buy it new and it always seems to me like a waste of trees. Hedges are perhaps the most ecologically sound fencing and don't have to cost a lot if you raise your own plants. However they take several years to become effective and you will need a temporary fence in the meantime. Walls are undoubtedly the most costly barrier, but also the most durable; a well built wall should last longer than you.

The materials you choose for your boundaries should relate to the house in some way and help to unify the whole picture. This doesn't necessarily mean using the same materials, but rather making them complementary.

In general long perimeter fences tend to use inexpensive material because you need a lot of it. However a continuous length of a single material can get monotonous, so it is common to use a variety of different materials. You probably can't afford to fence the whole garden with expensive stone walls, wattle hurdles, or bamboo fencing, but you could put a section in the most visible area, where it can really be appreciated. You could also have a combination of different materials in separate sections (part wall, part fence, part hedge). At the same time don't use too many different materials, otherwise things can get confusing. Change the materials where you want a different look (such as in different rooms), or in the corners or behind something.

Fences

These are the most common choice for boundaries in America, because they are quick and easy to build, don't take up much space and aren't too expensive (we have always had lots of forest). Fences are very versatile in that they can be solid and opaque, or open and transparent. Open fences have quite a different feel and use than closed fences. They don't cast as much shade, don't create frost dams or wind turbulence and tend to be more interesting visually. Solid barriers are better for privacy and can act as sun traps.

Fence designs tend to be fairly traditional and differ by region and what was readily available there. Certain styles have become are synonymous with certain places (bamboo-Japan, wattle hurdles-England, white picket-New England, grape stakes-Northern California) and it's usually best to use a style and material that fits in with your location.

There are a huge variety of fence materials and designs to choose from: woven willow, 1 x 8 boards, wooden pickets, wrought ironwork, split bamboo, corrugated metal and more.

I much prefer homemade fences to commercial ones, which tend to look too uniform. Making them yourself also gives you a chance to be creative and make something unique. You don't have to make enough to surround your whole garden, just put the handmade sections where they will most appreciated.

Fence color is something many gardeners don't think about. Dark colors generally work best, as light colors get dirty and need more frequent painting. If you don't want to paint the whole fence; you could just color the posts or even just the post caps. I generally avoid painting fences because once you do it, you need to re-paint every few years (remember Tom Sawyer). This can be difficult if you have plants growing on it. Also painted wood can't be recycled easily.

Board fences

The most common fences where I live are 1 x 8 Redwood or Cedar boards. In fact whole forests have been cut down to make good neighbors. The cheapest board fence I've seen was made out or old pallets. The boards on one side were taken off and nailed on to the other side. If you can get hardwood pallets this could last a long time.

If you are building a board fence it's a good idea to raise the boards a couple of inches off the ground, so they don't stay wet and rot. If you want the fence to go down to the ground (maybe to keep out pests), you can lay a single board horizontally along the bottom This is a bit of extra work, but means that there is only one board in contact with the ground to rot,

It pays to watch out for when people are replacing their old fences, as they will usually be happy to give it away (you might also try contacting a fencing contractor and offer to take an old fence away). These still contain a lot of usable wood, already weathered to a nice silver gray. Often all you have to do is cut off the bottom few inches of rotten wood (so what if your fence is only 5 feet 6 inches tall?) You can even regain these lost inches by using a horizontal board across the bottom.

A solid fence will take a battering in high winds, so it must be securely built and anchored. You can make it into a more effective semi-permeable windbreak by placing the boards on alternate sides of the rails. This allows some wind to go through the fence (though it also makes it slightly less private).

If you are worried about security, put the rails on the inside of the fence, so it harder to climb from the outside.

If you are really worried about privacy (perhaps you are an urban nudist) you can nail battens over the cracks between the boards, or you can overlap the edges of the boards.

If you have a problem with animals digging under the fence, you can dig a trench and bury gopher wire folded out from the base of the fence. You could even gopher proof a whole room in this way.

Picket Fences

These are one of the more formal and elegant wooden fences and are commonly used around the front garden to make a good impression. A picket fence can be open or closed. An open fence has spaces between the boards and so uses less wood. It allows some light to pass through, breaks the wind more effectively and you can see through it (plants can poke through as well) A closed fence has the boards butted together, which gives more privacy, but uses more wood and creates more shade.

You can buy picket fences in pre-made panels, but if you have a table saw you can make your own pretty easily. There is plenty of scope for creativity here; you can cut the tops of the boards into a variety of decorative shapes and can vary the height of the boards. They can be left unpainted, painted one color (to coordinate with the house), or you could paint things on them. When assembling the panels you should make the gap less than the width of the boards.

Old pallets can be used to make a picket fence, if you can get enough of them.

Grape stakes

A variation on the picket fence (often seen where I live) is made from old Redwood grape stakes. These are very durable, so you sometimes find old ones for sale inexpensively. New real grape stales are getting scarce these days, but you can still find the similar (but thinner) redwood palings. If you have a source of easily split wood (Redwood, Chestnut, Cedar) and a froe you can also make your own stakes. This isn't difficult and is very satisfying.

You can vary the transparency of a grape stake fence by how closely you space the palings. Very close together and it is almost opaque. Far apart and you can see right through it.

You can make a 4 feet high grape stake (or any other) fence deer proof by putting a 4 feet high fence of chicken wire parallel to it and 4 feet behind it.

Paling fence

A commonly used fence in England (and worth emulating) is made from strips of cloven chestnut held together with wire. This is an exceptionally versatile and useful fence because it can be moved quite easily (just roll it up and carry it away). It also uses less wood as it doesn't require any cross rails. This was once widely used to protect new hedges (from animals and wind) until the plants grew large enough to work by themselves.

If you are handy you can make paling fencing yourself from wire and coppiced Chestnut or old Redwood grape stakes or palings (or even sawn 1" X 3"). It is fairly straightforward to make (it would actually be a good business if you grew and coppiced your own Chestnut). A similar product is available commercially in this country, made with sawn redwood lath, though this isn't nearly as strong.

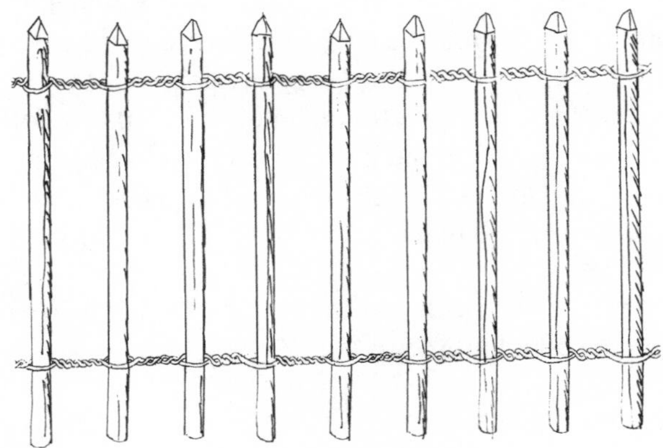

Corrugated metal

This can be used to create a secure and solid fence with a modern industrial look. Such a fence may take a battering in strong winds though, so needs very secure fenceposts and cross members. If combined with metal or concrete fenceposts, it is even fire resistant to some degree (though it will melt if the fire gets hot enough). Old corrugated metal (good enough for a fence) can sometimes be obtained very cheaply from junkyards.

Post and rail fence

These are widely used for keeping horses and other large livestock enclosed. They aren't very effective for much else though.

Home grown fence materials

A variety of home grown materials have been used for fences where wood isn't abundant. Split Bamboo (*Arundinaria*) is a favorite fence material in Japan and the intricate designs are a fascinating vernacular art form. In the southwest the woody ribs of the Saguaro (Cereus) have been used for fencing. Giant Reed (*Arundo donax*) was once used in France to make lightweight fence panels. With a little imagination Cattail, Bamboo, Bulrush and Reed might be used too.

Trellis

Lattice trellis is most often used for its visual effect, or for screening, but it can be used as a fence too. They are one of the best supports for vines, so long as they are strong enough to support the weight. Trellis is strong, stable, permanent and fairly easy to make (and repair).

Wire fencing

There is wire fencing to suit every situation. It can be several simple strands of wire (barbed or otherwise), chicken wire, chain link, hog wire and more. Wire fencing tends to be quite light visually, if also rather utilitarian. It can be covered with climbing vines to disguise it, in which case it becomes a fedge. Chain link can be disguised with wood strips (these make it into a good windbreak) or even pruned shoots from fruit trees.

If you use concrete fenceposts and wire fencing you can make a relatively fire resistant barrier (though it would melt if the fire got hot enough).

Barbed wire may be ugly and nasty (and bad Feng Shui), but it is also cheap and effective, which is why it runs for thousands of miles in some areas. In a humid climate it can be hidden very effectively with plants (they think it is a sturdy trellis just for them). Barbed wire decorated with Blackberries and Wild Roses would make a pretty formidable barrier.

Enhancing your fence

Ornamentation

Erecting the fence is just the start. Look upon it as a blank canvas, the starting point for some self-expression and let you imagination go to work. It can be decorated with artwork, vines, mirrors, old windows paint, old tools, trompe l'oeil or anything else you can think of.

Post caps

These don't merely give the fence a more elegant and finished look, they also protect the exposed end grain (which absorbs water more readily) so the post lasts longer. Caps can be made out of almost anything: wooden blocks (or stacks of blocks), elaborate finials, copper balls, birdhouses, hand picked stones and more. If you can't think of anything to use for caps, you could just bevel the tops of the posts to help them shed water more easily.

Fences from the garden

Brushwood fence

Brushwood fences (also known as dead hedges - for obvious reasons) were probably the first barriers ever made by humans. They can still be effective today and are relevant to us because they can be made at no cost, using unwanted material that might otherwise be burned. They also work as a quick screen.

To build a brushwood fence, a row of stakes are hammered into the ground on the desired boundary line. Large branches or limbs are trimmed to a single flat plane and the sharpened butt ends are stuck into the ground in a line. These are spaced close together so there are no large gaps between them. Additional stakes may be added as needed to give stability. Finally long supple shoots (Willow is ideal) are woven in and out of the branches and stakes to hold the whole thing together and fill any gaps.

Weeds and wild plants will soon colonize this kind of fence, as perching birds drop seeds in their droppings. Wind borne seeds are dropped when the dead hedge interferes with air flow. You can also sow plants intentionally (annual vines give an almost instant live hedge effect). Seedlings thrive in the protection of the dead hedge as there is no competition from living plants and they are safe from herbivores and strong winds. This type of fence will only last for a few years, but this is long enough for permanent plants to grow up through it, or to get a real hedge established.

Another brush fence

An even simpler way to use brush as a fence is to simply stack it sideways in a pile. The best way to do this is to hammer 2 rows of upright stakes into the ground about 18-24 inches apart, and stack the brushwood between the stakes, as high as you can go. As with the dead hedge, plants will grow up through the brush.

Tree stump fence

This was common in pioneer days when forests were being cleared to create fields. It consisted of a row of uprooted stumps with brushwood filling in any gaps in between.

Wattle hurdles

These traditional English panels are made from woven Willow or split Hazel. They are generally used as an accent around an important area, rather than around the whole garden. They look great but are pretty much impossible to find in North America (though Chinese copies are starting to appear). If you were motivated you could learn to make them yourself and perhaps create a business for yourself.

Wicker fence

This is like a combination woven hurdle, living Willow fence and brushwood fence. It is built using shoots of Willow (or other supple wood) woven between stout stakes pounded into the ground. If you use Willow for the stakes it will often take root and grow (if the soil is moist enough). These fences were once quite common in parts of the west where trees were scarce. I have also seen this done in modern gardens, by simply weaving fruit tree prunings around upright stakes.

Pole Fence

If you have enough poles, you can make a fence from peeled poles fastened to cross members, attached to posts, palisade style. If they are kept from contact with the ground and treated with preservative, even pine may last for a reasonable length of time. This is quite a bit of work, but if you have the right materials it wouldn't cost anything.

Fenceposts

Fenceposts must be made from rot resistant wood if they are to last for any length of time. Oak, Chestnut and Locust are the most durable, Cedar, Redwood and pressure treated softwood slightly less so. They are usually 8 feet long (with ¼ - ⅓ of the post going into the ground) and are spaced 6 – 8 feet apart.

Most pressure treated posts are now treated with the alkaline copper quaternary (ACQ), which is much less toxic than the old chromated copper arsenate. When placing a fence post I usually backfill the hole with soil (some people like to put some gravel underneath the post to improve drainage). Some people worry this won't be strong enough and use concrete to hold the posts more firmly. I might do this to anchor corner posts, or very exposed fences, but it also hastens rotting and makes it harder to pull the posts and reuse them (though you can sometimes smash it with a sledgehammer). If you do use concrete you don't have to mix it; you can just pour it into the hole dry. It will absorb enough moisture from the soil to set up (unless the soil is very dry).

In loose soil it may be easier to hammer pointed fenceposts into the ground, rather digging holes and planting them. They will also be more secure. Just make sure they are perpendicular when you hit them (an inexpensive post level will help).

If you are using pressure treated posts, don't put a cut end in the ground. The untreated interior wood will rot as rapidly as any untreated softwood. Always put the uncut pressure treated end in the ground.

Steel fenceposts are often used for wire fences. These are simply hammered into the ground, and can be installed very quickly. I often use them for temporary wire fences as they are fairly easy to remove and reuse. As a bonus they are also recyclable.

Grow your own posts

You can never have too many posts, but they aren't cheap to buy. If you have the space you could grow your own fenceposts by coppicing rot resistant trees such as Chestnut, Mesquite, Oak, Black Locust or Osage orange. Chestnut is superior to other common woods in that it doesn't have much sapwood. This means it can be used in the round, when only a few years old.

Most sapwood isn't very durable and a sapling may be composed of mostly sapwood. This is why fenceposts are commonly split out of larger logs (12" or so in diameter). There is then some heartwood in each piece to hold nails. To get posts size pieces out of a larger log just start splitting the pieces in half, until they are small enough to use. Don't try split a small piece off of a larger one.

In treeless (or fire prone) areas you can make virtually indestructible (though heavy) fenceposts from concrete and rebar. This is actually pretty easy and they really do last almost indefinitely.

Plants and fences

Fences can be made more attractive and productive by training climbing, rambling or espaliered plants over them (sometimes you may even put up a fence primarily to act as a support for climbing plants). This is a win win win situation; the plants receive support and extra warmth, the walls look better and are more secure and you get to harvest food. Akebia, Kiwi, Roses, Grapes, Passion Vines and thornless Blackberries all work well. After a while your fence may get so overgrown it starts to look like a hedge. You can add some trellis on top if you want extra height.

Some plants can be used to strengthen a flimsy fence and eventually turn it into a formidable barrier. These could be wild plants or useful cultivated plants such as grapes. Alternatively they could get so heavy they pull the fence down with their weight.

Interior dividing fences can be enhanced with plants quite easily, as they don't need to be protected from hungry deer.

Walls

Walls are expensive to build, but they are by far the most durable of all boundaries, in fact some of the oldest existing human works are walls. If you take this longevity into account, then they are actually the cheapest boundary in the long-term (of course you may not want to include the time you are dead into any cost benefit equation).

You should be absolutely sure you really want a wall before you expend all of that money and effort to build it. Maybe put up a fence first to make sure it is in the right place.

Stone or brick walls serve several functions as well as providing a beautiful boundary.

- South facing walls are sun traps (especially dark colored ones), absorbing heat during the day and releasing it at night. This can be significant in cool climates, where tender fruits are often grown as espaliers against walls. A sheltered south facing corner where two walls meet can get especially warm.
- Walls are the strongest windbreaks, though the enclosed area must be small otherwise they tend to cause turbulence.
- The mass of walls makes them a good choice for reducing noise.
- Walls are uniquely permanent and give a formal feel to the garden.
- A wall is totally fireproof and can slow a wildfire considerably. In fire prone areas you might consider using walls as part of your fire defenses.

Problems

The biggest problem with walls is their cost: they take a lot of materials, a solid foundation and labor to build. Modest height walls aren't that hard to build (I picked up the skill of making dry walls quite quickly) but they take a lot of hard work. Tall masonry walls are a much bigger project and not one for the inexperienced or timid. In earthquake prone areas they must be carefully engineered and reinforced with rebar. They also need a solid foundation that goes below the frost line (this can be 36" deep in some places), otherwise they can eventually become unstable.

Walls provide a great refuge for slugs and snails, especially the dry stone walls built without mortar.

When planting close to walls you may find that there is a zone of shallow, permanently dry, soil at the base of the wall. To grow plants near walls you have to enrich the soil with organic matter, plant away from the wall and perhaps irrigate too.

Types of wall

Stone – This is expensive to buy, so if you have stone on your property (or can get it free nearby) you are in luck. You will need a lot of stone to build a wall though (and I really mean a lot). A nice thing about dry stone walls is that in a hundred years time your great grandchildren will be able to dismantle your crumbling wall and reuse the stone to build a new one (if urban sprawl hasn't turned your remote homestead into a city lot by then).

Brick – If not too tall this is fairly straightforward to build (keep it plumb), though new bricks (and mortar) are energy intensive to produce.

Glass block – Not usually used by itself, but could be added to a wall for a modern look.

Concrete – Can work well for low walls, but making forms and pouring a tall one is quite a technical project.

Broken concrete – This can be dry laid like stone for a low wall (if you can get enough of it).

Concrete block – This is the cheapest kind of wall to build, much cheaper than stone or brick and faster to lay. It looks pretty urban industrial, unless you disguise it with a coat of stucco (or hypertufa) or evergreen vines. Of course you may like the industrial look.

Stud wall – Probably the cheapest wall I have built, this is essentially a stud wall covered with stucco. It should be built with pressure treated wood or salvaged redwood, wooden lath, tar paper and stucco wire. Compared to a masonry wall this type of wall is fairly light and not so vulnerable to earthquakes. I highly recommend them.

In cold climates you could put glass panels in a stud wall, to create a warmer microclimate on the north side of the wall.

Turf - I'm not going to try and convince you that this makes a very durable wall, but if you are removing a lawn you could use the turf to make an attractive low wall (for areas with lots of rain only).

Earthen walls - If you have your heart set on a wall, and have the right kind of soil, but no free stone, you might consider an adobe, superadobe, rammed earth or cob wall. I don't know anything about building with these, but there are books available that do. If you are interested in experimenting with these materials then a garden wall may be a good way to try them out. The idea of making free walls out of the earth is very appealing (though soil is heavy to work with).

Adobe bricks are made by packing soil and straw mix into a mold (8 x 16 x 4) and drying in the sun. Rammed earth is made by compacting soil in a form, leaving to dry for 24 hours and then raising the form and repeating the process. Cob walls are made by packing globs of clay soil together into one coherent sculptured mass. Superadobe is made by putting soil into tubular bags.

Earthen walls need a stone foundation to keep them dry and a roof to shed the rain, otherwise they may slowly dissolve.

Wall cap

Traditionally a stone wall was capped with larger stones. This cap has a decorative effect, but its main purpose is to protect the wall from the weather. It prevents water from getting into the wall, where the repeated freeze and thawing (and resulting expansion and contraction) could break it apart. Dry laid walls are usually capped with a row of larger stones laid on edge.

Cordwood wall

This is made of cordwood stacked in a single row and held in place with posts. Some even have a roof so they last longer and some are cemented together with mortar.

Retaining walls

A retaining wall can be made of stone, interlocking concrete block, poured concrete, railroad ties, wire cages filled with rocks, tires or wooden boxes filled with soil. It should lean in 2" for every foot of rise and there may need to be a drain or trap rock behind the wall for drainage. These walls must be strongly built as they have to hold back a considerable quantity of soil (which can be very heavy when it gets wet). A tall (over 36") retaining wall needs careful engineering and usually a building permit.

The posts of a wooden retaining wall should go into the ground to a greater depth than the wall is high. It should also be backfilled with gravel rather than wood, so it lasts longer.

Segmental retaining walls are made from commercially available concrete blocks that simply lock together. They are versatile and simple to install, but a bit manufactured looking.

A tall retaining wall can work as a stock proof boundary (most can't climb up or jump down) and is actually what is known as a Ha Ha. This is invisible from the vantage point of the viewer looking from above. They are much mentioned in English landscaping books, but I have only ever seen them in grand estate landscaping.

Plants on walls

In areas that have lots of rain throughout the growing season, a few plants will grow very happily in the free draining cracks of stone walls. Plants that are traditionally found on walls include Wall Lettuce (*Mycelis*), Wall flower, *Centranthus rubber, Galium verum, Dianthus, Campanula, Armeria maritima, Alyssum* and *Arabis* species. These plants can make a wall look really good.

I keep repeating this, but south facing walls provide a warm microclimate that can be used for growing plants that are marginally hardy in your area. In England it was common to grow espaliered tender fruits (Figs, Apricots, Pears) against them.

Vines can be trained up walls if you give them something to grab on to, such as wire and vine eyes, chicken wire or wooden trellis.

Low dry stone walls can have their center filled with soil and be planted like a rock garden planter. You often see these in the rainy west of England, with a hedge growing out of the top of them.

Some plants grow really well on retaining walls. Their roots can go right through the wall and into the soil, while the wall provides a warmer microclimate.

Ornamentation for walls

You can use most of the things I suggested for decorating walls. Large smooth walls can be painted with murals.

Making a wall look older

You can artificially age a new wall by spraying it with dilutes urine, yogurt or liquid fertilizer . This encourages the growth of mosses and lichens.

Hedges

In the right climate hedges are the most ecologically friendly and resource efficient way of enclosing land. They are made from living breathing plants (they actually consume CO2) and don't require the use of wood, stone, brick, concrete or wire. They are also largely self repairing (though they do require occasional maintenance).

Advantages of hedges:

- Hedges are one of the best windbreaks of all, because they flex and move and let some wind through. By doing this they create less turbulence.
- Hedges were first planted to keep animals out (or was it in?) If they are spiny enough they will also deter humans (how about planting a little Poison Oak in there as an additional deterrent?)
- A thick hedge can reduce noise considerably.
- If you use fruit bearing shrubs, your hedge can become a kind of linear food forest. This can be a source of soft fruit, herbs, salad greens and more.
- Hedges can provide mulch and compost materials, as well as coppiced poles, pea stakes and more.
- Hedges are beautiful and in areas with few trees they can be an important refuge for wildlife. In cities and suburbs they are particularly valuable as they act as sheltered corridors for wildlife movement.

Problems with hedges

One drawback with hedges is the time it takes to get them established (though in the scheme of things it really isn't that long, you just need patience). If you need an immediate animal-proof boundary you will have to provide an additional barrier for several years, while they are growing.

Another problem is that a vigorously growing hedge can take a lot of nutrients and water from the soil (and also create an area of shade). Their roots may spread sideways for twice their height, so you can't put intensive growing beds too close to them. This can be a problem in small gardens, where you need all the space you can get. One way around this is to put a wide path adjacent to the hedge.

In hot dry areas some hedge plants can be a potential fire hazard. In such cases you need to choose plants that are fairly succulent and not very combustible.

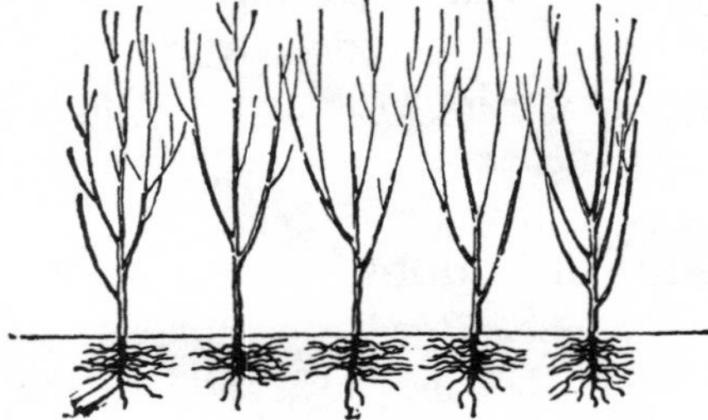

Formal hedges

These add interesting shapes to the garden and can be beautiful when well maintained. They have long been a mainstay of ornamental gardening, but considerable labor is needed to keep them looking good. They are generally made up of only one kind of plant and tend to be so uniform you can't see where one plant ends and another begins. Evergreens such as Privet, Box, Beech and Yew are most often used.

Formal hedges have fallen out of favor somewhat in recent years because they require frequent trimming to keep them looking good. When I was a kid, clipping the hedge was almost as frequent a task as mowing the lawn. The resulting trimmings are a resource in that they can be used as mulch material. In fact the plants may cut routinely just to provide this.

Of course is you are an obsessive compulsive workaholic you will consider this extra work to be an advantage rather than a disadvantage. It could give you a totally new outlet for your compulsion. You could even go in for topiary, which involves shaping the plants into all kinds of fanciful shapes (deer, peacocks, dragons).

Informal hedges

This kind of hedge sometimes consists of a single productive species, but more often it contains a number of different species. These are usually chosen for their suitability to the growing conditions and their edibility rather than for their appearance. The plants are mostly left to grow naturally, so it has a much wilder appearance. I like it, not only for its appearance, but also because it can be a useful source of fruit, nuts, mulch material and more. This type of hedge does require more room than a formal one, which might be an issue in small gardens.

Traditional British field hedgerows were planted using tough, vigorous, viciously thorny species such as Hawthorn and Blackthorn (a wild Plum). Over time (some hedges are hundreds of years old) other species would grow up within them from seeds dropped by birds or on the wind. These were usually encouraged as they made the hedge more diverse and useful.

Edible hedges

The most obvious of these would be a fruiting hedge of Blueberry, Pineapple Guava, Seaberry or Beach Plum). You could also try an edible foliage hedge, such as Linden (*Tilia*), Saltbush (*Atriplex*) or Moringa.

Forest hedgerow garden

This is a hedgerow that is treated like a forest garden and planted with a diversity of large shrubs, small trees, vines, perennials and anything else you can cram in. It is fairly tall so works best as a border (and windbreak) for the northern edge of the garden. See Wild ideas for semi-wild gardens.

Shape

Most hedges are straight, to minimize the space they take up and the number of plants required. However zigzag or winding hedges might give more valuable edge habitat and varied microclimate.

Planting hedges

When you plant a hedge you want the plants to grow quickly, which means the soil should be deep and fertile. If the soil is less than ideal you may want to dig a trench the length of the hedge and amend it with organic matter. The plants will also need sufficient moisture, which may mean irrigation in drier climates. A hedge won't thrive if there is too much shade either.

Plant the hedge when the soil contains plenty of moisture. Early winter is good in mild climates, early spring works best in colder areas. It is usually recommended that you use small seedlings when planting a hedge These may look puny to start with, but they will eventually out-perform larger container grown ones. This is good because they are also cheaper. For the economy hedge space the plants 9" apart in a row. For the luxury hedge you plant two offset rows of seedlings, 9" apart in the row, with 18" between the rows. If you are using bigger plants, space them anywhere from 2 - 5 feet apart (depending upon their size). Use sheet mulch to suppress weeds and conserve moisture until the plants get established.

A newly planted row of saplings won't start to behave like a hedge for several years. In the meantime you must erect a temporary fence to do the job. This could be anything that doesn't shade the new plants. Wire fencing and metal posts are good because they are easily re-used afterwards and don't cast shade or otherwise inhibit the plants. Chestnut paling (or Redwood snow fencing) is great if you can find it, as it also acts as a windbreak. Of course if you have already surrounded your entire garden with a secure perimeter fence this won't be necessary.

Care
You want your plants to grow quickly, so give them all of the water and nutrients they need and keep down weeds. After the first season the hedge is generally cut back hard, leaving only a few inches of growth. This encourages branching and rapid regrowth and results in a denser hedge. The hedge should then be trimmed once or twice a year to reduce shading and to encourage bushy growth.

Height:
The eventual natural height of the hedge will depend upon the plants used, the location and the climate. You can trim a hedge to keep it at a specified height, though it makes more sense to choose a plant that naturally only grows to the height you want.

Hedge maintenance
Hedges are not completely maintenance free. As they get taller over the years, lower branches may start to die off and holes may appear along the bottom. If you really need to keep out animals you will have to fix them. Any hole that appears in a hedge can be temporarily closed with a few cut branches. It can be filled more permanently by cutting part way through an adjacent stem, bending it horizontally to fill the opening and pinning it to the ground. During the next growing season vertical suckers will be produced along the stem and fill in the gap.

In England hedgerows are traditionally completely renovated every 20 years or so by a process known as laying. This is done when serious gaps start to develop in the hedge, or when it develops bushy or dead patches as a result of repeated trimming. The first step in layering is to remove any suckers or seedlings which deviate from the line of the hedge, along with any dead material. You then remove all other excess growth to leave a series of vigorous upright stems (known as pleachers), with bushy growth at their ends, These have their side branches trimmed off.

The pleachers are then bent over by cutting part of the way through the stem. The cut is somewhat tricky initially as you must cut deeply enough (¾ of the way through) to allow it to bend easily without breaking, but not so far that you sever it. The cut should be at a height of 2-5", and an angle of 45-60° (use a downwards cut). The pleacher is then bent down to an angle of roughly 20° (it looks better if you keep all of the angles the same).

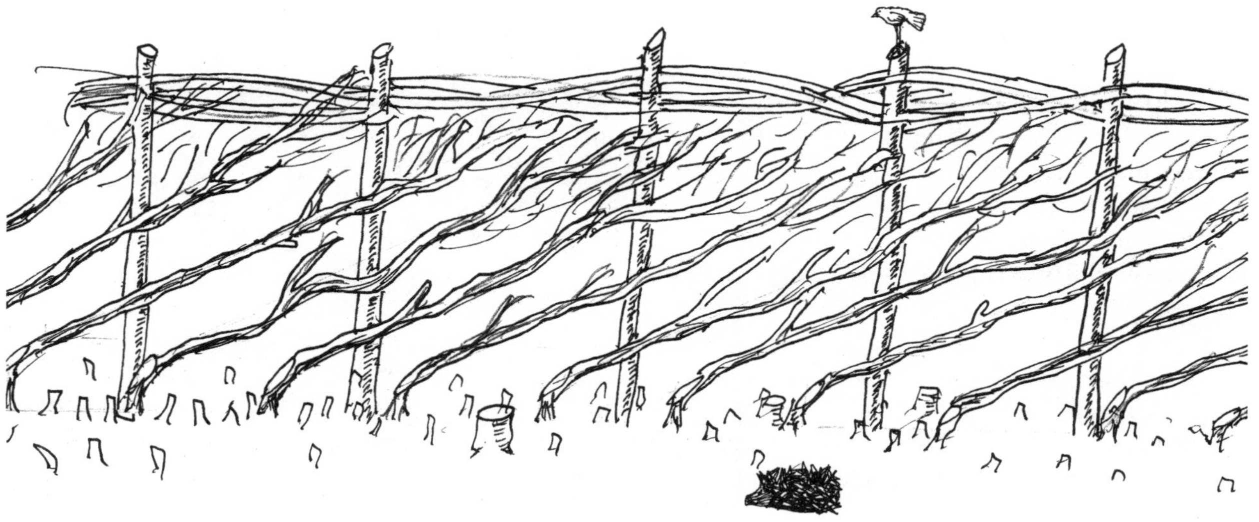

Very large gaps can be filled by laying pleachers both ways, or by rooting a pleacher to the spot by layering. You could also transplant a large plant into the spot.

The next step is to drive stakes down through the hedge and into the ground every 2-3 feet (sometimes existing saplings in the hedge can be cut at the appropriate height) to hold the pleachers in place. The final step is to weave flexible wands of Willow (or other wood) about 9-10 feet long (known as binders) around the stakes (and each other) to create a strong rigid fence.

During the next growing season vertical suckers will arise along the stem (due to the reduced apical dominance), and from the ground, filling out the hedge with vigorous new growth. The binders and the stakes will slowly rot in the hedge and disappear.

Another way to rejuvenate a hedge is to cut down everything and pile it along its length. New shoots from the hedge will find their way up through the dead branches and grow up to make a new hedge.

Plants for hedges

Native hedge
The cheapest way to create a hedge is to transplant small (hopefully useful) native seedlings from elsewhere on your property.

Fruiting hedge plants
Almost any vigorous shrub that is suited to the growing conditions can be used for a hedge, but it pays to use the ones that give tasty edible fruit too. Blueberries, Cherries, Currants, Hazel, Feijoa, Bush Cherry and Goumi are all potential candidates.

Thorny hedge plants
To deter deer and livestock (and humans) you can use thorny shrubs (the bigger and nastier the better). These might include Barberry, Blackberry, Black Locust, Caragana, Hawthorn, Honey Locust, Gooseberry, Osage Orange, Wild Roses (especially *R. rugosa*) and Natal Plum.

Evergreen hedge plants
These are popular because they hold their leaves year round, so always look the same. However there aren't many good edible evergreen hedge species. Feijoa, Natal Plum.

Drought tolerant hedge plants
Almond, Carob, Honey Locust, Black Locust, Hackberry, Pistachio, Pomegranate, Fig. Just be aware that plants with dry foliage can be a fire hazard.

Other plants to add
A hedge can have its own community of useful herbaceous species. Depending upon the climate these might include Comfrey, Red Dock, Sorrel, Good King Henry, Ramps and more. You could also interplant fruiting vines such as Blackberries or Passion Vine.

Other living fence ideas

If a hedge won't work for you there are several other options using live plants.

Fedge
This versatile barrier gets its name because it is a fence that resembles a hedge. It is a relatively modern idea and consists of a wire fence, over which climbing plants are trained. It deserves to be more widely used as it is a quick growing and very effective barrier, that will keep out all large animals (and small ones if you use a small wire mesh). It is also a good windbreak and doesn't take up as much space as a hedge.

A fedge may be used primarily as a boundary fence, or its main purpose may be to support climbing plants. Depending upon the plants it may be anywhere from 3 – 10 feet tall. Any kind of wire fencing will work, from barbed wire to chicken wire to concrete reinforcing wire. It will last as long as the fenceposts and wire, so make sure it is securely supported on strong posts.

Any climbing plants can be used for a fedge, though I prefer to use productive vines such as Grape, Kiwi, Passion Vine, Hops, Akebia or Blackberries. These can be used alone or in combination. Productive annual vines such as Cucurbits, Peas or Beans could be used for a temporary fedge (useful as a trial run if you aren't really sure whether you want a hedge).

Espaliers

These can be used to create a living fence or screen that is both beautiful and fruit. They are fairly transparent, so don't cast much shade. See Training trees for more on these.

Living Willow fence

Willow cuttings will root in any damp soil and can be used to make an almost instant living fence. Plant the longest shoots you have, at 10-inch intervals and overlap in a diamond lattice. Keep the soil moist and most of the shoots will root and start growing in spring. By late summer they will have formed a dense screen. If you have wild Willows growing nearby (you probably do), you should be able to cut enough straight shoots (the longer the better) for this. If you have any Basket Willow cultivars these are even better. This kind of fence will require some maintenance in spring, pruning, tying and bending.

You could also make a screen from two or three rows of fast growing Basket Willow cuttings. Cut them down to the ground every year to encourage new growth and to get material for crafts, mulch or other garden use.

Bamboo

A planting of living Bamboo can be a good fence. It is particularly effective if you have a sunken Bamboo barrier on either side. This keeps the runners confined to a narrow area and so makes the screen denser.

Prickly Pear

This has been used as a living fence in hot dry areas.

Ocotillo

Cuttings of this desert shrub will usually root if placed in a row and have been used to make a living fence (for desert areas of course).

Windbreaks

I already discussed how strong winds can be a problem in the garden, especially in colder areas. If your garden is exposed to the full force of the wind, you will have to provide some kind of wind protection.

Creating a windbreak isn't quite as simple as just erecting a fence or wall to block it out. Solid barriers such as these don't really slow the wind, they just deflect it, in much the same way a boulder in a river deflects water. This results in a low-pressure area behind the wall that sucks the deflected wind back to the ground, causing eddies and turbulence. The best windbreaks are actually semi-permeable, so some wind is deflected and some moves through them. The air filtering through the windbreak prevents a low pressure area developing.

It is important to put a windbreak in the best position, so it works with the land (just below the crest of a ridge is ideal). Also make sure your windbreak doesn't prevent the downward flow of cold air and thus create a frost pocket.

Windbreaks are usually placed where they will block prevailing winds, but it may sometimes be necessary to block particularly damaging winds that come from another direction (such as from north). In extreme climates there might be a windbreak around the garden and another one around the house.

A gap for a gate (or larger opening) should have another windbreak behind it as a baffle, to prevent it acting like a wind tunnel. Alternatively a paths could go through the rows of plants at an angle.

Living windbreaks

Trees and shrubs are make best windbreaks because they are naturally semi-permeable. Also their flexibility means they can absorb some of the winds energy without damage. Unlike non-living windbreaks they are also self-repairing if they do get damaged.

A good windbreak has defense in depth and slows the wind gradually, which creates less turbulence. Ideally it will consist of several (3-5) rows of plants, layered so there are short highly wind resistant pioneer shrubs to windward, coniferous trees in the middle and productive shrubs to leeward (fruit, nuts, fuel).

The low shrubs help to block the wind when the lower limbs on the trees die back. You might also have some trees that can be coppiced regularly, so they can fill in the bottom. In a small garden you may only have room for one row of windbreak plants. These will still be a big help, even if not as effective as a deeper barrier.

The size of a windbreak

The height of a windbreak determines how far downwind will be protected. It can fully protect an area for 5 times the height of the barrier and partially protect an area up to 20 times the height (depending upon how permeable it is). The length of a windbreak is also important; it needs to be at least 12 times as long as it is tall. If it is shorter than this the wind may simply eddy around the ends.

A problem with living windbreaks is that their extensive roots can take most of the nutrients and moisture from nearby soil. They can also cast unwanted shade. For this reason they can't be too near important crop growing areas (put a path or roadway between them).

Non-living windbreaks

Fences and trellis can also be effective windbreaks, though as I just explained semi-permeable ones are more effective than solid ones. If you need a fence to block the wind as well as give security, you could try nailing the boards on alternate sides of the rails (this is much simpler to construct than a louvered design, where the boards must be fastened at an angle).

The strongest windbreak for very high wind areas is a tall chain link fence with plastic or wooden strips woven between the links (I didn't say it was the prettiest). If the metal posts are securely anchored in concrete you will have a windbreak that could stand up to a hurricane.

Buildings can completely block the wind on the downwind side, so (if they also get sun) this often a good place for a patio. You can increase this sheltered area by extending hedges or fences out from the house. If you angle them downwind they can deflect the wind very effectively.

Walls also act as windbreaks, but can cause turbulence as described above. In windswept areas they commonly plant trees on the leeward side of a stone wall to make it more effective.

Berms as windbreaks

In high wind areas earthen berms come into their own, especially in conjunction with living windbreaks. A south facing berm stores the suns heat as well as slowing the wind, so creates a warmer sheltered microclimate. To be an effective windbreak a berm should be at least as wide as it is tall, with a triangular cross section. Trees or shrubs planted on top of the berm will increase its effectiveness.

Screens

Screens are primarily for visual purposes, so don't have to be as strong as fences. They can be used to divide up large areas into separate rooms and to shield private areas from view. They can also be used to hide unattractive parts of the garden, such as outbuildings, propane tanks, garbage cans and more. Conversely they are sometimes used to emphasize or frame particularly attractive places, such as sitting areas and ponds.

Types of screens

Materials for screens are usually the same as for fences and may be living or dead. They don't need to be as heavy though, as they just need to be strong enough not to get blown apart by the wind.

An open screen often works better than a solid one because it doesn't cast as much shade, even though it can still obscure whatever is behind it from view. Diamond lattice trellis works well (with or without plants). Simple screens can also be made from split Bamboo, Reeds, Willow shoots, or other small brushwood fastened into wooden frames.

A screen for a sitting area only needs to be about 4 feet high to afford complete privacy. Any taller and it may make the area feel too confined and block out too much sun.

Tall annual plants such as Sunflowers, Hemp (for you Dutch readers) or Corn, all work well as fast, temporary screens (perhaps while the permanent screen is growing). You could also use annual vines such as beans, peas, cucumbers or Sweet Peas.

Planter box screens

It is possible to create a completely portable living screen, using a long planter box with a trellis attached. Some of the more vigorous vines will quickly smother it in vegetation. You might also grow tall annuals, such as Sunflowers or Hemp. Just remember to keep the container well watered.

Animal fences

In a very large garden you might leave some areas unfenced to act as wild animal habitat, but if you are to have a productive garden you will need effective and permanent barriers. In fact in many areas one of your first concerns will be keeping herbivorous animals out of the garden.

Deer Fence

Deer are beautiful and entitled to their own wild lives, but they don't mix with gardens. If deer get into your garden they can reduce your precious plants to stubs overnight, and once they find food, they will return again and again. They must be kept out.

Deer aren't the brightest of creatures (there are no deer rocket scientists), but they do have a strong instinct to eat. If they see succulent leafy greens on the other side of a barrier, they will test it to see if it has any weak spots they can get through.

All kinds of arrangements have been tried to keep out deer. A double fence (each side 4 feet tall) can be effective if it is wide enough that they can't clear both at once, but narrow enough that they can't jump them singly. The protected inner fence can be used to support fruiting vines. A variation on this is one fence, with a parallel strand of wire the right distance apart. Apparently you can also lay the second fence on the ground in front of the first (you might try this if you are short of fenceposts). The theory is that this works like a cattle grid, as apparently deer won't go where they might get their feet stuck.

These double fence ideas are worth trying if you don't want your garden to look like a POW camp. You could have an attractive 4 foot tall open picket or paling fence, with another 4 foot fence five or six feet behind it (and not very visible) made from chicken wire.

Opaque fencing doesn't have to be as tall as a transparent one, because deer (rather sensibly) won't jump over something if they can't see where they will land.

The cheapest commercial deer fencing is the eight-foot tall plastic mesh. This is very effective and relatively invisible from a distance, so it is rapidly becoming the deer fencing of choice.

Deer resistant plants

The title of this box is probably an oxymoron, because there are very few truly deer proof plants. Just as you would yourself, these herbivores will eat almost anything if they are hungry enough. However for what its worth (which isn't much) the following plants are generally considered to be low on the gourmet deer menu. I say this isn't worth much because I have had several of the plants listed below eaten by deer, so don't stake your life on these recommendations. The only one of these suggestions that I might be totally convinced by would be a particularly vicious prickly pear.

Akebia vine	Alliums	Asparagus
Bamboo	Barberry	Black Locust
Bee Balm	Blueberries	Borage
Calendula	Camas	Chives
Chestnut	Comfrey	Currants
Echinacea	Eleagnus species	Elder
Fennel	Fig	Ginko
Gooseberries	Hollyhock	Juneberry
Lavender	Lemon Balm	Maximilian Sunflower
Mayapple	Mint	Nasturtium
Okra	Onion	Oregano
Passion vine	Pawpaw	Pineapple Guava
Pomegranate	Prickly pear	Prunus species
Rhubarb	Rosemary	Sage
Salal	Siberian pea shrub	Squash
Thyme	Willow	Wintergreen

If you have a major deer infestation, then I suggest using plants that can re-grow vigorously.

If you are a hedge fund manager or defense contractor looking for a deer fence for your tax shelter vineyard then the 8 feet tall steel wire mesh is the way to go (come to think of it hedge fund managers now legally pay so little tax they don't really need tax shelters). As an impoverished carpenter/writer I went with 2" mesh chicken wire attached to salvaged metal fenceposts. This is only 6 foot tall, but seems to be enough for the lazy, well fed deer around here. It probably wouldn't work in more extreme climates with less to eat and hungrier animals.

You can increase the height of any fence by attaching wooden stakes to the tops of the posts and fastening several strands of wire (or a strip of chicken wire) to them.

Deer are just as happy to go under a fence as over it, so make sure the bottom edge is secure too.

A thorny hedge will also keep out deer. Plant it on the inside of a fence and it will gradually transform even the flimsiest fence into a seriously impenetrable barrier.

Defense in depth

Gardening intelligently means not simply throwing money at a problem and surrounding your entire property with an eight foot high impenetrable barrier. You could emulate medieval castle builders and divide up the garden into several separate areas (hedges are good for this as they will be growing in a protected area). If a tree falls on your fence and deer get in, they will be confined to a limited area and won't have free run of your whole garden. If you have divided your garden into separate rooms, you have already gone a long way towards doing this. Use your strongest fences for the more important areas and weaker ones for less important places.

Rabbit fence

Rabbits are much smaller than deer, but can still do a lot of damage (curse you Beatrix Potter!). Their smaller size also means they are harder to keep out of the garden. They quite literally can't climb to save their lives (it's quite pathetic seeing them try), so won't usually try to get over a fence, but they are natural diggers and will try to go under it. To prevent this you have to bury the bottom of the fence in a trench, with the bottom 6" folded outwards. A rabbit will dig down, but when it reaches the horizontal folded fence it won't know what to do (there are no rabbit rocket scientists either). You can also do this with an existing fence, by fastening a strip of netting to the bottom.

Dog fence

This is mostly needed to keep these animals in rather than out. How thorough you need to be depends upon the dog. Some dogs are perfectly content to just run around inside a fenced area. Others will resent it as an affront to their canine dignity and won't rest until they have tunneled, jumped or squeezed their way out.

Gates

Whenever you have solid boundaries for security you need gates for access. The gate is another archetypal element, a portal or place of passage. As you move through the gate from one side to another you pass through a tension point, where things change.

As one of the most visible focal points in the garden gates are an important design element and make a statement about you and your garden. They are one of your best opportunities for ornamentation so make the most of it. There are lots of books with pictures of interesting gates and you may want to look at some to get ideas. Don't over-decorate though, make it compatible with the rest of the garden.

The location of gates is often pre-determined; they are placed where you need to pass through a boundary, or go between different parts of the garden.

Front gate

You get your first glimpse of the garden from the front gate (which may influence where you put it). It is the most prominent gate in the garden and so is usually the most decorative, It helps strangers find their way to your front door and is a transition point from the public area to a private one. The gate should be appropriate to the house and should have a wide path, with a firm smooth footing. The area around the gate should be inviting too.

Fences and gates should complement each other, but the gate should be easily identifiable. A high gate (which should still be slightly lower than the fence or wall) suggests privacy and it is harder to see who is arriving. A low gate you can see through is more welcoming and you can see visitors as they arrive.

Open gates are lighter and frame the view into the garden rather than obscuring it. An open (or low) gate isn't a good idea in a windy area because it can act as a wind funnel. A popular idea is to surround the front gate with an arch or trellis and train climbers such as Hops or grapes (no thorns please) over it.

The width of the gate depends upon the traffic. A wide gate will be needed if you want to take garden carts through it.

Front gates are sometimes painted a decorative color that echoes the house. Dark colored gates are less visible and so easier to see through. Light colored gates stand out more.

Other gates

These separate and secure different parts of the garden. You might choose gates that blend in with the rest of the fence, or gates that stand out as special features. You might also want a double wide back gate to allow truck access so materials can be brought in (though you could just have a removable fence panel.

Practical considerations

All gates need to be strong (ideally strong enough to swing on), well fitting and well maintained so they work well and don't sag with time. Two hinges work with a gate up to 4 feet tall and 3 feet wide. Larger gates should have 3 hinges. Prevent the sagging of large gates with a diagonal brace. A gate can be made self-closing with a counterweight.

Some people like to have a squeaky gate, as it lets you know when someone enters. A hanging bell can perform a similar function more elegantly.

Gate posts

These are an integral part of the gate and must be firmly anchored. They are most often made of wood and anchored in concrete, though they could also be metal, brick or concrete columns. The posts can be a decorative element with finials or caps. They could also form a part of an arbor.

Stiles

These provide a fast way to get over an existing fence or wall without using a gate. A wide variety of stiles have been developed, but all work on the principle that most humans are agile enough to climb over a stile (or thin enough to squeeze through) but most animals aren't.

Water in the garden

Open water is a unique element, unlike anything else you can put in the garden and you should have at least one water feature of some kind (and preferably more). You might even have a series of linked water features, starting at the house. This could begin with rainwater running off of the roof down rain chains into a basin, then trickling out into the pond (this gives you nice sound) and then through a rill to another pond, then to flow out of the pond and end as irrigation water for your crop plants.

Water brings life and increases biological diversity by providing a greater variety of habitats, such as ponds, marshes, bogs and more. This is particularly obvious in dry climates where it becomes a magnet for wildlife. Water attracts nearly everything: dragonflies, frogs, birds and many other creatures (I've often been buzzed by Hummingbirds while hand watering). One morning after accidentally running an overhead sprinkler overnight (this was before I invested in a timer) my vegetable garden was alive with dozens on Butterflies.

Water also has an instinctive appeal for humans, especially children. Of course they won't be satisfied with just looking at water, they find it an irresistible plaything and will want to play with it for hours.

Problems with water

Water can be a hazard to very small children because it is so fascinating to them. They will play around with it until something unexpected happens and have been known to drown themselves in a few inches of water, or even a bucket, so be aware and take precautions (see below).

Water also attracts less welcome visitors such as raccoons (they love to mess about in it as much as children), deer (they like to drink it) and mosquitoes (they like to breed in it). In warm weather Mosquito larvae will appear in any still water that stands around for more than a few days. In such cases you may have to take preventive measures, such as adding Mosquito fish.

Moving water

Moving water is even more interesting than still water. The problem with moving water is that you often have to make it move, which involves technology in the form of pumps, wiring and electricity. A solar pump or windmill could be enough to supply a trickle of water for a waterfall.

You could also use your well pump (or water mains pressure) to supply moving water. Just turn on the tap and run the water through your pond, bubbling fountain, rill or whatever. You would need a container at the end to catch the water so it can be used in the garden. You might also run it straight to an irrigation system, so that a waterfall or fountain runs whenever you are irrigating (giving a nice connection).

Water features

These can take many different forms, depending upon the situation and your needs. Whatever you use will become the focal point of its own area.

Barrels and tubs

Half a wooden whiskey barrel filled with water gives you an instant miniature pond. Its durable Oak wood and metal construction looks instantly at home anywhere in the garden. Galvanized horse troughs also work well. Old clawfoot tubs have been used as wetland planters and ponds, but unless very decrepit they are probably more useful when used as an outdoor bathtub.

Large open tubs of water were once placed in the garden as a place to quickly fill a watering can. This is much quicker than using a hose, just one dip and its full.

Sunken tubs

Almost any container can be sunk into the ground to become a small pool. It doesn't really matter what it looks like because it will be completely hidden. It doesn't even have to be waterproof as you can line it with pond liner. Plastic containers work very well as they aren't subject to corrosion or rot (just make sure no part is exposed to sunlight or it will deteriorate.

An advantage of sunken tubs is that the water temperature is more stable because the surrounding earth slows down temperature swings.

Birdbaths

One of the smallest ornamental water features (and an attractive focal point) is a bird bath. Birds like the water to be no more than 3" deep and have gently sloping sides and bottom. In hot weather a shallow birdbath may evaporate quickly.

Bowls

These are perhaps the easiest and simplest water features to create (even easier than barrels) and make a great focal point. All you need is some kind of bowl filled with water and a little imagination. You can increase the reflection of the water by making the interior of the container a dark color.

A water filled bowl will immediately add interest to any area. It could be placed on a table, on the ground, in a shady spot, in full sun to reflect light, or on a patio or deck. They can even be moved around the garden as you see fit. To impress visitors you can float flowers on the surface. They won't last long but are very pretty.

Any attractive waterproof container will work for this, though it should be compatible with the house and garden. It could be a large terra-cotta plant pot with the drainage hole filled up with caulk. It could be a basin carved from stone (expensive) or some form of cast concrete (see Concrete carving). Ideally it should be dark inside to better reflect the light. At its simplest it could be just an old garbage can lid, buried to its rim and covered with a layer of pebbles.

You can even grow water plants in these bowls. This could be a Water Lily for beauty or Watercress for edibility. You might even have a series of planted water filled pots.

All small and shallow containers need some looking after. In hot weather they warm up and evaporate quickly, while in cold winter weather they can freeze solid. If this could damage the container you should empty it and cover it (to stop it filling back up with rain), or just take it inside for the winter.

Bubbling water

Bubbling water makes such a nice kinetic sculpture, it may even justify using electricity to pump it. You can use almost anything for a bubbling fountain, all it takes is a little imagination. Old millstones were popular in English cottage gardens as an interesting focal point, but this was because they were laying around in the undergrowth. If you have to buy one it is quite a different matter. Better to use something you can salvage instead. See above for information on Moving water.

Canals and rills

These are shallow narrow channels of water and work best in formal settings (perhaps on a patio). In sloping gardens they can be used to move water from one area to another. They also give you a way to move irrigation water (or rainwater) across your property, while getting an ornamental effect as well. In a wet climate you could have a series of canals dividing the garden.

A rill can be made from concrete, a strip of pond liner, or even 3 Redwood boards caulked and nailed together. Then lay pebbles or gravel in the bottom.

A long canal filled with gravel and Cattails might be used as a gray water treatment marsh. Gray water goes in one end and slowly (use wooden blocks as baffles to slow the flow) moves along, getting cleaner as it goes.

Fountains
Fountains are beautiful, especially when sunlight glints off of the moving water. They also sound nice and are often used in urban gardens to mask the sound of the city. They were once widely used in desert gardens because they humidify and cool the air.

If you really want a fountain there are plenty of commercial offerings out there, or you can make your own out of plumbing fittings and imagination. Something as simple as a large ceramic pot can be good. Bamboo culms could be used as a spout, if you want a Japanese effect. A brass tap makes a cheap fountain. Some fountains get really elaborate, but they probably don't belong in this type of garden.

Wall fountains can work well in small gardens. They don't have to move a lot of water, a small trickle will supply the requisite splashing water sound.

Ornaments
Water is such a powerful element that it enhances anything it is combined with. A variety of sculptures or other ornaments might go in the water, might use water, or might just be affected by water. Tiles, glass, rock and pebbles all look better when wet and can be used to ornament any water feature.

Raised ponds
These fairly formal ponds are often incorporated into a patio or deck. If you only have room for a small pool then this type will probably work best. It's hard to make a very small pool look natural anyway.

It's pretty easy to build a raised formal pond. Use concrete blocks on top of a poured foundation, or even railroad ties. Use a pond liner to make it watertight and cover the top with stones or wide boards to hide it. Maybe make it 16" tall and use the edge as a seat.

Streams
I'm not really a fan of artificial streams. They add to the diversity of habitat and look (and sound) nice, but I think it's a bit frivolous to use all that electricity to slosh some water around.

Waterfalls
As with fountains these are as important for their sound as for their appearance. They probably work best in conjunction with a pond (and maybe a rill) and can help to aerate the water. Of course they also use electricity, unless you make a rain powered one.

Rain chains
These were traditionally used in Japan to lead water from gutters to the ground. They aren't quite as efficient as downspouts for capturing rainwater, but they are far more interesting and come alive in the rain. Linked rain chains are the cheapest and easiest to make, but the cup type is more effective and splashes less. All work best on houses with wide eaves.
Rain chains can be anchored at the base and end in an earthenware pot (or other container), or be free hanging.

Water gardens in containers
These aren't much different from other container plantings, except you don't have to water them nearly as often (and they use more water). They work great as ornamental features for the patio or deck.

You can use tall and striking plants like Cattail, Reed or Bulrush, shorter plants such as Arrowhead, floating plants such as Water Lilies and various marginal plants. In a large container you may have to put your plants on concrete blocks or bricks to bring them up to the right level in the water.

A wash
In dry climates you can make a wash to create another habitat. It should be placed where it will actually function as an overflow or swale in wet weather and will carry any runoff water down to a pond or rain garden.

Bog gardens
A bog garden provides a unique habitat for moisture loving plants and enables you to grow yet another set of edible plants. These grow rapidly in warm weather and can provide you with a lot of food.

The easiest place to put a bog garden is at the edge of a pond, where excess water overflowing from the pond will help to keep it moist. It can be simply an extra depression at the side of a pond, lined with pond liner and filled with soil (this should be high in organic matter). The water level can be allowed to fluctuate from being merely moist soil to being under an inch or so of water. The bog should be lower than the pond so nutrient laden water doesn't drain back into the pond.

Creating a separate bog garden is quite similar to building a pond. Excavate the soil to make a hole 15 inches deep and as large as you choose, then line it with pond liner. You don't need to use an expensive pond liner in this case, heavy duty plastic sheeting will work, because it will be completely buried and so is never exposed to damaging sunlight. It is normal to put some holes in the liner for drainage (to prevent stagnation. In gopher country you should also lay down gopher wire underneath the liner, otherwise these creatures will eventually feast on your succulent plants (this happened with my first attempt). Put 2 inches of gravel over the liner and then and lay down an old soaker hose to supply water when necessary. The soil is then returned to the bog, along with plenty of organic matter. If necessary use a mulch to reduce surface evaporation.

Natural swimming pools

Natural swimming pools are a hybrid of pond and conventional swimming pool and I see them as the wave (insofar as pools have waves) of the future. I imagine one day people will be horrified at the idea of swimming in a solution of deadly chlorine, just as we are today at the thought of showering with DDT. Instead of putting chemical poisons in the water to kill germs, natural swimming pools employ a filter bed of aquatic marsh plants to keep the pool water safe and clear.

This kind of pool is built like any other pool, using concrete or a flexible pond liner, but it is in two sections. There is the swimming pool itself and a separate marsh plant area, which is roughly the same surface area as the pool. The latter may be bounded by a low wall or it may even be a separate pond entirely. These pools do have a pump, but instead of moving the water to a filter system, they take it to the bed of plants for purification. These extract most of the dissolved solids (mostly plant nutrients) from the water and keep it clean, while microorganisms on their roots kill pathogenic bacteria. In some cases there may also be a UV sterilizing system.

The key to success with a natural swimming pond is to keep nutrients levels low so algae don't start to grow. For this reason the plants are usually grown in gravel or other inert growing medium rather than soil. This need to keep nutrients levels low can be a problem in some situations, because plants need nutrients to grow of course (though a few aquatic plants are adapted to low nutrient levels).

This kind of pool is still somewhat experimental and to build one you will need a lot more information. There are now several books available on building them and a few commercial installers you can turn to.

The site for a swimming pool should be private, in full sun, away from tall trees and sheltered from cold winds. It is usually adjacent to the patio area.

A swimming pool doesn't have to be very big, a plunge pool works great for cooling down on a hot day (it's the best way to cool down from a sweat lodge).

Ponds

A pond is an attractive, interesting and productive element and really brings the garden to life. Every garden should have a pool of some kind, whether it is only a few square feet, or large enough for boating. The magic of a pond is so powerful that it will be beautiful, useful and productive even if it looks completely artificial. The benefits of a pond include:

- Ponds are so beautiful they automatically become a focal point. They have movement, reflected light, tranquility and a luxuriant growth of plants.
- Ponds have psychological value because humans instinctively like to be near water. Witness the child's fascination with playing in water, or the calming effect of splashing water.
- There are more utilitarian values to ponds as they were once incorporated into kitchen gardens to keep ducks or fish (and as a source of irrigation water).
- I love ponds because they give me the opportunity to grow all kinds of fascinating new plants, especially edible water vegetables.
- Large ponds can be useful for fire prevention and suppression. Obviously a fire won't burn where there is water, so a pond can be an important part of your defensible space. They also hold water in a convenient place for fire fighting. To be useful for this, a pond should hold at least 5000 gallons of water or more and should be close to the buildings it is to protect. It should also be accessible by a good road. There should also be a sump so water can be extracted easily. This should be free of any vegetation that may clog a pump.
- A pond can be an effective water storage system, so long as evaporation isn't too high (deeper is better in this regard – though potentially more dangerous). For this it should be placed at the bottom of a catchment area (this could be a hillside, a roof or a clean paved driveway). Of course a fluctuating reservoir pond isn't very attractive.
- A pond absorbs heat during the day and releases it at night and so affects the microclimate around it.
- In warm weather a large pond can be used for cooling off, or even swimming, without all the hassle involved in maintaining a swimming pool.
- Pond mud is an excellent fertilizer, as are the various pondweeds and algae.
- Ponds increase the diversity of life in the garden. Last spring I dug a pond and my daughter introduced some rescued tadpoles. This spring the garden is full of croaking frogs. They don't care that it is completely artificial, they consider it their birthplace.

Warnings

A pond comes a close third behind the internet and television as a time waster. I don't need any more distractions, but my pond attracts me like nothing else in the garden. I often just sit and gaze at the water instead of getting anything done.

Another warning - Don't build a pond if you don't like the sound of frogs. They can be astonishingly noisy on warm spring nights.

My final warning is that ponds can be addictive, one may not be enough.

Designing Ponds

Ponds as ecosystems

Many modern ponds are treated like swimming pools and have pumps, skimmers, aerators, sterilizers and biological filters (these need to run constantly so can be quite expensive.). However all this technology isn't really necessary. If you use the right plants in the right numbers and maintain it regularly, your pond can remain clean and healthy all by itself.

Plants are the key to keeping a pond healthy naturally. The submerged oxygenators are particularly important because they release oxygen into the water (they also absorb soluble nutrients from the water). Floating plants are useful for removing the suspended nutrients that cause the algae growth that make ponds murky. All plants provide food and habitat for fish and other aquatic creatures.

A pond isn't static, it goes through distinct stages as organisms get established and nature takes over (there is often a stage of excessive algal growth in the first year). Small ponds are particularly vulnerable to minor changes having big effects.

I built my first pond as a learning experience, with the idea that it would allow me to learn about how ponds work, while growing and accumulating some interesting new plants (and other pond life). It worked out even better than I expected (and really does attract children).

Siting

The pond site should ideally be in full sun (6 hours a day minimum) and sheltered from strong winds that can cause excessive evaporation. It should also be free of overhanging trees, which cast shade, drop leaves into the water and perhaps damage the pond liner with their roots. Avoid Bamboos too, as their newly emerging shoots can penetrate the liner. In hot climates a pond should have a mix of shade and sun to prevent it getting too hot.

The bottom of a slope is a good place for a pond, because that is where water would naturally accumulate (though beware of frost pockets). Slopes lend themselves to running water features, such as waterfalls and streams and you could have several ponds connected by a stream.

A pond is such an attractive feature it is usually placed fairly close to the house, where it can best be appreciated. A large pond creates a flat area in the garden, which can be visually similar to a lawn (though more interesting).

Size

The pond should be in scale with the garden. A formal pond for a small garden might be as small as 2-3 feet in diameter. Bigger is generally better with ponds however and you might think of 8 feet as a minimum width and 3 feet as a minimum depth. Marginal water plants will spread out into deeper water and soon make the pond appear smaller. A natural pond in a very large garden could be big enough for swimming.

Shape

A pond could be composed of straight lines and have a formal feel, or it might be informal, with random curves to make it look like a natural pond. A very small pond doesn't provide much scope for using your imagination, as there isn't enough space for graceful curves. A large pond should have an irregular shoreline, with bays and promontories to create productive edge. It might also have at least one island (or a floating island platform) to create more edge and to provide a refuge for birds.

Depth

The larger the surface area of a pond, the greater the potential for heat gain and evaporation, so big ponds need to be deeper than shallow ones. The temperature of shallow ponds fluctuates too much for fish to be comfortable (warm water is not good for fish because it contains less oxygen). A deep pool also contains more water, so temperatures are more stable and there is less fluctuation in water level and quality. If your pond is fairly shallow you should have at least one deep area to give fish access to cool water in summer and provide a refuge from predators. This is also good place for deep-rooted aquatic plants.

The depth of a pond is usually determined by its size and the climate. In mild climates 18" is the minimum depth for a small pond (up to 50 square feet). In colder climates it should be at least 24-30 inches deep (this also works for a pond up to 300 square feet). If you want to keep fish such as Koi then it will need to be at least 36 inches deep (this is good for ponds over 300 square feet).

If you are growing plants in containers (usually plastic baskets) then the bottom of the pond should be level so the containers can sit flat (you vary the height of the plants by supporting them on bricks).

Overflow

A pond should have an overflow (spillway) to channel excess water from rainfall to where you want it (perhaps to a bog garden, a watercress bed or a swale). This spillway only needs to be 12 inches wide and an inch or two lower than the rest of the edge You could also have a L shaped pipe as an outlet.

Reducing the risk to children

If you have a pond there is always the possibility of some small child drowning in it. Statistics show that children under 3 are most at risk and that drowning most often occurs in other peoples ponds (which brings potential liability to add to the nightmare). Fortunately you can reduce the risk considerably by careful design.

To minimize the risk you should put your pond where it won't be seen from most places (if children don't know it's there, it won't attract them) It should be visible from the house however, so you can see if anyone is near it. You should have a secure fence around the pond to keep unsupervised children out (this is actually required by law in most places). This fence should be unobtrusive, so that it is a part of the garden rather than just a security fence. If well designed it may also help to keep raccoons from raiding your pond periodically.

The pond should consist of a series of shallow steps or shelves, so if a child falls into the water they can easily scramble out (there should be no steeply sloping sides). The shallow water zone (2" - 8" deep) is the most productive area of the pond anyway (the edge effect again). Unfortunately this also helps raccoons to get at your fish (fill it with plants to help prevent this).

Ponds are at risk from children to some extent. If you have children the edging and plants will have to be fairly robust or they will get loved to death.

Water sources

In hot dry climates the water may evaporate so quickly the water level recedes visibly each day. It's important that you have an adequate supply of water for your pond, so you can replace this regularly. If you have to re-fill your pond every few days and water is very limited, this might be a problem. In such cases you should evaluate whether you have enough water for a pond before you build it.

Ponds shouldn't receive runoff directly from roads, driveways or chemically fertilized lawns, because they may contain pollutants such as heavy metals, organic chemicals and excessive amounts of fertilizers (which will lead to algae growth). Wetland areas such as Reed beds can help to purify the runoff water before it enters a pond, and can be an important buffer zone. Frogs are a great indicator of water quality, if you have frogs your water is good.

Building a pond

Digging the pond

Before you start digging make sure there are no buried utility lines (gas, electric, water) in the way. Also decide where to put the excavated soil (this should be separated into topsoil and subsoil). Most often it is placed around the pond to give some variation in height, but you might want it elsewhere. If you are creating a pond on a slope you may have to build a berm, which is a good use of the excavated soil. Make it fairly wide or it won't look very natural.

Any pond, no matter how big, can be dug by hand, it just takes time. Mark out the outline of the pond with wood ashes or ground limestone and get digging. Dig for a half hour a day and it will eventually be done. Start by removing all of the topsoil and put it in one place, then dig out the subsoil. If the pond has several levels, you should dig out one level at a time, finishing each one completely before going down to the next. If you are renting a backhoe for other purposes, then by all means dig the pond at the same time.

Leveling

Water is always level, so make sure the perimeter of the pond is level too, otherwise it can be visually disconcerting. Level the perimeter by laying a long straight 2 x 4 from side to side and put a level on it. In a very large pond put a stake in the ground in the center of the pond at the correct level and use a long 2 x 4 with a level to check the perimeter.

Pond liners

Ponds are sometimes lined with clay, concrete, rigid fiberglass or plastic, but the most common are flexible liners of rubber, EPDM or vinyl. Avoid polyethylene sheet, except for a temporary pond, as any part that are exposed to sunlight will disintegrate in a few months.

It is not a bad idea to put a liner under the liner to prevent it getting punctured. Commercial liners are available but old discarded carpet padding, available from carpet shops works well. You might also use sand, cardboard or newspaper.

Estimating liner size

The length of the liner should be the length of the hole plus twice the depth plus 2 feet. The width of the liner should be the width of the hole plus twice the depth plus 2 feet.

For example if the hole is 8 feet wide x 12 feet long x 3 feet deep, the liner should be:

Length 12 + 6 + 2 = 20 ft.
Width 8 + 6 +2 = 16 ft.

A large pond may require more than one piece of pond liner. Separate pieces are connected with special double sided tape. You have to do this very carefully though, otherwise it may leak

Lay the liner in the completed hole and weight it down at the edges with rocks. Try and keep the liner as wrinkle free as possible. Then simply start filling with water. The weight of water will pull the liner down into position better than you could. The edge of the liner is then pinned down with wire pegs (use old coat hangers) and cut to shape. Don't trim the liner until the pond is filled with water and everything else is finished, you don't want to cut it too small.

I've never had it happen but apparently gophers have been known to bite through liners. If you worry about this you should lay down gopher wire underneath the liner (this is another expense though).

Clay as a sealer

Bentonite clay can be used as a natural pond sealer as it swells when it gets wet, making a waterproof seal. You will need from 2 - 8 lb. of dry clay per square foot, depending upon the soil. You scatter this over the entire surface of the excavation and work it lightly into the soil. Then you fill the pond with water and hope. Gravel is sometimes put over the clay to protect it from waders.

For ultimate convenience you can now get clay blankets where the clay is sandwiched between layers of landscape fabric. For no convenience at all you could dig clay from your own land and used it for lining the pond.

How much water?

To find out how many gallons of water there are in your pond, time how long it takes to fill up with water. Then time how long it takes the same hose to fill a 5 gallon bucket. Finally divide the first number by the second one.

If you are mathematically inclined, you can calculate the volume of the pond in cubic feet and then multiply by 7.5 to get the number of gallons.

Concrete ponds

A well made concrete pond is tough, durable (you never have to worry about gophers), easy to clean without damage and fairly easy to repair. It is also quite a bit more work to build.

A rectangular concrete pond is fairly straightforward to make; you just build a form, add reinforcing wire and rebar and pour. You can even use concrete blocks as the form.

A free form concrete pond is a little more complex. You have to excavate to the required shape, then lay down a layer of 4 inch reinforcing wire mesh. This must be carefully shaped to follow the contours of the pond and raised 2" in the air with small blocks of concrete called dobies.

To pour a free form pond you put stakes into the ground at various intervals and mark them at 4 inch depth. As you place the concrete you fill to the 4 inch mark to ensure an even depth of concrete (you could also use a stick marked at 4 inches). Remove these stakes as you go and fill in the holes. The concrete should be stiff enough to stick to the sides of the pond. Start by filling the bottom and then work up the sides (work from a board spanning the pond if necessary). If any wire touches the soil or sticks out of the concrete bend it back in as needed. Finish by troweling the concrete to a smooth finish.

Edging is usually considered a separate process and is done once the pond is fully cured.

Edging
The main reason most garden ponds look so artificial is because there is a clear demarcation between garden and pond, usually a ring of stones. In a natural pond there is no such clear boundary, plants grow in shallow water, mud or moist soil, advancing and retreating as the water level fluctuates. This edge zone is a very productive area.

Until I built a pond I always though the ring of edging stones to be a result of a lack of imagination. Now I have built one I realize it is simply the easiest way to keep the water and soil separate when using a pond liner.

If you don't like the stone edging you can disguise it in several ways. The simplest is to hide some of it with plants. You can also use more rocks and vary their size, putting some bigger ones on large shelves with the liner going up behind them, so the rock sits out in the water. Have these at various intervals, with plants and smaller rock in between.

The pond edge must be stable so the stones don't get dislodged and fall into the pond. This could create a mess, not to mention being potentially hazardous. Mortar is commonly used to hold the edging stones in place, though densely rooted plants can also work.

The ring of stones doesn't have to go all the way around the pond. You could have a bog area on one side, or you could create a beach of gravel (perhaps as part of the overflow). This would be a good place for children to play and provides easy access to the pond for small animals

Ornamentation
As with other elements a little ornamentation can turn an interesting pool into a garden jewel. You could use colored glass, tiles, sculptures and more.

Islands
If your pond is big enough for an island you can make one out of a pile of sandbags. Fill the lower sandbags with sand (it doesn't leach nutrients into the water) and the top bags with not very fertile soil. Then just pile them up so the top is just above the water surface and plant with marginal plants. The sandbags will rot in a few years, but by then plant roots should bind the whole thing together.

Base
Coarse sand or gravel may be put into the pond to hide the liner and make it look more natural. This also makes it easier for plants to get rooted. Don't use soil though, as it contains too many nutrients and would stimulate the growth of algae. It would also make the water muddy every time it gets stirred up.

Fence
As I mentioned earlier a fence is often legally required for safety. The best way to do this is to fence the whole pond garden room.

Fish
Any kind of fish will help to bring your pond to life. Even the small, rather drab Mosquito Fish are beautiful and fascinating to watch as groups of them weave around the pool. You may want to introduce larger, more interesting fish species too. Goldfish will eat insect larvae, algae and some plants and don't require much attention. They can live up to 12 years and grow to 16" in length. The best deal on fish are the feeder fish available for 19 cents each in your local pet store.

Having bigger fish means extra work to meet their needs. They need oxygen which can be provided by a waterfall or fountain (solar powered ideally). Dead leaves should be kept out of the water as their decomposition can consume oxygen. Fish also prefer some shade, so water plants should cover some of the water surface.

Bigger fish will attract the attention of raccoons, cats and herons, so will need a deep water refuge from predators. A simple refuge is a section of drainpipe in the deepest part of the pond. Terra-cotta work best, though plastic would also work if weighed down.

You could also cover the entire surface of the pond with black plastic netting (this also keeps leaves out), though this isn't very attractive. You might also have a more ornamental grid of bamboo or metal (this can work quite well in a formal pool).

If you have a really big pond and are motivated enough you could try growing fish to eat (grow your own sushi). As this involves caring for live animals it is a lot more work than raising plants (and beyond my area of expertise).

Animal pests

Mosquitoes

In warm weather any standing water will become a Mosquito breeding area. Within a couple of weeks of filling my new pond it was teeming with clouds of wriggling black larvae. The Mosquito control officer brought me some Mosquito Fish and they consumed them all in short order. I can't imagine how they managed to eat them all, or what they've been eating since. These fish can reproduce very quickly if conditions are right, though many die off over the winter.

It's said that Mosquito Fern (*Azolla filiformis*) can cover the surface so completely that mosquitoes won't breed in it. Of course you then have something that looks more like a lawn than a pond.

Dogs

Water loving dogs don't mix well with ornamental ponds, especially those with fish (some dogs will catch slow tame fish).

Raccoons

Raccoons have been nuisance in my pond, even without any large edible fish. They think it was made for them and wade around, knocking over any container plants that aren't firmly fixed in place (it's fortunate that water plants are so resilient). I can't imagine the damage they would do if they were pursuing fish as well.

Planting the pond

For me one of the biggest attraction of ponds is the unique growing conditions they provide. They give you an opportunity to try out some entirely new kinds of plants: submerged plants, free floating plants, emergent plants, marginal plants, bog plants and other moisture lovers.

The aquatics are some of the easiest plants to deal with. They never need watering, they transplant very easily (with some plants its just a matter of physically moving them) and many root readily from cuttings. The biggest problem is often controlling their excessive vigor.

Though water gardens are usually planted for ornamental purposes, there are a lot of useful aquatic plants. In fact some of the most useful of all edible plants are adapted to this habitat. See Water Plants for more on these.

Local conditions will dictate what species can and cannot be planted. Look around to see what grows locally before you attempt to introduce anything new to the pond. Also be careful what you introduce, as a number of aquatic plants have become pests when introduced into alien environments. Some (such as Water Spinach and Water Hyacinth) are actually illegal in areas where they can survive the winter.

As with any other garden design you need to ensure that the plants you choose are the right size for the growing conditions (in this case the pond). In warm weather many aquatics grow very quickly as they always have an abundance of water. Some can spread relentlessly and threaten to take over the entire pond. You could always create a larger pond at a later date to accommodate them, or give them their own water garden.

Most aquatic plants prefer fairly neutral water, not too acidic or alkaline and full sun (though many will take light shade). They also need adequate nutrients if they are to maintain their rapid growth.

Container planting

Most ornamental pond gardeners grow their plants in containers because they are easier to maintain (you just take the container out of the water). Dividing a plant in a container is a lot easier than dividing one that is rooted under two feet of water. This applies even more to plants with edible roots; you can just tip them out of the container on to the ground and pick out the roots. Using containers also makes it easy to keep aggressive plants under control.

The best container for aquatic plants is a wide plastic basket, which allows roots to grow freely and water to get into the growing medium. Water plants don't do well in conventional plastic pots because there is little exchange of water and gases between the soil in the pot and the pond. This lack of oxygen can encourage anaerobic bacteria, which give off gases that are toxic to plant roots. As these gases build up, the plants cease to grow well and may even start to decline. You can smell this if you take the plant out of its pot.

Fill the baskets with a sifted, not-too-fertile soil (I'm too cheap to use the specially formulated commercial mixes). Put the plants in the container and then cover the soil surface with a layer of gravel to hold it in place. Put the basket on bricks or flat rocks to bring it up to the desired depth from the surface.

It is also possible to use woven plastic mesh bags for planting (or squares of this material tied up in a bundle). These are good for edible tuberous plants that do better in soil, such as Arrowhead. You can also plant into sausages made from the legs of a pair of tights.

Direct planting

Some creeping pond plants do better if they able to root into a substrate of gravel, sand or subsoil. This allows them to creep as they like. To plant into the bottom of a pond you can put a plant in a square of burlap filled with a suitable soil mix. Fold up the edges of the burlap and tie together to make a small package. Soak the bag in water to exclude air before putting in the pond, so it will sink. The roots will come out of the bag and root into the gravel, while the burlap will slowly rot.

Control

Water plants have no limits to growth in that they get all of the water, nutrients and light they need. They may just keep growing until it gets too cold or they run out of room, which means they have the potential for getting out of control. If they get too numerous you will have to start removing excess plants. The floaters such as Water Hyacinth, Parrots feather and Azolla are particularly inclined to do this if given the opportunity. The best way to control them is by harvesting, either for food, mulch, green manure or compost.

You can prevent the spread of marginal plants by varying the depth of the water. Plants that grow in marshy conditions can't grow in deeper water.

Algae is a common problem in new ponds, when there are too many nutrients in the water and too much sunlight on the surface (the more the surface is shaded by plants the less algae you will have). Algae is unsightly and can clog fountains and pumps, but it isn't necessarily bad. It provides oxygen just like other submerged aquatics. It only really becomes a problem if it decays in the pond as it then consumes oxygen, so remove any excess algae and use it as fertilizer.

The best way to remove excess algae is to wind it up on a forked stick. Leave the algae by the pond so any creatures caught inside can get back to the water. You can also use Barley straw as an algaecide (you can buy this in the garden center for $8.00 a bag – or you could save a bit of a winter cover crop). Apparently this can't be used if you have fish though.

Planting around the pond

A pond shouldn't exist in isolation and it's important to pay attention to the land around it. Have a diversity of habitats surrounding the pond, each merging into the pond (and creating a variety of edge effects). An overflow can give you an area of wet soil adjacent to the pond (especially if you bury plastic to impede drainage) which can become a useful bog habitat.

The emergent plants around the margins of the pond can help protect it from pollution by absorbing nitrates and phosphates (and even killing pathogenic bacteria) before they enter the pond. Such plants need to be in a band at least 6 feet wide to have any effect on a large scale. The same plants can also be used for treating gray water.

Maintenance

A pond is one of the higher maintenance garden elements and even after it is filled and planted you still have to experiment and refine it to make it work well. Fortunately this isn't really work, in fact it is the kind of job your children (or grandchildren) may do willingly.

The most important aspect of maintenance is keeping the water clear (though this is by no means essential, I've seen some really cool ponds where the water looked like green pea soup). One of the commonest reasons for excessive algal growth (and murky water) is using garden soil in your planting containers. This contains a lot of nutrients and these leach into the water and stimulate algae growth (you will often see algae growing right onto the soil).

Water quality can be improved by growing submerged and floating plants, as they will absorb most of the nutrients in the water. There is a fine line here however, as too few suspended nutrients will means poor plant growth. It may sometimes even be necessary to add fertilizers to increase growth. If you are growing edible plants you won't want to add any kind of fertilizer that might contain pathogens (such as manure tea).

Pond plants can grow so rapidly in the right conditions that there is always the potential for one or more to get out of hand and threaten to fill the whole pond. Don't panic if this happens, just remove a proportion of the plants periodically and use them for mulch or compost. They are full of plant nutrients (Mosquito Fern even fixes nitrogen). In my pond the algae disappeared almost by magic in the spring of its second year. Ultimately you are always in control of what happens, because as a last resort you could empty the pond.

The working pond

A garden pond is not a natural pond, no matter how much you try and disguise it. To me it makes sense to concentrate on making your pond work as an efficient water plant growing system and not worry about its appearance too much (water and plants are beautiful no matter what you do). You might use a series of stepped concrete boxes, to create areas of even depth for planting with minimal shifting or tipping. This could have parts sectioned off for growing specific plants, as well as bog areas, deep water areas and more. There could even be channels or canals to take water to separate areas, perhaps ending in a sump at the bottom, from which irrigation water could be drawn.

Food ponds

The food pond is a pond specifically designed for growing edible aquatic plants. It is one of the best examples of edible landscaping in that it has all of the ornamental value of a pond, but can also produce a lot of food. Growing water vegetables can be quite fascinating and gives you another opportunity to increase your production of food with relatively little work.

A surprising number of the plants we grow as aquatic ornamentals are actually edible. In Asia a number of these are important vegetable crops and are widely grown in small ponds. These include Arrowhead, Lotus, Taro and Water Spinach.

Water vegetables can be useful as salad materials through the hotter summer months, when many traditional salad plants don't do well. This is almost foolproof vegetable gardening; as long as there is water in the pond they will grow.

The patio is a good place for a food pond, not because the pond needs much attention, but because it is such an interesting feature. This also makes it more convenient for harvesting.

Water vegetables can be grown in anything that will hold water, from a half barrel to a childs' paddling pool to a custom made concrete pond. A plastic paddling pool is one of the quickest and easiest ways to get started, if not the most attractive. This can be set up almost anywhere and could even be taken into the greenhouse for the winter (drain the water out before moving it).

You can create a pond bed for the vegetable garden without any digging, simply by using a 2 x 4 frame and a sheet of pond liner. Make sure this is perfectly flat so it will hold an equal depth of water all over. It doesn't need to be very deep as you only need a couple of inches of water to grow the plants. The water should be able to flow so it doesn't go stagnant. This means having an inflow (from a hose) and an outflow (exiting water can be used for irrigation).

If you get really serious about this you could make shallow concrete pond beds.

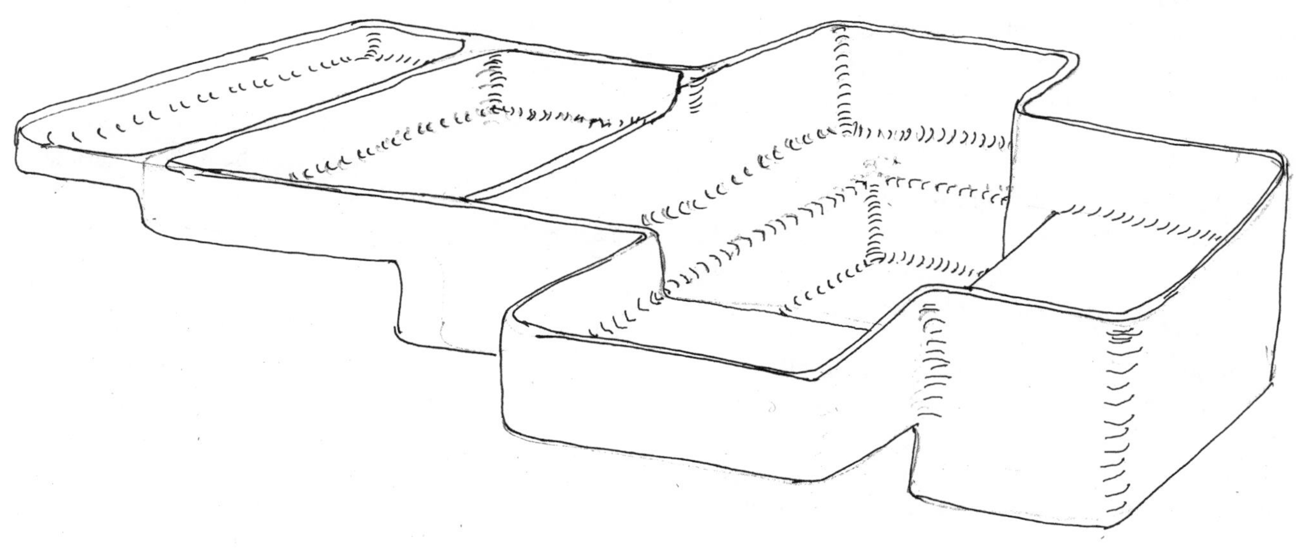

Caring for the soil

It's been said that the primary aim of organic gardening is to grow soil and that growing plants is secondary. As organic gardeners we strive to make the soil as biologically active and diverse as possible, and thereby. increase its ability to sustain healthy plant growth. Of course this is the very opposite of chemically dependent growers, who pretend that the soil is just an inert accumulation of minerals. Soil organisms (algae, fungi, bacteria, insects, plants) create topsoil out of mineral soil and really are the foundation of life on earth. We improve the soil by giving them everything they need to thrive (air, moisture and nutrients in the form of organic matter). If we do this well they will multiply rapidly and can transform even the most impoverished soil into a veritable, vegetable paradise (not overnight of course).

There are many ways to manage your garden soil and grow crops (biodynamics, mulching, double digging, chemicals, doing nothing), but not all of them are truly sustainable. Any time we disturb the soil we cause nutrients to be lost through oxidation and the increased activity of soil organisms. We also lose nutrients through the harvesting of crops This is why we have to continuously add organic matter and other nutrients to our vegetable gardens to maintain fertility.

The test of whether your system of gardening is really working is not whether it produces good crops, but whether you are creating soil or destroying it (along with how much you have to import and how much work you have to do). In the new food garden we try and use natural ways of enhancing fertility. We emulate nature in her use of plants and soil organisms to create soil and enhance fertility (nitrogen fixers, biomass plants, dynamic accumulators and the myriad of soil organisms). If we work with her she will work unceasingly to store and recycle plant nutrients in leaf litter, organic matter and humus. She will do this while we aren't even thinking about the garden.

In the ultimate garden no source of fertility (human manure, organic matter, yard waste, kitchen scraps, urine) would leave the land, it would all be cycled back through the soil, If you can close these loops your garden won't need any external inputs at all. Then your soil improving plants will be enough to increase soil fertility.

Improving the soil everywhere would be an impossible task in a big garden, fortunately it isn't necessary, or even desirable, Many useful plants are adapted to soils of moderate or low fertility and adding extra nitrogen or other nutrients would simply lead to unbalanced growth and an invasion of garden weeds.

For a more thorough treatment of improving soils for intensive vegetable growing refer to my book The Organic Gardeners Handbook.

Improving the soil

The first aim of a sustainable food producing system it to ensure that the soil doesn't deteriorate from our activities. Once this is accomplished we can devise ways to maintain and improve soil fertility in the areas that need it (which is not everywhere).

Organic matter

One of the biggest problems of chemically dependent farming is that it gradually depletes the reservoir of organic matter in the soil. This causes the soil to gradually deteriorate, which results in crusting, compaction, poor drainage, rapid drying, fewer earthworms and by the soil physically disappearing (this is particularly noticeable if you garden in wooden sided beds). It is essential that you replace the organic matter consumed in growing crops.

Organic matter is the single most important component in determining soil fertility and the most beneficial thing you can do for your soil is to add more of it. All organic matter is potential fertilizer for your plants and for all practical purposes you can't add too much. Only about 5-10% of the weight of compost actually remains in the soil as organic matter, so you must be quite diligent if you are to raise the soils organic matter level significantly. It also takes a long time; even with generous quantities of compost or manure it may take 5 years to increase it by 50%.

Mulching is the easiest way to add organic matter to the soil, and has the added benefit of keeping down weeds, conserving moisture and protecting the soil surface. The problem is getting it in sufficient quantity.

Green manures (especially grasses) also add organic matter to the soil if done the right way. This takes time, but doesn't involve the importation of large quantities of material. Green manures also protect the soil surface and help to conserve the organic matter already in the soil.

Always leave the roots of crops in the ground to decay (unless you are growing a root crop of course), as these form channels for air and water penetration. Roots make up 50% of the weight of some plants and so add an appreciable amount of organic matter to the soil. Of course you should also return as much of the above ground portion as possible. Either incorporated directly, or as compost or mulch.

Weeds improve the soil by adding organic matter an creating root channels in the soil.

Dead wood is beneficial for the soil as it provides food for soil organisms, especially fungi. Standing dead wood is also useful for wildlife.

In some cases what not to do is as important as what to do. For example we need to avoid digging where possible, as it oxidizes organic matter, encourages annual weeds and disturbs soil life.

Soil pH

Most crop plants grow best in a soil that is neutral, or slightly acid (pH 6.0 - 7.0), because the most nutrients are most available at this point. As the soil gets more acid, or alkaline, various nutrients become unavailable and some toxic elements may become more available.

You can determine the pH of your soil with a soil pH test kit. If done carefully it will be accurate enough for most purposes. If it indicates that your soil is very acidic, or alkaline, then you will have to correct it. This simple step can have more impact on soil fertility, than just about anything else you can do.

In most parts of the country the soil is most likely to be too acidic and you will have to add a liming agent to raise the pH. Ground limestone is the commonest of these, because it's safe to use, cheap and continues to work for several years. Others include Dolomitic limestone, ground oyster shells and wood ash. In arid areas you sometimes encounter alkaline soil, in which case you can lower the pH by adding peat moss, pine needle duff or sulfur.

As I mentioned previously you don't need to alter the soil over the entire garden, just where you want to grow the common crop plants. In the rest of the garden you grow plants that are adapted to the existing pH.

Soil Water

Water is an essential component of soil and makes up about 25% of its volume. It's very important that the soil contains the right amount of moisture, not only for good plant growth, but also for the soil life that is so vital for fertility.

Too dry: Soil organisms need water and if the soil is too dry they will be less active and slower to work their magic. Too much air can also oxidize organic matter.

In dry climates it is helpful to increase the moisture holding capacity of the soil by adding organic matter. Adding 1 pound of compost per square foot annually can increase the water holding capacity of the soil by 25% in 5 years. In some light soils (which of course need it most) you really have to work to build up the organic matter level, because they lose it quickly through oxidation, especially in hot weather (mulch can help reduce this loss). You should be adding organic matter to your intensive beds routinely as part of your soil-building program.

Too wet: Water is removed from the soil by plant transpiration, evaporation and gravity. If more water gets into the soil than gets out, then the soil becomes waterlogged. This displaces air and the resulting deficiency of oxygen slows down respiration, inhibits new root growth and causes existing roots to rot. Neither plants or soil organisms can thrive in wet soil.

Wet soils also tend to be cold and warm up slowly in spring, because evaporating water has a cooling effect. Simply draining off excess water has been known to raise soil temperature by as much as 6° Fahrenheit. If your soil is waterlogged you must remove the excess water before you do anything else. See Drainage for more on this.

Trace elements
If the soil pH is fairly neutral and contains lots of organic matter, you shouldn't have to worry too much about individual micronutrients. If your soil is poor then the best sources of micronutrients are compost and seaweed.

Soil compaction
Compaction reduces the amount of pore space in the soil, which means there is less air. This decreases the activity of soil organisms and can inhibit root growth. Compaction is a lot easier to avoid than to remedy, just keep to the paths (that's what they are there for) and off of the soil. If you must walk off the paths, put stepping stones (or log rounds) down, so you won't be stepping on growing areas. Heavy clay soils are more vulnerable to compaction than lighter ones, especially when wet.

You can loosen compacted soil with plants, particularly the annual or biennial tap rooted ones such as Chicory and Daikon Radish. Other useful plants include Borage, Buckwheat, Crimson Clover, Dandelion, Lupin, Phacelia,

Shallow soil
If your garden has very shallow soil you can grow your vegetables in raised beds or mounds. The soil will get deeper over time as you add compost and mulch and plant growth becomes more vigorous.

Soil life

The most fundamental principle of organic gardening is that everything you do should benefit the organisms in the soil. They are the key to fertility and the more diverse and abundant, the soil life, the less problems you will have. Life begets more life as plants live and die and decay, releasing nutrients for re-use. Over time the supply of readily available nutrients increases and so the soil gets more fertile (obeying the seemingly universal law that the rich get richer).

Most soil organisms are either beneficial or neutral, only a few ever become a problem and then usually when something is out of balance. A diverse microflora means that there are so many different species living in balance that no one gets out of hand. Logic says that when you upset the balance of these organisms you are asking for problems. This is why chemical gardening is so devastating to the soil. It would be nice if you could just add some soil life tablets (or a box of earthworms) to the soil and they would get to work improving it, but this doesn't work. If such creatures aren't already living there, it's because the soil can't support them for some reason. If you simply put a bunch of worms in an unsuitable soil, they will either die, or move on.

Actually it isn't generally necessary to add any organisms to the soil, most are already there in limited numbers. All you have to do is give them the things they need (which are pretty much the same things plants need) and they will multiply. Ensure there is sufficient air and moisture (not too much or too little), plenty of organic matter to supply them with food and a fairly neutral pH. Mulch also helps by providing organic matter, moderating soil temperature and conserving moisture. When you do these things, the life already in the soil will multiply rapidly and you will soon notice the improvement.

If your soil really doesn't contain many beneficial organisms the best way to introduce them is by adding compost. This acts as an inoculant, introducing new organisms, which will then multiply if conditions suit them. You can also move soil from fertile areas to impoverished soils to introduce soil organisms (when planting a tree in poor soil, you could take some soil from around a thriving tree). Of course you will be transplanting soil any time you plant something out of a pot, but life in a pot is difficult for soil organisms.

Earthworms are justly famous for their good work in the garden. They prefer a relatively neutral (6.5 pH), light, porous, moist, well-drained soil, with lots of organic matter. They love mulch as it provides food and moderates the soil temperature. They don't like constant cultivation and disturbance, especially in spring and autumn when they are most active. I've seen beautifully rich French intensive beds with very few earthworms in them, simply because there was too much disturbance.

Mycorrhizal fungi
The mycorrhizal fungi are the unsung heroes of the biosphere, so sing about them a bit. Sing about how these fungi form symbiotic associations with the roots of trees, expanding their reach many fold and giving them a more efficient way of getting nutrients (especially phosphorus) and water. They create a

web of mycelium that connects different plants (even different species) and can transfer nutrients from one plant to another. In return for these services the fungus receives the carbohydrates it needs for growth.

Inoculation

Though mycorrhizal fungi are already present in the healthy natural soil, they may not be present in sufficient numbers in the disturbed soil of gardens. In such cases inoculating the roots of your plants with a commercial inoculant may hasten the formation of these beneficial associations.

If you don't want to buy commercial inoculant you might try getting some rich forest soil and mixing it with your impoverished soil. There is some risk of introducing other less welcome organisms too.

Common fertility sources

My favorite materials in order of importance.

Kitchen waste and household garbage

I consider this the number one source of fertilizer for the garden because you already have it and must deal with it one way or another. It makes perfect sense to return this considerable store of plant nutrients to the soil rather than sending it to the landfill and then buying fertilizer. You might think that you don't produce enough of this to be worth bothering with, but in a year the average household throws away a half-ton of waste per person.

Vegetable scraps are rich in nutrients such as nitrogen and potassium and are easily dealt with. Animal based scraps can also be used, but you have to be more careful as they are attractive to scavengers. It is generally best to recycle paper, cotton, wool and the like, but if this isn't possible they can be composted too (so long as they are clean).

Worm composting is a good way to deal with the daily small quantities of kitchen scraps and is so clean and odor free that it has been used by apartment dwellers. Worms can also consume any other compostable household waste (paper, wool, cardboard, cotton, hair, cellophane and leather). Their nutrient rich castings are known as vermicompost and are perhaps the best plant fertilizer of all. They aren't usually available in sufficient quantity for adding to the garden as an amendment, so they are usually used to feed individual plants or to make compost tea. The drawback of worm composting is that it involves keeping live animals, which need special habitat and some (though not much) care.

If you don't want to go to the trouble of making a compost pile or worm bin, you can simply bury it directly in the garden. You can place these strategically around fruit trees (out at the drip line). Burial works well if you can stop animals from digging it straight up again (I lay down a piece of wire netting over the area to deter them).

Vertical mulching consists of digging trenches or holes 12" deep, 12" wide and 2-3 ft. away from the trunk of a tree and filling it with kitchen scraps and other organic matter. These can also be dug along the contour to act like a swale, intercepting runoff and allowing it to soak in.

You could also dig a trench the width of the bed, as if you were double digging (you can actually double dig slowly). Throw the kitchen scraps into this trench and cover them with soil dug from the next trench alongside it. Then fill this trench with garbage and cover with soil from the next one and continue this on down the bed (of course a worm bin might be less trouble than all of this). This can be a way of enriching the soil where you plan to put new beds, or plant fruit trees.

You can also compost kitchen scraps in a conventional compost pile. The problem here is that it's produced in small quantities steadily, whereas for composting you need large quantities at one time. You can't simply add kitchen scraps to the pile as they are produced. If you do it will simply become a feeding station for flies, rats, skunks, raccoons and stray dogs, which isn't good for you or the animals. One solution is to empty your kitchen scraps into 5 gallon buckets and cover them with a thin layer of shredded leaves or sawdust (to stop it smelling) and seal it with an airtight lid. As each bucket fills up store it in a cool place until you have enough material to build a pile.

Chickens are one of the best ways to deal with kitchen waste (they will turn it into eggs). Just leave it for them to pick through and anything they don't eat can be composted.

Urine

This comes second on my list because we all produce it every day. Human urine is a valuable fertilizer and like human manure it's a waste product that becomes a pollutant if it isn't used. You probably never realized that you are a walking plant fertilizer factory and that every day you are literally pissing away money. Urine is much easier to deal with than solid waste because it is usually sterile and so safe for direct use in the garden (a notable exception is that hepatitis can be transmitted through urine).

Who would have thought that good, old-fashioned pee, would turn out to be a cheap and easily available liquid fertilizer concentrate? The average quantity of urine produced by one person in a day contains about 12 grams nitrogen, 1.0 grams phosphorus, 2.5 grams potassium, 1.0 grams sulphur and 5.0 grams sodium (too much urine in one place could cause salt buildup).

Urine is normally diluted (4 parts water : 1 part urine) for use as a foliar feed or liquid fertilizer. Supposedly it may burn plants if used undiluted, though I haven't seen this. This same solution is also an effective fungicide. Urine can also be used as a source of nitrogen for the compost pile.

Plants

All green plants are rich in plant nutrients (that's what they are made of)) and so are an excellent fertilizer. Any vigorous and fast growing plant can be used as a source of biomass to supply carbonaceous material to make humus and supply nitrogen for plant growth. Depending on their quantity and composition, they can be incorporated directly into the soil, composted, or used as mulch.

- Weeds, lawn mowings, harvest trimmings, aquatic weeds, cover crops and any other green material can be used. Don't just think of the materials in your own garden though; expand you horizons and look further afield. Lawn clippings can be obtained from many apartment buildings, commercial buildings and more (often ready bagged).

- Landscapers will often give you their tree trimmings, lawn mowings, hedge clippings and other organic waste. In fact they are often looking for places to dump the stuff.

- Aquatic weeds often become a problem in streams, canals and lakes and have to be removed. They can be used as green manure or compost material.

- Some invasive plants (Japanese Knotweed, Kudzu, Ivy) can sometimes be obtained in quantity for use as mulch or for making compost.

- It is important to ensure that any vegetable material you receive from outside the garden isn't contaminated with weed seeds, diseases, pests, insecticides or herbicides.

- You may want to grow some plants specifically to supply greens for making compost, or for fertilizer. Good plants for this include Comfrey, Stinging Nettles, Sweet Clover, Sunflowers and Hemp.

Tree leaves

Tree leaves are an excellent fertilizer and mulch material and you can never have too many of them. You are lucky if you have enough leaves in autumn to warrant raking. Use them as mulch (you might run over them with lawn mower to shred), make into leaf mold, or simply add them to the compost pile.

Fallen tree leaves aren't very high in most nutrients (trees generally remove them before they drop), but they are one of the best sources of organic matter. In heavily forested areas, they will be one of your most important soil amendments and should always be returned to the soil. It is a crime to burn leaves and sending them to the dump (even to be recycled) isn't much better. They are too valuable to waste.

Contrary to popular belief, most leaves don't lower the pH of the soil significantly and it's easy to add lime if there is any problem. The presence of decaying organic matter may slightly inhibit the growth of some crops (if too fresh they may give off toxins), but the addition of organic matter far outweighs any temporary detrimental effect.

The best leaves are those from Oak, Maple and Beech, though any deciduous tree leaves may be used. Evergreens can be useful too, but you have to be more careful how you use them (see Mulch Materials for more on this).

If there are lots of deciduous trees around your garden, one of your autumn jobs should be to stockpile as many leaves as possible, so mark it in your diary. If you don't have trees of your own (or even if you do) then beg, gather, buy or steal as many leaves as you can from elsewhere. Some people even go so far as to get street cleaners to dump truckloads of leaves on their gardens (be aware that street leaves may have various pollutants on them).

If you have a power lawn mower you can run it over the leaves to shred them. The resulting chopped leaves are easier to handle, much less bulky, less prone to compaction and they decompose faster.

Chopped leaves can have a dramatic effect on soil fertility. Just put them on the surface as mulch and they will break down in one season. They can also be incorporated into the soil by double digging or rototilling and rot quickly when buried. The best time to do this is in autumn), as they then have all winter to decompose. If you have a lot of leaves this is a good way to prepare a large area for future planting.

Composting leaves

The simplest way to compost tree leaves is to pile them up in a heap and leave them for 2 to 3 years to break down. They take so long because they contain a lot of rot resistant lignin.

If you are in a hurry you can compost leaves in only 6 to 12 months. To do this the leaf pile should be as large as possible to help it hold moisture and heat. A container very helpful; as it keep the leaves together in a compact mass and stops them blowing around. A simple wire cage works as well as anything.

The leaves will break down faster if they are shredded as this increases their surface area, improves aeration and reduces their tendency to mat down. This can often be done while gathering, by running over them with a lawn mower. They should also be moistened thoroughly as they won't break down if they are dry. You might also add a little soil to the pile to add decomposing organisms, and a source of additional nitrogen. Urine, diluted 4 : 1 is ideal, if you can get it. As with other forms of composting, turning the pile occasionally will speed decomposition.

Leaves can also be used to make leaf mold. This valuable soil amendment holds 5 -10 times its own weight in water and is richer in nutrients than peat. In fact peat moss has been called an expensive and inferior, substitute for leaf mold (however there is no marketing organization promoting the use of leaf mold).

Leaf mold can be dug from any woodland, but you shouldn't take large amounts from any one area (and don't rob your own trees of all of their leaf fall). Woodland leaf mold is inferior to that you can make, because it tends to be acidic and may contain substances that inhibit seed growth. It is better to make your own. You can never have enough leaf mold for the greenhouse and garden so make as much as possible.

Compost

Compost is so important I discuss it is greater detail below. The problem with compost is that you have to make it, so there is almost never enough. In my garden it all gets taken up by the intensive vegetable garden. You can now often buy compost from commercial suppliers or from your local landfill (they now commonly compost a lot of their green waste). The latter may have lots of garbage mixed in though.

Wood ash

Wood ashes contain most of the elements that went into making wood, so are obviously a good plant fertilizer. Their nutrient content varies according to the kind of wood, but generally they are rich in calcium, potassium, magnesium and phosphorus, with varying amounts of sulphur, iron, copper, manganese, boron and zinc. They also make the soil more alkaline, so are considered a liming agent.

When using wood ashes it's important to know what has been burned to make them. If you have a wood stove for heating, make sure you only use clean wood and newspaper. Avoid glossy colored paper and any synthetic materials such as plastic, paint, or oil. They may contain substances that shouldn't end up in the garden.

I like to put my wood ashes through a ¼" screen to remove any pieces of charcoal, as these don't decompose very well in the soil (though see Biochar). Wood ashes should be kept dry until needed, so store in a watertight container.

Wood ashes are very soluble and leach from the soil easily. They should be scattered on the surface of the soil at the start of the growing season, or dug into the top 3 - 6" just before planting.

Animal manures

If you don't have enough compost (not many of us do), then aged animal manure is the next best thing. Not all people agree with this statement however. It's a sign of the diversity of organic gardening that some growers think animal manures are the best fertilizers of all, while others believe they are detrimental to the soil and should never be used.

Herbivorous animals eat plants, so not surprisingly their manure is an excellent plant food. Manure could actually be looked upon as a form of quick compost, produced by anaerobic fermentation in only a few days. It is most valuable as a source of organic matter, nitrogen and trace elements, but also contains a moderate amount of phosphorus and potassium. Farmyard manure (a mix of manure and urine soaked bedding) is even more useful, because urine contains nitrogen and potassium, while the bedding contains organic matter. The manure of young animals is less useful than that of older animals; because they need more minerals for growth, so digest their food more completely.

In many areas there are lots of horses and owners who have a manure problem. You can use as much manure as you can get when first starting a garden so it pays to establish a regular supply. This isn't difficult in most places, as horse owners are usually glad to get rid of it. It is often available free for the hauling and they will often load it into your truck for you. There is also a lot of other manure out there too. It's been estimated that American cows produce over two billion tons of manure annually.

Be cautious about using fresh manure as it may contain so much nitrogen it acts like a chemical fertilizer. It gives off ammonia and can burn the leaves and stems of any plant it comes into contact with. It may also cause excessive, sappy growth, lodging and delayed maturation of fruit. You can avoid this problem by applying fresh manure to the bed in autumn, to age over the winter and be incorporated in the spring. You can also spread it in late winter, to leach for a month or so before planting. Another way to use fresh manure is to make manure tea.

Another problem with horse manure is that it commonly contains viable grass and weed seeds. These may come from hay bedding, or from feed that has passed through the animal undigested (only chickens kill all of the seeds they eat). By using such manure directly you are very likely to be planting weeds. Aged manure left in a pile, may have heated up sufficiently to kill weed seeds in the center of the pile, but not at the edges. Dispersed manure may not have heated up at all.

Generally the best way to use manure is to get it fresh and compost it yourself. You then know that it hasn't lost nutrients through leaching and has been heated enough to kill weed seeds and break down potentially toxic chemicals.

Human manure

At one time human manure was considered one of the best fertilizers, which isn't really surprising considering the varied diet of its producers. Using it for fertilizer is a logical way to prevent the loss of valuable nutrients from the garden and to solve a waste disposal problem, but there are problems associated with its use. The most obvious problem in western countries is the serious social stigma attached. People think you are really weird if they find out you actually deal with your own waste. A more valid objection is that human waste contains dangerous pathogens (apparently vegetarian waste is less toxic than that of meat eaters), that make it unsafe to use without treatment.

In parts of the third world human waste is far too valuable as fertilizer to flush away. In China untreated human waste has been used as fertilizer for centuries, but there is a real danger of spreading disease in this way (which is why Chinese food is always cooked). More recently the waste has been piped into methane digesters and processed to provide methane for fuel and then used for fertilizer.

Ways of using human waste easily and safely should be a priority of agricultural researchers. This would not only provide enormous quantities of fertilizer, but would also save enormous quantities of water and reduce the pollution of our waterways, oceans and groundwater. See Humanure toilet for one simple way to do this.

Wood wastes

Sawdust, bark and wood chips are an excellent source of humus for building long-term soil fertility, but have a very high carbon to nitrogen ratio (as much as 400: 1). This means that if they are dug directly into the soil they will cause a temporary shortage of nitrogen. This happens because there is an explosion in the population of organisms that break down cellulose. These also require nitrogen and so they take it from the soil. The shortage is only temporary because the nitrogen is released again when the organisms die.

The best way to use wood chips (and other woody materials) is as a long lasting, weed suppressing mulch. When placed on the surface of the soil they don't stimulate the soil organisms that cause a nitrogen deficiency (or break down quickly).

Wood wastes (especially sawdust) can be composted if you mix them with a highly nitrogenous material, such as fresh manure, urine or even nitrate fertilizer. They can also be broken down by fungal mycelium and produce edible mushrooms at the same time. See Mushrooms and fungi for more on this.

Rock powders

The most commonly available rock powders include: basalt rock (calcium, iron, magnesium, phosphorus, potassium), granite dust (potassium and trace elements), greensand (potassium and trace elements) and colloidal phosphate (phosphorus).

There are several problems with these materials, probably the biggest is that they are mined, which usually causes environmental damage somewhere. Another problem is that you have to buy them, though they are usually fairly inexpensive). Yet another problem is that the nutrients they contain are fairly insoluble and are only made available slowly, by the action of organic acid and soil organisms. Only small quantities of nutrients will be available initially (only 2% of colloidal phosphate becomes available in the first year and only 18% ever). The rest will remain locked up in the soil.

Seaweed

The sea is a solution containing all of the elements on earth and consequently seaweeds contain all of the trace elements needed by plants (most micronutrient deficiencies can be resolved by applying seaweed). They also contain growth-stimulating hormones that may encourage plants to grow vigorously and increase their resistance to disease and pests. It is available as a powder or a (fairly expensive) liquid fertilizer.

Commercially produced liquid seaweed is widely used as a foliar feed, to remedy nutrient deficiencies, or simply to improve growth. Powdered seaweed is sometimes incorporated into the soil when first getting the garden beds established.

If you live in coastal areas you can gather the seaweed that has been cast onto beaches after storms (leave it in the rain for a while to wash off the salt). Fresh seaweed can be used like manure, applied at a rate of one barrow per 100 square feet. It rots quickly when dug into the soil.

The species most commonly used for fertilizer include: Kelp (*Alaria*), Giant Kelp (*Macrocystis*), Bladderwrack (*Fucus*) and Irish Moss (*Chondrus*).

Foliar fertilizers

Compost / manure Tea

This is my favorite liquid fertilizer as it can be prepared from locally available materials (I prefer to use worm compost), doesn't cost anything to make and supplies all of the most soluble nutrients found in those materials. It can also help to inoculate the garden with beneficial soil organisms.

Making this tea is quite simple, just fill a 5 gallon plastic bucket one third full of manure (or half full of compost) and top it up with water (larger quantities can be made with woven plastic sacks and 50 gallon oil drums. Cover the bucket with a tight fitting lid and let it sit for 7 -10 days (depending on how warm the weather). Then strain the tea into a bucket and dilute with 2 parts water to one part tea. Its only drawback is the foul sewage-like smell caused by its anaerobic decomposition.

Actively aerated compost tea

In recent years the making of compost tea has been transformed by the use of aeration. The foul smelling anaerobic compost tea can be replaced by actively aerated compost tea or AACT. This is made in a similar way to the old compost tea, except that air is bubbled through the liquid, resulting in an aerobic tea with only a mild earthy smell. Another big advantage is that it can actually multiply the number of beneficial organisms in the compost.

I use worm compost (vermicompost) from my worm bins for making AACT. It creates a nice loop whereby the kitchen scraps go to feed the worms and their waste is made into tea to feed the plants. The plants then go back into the kitchen.

To make this kind of tea you need to be able to bubble air through the liquid for the entire time it is brewing. You can buy commercially made aerating systems, but it is much cheaper to make your own. All you need is an aquarium aerator, a three-gang valve, some plastic hose and a 5-gallon bucket. If you have the right parts it probably doesn't take you any longer to make your own system than it does to take a commercial system out of the box and assemble it.

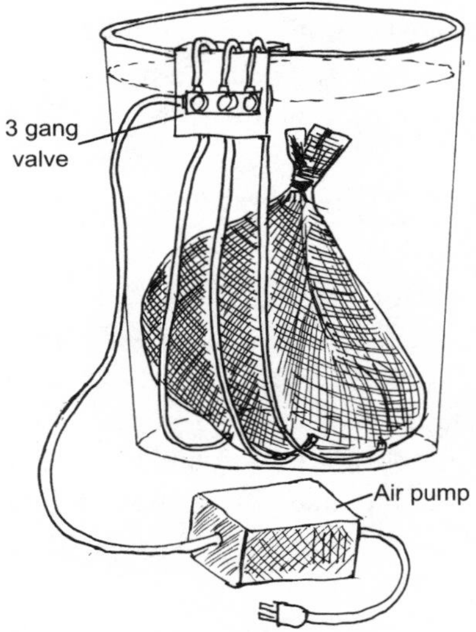

The compost (or vermicompost or aged manure) is put in a bag (a pair of old panty hose works great) to make a very large tea bag (this prevents the loose compost clogging the hose). Put this bag in the aerator bucket, fill it with water, put the lid on, switch it on and put it in a dark place at a temperature of 70 to 80° F. This is then left to bubble and brew for 24 to 48 hours.

The finished compost tea is diluted and used like traditional manure tea. If it smells offensive in any way then it didn't brew properly and you have made old-fashioned manure tea (you can still use it).

You can also take some exceptional garden soil, or fine, rich humus from the woods (watch the pH) and use this for actively aerated tea, to inoculate the garden with beneficial organisms.

The best plant teas

If a specific nutrient is in short supply you can use a plant that accumulates that nutrient. You can also mix different plants in one tea.

Comfrey – This is the most commonly used plant for making tea. It is best known as a source of potassium, but also contains nitrogen, phosphorus, calcium and magnesium.

Hemp – One of the best accumulators of phosphorus.

Stinging Nettle - A good source of nitrogen, phosphorus and iron.

Alfalfa - A source of nitrogen and phosphorus.

Horsetail - Biodynamic gardeners believe this plant increases resistance to disease.

Seaweeds - Rich in nitrogen, potassium and many trace elements (wash thoroughly before use to remove salt)

Yarrow - Rich in potassium and silica. Biodynamic gardeners say it increases disease resistance.

Grass - Lawn clippings are a good source of nitrogen.

Foliar feeding

This is a simple and effective way to supply plants with nutrients that may be lacking in the soil (or unavailable). It works because plants are able to take up small quantities of nutrients directly through their leaves (apparently this is 8 times as efficient as absorbing them through the roots).

The best way to apply foliar fertilizers is with a sprayer, as it enables you to wet both sides of the leaves for maximum absorption. The best time for foliar feeding is in early evening, because the nutrients are most easily absorbed during the night when the air is still, humidity is high and leaf stomata are open. Early morning is also good.

Plants only absorb nutrients through their leaves as they need them, so it's best to use frequent sprays of very dilute fertilizers. Too much foliar feed at one time is a waste of time and fertilizer (and could burn the plants).

Plant teas

Fresh plants can also be used to make a quick and easy foliar fertilizer, all you need is a good supply of foliage. You might even want to grow areas of plants specifically for use in this way.

The traditional method of making plant teas is exactly the same as described above for manure tea. You just fill the plastic bucket with as much foliage (Comfrey, Seaweed, Stinging Nettle) as it will hold, top it up with water, then cover and leave for 2 -5 days. This is used in the same way as manure tea and smells just as bad. You can also try making an aerated version.

Worm composting

Worm composting (or vermicomposting) gives you a simple way to kill two birds with one stone. It uses earthworms to dispose of all of your kitchen scraps and provides you with perhaps the best plant fertilizer/ soil improver of all. Vermicompost sometimes sells for $4.00 a pound, which gives you some perspective on its relative value and on the cost effectiveness of making it. It is also the best way to dispose of kitchen scraps without attracting rats, flies and other creatures.

The worms

Common earthworms are not used in worm bins, you need special compost worms (*Eisenia foetida*) (or *Lumbricus rubellus*) and these aren't found in large numbers in the soil. You can get such worms from an old compost or manure pile, from another worm bin, through the mail, or from a bait shop. They feed on decaying vegetable matter of almost any kind, except very acid materials such as Citrus peel) or those that heat up very quickly (such as grass clippings). I got my first worms out of an old, badly made, compost pile that had a lot of kitchen scraps. Their descendants have now been in the family longer than my youngest daughter (at least 9 years).

Making a worm bin

The worms need a suitable habitat in the form of a worm bin. The simplest type of bin is an old discarded plastic garbage can, with a series of holes punched into the bottom 4″ of the sides for drainage. The bottom is then filled with 6″ of sand or gravel to provide good drainage and water is added to provide humidity. A series of boards are set on top of the gravel (to keep it separate from the compost) and 3″ of bedding goes on top of this. The bedding is where the worms live and could be dry leaves, aged manure or leaf mold (torn newspaper if commonly used by city dwellers). This should be quite moist, like a wrung out sponge. Finally a layer of newspaper (or straw) covers the whole thing to hold in moisture and the lid is replaced. I like these plastic bins, because they are easy to obtain (I steal them from the town dump). I started out with one bin, but am now up to four.

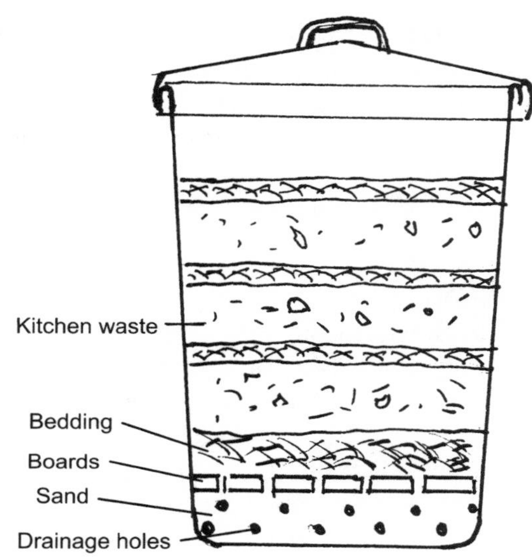

The best place for a worm bin is close to the kitchen, so it is convenient to quickly dispose of kitchen waste. If you have a mud room this could be a good place for it, as it should be protected from rain, pests and temperature extremes. It should ideally be kept within the range of 55 to 75° F. and out of direct sunlight. It could even be kept in the dark if that's more convenient.

Using the bin

The kitchen scraps are added to one side of the bedding at a time and covered with newspaper. The amount of waste that can be disposed of depends upon the number of worms and the temperature. The smaller the particles the faster they will decompose. It is best to give them too little food rather than too much (it's always easier to add more). Large quantities of food may heat up, or start to go anaerobic and smell. You may need to add water to keep it moist and add lime if the pH is too low. If you go away for a while and the worms run out of food they may die, but they will lay eggs that will hatch later. Obviously you should try to avoid this happening.

Mulch

Mulch is natures way of gardening. When you add mulch you emulate the growth of a forest, whereby trees drop their seeds and then cover them with a layer of fallen leaves. Every year another layer of leaves falls and decays, enriching and building the soil without disturbing it and recycling nutrients through the tree.

Mulching is also a fundamental part of the new food garden, as it gives us a way to add nutrients, suppress weeds and conserve water, while also reducing the amount of work we have to do. As soon as you put mulch down it goes to work and keeps on working.

The benefits of mulch

Soil building

Mulching is the easiest and most natural way to increase the fertility of the soil. Most organic materials break down quickly once they are in contact with the soil, because the humid interface between soil and air is the perfect habitat for decomposing organisms (this is evident when you look at an old fence post). This decomposing process is natures way of building soil, and a two-inch layer of shredded leaves will pretty much disappear into the soil in one summer.

When you stop digging and start mulching, the soil layers are no longer inverted or disturbed. Over time the structure of the soil is improved through the action of earthworms, mycorrhizae and other organisms and slowly returns to its natural state.

Weed suppression

Most annual weeds can only grow on disturbed bare soil, so simply by keeping the soil covered with mulch you can prevent most of them getting established. This is another example of going along with natural laws, rather than trying to fight them.

If the mulch material is free of weed seeds, it will eventually break down to form a weed free organic layer on top of the soil. Any weed seeds in the soil will slowly get buried deeper, out of harms way. If you don't allow any weeds to set seed and don't disturb the soil, you can almost eliminate the problem of annual weeds entirely.

Mulching also works on perennial weeds and can be used to clear land of major infestations, You just have to make sure it is thick enough and give it enough time (maybe two years or more). See Sheet mulching for more on this.

Water conservation

Mulch significantly reduces the loss of water from the soil (by as much as 50% in some cases) and is pretty much essential in dry climates. It shades the surface of the soil and increases the humidity of the air between the mulch and the soil. It also helps water to percolate into the soil, by slowing its movement.

Soil protection

Sunlight damages bare soil by burning up humus, oxidizing nutrients and killing soil organisms. A layer of mulch protects the soil surface and prevents these things from happening. It can also prevent soil erosion and reduce surface crusting and capping. It also protects plastic irrigation lines from the sun and so extends their lifespan.

Soil temperature stabilization

On a sunny day the surface of bare soil may reach 90° F, while on a cold day it may freeze. Organic mulch insulates the soil and slows down these temperature swings. It keeps the soil warmer in winter by reducing heat loss, and keeps it cooler in summer by reducing heat gain (it can reduce the soil temperature by up to 10° F.) Light colored mulches keep the soil cooler than dark colored ones

Organic mulch is so effective at insulating the soil that it can prevent the soil from warming up in spring. For this reason it is usually removed from intensive beds several weeks before planting.

Soil life

Mulch encourages beneficial soil organisms by providing organic matter for food, shading them from the sun, giving refuge from predators and providing places to live. It is one of the best ways to increase the number of earthworms in the soil.

Neatness

An attractive mulch can make the garden look neater and well cared for (I need all the help I can get). It also makes it less muddy in wet weather, and reduces the amount of soil splashing onto leaves (and hence the spread of disease).

Winter crop protection
A thick mulch (up to 12") of straw or other bulky material, can protect late crops and tender plants and help them to survive cold winter weather. It's a common practice to cover root crops with a thick mulch in late fall to stop the ground from freezing. This also keeps soil organisms (especially earthworms) active.

Cultivating mushrooms
Mulches of wood chips, sawdust, compost and straw can be inoculated with fungal mycelium to produce edible mushrooms. The mycorrhizae help to break down these materials more quickly and make them available for plant growth (that is symbiosis in action!) See Mushrooms for more on this.

Obtaining mulch
Almost any organic matter can be used for mulch so long as it is weed free and fairly odorless. The most easily obtainable materials include hay, straw, shredded tree leaves, aged manure and wood chips. In fact these materials are often available for free if you know where to look. In my neighborhood the ever present tree trimmers are happy to dump a load of wood chips on your property (you just have to ask before other homeowners). You may also be able to get lawn clippings or tree leaves. If you don't have any free sources you could grow some plants specifically to produce mulch material.

Its been suggested that 'garbage', such as kitchen scraps can be disposed of by spreading them under the mulch. This works well enough in theory, but where I live it would just be dug up again by rats, raccoons, dogs or other animals.

Mulch should be stored in a central area that isn't too visible. If you get mulch delivered this area should be fairly close to the driveway for convenience in unloading.

Make a habit of cutting weeds and woody brush regularly for use as mulch. Any time I do any pruning I cut the prunings up into smaller pieces and spread them as mulch. Any time you have a dense growth of weeds you should be thankful and look upon it as a source of mulch.

Applying mulch
To be totally effective in suppressing weeds a mulch must be laid down carefully and in sufficient quantity. Concentrate on one area at a time, the actual size of which depends upon the amount of mulch you have available (as well as your energy and the size of your garden).

Mulching large areas of the garden calls for a lot of organic matter. A cubic yard of mulch will only cover 160 square feet to a depth of 2 inches. You can spread it thinner if you put cardboard or newspaper (at least 5-6 layers) underneath it. These materials aren't normally used by themselves because don't look very nice.

Mulching doesn't work very well on sloping ground, because it tends to slowly move downhill (or rapidly downhill if assisted by water or birds). In heavy rain it may disappear almost completely. In these situations you should use shrubs and groundcover instead.

Mulch is slowly (or quickly) digested by the soil and needs replenishing regularly. How often depends upon the material and the amount of biological activity in the soil. Straw will only last a few months, while bark chips may last for four years.

Sheet mulching
This is a relatively recent innovation and gives you a way to transform untamed land into a garden in a matter of hours. It consists of several distinct layers of mulch and soil amendments, each layer intended to accomplish a separate task. See No-dig gardening for more on this.

Mulch materials

A good mulch material should be:

- Relatively long lived.
- Free or inexpensive.
- Available in abundance, preferably as a waste material.
- Heavy enough that it doesn't blow away.
- Free of weeds, weed seeds, pests, disease and chemical pollutants
- Attractive.
- It should enrich the soil with nutrients and organic matter.

Organic mulch materials

Tree leaves (2 - 3" depth) Deciduous tree leaves are my favorite mulch material, but unfortunately are not very plentiful where I live. They add humus and nutrients, encourage fungi in the soil and are usually free of weed seeds, pests and disease (as well as free for the gathering). If you can get them in sufficient quantity they can be used anywhere you want to enrich the soil, such as the garden growing beds. When used whole they tend to blow away or mat down (mixing with straw can help to prevent matting). A better solution is to shred them first, by running them over with a lawn mower (or with a weed wacker in a metal garbage can).

Broadleaf evergreens and the needles of coniferous evergreens can also be used as mulch, but you have to be more careful, as they contain toxic resins that make them resistant to decay. Broadleaf evergreens can be shredded to speed up decomposition. Conifers can lower the pH of the soil, unless you add lime to prevent this. Of course you can also make a virtue of their acidity and use them with acid loving plants such as Blueberries, Strawberries, Tea and various evergreens.

Pine needles mulch (called Pine straw) is widely used in the southeast and tend to stay in place in heavy rain better than other mulches. It is being produced commercially on plantations (presumably as a by-product of growing pine for lumber).

Wood chips (2 - 3" depth) These are hard to beat for availability, durability and cost (usually free). They are ideal for mulching paths and around permanent perennial plantings such as trees, but aren't suitable for intensive vegetable beds. They suppress weeds and conserving moisture but take a while to break down and add nutrients to the soil. Fresh wood chips may contain toxins that actually inhibit plant growth.

Sawdust (1 - 3" depth) Aged sawdust is usually preferred as fresh sawdust often contains toxic terpenes and tannins that can inhibit plant growth (this may be useful if you don't want plants to grow in an area). Sawdust is highly resistant to decay because it is very high in carbon, but when it does finally break down it is an excellent source of organic matter. When used as a mulch it remains on the surface and so doesn't cause any nitrogen deficiency problems.

Manure (1 - 3" depth) If you have an abundance of manure it can be used as a mulch. Composted manure is the best, as it will have heated up enough to kill any weed seeds and won't contain too much nitrogen. Aged manure is also good, though it may contain weed seeds. Fresh manure is least desirable as it often contains so much nitrogen that it burns plants, as well as weed seeds. Fresh manure is often applied to the soil in autumn, so some of the nitrogen can leach out over the winter (which makes it aged manure). Fresh manure might also be used as a sub-mulch underneath wood chips, to supply the nitrogen to hasten decomposition.

Compost (1 - 3" depth) Compost is a great soil amendment, but isn't very well suited to use as a mulch (it's generally too precious for this anyway). If you spread compost in a thin layer over the soil surface, many of its nutrients will be lost to oxidation and beneficial organisms will be killed by the UV rays in sunlight. It does make a good sub-mulch/inoculant underneath a more durable mulch.

Seaweed (2 - 3" depth) A rich source of trace elements, seaweed was once widely used as a mulch in coastal areas. It breaks down quickly into the soil, but doesn't add much humus.

Green plants (2 - 3" depth) These are rich in nutrients and humus, but decompose quickly when used as mulch. They need supplementing regularly if they are to keep weeds down. They are usually spread out in thin layers as they become available. You can just uproot the weeds and throw them down.

Bark (2 - 3" depth) This long lasting and attractive mulch material is widely used around shrubs and trees, but doesn't add much in the way of nutrients. It is sometimes used to cover a more nutritious but fragile mulch such as compost or manure. Shredded bark is probably the best looking mulch material, but you usually have to buy it.

Straw, hay (4 - 6" depth) These bulky materials are attractive and rich in plant nutrients. Potential disadvantages are that they can be a fire hazard in dry weather and you usually have to buy them.

Hay is made from whole dried grasses and weeds and contains most of the nutrients found in green plants. It is quite a good soil amendment and breaks down quickly, but usually contains weed seeds.

Straw is made from the stems of grain crops and isn't as rich in nutrients as hay, or as quick to break down. However it has a big advantage in that it is usually free of weed seeds.

Newspaper (6 - 12 overlapping sheets) This doesn't add nutrients to the soil, but is good for suppressing weeds. It is rather ugly and so light it may blow away if not weighted down, so is commonly used as a weed suppressing layer underneath other mulches. In most places it is readily available in quantity. Lay down 6 – 12 overlapping sheets and cover it with a more attractive layer of leaves, hay or other organic mulch.

Cardboard (1 layer of corrugated) This is like a heavy duty newspaper and can be used for suppressing tough weeds like Blackberries. Cardboard isn't quite as ugly as newspaper, but you will still want to cover it with a layer of more attractive material. The largest sheets of cardboard can be obtained from cabinet and appliance stores.

Inorganic mulch materials

Gravel (2 - 3") Gravel is sometimes used as a permanent mulch in hot dry climates, where there isn't much vegetation and organic matter burns up quickly in the sun. Dark gravel warms the soil, so is good for cold climates. Light gravel keeps the soil cooler and can increase light reflection onto plant leaves.

Plastic sheet This is commonly used by commercial growers for its weed killing, moisture retaining and soil warming properties. It is too ugly for regular use in the home garden though.

The color of the plastic has a significant effect on its properties as mulch. Black plastic increases the soil temperature by as much as 10° F and kills weeds by depriving them of light (even tough weeds like Blackberries). Clear plastic acts like a miniature greenhouse and can increase soil temperatures even higher (as much as 15° F.), but may allow weeds to grow underneath it (though it often gets hot enough to cook them).

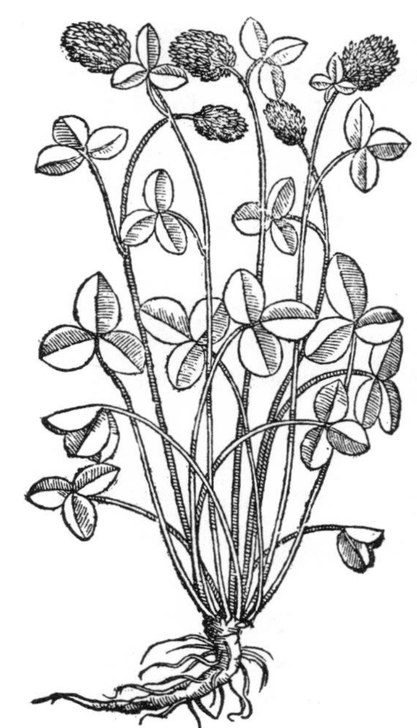

Using plants to grow fertility

In the last section I said that mulch was natures way of gardening but that isn't quite true. Ultimately fertility can only be increased by plant growth (mulch is simply a product of plant growth), hence plants are the most fundamental part of natures soil fertility program. You can use plants to maintain and build the fertility of the garden without importing any nutrients at all.

You may be surprised to learn that the soil/plant relationship is not a one way street, whereby plants simply take chemical nutrients from the soil. It is more of an exchange, whereby the plants give back carbohydrates and other nutrients to feed soil organisms. As generations of plants live, die and decay, their bodies feed soil organisms and organic matter builds up in the soil. This is why topsoil is so different from mineral soil and so much more able to support plant growth.

Selecting the right plants

The most effective fertility creating plants share many of the same characteristics. They germinate and grow quickly, have deep roots, produce a lot of biomass in a short time and grow well in poor soils. Many also contain nitrogen fixing bacteria in their roots. There are soil-improving crops for almost every conceivable growing conditions, cold, wet, acid, hot, dry, shady, or any combination thereof. It is important that you select the right species (and variety) for the conditions.

These plants may be divided into several categories, according to how they are used (though the same plants can often be used in more than one way).

Cover Crops

These hardy plants are planted in the fall to protect the soil over the winter. Their dense root network binds the soil together, preventing soil erosion and absorbing soluble nutrients so they don't leach away over the winter. In mild winter areas they continue to grow right through the winter, producing an abundance of organic matter and a leaf canopy that protects the soil from rain. In colder areas they will die back to the ground when it gets cold, but their roots continue to hold the soil together. In spring they grow rapidly from their established roots and produce a lot of biomass before they are incorporated. Cover crops can dramatically improve the structure of the soil over the course of one winter.

Green manures

Green manures are used to enrich the soil during the growing season and can be planted any time you have vacant space available. Like cover crops they improve soil texture; mine the subsoil for nutrients and break up compacted subsoil. Some also fix atmospheric nitrogen.

Deep rooted green manures can also be used to improve new areas of soil before the establishment of garden beds or woody plants.

Smother crops

These particularly vigorous and fast growing plants (Hemp, Sunflower, African Marigold), can overwhelm and smother almost all competition and are sometimes planted very densely to suppress out-of-control perennial weeds. Once these areas are under control the plants are incorporated into the soil, or used for compost or mulch.

Roots and fertility

Roots are less visible than the above ground plant parts and so are often overlooked, yet they are a very important factor in soil fertility. They may make up as much as 50% of the weight of some plants and add a significant amount of organic matter to the soil. When roots decay in the soil they leave behind channels for air and water penetration.

Of particular importance is the rhizosphere, the area of soil immediately adjacent to plant roots and extending out about 2 mm. This is the most biologically active part of the soil because it is rich in carbonaceous material sloughed off by growing roots (this may amount to 5% of all the carbon fixed by the plant). Plants actually attract and control the kind of organisms (bacteria, protozoa, fungi) that live in the rhizosphere by means of exudates from their roots. They give out nutrients (carbohydrates, proteins) to these organisms and get others in return. They also receive nutrient rich waste products from these organisms and when they die they get the nutrients in their bodies.

Spike rooted plants

These deep rooted species are useful for their ability to loosen compacted soils and draw nutrients up from the subsoil. Useful species include Horseradish, Chicory, Evening Primrose and Daikon Radish.

Living mulches

Plant growth is natures way of protecting and enriching the soil and if there is enough moisture available it should be our way too (if there isn't we have to turn to mulch). Living mulches are temporary groundcovers, used to cover the soil between widely spaced crops. These keeps down weeds, protect the soil surface and add organic matter (many also fix nitrogen too).

Clovers, Bugle, Nasturtium, Sedums and Strawberries have all been used as living mulch.

Accumulator plants

These are plants that have a special affinity for a specific nutrient and accumulate it in their tissue in greater quantities than most plants. They can be grown to make such nutrients more available (add them to compost piles or use for mulch or tea). Their deep searching roots mine for these nutrients down in the subsoil and bring them up to the surface, where they eventually become available to other plants.

Important accumulator plants

Alfalfa - N
Bracken Fern - K, P, Mn
Buckwheat - P
Carrot (leaf) - K, Mg
Chickweed - K, P, Mn
Chicory - Ca, K
Cleavers - Ca
Comfrey - Ca, K, N, Mg, P
Dandelion - Ca, Cu, K, P, Mg
Datura - P
Dock - Ca, K, P
Hemp - P
Horsetail - Ca, Co, Fe, Mg
Nettle - Ca, Cu, Fe, K, N, S
Plantain - Ca, Cu, Fe, K, S
Yarrow - Ca, K, P

Nitrogen fixing plants

This is an extremely important group of plants with regards to fertility. The best known nitrogen fixers are the herbaceous annuals and perennials of the Bean family (*Fabaceae* - sometimes referred to as legumes). These have a symbiotic relationship with Rhizobium bacteria that live in special nodules on their roots and fix nitrogen from the air. This nitrogen is shared with the host plant in exchange for nutrients and is released to the soil when the bacteria and plant dies. A good stand of a leguminous green manure can add several hundred pounds of nitrogen to the soil per acre annually.

Legumes might be annuals (Clovers, Beans), perennials (Alfalfa, Clovers, Lupins), shrubs (False Indigo or Caragana, Alfalfa, Clover) or even trees (Black Locust, Alder). See Soil improving plants for more on these.

Many woody plants (*Alnus, Eleagnus, Myrica, Shepherdia, Ceanothus* and more) form associations with nitrogen fixing actinomycete bacteria (these plants are said to be actinorhizal) and return extra nitrogen to the soil in the form of leaf litter. The *Frankia* species are particularly important and sometimes form a three way association with the host plant and a mycorrhizal fungus.

We can use the nitrogen-fixers to replace the nitrogen taken from the soil by growing plants and so they are an important part of the garden fertility cycle.

Inoculation

Nitrogen-fixing plants don't always supply nitrogen. If the soil is already rich in nitrogen the plants won't form nodules and there won't be any appreciable fixation. Other factors may also affect fixation, such as soil pH (it should be above 5.7), moisture level, soil aeration and availability of trace elements such as molybdenum, cobalt and boron. The key factor however is the presence of the right nitrogen fixing bacteria for the plant species. If this isn't present in the soil there won't be any nitrogen fixation al all. In such a situation the seed must be inoculated with the appropriate bacteria before planting.

Incorporation

In a conventional garden the green manures and cover crops are eventually dug into the soil, or the tops may be skimmed off and composted, while the roots are left in the ground. In the no-dig garden the tops are usually just cut down and left on the surface to decay.

The woody nitrogen fixers may be left to grow for years. These supply nitrogen through their leaf litter or when used as mulch.

Growing mulch materials

The garden is growing mulch all of the time of course, because any plant material can be mulch material. Some plants need to be kept under control by pruning and so supply mulch incidentally, others may be cut to obtain mulch material and some may be grown specifically to produce it. The most suitable plants for producing mulch grow quickly, produce lots of biomass, regenerate quickly after cutting and are easily propagated. Some even fix their own nitrogen.

If you never have enough mulch you could grow a stand of trees or shrubs to produce it. These plants should be harvested regularly because cutting stimulates the production of new growth, and ensures that the growth is not too woody or large. You could harvest branches and leaves at regular intervals, or the whole plant could be coppiced and chipped.

Mulch plants

The best species to plant specifically for mulch include:

Useful nitrogen fixing trees and shrubs include: *Acacia, Caragana, Ceanothus, Cytisus, Eleagnus, Robinia* and more. These can be coppiced regularly.

Fast growing non-nitrogen fixing species include Buddleia, Elder, Willow and Bamboo.

Many perennials can also be useful: Alfalfa, Comfrey, Globe Artichoke, Cardoon Jerusalem Artichoke, Rhubarb all produce large amounts of biomass.

Any fast growing, highly carbonaceous annuals can supply useful mulch. Sunflowers, Corn Sweet Clover, African Marigold, Hemp. These are usually grown for another purpose but then used as mulch afterward.

If you have any problem plants in your garden, that grow too easily and quickly despite your best efforts, they may be trying to tell you something. In my garden Scotch Broom grows through the summer without any irrigation and with a vigor that is nothing short of amazing. After years of fighting to keep it off my land, I suddenly realized I should be encouraging it and using it! Buddleia is another very vigorous grower.

Woody material works better as mulch and breaks down faster if shredded first. I have recently rediscovered a small electric chipper I bought at a garage sale about ten years ago and promptly forgot about. It gives me an easy way to chip the small brush (up to an inch in diameter) that is produced so abundantly.

Wild plants can be another source of mulch and grow well without anything from you. You might think about retaining some existing plants just for this purpose. When I cut all of the old Elderberry bushes on my property to the ground, they came back re-invigorated and sent up masses of vigorous new growth (12 feet in one summer).

A Comfrey fertility bed

This fast growing, vigorous and independent plant is ideally suited to growing in a fertility bed. It is very easily grown from root cuttings, planted 24 inches apart in offset rows. For maximum productivity it should have full sun and a deep fertile, moisture retentive soil. Mulch the newly planted bed to conserve moisture and keep down weeds until it gets established. Depending upon growth you should be able to cut it once or twice in the first year.

For maximum growth the Comfrey bed should be kept well watered (gray water is good) and fertilized with anything you have available. Urine is good because it is high in available nitrogen and free. Once Comfrey gets going it is very vigorous and can compete against most weeds. You can cut the leaves (an inch above the ground) whenever there is enough growth to justify it, which should be 5 or 6 times in a season. Also cut off any flower heads that form.

To increase the size of the bed, simply remove the crowns by cutting through the newly harvested plants with a spade 3 inches underground. Divide these to leave at least one growing point on each piece and replant. The severed roots remaining in the ground will re-sprout and become new plants, making the original bed even denser.

Comfrey leaves can be used as mulch, in the compost pile or directly as fertilizer. The wilted leaves are a nutrient rich substitute for compost and are very useful for growing potatoes and other hungry crops.

Compost

Compost is one of the cornerstones of traditional organic vegetable gardening for a variety of reasons.

- It is the best source of organic matter and humus, for the garden. It is so valuable that the pile has been called the heart of the intensive organic garden.
- It contains every nutrient that plants need, including all of the micronutrients.
- Compost is full of beneficial microorganisms. A teaspoonful of compost may contain 1 billion bacteria, 2500 protozoa, 300 feet of fungal hyphae and 150 nematodes. A half inch layer of compost can be used to inoculate poor soil with these organisms. If you also add a suitable food source (and have some luck) they will multiply in your soil.
- Composting is a great way to dispose of any organic waste from the garden and house.
- Compost suppresses a variety of soil pathogens, including those that cause Damping Off.
- The composting process breaks down toxins such as pesticides and can bind heavy metals to make them unavailable to plants.

Composting as recycling

In recent years we have begun to realize the importance of recycling wastes and composting is particularly useful in this regard. It allows you to take materials that would otherwise end up in the landfill and recycle them into a product your garden needs. The most commonly composted household materials are kitchen scraps, but almost any organic material can be composted (so long as it hasn't been treated with toxic chemicals).

City people often think that compost making must be a smelly affair. They assume that rotting vegetation, food scraps and manure must smell and attract flies and vermin. However rotting isn't composting; there is a big difference between a well-made compost pile and a heap of garbage. In fact composting is actually the best way to dispose of organic waste without creating these problems.

Building a compost pile

There is no great mystery to making compost, all you have to do is combine all of the materials in the right proportions of carbon rich materials to nitrogen rich materials, and keep them moist. The artificially warm and humid environment created inside the pile simply accelerates the process of decay that goes on in nature all the time. You don't even have to be too precise with the proportions. A pile with too much nitrogen will simply vent off the excess, a pile with too much carbon will just work more slowly (adding nitrogen rich urine can help this).

Some gardeners don't like hot composting, arguing that too much of the organic matter is consumed by soil organisms and doesn't end up benefitting the soil. They say if you must compost you should use cool piles (made with more carbon and less nitrogen), even though they take longer to work and don't kill weeds seeds and pathogens as thoroughly.

Start building a pile by laying down a 6" base layer of somewhat woody material, such as small brush, or Brassica or Sunflower stems. This defines the bottom of the pile and improves drainage and aeration. Cover this with a 4 " deep layer of weeds, green manure and any other green plants, followed by a 2 - 3" layer of manure (horse manure is the easiest to find in quantity). Follow this with a 3" layer of wetted straw or dry plants and finally a thin 1" layer of soil. If any of these layers are dry you should moisten them thoroughly as you lay them down.

Repeat these four layers (greens, manure, straw, soil) alternately until the pile is of the desired height (4' - 5' is good). Concentrate on building the sides of the pile, keeping them as nearly vertical as possible and the inside will take care of itself. When you get near the top start to slope the sides inwards to give a slight peak (a steeper pitch is good in wet climates). Some gardeners finish off the pile with a thick layer of straw.

It isn't really necessary to turn a well-made and well-maintained pile, but it speeds up the composting process and ensures that the whole pile heats up uniformly. If you don't turn a pile, the outer 10" layer of the pile won't heat up sufficiently to decompose, or kill pathogens and weed seeds. When a pile is used, this outer part can be stripped off separately and composted again.

If you turn the cooling pile it will heat up a second time as more air is supplied and the goodies in the outer layers are consumed. It won't get as hot as it did the first time though.

For more information on how compost works refer to my book The Organic Gardeners Handbook. Of course it's very convenient for me to suggest you buy another of my books, but I don't want to repeat myself too much here.

Planting the compost pile

You can recover some of the nutrients that inevitably leach out of a compost pile by planting vigorous vegetables such as Squash or tomatoes alongside it.

Pests

If your idea of composting is to throw a bucket of food scraps out onto a pile every few days, you are going to have problems. Such a pile won't heat up very much because it isn't really a compost pile, it is a supermarket for rats, skunks, raccoons, dogs, bears, flies and other wildlife. A properly made pile will heat up quickly, and there should be no problems with foraging pests. Meat, bones and other animal products are the commonest cause of problems so are often kept out of the pile (though any recognizable food waste is a potential lure). A cap of soil or straw will keep flies out of a pile, until it starts to heat up.

Using compost as an inoculant

Compost plugs can be used to inoculate impoverished soil. You simply grow plants in pots full of compost and then plant them out in the poor soil. Of course you could simply put a handful of compost in the hole when planting. You then mulch around the plant to protect it (and the compost). With a little luck the microorganisms will migrate into the soil around them.

Growing compost materials

Any plant can be composted of course, but some plants can be specially grown to supply the high volume of material needed to make a compost pile. A good compost plant grows quickly, produces lots of biomass, regenerates quickly after cutting and is easily propagated (some also fix nitrogen). Sunflowers, Comfrey, Corn, Sweet Clover, African Marigold and Hemp and all particularly useful.

If you really get into this you could grow some plants to produce green high nitrogen materials and others to produce the more woody highly carbonaceous stuff.

Where to grow compost and mulch crops

You could have a designated area for growing mulch and compost crops. This could be fertilized with urine and irrigated with gray water. It could be a polyculture of several different species, each providing a different and complementary benefits. For example you might choose a nitrogen fixer, a deep (or fibrous) rooted crop and a producer of abundant organic matter, (perhaps Bell Beans, Barley and Sunflowers) and a dynamic accumulator. You might also have an area for woody shrubs, such as Broom of Willow.

You don't necessarily have to devote valuable growing bed space to growing these crops; they can be planted in any suitable vacant area. They could also be grown as groundcovers, temporary windbreaks, screens, hedges and more. Smaller plants like comfrey can be grown underneath fruiting trees and shrubs. Annuals can be used as a temporary groundcover. See Alley cropping for another way to grow mulch.

Biochar

Biochar has been in the news recently as a possible way to combat global warming. It's been suggested that we could grow biomass and turn it into biochar, thus locking away the extra carbon and improving the soil at the same time. To me this sounds like wishful thinking, in that I can't imagine any way we could do this on the required massive industrial scale. I only mention biochar here because of its potential for home garden use.

In the Amazon rain forest native tribes once created very fertile gardens by adding charcoal to the soil (probably by a process of slash and char). These soils are still unusually fertile after hundreds of years and are known as "terra preta de indio". It isn't quite clear exactly how charcoal benefits the soil because it doesn't contain many available nutrients, but it may somehow stimulate soil organisms, especially mycorrhizal fungi. It also increases cation exchange capacity (which improves nutrient uptake and decreases leaching), raises soil pH and has other benefits.

Though I can't quite see the logic of burning wood to reduce global warming, I can see the logic of turning that pile of wood or yard waste into useful charcoal, rather than simply burning it. If this can increase your soil fertility and prevent about 50 percent of the carbon from entering the atmosphere, then it may be worth experimenting with.

Making biochar

Making charcoal is a skill to be learned like anything else. If you really get into it you could grow your own biomass and char it in an oil drum kiln (this is the simplest and cleanest way). Coppiced Willow or Hazel could be grown for this (though artists might want to steal your fine willow charcoal for their own nefarious purposes). There are even stoves you can cook with and produce biochar at the same time. Do it on a big enough scale and one day you may be selling carbon credits to Exxon.

Any plant material (prunings, poles, brushwood, straw) can be used to make charcoal, but wood is most often used. The best wood is dry hardwood of a uniform thickness (the latter is important because you want it all to char at the same rate).

To make charcoal you need to be able to control the air supply of the burning wood, which slows the rate of burn. Large quantities are usually made by burning the wood in a trench. Small quantities of charcoal can be made more easily in an oil drum kiln.

To make charcoal in quantity you dig a trench and fill it with wood, then start a fire in the normal way. Leave it to burn until the early white smoke (which contains a lot of moisture) disappears. You then cover the fire with a layer of soil to deprive it of oxygen. It will then smolder and char rather than burning up completely. When all of the wood has turned to charcoal you spray water on the fire to extinguish it.

When the charcoal has cooled sufficiently it can be broken down to gravel size pieces or less (beware of inhaling the dust). The best way to do this is to put the charcoal in a metal bucket and crush it with a heavy wooden post. It is then composted (or soaked in compost tea) to add nutrients and beneficial organisms. You then incorporate it into the top few inches of soil, adding up to 1 lb, of charcoal per square foot.

If you use a wood stove you might make a habit of collecting any pieces of charred wood for adding to the garden.

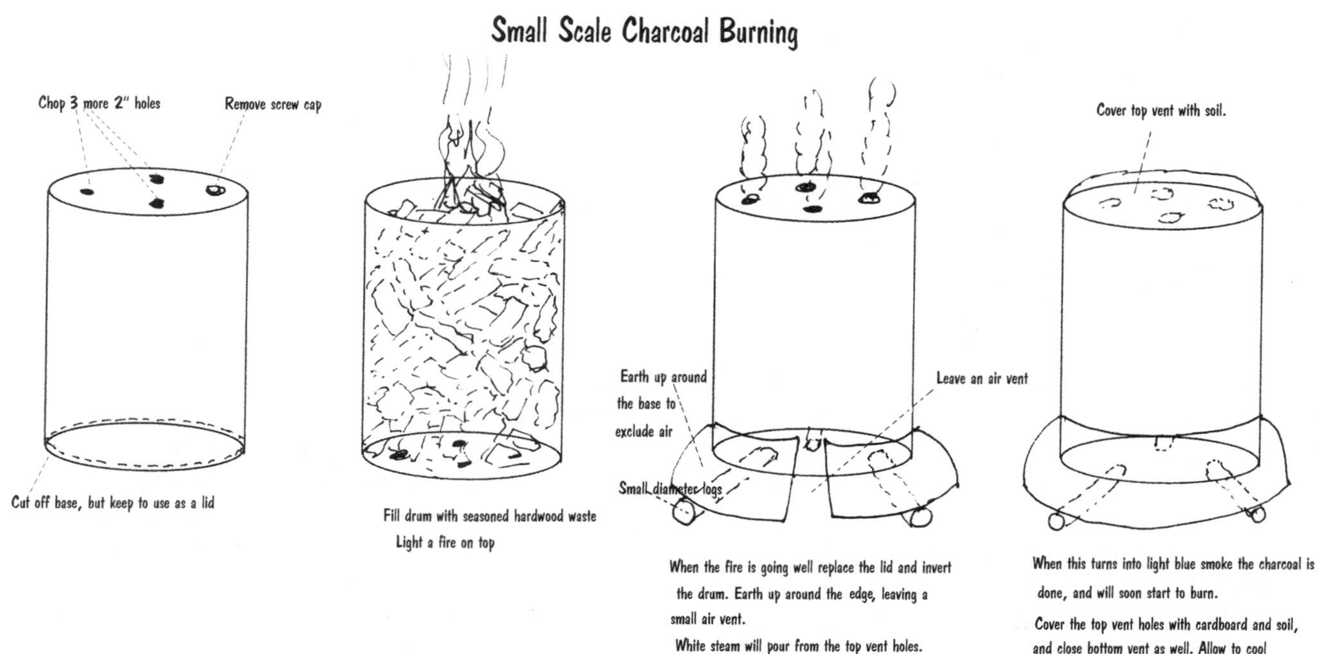

Water and irrigation

The axiom water is life is nowhere more apparent than in the garden. With abundant water you have a luxuriant green jungle, without it you have a brown desert. All garden life needs water, not only plants but also birds, insects, earthworms, fungi, algae, bacteria and everything else.

It seems self evident that a garden should only use the amount of water that is sustainable for its location, but this is far from the case at present. People moving to Arizona and Nevada often expect to be able to grow the same kinds of gardens they had when they lived in New Jersey or Oregon. In many places these green oases are totally dependent upon rapidly diminishing groundwater supplies.

Many gardeners use a lot of water to keep their gardens alive, but in the future this may get so expensive that habits will have to change. I have talked to people who already pay $200 a month for water to keep their gardens alive through the summer. Change is already starting to happen in some places: just yesterday I saw an astro-turf lawn being laid in someone's garden, California recently approved the use of gray water in the garden without a permit.

The amount of water your garden needs will depend upon the climate (among other things). In California the conscientious gardener is more limited by water than any other factor. I adhere to the idea that you should only use as much water as falls on your land (or should I say is absorbed by it) as rain. However in our climate we get no rainfall at all for the warmest 6 months of the year. If we are to grow enough food to feed ourselves we need some way of storing rainfall for use during this time. This is most often stored in reservoirs and sold to us by the water company. It can also be stored in the ground and pumped to the surface through a well, or it is stored in a tank, ready for immediate gravity fed use.

Irrigation increases the range of plants you can grow successfully in dry climates and thereby increases the productivity of your garden. It isn't hard to justify using irrigation water in our gardens if they produce food in return. We grow food using much less water than commercial growers, so even when we are using water in our gardens, we are saving it elsewhere. Used thoughtfully a little irrigation water can go a long way.

Irrigation has been a mixed blessing. On the one hand it has enabled us to grow food in places where we otherwise couldn't, but it has also encouraged us to develop totally unsustainable landscapes and agricultural systems. In industrialized countries we have become incredibly wasteful with our water resources. It may seem ridiculous to talk about peak water as we talk about peak oil, but the era of cheap and abundant water is just about over. In recent years fresh water is becoming increasingly expensive and restrictions on its use are becoming more frequent. When global warming really starts to affect weather patterns, what we think of as drought may become normal in many areas.

Water sources

Tap water

In cities your water usually comes out of a tap. This is the ultimate in convenience, though of course you have to pay for it. This is very clean and already under pressure, ready for use in irrigation. It is getting more expensive all the time though and often contains a lot of chlorine (leave it in open tubs for this to dissipate).

River or creek water

This is often used in remote areas, though it is not always legal to take it. If it is to be used in a drip system it will need some serious filtering.

Well water

This is generally of good quality because it has been filtered through the soil. If you live in the vicinity of a potential source of pollution (industrial site, landfill, toxic waste dump, gas station) it may be a good idea to test your well water for chemical and biological pollutants. Nitrates and phosphates are the commonest problems on agricultural land. Many rural wells are now contaminated with MTBE, perchlorates and other industrial chemicals. Of course you may have to use this water anyway, if that's all you have (though you could also make a serious effort to collect rainwater).

Rainwater

The best source of irrigation water is that which nature drops on to your garden as rainfall. This is very clean and contains no dissolved salts or other potential problems. It may even contain traces of plant nutrients such as nitrogen and sulfur.

In the most blessed areas rainfall comes regularly and abundantly during the warm months. In such areas you don't even have to think about water, it just falls and soaks in to the ground (you may even have to think about ways of getting rid of excess water). In dry climates you have to think about rainfall very carefully. It makes no sense to be trying to get rid of rainwater one month and then having to pay a hefty water bill to keep your plants alive a few months later .

Drainage

Drainage means making sure that water goes where you want it to go and doesn't go where you don't want it. In planning for drainage you need to look at the site from the viewpoint of a drop of water and figure out where it will travel. As long as the land is sloping any surface water will keep moving. When it levels out (or becomes a hollow) the water will stop moving and start to accumulate.

It is important to keep water decentralized by directing its flow in different directions. Many small flows can be dealt with much more easily than one big flow. In some cases it may be important to get water away from certain parts of the property, so it doesn't cause damage. At other times you may want to direct it to where it can do the most good.

Surface water is usually dealt with by grading, which means creating a slight slope so any runoff moves in the direction you want it to. It doesn't take much slope to direct water and in an established landscape it may not even be obvious that there is one. Of course you also have to give that water somewhere to go, whether a pond, a wetland, a wash, a retention basin or a swale.

Don't do any grading unless it is essential (and be especially careful about not altering the grade around established trees). If you must do it, then do it right because you can't change it easily once the garden is built and planted.

Subsurface water can be removed with perforated pipe drains (remember that counter-intuitively the holes go to the bottom, not the top). However it is best to avoid drain pipes if possible, they are much less reliable than grading. Pipes should slope 1/8" per foot minimum.

If an area is very wet you might leave it alone as natural vegetation (probably the best idea), or you could plant specially adapted crops (such as basket Willows). You might also excavate it to form a pond or marsh.

Erosion control

Any time water moves over bare soil there is the potential for soil erosion. This is most commonly seen on overgrazed hillsides, but can occur on any poorly vegetated slopes. The angle of the slope, the amount of vegetation, the type of soil and the amount of rainfall will determine how serious the problem is. It doesn't take a genius to figure out how to prevent erosion, you just have to keep the soil covered and stop the water from moving.

The best way to prevent erosion is to keep the soil covered with a variety of native plants: trees, shrubs, groundcovers and perennials. Several species growing together work better than a single species, because they have different root depths and different levels of cover. Use mulch to cover any bare soil between the plants until they get established (this will occur much more quickly if they are irrigated in dry weather).

You can also stop the water moving by creating obstacles, such as swales (these are often planted with native species), hay bales, berms and terraces. On steeper slopes you can use a brush mat mulch, held in place with wires and stakes.

Check dams

These are not dams in the traditional sense in that they don't impound water. They are placed across an eroding gully to slow down the flow of water, so it drops its load of sediment and has a chance to soak into the soil. A simple check dam might be a wall of hay bales, rocks or gabions, or even a pile of wood chips (for a small gully). Over time the sediment intercepted by the check dam can accumulate and create a flat level area of deep rich soil. Native Americans often made gardens in these places because the soil can be richer and moister than elsewhere.

A series of small check dams less than 2 feet tall (with the base of one on a level with the top of the next) works better than one large dam. Each should be embedded into the sides of the gully and should have a low spot for water to flow over. There should also be an apron of rocks to break the flow of any falling water so it doesn't cause erosion.

Rain

Celebrate the rain

Growing up in England, rain was more of a topic for complaint that celebration, but absence makes the heart grow fonder. Since I have lived in California and seen what a low rainfall landscape looks like, my viewpoint has changed completely. Rain brings life and the fact that it is raining is nearly always good.

To increase your awareness of the rain that falls on your garden, you could use it to make a living sculpture with a series of linked water features that come alive every time it rains. Gargoyles and rain chains on the roof, could pour water into tubs and bowls, which then runs along canals or rills and over a waterfall into a pond and finally out through a spillway into the soil. This could really help to brighten up the winter rainy season. In areas with year round rainfall it can be even more appreciated as some of it will fall in the summer when you are out in the garden.

Rainwater infiltration

In the past rainwater was looked upon as an inconvenience, a waste product to be disposed of as quickly, efficiently and safely as possible. Things have started to change as water has become more expensive and in dry climates improving rainwater infiltration should be a high priority. To do this you need to understand how water moves across your land and where it goes.

In most cases the land will already retain most of the water that falls on it, without any problem. You just have to deal with those areas where it runs off or causes erosion for some reason. Go out in the rain and these places should be obvious because you will see accumulated water running downhill.

Soil varies enormously in its ability to absorb water. A couple of days ago we had 5 inches of rain overnight in an early fall rain, yet when I dug around I found places where the ground was still dry only 3 inches down. When rain falls very rapidly on to sloping ground, it quickly saturates the surface soil until no more can enter (until it has percolated down). Further rain then just runs off straight downhill. To prevent this you need to make the water stand still long enough to soak in.

Enhancing rainwater infiltration

Nature has always taken care of rainwater infiltration on your land and will continue to do so unless you mess it up by creating bare soil, paths, driveways and roofs. These become a problem because they allow water to accumulate in volume and move quickly. Of course when you start landscaping you will often do these very things, and may have take steps to prevent erosion and enhance infiltration (almost the same thing). Water becomes a problem when it accumulates in volume and starts to move.

In very dry climates water is too precious to just let it run off down storm drains, so you need to enhance the soils ability to absorb it. You do this by creating obstacles to slow down the flow, so it has time to soak into the soil. You may also want to redirect the natural flow of water, so it soaks into the soil where it can be of the most use. By giving runoff water somewhere to go, you prevent it becoming an erosion problem lower down. You should also have a provision for handling any overflow water that makes it through the whole system.

Water travels from the highest to the lowest spots by the most direct (steepest) route downhill. It moves more quickly on slopes and slows down or stops on the flat. Your aim is to slow down the water flow long enough for it to soak in to the soil, or to direct it to low spots where it can soak in.

Steep or unstable slopes should never be encouraged to absorb water, as it can cause them to slide. Instead water should be drained away from these areas.

Permeable paving should be used in most places as it allow water to go right through it. Impervious surfaces are used when you want to concentrate and collect the water (and have somewhere for it to go).

Vegetation
The most fundamental way to encourage water to percolate into the soil is to ensure that the ground is covered with vegetation. This slows down the movement of water (both as it falls and on the ground) and slows it down until it has a chance to soak into the ground. Rainwater rarely runs off of thickly vegetated slopes.

Swales
A swale is a low wide ditch that runs around the contour of a hill. Its purpose is to intercept rainfall and hold it in place until it percolates into the soil They work best on low to moderate slopes with light soils. A good swale may catch so much water it creates its own ecological niche that is able to sustain more plant life than the surrounding slope.

Building a swale
A swale can be a long continuous trench, or it might be a series of short bow shaped swales. If you carefully follow the topography of the land and watch where runoff flows, you may find that small, strategically placed swales, only a few inches deep are sufficient to intercept all of the runoff and allow it to soak in.

The size of the swales and their distance apart will depend upon slope angle, the porosity of the soil and the rainfall pattern. The steeper the slope, or the heavier the rainfall, the deeper and closer together the swales should be. Obviously you don't need to plan for a deluge of biblical proportions, but you should arrange for any overflow from a swale to have somewhere to go. The bigger the swale the more water it can hold and the longer it will work effectively before getting filled with soil. It should probably be slightly deeper than you anticipate, to allow for the fact that they will fill with sediment over time.

A shallow swale can usually be dug fairly quickly with a spade or shovel. Just throw the soil to the downhill side to form a berm. You can compact this berm with your feet but should leave the soil in the swale loose so water can soak in easily. The bare soil of the newly built swale should be covered with mulch to protect it until plants get established.

Over time silt and organic matter may accumulate in the swale and turn it into a level terrace. If you don't want this to happen you will have to clean it out occasionally.

A swale must be accurately placed along the contour to work well. If it isn't then water will run down and accumulate in the lowest spots (and possibly overflow). The simplest tool for finding the level contour is the A-frame level (a large simple tripod with a plumb bob in the middle), though a water, builders or laser level will be more accurate and faster.

Diversion swale
A diversion swale slopes slightly downhill so water moves along it As the name suggests it is used to catch runoff from a slope and divert it to where you want it (perhaps a pond, a retention basin, or to other earthworks). Such a swale may resemble a creek bed during rain. These are usually planted with low groundcover such as grass to prevent erosion (larger plants such as shrubs could impede the water flow). In very dry climates you might channel water along a shallow diversion swale so it terminates around a fruit tree, where the water can soak in where it is needed.

Berms
Another way to control and direct water flow on low slopes is to use berms. A fairly stable berm can be made using brushwood, manure and topsoil. The brushwood is piled up along the contour (this is a good way to get rid of unwanted woody material), in a pile that is four times as wide as it is high. This is then covered with a layer of manure (the extra nitrogen helps it decompose) and then a layer of soil (get this from the uphill side to create a swale). This kind of berm is essentially a slow compost pile and will settle considerably as it decomposes (by up to two-thirds its height). The next step is to plant something on it to stabilize it. This could be any suitable useful plants.

Light runoff may be stopped with fairly rudimentary berms, made by placing logs or brush across the contour. Use stakes to anchor the logs or partially bury them. If you have lots of wood chips, they could be used to make a water-intercepting berm that eventually breaks down and enriches the soil. All of these will accumulate the silt that is washed downhill and slowly decompose to add humus to the soil. If there are no logs or wood chips then rocks can perform the same function. If you don't have logs or brush or rocks you live in a seriously barren place (hopefully you have some rainfall to collect). In such a place you can dig trenches (swales) and use soil for the berm.

Paths, fences, growing beds and hedges can all be placed along the contour to slow down moving water and give it time to soak in.

Rainwater retention basins

These are mostly used in urban areas where there are large areas of impervious paved surfaces shedding large volumes of runoff water. These basins catch and hold this water and allow it to sit until it soaks into the soil. They are occasionally used in gardens to enable runoff from the roof or driveway to soak into the soil rather than entering storm drains. When I built my house I grumbled about having to pay an engineer for calculations on how to deal with runoff from the roof, but now I appreciate the reason for them.

The placement of a retention basin is largely determined by the soil and the topography of the land. The area should be relatively flat, otherwise considerable earth moving may be needed. Ideally it should also be sunny for maximum plant growth. It doesn't have to be close to the house, because water from the roof can go along a pipe or canal to the basin,

The size of the basin depends upon the amount of runoff it has to deal with and how well the soil drains (dig a hole 6" deep and fill with water, it should drain away within 24 hours). The basin should be at least twice as long as it is wide, with a minimum width of 10 feet. To collect the water coming from a roof might require a basin roughly the size of the roof. The basin is an evenly sloped level shallow depression 6-18" deep.

The basin receives water every time it rains, so the moisture level will fluctuate constantly. It may be totally dry or it may be temporarily submerged under water. It shouldn't contain standing water for more than a day or two, otherwise mosquitoes may start to breed.

In areas of very high rainfall there may be several basins in a series, one draining into another. There should be a spillway to channel the excess water if they all get completely full.

The retention basin can be looked upon as another kind of habitat and planted with suitably adapted useful species. The vegetation must be tolerant of temporary flooding and a wide range of moisture levels from dry to saturated. Put plants with higher water needs at the bottom of the basin and more drought tolerant ones at the edge. In very wet areas you might have to use water tolerant species such as Gotu Kola or Water Purslane. In dry areas trees are often planted around the basin to take advantage of the accumulated water. The vegetation is normally cut every spring and used as mulch or taken away for composting.

French drain (Soakaway pit or dry well)

A French drain works like a retention basin, but is hidden in the ground. Its purpose is to hold runoff water until it can percolate into the soil. It consists of a big hole filled with rock (it is usually covered with landscape fabric to prevent it slowly filling with sediment). The voids between the rocks fill with water during heavy rain, and hold it until it can soak into the soil. There should also be an overflow to channel excess water away if it fills up.

Rainwater storage

Rainfall is often erratic even in humid areas; it might rain for weeks and then be dry for weeks. It may dump 2 inches of rain in an hour and then be dry for a month. If you are to have this water available when you need it, you have to store it in some way.

An inch of rain equals .623 gallons of water per square foot, so an inch of rain falling on an acre of land gives you 27000 gallons of water. The average winter rainfall at my house is around 50 inches, which means my 2.5 acres receives over 3 million gallons of water every year.

The only way to store large quantities of water is in the soil. This is known as passive storage because it doesn't require any active piping, pumps or tanks. On good soil this happens naturally without your involvement, but on poor soil you might have to help the water to infiltrate into the soil.

The soil is an enormous sponge that can absorb and holds huge quantities of water almost indefinitely with no evaporation. Water held by the soil doesn't go stagnant, breed mosquitoes or cost anything to store;

it just sits there, available for plants to use in the hot dry days of summer. Many trees, shrubs and perennial plants can send down roots far enough to tap into this ground water, so we don't even have to pump it out of the ground. My established fruit trees go through 6 rainless summer months (and fruit heavily) just on the rainwater held by the soil.

The easiest way to use rainwater is to let it percolate into the soil and then pump it back out via a well. Of course this is how most rural properties get their water. If you don't have a well, or live in a city and have to rely on expensive tap water, you should investigate active storage systems.

How much water can you collect?

To estimate how much rainwater you can collect from your roof, multiply its footprint (looking down directly from above, not its actual surface area) in square feet by the average yearly rainfall in inches. Divide this number by 12 to get the number of cubic feet of water. Then multiply this by 7.5 to get the number of gallons.

For example, my roof is approximately 800 square feet and we get about 50 inches of rain per year. This works out to 40000, which divided by 12 equals 3333. Multiply this by 7.5 and you get 25,000 gallons of water. If only storing it were as easy as calculating it!

Runoff from larger surfaces such as roads, paths and hillsides might also be collected. Rainwater knows no boundaries, so you might even be able to collect water from neighboring land. A paved driveway could be shaped to collect water and deliver it to a pond or tank. Be aware that driveway runoff may be contaminated unless you take precautions. Concrete is the best material for this and it should be kept clean, with no oil or other chemicals on it. It is possible to clean dirty water with wetland plants or even fungi, but this is perhaps a little too complex for the moment.

Active storage

Water in barrels, tanks or ponds is called active storage because it is immediately available for use This should ideally be stored high up on the property, so it can be gravity fed to where it is needed, without electricity or pumps. The drawback to active storage is that it usually costs money and to store a lot of water can cost a lot of money. The strategy you adopt will depend upon your climate, rainfall pattern and the depth of your pocket.

In dry areas with rain throughout the growing season, storage is pretty simple. All you need to do is store enough water from recent rains to see you through any rainless stretches. If you run out of stored water you will just have to resort to tap water, no big deal. A few rain barrels might be all the storage you need, or perhaps an old discarded hot tub or a couple of old water beds. Concrete or galvanized metal culvert sections can also work well.

Rainwater collection is particularly useful in arid areas that get infrequent but heavy summer showers. In such areas rainwater can provide for most of your irrigation needs.

I live in an area that is more problematic. We get massive amounts of rain in winter (40 - 100 inches) and none at all in summer. In this situation a storage system has to be big to have any significant effect. Large tanks are expensive to buy, though they may save you money in the long run if you pay monthly water bills. It is possible to make your own tanks out of concrete or ferrocement.

One of the cheapest ways to collect a significant amount of rainwater is in an above ground swimming pool (the vinyl may leach toxins into the water so don't drink it). A more durable alternative is a hole or trench in the ground, lined with pond liner. This should be covered in summer to reduce evaporation and to keep out mosquitoes and children.

Even bigger storage would be a pond or reservoir, which can be of almost unlimited capacity. This doesn't have to be very complicated, it can be simply a large hole in the ground lined with pond liner (essentially a swimming pool). Keep the depth fairly shallow and you don't have to worry about the sides collapsing. In some areas there are restrictions on doing this, so you may want to check with your local building department (it could also present the same drowning hazard as a swimming pool)). Also be aware that large water storage brings with it the possibility of large problems.

Water storage should be placed as high up as you can get it (for gravity flow). It should also have an overflow to carry away any excess water and dispose of it safely (this could be an overflow pipe attached to a perforated pipe, or section of soaker hose.

Rainwater collection systems

Rainwater that lands on buildings is easily collected for garden use, as it falls high up and can be gravity fed to a storage place without the use of pumps. A rainwater collection system usually includes:

- A clean catchment area. In most cases the roof already fills this requirement, it is relatively clean and comes with ready made piping in the form of downspouts. You could also collect rainwater using waterproof fabric awnings.

- Pipes and gutters. These must be large enough to collect the maximum flow of water without overflowing and deliver it to a storage tank. These should be kept free of leaves and other debris that might clog them and cause them to overflow. You can even push water uphill somewhat, so long as the top of the tank is lower than the gutter.

- A storage tank. This should be covered to reduce evaporation and should have screened vents to keep out insects. It should also have an overflow to direct excess water into the soil. It should be dark inside to prevent the growth of algae. The inlet for the tank should have a screen to remove any debris.

Gray water

Gray water is any water that has been used in the house, but doesn't contain sewage (water containing sewage is known as black water - like the security company). Gray water may actually contain minute quantities of sewage, as well as bacteria, viruses and a variety of chemicals so it isn't completely harmless. However once the water enters the soil, bacteria quickly break down any toxins and render them harmless.

In the years from 1996-1999 the average indoor water use in the United States was around 70 gallons per person per day. In dry climates it is just plain crazy to use this water once and then let it drain away, when it could be your biggest source of free water (you already paid for it). This water is already piped and with a little modification of your plumbing (and some of your more wasteful habits) at least half of it could be re-used quite easily.

The state of California has just recently seen the logic of gray water re-use and decided to allow it without requiring permits or expensive systems. Even government bureaucrats can see sense sometimes.

It isn't always necessary or desirable to use gray water in the garden. In areas with ample rainfall all summer it's better if it goes into the leach field to recharge the groundwater. There is also no point in using gray water in winter, when plants don't need it. In fact you should switch your system so gray water goes into your septic system at this time (this is legally mandated in California). Otherwise you may just end up waterlogging your soil and cause runoff and pollution.

Gray water should ideally be kept below the surface (usually under mulch) where the bacteria in active soil can break down the toxic chemicals into their component parts (many of which are plant nutrients).

Gray water may contains some thing plants don't like and generally its better to use it on perennials and shrubs (Willows, Bamboo or Blackberry) rather than annual crops. You might also use it to irrigate fertility crops, such as Reeds or Comfrey, grown in their own special bed. In most places winter rain will prevent any buildup of harmful salts.

If you intend to use gray water for irrigation you can minimize its toxicity by altering your washing habits. Be careful which soaps, shampoos and detergents you use: no boron, high sodium, bleach, water softeners, perfumes or lanolin. Some of the eco-detergents appear to be pretty much harmless to plants, though they do make the water more alkaline.

Purification of gray water

Gray water is usually used for watering the garden directly, but it can also be purified for use in ponds. The best known way to do this is with a gray water treatment marsh. This consists of a shallow (12"-18") pond filled with gravel (to prevent mosquitoes breeding) and planted with marsh plants, such as Cattail, Bulrush (Tule) and Reed. These plants have the ability to supply oxygen to their submerged roots, which enables various species of bacteria to grow around their roots. These are able to break down various pollutants and convert them into plant foods. These marshes don't work in winter because the plants are dormant, but this isn't usually an issue as we generally have plenty of water at this time. Another problem with such systems is that the plants use a proportion of the water for their own purposes.

Over complexity is one of the banes of modern life and we should beware of introducing it into the garden. A gray water treatment marsh feeding a pond is a wonderful thing, but it is usually simpler to just use the gray water directly for irrigating plants (perhaps alternating with irrigation of fresh water). You can then use the clean water you saved to supply a pond

Mycofiltration

Some fungi can be grown in wood chips and the whole mycelial mass can act as a filter to purify water. This system is simpler and cheaper than a treatment marsh and doesn't consume as much water (it does require some expertise though).

Gray water irrigation

If you produce a lot of gray water you should re-organize your household use of water so that it can be more easily re-used when it comes back out.

The cleanest gray water is that wasted while waiting for the hot water tap to get hot. The next cleanest comes from the shower and bathtub, then the washing machine (make sure you use eco-friendly detergent) and finally the kitchen sink. The latter is rich in nutrients, but very dirty (from grease and oils and food particles) and has the potential to cause problems. You could have 2 sinks in the kitchen, one for relatively clean tasks like washing vegetables and another for the dirty jobs. You could also wash your vegetables in the garden sink outdoors. This fairly clean water can go directly onto the garden

You may want to draw up a plan of how the gray water is to be used. Draw out where you are tapping into the house plumbing, where the pipes will go and which garden areas they will supply. This isn't complicated, but it helps you to visualize what needs doing and where. How to get the pipes from A to B (through the foundation?) How to get gravity flow. Where to bury pipes so you don't trip on them or see them (and can drain them in winter). A plan may also help you find them again in a few years time.

An easy way to re-use gray water is to build an outdoor shower or bathtub. This allows you to re-use the water in hot weather when you need it most. Another easy way is to direct your washing machine water into the garden. You might have several perforated pipes buried in different locations and simply move the discharge hose as necessary.

It is very important that gray water is used immediately and not stored for any length of time, otherwise bacteria will start to grow and it will smell bad.

I have found two useful books on using gray water for irrigation, written by two inspired individuals, Art Ludwig (Branched Drain Greywater Systems: A Supplement to Create an Oasis with Gray water, Oasis Design 2000) and Robert Kourik (Gray Water Use in the Landscape, Metamorphic press 1988). Both systems start with a diverter valve that allows you to run water either into the septic tank (in winter when you don't want it in the garden) or out to the gray water system in summer.

Surge tank and hose

Robert Kouriks system consists of a pipe that runs the water into a surge tank (a 50 gallon polyethylene drum works well). There is a washable screen to remove any solids. The bottom of the tank has a tap connected to a hose, which runs the water to any one of a series of buried 10 foot long perforated pipes that act like mini leach fields. You could also just run the hose to mulch basins surrounding trees.

Branched drain

Art Ludwig came up with the branched drain idea, as a foolproof no-maintenance system. This simple system relies on gravity and uses large enough pipes (1 ½ minimum) that they don't get clogged. The gray water is diverted through a series of branched pipes that split the flow and direct it to different areas of the garden. It then flows out into mulch basins (often around trees). The mulch keeps the gray water covered and prevents many problems.

Ludwig recommends that the discharge should be in the air, so solids don't accumulate and back up to block the pipe. There should also be clean outs where necessary, in case something does get clogged.

Assembling your gray water system

When you are ready to assemble your system you should cut and lay all the pipes out on the ground in place and dry fit all the connections. This will help you to work out any problems. Plastic pipe is pretty easy to work with, but its still best not to glue anything until the end. Expensive fittings such as valves can be glued with silicone caulk rather than glue (this allows them to be taken apart and reused if necessary).

Watering plants

If you live in a climate where ample water is supplied by rain you are lucky (though you might not think so when it rains on your garden party). Any dry spells that do occur are usually short and you can do the necessary watering by hand without too much trouble. For longer dry spells you could use a portable sprinkler or oscillator.

In dry climates things are very different and much of your garden work can consist of simply keeping your plants alive. The quantity of water you have available will determine how many plants you can grow and how much food they will produce. In such circumstances watering a large garden by hand is totally impractical and even portable sprinklers can take a lot of time. In such situations we can turn to technology (albeit a simple one) in the form of drip irrigation.

Water requirements of plants

This varies enormously of course, some plants live in water all of their lives, some desert plants don't need watering at all. Native plants can survive on what nature provides, vegetable crops generally need a constant supply of water. Newly planted plants need watering more regularly than established plants, because they haven't developed an extensive root system.

Of course the weather also has a big effect on the amount of water your plants use. They need a lot more water in hot sunny windy weather, than they do when it is cool and humid.

Soils and water

The type of soil affects how often you need to water, as well as how you water.

Sandy soil: Water moves through sandy soil easily, so it fills up or dries out fairly quickly. Such soils don't have a large reservoir of water, so must be watered frequently in dry weather to keep plants supplied. Offsetting this to some extent is the fact that roots can penetrate more easily and deeply in search of water.

Clay soil: Water moves through clay very slowly because of the small pore size, and often puddles on the surface or runs off downhill. For this reason you should water a clay soil slowly, using lower flow drippers and leaving them on for longer. Clay soils can hold as much as 40% water at field capacity, so don't need watering as frequently as sandy ones. Water also drains from clay soil slowly, which can be a problem in wet climates.

Silt soil: These have characteristics somewhere between those of sand and clay.

When to water

It is important to learn the subtle signs that indicate plants are in need of water. As the amount of available water declines, plants start to lose the sheen on their leaves. As their stress increases they sag slightly instead of standing rigidly upright, and leaf edges may start to curl. Then the leaves and growing tips wilt and go limp. If they still don't get any water the leaf areas start to die and don't recover even when watered. Ideally you should never allow any water stress to occur, because it slows down growth.

Wilting isn't always a sign that plants need water, in very hot and sunny weather they will often wilt intentionally to reduce water loss. However they recover quickly as soon as the temperature drops. Wilting can also be a sign of disease.

The evapotranspiration rate is a measure of the rate of water loss from the soil from combined evaporation and transpiration. If you know the evapotranspiration rate then you know how much water the soil is losing and how much you need to apply to keep the garden growing. Computerized smart controllers use this information and adjust watering accordingly. These are most useful where the weather changes frequently, less so if it is predictably hot and dry all the time.

Many trees and shrubs only need irrigation for the first year or two. Once they get established and develop a good root system they can find water deep underground.

Checking soil moisture

Check the moisture level of the soil by digging down to the depth of your index finger (about 4″) and picking up a small amount of soil. If the soil is so dry it won't squeeze into a ball, then it needs water.

Canary plants

Some plants are much more prone to wilting than others, especially those with big thin leaves, such as Sunflowers (the best), Grapes, Mallows, Cannas and the Cucurbits. You can use these plants as early warning "canary plants" to indicate when the soil is getting dry and water is harder to obtain. These plants will nearly always wilt in the hot afternoon sun, but soon recover when the temperature drops. If they don't recover quickly it tells you that water is getting harder to obtain and you will need to irrigate soon. Spot plant these species around the garden to give you a quick visual cue of the state of soil moisture in different places.

Irrigation options

Hand watering

Old fashioned hand watering has always been the best way to water plants and will continue to be until someone invents the hydrobot smart irrigation robot. It is very responsive so each plant can get exactly the quantity of water it requires under the circumstances. It also gets you out into the garden and in contact with each plant in turn, which helps you to notice when problems arise. The big drawback is that it takes a long time to thoroughly soak the soil and not just dampen the surface (leaving the soil dry an inch down). Hand watering works best in small gardens in humid climates that have lots of rain throughout the growing season (i.e. when you don't have to do much of it).

If you only have a few plants they can be watered with a watering can. This can be filled anywhere, but traditionally there would be a large tank of water in the garden to dunk them in (this is quicker than filling from a tap). Larger areas are most effectively watered with a hose and some kind of spray nozzle or wand (though you can make an accurate spray by simply putting your thumb over the end of the hose.

To get an idea of how much water a hose is putting out, time how long it takes to fill a 5 gallon bucket. As a rough idea a ½" hose can move 240 gallons of water per hour. A ¾" hose can deliver 480 gallons per hour. On average it takes me about 45 seconds to fill a hose, which works out to about 400 gallons an hour.

Portable sprinklers

Areas that are too large for hand watering can be irrigated with a portable oscillator or sprinkler. These can be adjusted to water different sized areas and at their maximum setting can cover quite a big area. They can save a lot of work, but waste a lot of water from evaporation, wind, and by watering the whole area whether it contains crop plants or not. They are most useful in humid areas to get you through extended dry spells, where the cost of a permanent irrigation system isn't justified.

Clay pot irrigation

In India and elsewhere clay pots are buried in the ground alongside plants and filled with water. The water slowly seeps out through the porous clay and keeps the plant supplied. You can use large clay plant pots for this, if you seal up the drainage hole (use caulk) and cover the top with a board or slate. More modern alternatives are perforated tin cans or plastic milk jugs (punch a few holes in the bottom and cover the opening with a piece of mesh, held in place with a rubber band, to stop insects falling in). You then bury them up to the neck and fill as needed.

A similar setup consists of a 5 gal plastic bucket with a ⅛" hole at the bottom edge. The water will slowly drain out and drip irrigate the plant. These are quite portable and can be moved around as needed (have a plug so you can close the hole for carrying the bucket). They are useful for isolated plants that only need occasional watering and don't justify a drip line.

Underground sprinkler systems

These are used in conventional gardens for lawns and groundcovers, as they quickly deliver a large volume of water to a wide area. They can be adapted for watering vegetable beds, but waste a lot of water and don't work as well as a drip system. If your garden already has one of these installed you can easily convert it to a drip system by removing the sprinkler heads and attaching drip lines. You can still use all of the piping, valves and timer.

Sprayers and Micro-sprinklers

These use less water than conventional sprinklers, but more than drippers. They wet the ground over a wider area than a drip system and are useful for watering small areas of closely spaced plants. They are also good for watering summer salad beds as they also have a cooling effect. A drawback with micro-sprinklers is that they are quite fragile and easily damaged or displaced. Another problem is that they should not be on the same circuit as drippers.

Soaker hose

This is made from recycled tires and oozes water down its entire length. It is good for growing vegetable crops because it wets the soil fairly evenly and is easy to move around. It can be buried under the soil surface so the surface doesn't get wet and grow weeds (this also reduces U. V. exposure).

There are some drawbacks so soaker hose. It's easily damaged (I have speared it with a fork more times than I care to remember - fix it with a hose repair kit). Another drawback is that it loses porosity over time, due to clogging from hard water, algae or small particles (a good filter will help to prevent this). This means different hoses often have different degrees of porosity, and you can't join them together because they won't water evenly. Also a run of soaker hose can't be much longer than 50 or 75 feet, as the pressure from start to end will vary too much.

Your soaker hose will last longer if you roll it up and store it inside for the winter (put it somewhere rodents won't chew it).

Garden plumbing

For maximum efficiency you should have water sources at convenient locations around the garden. Nothing saves frustration (and ensures efficient watering) like having water right where you need it, when you need it. You can waste a lot of time walking 50 yards to connect the hose and turning it on, then dragging it back to the dry plants, watering, then walking back to turn it off. This is a sure way for plants to get neglected.

The plumbing system usually consists of PVC pipe (though see Plastics in the garden) buried at least 12" underground. Ideally you will run these along the edge of paths, so you know where they are located (and can dig them up without disturbing paths or plantings). The risers coming out of the ground should be metal and should be attached to wooden posts.

In a large garden you may have several hydrozones (areas of plants with similar water requirements), each with its own set of zones and centered on a water source. Some of these will be high water use (near the house) and some will be low water use (further away). The areas between the zones will be categorized as low water use.

The time to install water pipes and faucets is right at the beginning, while there is nothing to disturb.

You can ornament your taps with various cast bronze figures. I used to think these were rather kitsch, but they are actually useful if you have weak hands or arthritis, as they can be easier to turn (if you choose the right one).

Drip irrigation

If you live in a dry climate you will probably turn to some kind of drip system eventually (they were first developed in Israel as a way to minimize water use). A good irrigation system should supply water to your plants without wasting any to evaporation, wind or watering weeds. It becomes the vascular system for the garden and can keep your plants growing at maximum productivity while requiring a minimum of water and attention.

These systems can vary in complexity, from a simple stand alone manually operated circuit above ground, to multiple automated circuits, with timer, control valves and underground piping. They take a while to set up, as there are many small pieces, but they are simple enough to put together. Once this is done they are economical and labor saving to use. I recently put together a fairly complex system, with 5 zones and an automatic timer, over the course of a few days (and that included hand digging all the trenches). My total cost was somewhere around $500 for parts.

In a very dry climate setting up an irrigation system may be an early priority. You set up the piping system in the early stages of garden building, but don't put the drip lines in until the beds are complete (you can even put the line into a fully planted bed).

If you are interested in drip systems I suggest you examine the commercial literature to see what is available. Then check out the various systems in hardware stores, garden centers and more specialist stores. The big manufacturers of irrigation equipment have some very informative free manuals and online tutorials on how all of this stuff works.

The advantages of drip systems

- They can reduce water consumption by up to 50% because water only goes where it can be used by your plants. If you have to pay for water the saving in water alone is often enough to justify such a system.
- Water is delivered slowly so there is no runoff or erosion.
- They can increase yields because plants always have water easily available.
- They work with low water pressure (20-40 psi).
- There is less disease because foliage doesn't get wet.
- There is less weed growth because most of the soil surface remains dry, only the part around the plants gets wet.
- If you use an irrigation controller it can reduce the amount of time you have to spend on watering to almost nothing. All you need to do is program the

controller (the complexity of this depends upon the particular controller, some are simple, some not so simple). Then all you then have to do is keep an eye on it and make sure it is working.

- A drip system can help you to use your time and irrigation water more efficiently and so is a very valuable tool for dry areas.
- In hot climates they are the only practical way to water plants in containers.

Reality and drip systems

The advantages of drip systems are quite real, but they have to be both planned and used very carefully, otherwise their advantages can disappear, The biggest problem occurs when you automate your system with an irrigation controller. This is very convenient (the ultimate modern virtue) in that you can just set the timer and forget about watering for the summer. Unfortunately the trade-off is often significantly greater water use (an average of 50% more). This is because they water to a schedule, rather than to the needs of the garden. When I first read that irrigation systems can increase water use, I didn't believe it would apply to me, but it did. It is very important to adjust the watering schedule as weather patterns change.

This technology can also take you a big step away from your garden. It enables you to forget about watering and go do something else, rather than getting out in the garden where you will notice problems as they occur.

Other problems with drip systems include:

- Emitters can get clogged easily and stop working without it being apparent. To reduce clogging always use a good filter system and be meticulous about cleaning it.
- These systems are quite fragile and are easily displaced or damaged by careless walkers, rodents and sunlight (they can be covered with mulch to protect them from sunlight). String trimmers are a major hazard.
- They are made from plastic and eventually become garbage (polyethylene can be recycled but not PVC).

Planning a drip system

Drip systems are most useful for permanent plantings such as trees, shrubs and perennials. Usually you use individual drippers for watering widely spaced plants and drip emitter line for watering areas of closely spaced plants. These don't usually work together, so you need to keep them on different circuits (which is simple enough).

The best way to water the vegetable garden is with drip emitter tubing. This should definitely be on its own separate zone, as it needs more responsive watering, depending upon the crops and stage of growth.

Start planning your system by drawing out an irrigation plan on paper, showing all of the areas to be irrigated, the vegetable garden, front entrance garden, fruit trees, individual trees and various other growing areas. Basically you need to know how much water the plants require, so you know how many drippers to provide and how long to run the system. The water requirements of plants will be affected by slope, sun and other factors. The plan should also show where to put the timer and control valves, as well as where the water supply is coming from.

I already advised dividing larger gardens into separate hydrozones. The number of zones will be determined by the size of your garden and how much water each area requires. The size of each zone might be decided by flow rate (how many gallons of water can you supply to an area), by length of run (200 feet is maximum for ½" pipe)) or by location (the plants in a specific microclimate). Each zone must be small enough for the water supply to handle, with some room to spare for expansion.

Length of pipe

This is important because water pressure drops with distance. For example 200 feet of ½" pipe can supply 240 GPH, but if you double the length of the pipe to 400 feet it can only supply 160 gph. Normally the maximum length for ½ inch pipe should be 200 feet. If you need to go further than this you should use larger ¾ or 1 inch pipe to get to the center of the garden and branch off from this with ½" pipe.

Pipe size	Gravity flow	20 psi
½”	7 gpm 42 gph	14 gpm 840 gph
¾ “	11 gpm 660 gph	23 gpm 1420 gph
1”	16 gpm 960 gph	37 gpm 2220 gph

Flow

The size of an irrigation zone may be determined by how many plants your piping can supply. The volume of water you can deliver depends upon the size of the pipe, its length and the pressure of the water. To get an idea of the flow rate from a tap, you should time how many seconds it takes to fill a 1 gallon bucket and then divide that number into 3600 seconds (an hour). This will give you the number of gallons available in an hour (the maximum flow rate for an irrigation line is generally considered to be 75 percent of this). It's not a good idea to use a line to its absolute capacity right from the start, as you need to be able to add drippers as the plants get bigger.

The flow rate (measured in gallons per hour) will determine how many drippers you can put on a system (or how much in-line drip emitter tubing you can use). For example if you need 240 1 gph drippers on a circuit then your supply line needs to be able to supply 240 gallons of water per hour.

How many drippers?

One rule of thumb says that established plants should be watered for one hour per week. To achieve this you need to make sure each plant has enough drippers to supply the necessary amount of water in an hour (of course you could run it for as long as you like).

It's impossible to give precise advice about how much to water plants, because this varies according to the climate and the species of plant. Some plants like an evenly moist soil, some like the soil to dry out between watering. Some plants suffer if they don't get enough water and some suffer if they get too much water. If you really want a precise figure then try this: Give established trees 10 gallons per week per inch of trunk diameter. Newly planted trees need less as they have more compact roots, so give them 6 to 8 gallons a week per inch of trunk diameter. Give small shrubs 4 to 6 gallons per week and bigger ones 10 to 12 gallons.

If you need more drippers, or a longer run of pipe than your flow rate will allow, you can split the area into two zones and supply them both with a larger pipe. Alternatively you might use lower flow drippers (perhaps ½ gph) and simply run the water for longer.

Drip system components

Specialist irrigation shops are usually more expensive than do-it-yourself stores because they sell higher quality components to professional contractors. This is more durable than homeowner grade stuff and should last a lot longer.

Filter

A good filter is essential when using a drip system because the drippers have a very small aperture and if they get clogged with grit or debris they become useless (most are very hard to clean). Use a good, easily cleaned Y filter with a 150 mesh screen for clean municipal water. Dirtier well water (or pond water containing algae) may require a higher mesh filter.

Backflow preventer

This is a one way valve that only allows water to travel in one direction. It is necessary (even legally required) when connecting to a potable water source, to prevent dirty water flowing backwards and contaminating the water supply. Anti-siphon control valves don't work as well, nor does a vacuum breaker attached to the hose.

Pressure regulator

This reduces the house water pressure down to 15-30 psi (higher pressure can cause drip fittings to malfunction). Cheap regulators are fixed, more expensive ones are adjustable.

Supply lines

The supply lines that carry the water to different parts of the garden are usually either rigid PVC laid underground (best) or flexible polyethylene. The latter has the advantage that it doesn't have to be buried. In cold climates you usually drain the system for the winter to prevent damage.

PVC is not a very environmentally friendly material and it would be nice to avoid it. I used it for my garden because it was cheap, but it felt a bit strange dripping all that glue on to my lovely organic soil.

If you only have a few short runs ½ inch drip line will be sufficient. If you have a lot of long circuits make sure the main supply lines are big enough (at least ¾ ¾" and maybe 1"). Also be sure to get enough pipe. It's often cheaper the more you get; so try and get it all at once. You often end up using more than you anticipated because you have the trench open and if you might want something else at some point in the future, now is the time to lay it.

Drippers

These are used for watering individual plants. They plug directly into the ½" supply lines and can be spaced anywhere on the line. They are quite flexible in that you can add extra drippers as plants get bigger and need more water. You can also switch them for higher flow drippers (just don't have both types on the same circuit). Flag drippers are good if the water isn't very clean as they can be taken apart and cleaned if they get clogged.

On sloping ground you may need pressure compensating emitters to get an even flow (otherwise low spots may get more water than high ones).

Drip emitter line

An alternative to individual drippers is to use hose with built in emitters. Drip emitter line is most often used for closely spaced small plants such as vegetables and groundcovers, but short lengths can be attached to ½ inch pipe to water almost anything. I use this combination for most of my garden. There is also ½" drip emitter tubing for greater flow.

Soil staples

These are used to pin the flexible hose down and keep it from moving around. You can buy these, but I often make them myself from scrap wire (bend it around a ¾ pipe to get a nice even curve) .

Tools and accessories

You will need a hole punch for attaching drippers and a knife or secateurs for cutting the pipe. A fishing tackle box is great for keeping all of your small parts together and organized.

Irrigation controller

This is used to turn the water on and off at pre-determined times. This saves work and ensures the plants get the water they need, when they need it. It connects to the control valves via low voltage wires. Some types require a battery backup so you don't lose programming information if the power goes off, others don't.

During my research for a controller I found a fantastic source for reviews of products at Amazon.com. Whatever they sell they allow buyers to comment on the product, so you get the real world views of ordinary people on most products. Of course it being the internet you get wildly differing viewpoints on the same thing.

Control valves

Full automation requires a control valve for each watering zone. These are usually combined in a manifold that is placed near the water source and timer (usually in a box below ground). You can also have manual controls for any circuits you only use occasionally.

An extra control valve is normally added to the manifold to turn the water supply on and off at the same time as the chosen circuits. This ensures that water won't be wasted if there are leaks anywhere in the system, or if a control valve get stuck open.

The valves run on 24 volts and are connected to the controller or timer with 18 gauge wire. The whole thing is very simple to put together and well within the capabilities on any reasonably competent individual (I'm electrically challenged and I found it easy).

Installation

Trenching

Pipes for drip systems don't need to be buried in trenches; they can run along the surface under mulch. These should be anchoring firmly though, so they don't move around as water pressure changes, or get tripped over.

Even though it's not essential, I like to bury the main supply lines underground and out of harms way. Run these to the main areas of the garden and put in risers as necessary. The main water pipe are usually buried 18" deep, with branch lines only 12" deep. In areas where there is any possibility of freezing it is nice to be able to drain them easily in winter.

If you decide to bury your pipes then digging trenches should be an early priority. It's a lot easier to build a patio over a water line than it is to run a water line under a patio. As I've mentioned before, any time you start digging you should be aware of the possibility of hitting buried water, gas or electric lines. Also try not to disturb the roots of important trees.

If you run the pipes along the edge of the paths, you will know where they are and it will be easier to get to them if necessary. On a hillside you should run a line straight uphill, and tee off of it with lines across the contour (if you don't refill these completely they can even do double duty as swales).

If you are hand digging a trench in hard dry soil don't waste your time chipping away at it. Just dig down a couple of inches along its entire length and fill the depression with water. When this soaks in it will make watering infinitely easier. Dig out the moist soil and repeat the process as often as necessary.

It is important to make an accurate plan of where all of your buried water lines are located. This will simplify your life at a later date, or that of the next occupant of your garden.

If you are digging a trench around your garden for water, you could install some vertical gopher wire and make a gopher free zone. See Caring for the forest garden for more on this idea.

Don't refill trenches until you have tested the system for leaks, otherwise it will be impossible to find them. Make sure you fill a downhill trench fully, if you leave a depression water may run down it and cause erosion. In fact you should over-fill the trenches so they are a slight hump. They will soon settle down to flat.

Assembly

Lay out your pipe and then glue it together. Incidentally don't leave your glue can on unstable soil with the lid loose. I guarantee you will knock it over.

Assemble the backflow preventer, control valve, filter, and pressure regulator and if necessary the control valves (make sure you install them so the water flows in the right direction). Use Teflon tape on any threads. The supply pipe then goes into this.

Unroll flexible polyethylene pipe carefully, don't just pull it from the inside of the coil or it will never go flat. If it is very stiff you can leave it in the sun for a while to soften up. Soil staples will be a big help in holding it in place.

In very cold climates you need to be able to empty the system so it doesn't get damaged by freezing. The easiest way to do this is to have all of the pipes sloping downhill, so they can drain by gravity. You them just need screw off openings at the lowest and highest points. If you can't use gravity you will have to blow out the pipes with a compressor, which is more work.

With larger plants you will run the drip line to the tree, but with smaller plants you may well put the drip line in first and then plant around it.

When all of the pipe is fully assembled you must flush the system before closing the ends. This is important, as if you leave any debris in the tubing, the only way it can get out is through the drippers. If it can't get out then it will clog them. Don't install the drippers until everything has been flushed thoroughly.

When installing the drippers the barbed end goes into the pipe. Drippers should go directly in to the ½ inch tubing where possible, don't run them from ¼ inch tubing. On a slope the drippers should be placed on the uphill side of the plant, so water flows down towards it.

When everything is working satisfactorily you may want to cover the tubing with mulch. This helps to reduce loss from evaporation, protects it from the sun and looks better. The drawback to this is that it is harder to see whether it is working properly, or if there are any leaks.

Alterations

If you decide a dripper is in the wrong place, pull it out with pliers (it is barbed so this isn't easy) and fill the hole with a goof plug. Then punch a hole in the right place and install a new dripper.

Repairs

If a tube gets damaged (by weed wacker, gopher or whatever) just cut out the damaged section and re-connect with a short piece of pipe and two couplings.

You can sometimes clean a clogged dripper with a paper clip. If this doesn't work then replace it (they aren't exactly expensive). As I mentioned previously, flag drippers are designed to be easily cleaned, so if your water is particularly dirty, you might want to go with these.

Using drip irrigation

A well functioning automated drip system does its job without your attention and tends to become almost invisible. The big advantage (it doesn't need your input) is also its biggest disadvantage, in that you become less involved with that aspect of the garden and pay less attention to it. I was quite amazed at how this happened in my garden after I automated my irrigation. I didn't give the plants as much individual attention and as a result I lost several plants

When you first get your system going you must watch it with an eagle eye, to see if you have missed any areas Watch for leaks whenever it is turned on (this isn't easy if it is covered with mulch). Watch for wilted plants, which indicate water isn't getting through to them (usually because a hose has become disconnected or a dripper isn't working properly). If you find one, check to see if the soil is moist around it. Also make sure it is putting out enough water, which varies according to weather and time of year. At the same time you don't want to be putting out too much because this wastes water.

You can check if the system is applying enough water with a soil probe (this is a tube you push into the ground to get a core sample of soil). If the soil is wet all the way down there is enough water. If it is dry a few inches down you haven't applied enough for it to soak in fully. The top 3-4 inches of soil should be allowed to dry out before you water again.

Learning to program your timer is often easier said than done, however it's worth spending some time to become familiar with it. The system will work better if you can easily make adjustments as needed.

The system will need some annual maintenance to keep it working well. If there is any possibility of freezing over the winter, you must drain the whole system in fall. In spring you should check the entire system, clean the filter and flush the supply lines before starting it up. Over the winter pipes can get broken, drippers can come loose and delicate parts like micro-sprinklers may cease to function properly.

Drought tolerant food plants

A few common crops are surprisingly drought tolerant and can grow with no irrigation, even in very dry climates.

Hardy:

Asparagus	Eleagnus	Oregano
Sage	Fennel	Walnut
Chestnut	Stone Pines	Day Lily
Gingko	Bayberry	Rugosa Rose
Caragana	Hollyhock	Mallow
Mulberry	Onions,	Broom
Jujube	Carob	Orach
	Pistachio	

Less hardy:

Pomegranate	Fig	Olive
Rosemary	Almond	Grape
Prickly Pear	Loquat	Carob
Bay	Origanum	Ice Plant
Marjoram	Sedum	Tomato
Watermelon		

Water conservation

There is a water crisis looming in much of the United States. This isn't brought on by global warming (though this may make it worse) but simply by our refusal to accept any limits on consumption, We seem unable to grasp the fact that fossil groundwater is not the same as water that falls from the sky; it is a limited resource. Increasing population growth and industrial agriculture means that in many areas water is being removed from the ground faster than it is being replenished and vital aquifers are being sucked dry. At some point in the not too distant future there will be no more cheap water (or emerald green golf courses in the desert). Some of those desert housing developments may one day become ghost suburbs (complete with ghost Starbucks and ghost Walmarts).

The good news is that we waste an incredible amount of water and that with only a few minor changes to habits and plumbing systems we could dramatically reduce our consumption. In the western United States almost half of household water use goes onto gardens and most of that is used to keep lawns looking green. Simply flushing all of those toilets uses up to 8 billion gallons of water daily.

Because you will be growing a lot of food you can justifiably use more water than would be acceptable for an ornamental garden. Nevertheless you should still take steps to use your water resources as efficiently as possible. Here are a few ideas on reducing water consumption in the garden (taken together they could save a lot of water).

Practical ways to reduce water use

There are many ways you can reduce the amount of water your garden requires, here are a few:.

- Mulching is one of the most important water conserving techniques and can reduce garden water consumption by as much as a third. It does this by shading the soil from direct sunlight (this reduces evaporation by 50%) and by eliminating thirsty annual weeds.

- If used carefully a drip irrigation system can reduce garden water consumption by 50%.

- Group your plants according to their water needs (this is called hydrozoning). You can have areas for moisture loving plants and separate areas for the more drought tolerant crops. This enables you to more easily adjust your watering to the crop.

- Use all of the rainwater that falls on you land, by storing it either in the soil or above the ground. The soil is your cheapest water storage medium and one of the best (if not the most obvious) ways to conserve water is to add organic matter to the soil. A soil that is high in organic matter absorbs water like a sponge and holds it until your plants use it.

- Any water that lands upon your roof (or clean paved surfaces) could be captured and stored for irrigation.

- Get the maximum use out of your household water by using it twice. Once in the house and a second time in the garden as gray water.

- Make sure there are no leaks in any garden plumbing, pipes, faucets, hoses or irrigation lines. Any leak that goes on 24 hours a day can waste a lot of water.

- Plant (or transplant) trees and shrubs in fall, to give them all winter to get established before they are faced with dry weather. Don't transplant in summer when plants will require extra irrigation to get established.

- If water is always scarce you should use drought tolerant species for most of the garden. These might be native plants or those from similar dry climates around the world (Fig, Olive, Grape).
- You can cut down on water consumption (and work in general) by working a smaller number of beds very intensively.
- Though the rich soil of intensive raised beds holds a lot of moisture, their raised profile increases their surface area and so also increases water loss. In hot, dry climates the beds should be flat to reduce evaporative losses. In extremely arid areas they may even be sunken.
- You could forget about raised beds altogether and plant your crops in widely spaced rows. This gives each plant a larger area to obtain water (and nutrients), so there is much less need for irrigation. This is how gardens were mostly grow before everyone had piped water for irrigation.
- If water is very scarce don't use cover crops or green manures in summer. They can take a lot of water from the soil even before you plant your crop (use a mulch instead). Be sure to remove old crops when they start to decline, as they will continue to take water out of the soil. Also keep the garden well weeded, as these remove moisture from the soil too.
- Dry winds can take a lot of moisture from the soil, so make sure the garden has an efficient windbreak.
- Don't water your plants in the heat of the day, as a lot of the water will be lost through evaporation. Water in early morning or in the evening (this is a good idea even with a drip system.
- Don't deprive plants of the water they need for proper growth. It's much better to have a few healthy and productive plants, than a lot of water stressed unproductive plants.
- Water large plants individually, rather than wetting the entire bed (perhaps sink a perforated can by each plant).
- Use a timer to shut off irrigation water after a pre-determined time. That way you don't forget about it and leave it on longer than necessary.
- In areas with wet winters and dry summers you should grow your main staple crops in spring, while there is still plenty of water in the ground from winter rains.
- Plant a dry garden that produces without irrigation. See Drought tolerant dry gardens for more on growing vegetable crops without irrigation.

Building the garden

Designing a garden is an interesting intellectual exercise, but building a garden is a physical one. Gardens are not made 'by saying oh how beautiful and sitting in the shade' (as Rudyard Kipling once observed). They only come into being when someone goes outside, rolls up their sleeves and gets to work (that someone should be you). This can be a problem because the average middle class American is not only unwilling to do hard physical labor, they are often so out of condition they are unable to. Work that a day laborer can do all day long could put the average office worker in bed for a couple of days.

Gardening is a labor of love, with the emphasis on labor, it involves hard work, digging, sowing, propagating, mulching, pruning, harvesting and sweating. Manual labor is regarded as demeaning in our consumer culture, fit only for those at the bottom of the ladder with no other choices. Smart people don't sweat and get dirty (or at least not when it has a productive purpose). Many famous garden writers (who should have known better) rarely lowered themselves to actually do much physical work, confining themselves instead to the more cerebral and refined aspects of gardening.

To be a real gardener you need to embrace physical work and enjoy it. It is what our bodies were designed for and you ignore that fact at your peril (use it or lose it). The non-gardener can never really understand the truly passionate gardener, working into the twilight hours, undeterred by aching back, heat, scratches, sunburn, splinters, cracked skin, insect bites, Poison Oak rash, sore muscles and more.

A garden is more than a place, it is a process, a symbiotic interaction between the gardener, the land, the plants and the rest of the natural world. An important factor that made the old cottage gardens such special places was that they were created, maintained and loved by the people who lived in them. They were the result of the devoted attention of an involved gardener (or a series of them) over many years.

Gardening is like parenting in that it is mostly learned on the job. You don't need to be a parent to have a child and you don't need to be a gardener to have a garden. This is the beauty of doing things yourself, you start out a complete novice but by the end of the job you actually know what you are doing. Do the same job a second time and you are almost an expert.

Organization

Of course it isn't enough to just put in hours of work, if you run around like a headless chicken. You have to be organized so the work you do is effective and a little paperwork can help you with this, Make a list of all the things that need doing, in the order they need doing. Some must be done immediately; others must be done in a certain order, or at a certain time. You also need to get materials and plants, some of which are only available at certain times of the year.

It isn't possible to do everything at once, so start small and close to the house. One of my first priorities would be getting a few intensive vegetable beds established. You will also want to get working on the garden living area, along with the large plants that make up the garden framework. A selection of fruit trees should be planted early on, as they won't start bearing for several years.

Build the garden one section at a time, at least to the point where all the major plants are in the ground and growing (even if the hardscaping isn't complete). The garden will grow quickly if you keep working at it. As you increase the number of areas you also increase you workload of course, so make sure these additional areas are as low-maintenance s possible.

There are other projects to work on at the same time you are building the garden sections. A fence to keep out deer is a big one. Propagating plants should always be a high priority, but it is especially important if money is limited. In dry areas you will want to get the irrigation system going, before the available moisture is gone from the soil in early summer. If you have to pay for water a rainwater collection system may be important.

Plants are living things and you have to take their needs into account. For best results some things must be done at certain times There is a limited window for moving plants, planting bare root fruit trees, sowing seeds, grafting and other forms of propagation.

If you are short of money you could concentrate on the projects that are labor intensive, but don't require much in the way of materials or money. For example digging. As you get materials or money you could come back and fill in the missing pieces.

Cooperative gardening

A good way to get your garden going is to organize a cooperative gardening group. Get together with a few like-minded people and rotate working a day in everyone's garden in turn. You get to talk about gardening and related subjects, share skills, plants, food and fun. You can also get vital advice from more experienced members of the group.

Time

The most precious resource you have is time. They say that time is money and it's true that the more time you have, the less money you will have to spend. It's nice if you can give yourself a block of time to devote entirely to getting the garden established.

Most gardeners are limited by the amount of time, energy and muscle they can devote to their gardens. For a part time gardener the amount of work can seem a little overwhelming. If this is the case you should work in stages as time and money allow. Start close to the house with the items that give the most return for the least effort and do something regularly. One way to encourage this is to give yourself a weekly project.

If you have the resources and energy a lot of the garden can be built quickly in a few weeks, but more often it is created slowly over a number of years. The important thing is to do the right things at the right time (such as planting trees in the right places), so you are making progress and the garden is moving forward.

When to work

Winter - In our mild climate winter is the best time to create new parts of the garden. The cool weather is conducive to heavy outdoor activity and there is plenty of moisture in the soil. It's also easier to evaluate trees (and work on them) when they don't have any leaves. Plants are dormant at this time, so it is also the time to move (and prune) them. Late winter can get busy, especially if you leave everything until the plants start to wake up.

Spring – Where winter work isn't practical the cool weather of spring is a good time to create the garden. The first beautiful spring days just drag you out into the garden anyway, so you may as well do something useful. Unfortunately this is usually the time of maximum garden activity anyway, so there's may not be much time to spare for new things.

Summer – This is the time to enjoy your handiwork. There is already enough to do maintaining the established gardens and laying in the hammock. Every summer I get a mental block at some point, when I can't get anything done. The heat drains away enthusiasm and makes heavy garden work seem even heavier. To get anything done at this time of year I have to get up at sunrise while it is still cool (this is actually my favorite time to be in the garden).

Autumn - In colder climates where winter work is limited, the autumn is often the best time to work on new garden projects.

Some things to do in the garden

In case you couldn't come up with your own list of stuff to do, I've made one for you.

Plant a vegetable garden
Plant fruit trees
Plant fruiting shrubs
Plant perennial vegetables and herbs
Create a patio
Build a windbreak
Build a pond
Build a greenhouse
Set up an irrigation system
Set up rainwater storage
Set up a gray water system
Create a rain garden
Create a wild garden
Build a worm bin
Dig a fire pit

The order of work

The following is a rough schedule of how you might prioritize the work.

1) Clean up the site, remove anything that won't stay. Try and reuse anything you can.

2) Tree removal should be done early on, while the garden area is still clear. This is much less stressful when you don't have to worry about hitting anything. Dropping a tree between your gazebo and fruit laden Karmijn De Sonnaville is no job for the timid and may end up requiring expensive professional help.

If you are planning on renting a backhoe this gives you an easy way to remove trees, you just push them over (taking out the roots and all). It can also make short work of shrubs and their roots. This should be done just before the backhoe leaves, because if you do it earlier you won't be able to do any more work until you clear the trees away (though you could use it to move them). Be sure to save any useful logs, poles and brush for building the garden.

3) Remove persistent weeds such as Blackberries and Poison Oak/Ivy (again the backhoe can help if used carefully). You will never have rest until persistent perennial weeds are under control, so don't just take out all the above ground parts and ignore the rest.

4) Mark out where the most important elements will go and locate any underground utilities.

5) Trenching for water pipes and other utilities should also be done at this time, before tree planting or anything else gets in the way. Then lay the pipes and conduit and pull any wires, so you can fill in the trenches (after testing water lines of course).

6) Earthworks (ponds, swales, rainwater infiltration, terracing, drainage, grading) come next. If you are renting a backhoe it is important to get this organized, so you can complete all of the heavy work while you have the machine. Once you have filled the place with trees shrubs and other elements, there may be no room for such a large machine to work.

7) Before you can do any planting the growing areas must be securely fenced to keep out deer and the like. It is possible to cage plants individually, but if you will eventually put up a fence anyway this would be doing things twice, which doesn't make sense.

Once the fence is in place it may limit your access to the garden. If this is a problem you might have a removable panel you can take out as necessary.

8) In windy areas you will have to provide your main living and growing areas with wind protection.

9) Pathways must be cleared early, so you have easy access to all parts of the garden with your tools and wheelbarrow. Don't put down any paving until near the end of the job, when it won't get messed up.

10) Fruit and nut bearing trees, shrubs and vines are a fairly high priority because they take a while to get established and start fruiting. You will want to get them into the ground as soon as possible. They need fertile soil so you may have to improve the soil before planting.

Bare root tree planting (and most transplanting) has to be done while the plants are dormant, which means during the coldest months.

11) The hardscaping comes next. Work on building patios, decks, stairs, arbors, pergolas and more.

12) Any utility work should be done now, Installing lights, outlets, faucets, etc.

13) To successfully grow vegetables and fruit you need a fertile soil, hence soil building is always a high priority. Once the growing areas are defined you can start to work on this. Don't do it any earlier as you don't want to waste effort and amendments on areas that will become paths or patios.

14) Plant small plants.

15) Plant ground covers.

16) Finish the irrigation system.

17) Mulching is one of the final steps, but a crucial one to reduce maintenance and build soil fertility.

18) Complete the furnishing and any ornamental stuff and then pat yourself on the back. You are ready to start gardening!

Working

When it comes to actually getting the work done people have different ways of working. A friend has to do everything perfectly as he goes along and can't tolerate leaving any mess. I tend to go over an area and do the major changes and then go back at a later date and refine it.

Efficiency

If you are doing most of the work yourself you need to work efficiently to get the most accomplished. Here are a few suggestions for increasing your efficiency.

Get organized and do things in the right order. Don't work against yourself.

Scan your to-do list and get the materials you will need to complete these tasks before you start. You will then have them on site when you need them.

Keep your tools in a convenient and easily accessible place, close to where most of the work happens. You will then know exactly where to go to get them. Wandering around the garden looking for a tool is frustrating, wastes time and causes you to lose focus.

Keep some hand tools (secateurs, trowel, knife) in a bucket close to the door, so you can pick them up as you go outside

Some jobs can be done more easily and quickly if you rent the right tool. If you can afford it then go easy on yourself and rent that ditch digger. If you object to all that noise and pollution you could hire some laborers for the day (just make sure they have green cards, workers compensation, are bonded and licensed and you get their fingerprints).

Power tools can speed up the work so much they are almost indispensable in some situations (I can't imagine cutting up a tree with a handsaw, though I suppose they once did), however this comes at a price. I recently read that using a 2 stroke chainsaw for two hours creates as much pollution as driving 2500 miles. Electric tools may be less portable and less powerful, but they are also much less polluting. Propane is now another alternative to the smelly, dirty 2 stroke.

You will also need the right work clothes, hat, sunscreen, boots and gloves. I find my work brain doesn't start to function until I put my boots on.

Safety

Gardening can be (often is) hazardous to your health. I have cut my hand with secateurs, speared my boot with a spading fork (happily missing my foot), crushed toes and fingers under rocks, jammed large splinters into my hands (and countless thorns), slipped and jammed a wheelbarrow handle into my ribs, and incurred countless cuts and scrapes. Happily as organic gardeners we avoid a lot of toxic chemicals, but we still have various fine dusts (vermiculite, wood ash, concrete) that are best kept out of our lungs I have never seriously hurt my back lifting, but I'm probably in the minority. In spring the majority of over-enthusiastic gardeners over-work unfit bodies and end up with sore muscles for a few days, or worse. Don't overtax yourself.

I mention the above things to forewarn you, but realistically nothing I can say will make them happen any less frequently. The more work you do, the more you will injure yourself. All you can do is develop the stoic attitude and the colorful vocabulary of a rustic son of the soil (sorry to be sexist, but earth goddesses just shouldn't curse).

Cleanup

Clean up the site thoroughly before you start work on a section of garden. Remove everything that won't remain: old furniture, debris, lumber, wire fencing and more. Put anything you can reuse at some point in a safe place and take the rest to be recycled or dumped. Any demolition should be done at this time too (save any stone, brick, usable lumber, broken concrete and anything else that can be re-used). If you need to move something, then move it once, to where it will remain or off the site. Don't keep moving things around.

Don't be afraid to cut established woody shrubs down, it can make working in the area easier and will often re-invigorate them. When digging the foundation for my house the backhoe driver demolished everything in his path. It looked like he had removed every living thing from the entire house area, but the following spring shoots emerged from hidden roots all over the place. Chestnut, Elderberry, Redwood, Walnut, Blackberry and other plants came back vigorously.

Marking out

Mark out where important new elements will be placed, using a 100 feet tape measure, string and stakes. Mark out the location of curved elements such as paths and fences using a line of ground limestone. If you need a nice clean arc or circle, use string and pegs.

Laying out on the ground in this way gives you a much better idea of your layout, so you can evaluate what you have and correct any problems easily. Find a high vantage point (hill, roof, tree) to get a better view.

As you mark things out on the ground new ideas may emerge and you might have to change your plans.

Moving the earth

Earth is heavy and there is a lot of it. You are small and there isn't much of you. A backhoe is strong and doesn't get tired. Moving earth is easier with a backhoe. A backhoe uses fossil fuel, is noisy, smelly, compacts everything and isn't very sensitive. If you don't want to use a machine you could hire some people to do the heaviest work by hand.

If you have any earth moving to do, it will be one of your first tasks because everything else goes on top of the earth (try moving soil from underneath something). There is also plenty of room to work when you first start, whereas once you get planting and building it may become completely inaccessible to machinery.

If you are renting a backhoe (or hiring someone to do the job) you need to get organized. You need to know exactly what you want to accomplish (where to dig, where to put excess topsoil and subsoil, which trees to remove, what trenches to dig, how to get around the site) while you have the machine. Don't be left with a couple of yards of earth to move after the machine has gone.

Be warned that heavy equipment operators often have their own opinions about what you should do and are notorious for flattening everything in their path (it's so easy). Keep a very close eye on them, don't let them tell you what to do and never, ever, leave them alone for longer than 5 minutes. If you do you may return to find a soccer field where there used to be a wooded hillside. Even when not deliberately flattening things they are compacting the ground, tearing bark off trees and worse.

Any shaping of the earth (terraces, swales) should be done by moving the subsoil rather than the topsoil. The topsoil should be skimmed off, the subsoil shaped, and then the topsoil should be replaced. Of course this is more work, but your plants will do much better in topsoil, than they will in subsoil. Also don't leave topsoil in a pile for too long as it will deteriorate

> **Caution: Buried utility lines**
>
> Before you do any digging into the earth (especially with power equipment) you need to know where any underground utility lines are located. You can call and check that there are no buried utility cables or pipes from the street, but those on your property are your problem. Hopefully your plans will tell you where they are, but you may have to figure it out for yourself by a process of deduction (if the electricity arrives on your land here and enters the house there, then the underground cable goes between the two). This is a serious business because what you don't know could kill you. It's bad enough to break a gas line or water pipe (I once broke the sprinkler line for an entire condominium complex), but slicing through the electric service cable could be the last mistake you ever make. I saw someone do it once, but luckily he had just switched from a metal digging bar to a wooden handled shovel.
>
> If you are using heavy equipment you need to make sure it doesn't run over the septic system or other delicate areas. A heavy backhoe can do a lot of damage to a leach field.

If you are going to remove a lot of soil from one area, you should decide where to put it before you start. You don't want to move it twice. Coordinate any earth removal (ponds, swales, basins) with berm or terrace building, so soil can be transferred straight from one place to the other. In this way you can be doing two things at once. If you don't need any soil you may have to spread it out thinly somewhere.

You may have noticed that when you move soil it takes up more space than it did before. This happens because loosening the soil creates more pore space, so it has a greater volume (up to 25% more). This effect never goes away entirely, but may eventually settle back to be only 10% more.

As soil dries out it becomes much harder to work, so do your digging while it is moist. This isn't much of an issue if you are using heavy equipment, but it is if you are digging by hand. If the soil is very dry you might want to run a sprinkler on an area the day before you dig. Wet soil is also a problem, as it can be compacted and damaged by careless cultivation (it also sticks to tools). Wait until it had dried out before digging.

When constructing any kind of drainage earthworks it is essential to slope everything so it drains to where you want it to go. You should also take care not to leave any bare soil, as it is prone to erosion and degradation. Cover it with a mulch of straw or wood chips, until plants can get established.

Trenching
If you plan on burying water lines, electrical conduit, drainage pipes, or making gopher or bamboo barriers, you can save a lot of work by renting a ditcher for a day and doing it all at once. This means getting everything cleared and marked out in advance, but is very worthwhile. Often more than one item can go in the same ditch.

Irrigation pipes should be laid in the trench and glued up with risers (fasten them to a wooden stake) and capped off . You can then test the lines for leaks before filling them in (it's almost impossible to find a leak in a buried pipe, unless the moisture comes to the surface). You can finish the plumbing and irrigation after the beds are established.

Electricity isn't normally a high priority, but if you think you may want power out in the garden (for lighting, the greenhouse, shed, work area or fountain) now is the time to lay any conduit and wires. Its safest to put electric lines in conduit and bury it below digging depth. Low voltage surface wires can run alongside walls or paths, where they are somewhat protected and hidden.

Windbreaks
If there are strong winds in your area, one of your first priorities will be finding ways of reducing them (most plants won't grow well if continuously battered by the wind). The usual strategy is to build a fence for immediate effect (this is often needed to keep out deer anyway) and to plant young trees and shrubs behind it. As these grow they will eventually take over and perform the task more effectively. See Windbreaks for more on this.

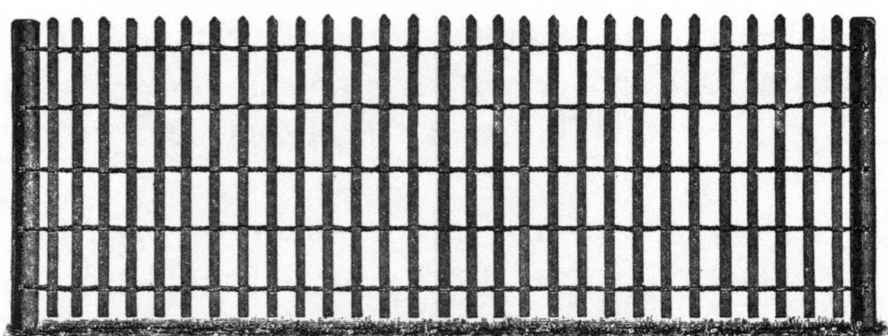

Fencing
In rural areas fences are often essential to keep out deer or other animals. This is often a high priority because there is no point doing any planting if deer can just walk in and dine on them. If you are on a tight budget the first fence will have to be simple and inexpensive. In the future you can gradually replace it with a more durable and attractive fence or wall, or you could grow some spiny hedges. See Boundaries and dividers for more on this.

Plant stuff
Clearing weeds and unwanted plants
Before you clear away any vegetation you should know what it is, so make a habit of identifying every plant before removing it. You may want to keep especially useful or interesting plants, or move them.

Large areas of dense brush and perennial weeds can be attacked with a brush cutter (a string trimmer with a brush cutting blade). This will make short work of the above ground parts (and irrigation hoses, tree trunks, prized plants and legs) but some plants can grow from root cuttings and these will soon send up new shoots. These should be removed promptly as they will be much weaker for a while (they will recover if left for too long). Be aware that some creeping weeds will try and creep back in and need to be kept out with a barrier of some kind.

If you have a lot of woody plants you could pull them out of the ground by (most of) their roots with a woody weed puller. Unfortunately these are a little expensive if you only have a few plants to remove.

The shade of the tree canopy and shrub layer is very effective at suppressing weeds (most of which need sunlight). If you remove trees be prepared for an explosion of weed growth on the now sunny forest floor. When you remove plants you inevitably disturb the soil. Don't leave this bare as you are not only exposing the soil to degradation, you are also setting the garden up for a succession to start, beginning with the annual weeds. Cover disturbed soil with mulch to prevent this happening and to protect it from the elements.

Poison Oak/Ivy

I consider myself an expert on getting Poison Oak rash (Rhus dermatitis). If you are susceptible then any time you work near the plant you stand a good chance of contacting it and developing the rash. I have found the best way to reduce the severity of its effects is also the simplest. Apparently it takes at least 20 minutes for the oil (urushiol) in the plant to bond with your skin. This oil is broken down by water, so if you wash frequently you can greatly reduce its impact. Any time I knowingly brush against a plant I wash the area thoroughly within 15 minutes. I also rinse my hands every so often, because any oil on your hands can be transferred to other part of your body. Since I started doing this zealously I haven't had a serious case of Poison Oak.

Persistent weeds

It is essential to deal with persistent weeds early on. Don't ignore them hoping they will go away because they won't. They will come back to haunt you for as long as the conditions suit them, and will cause you far more work than if you got rid of them in the first place. The best way to deal with them is in one manageable section at a time. Get them cleared up before moving on and go back occasionally to check for survivors and new seedlings.

Plants such as Blackberry and Poison Oak can give you sympathy for chemical gardeners. In fact I have to admit I did once (in another lifetime) try an herbicide (glyphosphate) in frustration at repeated bouts of Poison Ivy rash. I carefully applied it to some Poison Ivy and sat back waiting for it to die. Much to my surprise (and disappointment) the plants never even noticed the stuff (and I thought it killed everything it came near). Eventually I found that a much better solution was to wear rubber gloves and pull the plants out by their long roots during wet weather.

There is actually a very safe herbicide that is effective against Poison Oak, ammonium sulphamate, which quickly breaks down into the chemical fertilizer ammonium sulphate. This is one chemical herbicide I would use, but unfortunately it is illegal in California (and elsewhere) because it hasn't been registered as an herbicide. I'm guessing this is because Presumably because it is a fairly simple chemical that can't be patented and so there isn't enough profit in it for the chemical companies.

If you are removing a lot of weeds clear them up as you go (or chop and spread them as mulch). This makes walking easier and reduces the risk of tripping.

Sheet mulch kills weeds by depriving them of light and is one of the best way to get weeds under control. You can also use plastic sheeting to cook them out. Black plastic increases the soil temperature by as much as 10° F, while clear plastic can increase soil temperatures even higher (as much as 15° F), but may allow weeds to grow underneath it (if it doesn't cook them). Woven plastic sheeting is the most durable

A chicken tractor can be used to clear and fertilize land. It is a movable chicken run that allows the birds to eat everything inside it. Once everything is gone it is moved to the next area.

Goats and pigs can be useful living weed eaters, but of course they entail work keeping livestock.

Plant something

Once you get an area cleared of weeds you need to cover it with something. If you leave it bare it will grow new weeds. If you aren't ready for a permanent planting, you could plant a temporary groundcover (preferably a nitrogen fixer), which may last up to 2 years. For a very short term solution you could use mulch.

Burn piles

The fastest way of disposing of debris when clearing large areas is to burn it. However this is also very wasteful and polluting. You could heat your house for weeks on the firewood burned in one good burn pile. There are also better ways to use this material (berms, mulch, barriers).

If you really must have a burn pile make sure it gets hot, for cleaner combustion and less pollution. Don't put any green or wet branches on until it is really burning fiercely and never put loose leaves (brown or green) on it.

As an alternative to burning you might want to experiment with biochar (see Biochar) for possible soil improvement (this is a little more technical though).

Trees

Existing large trees can present a dilemma for the ecological gardener. On the one hand they can be a problem because they cast a lot of shade and compete for nutrients and water. On the other hand you should cherish them because they are beautiful and precious and took a long time to grow. If your garden is heavily wooded you will have to think creatively about the best way to make it productive without clear cutting it.

How you regard your trees will also depend upon their relative abundance. If you live in a relatively treeless area you will treasure them much more than if you live where they grow like weeds.

Any tree work should be done early in the construction process, when there are less things around to damage. I once cut a tree that fell in the complete opposite direction than I had anticipated, and came so close to crushing my truck that a side branch dented the hood (that was before I discovered rope).

Temporary tree removal

Growing up in a country with barren moorland where dense forest once grew I have a particular appreciation for Americas lush forests. I have always felt pangs of guilt when removing trees, because the world doesn't need less of them. However if you want to grow food in your garden you need sun above all else, and if trees are preventing you from doing this you have to do something. Fortunately there is a solution to this, in the form of coppicing.

Coppicing gives you a way to temporarily remove some species of trees (mostly deciduous trees) without killing them. It allows the tree to live on at a more shrub-like size and can work out very well in some situations. It keeps some height and shape to the garden (the shoots grow quickly) and you eventually get useful poles for firewood and garden use. If you move, or decide not to do any more gardening, the trees can simply be allowed to grow back. I have done this with some Redwoods in my garden because killing trees that could still be alive in the year 4000 A.D. just doesn't seem right. See Coppicing for more on this.

Tree removal

Removing large trees can be a daunting task, so don't do it unless it is absolutely necessary.

If you have a backhoe on site the easiest way to remove modest size trees is to push them over. This brings the roots out of the ground as well, which can save a lot of work. Once they are down the hard work of removing them begins (I look upon this as penance for cutting them down in the first place).

If you must cut trees with a chain saw, cut them high up (ideally 8 feet) so the stump can be used as a lever to get the roots out. If you cut it down low it will be much more difficult to get out, so don't forget!

If you cut trees on your property you should make use of them, especially if they are hardwood. Trees are a valuable resource, not trash to be disposed of as quickly as possible.

Better quality trees could (and probably should) be milled for lumber (there are specialist contractors who do this). A durable wood like Oak or Chestnut could also be split for fenceposts (you can never have too many of these). Large branches can be used for posts, rustic trellis and more. Nice long poles with a fork at the end make great supports for heavily laden fruit tree branches. Logs can be used for walls or retaining walls, rounds can be used for steps and paving.

Inferior logs can be used for firewood (if you don't need it, then sell it or give it away). Any hardwood above 3" in diameter could be used for growing mushrooms such as Shiitake (See Mushrooms).

Brushwood is another useful resource and can be used for berms, fences and windbreaks. It can also be chipped and used for mulch or growing mushrooms (you might chip hardwoods specifically for this, cutting them in winter when they have no leaves).

Removing trees drastically alters the ground beneath them by allowing sunlight through. This immediately causes Blackberries and other pioneer species to spring to life. Without the protection of overhanging branches the soil on slopes may become vulnerable to soil erosion in heavy rains. Make sure it is protected by mulch or groundcover plants.

Stump removal

If you left a tall trunk sticking out of the ground, removing a tree stump will be much easier. Just attach a chain from the top of the trunk to your truck, undercut the roots and yank it out (warning - this may void the warranty on your truck). If you value your truck you might prefer to use a come-along. If you didn't leave a tall trunk you will have to laboriously dig it out (or leave it).

In days of old you could buy dynamite and blast those stumps out, but this is yet another convenience we have allowed terrorists to deprive us of.

Stumps can simply be cut down low and left in the ground, though you might object to their appearance. Pine stumps can rot in as little as 3 – 4 years and there are ways to hasten this. More durable stumps might be carved into seats or pedestals for ornaments.
It is possible to remove stumps and grow edible fungi at the same time, by using such species as Shiitake, Oyster Mushrooms or Maitake. You drill holes in the freshly cut stump and implant wooden dowels impregnated with the spawn. This has to be the most elegant and productive way to get rid of stumps, if not as quick (or as much fun) as dynamite. See Mushrooms and fungi for more on this.

Planting

Generally planting is best done while the plants are dormant, from late fall through early spring.

Finding the right place

If you don't already know where you are going to put a plant, you need to spend some time working it out. I already discussed this in detail in Where to plant, so I won't repeat myself here.

Planting trees and shrubs

The plants that take a long time to start producing (trees, shrubs and perennials) need to get into the ground as early as possible. If you know where they will be situated (and can look after them) then by all means start planting. Don't be too hasty and plant them in the wrong place though.

Planting is a fairly straightforward procedure, but there are still right and wrong ways to do it. There are definite rules governing the best way to plant a tree and you should abide by them. However I have probably broken every one of these over the years and still have lots of thriving trees (they really do want to grow).

Planting holes

There is a gardeners saying "small tree, big hole" and while this isn't the most pithy of sayings, it is useful advice. The hole should be at least twice as wide (or even 3 times as wide) as the size of the root ball (as much as 2 -3 feet wide). This gives the roots some nice loose disturbed soil to grow sideways into while they are getting established. If you want to make the ultimate hole you can also make it square rather than round, as this gives even more loose soil. A large hole also minimizes the chance of air pockets being left around the roots.

Small tree, big hole only applies to the width of the hole though, not its depth. It should only be deep enough so the root ball sits at the same height as it was when originally planted (the groundline). If you dig a deeper hole and then refill it with soil, there is a danger the plant may sink as the soil consolidates underneath it. When the tree is planted the bud union should be at least 4" above ground level. Planting too deep or too high can cause problems with drying out or waterlogging.
A hole for a bare root tree should have an undisturbed mound or cone in the bottom, rather than being flat.

When digging the hole try not to compact the sides, as this can prevent roots growing sideways into the native soil. If the texture of the soil is very poor (clay) then gently crack open the bottom and sides of the hole for easy root penetration.

When digging the hole it is good (and no more work) to put the top soil on one side and subsoil on the other. You can then put the subsoil back in first. It's also not a bad idea to put all of the soil on a tarp or piece of plywood so it doesn't get mixed in with existing vegetation.

Gardeners used to be advised to amend the soil in the planting hole with a variety of nutrients, in the belief this gave the tree "a good start". This is now discouraged as it is believed that if there are a lot of nutrients concentrated around the roots, the tree won't send out vigorous new roots to search for them. It's much better for the nutrients to be naturally spread out thinly throughout the soil. One situation in which you might amend the hole is in very light, free draining soil. In this situation you might want to add some organic matter to increase its moisture holding capacity directly around the tree.

Acid loving plants such as Blueberries will benefit from acidifying agents.

If Gophers are a problem in your area you will have to plant in a wire mesh gopher basket. If you don't do this, you might well lose the tree at some point.

Planting methods

Container planting

Plants grown in containers don't usually perform as well as bare root plants, but they are more convenient. They can go in the ground at any time of year and don't need pruning before planting. You can also plant them at your leisure; so long as you keep them watered they can stay in their pot for weeks. It's a good idea to water them a few hours before planting as the root ball stays together better when it is moist (a dry ball will often crumble).

Planting from containers is pretty straightforward. Take the plant out of the container, being careful not to break up the root ball or lift it by the trunk. If the plant is root bound gently loosen, separate and unwind the encircling roots, so they can grow away from each other. Then place the tree in the hole, in the right position (you dug the hole so it will sit at the same height it was originally). Finally fill in the hole with the excavated soil, making sure it is packed in firmly (use your heel) so there are no air pockets.

Ball and burlap planting

A variation on container grown plants, this is usually used for larger plants, or those that can't be bare-rooted (such as conifers and evergreens). Plant them as you would container plants, being extra careful not to damage the root ball (it can be damaged by rough handling). The burlap is left on the ball, as roots can grow through it and it will eventually rot. The top of the burlap should be loosened once it is planted, as it has been known to constrict the growing plant. You might also want to cut away (or bury) any protruding burlap, to prevent it wicking moisture away from the root ball.

Bare root planting

Bare root trees are shipped in winter while dormant without (as the name suggests) any soil around them. Most specialist mail order nurseries ship plants bare rooted, not merely for lighter shipping convenience, but also because such plants usually outperform container grown ones (even if smaller initially). The catch is that they can only be moved during winter while they are dormant.

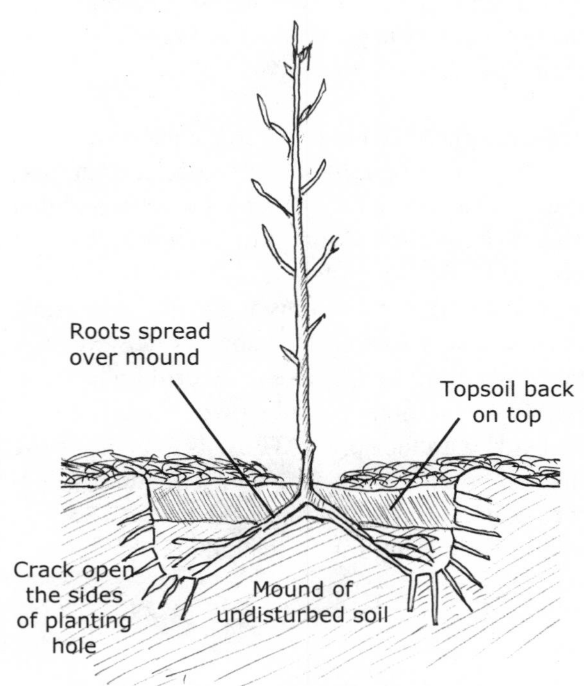

Bare root trees should be taken out of their packaging as soon as they arrive and you should make sure the roots are moist. If they don't dry out they will be happy for a week or more. If you can't plant fairly promptly you should heel them in, which means digging a trench, putting the roots in the trench and covering with moist soil. Treated in this way they can be left for several weeks (watch for gophers - my Emerald Beaut plum had half its roots eaten before I even got it planted). Don't forget about them though, once the weather warms up sufficiently they will start growing, so you should get them in the ground as soon as possible.

It is customary to prune bare root trees before planting, to balance the top and root system. However this has often been done already when you buy your plants. You should also cut off any kinked, twisted and otherwise damaged roots. Leave any long roots alone though, just make the planting hole big enough to accommodate them. The roots are sometimes soaked overnight in water prior to planting (not too long though).

A hole for a bare root tree should have a cone shaped mound in the bottom. Spread the roots out over this, so the tree sits slightly higher in the soil than it was originally. Make sure that any encircling roots are loosened and allowed to hang down. Separate the roots so they spread out to cover as much of the hole as possible and don't mat together.

With the tree in place half backfill the hole (with the subsoil), pull slightly on the tree to fill in any air pockets and then tamp tightly (I often use a stick to compact between the roots). Finally fill up the rest of the hole (with topsoil) so the tree settles down to its original soil level. Make sure you don't cover the graft union (it should be at least 4" above soil level) or you may end up with a different tree.

They say a bare root tree should be planted with the biggest root going into the wind to help anchor it. They also say the upward side of the graft should be away from the sun, to the north of the trunk.

Final steps

When you have finished planting your trees there should be a slight basin around the trunk to hold water. You should then water the soil thoroughly by filling the basin, not only to give the tree water, but also to settle the soil around the roots. On sloping ground you might have to build a dam to achieve this.

Staking trees is largely frowned upon nowadays, as flexing in the wind is thought to encourage a stronger trunk. Staking should probably be done in very windy sites (use a piece of old rubber hose to attach the tree to its stake), otherwise they can get rocked almost out of the ground. Even then the stake should be short (or placed at an angle) to allow the top of the tree to flex.

Mycorrhizal inoculants

Trees grow better when they associate with mycorrhizal fungi, but it isn't usually necessary to inoculate them. Most soils already contain the spores of suitable species just waiting for the right root to come along. If your soil is very poor you might throw in a shovel full of soil taken from around a tree that is thriving. You can also buy commercial inoculants.

Protection

In some situations you may have to protect newly planted trees from rodents and other pests. I already mentioned gophers, but other rodents (mice and rabbits) can be a big problem in winter and early spring as they gnaw the sugar rich bark. If they girdle the tree it will die unless drastic measures are taken (like bridge grafting). You can protect trees with commercial rabbit guards or wire mesh tubes. Bury them 4 inches deep and scatter gravel around the base to make it harder for them to dig.

Mulching

In the more protected inner zones you will lay down a mulch of wood chips, bark, straw, aged manure or compost helps to reduce competition from weeds, conserve moisture and provides slow acting nutrients. If weeds are very bad you might use a layer of cardboard or newspaper under the mulch.

In the outer zones you might want to scatter a layer of fertilizer around the trunk, then lay down a layer or cardboard mulch (keep it at least 6" away from the trunk). Cover this with a layer of wood chips out to the drip line.

Labeling

An important final step is to fasten a durable metal label onto the tree and mark its location and name on your garden plan. This ensures that you (and others who follow) will know what it is.

Strips cut from aluminum drink cans make good labels, just write on them with an old ball point pen.

After Care

Your job isn't finished when the newly planted tree is labelled and recorded in your book. It will need a whole growing season to adjust to its new situation and must be looked after until it is able to survive independently.

One of the most important tasks is to keep the area around the crown free of all vegetation, as the young plants can't compete against weeds very well. The easiest way to do this is with a thick mulch.

In dry areas it is essential that you keep a newly planted tree well watered until it is well established.

A newly planted tree won't need fertilizing in its first year. In future years the decomposing mulch should provide the tree with all of the nutrients it needs. If you feel your trees would benefit from additional nutrients, then spread some slow acting organic fertilizer on the soil surface around the tree. Water will leach the nutrients down into the soil over time. If you need a faster response use a liquid fertilizer or foliar feed.

It will soon be fairly apparent if a tree is happy, it will put on lots of vigorous green growth. At least 12" annually and up to several feet in a hospitable climate.

If any fruits appear in the first year they should be removed so the plant can devote all of its energy to vegetative growth.

Planting perennials

This is pretty much the same as for planting trees, but on a smaller scale and more straightforward, as you don't need to be as meticulous. Like trees these should also be planted at the right depth.

Plant propagation

The most cost effective and rewarding way to get plants is to grow them yourself, either from seed or by the various means of vegetative propagation. Propagating plants should be a high priority in the initial stages of creating the garden, as the plants you produce will play a crucial role in filling it with productive vegetation. Time spent on this is never wasted and you can't start too soon.

An early priority should be establishing a nursery and propagation area, so you can get plants growing right now. I really urge you to start experimenting with propagation; there aren't many activities that are as interesting or productive. Propagating plants is an ongoing process in my garden and as a consequence I always seem to have more plants than I need.

I suggest you go on a spending spree and get as many different tree, shrub and perennial seeds as you can find (and learn the right way to germinate each kind). Also buy as many different plants as you can afford, paying particular attention to the easily propagated species. You should also beg, steal or borrow cuttings and other propagation material. By doing this you can have plants growing while you are still getting the garden organized. See Maintenance for more about propagation.

Deadheading

Don't allow perennials to produce seed if you don't want seed. It wastes energy that could go into vegetative growth.

Soil stuff

Soil improvement

One of the biggest projects for the first year (and several years thereafter) is improving the soil in the crop growing areas. I already discussed this in the section on Soil improvement so I won't repeat myself here. Instead I am just going to give a few more suggestions.

Once you have marked out the location of improved planting areas the initial improvement should be fairly broad scale: rototilling, planting soil-improving crops (especially legumes), adding nutrients. You don't need to worry too much about wasting fertilizers on paths, because you will remove the good soil from the paths as you create them. If you don't need a newly marked out bed immediately, you should sow a long-term green manure crop to improve the soil.

Stimulating the life that's already in the soil should be one of your first priorities, as it will give you the biggest return for the effort invested. Adjust the pH, add organic matter, aerate if compacted and use mulch to protect the soil from harsh sun and to conserve moisture.

The more organic matter in the soil the more water it can hold. Find a source of compost, aged manure, tree leaves or wood chips. The more you can get, the better your garden will be (and sooner).

If you are of a scientific inclination you may want to test the soil, so you know what you are working with and (most important) if there are any serious deficiencies.

The Newness factor

It will take a few years for your new garden to transform into your vision of the perfect garden. If you planted your trees and shrubs at the proper spacing, they will look very sparse for a while. If possible it may be a good idea to keep some existing plants temporarily, so long as they don't cast too much shade. These can be removed in a few years, once your plantings have achieved some height.

It will be at least 5 years (depending upon the climate) before the garden plants start to develop much height. You can add instant height with wooden screens, poles, obelisks, arbors and trellises, covered in vines such as Cucumbers, Morning Glory, Pole Beans, Squash or Scarlet Runner Bean.

You can use perennials and fast growing shrubs to quickly fill in vacant spaces. Often you will be able to move them when the trees are big enough (look upon it as a way of multiplying your stock of plants). .

You can also use fast growing tall annuals like Sunflower, Corn, Amaranth and Hemp to add height. Of course you have to use such plants carefully so they don't adversely affect any of the permanent plantings.

You may also want to fill up bare areas with green manure plants of various kinds, to improve the soil as you go.

Creating growing beds

Growing beds can be created in a variety of ways and could be highly intensive or very low-maintenance. They can have a range of uses, from intensive annual crops to perennial vegetable crops to a full shrub and tree-based polyculture.

Nothing is set in stone in gardening (except for walls and some paths) and you can easily convert conventional intensive beds into no dig beds (just stop digging them). You could build up soil fertility fairly quickly by conventional intensive cultivation (to increase its depth, eliminate compaction, add organic matter and other nutrients) and then switch over to mulching.

Intensive beds

Traditional intensive beds can be quite labor intensive to create if you have to get into double digging. If your soil is fairly good to start with, the job is much easier and you can create growing beds fairly quickly.

1) The first step is to remove any existing vegetation by skimming it off with a spade. You can either take this away and compost it, or bury it while digging. Either way involves quite a bit of work, but it only has to be done once.

2) Mark out the shape of the beds with string (if straight) or use a trail of ground limestone (if curved).

3) The amount of cultivation you have to do is largely determined by the quality of your soil. In a rich light soil all you have to do is spread a layer of organic matter on the surface and incorporate it with a fork. A heavy compacted soil might need a full double digging treatment and the incorporation of lots of organic matter. Whatever you do it is important to remove the roots of any perennial weeds you come across. If you don't remove them, they will reappear and be even harder to remove from amongst your growing plants.

4) When you have finished digging the beds you should remove the topsoil from the paths and throw it onto the beds.

5) The final step is to shape the beds with a rake.

Other kinds of beds

Tilled mulched beds
If you have a large area of poor soil you could spread a thick layer of tree leaves (and rock powders and any other amendments you deem necessary) on the ground and go over the entire area with a rototiller (make two passes to get to the maximum depth. Then mark out the shape of the beds with ground limestone and shovel the loose soil from the paths onto the beds. Finally plant and apply mulch on the beds.

New garden areas
When establishing a new garden area you should start with plants that can survive and compete with native vegetation (potatoes are ideal). Irrigate, mulch between them and weed as necessary. Once the area is under control you can add other plants.

Using potatoes to create beds
Potatoes are such vigorous and easy to grow plants they can be used to start a new garden on grass or weed infested land. Even perennial weeds will succumb to the combination of a thick mulch, deep shade and the considerable soil disturbance of planting and harvesting.

You can create a new bed by simply cutting down all of the vegetation and laying the seed potatoes on the ground. These are then covered with a 3″ layer of mulch (compost, straw, chopped leaves, aged manure). As the plants get taller you add more mulch until it is 8″ to 12″ deep. This is necessary to suppress the existing vegetation and because tubers only form above the seed potato.

Another method calls for marking out the areas for beds and paths, then skimming the turf from the paths and inverting it on the beds. Then the beds are covered with a wheelbarrow load of manure for every 50 square feet. Finally the soil from the paths (and elsewhere if possible) is thrown on top of the beds. You then sow your potatoes and cover with a thick layer of mulch.

No dig gardening

Nature doesn't do very much digging and we shouldn't either. Cultivating the soil often does more harm than good, not to mention being one of the most physically demanding of all gardening activities. In the temperate zone our model for the garden should be a deciduous forest, where falling leaves spread a layer of organic matter on the soil every autumn. Over time earthworms and other soil creatures turn this leafy mulch layer into well structured and fertile soil. We can emulate this process by sheet mulching, which provides fertility, covers seeds and suppresses weeds, all without digging, composting, fertilizing or weeding.

There are some disadvantages to mulching your whole garden, perhaps the biggest being that it requires a lot of organic matter. If you live in a city you may not be able to get enough mulch unless you buy it. Another problem is that it takes longer to build up your soil using no-dig methods and it isn't as productive as more intensive gardening practices (it is less work though). Heavy soils that are low in organic matter may slowly get compacted if you keep walking on them (the solution to this is to not walk on them of course). Also if slugs are a problem in your garden, mulch gives them lots of places to hide and can make them even more of a problem.

Conventional cultivation destroys organic matter (the additional oxygen encourages an explosion of soil organisms that consume it), which then has to be replaced to maintain fertility. In a no-dig system this doesn't happen so soil can build up naturally by the growth and decay of plants.

Sheet mulching
Sheet mulching gives you a way to quickly create an instant garden without disturbing the soil and with a minimum of work. You simply cover the whole area with mulch, so the only plants that grow there are the ones you want.

Sheet mulch performs several functions that make it useful for establishing a new garden. Most importantly it kills perennial weeds by depriving them of light and can turn a weed patch into a garden in a few hours. Equally important it acts like a compost pile and enriches the soil with organic matter, nutrients and microorganisms.

Cardboard generally works better than newspaper for persistent weeds, but newspaper is often easier to obtain (I feel guilty exposing the soil organisms to Rupert Murdochs lies, but I'm not going to separate them out). You can use the whole newspaper nowadays even the color parts, though I would discard the glossy inserts. You probably won't have enough newspaper from your own house (unless you are an avid consumer of advertising and propaganda), but you could get it from a recycling center or from gullible neighbors and friends. You may be able to get large sheets of cardboard from a furniture, window or cabinet store.

The drawback of sheet mulching

Though you create a sheet mulch garden in only few hours, there is a lot of preparatory work to do beforehand. You need a lot of material to cover a large garden and have to collect it all together and get it to the site.

How to do it

I will now describe the various steps for creating an idealized sheet mulch garden. You may find that you don't have enough materials to include every layer. This doesn't matter too much, so long as you have the cardboard / newspaper weed barrier layer and a weed free top mulch layer it should work out fine.

- The day before you create the garden, you should water the area to thoroughly soak the soil. The ideal tool for this is an oscillating sprinkler as it can be set to slowly soak a large area.
- The first step is to cut down or flatten all of the vegetation so it is completely flat. Dig out any small trees or shrubs, as they can send up suckers.
- If the soil is heavy you should fork it lightly, by pushing your spading fork into the ground and levering it back and forth. The resulting cracks allow air and moisture to penetrate.
- The next step is to scatter thin layers of any fertilizers you think necessary (kelp powder, wood ashes, ground limestone, greensand, rock phosphate and any other rock powders).
- Next put down a thin ½″ layer of compost. This is a highly concentrated source of beneficial soil organisms and is used as an inoculant for poor soils. This should always go underneath the mulch and close to the existing soil where its valuable microorganisms (and nutrients) can find a suitable home, protected from harsh sunlight.
- Then cover the entire area with a layer of carbonaceous material such as straw, hay, dried leaves, weeds or wood chips.
- This is followed by a layer of high nitrogen material, such as manure or kitchen scraps, to speed decomposition of the carbonaceous material. The closer the C : N ratio to 30:1 the faster it will decompose and enrich the soil.
- The layer of newspaper or cardboard that follows will slow water infiltration, so the whole area should be thoroughly watered again before laying it down.
- The cardboard or newspaper layer is used to suppress perennial weeds and isn't really needed if you don't have any weeds to worry about. Lay down a layer of cardboard or 5-6 layers of newspaper to completely cover the whole garden area. If you are using newspaper it helps if you wet it, by soaking it in a garbage can of water. It then lays flat and sticks together, rather than blowing away. Each layer should overlap by at least 6 inches, except when you have to go around existing plants (give them a few inches of space). It is important that this layer completely covers the whole garden area, so you don't give the weeds breathing space and a chance to regroup. You want the plants dead before the paper weakens and disintegrates (newspaper only takes a couple of months, cardboard might last a year).
- Another layer of nitrogen rich fertilizer (manure is ideal) goes on top of the paper.
- Finally there is a 3" layer of weed free (this is important) organic material, such as straw, shredded leaves, wood chips or bark chips. This holds down the previous layers and looks a lot better than scattered newspaper or cardboard. It should be watered thoroughly as you spread it to ensure it is evenly moist. The bed is then ready to plant.

Make your bed

Sheet mulching is usually applied to the entire area and then you just define the growing areas and paths afterwards. However if you know where your paths are to be placed beforehand, you don't need to put down all of the fertilizing layers in those areas. You could just put down the paper layer and a final mulch layer.

Planting the sheet mulch Garden

You can plant into the sheet mulch as soon as you have finished laying it down. There is no need to wait for anything to break down. The first plants to be grown in a newly made bed should be fairly vigorous and able to take a little abuse. Potatoes are perhaps the best crop, not only because they are able to take care of themselves, but also because they help to improve the soil. Vigorous transplants such as Tomato, Cucurbits or Brassicas also do well. If you are going to sow seeds, the large vigorous types, such as Peas and beans, work best.

Seeds and small plants are usually planted on top of the paper layer, directly into a hole filled with compost (replace the mulch after planting). Larger plants (seedlings, divided plants, cuttings, plants from pots) are normally planted into the soil below the paper (dig down, cut an x in the paper and plant through it).

Adding mushrooms

If you have read anything about cultivating mushrooms you may have noticed the similarity between a fungus bed and a sheet mulch bed; they are almost the same thing. You could inoculate the top mulch layer with mushroom spawn and not only get another crop, but also break down the carbonaceous material into soil more quickly. See Mushrooms and fungi for more on this.

Living with the garden

Gardening is a continuous learning process (this is one of its greatest appeals) and this type of garden will teach you more than most. A lot of this stuff is fairly new and hasn't been done very much, so you often have to learn as you go. I learned long ago that being a good carpenter is all about knowing how to fix your mistakes and the same applies here to some extent.

The garden isn't finished just because it is built and planted, in fact this is where it starts to get interesting. Even if you created a garden that totally looked after itself, you would still spend time working in the garden, because it is enjoyable. It is the kind of work you will be doing that concerns us here.

If you designed and planted the garden properly, you should have eliminated a lot of the tedious and repetitive tasks of conventional gardening. You will then be left with the interesting and enjoyable tasks: harvesting, creating art, messing about with water, adding interesting new plants and whatever else you feel like doing. Neither you nor the garden should be the slave, it should be a symbiotic partnership from which both benefit.

The amount of work the garden requires will vary according to the time of year, with summer being much busier than winter. As the garden matures it may take less work, but if you are like me you will just keep adding more stuff to keep it interesting.

If you are spending so much time in your garden that it becomes a chore, you should take a break and go do something else. A short break will recharge your batteries and you will return as enthusiastic and excited as ever. Gardening should be pleasurable.

Unnecessary maintenance

Conventional gardens require a lot of upkeep, with endless repetition of the same tedious tasks (mowing, edging, trimming, pruning and more). This is necessary because they ignore the way nature works and attempt to impose human ideas on her. If you want to minimize the work you have to do, then you must learn to work with nature and find ways of doing things that she approves of.

If you find yourself doing the same jobs over and over again just to stay in the same place, you should think about what you are doing and how you might change things. Often we unthinkingly work to maintain some arbitrary human standard of order and neatness that has no relevance to the natural world. I read one book that described how to keep the bark of your Birch trees nice and white by scrubbing them with soap and water. A lot of this can be traced back to the bourgeois tradition of having a hired gardener. If you are paying someone to work for you then you want to keep them busy doing something. Of course it is equally possible those hired gardeners established these standards themselves, in order to make themselves indispensable and so keep themselves employed.

Poor choice of plants can increase your maintenance considerably. If you want an area to be low-maintenance then you need to use locally adapted species that aren't so weak they need to be encouraged, so strong they need to be discouraged or so tender they need to be protected. Don't give these plants extra water or fertilizer either, as it will just make them grow faster, get bigger and they may require work to keep them under control (it can also help some plants to out-compete others).

Gardens are artificial creations and will always need looking after to some degree. How much work they require will depend upon the kind of garden it is. A native garden requires nothing from you (once the plants are established), whereas an intensively planted vegetable garden requires a lot of care. You have to find the right balance between how much work you want to do and how much food you want to produce. We could minimize the time we spend on maintenance by planting tough unproductive groundcovers and other plants (most modern gardens do this and then throw in a lawn to suck up the rest of the available resources). As you know such gardens aren't very interesting and don't produce very much. If we want a productive garden we have to choose productive plants and look after them properly, which requires work. The intensive vegetable garden takes more work than a lawn, but its productivity is much greater.

Necessary maintenance

You can't just buy the plants you want, stick them in the ground and forget about them, you have to look after them so they grow and thrive. Plant growth is always limited by some factor, whether water, fertility, sunlight, shade, competition, weeds, temperature (too hot or too cold) or something else. Maintenance means ensuring that none of these factors affect your plants too much.

The daily walk

There is an old Chinese saying "the shadow of the farmer is the best fertilizer". This means that your care and attention is more important in getting things to grow than anything you put in the soil. Make a habit of walking around the garden every day and write down what needs doing (saving seed, staking plants, pruning, harvesting). If you are observant you might catch those Gooseberry Sawfly before they defoliate your plants, rather than afterwards.

Learning how to look and understanding what you see, is one of the most important skills of the gardener. As you walk around the garden ask yourself what is working well and what isn't (make notes in your journal). Observe how your plants are doing, which combinations work and which don't. If something works well then think about how you could improve, repeat or extend it. If it isn't working then find out why not, and look for a way to make it work (or give up on it).

Check potentially vulnerable elements (fences, dams) regularly for problems (especially after storms), Deer have a way of finding any weak spots in a fence and will come back again and again if there is food for them.

I make a habit of pulling a few weeds when walking around. In fact it's nice if your daily walk can be extended to include a few minutes of maintenance at the most urgent task.

I usually walk around the garden in the evening after I get home from work. I look upon these walks as a pleasure and look forward to them. There is always something interesting to check on. In summer this walk should include a basket for harvesting anything that is ready to use, as well as pen and note pad.

Two or three times a year you should walk around the whole garden and evaluate where you are and what needs to be done next (propagation, clearing, reducing shade. On your early winter walk you write down what needs doing while the plants are dormant (moving, dividing, pruning, crown lifting). Also check all of your trees to ensure the gopher baskets haven't been buried (which allows gophers to go over them).

Journal

It really helps to keep a journal of your everyday gardening activities, planting, harvesting, fertilization, the weather and more. This is also the place to write down your relevant observations (not what you had for lunch). This could include the dates when weeds and pests appear, when the first fruits ripen and when different flowers bloom (with enough information you could eventually time your vegetable planting to the bloom sequence). In years to come this journal will become an invaluable aid to maintenance as it gives you a better idea of when to do things and when to anticipate problems.

Most commercially available 'garden journals' are designed to be pretty, rather than functional. Make your own by printing out some master pages, divide them up into months and make as many copies as you need. I write in the same monthly sections until they are full, just noting the year as well as the date (I change my color pen every year). In this way everything I did in the same month over the years is all visible at once. Keep these pages in a binder and put the journal in the tool shed (with a pen). If you can't get it together to make a journal, you could have a large calendar on the wall and make notes on that.

If you really want to get into record keeping you could also print out plant information sheets for each species in the garden. You can then keep records of flowering, fruiting and harvest dates, pests, propagation techniques and how well it does. You could have separate subsections, or even blank pages, for each variety. If you know the dates of flowering and harvest for each fruiting species in your garden, you can predict fruiting times quite accurately.

In this digital age you can also take lots of photographs and create a visual record of the garden. This can be a great learning tool, as you can see what the garden looked like on any given day (digital photographs have the date they were taken on them)/ This can help in your design efforts, as well as being a comfort on cold winter nights. You could even put it on-line for others to see and be inspired by.

Chalkboard

It is helpful to have a prominently placed chalkboard in your garden shed, where you can write down tasks to do as you think of them (the less organized you are, the more helpful this is). When if you have a few minutes to spare in the garden you can then go directly to the most urgent task.

General oversight

The time required for maintenance varies considerably through the growing year. There is a lot more to do in the warmer months when plants are growing fast, pests are active and the soil dries out rapidly.

If you have divided the garden into separate rooms or sections, you might spend a day (or evening) maintaining each area in turn.

Over time you will refine your garden and develop the techniques that work for your particular situation. When you get to this point you are ready to start helping others with their gardens (perhaps in exchange for some help in yours).

Some of the ways I have killed trees

- I didn't put it in a Gopher basket.
- I forgot to water the young tree (this didn't work with Almond.)
- I allowed deer into the garden (even if they don't kill it they will destroy its shape and stunt its growth).
- I removed the bark with a brush cutter (this can remove the trunk of a small tree).
- I used a chain saw (this doesn't work with trees that coppice).

Plant tasks

Plant problems

You can easily tell when a plant isn't growing well; it grows slowly, it doesn't have much new growth and existing leaves may turn brown and die. Poor growth may be caused by lack of water or a specific nutrient, too much shade, root damage, pests, too much competition or something else. You need to find out what the problem is and correct it

Sometimes everything you plant seems to have a problem and it's easy to get discouraged. However there is a solution to every problem, you just have to find it. The nice thing about gardening is that no matter how incompetent you are and how badly things go wrong, you always start next year with a clean sheet. Gardening is an activity for optimists; next year will be better when you implement your new plans and get the timing exactly right.

Planting

Planting is a never ending process in the garden. You keep finding new and interesting plants you just have to grow. You also have to replace plants that die, are harvested or prove unsuitable. Of course the vegetable garden is one long round of planting and replanting.

How and when you plant depends upon what type of plant you are dealing with. Bare root plants can only be planted while they are dormant (and available). Container plants can go in the ground at any time, even when in full growth. Winter is generally the best time to plant, because there is plenty of moisture in the soil and you don't have to keep watering.

Moving plants

Transplanting is an important skill, as you will be continuously moving plants around your garden, as your ideas change and plants grow. The amount of care you need to take depends upon the species. Some easily moved perennials almost seem to benefit from it, while others don't like any disturbance at all.

Late fall and winter are the best times to move plants, as they are dormant and the ground is at its wettest (though some may be hard to locate at this time - mark them in summer when in growth). If you take extra care it is possible to transplant many plants when in leaf in summer. You just have to take a large enough root ball and give them enough water. However I find that in our hot dry climate it takes a lot of water to keep them moist until they recover, so I prefer to do my transplanting in winter, while the soil is wet. The very worst time to try and move something is when new leaf shoots are emerging, they will almost always die back.

All gardening rules are made to be broken and this includes warnings about not moving certain plants. Plants want to live and grow; they won't usually just curl up and die if you move them. Of course moving them may set them back so much that they will take a few years to recover.

Moving trees and shrubs

If a plant is obviously in the wrong place you can either move it or cut it down. If you are thinking of moving it, you should do it as soon as possible because younger trees recover much better. Once a tree gets past 2" in diameter it becomes much harder to move. Conventional wisdom says that for every inch of trunk your root ball should be 12" across. As you probably know root balls are heavy, which means anything with a trunk bigger than 2" is going to take a lot of work. This means that a tree with a 6" diameter trunk should have a root ball 6 feet in diameter!

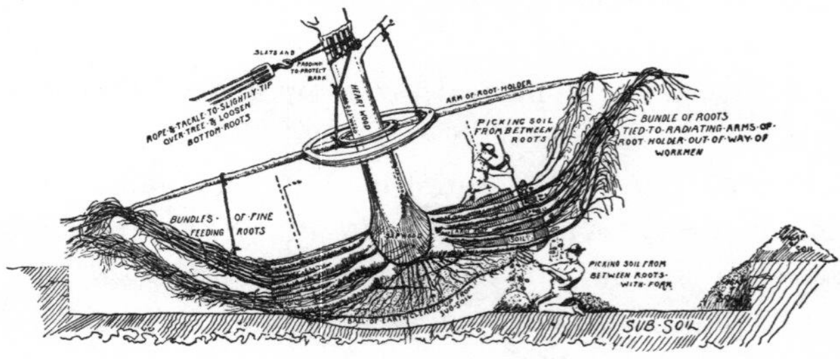

It is possible to move larger trees if you treat them very carefully (and if you can physically move it). A large tree should be root pruned 6 months before you intend to move it, by digging a trench down 2 feet and 12" less than the size of the root ball. After digging the trench you should refill it with soil. This will stimulate the growth of fibrous new feeder roots even before it is moved. The tree can then be moved while dormant from late autumn to late winter. Water the root ball the day before transplanting. When digging you should note the orientation of the plant and mark the north side.

Dig the hole before you start working on moving the plant, so it can go straight back into the ground. Make it the same depth as the root ball, so it will sit at the same level it originally was) but ideally twice as wide (that 6 feet wide root ball would require a hole 12 feet wide). In heavy soil you might want to loosen the sides of the hole, but leave the bottom alone. If the soil is dry you should water the hole thoroughly. The top of the tree is usually pruned to reduce water loss.

Start excavating the tree by digging the trench around the root ball. This ball should include most of the new feeder roots that have just grown. You dig down and under the root ball, until you can tilt the tree over and get a tarp underneath it. You then lift the tree out of the hole with the tarp and move it to its new home. It's tempting to lift the tree by that convenient handle known as the trunk, but it's a bad idea (like lifting with your back instead of your knees).

When you put the tree back in the ground, it should face the same direction as it was before. It should then be well watered until it has fully recovered.

I would only go to all this trouble with a tree that was very important, I have transplanted 2-3" diameter trees almost bare root. One of these is now 8" in diameter, so has recovered pretty well. If it has to move or die, you can just do your best.

Filling in

Gaps appear in the garden all the time as things are harvested. These can be filled in immediately with plants from the nursery bed or greenhouse, or from fast growing direct sown seed. I often transplant volunteers from paths and elsewhere, as these can't always remain where they are. You might also sow a few seeds around a plant a few weeks before harvesting. Any large open spaces that aren't needed immediately can be planted with a fast growing green manure plant such as Phacelia, Mustard or Buckwheat.

Holes created when digging out plants, can be filled with kitchen scraps, to enrich the soil. If there is the possibility of animals digging it up then cover it with chicken wire until it decomposes.

Control

When the garden really gets going, keeping things under control becomes one of the main maintenance activities. Left to themselves most gardens lose species as weaker ones succumb to changing growing conditions, or competition from the stronger ones. One of your jobs is to encourage the weaker ones and rein in the stronger ones.

Editing and removing

If the garden gets so full you don't have enough space for new additions, you have to start looking at the garden in a different light. Inevitably some plants are tolerated because they grow well, even though you don't use them very much. Such plants often take up increasing amounts of space every year and compete with more useful plants. Remove any plants that aren't paying their way in some manner (the definition of this is up to you).

If you decide to thin out an area (to get more light, or to reduce water stress and competition), you should start by removing the least useful or productive plants Sometimes you can transplant unwanted plants rather than destroying them.

If a creeping plant starts to run where you don't want it, dig it up and transplant it (or pot it up and sell it). Running Bamboo canes can be cut for garden use or the new shoots may be harvested and eaten.

Ugly overgrown or misshapen shrubs and seedling (not grafted) trees can be transformed and re-invigorated by cutting them down to the ground. They will send up nice, straight, vigorous new shoots.

You can tell whether a plant is dead or just dormant by scraping at the bark. If the inner bark is green it's alive and dormant, if it is brown it's probably dead. A dead branch is brittle and snaps easily, a living one is supple and bends rather than breaking.

Trees that cast too much shade can be coppiced or pollarded. (See Trees for more on this).

Crown lifting

Some areas of the garden will gradually get shadier as the taller plants grow and spread out, cutting off light to those below. If a wooded area starts to feel claustrophobic, you can prune out some of the branches to let more light through. You have to do this methodically though, if you just remove them randomly it won't be long before they grow back (often even thicker).

The best way to get more light underneath a tree is by crown lifting, which consists of trimming off the lower branches so the crown starts higher up the tree. Only about half of the crown should originate in the lower two thirds of the trunk, the other half should be in the top third. These lower branches are less likely to grow back as they receive less light and aren't as vigorous (most would eventually die naturally).

You have to be careful about crown lifting in very windy areas. By putting more of the foliage higher up, you can make the trees more vulnerable to breaking in high winds.

Make sure you trim off the limbs properly. The biggest mistake you can make is allowing the branch to fall before you finish the cut. This rips a strip of bark from underneath the branch and proudly proclaims that you are an amateur who doesn't know what they are doing. All you have to do to prevent this happening is to undercut the branch a little, before cutting from the top.

Frost protection

In some cases you can protect tender plants over the winter, making it possible to keep then alive in climates that would otherwise be too cold for them. In Japan the wrapping of trees has been elevated to an art form (like many other everyday activities) and the wrapped plants become garden ornaments in their own right. This makes a lot of sense if they are to be in a prominent place for many months of the year.

In citrus growing areas gardeners often have to come out on cold nights and cover their trees to protect them from light frost (cotton sheets work best). A harder frost can be kept at bay by putting an incandescent light bulb under the sheet to supply a little additional heat. On a bigger scale you could light fires near the trees.

Commercial citrus and strawberry farmers protect large areas of crops by running sprinklers all night. As the water turns to ice it gives off heat and so prevents the plants from freezing. This has been effective at protecting Citrus groves down to 15° F. In an emergency you could emulate them and leave a sprinkler on for the coldest part of the night (don't turn it off until all of the ice has melted).

Incidentally don't remove frost damaged branches from plants until spring. Sometimes only the leaves are killed, the branch may survive and sprout new ones. They can also help to protect the rest of the plant below. Likewise is a tree appears to be dead, don't yank it out of the ground immediately, wait until spring. I have had several trees come back from the dead.

Some tender plants can be dug up in fall and stored in a frost free place for the winter (Dahlia, Gladiolus and Geranium are often treated in this way). If you aren't sure whether a plant can make it through the winter outdoors, take out insurance. Pot up some cuttings or divisions and keep them in the greenhouse for the winter.

Fire Maintenance
In a hot dry climate it is important to maintain your fire breaks and other defensible space in case of wildfire. This means keeping the area around the house clean and tidy, with no dry grass, leaf litter or dead plants. Keep the roof and rain gutters clear of plant debris that could catch flying embers. Remove any unwanted, dead or overcrowded vegetation to reduce fuel load. Keep the plants that are close to the house low and well watered. Remove low hanging limbs from trees.

Harvesting
Harvesting is a continuous process throughout the growing season and in mild climates it can continue year round. The aim of harvesting is to maximize the harvest by keeping the plants productive for as long as possible.

All crops must be harvested at the right time for best flavor, but this is especially important with the less domesticated plants. Herbs are best harvested just before they flower. Roots are at their best while they are dormant and contain the maximum nutrients. Greens are usually best while still young and growing rapidly, before they get into flowering mode. Perennial greens are best in spring (again before they start to think about flowering). Fruit should be ripe (or at least at the point where it can ripen off the tree). Mushrooms should be harvested as soon as they are fully expanded (for biggest harvest, best flavor and for easier identification),

Some plants can be harvested one leaf at a time, without significantly affecting them (Chard, Kale, Amaranth, Giant Lambs Quarters).

In some cases you need to think about pests too. I have several young Walnut trees that are producing nuts, but I never get any because the Squirrels are there before the nuts are fully ripe. Same thing with my Hazels. In Japan they harvest perfect fruit by enclosing each fruit individually in a paper bag.

Storage and preservation
The garden will intermittently produce a glut of food all at once, far more than you can use. If you are aiming to live off of the food from your garden, you need some way to preserve this for later use. The traditional staples (potatoes, carrots, cabbage, beans, field corn) are fairly easy to deal with, if you have the right storage conditions (a root cellar is the ultimate solution). Other foods may need to be canned, dried or frozen. These require special equipment and some fairly basic skills (these aren't difficult to learn).

Using the food
The challenge with the more unusual foods is finding ways to incorporate them into your diet on a regular basis. As I said before, if you don't eat them they don't count.

Mushrooms
Saprophytic mushrooms grow wherever they find suitable organic matter to grow on. When this has been broken down they move on. You can encourage them to keep growing in the same place by periodically giving them fresh organic matter (straw, compost, wood chips).

Plant propagation

The ability to propagate plants is one of the most useful, satisfying and profitable of all the gardening skills you can acquire. At its simplest propagation means sowing seeds and dividing perennials. You can then go on to taking hardwood and softwood cuttings and layering. As you get more experienced you can get into the various forms of grafting, budding and raising your own rootstocks.

Propagating your own plants really impresses the uninitiated (they say you have a green thumb), but the biggest secret about propagation is that it is easy (don't tell anyone I told you though, it would spoil the mystique). Propagation is largely about timing and if you get that right it is pretty straightforward. The only special talent you need is patience. The most important thing about propagation is to do it now.

I make a habit of taking hardwood cuttings from suitable plants in early winter (you can often combine this with pruning). I also usually do a couple of rounds of softwood cuttings in early summer and a round of layering in spring. I also pot up suitable suckers and volunteers whenever the opportunity arises. Far from being work, these activities are interesting and very rewarding.

Some plants are almost foolproof when it comes to propagation (Currants, Gooseberries, Blackberries, Willows, Grapes, Comfrey, Poplar, Horseradish), all you have to do is cut up a stem or root and stick the pieces in the ground. If you can manage to put them in the right way up they will grow into new plants in a few months (no green thumb required).

I'm always experimenting with unusual edible perennials, which aren't readily available. These plants are often fairly expensive to buy, but I keep my costs down by buying only one plant (or two if needed for pollination) of each variety and propagating them myself.

If you propagate methodically and things go well, within a couple of years you will have plants worth many times what you originally paid. In fact you can easily recoup your initial investment by selling off surplus stock.

Starting plants from seed

This is the commonest method of plant propagation of course. I dealt with growing vegetables from seed at great length in The Organic Gardeners Handbook. Most of that stuff is also relevant to growing other plants as well, so I am not going to repeat myself here.

Growing perennials from seed can be harder than starting annuals, because they are more temperamental. The seeds of many temperate zone species have a built in dormancy period, to prevent the ripe seed germinating just as winter starts. This dormancy period must be overcome by stratification before the seed will germinate and even then germination may be erratic (especially if the seed isn't fresh). This isn't necessarily a big problem though as you don't usually need a lot of plants.

The simplest way to stratify seeds is to plant them outside in fall in a nursery bed and leave them over winter (protected from rodents and birds).

If you don't get your seed until mid winter or early spring, you may have missed the natural stratification timetable and will have to do it yourself indoors. The basic method is to mix the seed with some damp vermiculite and put it in a plastic bag in the fridge (not freezer). Leave it for 6-12 weeks and then plant it in a warm place. Some seeds with hard seed coats germinate better if the seed coat is scratched or nicked to allow water to penetrate. A few even need treatment with acid, to simulate the journey through an animals stomach. Each type of seed is different so you have to find out exactly what they need.

If you are sowing the seed of warm climate plants, don't make the mistake of starting them too early. They won't germinate well if it's too cold and may eventually rot. Be patient and wait until it gets warm enough and they will germinate and grow rapidly.

Most fruit trees don't breed true from seed, which means the resulting tree will have fruit that is quite different (and usually inferior) from its parent.

Seed saving

Saving seed was once an integral part of growing your own annual food crops. If you wanted to plant seed, then you had to save seed. Only relatively recently has it become the norm for gardeners and farmers to buy seed every year. Saving seed from most common vegetable crops is actually pretty simple and very worthwhile. You can also save seed from perennials and any fruit or nut bearing plants (though the offspring may sometimes surprise you).

Your garden will produce a lot of seed if you allow your plants to do what nature intended. Occasionally you have to assist them, but often they do it whether you like it or not. All you have to do is gather the seed when it is ripe, dry it thoroughly and store it. I don't particularly care if the seed isn't 100% pure, because it is just for my own use (if I plant a lettuce seed I'm pretty happy is a lettuce plant appears).

I save seeds any time the opportunity arises. I just go out into the garden every so often with some paper grocery bags and collect whatever is ripe. The seeds go in the warm greenhouse or shed to dry and are then cleaned (with the help of a series of different sized sieves and some old fashioned winnowing). The clean seed is then stored in paper envelopes in a cool dry place (with a description and the date written clearly on them). It is most important that the place be dry, as the biggest enemy of stored seeds is moisture.

Saving your own seed results in you having far more seed than you need for planting. This leaves you with lots of seed to give away, trade, sell, or simply scatter around the garden. Many edible seeds (Brassicas, Sunflowers, Radish) can be eaten as nutritious seed sprouts.

Deadheading

Don't allow prized perennials to set seed unless you want seed. It takes a lot of energy and nutrients that could have gone into vegetative growth. Some plants may even die after producing seed.

Volunteers

Often nature will offer you the seedlings she considers best adapted to the growing conditions, the self-sown offspring of your crops. If you regularly allow plants to produce seed for saving, some will commonly fall before you collect it. By allowing your best plants to self-seed you can build up a reservoir of useful seeds in the soil, giving another layer of productivity to the garden. Some annual crops can produce so many seedlings you don't ever have to plant them again.

As the garden increases in diversity you will find more and more interesting volunteers. Often there will be a thick carpet of seedlings where the seeds fell. You might allow these to grow where they fall and thin them to leave the most vigorous plants, or you could transplant some to a more convenient spot. Often I just let them get big enough to harvest and then eat them.

Reliable volunteers in my garden

Tomato, Tomatillo, Lettuce, Cilantro, Parsley, Carrot, Kale, Giant Lambs Quarter, Amaranth, Orach, Strawberry Spinach, Chard, Chicory. Cornsalad, Chia.

Calendula, Morning Glory, Alyssum, Hollyhock.

Apricot, Chestnut, Walnut.

Many fruit trees also self-sow readily, though (as I mentioned above) the resulting fruit will often be different from the parent plant. If a lot of fruit falls in the garden you may well have volunteer tree seedlings appearing. A few species (Apricot, Cherry, Chestnut, Lemon, Peach) can produce fairly good seedling fruit and if you have the time, space and the inclination you could plant large numbers of seeds and see what comes up. These seedlings could also be used as rootstock for grafting (they will produce full size trees of course).

I'm always on the lookout for interesting volunteers and I mark the location of anything interesting with a flag so I don't accidentally remove it. These kinds of volunteers are one reason for not wiping out weeds blindly without first identifying them.

You can also plant fruit pits or seeds around the garden. Sometimes interesting things appear.

Vegetative propagation

Vegetative propagation gives you the means to obtain more plants than you could ever use with relatively little effort. You can even obtain plants from the wild without significantly impacting a single wild plant. Be aware that propagation techniques are sometimes very specific to individual species and you need to find out the best way to treat each one.

Cuttings

You can get cuttings from your own plants, from friends and neighbors or by more illicit means. In England there is a gardeners joke that hints at an old tradition among the plant obsessed:

Question: When is the best time to take cuttings?
Answer: When no one is looking.

If your conscience stretches to this you should always do it with the same consideration you would give your own garden. There shouldn't be any visible damage and it shouldn't be apparent that any plant parts are gone.

Hardwood Cuttings

These are usually taken after the leaves have fallen in late autumn. Use healthy dormant growth of last years wood to take cuttings 10 inches long and as thick as a pencil. They can be planted in pots, a nursery bed or the ground and are pushed into the ground, leaving only a couple of inches sticking out. By the spring they will have rooted and will put out new shoots.

A few species (Salix, Populus) have dormant root buds along their length and root very easily. However most plants can't grow roots until they have formed callus tissue over the cut, because the callus produces the roots.

Softwood cuttings

A lot of species can be grown from greenwood cuttings if you cut them at the right time and give them the right conditions. A few are less accommodating and demand extra attention, maybe even misting, bottom heat and more. Even most of these will work out if you give them exactly what they want.

Softwood cuttings are usually taken in early summer when a plant has produced a significant amount of new green growth. The simple way to root these cuttings is to trim off most of the leaves and put the cuttings in a plant pot full of moist peat moss. Cover it with a plastic bag to keep in the humidity and put in a warm place with filtered light. Keep it moist and within a month or two many of the cuttings will be well rooted and can be potted up individually.

Softwood cuttings work with herbaceous plants as well as woody ones. You can get a whole second generation of Tomato or Basil plants by rooting suckers from your first generation.

Root cuttings

The species that can be grown from root cuttings may be propagated in large numbers very easily. These include members of the *Amelanchier, Caragana, Robinia, Populus, Prunus, Sassafras, Rhus. Rubus, Sambucus* and *Vaccinium* families,

Root cuttings should be taken from fairly young and vigorous roots that are at least pencil thickness. Make the cuttings 4 inches long, cutting cleanly so there is no crushing or other damage that could invite rot. Cut the top (sky end) of the root flat and the bottom (ground end) at a slant, so you will know which end is up. You can take root cuttings pretty much any time, but the best time is when they are dormant and full of nutrients.

The best time to root cuttings is in spring as the soil is warming up, so store them in bundles for the winter in moist peat moss, sawdust or sand in a cool (40 degree) place. By early spring many will have produced buds and roots, so untangle them and remove most buds, leaving only the biggest one. You can plant the cuttings in pots or a nursery bed, or plant directly in the field (you may lose a lot more this way though).

Layering

Another simple and almost foolproof propagation method. The best time to do this is in early spring before buds open, but you can do it any time so long as the soil is moist.

To layer a plant select a flexible dormant shoot of last years wood and bend it sharply 12 inches from the tip. This may cause some of the fibers to crack, but this is okay as you need to wound the shoot anyway. If it doesn't then scrape some of the bark from underneath the bend (this isn't essential but can help root formation). You bury the bent part of the shoot in soil by digging a slight hole, holding the stem down and dropping the soil on top (compact the soil on top of the branch). If it tries to pull out of the ground you can use a soil staple or bent stick to hold it down (this can also help to mark it). As the tip grows you tie it to a stake so it grows upright. All you have to do then is ensure that the soil doesn't dry out completely and wait.

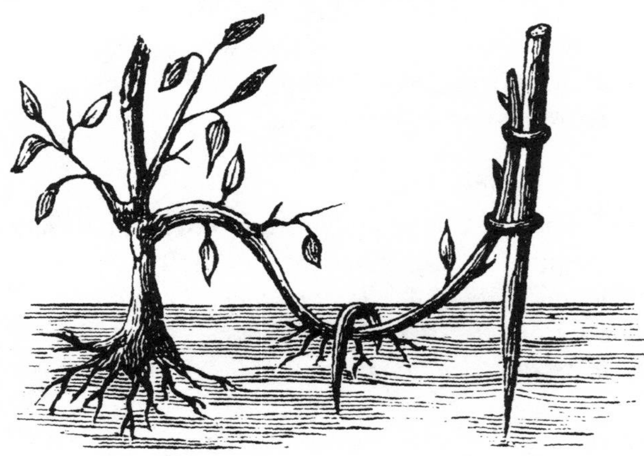

I like layering as it is so simple and easy. Just spend an hour or so in spring, going around burying branches. Go around again to stake the growing shoots upright and forget about them for a year. Next year you just go around and detach all of the new plants (and do some more).

Division

Dividing basically consists of splitting up plants. Sometimes you do this carefully with your hand, sometimes you do it brutally with a spade (it depends upon the species).

Dividing plants is a satisfying activity, because it accomplishes two things at once. You rejuvenate overcrowded plants (many perennials need dividing every 2-3 years) and you end up with more plants than your started with. I just finished a big effort to plant out everything I had remaining in pots. This also involved moving some plants that were in the ground. By the time I had finished dividing these I had more new plants in pots than I started with.

Grafting

Most common fruit trees are grafted or budded to ensure they have a suitable rootstock. It is sometimes possible to graft an improved cultivar onto a closely related wild rootstock, to get a larger plant much more rapidly. This isn't often done though, so should be considered experimental. Grafting is pretty straightforward if you know what you are doing. I don't have room to go into detail here, but there are plenty of good books on the subject.

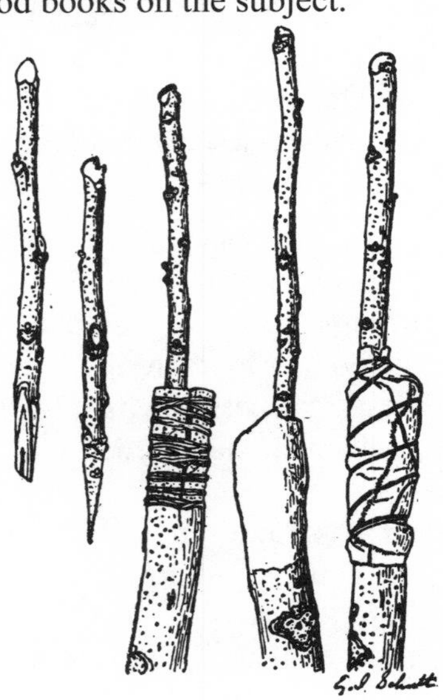

Suckers

No I don't mean people who vote against their own interests in elections because some clever ad campaign pushed the right buttons, I'm talking about the shoots that emerge from the roots of some trees and shrubs. Plants that send up suckers are easily propagated. You simply detach the rooted sucker while the plant is dormant and replant it. This won't work with a grafted tree though, as the sucker will emerge from the rootstock (though it could be used as a rootstock for grafting).

The nursery bed

Once your newly propagated plants are growing well, you move them to a protected nursery bed. They are then left there until they are big enough to plant out. A nursery bed can also be used to raise seedlings in warm weather. Simply sow a few seeds of whatever you want in the bed, safe from birds, insects and other perils. It can also be used to stratify seed over the winter, just sow them in fall to germinate the following spring.

The nursery bed is also useful as a holding bed for volunteers transplanted from the garden. It can also be used to grow on some of those tiny mail order plants that are often little more than rooted cuttings when they arrive. Put them in the nursery bed for a year to increase in size (and perhaps take some cuttings from them).

Weeds

A weed is an anthropocentric concept and basically means any plant that is growing where we don't want it to. Amaranth or Purslane may be growing in our intensive beds as crops, or they may be there uninvited as weeds. If we eat the plants that grow as weeds are they still weeds, or are they only weeds when they are a problem?

Annual weeds are a particular problem in the vegetable garden because they have evolved to grow in moist, fertile disturbed soil. They are also able to germinate quickly and have a greater ability to forage for water and nutrients than our chosen crop plants. This means they can out-compete our crop plants every time.

For ornamental gardeners weeds commit the even bigger crime of being unsightly and spoiling the carefully created illusion of perfection. I don't have this problem, I enjoy seeing vigorously growing plants and some weeds are just as beautiful as anything we might choose to grow (look at a Dandelion). If you have a problem with weeds you might want to re-evaluate your priorities and figure out where the problem really lies. Are you worried about what the neighbors might think? Are you obsessively neat? Do you feel inadequate in some way and feel the need to prove yourself by picking on small defenseless weeds?

Weeds can be a good thing in that they increase the biodiversity, productivity and usefulness of the garden, with no effort on your part. Perennial weeds are particularly useful for taking nutrients from the soil and converting them into organic matter and can be grown in their own fertility bed. Many weeds are edible or have other uses too (see Wild plants and weeds for more on this).

Control

If weeds are to be a useful component of your garden, rather than a headache, you have to keep them under control. You can't just let them do what they want. While a few weeds are a beneficial addition to the garden, too many are decidedly detrimental.

How you deal with weeds depends upon where they are found. Only a few useful weeds can be tolerated in the intensive growing beds, or the ornamental front garden, but there is plenty of room in the rest of the garden.

The first rule of weed control is don't let them set seed. The old saying is one years seeding means nine years weeding.

The second rule is don't deal with the weeds, deal with the reason why they are appearing. The best way to control weeds is the same whether it is a clump of Chickweed or a Cottonwood tree: don't give it a niche to grow in. Annual weeds are a problem in conventional gardens and farms because the repeated cultivation means there is always plenty of bare disturbed soil. Nature abhors bare soil because it leads to soil degradation and uses annual weeds to cover and protect it.

When it comes to weeding those who don't learn from history will be condemned to repeat it. Don't spend an hour weeding and then just leave the newly disturbed soil to grow more weeds in a few weeks. After weeding you need to change the growing conditions that favor weeds, by planting something or laying down a mulch (preferably both). Annual weeds won't even try and germinate if the soil is covered.

Perennial weeds are opportunists and appear wherever the conditions are suitable. Remove these while they are small and can still be dealt with like annuals. Once they establish a deep root system they become much harder to eliminate. Established perennial weeds are best controlled by a combination of mulch (cardboard works well), digging and (sometimes) cutting.

A few pernicious weeds (Bermuda grass, Bindweed, Ground Elder) can't be tolerated at all and should be eliminated by any means necessary. If they get established they will be permanent as long as you have a garden. To get rid of them you will have to alter the habitat completely.

You can keep weeds under control by harvesting their growth to eat or use for mulch (this also prevents them seeding). Every time a flush of weeds get to a reasonable size it can be cut down, chopped up and scattered on the soil surface.

Compost

If you use compost in the intensive vegetable garden, or as a soil inoculant, then you must regularly take time to build some piles. The first rule of compost is that you have to make it (or buy it) before you can use it.

Soil fertility

In the mature garden the nutrients for plant growth will mostly be supplied by the decomposing mulch and by nitrogen fixing plants. However in the early stages it may be necessary to build up the soil with doses of organic matter, rock powders, seaweed and other amendments.

Most of your fertilizing efforts should be concentrated on the plants that really need fertile soil, the areas around the house, the intensive vegetable garden and the fruit trees. Other areas are best left in a natural state, as fertilizing the soil can have unintended consequences. It makes the plants that respond to fertilizer grow faster, which includes many of the plants we think of as weeds (most thrive in nitrogen rich soil). It gives these plants an advantage over plants that have evolved other growth strategies. It may also cause nutritional imbalances that can lead to sappy growth, pests and disease problems.

All material from the garden should go back into the garden: weeds, prunings and any other plant debris. Kitchen scraps should always be returned to the soil via, composting, vermicomposting, mulching or simply burying it in the ground. If you get really serious about this a composting toilet can close another circle and prevent a lot of nutrients being lost though harvesting. See Soil improvement for more on this important topic.

Maintain the mulch

An important annual maintenance activity is putting down a fresh layer of mulch around all of your permanent plantings. This conserves moisture, prevents annual weed growth, feeds the soil and covers the seeds. You should also take any other opportunity to add mulch as it arises (it is the best way to dispose of any organic material: weeds, harvested crops, prunings and more).

A freshly laid mulch is very loose and will often get scattered by birds, skunks and other foraging creatures, especially if it hides a lot of tasty soil life. Mulch on a slope tends to move downhill from the action of birds and heavy rain. If the mulch layer gets too thin it won't be as effective, so fix it.

Watering

In dry climates watering is the most important maintenance operation. Water is not only necessary for the plants in your garden, it is also important for the health of the soil and the organisms that live in it. See Watering for more on this.

Irrigation can cause an imbalance that favors those plants that can grow rapidly with extra water over those that are tolerant of drought.

Vacation watering

If you are not to become a slave to your garden you need to be able to take time away in summer without worrying about your plants. In dry climates this usually means having someone come in and do the watering for you. I like to minimize the chance of problems by making the job as simple as possible. I put my drip systems on a timer, move potted plants to a shady convenient place and connect up the hose. Then the job is mostly about keeping an eye on everything and making sure it all keeps working.

Once when I didn't have anyone to water for me (or a drip system), I put all my potted plants (even flats of seedlings) in the pathways of the vegetable garden and watered everything for an hour a day with an overhead oscillating sprinkler on a timer. This was somewhat wasteful of water but not only kept everything alive, the plants grew rapidly.

Cleanup

According to Feng Shui it is important that the harmonious garden be free of mess, which suggests work left undone and hence is not restful (it also slows down the chi). You garden will need an occasional cleanup for it to look its best. This really can make a big difference in how it feels.

Don't think of plant debris as being mess though and don't clear it away to leave bare soil. As I have said elsewhere human concepts of tidiness have no place in the natural world. Leaf litter and dead plants are important because they provide food for soil organisms, protect the soil from the elements and can even help to protect tender plants from frost. They also provide a place for many creatures to survive the winter. This can be good or bad, depending upon the creature. After a tree is finished bearing fruit you may want to clean up underneath it for disease and insect prevention.

Animal challenges

Every garden has its share of pests, but most don't do enough damage to warrant doing much about them. Only a few pests are problematic enough that you have to take decisive action to deal with them.

It would be nice if you could simply ignore all wild creatures and just let them live their wild lives, but this won't really work. Deer and rabbits can strip plants overnight. Gophers will slowly work their way around your garden, devouring anything in their path: fruit trees, shrubs, perennials and annuals. Birds will strip your trees down to the last cherry, blueberry or mulberry. Squirrels love walnuts and hazelnuts (they are busy harvesting chestnuts as I write this) as well as some vegetables. Raccoons will pick your ripe corn the night before you do. In my garden quail will eat any succulent vegetation in summer (purslane doesn't exist because they eat it all), while in winter they go for Brassicas.

Dealing with pests

Don't look upon all wild creatures: birds, insects and reptiles as a potential enemy, they aren't. The more diversity you have in the garden, the less pest problems there will be. The creatures we consider pests are an important part of the food chain and we shouldn't really try to eliminate them.

Since its messy to crush a gopher underfoot and Ortho hasn't brought out a "coon killer" spray yet, I find the best first line of defence to be a secure fence. Some people around here get so frustrated at the continuous depredations of deer, gophers, jays, quail and raccoons that they eventually enclose their entire vegetable garden in a cage. This can certainly increase your peace of mind and results in a lot less lettuce losses in the garden (it also makes you feel less murderous to the animals).

Another good strategy is abundance; having so much food available at any one time that any losses aren't important.

The best way to deal with most insect pests is by encouraging their predators. This means having as much biodiversity as possible: trees and shrubs for habitat, open water and a wide diversity of food plants.

The neatness so prized by many gardeners often makes pest problems worse, by making it easier for pests to locate their desired plants. The most obvious example of this is a nicely weeded bed, with only bare soil and crop plants. Not only can the slugs easily find the crop plant, but there is nothing else for them to eat there.

A simple way to deal with some fruit eating pests is to pick the fruit before it is fully ripe and let it ripen off the tree.

Income

The garden saves you money by providing you with food and other things (at least if you don't keep buying stuff for it), but it would be even better if it could help to support you financially. There are actually quite a few ways it could do this if you are enterprising enough. Usually the hard part isn't producing something to sell, but finding somewhere to sell it. Craigslist.com might be a good start.

Vegetables
A large vegetable garden can produce a lot of food over the summer months and you could sell the surplus for income (this is a cottage garden tradition in fact). You could also arrange to grow vegetables for a few neighbors for a pre-arranged weekly fee. This could be a good way to learn the ropes if you want to eventually become a real farmer.

We need to develop a new kind of gardening that is somewhere between market gardening and traditional home vegetable gardening. Producing food doesn't just have to be the domain of the farmer with hundreds of acres, or even the market gardener with 2 or 5 acres. It's been estimated that you could make a living from intensively cultivating only ⅛ of an acre. You just need to use the right techniques and the right crops (Tomato, Lettuce, Garlic and others). You might also concentrate on the more expensive luxury crops.

Fruit
You could also sell fruit (which takes even less work than vegetables), in fact this could be a good way to dispose of the over abundance of fruit that comes from getting too interested in fruiting plants. A few productive fruit trees can give you a lot of fruit in a short time. Make sure you choose the best-flavored highest quality varieties and you should have no trouble selling any fruit you can produce. You could also dry fruit for selling later when prices may be higher. To add even more value you could make preserves or pies.

Salad mix
Salad mix is a high value intensive crop that doesn't require much space to grow. I have known a couple of people who made a good living growing edible flowers for chic restaurants (one even sold her weeds).

Berries
A high value crop of berries will only take a couple of years to get going. As with tree fruit you could sell fresh or dried fruit, or make preserves or pies (sell to coffee shops).

Herbs
This could be culinary herbs, but it may be more profitable to go for the more specialized medicinal herbs (fresh or dry). You could grow and dry herbs for making tea, or get equipped to make your own tea bags (make your own tea blends and put them in fancy boxes). You could also add value to your medicinal herbs by making salves, tinctures, essential oils and more.

Mushrooms
Mushrooms and other fungi might be grown on a small scale, indoors or out and could provide you with a high value crop. If you are successful at this, you might also sell spawn of various edible species so people can grow their own.

Chickens
Grow your own chicken feed and sell eggs.

Seed sprouts. Micro-greens
Save your own seeds and use them to grow these.

Cut flowers
Another easy one.

Food stall
You could also sell all of the above foods (and other products) at your local flea market, or set up a roadside stand.

Craft materials
Basket Willows are easy to grow and are in demand from crafts people. Bamboo canes could be sold to gardeners and for use in crafts, There are also other craft products you could grow: dried flowers, dye plants, coppiced shoots and more.

Bamboo
Bamboo is easy to grow yet plants are expensive to buy. It wouldn't take long to build up enough stock to sell. You could even offer an invasive bamboo removal service (then pot it up and sell it). You could also produce canes for gardeners.

Ornamental plants
Hobby ornamentals such as Dahlias, Orchids, Begonias, Iris and others offer a lot of scope for sales. You have to be interested in the plants of course.

Chickens
Grow your own chicken feed and sell eggs.

Honey
Bees help out with pollination in the garden and can provide you with honey without asking for much in return.

Wine
Many fruits can be used to make wine, not just grapes. There would no doubt be a market for some of the more unusual ones. Get adventurous and add herbs, flowers, fruits, etc.

Smoking materials
You could grow the herbs to make your own herbal smoking mixtures. You could make some with a base of tobacco for cigarette smokers (due to tax laws this is no doubt illegal though), and some without. You might also try making herbal smoking mixtures from Bearberry, Mullein, Coltsfoot, Mint and other herbs. I would find this quite fascinating, if it wasn't for the fact that I don't like to get smoke in my lungs.

Seeds
Sell your own locally produced and adapted seed from heirloom and unusual varieties. If you save your own vegetable seed you usually have a surplus anyway.

If your garden contains a lot of unusual edibles, you could allow them to produce seed and collect it for sale.

Seedlings
If you are already growing vegetable and herb seedlings for your own use, you might also grow extra plants to sell.

If you have useful plants that produce short lived, large seeds (Chestnuts, Hazels, Walnuts) you could grow seedlings for sale. You might also be able to pot up self-sown seedlings.

Propagating plants
Many plants are easily raised from cuttings, layering and division. You could make money every year by propagating food plants, especially the more unusual cultivars. If you get into propagating perennials and woody plants from seed then there is no limit to what you can do. If more people did this many useful plants could become better known and more widely available. Craigslist.com is a fantastic resource for selling plants as it can put you in touch with buyers of even the most obscure things.

Gardening supplies
If you have a big truck you could find a good source for manure, compost, mulch, shredded bark and supply less mobile gardeners with these important materials. You might also find a source of used fence boards (contact fencing contractors) and other recycled stuff.

Garden advisor
We need a new type of hands-on gardener/small farmer/consultant, ready to share knowledge with neighbors and help them to grow more of their own food and make city neighborhoods blossom.

You could take this one step further and advise people on decreasing their consumption and greening their homes and lives. To help them to integrate not only growing the new food garden, but also insulating the house, photovoltaics, solar hot water, vegetable garden, edible landscape, greenhouse, gray water treatment, rainwater harvesting, composting toilets and more.

Once your garden is sufficiently developed you could teach others how to plant and maintain this kind of garden. This could tie in well with selling surplus useful plants. Don't do this until you have gained sufficient knowledge though. There are many more people who like the idea of being teachers, than there are people worth listening to.

Plants

The rest of this book deals with specific groups of plants and their uses. I haven't really emphasized the more commonly grown plants, except when they can be grown in more unusual ways. This is because they are so familiar and so much information about them is already available.

Trees

When I first started gardening I didn't give much thought to trees, I simply accepted whatever trees nature (or previous owners) had provided and planted my annuals and perennials around them. It took quite a few years before I got around to planting many trees myself (no doubt it was something to do with being a renter all those years). Food bearing trees actually add a whole new dimension to the productive garden and now I can't really imagine a garden without them.

Fruit and nut trees are the most productive plants we can grow in terms of what they produce for what they demand from us. They require less work, skill and commitment than vegetables and often largely look after themselves. Many just keep on producing food almost every year. All they require is occasional attention, mostly in winter when there is often little else to do in the garden anyway. My chestnuts quite literally produce food with no work at all.

Trees mostly produce fruits and nuts, which complement the produce of the annual vegetable garden perfectly. They can also provide us with other useful materials: lumber, firewood, poles, mulch, compost material and more.

The best thing about trees is that they aren't just crops of course, they also some of the most beautiful plants as well as some of the most versatile in their uses in the garden. They give privacy, shelter, shade and make up the framework of the garden. See Landscape uses of trees for more on this.

Planning tree crops

Trees are a long-term investment and you should plan them carefully. Incidentally don't take anything you read about plants in books for granted (except what you read here of course). I just read a book saying Greengages don't produce well in hot climates. That's not my experience at all, in fact I really can't imagine how any tree could produce more fruit than my Greengage. I've now grown so many plants that supposedly don't like hot weather (Blueberries, Black Currants, Raspberries) that I'm starting to wonder what hot means. Another book warned against planting any fruit, anywhere in the garden.

Flavor – I consider this to be the most important criteria for selecting varieties of any fruit crop. If I am going to go to all of the effort of planting and tending trees for their fruit and then waiting several years for the first reward, I expect the resulting fruit to be exceptional. Simply as good as that I could buy isn't good enough, Fortunately this is mostly a matter of genetics, if you select an exceptional tasting variety you will be more than half way towards a delicious harvest. It works too, my apples, mulberries, nectarines and plums are the best I've ever had.

Climate - This is one of the most important factors in determining what you can or can't grow (and how it will taste). The zone hardiness map of the USDA will tell you what zone you are in, and most plant catalogs indicate the zone requirements of their plants.

Most common tree fruits are cultivated all around the world and they have undergone extensive breeding to adapt them to different climates. This means that there are varieties adapted to almost every imaginable situation. You have to determine which ones will best suit your needs, taking into account all of the various factors. It is important that you get varieties that can tolerate the winter in your area (small local nurseries usually sell such varieties).

Bloom time - The time of year your trees bloom can be important. If they bloom so early the flowers are killed by frost every year you won't get much of a return for your effort.

Chill factor - In areas with very mild winters (above zone 7) some temperate fruit may not do well because it isn't cold enough. A certain amount of cold weather (below 45° F.) is needed for the trees to go dormant and if they don't get this rest period they may leaf out late, produce few flower buds and not fruit well. The number of hours they need to rest is known as the chill factor and varies as much as hardiness. If you have this problem, you should choose low chill varieties and plant them in the coldest microclimate you have.

Heat units – Heat is necessary to ripen fruit and is measured in heat units. The hotter it is, the more heat units and the faster fruit will ripen. Without enough heat the fruit may never get sweet, because it doesn't contain enough sugar. It might also take so long to ripen that it gets damaged by frost before it is fully ripe.

Maturation date – The maturation time from flowering to harvest varies considerably, with most crops having early, mid and late season varieties. If you are planting 4 plum trees you don't want them all to ripen fruit at the same time, so you choose varieties that will ripen one after the other. This gives you a steady supply of fresh fruit for weeks. One advantage of using dwarf trees is that you can have a large number of varieties with different maturation times.

Rootstock

Though these are best known for affecting the size of trees, this isn't all they do. They also affects tolerance to soil conditions, pests and more.

Tree size

Trees need plenty of space, not only for their own sake but also because they affect everything else around them. The size of a tree and the size of the garden may determine where you can put it (or if you can fit it at all). In small gardens most trees are placed to the north side, where they won't cast unwanted shade. Of course you should also think about whether they will shade someone else's garden and if they care.

Thanks to the wonders of dwarfing rootstocks you can now decide how big a tree you want for most of the common fruit trees (see Choosing fruit trees). You can get the same variety of tree in different sizes, which gives you a lot of flexibility in designing with trees.

Large trees (40 ft. +) Climax forest trees can get very big and don't really fit in to the food garden unless it is very big. I suppose you might be able to squeeze some in on the northernmost edge of the garden, where they won't cast too much shade.

Some of the large nut producing trees can be incredibly productive (that massive amount of foliage can produce a massive amount of food). A mature Chestnuts tree can produce 250 pounds of carbohydrate rich nuts almost every year. Some trees can also produce valuable timber (Walnut and Black Cherry are particularly prized). You might want to ensure that these trees grow straight and tall with one trunk (to be valuable for lumber), or crooked with many stems (to make sure they aren't).

Rootstocks

Apple
Antonovka: 25-35 feet Cold hardy (also produces good fruit)
MM 111: 20 feet Vigorous, most soils
M 25 to 25 feet
M 106: 15-20 feet Precocious, heavy bearing
M7A: 15 feet Precocious
M 26: 12 feet. Precocious, hardy, heavy bearing, most soil
M27: 6 feet Very precocious
Seedling: (any seed) 30 feet vigorous, slow to bear,

Cherry
Colt: 12-20 feet Precocious, hardy, not drought tolerant
Gisela is much smaller at 10 feet

Pear
Seedling: (seed from Bartlett), Most soils
OHXF: 15 feet Precocious, hardy, Fire Blight resistant

Almond, Apricot, Peach, Plum
Citation: 15 feet Tolerates wet soil, reduces canopy more than height, needs irrigation.
Lovell: Produces a standard sized tree but longer lived and hardy
Myrobalan 22 feet
Pixy 12 feet
St. Julian A: 15 feet

Medium trees (25 - 40 ft.) Full height fruit trees (known as standards) are more useful for landscaping than the smaller trees, because they look like trees rather than tall bushes. They can be useful in the large garden, but cast a significant amount of shade, which limits their use in small gardens.

Standard Cherry, Pear and Apple all grow into medium sized trees that bear a lot of fruit at one time. This is good for sale or processing, but isn't what you want for fresh eating (one solution to this would be to graft several varieties on to the tree, so they fruit at different times). They are also longer lived than most dwarfed trees (100 years, as against 30 years for some dwarfs). Of course they are also more difficult to harvest and require an orchard ladder, a pole picker and some energy.

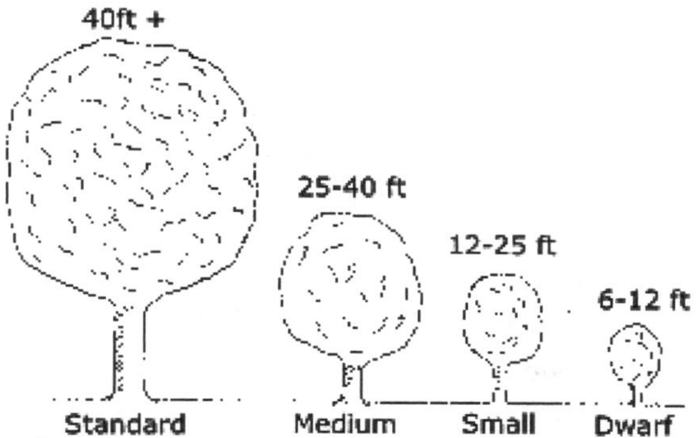

Small trees (12 - 25 ft.) They can be used as the top layer of a low forest garden or as an understory layer in a larger one. The big virtue of these small plants is that they don't take up a lot of space, so you can have a number of varieties, each with a different maturation date (early, mid and late varieties). This can extend your harvest season considerably.

Most fruit trees on dwarfing rootstocks fall into this category. There are also quite a few naturally small fruit trees that are worth experimenting with, including Pawpaw, Amelanchier, Medlar, Fig and Elder.

Dwarf Trees (12 ft. -) Trees whose rootstocks make them 50-80% smaller than standards are known as dwarfs. These don't really add a lot to the garden visually, they are just a crown of foliage at head height that obscures your view of the garden (which is okay if you need a screen to hide something). They are commonly used for cordons, espaliers, fans, arches and can even be used for tall hedges (alone or with fruiting shrubs).

In recent years there has been a trend towards smaller size fruit trees in the home garden (and in commercial growing) because they have several advantages:

- They mature faster and start to bear at a younger age.
- They yield more for a given area because you can have more trees.
- There is room for more varieties, which helps to stagger the harvest period.
- They are closer to the ground so are easier to prune, spray, net, protect from frosts and harvest.

Width of trees

It is important to know the ultimate width of the mature tree when planning, so you can space them properly.

Buying trees

I have bought a lot of trees over the years, from local garden centers, specialist nurseries, large mail order nurseries, home improvement centers and even big box stores. I have rarely had any problems from any of them (my inexpensive Costco trees have done exceptionally well). The big difference in these places is in the variety of species and cultivars available. Generally the bigger stores only carry the most common varieties, whereas the smaller places have a greater selection. To get the more unusual species and cultivars you have to go to the more specialist mail order places (though more than once I have bought something and they have then turned up cheaper and bigger at my local garden center). The internet is the ultimate resource for locating the more unusual stuff of course.

Trees are available in several different ways, depending upon the species, time of year and where you get them.

Bare root plants

Deciduous plants that go fully dormant (most common fruit and nut trees) can be obtained bare rooted. This is the cheapest way to obtain plants because they are relatively compact and there is no weight of soil to be shipped (this is the only way you can get bigger trees through the mail). The disadvantage (and not a very big one) is that they are only available for a short time in winter (they arrive at my local garden centers some time in January and are pretty much gone by the end of February), so you have to be prepared for them. They should be planted as soon as possible after receiving them.

Container grown plants

Container growing is used for plants that can't be sold bare root, such as conifers and some broadleaf evergreens (Citrus and Avocados come like this). The plants are grown in successively larger containers and can be obtained and planted at any time of year. Be aware that some garden centers pot up their unsold bare root trees when they start to leaf out and sell them at a higher price than the bare root trees. These are available after bare root season, but they are best avoided.

Container grown plants tend to be relatively small (or expensive) because of limitations in the size of the container that can be transported economically. Once you get them home they can be kept in the container for a while, so long as you remember to water them.

Ball and burlap

Conifers, evergreens and larger deciduous trees are sometimes available balled and burlapped and tend to be less expensive than container grown plants. They are grown in a nursery bed and dug and burlapped in winter. They should be planted as soon as possible.

Cultural practices

Soil

Fruit trees will grow faster and be more productive when growing in a deep, loose, well-drained and fertile soil with full sun. These are such important plants that they are usually given the best locations in the garden.

Some gardeners advise improving the soil for several years before planting fruit trees, others say you should get the trees in the ground as soon as possible and improve the soil with mulch. It really depends upon the soil. If the soil is fairly good I would just plant the trees. If it is heavy and compacted the trees could benefit from a double digging and the incorporation of organic matter before planting. If the soil is very poor you could plant a deep rooted green manure crop on the site (Alfalfa, Sweet Clover), along with a tap rooted plant such as Radish or Chicory. Leave this at least one growing season before planting the trees.

Ideally the soil should be well drained because most fruit trees don't like to have wet roots, particularly in winter. In very poorly drained soils you might have to plant the trees on small mounds. Selection of proper rootstock can also help, as some are more tolerant of wet soil than others.

Fertilization

When trees are fruiting regularly and heavily they take a lot of nutrients from the soil and you need to replace them to maintain fertility. The best way to do this is with a layer of permanent mulch (this will also suppress weeds of course). I also give them the wood ashes from my fireplace.

Nitrogen can also be supplied by interplanting nitrogen fixing trees and shrubs between the food bearing trees. There might also be a groundcover of Comfrey to supply phosphorus.

Irrigation

Your trees will need regular watering until they are established enough to obtain it for themselves. If you live in a climate without sufficient natural rainfall it makes sense to use drip irrigation. This significantly reduces the amount of water needed, as well as the amount of work you have to do. Drip is perfect for trees because you only need set it up once (unless you try and use a brush cutter near it). It also allows the trunk and leaves to stay dry and so reduces the incidence of disease.

You want the irrigation water to penetrate the top 2 feet of soil underneath the trees canopy, as this is where the majority of feeder roots will be. You don't want too much water near the trunk as in some cases it can contribute to rot. I prefer to water my trees with a ring of drip emitter line, connected to ½" poly hose. You can also use a series of drippers.

You don't necessarily have to give older plants more water than smaller ones, even though they obviously use more. This is because they have a much bigger root system and can search for their own water much more effectively.

If you don't have a drip system you could water a young tree with five gallon bucket, with a small hole in the bottom edge. Fill it up and will slowly leak out.

Mulch helps to reduce the amount of water a plant requires, by reducing surface evaporation and suppressing moisture robbing weeds.

Weed control

Young trees are shallow rooted and can't compete for water or nutrients very well. For this reason it is vital to keep weeds and grasses under control at least out as far as the drip line. Mulching is the best way to do this, as it also conserves moisture and protects the soil.

Hoeing isn't a good way to remove weeds around trees because it can damage their shallow roots.

Pruning

I am not a big fan of pruning and prefer to let plants grow naturally when possible. Pruning tends to become one of those self-perpetuating activities, once you start doing it, you need to keep on doing it. It can become quite a chore if you have lots and lots of large trees. On the other hand if you only have a few small trees it can be quite therapeutic (it also gives you a gardening activity to do in winter). A light annual pruning can help make the garden more productive, just don't get carried away (too little is better than too much).

Pruning may be done to accomplish several things:

- It is used to keep trees at the desired size. Dwarfing rootstocks rarely accomplish this without a little pruning help
- It lets more light into the canopy of the tree, so the lower leaves aren't shaded by upper leaves (that's why fruit growers talk about a vase or goblet shape.
- It can increase fruit size and deter annual bearing.
- It removes dead and misshapen branches and suckers (it is particularly important to remove those from below the graft line).
- It may be used to shorten overly exuberant growth, so you don't have long slender branches that bend or break under a heavy load of fruit.
- It can reduce or encourage vigor (summer pruning reduces vigor, winter pruning increases it),
- It can encourage the formation of flower buds.

No pruning

Unpruned trees commonly produce more fruit than pruned trees, though it is usually smaller and less attractive. They may also become biennial bearing. Enthusiastic thinning can help to correct both of these problems.

The tip bearing species (those that bear their fruit on new growth) respond best to not being pruned. These include the Citrus, Persimmon, Mulberry, Fig, Pomegranate, Olive and more. Other minimal prune plants include Apricot, Medlar, cherry, plums and Juneberry

Pollination

It is important to think about pollination when placing your trees. Plants that require cross-pollination must have a compatible plant flowering at the same time and close enough for pollination 50-100 feet. There should also be pollinating insects available to do the work (attract them with flowers if necessary). This is absolutely vital, a tree could be 20 years old and thirty feet tall, but it won't produce any fruit if it doesn't get pollinated.

Most fruit trees are pollinated by bees of some kind. A bee attracting groundcover such as Clover is sometimes planted to help attract them to the trees (it also adds nitrogen). Most nut trees are wind pollinated, which is usually pretty straightforward.

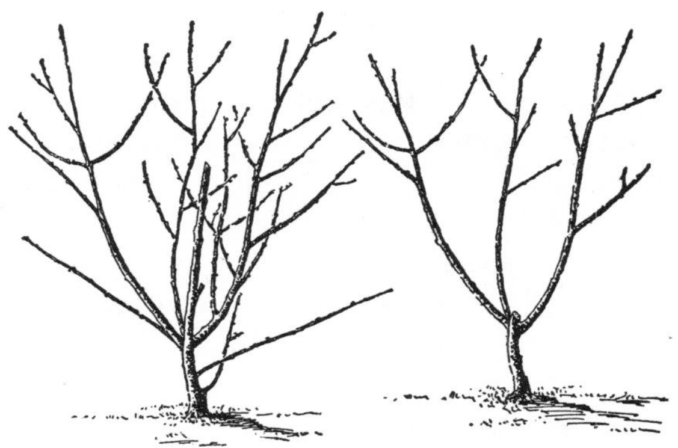

Sour Cherries, Figs, European Plums, Peaches, Walnuts, Citrus, some Apricots and a few Apples are self-pollinated (though some will bear more heavily if cross-pollinated). This means you only need to plant one tree to get fruit.

Most Apples, Sweet Cherries, Japanese Plums, Pears, Filberts, Chestnuts and some Apricots require cross-pollination, which means you need at least two compatible varieties to get fruit.

If space is very limited and you need 2 plants for pollination you could try planting 2 trees in the same planting hole. You might also get a tree that is grafted with two or more compatible varieties.

If for some reason a tree doesn't have the pollinator it requires, you could get some flowering branches from elsewhere and put them in a bucket of water out by your tree (ideally high up) for the bees to visit. In some cases you might even hand pollinate.

Fruit thinning - Sometimes a tree will set so much fruit that the branches are almost entirely covered in small fruit. In such cases you must thin drastically to increase fruit size and to deter biennial bearing. This is a somewhat tedious task, but not totally unwelcome because it means you will have ripe fruit in the near future. This spring my daughter was shocked to see me pulling dozens and dozens of tiny peaches from a tree. I explained to her that a tree has only so much energy for making fruit and it will use all of that energy no matter how many fruit are on the tree. Less fruit means bigger fruit (she would probably have liked one giant Peach). She understood it later when the fruit grew to 3 times the size of last year when I didn't get around to thinning at all.

Thinning excess fruit prevents the tree draining itself of resources completely. When this happens you will often get very little fruit the following year as it works to rebuild its resources. This can lead to biennial bearing, whereby you only get a good crop every other year. This could be okay if you had other trees to bear in the alternate years (with my luck they would all bear in the same alternate years), but it is better if they all bear some fruit annually.

It's natural for some fruit to drop naturally before it gets ripe, especially if the tree has a heavy load. Birds will also peck fruit and dislodge it from the tree.

Pests and disease

I have to admit I haven't had a lot of experience with any serious pests, such as codling moth or Fire Blight. The worst I have had to deal with have been jays. My trees seem to just do their own thing and produce fruit.

An easy way to protect your fruit from birds and insects (and get perfect fruit) is to grow them in waxed paper bakery bags. This works with all kinds of fruit from apples to grapes. Wrap the bag around the fruit and staple each side to enclose it tightly and keep out insects.

If diseases such as Fire Blight and Peach Leaf Curl are a big problem in your area, you may want to use varieties that are naturally resistant.

Removing fallen fruit and diseased leaves can reduce pest and disease problems.

If you allow chickens to free range under your fruit trees, they will eat a lot of insect pests and clean up dropped fruit (though they may also eat some of your other plants too). They will also help to fertilize the trees.

Gophers are a big problem in my area. I have found trees laying on the ground, with their roots almost completely gone. I have seen trees that had half their roots eaten, so they almost fell over but then recovered and kept on growing at a crazy angle. Gophers can even kill quite mature trees by ringing the bark. The best way to defeat gophers is to plant the tree in a wire basket. This is an extra hassle, but I would never plant another tree without one. I should add that I have re-rooted trees that have had almost all of their roots eaten. I simply put them in a pot and kept the soil constantly moist.

When gophers get really active you might (if you are of a paranoid inclination) feel that forces out there are out to get you and ruin your garden (not without some justification).

Netting - This is often the only practical way to keep birds from stripping all of the fruit from Cherry, Mulberry and Blueberries, or damaging much of the fruit on other trees. This can be quite a project if the tree is large. With small trees it is a lot easier. It is easiest with espaliered trees grown against walls.

Support – In a good year the branches of Plum and Peach trees may be so heavily laden they break under the weight (especially when they get some additional stress such as high wind, rain or climbing raccoons). The usual way around this (apart from heavy thinning) is to support the branch with a sturdy pole with a Y at the end. You can make these from the crotch of a small tree, 2 x 4's or any suitable poles (look out for them when cutting brush). When arranged around an old tree these props can be quite ornamental.

Harvesting Fruit trees take several years to start bearing, so the first ripe fruit is an exciting event. You finally get to taste what the fruit is really like. Even more exciting is the first real harvest, where you finally have more fruit than you know what to do with. When you get to this point you don't have to harvest every single piece of fruit. You can leave some for wildlife. Even that which falls to the ground and decomposes isn't wasted, as its nutrients will go back into the soil and quickly be taken up by the tree or soil organisms (though you may have to worry about some pests and diseases overwintering in this way).

Cleanup

Any abundantly producing tree can drop a lot of messy fruit. If this is directly on to the soil it isn't a problem, but if it is a paved surface it could be. It can stain the surface, and may be a slipping hazard too (on a public street this also brings potential liability).

Training trees

Espaliers, fans, cordons, stepovers, arches, tunnels are all attractive garden features as well as being a way to produce fruit in small spaces. They are often used against walls where their decorative effect is particularly desired, or in cool climates to give the fruit extra warmth. Of course training trees in this way is more work and could hardly be described as natural or low-maintenance. They work best for gardeners with small gardens and without enough to do.

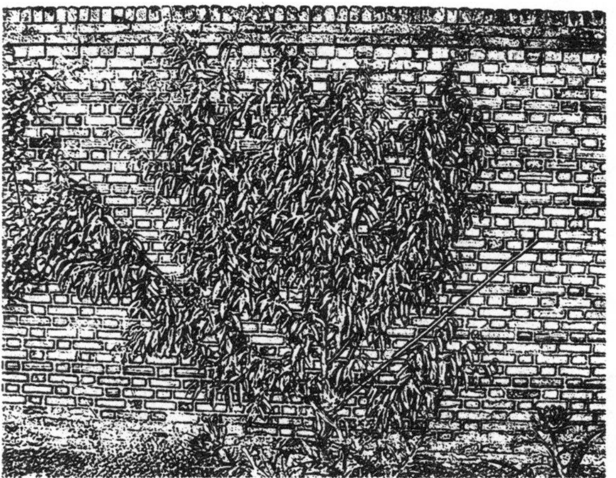

Common tree fruits

Probably no other plants in the garden give so much for so little work as the fruit trees. Plant them once, give them a little care and they will reliably produce fruit for years to come. Every garden should have its full complement of suitable Apple, Apricot, Cherry, Peach, Plum and Pear varieties (and more).

Fruit trees don't just produce food, they are also some of the most beautiful plants in the garden and add year round interest in the form of continuous seasonal change. First you get flower buds, then flowers followed by leaves, then small fruit, then ripe fruit (a highlight of the summer), then the leaves drop. In this way they don't only feed us, they also help to connect us to the yearly cycle of the garden.

I don't intend to go into great detail about the various aspects of fruit growing, as that would be repeating what is already available in many books (find a book that covers fruit growing in your particular climate). Instead I'll just give a few observations and comments on my experiences and mention a few things to consider when selecting your trees. I should probably add that I live in an area that is particularly favorable to fruit growing. If I make it all sound easier than you find it to be, this is probably why.

Apple (*Pyrus malus*) Zones 3-9

The most widely cultivated temperate zone fruit, a huge number of Apple varieties have been produced over the years. There are varieties for eating fresh, varieties for cooking and varieties for making hard cider. There are also varieties for every temperate climate, from frigid Russia to warm Israel.

The Apple is tasty, fairly easy to grow and reliably productive and at one time almost every country garden had at least one tree. In colonial times Apples were grown almost entirely to make hard cider and they were one of the most profitable crops. I have never been a big fan of commercial apples, but a home grown Golden Delicious at its peak is one of the biggest treats of the garden year.

Apples thrive best in cool moist temperate climates and most need a significant amount of winter chill. They don't need a very fertile soil, though it should be well drained and have lots of sun (especially for the sweeter varieties). They usually need some annual pruning and fruit thinning.

Young Apple trees grow quite quickly, but this slows considerably when they come into full bearing. A standard tree can live for a century or more and develop an attractive gnarled appearance with age.

Most apples require cross-pollination though there are some self-pollinated varieties. The fruit matures in anywhere from 70 - 180 days, which can be as early as July or as late as November. If you plant a few different varieties you can have fresh apples for months. Careful storage can extend this even further.

Apples were the first fruits to be grown on dwarfing rootstocks and are now available in wide range of sizes.

Apricot (*Prunus armeniaca*) Zones 5-9

This species is more exacting in its requirements than most common tree fruit and so is less commonly grown. It flowers earlier than any other common fruit and consequently fruit set is often poor due to bad weather. In areas with high humidity Apricot is often afflicted by pests and diseases, which is why it is mostly cultivated commercially in the warmer drier western areas. It needs warm summers to ripen its fruit to perfection.

Apricots like the same conditions as the related Peaches; light, fertile well drained soil, with good air circulation (avoid frost pockets).

Apricot is one of the prettiest common fruit trees and is quite spectacular when in bloom in spring. It doesn't get very big, a standard tree is usually not much more than 25 feet in height, and dwarf trees may only be 6 feet tall. It is quite a wide spreading tree and is often as wide as it is tall. It does well as an espalier and in cold climates is often grown against a wall for extra warmth.

Some Apricot varieties need cross-pollination and some are self-fertile (though for heaviest crops they all benefit from cross-pollination). The fruit ripen in 100-120 days, which makes it the first of the common fruits to ripen (July in my garden). A fully ripened apricot doesn't ship well, so for the best flavor you have to grow them yourself. The fruit is good cooked, fresh or dried.

There aren't a huge number of Apricot cultivars available. There are some that do well in cooler climates. A few have edible seeds as well as flesh and are known as Sweet Pit Apricots (see Nuts). I've had good success with Apriums, a cross between Plum and Apricot that closely resembles an Apricot, but isn't quite as fussy.

Cherries (*Prunus* species) Zones 4-9

There are two kinds of Cherry, Sweet and Sour. All ripen in about 100 days.

Sweet Cherry (*Prunus avium*) - This species produces the best fruit but is more particular about growing conditions. They need considerable winter chill, but don't like very cold winters, late frost, very hot summers or high humidity. They grow best in the western states where they suffer less from pests or disease.

Sweet Cherry trees are quite vigorous and grow quickly when young, to become the tallest of the common fruit trees (to 50 feet or more). Dwarfing rootstocks are now available to keep them to a more practical size.

Most Sweet Cherries require cross-pollination, so you will have to plant several trees (or one of the few self-pollinating varieties).

This species bear fruit very reliably, but you won't get much if you don't deal with birds. Cherries are one of their favorite fruits and they will strip a tree completely if given the opportunity. It's said that they don't go for the yellow fruit as much, because it doesn't look ripe.

Sour Cherry (*Prunus cerasus*) - The fruits aren't as good as sweet cherries for eating raw, though they aren't necessarily sour. They are commonly used for juice, pies and commercial canning. They are more adaptable than the Sweet Cherries and less prone to pests and disease, and can be grown almost anywhere in the country. They are not nearly as tall as Sweet Cherries and they are usually self-fertile

Fig (*Ficus carica*) Zones 8-10

In the right climate the fig is an ideal low work plant for the productive garden. It requires little attention once established, grows in almost any soil (so long as it is well drained), is very drought tolerant and sometimes produces two crops a year, one in early summer and one in fall.

The fruits of the Fig are good fresh or dried (in dry climates they dry on the tree and then drop). Dried fruit are particularly useful because they can be stored for long periods.

Figs are native to hot dry areas but there are also cultivars for colder climates. These need protection where winters get seriously cold (10° F), otherwise they may be killed back to the roots (these will often re-sprout though).

Gophers are particularly fond of Fig tree roots and will kill trees of any size if they aren't very carefully caged.

Fig can be grown as a single trunk tree up to 20 feet in height, or as a multi stemmed shrub up to 20 ft. wide (bear this in mind when deciding on where to put it). The large leaves make this a very attractive plant and it can be used as a screen, specimen shrub, or even a hedge. The fresh fruit may drop and make a mess on paved areas.

Fig is easily propagated vegetatively from cuttings. When a winter storm dropped a large branch on my young tree and smashed it to pieces, I just stuck all of the pieces in the soil. They almost all rooted and grew into new plants.

Peach and nectarine (*Prunus persica*) Zones 5-9

A soft and succulent ripe Peach, still warm off the tree, is one of the ultimate treats of the summer garden. Store bought fruit doesn't even come close. A nectarine is almost identical to a Peach, except that it has lost its fuzzy coating (which many people find to be a big plus).

I am fortunate to live in an area that is very favorable to Peach growing and I find them to be fast growing, vigorous and highly productive. There is the ever present Peach Leaf Curl, but I find I can ignore it entirely. Even though the plants are sometimes afflicted quite badly, they are so vigorous they just put out more leaves and plenty of delicious fruit. Some curl resistant varieties are now available.

Peaches don't like very cold winters (below –20 F), or very mild ones where they don't get enough chill hours (though there are some low chill varieties). They are best planted in a warm, sunny spot that is sheltered from cold winds. Beware of frost pockets because they flower almost as early as the Apricot (February in my garden). They can be grown in cooler areas if you choose the variety carefully and plant in a warm sunny microclimate. However warm summers will produce the best fruit.

Peaches are self-pollinated and so are very reliable producers of fruit (more than any other tree fruit in my garden, they haven't missed a year yet). In fact they usually set so much fruit they need to be thinned to avoid overbearing and breakage of branches. I spend more time thinning the excess fruit than on any other Peach task.

If you don't pick the ripe fruit regularly, they can drop and make a slippery mess on paved surfaces.

Some peaches come fairly true from seed and apparently it is possible to grow Indian Blood Peaches from seed to fruit in as little as 5 years.

Pear (*Pyrus communis*) Zones 5-9

The Pear is related to the Apple and almost as easy to grow. It is an attractive and long lived tree, and can eventually get quite big (60 feet or more), though most are now grown as dwarfs. It works well as an espalier or cordon

Pears can tolerate extreme cold (to –25 F), but require warmer summers and more sun than the apple. They are also more drought tolerant and less fussy about the soil.

Pears commonly require cross-pollination, so you need at least 2 compatible trees. The fruit ripens in 120-160 days, though it if often harvested before it is fully ripe and ripened off the tree.

Fire Blight is a serious disease that can kill Pear trees (though some varieties are resistant).

Asian Pears (*P. pyrifolia*)

These are grown in the same ways as the above, though the fruits are more apple-like.

Plum (*Prunus* species) Zones 4-10

A tree ripened plum is another of the great treats of the summer garden. I find Plum trees to be very low-maintenance, they just sit there looking pretty and produce fruit in most years. The trees tend to be smaller than other common fruit trees and so fit well in the smaller garden, or in odd corners. They also drop lots of messy fruit, so don't plant near paved areas.

Plum trees are very vigorous and hardy and rarely bothered by disease or pests. My biggest problem has been their tendency to produce too much fruit. A heavy load of fruit will break branches if not supported. Some fruit drop naturally before it is ripe, but you usually need to thin the fruit enthusiastically. The fruits ripen in 140-180 days. They usually flower early and are sometimes hit by frost.

The lighter colored varieties seem to be less attractive to birds than the darker ones (maybe they don't think they are ripe enough to bother with).

You have several choices when choosing which Plums to grow.

European Plums (*Prunus domestica*) - These can be grown almost anywhere, but are particularly well suited to cool climates. They are usually self-fertile.

Japanese Plums (*Prunus salicina*) - These vigorous trees are better suited to warm climates than the Europeans. Most varieties require cross-pollination.

American Plums (*Prunus americana*) - These rugged Plums may do well in areas where the others don't.

Pluots - These are a cross between an Apricot and a Plum that resembles a Plum. They can be very good.

Less common tree fruit

Avocado (*Persea Americana*) Zones 10+

My one regret about where I live is that it is too cold for Avocados. I could probably get a tree to survive (some can tolerate 20° F.), but it would be unlikely to produce any fruit because the flowers and immature fruit are easily damaged by frost.

The Avocado is unlike most other fruit in that it is rich in fat and protein. It is usually treated like a vegetable in the kitchen.

A large tree (to 60 feet or more) with dark green shiny evergreen leaves that cast dense shade. It sheds leaves constantly and any ripe fruit that are left on the tree too long (dogs enjoy these windfalls). It is common to pick the fruit before it is quite ripe and allow it to ripen off the tree.

Citrus (Citrus species) Zones 9-10

In warm climates these attractive evergreen trees are common low-maintenance garden fruit. They have shiny dark green leaves and fantastically fragrant white flowers (put some near your patio so you can appreciate their scent and protect them from frost). Most are self-pollinated and fruit prolifically.

All of these species need full sun and hot weather if they are to produce sweet fruit. They are easy to grow in the right climate, not so easy if it isn't suited to them. Lemons and Limes don't produce sweet fruit of course so don't need as much heat.

Citrus prefer well drained, moist, fertile soil and like mulch. Established trees are fairly drought tolerant, but need a constant supply of water if they are to produce well.

Citrus are not frost tolerant and if temperatures drop much below freezing they must be protected (there are various ways to do this). In marginal areas they must be grown in the warmest protected microclimate in the garden. In colder areas they can be grown in large tubs and brought indoors for the winter. The grapefruits and limes are the most tender, followed by the oranges. The mandarins and lemons are the most hardy.

The hardiest and most reliable Citrus varieties include:

Owari Satsuma - This delicious seedless mandarin is one of the hardiest species and has been known to survive temperatures as low as 15° F (though not for long). It ripens in December.

Meyer Lemon - A cross between a lemon and a mandarin, this variety is has been known to survive temperatures as low as 18° F. It flowers and fruits over a long period, so you can get fruit almost year round (a wonderful asset in any fruit).

Washington Navel - A fine flavored orange as well as one of the hardiest Oranges. It can survive down to 24° F.

Moro Blood Orange - Has dark purple flesh with a unique flavor. Hardy to 27° F.

Bears Lime
The hardiest lime (to 28° F.)

Eureka - The classic commercial lemon.

Lisbon - The fruit of this Lemon is similar to Eureka, but the plant is more vigorous, hardier and generally easier to grow.

Cornelian Cherry (*Cornus mas*) Zones 4-9

This species is related to the ornamental Dogwoods and is equally attractive. The fruit looks like a sour cherry and can be very good. Though partially self-fertile it produces more fruit if cross-pollinated. It is easily grown from seed and the fruit is okay, but named varieties are better. These can be propagated from semi-ripe cuttings, hardwood cuttings, suckers or layering.

Jujube (*Zizyphus jujuba*) Zones 6-10

Attractive enough to be used as a specimen plant, but usually grown for its edible fruit. The ripe fruit starts out resembling an apple, but it slowly shrivels and gets sweeter until it is more like a date (it is also known as Chinese Date). It has a nice habit of producing fruit over a long period.

A fairly small tree (15-30 feet in height). It is propagated by seed or hardwood cuttings (not easy). Jujube spreads by means of suckers and these can be detached and replanted (these will be the rootstock of course – you could graft them with scions from the original plant). Some varieties are self-fertile but most need cross-pollination.

Jujube will grow in poor soil and is hardy down to –20° F. It needs hot summers to ripen fruit. It is fairly drought tolerant, but is more productive when growing in moist soil.

Juneberry (*Amelanchier laevis*, *A. canadensis*) Zones 3-9

Though some Amelanchier species are bushes, these two definitely qualify as trees. They are quite spectacular in spring when covered in white blossom. The sweet fruits are used like Blueberries and are very good (birds enjoy them as much as Blueberries). Obviously the fruit are harder to harvest when they are carried higher up.

Juneberry will grow in full sun or part shade. Some species are extremely hardy (-40 F), but they also do well in warm climates. They are self-fertile.

Loquat (*Eriobotrya japonica*) Zones 6-10

I prize this tree because it flowers in winter and produces the first tree fruit of the spring. It is also quite an attractive tree (to 25 feet) with large evergreen leaves. The fruits contain several very large seeds, but the flesh is tart, juicy and delicious.

Loquat isn't considered very hardy, but survives and fruits in my garden where it is exposed to some frost every winter (it will tolerate 15° F, though the flowers may be damaged). My plants are self-sown seedlings dug from another garden but they still produce good quality fruit.

Mulberry (*Morus* species) Zones 5-10

A tough, drought tolerant tree the Mulberry will grow with very little attention. It doesn't produce flowers until late in the spring and so avoids potential damage from frost. Some Mulberry species are monoecious (and self-fertile) and some are dioecious and require cross-pollination (only the females will produce fruit of course). A few are parthenocarpic and produce fruit without pollination. They are all wind pollinated. Unlike most fruit trees it can be propagated from cuttings.

These fast growing trees are commonly used around the Mediterranean for creating shade. A couple of rows of trees can be pruned and trained to create a green ceilinged room. Fruitless varieties are used for this of course as the fallen fruit would make a mess (don't put fruiting varieties over paved surfaces).

Birds love Mulberries even more than Cherries and if you don't keep an eye on them they will take every fruit on the tree. I have a Black Beauty that hides its delicious fruit under the leaves, but they still find them eventually. Wild Mulberries are notorious in some areas because birds eat the fruit and drop purple droppings on patios, paths and even (horror) cars.

The quality of fruit varies considerably, some seedlings are not very good, some cultivars are delicious (the good ones can be propagated vegetatively). Dried Mulberries are an important food in Afghanistan and are said to be as nutritious as Figs. Ornamental Mulberries are usually male so they don't produce messy fruit

White Mulberry (*M. alba*) Commonly self-fertile. The fruit is very sweet

Red Mulberry (*M. rubra*) This native species can grow to 50 feet

Black Mulberry (*M. nigra*) Generally this species has the best flavored fruit. It likes hot summers, mild winters and full sun and is a very reliable low-maintenance fruit producing tree.

Olive (*Olea europaea*) Zones 9-10

Olive is adapted to the Mediterranean climate of hot dry summers and mild winters. It is hardy to about 10° F, though the flowers can be injured by frost. An attractive tree it is sometimes used as a specimen plant. Don't plant near paved areas as the oily fruit can stain them.

The fruit are too bitter to eat raw and must be soaked in brine to make them edible. This isn't difficult, but it has to be done carefully and takes time. Of course olives are also used throughout the Mediterranean as the source of cooking oil.

Olives are said to live up to 1000 years. At the rate my tree is growing it should be a modest sized tree by then (it is slow-growing). It is quite precocious however and has already started trying to produce fruit. Most trees require cross-pollination (by the wind), though a few are self-fertile.

Pawpaw (*Asimina triloba*) Zones 5-9

The native American Pawpaw is a small (to 25 feet) attractive tree with large leaves and clusters of fruit. The large fruit has large seeds surrounded by a soft sweet pulp and is sometimes known as a Michigan Banana. Pawpaw is very hardy and can tolerate temperatures as low as –20° F, but needs warm summers to produce good fruit. It also needs consistently moist soil, so will need irrigation in dry areas.

Attractive enough to be used as a specimen tree it can also be used for a tall hedge. It often grows naturally as an understory tree, so doesn't mind some shade.

Pawpaw is quite slow-growing when young and doesn't like transplanting. It is fairly easy to grow from seed, but the quality of seedling fruit is variable, so most trees are grafted. If you cut the plant back to the ground it will send up suckers. These will be from the rootstock of course and could be used for grafting.

Pawpaw is not self-fertile so you will need two trees to get fruit and insects to cross-pollinate them (a small number of flowers could be hand pollinated).

Persimmon, Asian (*Diospyros kaki*) Zones 6-10

Persimmons are among the most ornamental fruit trees, with attractive leaves, bark and fruits. After the leaves drop the fruits continue to hang on the trees like orange Christmas ornaments.

Persimmons can be divided into astringent and non-astringent varieties. The former must be allowed to become very soft and ripe before they are good to eat. The latter can be eaten while still firm. Many people don't like Persimmons because they haven't had them at the right stage. The fruits really do have to be properly ripe to be good.

Persimmons are notorious for making a mess on the ground underneath them, so don't plant near paved areas.

These trees are hardy to 0° F and quite drought tolerant. Most cultivars are self-fertile.

Persimmon, American (*Diospyros americana*) Zones 5-9

These trees are bigger are hardier than the above, while the fruits are smaller. These are also better flavored, though they too have to be fully ripe to be good. Unlike their Asian cousins most American cultivars need cross-pollinating, though a few are self-fertile. Considering this and the fact that the fruit is very variable, it's best to plant a good cultivar rather than a seedling.

There are also hybrids between the American and Asian species, that combine the large size of the Asians with the hardiness of the Americans.

Quince (*Cydonia oblongata*) Zones 5-9

In the right conditions (full sun and well drained fertile soil) this easy to grow and independent little tree doesn't take much looking after. In my garden it is almost completely ignored, yet it still produces fruit reliably every year. It is self-fertile so you only need one variety.

Quince looks rather like a large, fuzzy, slightly misshapen pear. It is not usually eaten raw as it is dry and slightly astringent, though the flavor is good. It is commonly cooked in preserves and is particularly good when added to apple pie.

With its beautiful spring bloom, attractive shape and interesting yellow fruit, the quince is one of the more ornamental fruit trees. It also espaliers well and is very attractive when grown in this way.

Wild fruit trees

Quite a few wild fruit (and nut) trees are worth exploring as no-maintenance sources of fruit. We could propagate superior individual wild plants or even breed improved varieties. This has already happened in the case of the Juneberry, Mulberry, Pawpaw and Persimmon. Other potentially useful species include:

Beech (*Fagus* species)
California Nutmeg (*Torreya californica*)
Chokecherry (*Prunus virginiana*)
Hackberry (*Celtis* species)
Hawthorns (*Crataegus* species)
Oaks (*Quercus* species)
Silverbells (*Halesia* species)
Tupelo (*Nyssa* species)
Wild plums (*Prunus* species)

Of course you don't have to confine yourself to native wild species. You can also search for plants from similar climates in other parts of the world. You just have to be sure a plant isn't going to be invasive.

Nut Trees

In many ways nut trees are similar to fruit trees (botanically speaking they are fruit) and their propagation, planting and care is pretty much the same. Probably the biggest difference is that most common nuts are produced on large forest trees and are too big for all but the largest gardens. Another difference is that most are wind pollinated.

Many nuts are high in protein and fats (nutrients lacking in many vegetable foods), as well as minerals, vitamins and anti-oxidants.

The large nut trees need a deep fertile soil for best growth (most are tap rooted) as they can get quite enormous given enough time. Some species take a while to start bearing, but don't let this discourage you. Plant them and forget about them for a few years. Grafted trees start bearing a lot earlier than seedlings.

Most nut trees are tap rooted so give them a planting hole that is deep enough to accommodate the root. Don't bend the taproot sideways to fit it in the hole.

Large nut trees should have a clear area underneath them so you can gather the fallen nuts (this is the only practical way to harvest them). Chestnuts create fairly dense shade anyway.

Nut trees respond to having nitrogen fixers around them even more than fruit trees.

The most important nuts

Sweet Chestnut (*Castanea sativa*) Zones 5-9

One of my favorite trees, Chestnuts grow quite rapidly and a mature tree can reach 80 feet or more. They are hardy to about –20° F, but their preferred climate is Mediterranean with mild winters and hot summers. They are very drought tolerant and have pretty much naturalized in gardens around where I live.

Unlike most common nuts, chestnuts are high in carbohydrates rather than protein or fat and in the kitchen they are treated more like a cereal than a nut. They produce a crop of nuts regularly (in my garden they haven't missed a year yet) and can be amazingly productive. The fresh nuts deteriorate quickly, but they can be dried for long term storage.

Chestnuts are easily grown from fresh seed, but this loses viability rapidly as it dries out. Self-sown (and squirrel sown) seedlings appear all over my garden. These grow very rapidly in the right conditions, but may take 10 years to start bearing much fruit. Grafted trees bear at an earlier age.

Chestnuts are cross-pollinated by the wind, so you need more than one tree to produce fruit.

Chestnut wood is very strong and rot resistant and has been called the most useful wood of all. The trees produce little sapwood and so are rot resistant even at a young age. They are often coppiced to provide poles for garden use. They grow very rapidly when treated in this way and can be cut every 3-10 years (depending upon the climate and the size poles needed). You could coppice any trees that get too big for the garden.

Some people don't like having Chestnut trees in the garden because of their painfully spiny husks (even my dog is reluctant to go underneath the trees). If you want to use the area underneath the trees, these should be raked up as they fall and composted (they break down very quickly). These spines serve an important function in that they effectively prevent squirrels from eating the nuts before they are fully ripe.

Unfortunately it isn't possible to grow European or American Chestnuts in the eastern part of the country because they are susceptible to Chestnut Blight. This introduced disease wiped out almost all of the American Chestnuts in its native range (this has been called the greatest ecological disaster in American history). Fortunately we can still plant the smaller Japanese and Chinese Chestnuts, as they are resistant. (they are attacked by Chestnut Weevils though).

Pecan and Hickory

These beautiful and stately trees are fairly slow-growing, but can eventually reach over 100 feet in height. When mature they are spectacular shade trees, as well as excellent lumber.

The wild nuts have very good flavor, but their thick shells are hard to crack. Many improved cultivars have been selected for their thinner shells.

These species are easily grown from fresh seed and often self-sow. Seed should be planted immediately, in a place that is protected from rodents. They produce a taproot and don't really like transplanting, so use a deep container or sow directly in the garden.

The most useful species include:

Shellbark Hickory (*Carya ovata*)

Shagbark Hickory (*Carya laciniosa*) Zones 4-9

These species can be identified by their characteristic shaggy bark. It has been suggested this may have evolved to deter nut-loving squirrels from climbing the trunks to eat the unripe nuts. Both species produce fine flavored nuts and are occasionally cultivated in northern areas. They are very hardy and are sometimes crossed with the Pecan to produce more cold tolerant hybrids. The Shagbark Hickory also produces the best wood for tool handles of any common tree.

Pecan (*C. illinoensis*) Zones 6-9

The Pecan is the largest *Carya* species and in its native habitat it has been known to reach 200 feet in height. It is the most valuable cultivated native nut tree and many cultivars are available. It is not very hardy though and needs a long growing season.

Almond (*Prunus dulcis*) Zones 6-9

This small tree is related to the Peach and Plum and differ from most nuts in that it is pollinated by bees. Generally you need two varieties for cross-pollination, though a few are self-fertile. Almonds are quite spectacular when blooming in spring and in the right conditions they can be very productive.

Almond likes hot dry summers and well drained soil. It is very drought tolerant - I went away one summer and forgot to tell the house sitter to water the Almond tree sitting in a pot away by itself. When I came back two months later it looked like a dry stick, yet when I gave it water it leafed out like nothing had happened. It is now close to 20 feet tall and none the worse for the experience. Of course this doesn't mean you should neglect the trees, they will produce a lot more nuts if watered occasionally.

Harvest the nuts as the dried up fruits start to split open. Leave them too long and Squirrels may get them. Remove the nuts from inside the husk and dry them until fully dry.

Walnut, Persian (*Juglans regia*) Zones 3-9

Walnut trees are prized for both their edible nuts and their beautiful wood. It used to be said that farmers should plant walnuts as an investment for their grandchildren's college fund. Unfortunately this isn't for their nuts, but for their valuable wood. Grow a nice straight Walnut and it could grow big enough to be very valuable one day (though you won't live to see it). They also make great shade trees.

The nuts are delicious as well as high in protein, fat (especially omega 3 fatty acids) and minerals (notably calcium).

Walnuts are notorious among gardeners for secreting allelopathic substances that inhibit the growth of some neighboring plants (Alfalfa, Blueberry, Apple, Tomato, Potato and others). They may also be home to aphids that secrete honeydew onto anything beneath them

There are quite a few improved cultivars available. These tend to be more precocious (they bear at a younger age) and have thinner shells.

Related species:

Black Walnut (*J. nigra*) - The nuts are harder to shell and smaller than the Walnut, but have very good flavor. The trees are also more allelopathic.

Butternut (*J, cinerea*) This species is hardier than Walnut, but the nuts aren't as good.

Heartnut (*J. ailanthifolia*)

This Asian species is smaller than most other Walnuts and shorter lived. The nuts are similar though.

Other nut species

Gingko (*Gingko biloba*) Zones 5-9

This tall tree is a living fossil, notable as the only surviving member of a group of plants that lived 150 million years ago. The other notable thing about Gingko is the stench of the flesh around the seeds, which smells pretty nasty as it decays. The female trees (it is dioecious) produce tasty nuts after pollination by a male tree. These are cooked and eaten in China and Japan (apparently they are somewhat toxic when raw).

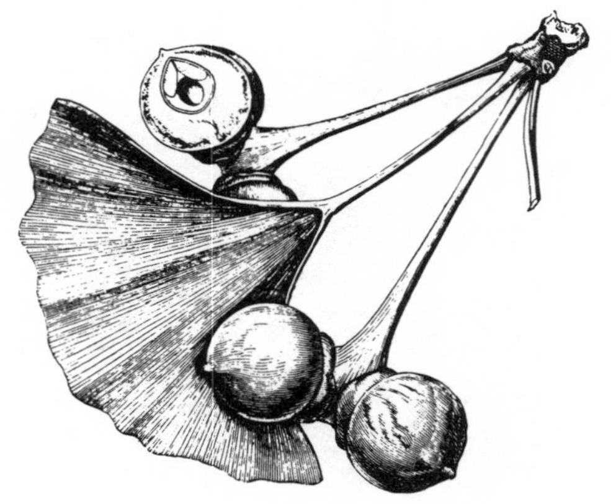

The leaves have been found to have a beneficial effect on brain functions, heart disease, blood vessels and more.

Ginko can be propagated from seed or softwood cuttings (the latter is preferable as you then know the sex of the plant).

Oak (*Quercus* species) Zones 3-9

These are related to the Chestnuts and like them produce nuts (acorns) that are high in carbohydrates rather than protein. Unfortunately they are also high in tannin, which makes them inedible unless specially prepared by leaching with water. We don't really think of acorns as food, but they have been an important staple for indigenous people around the world. Their use was so widespread and important in the past that Oaks have been called the ancestral food of humanity.

I don't really imagine many people will want to harvest and process their own acorns, when there are so many easier crop. However I wanted to make you aware of them because of their high food value. If you are interested in this I wrote extensively on their preparation in my book 'The uses of wild plants'.

If you have any woodland you might already have Oaks growing (I do in California, I did 3000 miles away in Connecticut and I did 6000 miles away in England) and might want to experiment with them. The edibility of acorns varies considerably, some are large and relatively low in tannin, some are small and inedible. My garden contains a lot of Tanoak (*Lithocarpus densiflorus*) which produces very good acorns, so I try to look after them.

Pistachio (*Pistacia vera*) Zones 7-9

This small (to 30 feet) tree is native to mountains of the Middle East and is adapted to hot dry summers and cold winters (it needs considerable winter chill and is hardy to 0° F.) It is very drought tolerant and actually doesn't like a lot of moisture.

Pistachio is dioecious so male and female trees are needed to produce the delicious nuts. 1 male is enough for 10 females, though often pollination is poor.

Pistachio can be grown from fresh seed (soak first to remove inhibitors), but you won't know the sex of the seedlings. Seedlings may be grafted with a improved cultivars (you will then know what sex they are).

Pine nuts (*Pinus* species) Zones 3-9

These nut bearing conifers are ornamental, as well as producing nutritious (they are high in fat) and delicious seeds. They are also drought tolerant and self-fertile. The problem with growing them is that it may take 10 years before you get your first pine nut. I bought two Italian Stone Pines as potted Christmas trees several years ago and they are now just starting to take off (it will be a few years yet before I get any nuts though). The best species include:

Italian Stone Pine (*Pinus pinea*) – This European species is the original source of Pignolia seeds or pine nuts. It grows up to 60 feet tall with a characteristic spreading top, which is why it's sometimes known as Umbrella Pine). It is hardy to 0° F.

Korean Stone Pine (*P. koraiensis*) – This Asian species is also very hardy and very good. It is the source of the Chinese pine nuts sold in grocery stores.

Pinon Pines (*P. edulis, P. monophylla, P. cembroides*) These small native southwestern trees could be grown for their delicious nuts, Sometimes you can find them sold as Christmas trees. If you grow them from seed you will have to be very patient.

Stone Pine (*P. cembra*) This slow-growing species is found across Northern Asia. It is hardy to –50° F.

Sweet Pit Apricot (*Prunus armeniaca*)

Zones 4-9

This species produces edible apricots, but it is mostly grown for its Almond-like edible seed (these need roasting to make them edible). These seeds are best known as an important part of the diet of the Hunza, a long lived people from the Himalayas. See fruit for more on Apricots.

Squirrels

Squirrels go with nuts like beer goes with pizza. If you want to grow almost any kinds of nuts and have these rodents around, you have a problem. They may well take every nut on a tree as soon as it becomes ripe, or even before. They will take even more than they can eat immediately because they store them for the winter. It may be possible to keep squirrels from isolated trees with a suitable trunk guard (made from cone shaped sheet metal), but they are intelligent, resourceful and highly motivated creatures.

To their credit squirrels also plant many nut trees, when they bury them for the winter and then forget about them. The Chestnuts and Walnuts on my property were most likely planted by squirrels. Which I suppose raises an ethical question about who they actually belong to, and who is the pest. I consider other fruit trees mine simply because I planted them, so what about those the squirrels planted? I transplant small self-sown seedlings to suitable locations, or give them away.

Monkey Puzzle Tree (*Araucaria araucana*)

Zone 6-9

Though rarely grown for its nuts in this country, this large and spectacular South American tree has been an important food source in its homeland. The large, tasty, oil rich seed is produced in a large cone. This species grows well in mild maritime climates, but is actually hardy to 0°. It likes full sun and well drained soil and is salt tolerant. Unlike many nut trees it doesn't cast a lot of shade.

Monkey Puzzle is dioecious, which means there are pollenizing male trees and fruit bearing female trees. The usual ratio in a planting it one male to every 6 females. Seedling trees may take 10 years or more to start producing seed.

Tree Hazel (*Corylus colurna*) Zone 5-9

This species is cultivated like the closely related Hazel, but really is a tree, sometimes reaching to 75 feet in height. Its wood is prized for cabinetmaking. You need to plant at least 2 varieties to ensure cross-pollination.

Edible pod trees

These aren't commonly thought of as crops, but they have potential because their pods are rich in sugar and (most) fix nitrogen in the soil.

Carob (*Ceratonia siliqua*) Zones 9-10

This attractive wide spreading tree can grow to 50 feet tall, and has dense foliage that makes it useful as a shade or windbreak tree. It doesn't like cold weather (no lower than 20° F), but it is heat, salt and drought tolerant (in fact it doesn't like a lot of rain). Like other leguminous pod bearers it can be very productive.

The large nutritious pods can be used to make a chocolate substitute, or their sticky sweet interior can be eaten straight out of the pod. They are also used as fodder for animals.

The trees are dioecious and only the females produce pods. If you grow them from seed some are likely to be male and won't produce pods. A few varieties with superior pods have been selected but they are hard to find. In fact many improved cultivars are actually male so they don't produce pods (damned messy things.)

Honey Locust (*Gleditsia triacanthos*) Zones 4-9

The trunk of this species is covered in pronged spines, which make climbing impossible. It's been suggested that this is an adaptation to prevent the sweet immature pods from being eaten by squirrels before the seeds are ripe. The immature pods have been eaten raw, or cooked as a vegetable. The mature pods are inedible, but contain a sweet inner pulp that contains about 30% sugar.

Fast growing Honey Locust will grow in almost any soil and tolerates drought, saline soil, disease, insect pests and air pollution. It is propagated from seed or cuttings (hard, green or root), while scions of choice varieties can be whip grafted or budded. It doesn't like transplanting though and doesn't fix nitrogen. A few improved cultivars have been produced (notably Calhoun and Milwood), but they aren't easy to find.

Mesquite (*Prosopis juliflora*) Zones 7-9

The Spanish name for the plant is Algaroba, which is the same as for Carob because the flavor of their pods is quite similar. The inner part of the pod is rich in protein, sugar, calcium and iron. Native Americans ground and sifted the pods to make flour, which was used for drinks or baking bread.

Mesquite can be grown from seed, which should be scarified with acid, or nicked with a file, prior to planting to allow water to penetrate the tough seed coat and hasten germination. It will grow in any well-drained soil.

Mesquite coppices easily and could be grown for poles, fenceposts or firewood (it is widely sold for use in barbecues). It makes a good spiny hedge plant too.

Screwbean (*Prosopis pubescens*) Zones 7-9

This related species can be used in the same ways and produces even better pods.

Syrup producing trees

The Sugar Maple (*A. saccharum*) is the best known syrup producing tree (it's the source of most commercial Maple syrup) but quite a few other trees can be tapped in the same way. The key factor in determining your success is whether your garden has the right growing conditions, as sap is produced best when warm days follow cold nights.

A big tree is needed to produce a significant quantity of syrup without harm, which takes a long time to grow. It's not really practical to grow your own syrup trees, though you might plant them for your grandchildren (varieties that produce sap with a higher sugar content have been found). Usually you just take advantage of trees you already have.

Useful syrup producing species include:

Maples (*Acer* species) The best include *A. negundo* and *A, platanoides*.
Red Alder (*Alnus rubra*)
Black Birch (*Betula lenta*) - Has a Wintergreen flavor.
Walnuts (*Juglans* species)
Cider Gum (*Eucalyptus gunii*) – The syrup produced from the sap of this Australian species was fermented to produce an alcoholic drink, hence the common name.

Other uses of trees

Trees don't just produce food of course, they produce other useful things too.

Christmas trees

Growing your own Christmas trees is easy enough, just plant a bunch of seedlings, or even seed, of the desired species. Favorite species vary depends upon where you live, but include Nordmann Spruce. Douglas Fir and Scots Pine.

Put your Christmas trees in fairly poor soil, in a sunny, out of the way place (you don't want them to be part of the landscape because you will eventually be cutting them). Also don't give them too much water or nutrients because you don't want them to grow too quickly, you want them to stay compact

You don't have to kill a Christmas tree when you cut it down. If you only cut the top two thirds of the tree the portion remaining will re-grow a new top. This won't create a very attractive tree though, so its best if this doesn't frame the entrance to your house.

Fenceposts

You can never have too many fence posts and they are getting expensive to buy. You can grow your own from fast growing and rot resistant Black Locust and Chestnut. The latter is particularly prized as it has little sapwood so can be useful even when fairly small. See Fences for more on this.

Firewood

If you use firewood and have the room you should think seriously about coppicing trees for fuel, I used to think growing firewood was a bit impractical until I cut some Monterey Pine firewood that had only seven growth rings. If cut when only six inches in diameter the wood doesn't even need splitting.

Good candidates for firewood plantings include Acacia, Black Locust, Mesquite, Red Alder (these all fix nitrogen), Chestnut, Eucalyptus, hybrid Poplar, Honey Locust, Linden, Ash and Oak. Just choose a species that grows like a weed in your area and coppices readily.

Once upon a time in Europe, smaller diameter branches were bound into bundles known as faggots. It may well be time to revive such a practice, though probably under a different name (burning faggots just isn't acceptable).

Furniture
I'm not talking about using wood to make furniture here, though you could do this if you choose. I'm talking about manipulating growing trees into shapes that can be used as furniture. This is sometimes known as arborisculpture and can be used to create some really beautiful pieces. As you might imagine it takes some time to grow a chair, but it isn't very difficult. Arborisculpture can also be used to make bridges, arbors and even tree houses.

Seeds and seedlings
You could gather seeds from your trees to sell, or you could pot up seedling trees and sell those. My garden produces lots of Black Walnut and Chestnut seedlings. See Income for more on this.

Lumber trees
Many hardwoods are highly prized for cabinetmaking and if you have a good specimen it could be of considerable value. However I am more concerned with encouraging you to plant trees rather than to cut them down for profit, so I will say no more about this. Planting such trees isn't a get rich quick scheme by any means, in fact it's more of a stay poor permanently scheme, as you probably won't see any benefit from it at all. It's something you would do for your great grandchildren, though the concept of property staying in one family that long is long gone.

If you have a crooked young Walnut (or other hardwood) tree and want to make it straight, just cut it down to the ground. The new coppice shoots that emerge will be fairly straight. Remove all but the best one of these and allow it to grow into a new tree.

Important fine hardwood species include
Black Cherry (*Prunus serotina*)
Black Walnut (*Juglans nigra*)
Walnut (*Juglans regia*)

Empress tree (*Paulownia tomentosa*) Zones 7-10
This very fast growing (12 feet annually) pioneer tree is a good shade tree, bee plant and ornamental (it has beautiful blue flowers and large leaves). The wood is strong but very light (1/2 the weight of Pine) and is prized for cabinetmaking, carving, musical instruments. The leaves can be fed to livestock.

Nitrogen fixing trees
These enrich the soil with their annual fall of leaf litter and are often important pioneer and nurse trees. They are an important source of fertility if you are trying to create a low input system and should be planted all over the garden.

Black Locust (*Robinia pseudoacacia*)
Acacia (*Acacia species*)
Alders (*Alnus* species)
Black Birch (*Betula lenta*)
Paloverde (*Cercidium* species) Syn *Parkinsonia* spp
Redbud (*Cercis* spp)
Carob (*Ceratonia siliqua*)
Mesquite (*Prosopis juliflora)*
Mimosa Tree (*Albizia julibrissin*)

Coppicing

No treatment of trees in landscaping would be complete without mentioning coppicing. This useful technique is relatively little known in this country, but is widely used in Europe and elsewhere. This is no doubt because we have always had such an abundance of forest resources we haven't had to be very economical with them.

Coppicing takes advantage of the fact that when you cut a deciduous tree down it doesn't necessarily die. The roots commonly remain alive and send up a ring of vigorous new shoots around the stump (known as a stool). If these are left alone (and not eaten by deer) they will grow vigorously until they start to compete with each other. The strongest shoots will eventually shade out the weaker ones and grow into a new trunk (or several), just as large and robust as the original.

Coppicing consists of cutting these shoots when they get to a useful size, which can take anywhere from 1 –30 years depending upon the species, climate and what you want to do with them. After cutting the stool sends up another crop of shoots and the process begins all over again.

Coppicing gives you another level of control over the growth of trees, as it gives you the ability to remove a tree that is casting too much shade without killing it. In fact you have the option of eventually allowing it to return. If you are clearing land for a garden you can choose to coppice some of the existing trees (or shrubs) rather than removing them entirely. You can then allow them to grow to whatever size you choose and get a useful crop of poles or mulch from them.

Coppicing is also the best way to get maximum production of wood from an area (much faster than starting from seedlings again). The new shoots are growing from well established roots and get plenty of sunlight, so growth is extremely vigorous (some may grow 14 feet in a season). It is a very practical way to growing firewood and gives larger yields than cutting mature trees and replanting.

Coppicing works best with fairly small trees and may not work at all with very old ones (the large unprotected surface area of the cut stump may invite rot).

Using coppice in the landscape

When a tree is coppiced you dramatically reduce its size and change the way it is used. The problem with using coppice in ornamental areas of the garden is that it is never the same size two years running. It is either getting larger rapidly or it is suddenly cut back to the ground. This is why it is usually placed out in the semi-wild garden.

Coppicing for fun and profit

Coppicing is destined to become much better known in this country as a way of producing firewood. With the price of a cord of Oak firewood already reaching $350 in some places, it won't be long before firewood plantations become a viable form of farm. A nitrogen fixer such as Black Locust, that also produces good firewood is particularly useful for this, as it can even supply its own fertilizer.

Creating and using a coppice woodlot

You can coppice many of the existing trees in your garden, but if you want to grow a specific product you will have to use the right species. To grow it on a large enough scale to support a craft business you would have to grow your own plantation (known as a copse).

Planting

You plant trees for coppicing just as you would any other trees, the main difference is that you plant them closer together and so have many more trees (a plantation of basket Willows might contain 20,000 plants per acre). This is where the trees that are easily propagated (from large nuts, suckers, layering or cuttings) have an advantage.

Spacing

Plants for coppicing are spaced much closer together than in conventional forestry, because they don't grow as large (the space is determined by their diameter at cutting time – when their crowns should just touch).

In dry climates coppiced plants should be spaced further apart so they can obtain water from a greater volume of soil.

Where

A coppiced plantation might consist of a single species, mixed species, or coppice with standards (full size trees mixed in with the coppice to grow lumber). It could even be grown in the form of a hedge, to serve as a screen.

Care

The young growing plants need weeding (a mulch can help a lot) and protection from deer and other browsing animals. In dry climates they may also require irrigation to keep them growing rapidly.

Cutting

It's important that the trees are well established before you begin regular cutting. They should be allowed to grow for 4-6 years before the first cutting, to give them time to produce a vigorous root system.

The frequency of cutting depends upon the speed of growth (which depends upon species, soil fertility and climate) and what you want to produce (shoots, poles, fenceposts, firewood). Long-term coppice may be harvested every 10 - 15 years, while short term coppice might be harvested every 4-5 years. Willow for basket weaving is commonly harvested every year or two. If coppice is left for too long (15+ years) the taller shoots will start to shade out the shorter ones and growth will slow down.

Coppice grown for fenceposts is usually allowed to get to 12" in diameter. This ensures there is enough volume of rot resistant heartwood when it is split into post size pieces. If you just cut round posts when they are 4" in diameter they would consist mostly of sapwood, which isn't very rot resistant and wouldn't last very long.

When

The trees are cut any time after they drop their leaves in autumn, right up until growth starts again in spring. You could cut in summer too, but the leafy branches get in the way and contain nutrients that are best left in the root (and may also encourage fungal attack). If you are cutting them for animal feed or biomass this is usually done in summer of course.

Usually a whole area of copse is cut at once, to ensure maximum light for regrowth. You can cut individual plants, but they may be shaded by their neighbors and so won't get as much light (or grow as rapidly)

How

Cut the stems carefully and cleanly (keep your tools sharp) to minimize injury and chances of rotting (don't tear the bark). Smaller stems were once cut with an axe or billhook, but now this is most often done with a chain saw The stems should be cut close to the stool, which is only 4 - 6" above ground level. (Watch out for stones embedded in the stool). Tradition says the cut should slope away from the center of the stool, so water drains outwards and doesn't pool in the center (which could cause rot).

Uses

When coppice was cut in the past every part was used for something. The poles were sorted by size for use as tool handles, garden supports, walking sticks, fishing poles and more. The poles of some species were split lengthwise for weaving wattle hurdles and baskets and for barrel hoops. The smallest twigs were used by gardeners as pea and bean supports. Leftover brush or wood was bound into faggots and used for firewood.

Any time you coppice you get a lot of woody material that is good for mulch. In fact this could actually be a primary reason to coppice (use Basket Willow or a nitrogen fixer such as Alder). If the material is only an inch or so in diameter it can be chipped in an electric shredder. Larger material could be used for berms.

Regeneration

The spring after cutting the plants will send up vigorous new shoots. Protect these from deer and the whole cycle will begin again. Not only doesn't coppicing harm the tree, it can actually prolong its life span significantly. If a plant dies after being coppiced (it occasionally happens) it can be replaced by layering from the next plant over. The coppiced trees can be converted back to full size trees by allowing the strongest sucker to grow and removing all of the rest.

Other Forms of regrowth

Pollarding

Livestock (and deer) relish the new growth of a coppice and will eat it readily. If it is not possible to fence them out then pollarding (or polling) can be used instead. Pollarding consists of cutting the top off the tree, leaving only the trunk, about 6 – 10 feet tall. This causes the tree to send out a cluster of shoots just as with coppicing, but these are on the top of the trunk, out of the reach of hungry herbivores.

Pollarded shoots can be used just like those from coppiced plants, though the poles aren't as straight. They were traditionally used for animal feed, though you could also use them for mulch.

Pollarded trees have a very distinctive appearance and were once commonly used as boundary markers.

Suckering

A few species (*Robinia, Sassafras, Tilia, Ulmus*) send up new shoots (suckers) from the roots, rather than the stump, a process known as suckering. These can be cut when they reach a suitable size, in the same way as coppicing. Rooted suckers can also be detached from the parent plant (while dormant) and transplanted to give you a new tree.

Species for coppicing

In Britain several tree species were traditionally coppiced to produce the raw materials for important crafts or industries.

Chestnut

One of the most versatile and important coppice trees, its durable wood is used for fenceposts, split rail fencing, paling fencing, as well as poles and trugs. As many as 300 - 400 stools can be grown on an acre of land and can be cut every 8 - 20 years. Unfortunately coppiced plants don't usually produce many nuts, because they are just getting big enough to be productive when you cut them.

Hazel

In Britain the long slender stems of the coppiced Hazel (*Corylus*) shrub were commonly split lengthwise and used for weaving wattle hurdles. Larger stems were used for firewood and charcoal. It is cut on a short rotation of 5-10 years and there may be 800 stools per acre. If left long enough between cuts it will also produce edible nuts.

Willow

In times past baskets were some of the most widely used household containers and weaving them was a major cottage industry. To supply their raw materials basket weavers would often grow improved Willow cultivars in special Willow gardens conveniently located near their houses.

Willow is easy to propagate from 12" hardwood cuttings, planted 12 - 24" apart in wet soil. Harvesting begins 3 years after planting and may be carried on every 1 - 3 years for 70 years or more.

Oak

In England this was once widely coppiced to provide firewood and for making into charcoal.

Useful American species

Any deciduous tree that sends up sprouts from the stump can be coppiced. The following species should all work well:

Alder	Basswood	Beech
Birch	Black Locust	Cherry
Eucalyptus	Hackberry	Hazels
Hickory	Honey Locust	Oak
Maple	Mesquite	Pawpaw
Persimmon	Plum	Poplars
Redwood	Sassafras	Willows

Using coppice products in the garden

Coppicing enables us to grow a variety of useful garden materials cheaply and relatively quickly.

Fenceposts - Black Locust, Chestnut and Oak are all good for this and can be grown in a few years.

Poles - There is a constant need for poles of various sizes in the garden. We might use 6-inch diameter poles for arbors and pergolas, 4-inch poles for fenceposts, 2-3 inch poles for lighter fenceposts and tree branch supports. Smaller poles might be used for rustic trellis, arches and plant supports.

Pea sticks – These are used to support vines (traditionally peas) and any tall plants that may get top heavy and fall over. See Temporary plant supports for more on this.

Wood chips - Any coppiced plants can be a source of wood chips for mulch. Don't let them get too big, they need to be small enough to fit your chipper.

Wattle hurdles - These traditional English panels are made from woven Willow or split Hazel. They were originally used for making pens to hold sheep, but are now more often used as decorative panels in the garden. They are fairly simple in design, but take a considerable amount of skill and experience to make well.

Fencing - Paling fences, split rails. See Boundaries for more on these.

Fuel - Firewood, faggots charcoal, biochar, biogas, alcohol. Trees could be grown to produce cordwood or poles for binding into bundles. They might also be grown on short rotations and chipped whole for use as fuel or turned into biochar for soil improvement.

Miscellaneous - Tool handles, rustic furniture, bird tables, walking sticks, gates and more.

By products - wood ash, leaf mold.

Basketry - The material obtained by regular coppicing is superior to that cut from the wild, because it has grown faster under optimal conditions. It may also be a superior cultivar, that has been bred for its special properties.

Mushrooms - Shiitake, Maitake, Oyster Mushrooms and more can be grown on 6" diameter coppiced logs of Oak, Chestnut, Alder and other species. Plugs of spawn are inserted into holes drilled into the logs. These take about two years to start fruiting and then continue for several years. See Mushrooms for more on this.

Shrubs

Shrubs are an integral part of the new food garden and have a unique role to play (they fill the gap between trees and herbaceous perennials - often literally). They can be highly productive, fast growing, independent (and often drought tolerant) and you should utilize them as much as you can. They are smaller than trees and considerably more accommodating for use in small gardens. However they vary in size and shape and growth habit (some can form large thickets). Like trees they take a while to reach maturity, so must be planned for in advance (though if they start to get too big, you can always coppice them).

Bush Fruit

I don't mean fruit that can be found growing in the bush, but rather fruit that grow on bushes. Also known as soft fruit, the Blueberries, Currants, Gooseberries, Blackberries and Raspberries have a special place in the productive garden for several reasons:

The bush fruits are amongst the tastiest treats the garden has to offer and almost everyone likes them. They are nearly always expensive to buy because they are perishable and don't ship well. Planting them can be a significant step in maximizing the productivity of your garden and you should plant a variety of species.

Many bush fruits are also uniquely nutritious, containing vitamins, minerals and some unique antioxidants and other phytonutrients. Some species are worth growing just for this, even if they aren't particularly tasty. Just use them for juice in a cocktail or mix them with tastier berries such as Blackberries or Blueberries.

Many species require no attention once established and can be very productive. The harvest period is relatively short, but it can be extended considerably with different species and varieties. They are also easy to preserve by freezing, canning or drying.

Care

Most bush fruits are easy to grow, if you pick suitable varieties for the growing conditions. Once established they practically look after themselves and produce abundantly. Your main task is often preventing birds from eating them.

Many species are adapted to cool moist climates and if you want to grow them in hotter areas you must give them plenty of moisture and light shade.

Most shrubs respond well to vigorous pruning or even coppicing. Cut them down and they will sprout up again vigorously. Most species are easily propagated from layering, cuttings or division and take only a couple of years to start producing well.

Small berries such as Blueberries and Currants are most efficiently picked using a berry comb/picking rake. This can drastically reduce the time needed for harvesting.

Bush fruits are sometimes planted around fruit trees to give a temporary crop until the trees really get going. You can then move them somewhere else (or take cuttings from them).

Fruit cages

Don't delude yourself into thinking you can get a good crop of Blueberries (and to a lesser extent other berries) without protecting them from the birds. This needn't be a very complex or expensive affair. A wire or plastic mesh fence may already enclose the walls. In such a case you just need to string some wires between the fenceposts and drape some netting over the top.

Common bush fruit

Some of these plants are among the best low-work sources of food available anywhere. They produce food reliably year after year, often with little attention from you. The best species include:

Blackberries (*Rubus* species) Zones 5-9

The Blackberry is the ultimate bush fruit for all around ease of cultivation, flavor and productivity. They are particularly outstanding for fruit pie, alone or with apples or other fruit. They are also very easy to store by freezing and can also be made into preserves. The only argument I can think of for not growing Blackberries is if you already have an abundance of wild ones growing nearby.

This is a plant where a small amount of work can reward you very well. Even the cultivated Blackberries retain a lot of wild vigor and are very independent (so much so they can sometimes become invasive). They do best in a rich, moist soil with full sun and in ideal conditions some cultivars can produce stems 2" thick and 20 feet long. They are all self-fertile so only one variety is needed for fruit production.

Blackberries are easy to propagate because the flexible stems naturally root at the tips of canes and create new plants every year (this makes them quite mobile). They also send up suckers from the base of the plant and can be grown from cuttings.

The wickedly thorny stems make them useful as security barrier plants or to reinforce a fence (think of them as vegetable barbed wire). Don't put them anywhere the vicious thorns might come into contact with living flesh, such as near paths or gates. There are now quite a few very productive thornless cultivars that work much better in heavily traveled locations. These can be grown on fences, arches and even pergolas.

Deer love all *Rubus* species and will eat all but the most viciously spiny parts (and there they will carefully nibble the leaves off). The thornless types are a deer dream come true

Raspberries (*Rubus* species) Zones 3-9

These are so closely related to the Blackberry that there are hybrids between the two. The fruit tastes every bit as good as Blackberries, though their flavor is quite different. It's said that Raspberries don't like very hot weather, but all three types (red, black and yellow) have done fine in my garden.

Raspberries have a different growth habit than Blackberries. They don't root at the tips, but instead spread by means of underground roots and form dense colonies.

Everbearing Raspberries fruit on one and two year old canes and can give 2 crops a year.

Hybrid Bramble berries Zones 5-9

These are crosses of various *Rubus* species and can be even better than their parents. Delicious, vigorous and productive, they include Loganberry, Ollalieberry, Marionberry, Tayberry and more. There is also the beautiful Japanese Wineberry, which is one of most ornamental of fruits.

Blackcurrant (*Ribes nigrum*) Zones 3-8

This European favorite is very much under appreciated in the United States and deserves to be more widely used. This is partly because they are plants of northern climates and do best in cooler areas. The other reason is that it has long been illegal to grow them in many states, because they are an alternate host for White Pine Blister Rust.

Blackcurrants are tart and not very good raw (or should I say they are an acquired taste). However when cooked and sweetened they make outstanding fruit pies or preserves. It makes my mouth water to think about them, they are totally addictive.

Blackcurrants are hardy, very productive and easy to grow, though they don't really like hot weather (give them some shade in warmer climates). They are also easy to propagate, just stick hardwood cuttings into the ground in fall and you will have plants by spring.

These plants aren't fussy as to soil type so long as it is moist. They like a mulch to keep it cool though.

Blackcurrant fruits are very rich in vitamin C and are one of the best sources of antioxidants.

Jostaberry is a delicious cross between the Blackcurrant and the European Gooseberry with larger fruit than a Blackcurrant and no thorns.

Redcurrants, Whitecurrants *(Ribes Rubrum)* Zones 3-8

These are closely related to the Blackcurrant, but have quite a different flavor. They are easy to grow, self-fertile and do well in warm climates (if given light shade). They are also very ornamental, with beautiful translucent red, pink or white berries. These varieties can be grown as specimen plants, as a hedge and in a forest garden. They tolerate more heat and shade than other *Ribes* species.

The fruit is quite tart, even when fully ripe. They work well when mixed with sweeter fruit in pies and compotes.

Missouri Currant *(R. odoratum)* - This native

American species is very independent and tolerant of cold, heat and drought, though it is more productive if given better conditions. It spreads vigorously by means of suckers and forms large colonies.

This species is propagated in the same way as the related Blackcurrant. It is partly self-fertile, but produce more fruit with cross-pollination.

The ripe fruit can be used like that of Blackcurrant. It is actually better than Blackcurrant for eating raw, but not as good when cooked.

Gooseberries *(Ribes species)* Zones 3-8

This relative of the Blackcurrant is much more highly esteemed in Europe than the United States. As a consequence there are not many varieties available in this country.

Gooseberries are sometimes trained to have a single stem and a bushy top, so they are more ornamental. They are also thorny enough to be used as a barrier hedge.

Gooseberries do well in poor soil, but need regular moisture. Like other *Ribes* species they prefer light shade in hot climates They are easily propagated from hardwood cuttings, softwood cuttings or layering.

European Gooseberry *(Ribes uva crispa)*
This species has the best flavored fruit, but many cultivars don't do well in North America.

American Gooseberry *(Ribes hirtellum)*
This species does better in North America but the fruit isn't as good as the above. Some hybrids between the two are available.

Highbush Blueberries *(Vaccinium corymbosum)* Zones 3-10

The familiar Blueberries are not only delicious, but also rich in antioxidants and other special nutrients. They can also be amazingly productive, which is good because you can never have too many Blueberries.

Blueberries are attractive shrubs and make good hedges. They have nice fall color and colored bark.

The most important thing about growing Blueberries is that they need an acid soil (pH 4.0 – 5.0) for good growth. Provide this by adding peat moss or sulphur and mulching with acid material such as Pine needles (maintaining the necessary acidity can be an ongoing thing). It is also important to keep the soil moist for maximum productivity. Most Blueberry species are adapted to cool northern areas and in very warm areas they may appreciate light shade.

The other important thing to remember about Blueberries is that they are one of the all-time most favorite foods of birds. If you want to get a reasonable harvest they should be located fairly close to the house and netted when the berries are ripening. Alternatively they could be grown in a fruit cage (this isn't very ornamental though).

Blueberries are partly self-fertile, but produce more fruit with cross-pollination.

Other useful Blueberries include:

Rabbiteye Blueberries (*V. Ashei*) - These are more heat tolerant than the above and can be grown in hotter climates. They also tolerate less acid soil. Some Rabbiteye varieties can get quite tall (to 12 feet or more).

Lowbush Blueberry (*Vaccinium angustfolium*) These are smaller, sweeter and less productive than the above. See Groundcover for more on this.

Hazel, Filbert *(Corylus avellana)* Zones 3-9

This delicious and uniquely flavored nut is a fruit from a botanical standpoint, if not a culinary one. These attractive shrubs are the smallest plants to produce a significant commercial nut crop. Because of their compact size they can even be fitted in small gardens and so are very popular in parts of Europe.

The Filbert is an important nut producer in Northern Europe because it thrives in colder conditions than any other commercial nut crop (though it flowers early, so frost can sometimes damage the flowers). They actually prefer cool weather and don't like very hot summers.

These species will grow in part shade but prefer full sun for a good part of the day. They like well-drained but fertile soil. They are quite drought tolerant, but produce better with regular moisture.

Hazel is usually grown from stratified seed, though you can just plant the fresh nuts outside in the fall to stratify naturally. They are most easily propagated by separating suckers from the parent plant, layering or root cuttings (each with 2 buds). These species are monoecious, but many are self-infertile and you will get much better fruiting if you plant two varieties. They are cross-pollinated by the wind

Squirrels were born to eat Hazel nuts. If there are any Squirrels present in your garden (are there any without them?) you won't get many nuts if you don't take precautions. In extreme cases this may have to be a complete cage.

Filbert Blight can be a serious problem for gardeners in the eastern part of the country

A vigorous and densely growing shrub, Filbert can be used as a hedge, screen or specimen plant . In England it is commonly coppiced to produce long thin shoots. These are split and used to make wattle panels for fencing.

Less common bush fruits

There are a lot of less well known fruiting shrubs that can provide food, drink and more, as well as looking good. I don't have room to go into much detail here but I do want to make you aware of some of the best options.

All of the below are relatively easy to grow and most require little attention. However their fruit varies in quality considerably. Some are really good, others have to be carefully prepared to be considered worth eating. One clue as to how good they are is how many cultivars have been produced.

Beach Plum (*Prunus maritima*) Zones 5-7

This has been gathered from the wild more often than it is cultivated in gardens, but a few improved cultivars are now available. They are cross-pollinated so you need to plant two varieties to get fruit.

This attractive shrub grows to 6 feet in height and spreads to form a dense clump. It can make a good hedge plant or screen. Any branch that touches the ground can root and become a new plant (which is worth knowing). Like many coastal plants it isn't very hardy.

This species is prized on its native Cape Cod for making Plum jam, but it is usually too tart to eat raw.

Bush Cherries Zones 3-5

Nanking Cherry (*P. tomentosa*)
Japanese Bush Cherry (*P. japonica*)
These hardy species can tolerate heat, drought, light shade and cold winters and can be very productive if pampered a little. The fruit is eaten fresh or used for juice, Most need cross-pollination to produce good crops.

These species can grow up to 10 feet tall and make an attractive flowering and fruiting hedge. They sucker freely and spread to form dense colonies.

Chokeberries (*Aronia* species) Zones 3-9

This independent native American species produces fruit reliably in my garden without much attention from me. In fact it almost always seems to have fruit on it, because it produces them so easily, holds them so long and because neither I nor the birds really like them. It is also attractive enough to be grown as an ornamental.

The fruits are one of the richest sources of anti-oxidants ever found. Unfortunately they aren't very good raw, but can be cooked with other fruit in pies or preserves. They are used commercially for juice, which is extracted from the berries by steam extraction or mashing. This tastes best when mixed with an equal amount of sweeter juice, such as apple juice.

Serviceberry *(Amelanchier alnifolia)* Zones 3-9

I already mentioned this productive and tasty native American species in the section on trees. Much of what I said in that section also applies to this shrubby species.

Serviceberry is quite spectacular when flowering in spring and is sometimes grown purely as an ornamental. This is a little silly because the fruits are very good. They look somewhat like Blueberries, but have their own distinctive flavor. A number of productive improved cultivars are available. It is self-fertile so you only need to plant one variety.

This extremely hardy plant can be grown in full sun or part shade. In some areas of the east Juneberries are plagued by pest and disease and don't grow well. In most other areas it is quite trouble free, except that birds love the berries.

Chilean Guava *(Ugni molinae)* Zones 8-10

I love these berries raw, and consider them one of the best flavored fruits in the garden. They remind me of strawberry ice cream. Apparently they were a favorite of Queen Victoria too, so she is in good company.

This species actually does well in part shade, which makes it particularly useful for forest gardens. It likes a fertile, well drained soil and tolerates salt. It can be grown from seed, semi-ripe cuttings, hardwood cuttings or layering. It isn't very hardy however and won't survive long cold winters.

Elder *(Sambucus nigra)* Zones 4-9

Elder is a common weedy shrub or small tree of cooler northern areas. It will grow in sun or part shade, isn't fussy about the soil and is extremely hardy. Quite a number of improved fruit bearing cultivars are available and these are becoming popular as garden crops in colder areas.

These fast growing shrubs are quite ornamental with attractive flower umbels and purple fruit. Some varieties even have variegated foliage. They have been used as hedges, screens and specimen plants.

The flowers can be added to salads, fried in batter, or used for tea. The blue berries have been used for wine and mixed with other fruit in pies, They even contain a substance (3-rhamnoglucoside) that is very beneficial for the eyes.

These fast growing plants are also a good source of biomass, mulch or compost.

Fuchsia *(Fuchsia species)* Zones 7-9

Though these species are widely grown as ornamentals, most people aren't aware that the fruits are edible and sometimes quite good. Many varieties don't produce fruit because of poor pollination.

They aren't very hardy and need regular moisture and fairly fertile soil. They are usually propagated from semi-ripe cuttings.

The best species include:
F. magellanica
F. splendens

Highbush Cranberry *(Viburnum trilobum)* Zones 3-9

This shrub is cultivated as an ornamental for its pretty flowers, attractive berries and red fall foliage. It also makes a good hedge or screen. It likes moist soil with sun or part shade. Very hardy and self-fertile, it can be grown from seed, cuttings or layering. The berries often remain on the bush well into winter and may be improved by repeated frosts.

The sour fruit is rich in vitamin C and taste somewhat like Cranberries. They can be used in preserves, jelly (they are rich in pectin), sauces and juice cocktails. Plant breeders have worked to improve the fruit and a number of superior cultivars are available.

Honeyberry *(Lonicera caerulea)* Zones 2-8

For the food gardener there are two distinct types of Honeysuckle, The vigorous ornamental vines with their lovely scent don't produce edible berries (some are actually poisonous), so are only of limited use. Of much more interest for us are those that bear tasty Blueberry-like berries in late spring. In recent years they have been differentiated by the name Honeyberry, no doubt because they are a form of Honeysuckle (the berries aren't particularly honey-like). These vigorous and hardy plants are very easy to grow and deserve to be more widely used. They bear the first berries to ripen in my garden in spring.

Honeyberry prefers fairly rich and moist soil. It needs full sun in cool climates or part shade in hot ones. It is propagated from hardwood or semi-ripe cuttings.

Though the above species is from Asia, there are several similar edible native American species, including the Waterberry (*L. villosa*) and the Twinberry (*L. involucrata*).

Pineapple Guava *(Feijoa sellowiana)* Zones 8-10

Not very hardy, the Pineapple Guava needs full sun and a warm sheltered spot. In an ideal climate it is very easy to grow and may reach 10 feet in height. A nice feature is that it fruits late in the year, after most other fruits are done.

This evergreen self-fertile shrub has beautiful flowers, nice foliage and tasty fruit. It can be trained to grow into a small tree (to 12 feet), but more often it grows as a tall multi-stemmed bush. With a little pruning it makes a good hedge (big or small) or windbreak. It tolerates some shade.

Hardy to 15° F, it prefers fairly cool summers. It is quite drought tolerant, but fruits better in moist soil. Propagate from seed or cuttings.

Pomegranate (*Punica granatum*) Zones 8-10

With its red flowers and large orange fruit this self-fertile shrub is as ornamental as it is edible. It is native to the Middle East and prefers areas with hot summers and mild winters (it doesn't need much winter chill). In cooler climates it might be grown against a wall to give it extra heat. It prefers moist, fertile soil with full sun.

In the right conditions this it is a drought tolerant and very low-maintenance plant and can be grown as a shrub or a small tree (up to 20 feet high).

Pomegranate can be grown from seed, semi-ripe cuttings, hardwood cuttings or layering.

Salal (*Gaultheria shallon*) Zones 6-9

This west coast native is a small to medium sized shrub (4 feet in sun, up to 10 feet in the shade) with leathery evergreen leaves and edible Blueberry-like fruit.

It can be grown as a hedge (part shade) or groundcover (in sun). It is quite happy in poor, acid woodland soil and in my garden it grows without any attention whatsoever.

Wolfberry, Goji Berry (*Lycium barbarum, L. chinense*) Zones 6-

This leaves and fruits of these species are widely eaten in China and a number of improved cultivars exist. The berries are one of the best (maybe the best) sources of anti-oxidants and they have become a trendy new health food in recent years (the dried berries sell for $16.00 a pound in our local natural food store). In Chinese medicine they are said to give long life.

Unlike fussy health plants like Ginseng, this vigorous plant is easy to grow and has naturalized in some areas. It can be grown from seed (get some from the dried berries), tip layering or soft cuttings (these are very easy).

The newly emerged foliage is sometimes eaten in spring. The berries can be eaten fresh or dried for later use.

Sumach (*Rhus glabra*) Zone 2

This attractive, fast growing and hardy plant is commonly planted as an ornamental. Native Americans used the fuzzy fruit clusters to make a kind of lemonade (they steeped them in cold water for a few minutes). This fast growing plant can also be a good source of biomass for mulch.

The related *R. integrifolia* and *R. ovata* can be used in the same ways.

Wild fruits and nuts

Quite a few wild shrubs are worth exploring as no-work sources of fruit. We could propagate superior individual wild plants or even breed improved varieties. Of course this has already happened in the case of the Blueberries, Blackberries, Juneberries and others. Other potentially useful species would include:

Barberry (*Berberis* species)
Black Haw (*Viburnum prunifolium*)
Bladdernut (*Staphylea trifolia*)
Buckberry (*Lycium* species)
Chinkapin (*Castanea pumila*)
Bush plums (*Prunus* species)
Hollyleaf Cherry (*Laurocerasus ilicifolia*)
Huckleberries (*Gaylussacia* species)
Oregon Grape (*Mahonia* species)
Silver Buffaloberry (*Shepherdia argentea*)
Silverberry (*Eleagnus commutata*)
Wild currants (*Ribes* species)
Wild roses (*Rosa* species)

Of course you don't have to confine yourself to native wild species. You can also search for plants from similar climates in other parts of the world. You just have to be sure a plant isn't going to be invasive.

Other useful shrubs

There are also useful shrubs that produce edible leaves, tea, culinary flavorings and more.

Edible foliage shrubs

Not many temperate climate shrubs have useful edible foliage, but there are a few. These are so potentially useful that it's worth experimenting with them. Some of these are actually trees, but when grown for their edible leaves they are coppiced to keep them to a reasonable height for harvesting. This means they can be treated like shrubs in the landscape.

Basswood, Linden (*Tilia* species)

These species produce edible leaves (*T. cordata* is the best) and are very good if gathered when they first unfurl. They are actually fairly tall trees, but when grown for food they are coppiced, to maximize leaf production and keep the leaves at a convenient height for gathering.

Beech (*Fagus grandifolia*)

The leaves of this large forest tree can be eaten in spring when they first open. It could also produce edible nuts if it got big enough, but this won't happen if you are coppicing it for leaves.

Cabbage Tree (*Moringa oleifera*)

This tropical tree produces exceptionally nutritious edible leaves and seedpods and has the potential to be an important vegetable crop.

Though Moringa is actually a tree (it can grow to 40 feet in height) it doesn't grow as one in temperate climates. This is because it isn't very hardy and dies back to the ground if hit by hard frost. The roots will usually survive in the ground though (so long as they aren't frozen) and will send up vigorous new shoots in spring. For this reason it grows as a shrub in cooler climates. It can easily be grown from seed (give it plenty of warmth) or hardwood cuttings.

This species can be grown as an edible deciduous hedge and kept at 4-6 feet in height.

Sourwood (*Oxydendrum arboreum*)

This species produces sour tasting leaves, hence its common names Sourwood or Sorrel Tree. I have never grown it though.

Fragrant Spring Tree (*Toona sinensis*) Zones 6-9

The aromatic young leaves of this small tree are commonly used for food in China and it is widely cultivated there. It is fairly tender and is killed back to the ground by hard frost, but it will usually grow back from the roots in spring. It is easily grown from seed and grows very rapidly. It can also be propagated from root cuttings (I moved some trees and re-emerged in the places I moved it from).

Mediterranean Saltbush (*Atriplex halimus*)

This shrubby evergreen relative of the (not very common) garden vegetable Orach is easy to grow but hard to find. The tender, mildly flavored leaves and growing tips can be eaten raw or cooked (though like the related Spinach they contain oxalic acid).

It can be grown from seed easily enough if you can find it, but softwood cuttings are quicker (if you can find a plant to take them from). Saltbush is drought and salt tolerant and hardy to zone 7.

If you can't find this species you may have better luck with the similar American species Four Wing Saltbush (*A. canescens*), which can be used in the same way.

Lemon verbena *(Aloysia triphylla)* Zones 8-10
In a suitable climate Lemon Verbena can grow into a small tree. It isn't very hardy though and a hard frost will kill it back to the ground (it will send up new shoots the following spring). In colder climates it is usually grown as a container plant (it does well in containers) and taken indoors for the winter.

The Lemon scented leaves make excellent tea, either fresh or dried.

New Zealand Flax (*Phormium tenax*) Zone 7-9
This large (to 8 feet) clumping plant species will grow in full sun, but also tolerates deep shade, as well as saline soils and wet or dry conditions. The flowers are a good course of nectar and the seed is edible.

New Zealand Flax is most notable for its incredibly tough and flexible leaves. These are one of the best materials you can grow for tying up plants. The leaves will take a tight knot and are so tough its very hard to break one with your hands. It didn't surprise me to learn that they were once used for making rope. It is now mostly grown as a low maintenance ornamental.

Myrtle (*Myrtus communis*) Zones 9-10
This attractive and fairly hardy evergreen shrub is widely grown as an ornamental. The aromatic leaves are an important culinary flavoring and can be used like Bay leaves. Try adding a few twigs to the barbecue, as you would Rosemary.

The drought tolerant Myrtle prefers hot summers and mild winters. It doesn't need a very fertile soil. Propagate from softwood cuttings in summer, hardwood cuttings in winter, or seed.

Myrtle is related to Chilean Guava and like that plant it bears edible berries.

Tea (*Camelia sinensis*) Zones 7-10
As the name suggests this is a very good tea plant, because it is the original Tea! As the Latin name indicates it is a form of Camelia and quite attractive. With its shiny evergreen leaves it can be grown as a hedge, background shrub or a small tree (obviously harvesting is easier if the plant isn't too tall. It is quite slow-growing.

People think that because tea grows in India and Sri Lanka that it must be a tender tropical plant but this isn't the case at all. In those countries it is grown in cool highland areas, and is actually hardy to about 0° F.

Tea prefers some shade in hot climates. It likes moist acid soil and doesn't like to be dry. In a suitable climate it isn't any harder to grow than the related Camellia.

Tea is made from the new leaves growing at the tip of each branch. When it is growing well you can harvest several times in a season.

Rose of Sharon (*Hibiscus syriacus*) Zones 5-9
This attractive shrub is commonly grown as an ornamental, but the young leaves are edible and can be eaten raw or cooked.

Roselle (*Hibiscus sabdariffa*) Zones 9-11
With its edible leaves and beautiful (edible) flowers this species is a useful ornamental for milder areas. It is a perennial, but not very hardy plant and in colder areas it must be grown as an annual. It is easily grown from seed, so long as it is warm enough. The flowers make excellent tea.

Willows (*Salix* species) Zones 3-9
These are really tree species, but coppicing keeps them growing at shrub size, so I have placed them here. They are not edible, though they do have medicinal properties as a painkiller. Their chief use is for basket weaving and selected cultivars are cultivated commercially (and on a home scale) for craft supplies. In some parts of Europe Sally (willow) gardens were once a common sight, grown to supply materials for the basket makers living in nearby cottages.

Almost any Willow cutting will root and the long shoots can be used to create living arches, arbors and even plant supports.

Saw Palmetto (*Serenoa repens*) Zones 9-10

This vigorous weedy little palm is useful as a source of small palm hearts and for its medicinal berries (they are beneficial to prostate health).

This species is easily grown from seed and does well in most soils (so well it is often considered to be a weed). Though hardier than most Palms it is still pretty frost tender and can't stand prolonged cold. In the north it is sometimes grown as an indoor plant.

Rosemary (*Rosemarinus officinalis*) Zones 7-10

This vigorous evergreen shrub is an important culinary herb and can be used fresh year round. It is also a valuable, drought tolerant landscape shrub and one of the few things deer will rarely touch (I grow it outside my deer fence). The pretty blue flowers are a favorite of bees.

Rosemary isn't very hardy and won't survive outdoors in very cold areas. Fortunately it grows well in pots.

Rosemary makes a good windbreak / hedge for the barbecue area. You can then just clip a few branches and toss them on the barbecue when cooking.

Flowering shrubs

A few shrubs make it into my garden not because they have any special uses, but just because I like them (call me old fashioned if you must).

Butterfly Bush *(Buddleia davidii)* Zones 3 -9

How can anyone not like this unassuming shrub. It isn't of any particular use that I am aware of, but it is a fantastic nectary plant, As the common name suggests it is particularly good at attracting butterflies (and hummingbirds, bees, wasps and other nectar loving creatures). Plant it near your sitting area and you can watch its flying blossoms.

Butterfly Bush is an extremely hardy and drought tolerant plant (even weedy) and often naturalizes. It can be planted in any neglected spot where you want a vigorous shrub. It tends to get straggly if left to its own devices so is pruned frequently in ornamental gardens (it can even be cut right down to the ground). This ties in well with its use as a fast growing source of biomass, just cut it and chip it every couple of years.

Roses (*Rosa* species) Zones 2-9

The quintessential aromatic, beautiful and sensual cottage garden shrubs, Roses can become addictive and some people fill their entire gardens with them. I used to disdain roses as symbolic of unproductive, resource consuming gardens, but I have to admit they have been growing on me of late. I still don't have any time for the fussy kinds, but I do admire the vigorous and enthusiastic shrubs and ramblers (these can often be propagated from cuttings).

Few plants are as vigorous or tough as the wilder roses. They have many landscape uses, as hedges, windbreaks and screens. They can be trained as climbers to soften trellises, walls and buildings. Some even tolerate part shade.

Roses are not just ornamentals however, they have many uses as food and medicine (hips) flavoring (petals), cosmetics, perfumes, potpourri, cut flowers and more.

Rose flowers are self-fertile and are followed by Rose hips, which taste like apples and are very rich in vitamin C. The larger hips (*R. rugosa* is one of the best) are particularly useful, just cut them in half, scoop out the seeds and rinse off the hairs. They can be dried for tea, cooked in jam and soups and more.

Sages (*Salvia* species) Zones 3-9

Some of the shrubby Sages are useful for filling in vacant areas of the garden. They are aromatic, drought tolerant, pretty and attractive to insects.

Lilac *(Syringa vulgaris)* Zones 3 -9

For an expat Brit like myself Lilac is the essence of summer (even though it flowers in spring in my garden). The flowers can be eaten like those of Elder.

Lilac is also a good indicator plant, to tell you when spring is here and its time to start direct sowing vegetables in your garden. You might even plant it at the entrance to your vegetable garden for this.

Nitrogen fixing shrubs

Though any vigorous shrub can be used as a source of biomass, only a few fix nitrogen. These species have a symbiotic relationship with nitrogen fixing organisms which enables them to grow in very poor soils, where there is less competition. You can harvest branches and leaves from these plants at regular intervals and they will regenerate fairly quickly. The foliage can be used for composting or animal feed, the stems can be used for mulch.

These species are so important they are often grown purely for adding fertility. However if you can also get a useful crop so much the better.

California Lilac (*Ceanothus* species) Zones 7-10

Most of these species are very drought tolerant and also fix nitrogen. The leaves of *C. integerrimus, C. sanguineus and C. velutinus* have been used for tea.

New jersey Tea (*C. Americana*) Zone 3

This is a good tea plant (as you might safely assume from the name).

Autumn Olive (*Eleagnus umbellata*) Zones 3-9

The fruits of the best varieties are good when fully ripe (eat them seed and all), but don't stay that way for long.

Autumn Olive is quite an attractive plant and makes a good hedge or specimen plant. It is mostly self-fertile so you usually only need to plant one variety. It is so easy to grow that it is considered invasive. It can grow in poor soil because it hosts a nitrogen fixing bacteria.

Goumi (*Eleagnus multiflora*) Zones 6-9

Hardy, drought tolerant, nitrogen-fixing, self-fertile and it produces berries rich in vitamin C. I won't pretend the fruits are delicious, but they aren't bad when fully ripe.

A relative of Autumn and Russian Olive this species grows to about 8 feet and can be used as a hedge. It can grow in full sun or part shade and tolerates poor soil because it fixes nitrogen. It is also a good source of biomass for mulch.

Russian Olive (*Eleagnus angustifolia*) Zones 3-9

These very hardy plants can tolerate drought, poor soils (they fix nitrogen), salt and more. They are actually so independent they are banned in some states for being invasive.

The fully ripe fruits can be quite good and some improved varieties are known as trebizond dates. It is self-fertile so you only need one variety to get fruit.

Eleagnus x ebbingei

This large hybrid shrub is grown as an ornamental, but produces tasty edible fruit too. It isn't self-fertile so you will need another cultivar to produce fruit.

Sea Buckthorn (*Hippophae rhamnoides*) Zone 3-9

This species was widely cultivated in the Soviet Union and eastern bloc countries for its vitamin C rich berries. Over the years many improved cultivars were produced and some of them are now fairly widely available. These are a little too sour to eat raw, but have a nice flavor. They are most often used to make a juice drink (sweetened and diluted with water).

Sea Buckthorn is very hardy and easy to grow. It prefers full sun though it will tolerate part shade. The plants are dioecious and you need both male and female plants to get fruit.

This attractive species can be used as an ornamental for its silvery gray foliage and orange berries. It can reach 10-15 feet in height in hospitable climates and sends up suckers to form dense colonies.

The fruits are hard to harvest as they stay firmly attached to the branch. Sometimes the whole branches are cut off and frozen, so the berries can be brushed off and collected.

Siberian Pea-Shrub (*Caragana arborescens*) Zones 2-8

This nitrogen-fixer may grow anywhere from 6-12 feet tall and can be used for a hedge, screen, or windbreak. It is also useful as a source of nitrogen rich mulch or compost material.

The small edible seeds have been eaten by humans, but are more often fed to chickens.

Propagate from seed, semi-ripe cuttings, root cuttings or layering. Siberian Pea Shrub will grow in poor soils and is quite drought tolerant.

Scotch Broom (*Cytisus scoparius*) Zones 4-9

This shrub is condemned as an invasive weed where I live and I have always conscientiously kept it out of my garden (it self sows like crazy). However it always somehow seemed wrong to be pulling up such an astonishingly vigorous species when there was little else that could survive in its place (how can it grow like it does without any apparent source of water?) So I have recently been rethinking this policy and I have decided to grow it as a compost material or mulch crop. It is easily grown from seed and can take all the abuse you can give it.

Silver Buffaloberry (*Shepherdia argentea*)

Closely related to the *Eleagnus* species, but the abundantly produced fruit isn't as good (they are okay if cooked and sweetened). It isn't self-fertile so two plants are needed to produce fruit. Propagate from fresh seed or semi-ripe (or hardwood) cuttings.

Tree Lupin (*Lupinus arboreus*)

This small shrub is a good nitrogen fixer. It can be grown from seed or soft cuttings.

Bush Clover (*Lespedeza* species)

This shrubby relative of Clover is a valuable nitrogen fixer and animal feed for cool areas. It is easily grown from seed/

Wax Myrtles (*Myrica* species)

Some of these species can grow to 25 ft. in height and 10 feet wide, Their aromatic leaves can be used as a culinary flavoring like Bay. The berries have a wax coating that has been used to make candles.

These species can be propagated by layering, semi-ripe cuttings or suckers. Ripe seed may be sown immediately in moist acid soil, or stratified at 35° F for three months. They are able to grow on very poor soils, because they fix nitrogen by means of bacteria in root nodules. Some species are popular drought resistant ornamentals. They are dioecious, so male and female plants are needed to produce fruit.

Bamboos

These large woody grasses are the shrubs (or sometimes trees) of the grass family, so this seemed like as good a place to put them as anywhere. Some of the most useful and versatile of all plants, bamboos are a worthwhile addition to your garden: for their beauty, useful poles and edible shoots.

Bamboos generally prefer rich moist soil and are propagated from pieces of rhizome (they rarely produce seed).

There are two distinct types of Bamboo, the running species and the clumping species. The running species are the most hardy and the most invasive. The clumping sympodial species are easier to control, but are mostly tropical and much more frost tender.

The big drawback of most temperate Bamboos (and why so many people dislike them to the point of fear) is that in ideal conditions (warm, moist with fertile soil) they send out long roots and throw up shoots at regular intervals. They can be very invasive and will go anywhere the soil is sufficiently moist. They have even been known to emerge through driveways, which is bad enough if it is your driveway, but worse if it is your neighbors (they don't respect property boundaries).

Some Bamboos really do have a life of their own. When I lived in Connecticut I planted a single small piece of root and attached 3 ft. tall culm I had dug up from some waste ground (I just love Bamboo). I went back 10 years later and the 20 ft. tall culms were all over the garden. I imagine the present owners cursing the idiot who introduced it as out of his mind.

You can keep running Bamboo under control by planting it behind a barrier of concrete, sheet metal, thick 80 mil plastic Bamboo barrier or an open ditch. All of these should go down at least 24 inches, otherwise the roots could go underneath them. An added benefit of using these is that they may also keep gophers out of the area.

You can also slow down a vigorous stand of Bamboo by cutting and eating any new shoots that appear where you don't want them. You can also just cut all the culms as they appear (though it may take a while before they give up). Where I live Bamboos only really thrive when irrigated through the summer, so withholding water slows them down dramatically.

You could actually put their invasive nature to use, as their dense spreading root network makes them good plants for erosion control in moist soil (just make sure it doesn't spread where you don't want it).

Viewed subjectively Bamboos are fantastic landscape plants for use as windbreaks, screens, specimen plants, hedges and more. Some may grow to 60 feet given the right conditions and a little time. In which case they are more akin to trees in their landscape uses. Many people prefer to stick with the better behaved non-invasive clumping species. These are also better in gopher country as they are easier to protect (gophers love the shoots).

A Bamboo grove is beautiful, shelters wildlife, acts as a windbreak, sounds nice and provides food (in the form of shoots), compost material and valuable poles for general garden use. The main requirement for a grove of Bamboo is enough space so they can run wild. They also need plenty of water for good growth. Fertilize it from your composting toilet and give it water from the sink and shower (or gray water system). Deer won't usually eat it.

Bamboo has a huge range of garden uses (canes, poles, fences) depending upon the species. The size of the culms (stems) varies enormously, they can be ½" diameter and 6 feet long, or 7" in diameter and 40 feet long. These need at least 3 years to mature before they are ready to use.

Some Bamboos are fairly drought tolerant, but most grow much better when well watered. In my experience they are perfectly happy with gray water.

Edible Bamboos

Bamboo shoots vary greatly in their value as food, though generally the bigger shoots, the more useful they are for food (though some have better flavor than others).

Gathering

Bamboo shoots are harvested when they first emerge in spring or summer. They can be detected even before they break the surface by feeling for the bulge in the soil as they push up. Sometimes soil is piled up on top of these to keep them white and tender for longer (once light hits them their flavor and texture starts to deteriorate). The best edible species include:

Running species:

Phyllostachys dulcis – Sweet Shoot Bamboo
P. aurea - Golden Bamboo
P. aureosulcata - Yellow Grove Bamboo
P. edulis - Moso Bamboo
P. vivax - Giant Timber Bamboo
P. nuda - Green Bamboo
Semiarundinaria fastuosa - Temple Bamboo

Clumping species:

Bambusa burmanica - Burma Bamboo
B. oldhamii - Giant Timber Bamboo
Dendrocalamus asper - Giant Bamboo
D. beecheyana
D. giganteus

Preparation

The shoots are peeled by slitting them lengthways and removing the tough outer layers. The remaining edible white inner part can be sliced and used raw if it tastes good, but most are bitter at this stage and must be cooked. These are put in boiling water and boiled for 10 minutes, then this water is discarded and they are put in more boiling water. They are then cooked until tender.

Climbing plants

Climbing plants are particularly useful in the garden because they allow you to increase productivity by using vertical space that would otherwise be empty. They are especially valuable in hotter climates, as they can be used to create the shade that is so essential for comfort. Their exuberance and appearance makes them one of my favorite groups of plants. See Where to plant for ways to use them in the garden.

Climbing plants grow rapidly once established, because they don't waste a lot of energy creating a structural skeleton for themselves. This lack of structure means they need something to hold them up and they have developed various methods for holding on to their supports.

The twiners simply grow in a clockwise (or is it anti-clockwise?) direction and twine themselves up around anything that gets in their way (including each other). Hop, Kiwi, Akebia, Beans and Malabar Spinach all grow in this way.

The clingers (Ivy, Virginia Creeper) cling to walls or trees by means of roots or sticky tendrils. These species are the most effective plants for training directly on to walls, but I don't know of any useful species in this category.

Tendril bearing plants grab on to small twigs with their tendrils. They include the Passion Vine, Peas and Cucurbits. These may also twine around their supports to some degree.

The sprawlers don't actually climb, so much as grow through other vegetation. Some (Blackberry, Rose) use thorny stems, other have Velcro-like hooks to get traction. These species often need encouragement to go where you want them, in the form of tying in. They grow best on wide supports that aren't very high.

Care

The young plants may need some encouragement to climb where you want them to, but once they get a going there is usually no stopping them.

Vines can put out a lot of top growth on relatively compact roots, so need plenty of nutrients for good growth. For maximum productivity you may want to feed heavy bearing plants regularly and make sure they get enough moisture (all of that top growth can use a considerable quantity of water). They also benefit from mulch because they don't always cover the soil very well.

Ideas for support

The fact that these plants climb can up almost anything (with a little help) makes them uniquely useful in that they become a part of a structure. In the wild they are usually supported by other plants, but in the garden you can support them by a variety of means.

Fruiting perennial vines must have a strong and stable supporting structure, as every year they get heavier, while the support can only get weaker. Wind is also a consideration and can blow over a weak support structure, especially if loaded with a heavy crop of fruit. In very windy areas it may be necessary to use guy wires to give them the necessary shear resistance.

Of course you want the fruit to be accessible, so don't make your support too tall,

Permanent plant supports

Buildings
Buildings and climbing plants go together well, the plants benefit from a very secure support, while the buildings generally look better with plants growing on them (it makes them a part of the garden). The key is to give the plants something to hold on to (most can't climb a bare wall). This could be wire or plastic netting, individual wires or wooden trellis. This is usually designed to hold the plants away from the wall, so air can circulate behind them. Existing downspouts are probably the easiest way to get some plants to climb (though perhaps not the best idea in the long run).

Pergolas
See Overhead structures.

Arches and tunnels
See Overhead structures.

Arbors
See Overhead structures.

Ropes or wires
See Overhead structures.

Beams
See Overhead structures.

Obelisks
These can range from the very formal painted wood obelisk with a finial on top, to the rustic woven cone made from Willow shoots and grape vines. They not only look good, but are a practical, versatile and easily moved support.

Wire Fencing
One of the easiest ways to support climbing plants is with a wire fence, A fence upon which vines are trained is sometimes known as a fedge because it is a fence that resembles a hedge. See Boundaries for more on these.

Concrete reinforcing wire, chicken wire or hog wire can all be used to support climbing plants (it keeps the fruit low down where it is easy to harvest). Don't think of this as only suitable for low-growing vines though, it could be 10 feet tall and used for vigorous species such as Grapes and Kiwis. You just have to make sure you have enough square footage of fence to support the fast growing plants (and that the posts are strong enough).

Wire can also be rolled into cylinders to make columns of vegetation. If these cylinders are tall (you can make them any height by folding the wire along the short dimension) they will need the support of a post inside them. These look quite utilitarian when you first set them up, but are soon obscured by vegetation. In full growth the tall growing pillars can be very ornamental. They work particularly well with annuals such as beans and peas.

Posts
Vertical posts make good, long lasting supports for tall vines.

Permanent support posts could be installed at strategic places around the garden. These could be 4″ x 4″ fenceposts, ten feet long and sunk 24″ into the ground. Put metal eyes in them and you can put string (or galvanized wires) between them as needed.

Metal
Steel rebar is another support option, that is not only very strong, but versatile too. It can be wired (you can then take it apart and re-use the bars) or welded to make a variety of useful (and very strong) arches, domes and other structures.

Copper water pipe is another popular choice for arches, though it is getting quite expensive.

Lattice trellis
This can be used to create gazebos, fences, sunshades, sitting areas and sculptures. These are not only attractive in themselves, but also provide great structures for growing plants. A substantial trellis covered in vines can define a transition from one area to another, act as a screen and give the garden temporary height until the trees catch up. It makes one of the best garden dividers because it gives you a light open feeling (and uses less wood than a solid fence).

Making trellis
If you have a table saw you can make as much lath as you want by ripping 2 x 4 or 2 x 6, into ½ x 1 ½ strips. The openings may be square or diamond shape and may vary from 4-10" in size. The easiest way to connect these is with a pneumatic stapler, but 2 brads will work also. The finished trellis can be mounted to a wall or to posts.

Trees
Trees can be used as supports for herbaceous vines that die back to the ground every year. Woody vines don't work so well because they don't come back down, they just keep getting bigger and taller every year.

If you want to use trees to support your vines you need to use established trees. Obviously you can't grow them up saplings and they can't be so tall there may be a problem harvesting. You could use existing native trees, as this enables you to get a crop from them.

Steel mesh
In Europe when plants are increasingly being used for the façade greening of large buildings, they often use stainless steel mesh as a support. This is completely weatherproof and very strong (and expensive).

Nothing
Some climbing plants can work well when allowed to ramble over the ground as groundcover. Just make sure that they don't go anywhere they aren't wanted and get out of hand. They can also be trained over ugly objects to hide them (perhaps by covering them with netting).

Temporary plant supports

Stakes, poles and canes
Bamboo canes are probably the most widely used supports for annual crops and are commonly available in garden centers. If you have the space it's worth growing your own Bamboo. If you do you might want to leave some of the side branches on the canes, as these provides good holds for tendril producers like peas.

For stakes I mostly use ¾ x ¾ Redwood strips, ripped from old fence boards (you can use any other wood for this). You could also use any long straight sticks from the garden (perhaps fruit tree prunings). They don't have to be particularly durable as they are the original disposable poles, they just go back into the soil.

Poles can simply be stuck in the ground individually for single plants such as tomatoes, or they may be tied together in a variety of ways for greater stability. Teepees are easy to make, very stable and quite decorative, either alone or in a group.

Some crops weigh a lot and require a strong and stable support structure (they may also need to be braced for stability). Stronger support structures can be made from 6 to 8 foot poles of bamboo, scrap wood, or even metal pipe, stuck into the ground. These can be lashed together into various configurations.

Netting
This is often used in the annual garden for growing peas and beans. The thicker plastic deer fence mesh is good for this as it is more durable and animals are less likely to get tangled in it. Of course netting also needs a sturdy frame to support it.

Brushwood
For smaller vines such as beans and other annuals, you can cut brushwood supports from shrubs and trees (or even use suitably shaped fruit tree prunings.) Simply plant a branch securely upright in the ground and it will soon be covered in foliage. These work very well, cost

nothing and blend into the garden better than wire cages.

Traditional English pea sticks were made from the slender but sturdy branches of Hazel (they were a by-product of coppicing Hazel), though many other woods would be just as good. They are about 5' tall and are trimmed of branches on two sides so they are flat (so they can be inserted into the soil in close rows). They were planted about 20" into the ground for stability.

If you want a more unusual effect try bending or weaving supple poles such as Willow (Salix) or Vine Maple (Acer) into arches, domes or elaborate ornamental trellises.

None of these brushwood supports will last very long in the ground, but it doesn't really matter. They just go back into the soil from whence they came.

A frame
Used for climbing annual vegetables such as Cucumber, this is pre-fabricated from 2 frames attached with hinges (need a stop to secure it at the appropriate angle). This is easy to use and easy to fold up and store when not needed.

Wire cages
Tomato cages can be used for a variety of crops. I make my own four foot tall cages from 4" concrete reinforcing wire (these may need staking to stop them falling over). These cages can also be opened up and spread them across the bed like semi-cylindrical wire cloche frames. The plants will grow up through the mesh and sprawl over the top.

Miscellaneous supports
Basket teepees can be made from long straight prunings and flexible vines from your garden. They work well, look great and are easy to make.

Metal spirals make ornamental and useful supports. If you are strong enough you can make them yourself by bending thick wire around a pipe of suitable diameter.

A good support for pole beans and other annual vines are corn or Sunflower stalks. You can grow the beans and corn together in a three sisters garden, or you can just leave the stalks in place after harvest and plant around them.

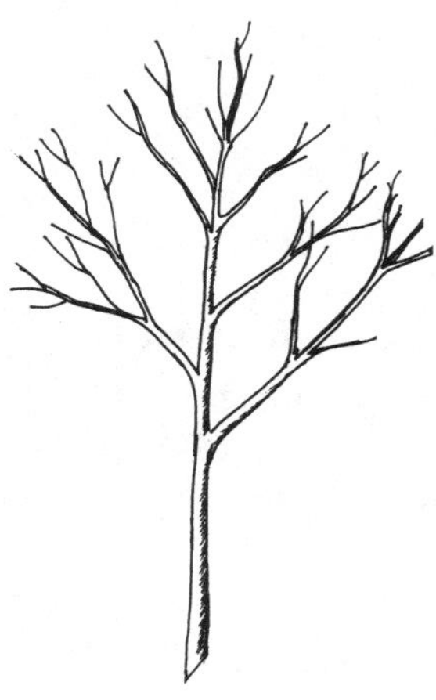

Annual species
Annual vines grow better when given some support to keep them off the ground. Also their fruits stay cleaner and are less prone to rot.

Most of these following species are commonly grown as vegetables, but they can also be used for their ornamental properties. They are particularly useful for providing summer shade, as they vanish completely in winter (when you want the sun). They can also be used to give a fast growing screen.

Malabar Spinach (*Basella alba*)
This tropical perennial is grown as an annual spinach substitute for hot climates. With its glossy leaves and small pink flowers it is pretty enough to go in the ornamental garden.

Malabar Spinach can be grown from cuttings or seed. It needs a moist fertile soil and a long, hot growing season to be productive (in cool weather it will grow very, very slowly).

Balloon Vine *(Cardiospermum halicacabum)*

This fast growing annual vine is most often used as an ornamental, but its foliage can be used as a potherb.

Peas and Beans

These familiar garden vegetable produce a lot of biomass and food, as well as being quite ornamental. Of course they can also host nitrogen fixing bacteria and so improve the soil too.

Hyacinth Bean *(Dolichos lablab)*

This tender tropical perennial is usually grown as an annual in temperate climates. It is attractive enough that it is most often grown as an ornamental in this country, but the young pods and immature beans are edible when cooked. It's easily grown from seed in most soils and has been used as a green manure and cover crop (it fixes nitrogen).

Luffa Sponge (*Luffa angulata. L. cylindrica*)

These vines produce Squash-like fruits, that can be eaten like zucchini while young, or left to mature into the familiar vegetable sponges (keep the seeds for replanting).

Melons, Squashes and Cucumbers

(*Cucurbita* and *Cucumis* species)

If you are a vegetable gardener you probably know these well. Most vegetable gardeners don't take advantage of their potential as productive ornamental vines though. In fact many varieties are selected to grow as bushes rather than vines. The vines are much more versatile and can be trained over trellis, tripods, fences and even onto arbors. Getting them up off the ground helps to keep the fruit clean too.

Morning Glory (*Ipomoea* species)

One of the few plants I mention in this book that isn't edible, but with its art-nouveau elegance it is one of the most perfectly beautiful plants to be found anywhere. Morning Glory will grow in any reasonable soil as long as it gets enough moisture and sun. You could grow it with less attractive productive vines to jazz them up. It self-sows readily in my garden and produces flowers all summer long.

Sweet Potato (*Ipomoea batatas*)

This species is actually a perennial, but is grown as an annual in most of the United States because it is too tender to survive outdoors. It has never survived the fairly mild winter in my garden; it has always been killed by frost.

Sweet Potato is usually grown from shoots taken from a tuber in spring. It is an attractive and vigorous plant and can produce a lot of foliage in a summer. It could be used as a temporary annual groundcover or trained to cover a screen.

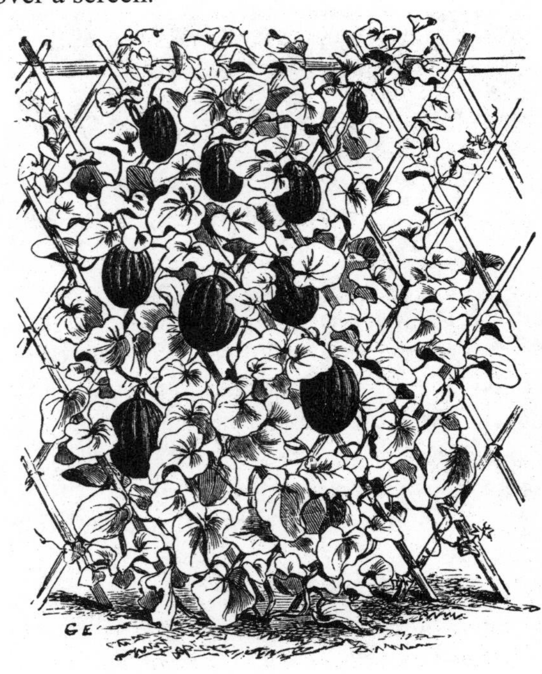

Sweet Pea (*Lathyrus odoratus*)

This is the famously scented Sweet Pea, which deserves a place in the garden just for its scent and beauty. It isn't edible though.

Scarlet Runner Bean (*Phaseolus coccineus*)

This beautiful vine, with its red, white or pink flowers, is usually grown as an annual, but is actually a tender perennial and may overwinter in mild winter areas. It is an excellent vegetable, especially if you get cultivars selected for food rather than flowers (which is not always easy in this country). It also fixes nitrogen.

Scarlet Runner bean is a very vigorous plant and is one of the best for caves and teepees for childrens gardens.

Nasturtium (*Trapaeolum majus*)

This pretty flower is very popular as an ornamental, yet it is also one of my favorite edible flowers. Unlike many edible flowers that add color but not much else, these add flavor too and are great in salads. The leaves and immature seeds are also good.

Some Nasturtium varieties climb enthusiastically, others just trail and are better suited for use as groundcover (or to hang down a wall). If you want a climber then it is important to choose the right variety.

Nasturtiums are easily grown from seed; and do well in fairly poor sunny locations. In the right conditions they self-sow readily.

Canary Flower (*Trapaeolum peregrinum*) This pretty climber can be used in the same ways as Nasturtium.

Herbaceous perennial species

These produce an abundance of foliage in summer but die back to the ground completely in winter. If you take away the dead vines no trace of the plant remains above ground. They can be used like the annual vines to provide summer shade that disappears completely in winter (when you need sun). Of course being perennial they will do it all over again next year.

Groundnut (*Apios tuberosa*) - This attractive native vine produces scented Pea-like flowers and a string of edible tuberous roots. It prefers part shade and needs moist soil (it won't thrive in dry soil) for good growth. It can even tolerate flooding.

Groundnut is easily grown from seed or from individual tubers (these are used to propagate selected varieties). It can take least two years to produce large tubers.

Chinese Yam (*Dioscorea batatas*) Zones 5-
The foliage of the Chinese Yam is quite attractive so it is sometimes grown as an ornamental. The not very impressive flowers are supposed to smell like cinnamon, which is why it is also known as Cinnamon Vine.

I planted this vigorous and independent vine 5 years ago and it has persisted ever since with no attention from me. It even spreads by means of bulbils that develop in the leaf axils along the stem (I'm not quite sure how these get half way across the garden, but they do).

Hop (*Humulus lupulus*) - This perennial vine is best known and loved as the plant that gives beer its flavor (the wonderfully aromatic female flowers are used). If you make your own beer it is worth growing Hops, as they are easy to grow but expensive to buy. If you don't make beer you might grow them for their edible leaf shoots. Gathered when a few inches long in spring, they are prepared and eaten like Asparagus.

Hop can be grown from seed, but specific varieties must be grown from root cuttings or division. If you have any interest in using the flowers for beer, you will want to use a specific variety, as it's important to know the exact qualities of the flowers. If you brew beer you may be familiar with some of these famous cultivars.

Bullion- Bittering hop with an earthy resinous aroma .
Brewer's Gold - Has a spicy resinous aroma.
Cascade – All purpose.
Fuggle - Aromatic.
Kent Golding - Aromatic with a sweetish flavor.
Hallertauer – The classic German lager hop.
Nugget – A bitter Hop.
Saaz - The classic Bohemian lager hop.
Willamette - Similar to Fuggle, but more fruity.

Hop is very independent once established and may outlast you and your garden (I've seen it growing in a ghost town in eastern California that was abandoned in the 1940's). However for best growth and productivity it requires rich, moist soil and full sun.

A very vigorous climber, Hop can grow more than 25 feet in a season (they need a substantial support to climb on). They can be useful as a deciduous screen, or summer shade plant.

Maypop. Passion Vine (*Passiflora incarnata*) Zones 5-9

The Passionflower produces spectacular flowers as well as tasty edible fruit. Most edible Passion Vines are very tender and can't stand any frost, but Maypop is unusual in that it is hardy down to 0° F. It disappears completely in winter leaving just a few brown threads and pops up again the following spring. It still needs hot weather for good growth though.

Maypop is easily grown from seed and spreads by means of suckers (these can also be used for propagation). It grows vigorously enough (up to 20 feet in a season) to be considered a weed in its native land The flowers need cross-pollination to bear fruit (small numbers of flowers can be hand pollinated to help fruit production).

This vigorous vine needs a sturdy support structure. A tall chain link fence works great and is soon transformed into a fedge.

Mashua, Tuberous Nasturtium (*Tropaeolum tuberosum*) Zone 8

Perhaps the perfect deciduous vine, it is vigorous, productive, easy to grow, completely edible and beautiful enough to be widely grown as an ornamental. It is another of the Andean tubers, from the same region as Yacon, Oca and Potato.

The raw tubers have a pungent flavor like the related Nasturtiums (or Horseradish), but this completely disappears when they are cooked. The leaves are also edible and have the characteristic Nasturtium flavor. Like other Andean tubers, it comes from the tropics and so most varieties are day-length sensitive.

Perennials

Kiwi Vine (*Actinidia deliciosa*) Zones 7-9

These deciduous vines grow amazingly fast once established, but need a few years (5 or more) to get established before they start to produce much fruit. The plants are dioecious so you need female plants to bear fruit and a male plant to pollinate them (a ratio of 8:1 works).

A nice feature of Kiwi vines is not just that they produce a ton of fruit (though they usually do), but that they produce it late in the year (November and December) when fresh fruit is otherwise scarce. Also you can harvest them before they are fully ripe and store them in a cool place until needed. You can then bring them into a warmer place to ripen as you need them. When treated like this they may even last until March.

A. arguta - Hardy Kiwi Zones 5-9
A. kolomitka Arctic Kiwi Zones 3-9
These species differ from their fuzzy cousin in being a lot hardier, so they can be grown in colder climates. Also their fruits are a lot smaller and have a smooth skin that can be eaten. Their flavor is equally good though. Like the above they can be slow to get started, but once established they are vigorous climbers. The plants are more precocious than the above and start bearing at an earlier age.

The Arctic Kiwi does better with light shade in hot climates (I killed my first plants by giving them too much sun and not enough water).

Akebia Vine (*Akebia Quinata*) Zones 4-10

This vigorous vine is usually grown as an ornamental for it's attractive lobed leaves and (not very impressive) vanilla scented flower. However it can also produce edible fruit if two varieties are grown for cross pollination. It is hardy enough to withstand light frost

It grows best in moist soil with part shade, but mine still thrives in full sun and with no irrigation all summer (this may explain why it isn't very productive).

Strawberry (*Fragaria* species) Zones -10

I know you are thinking how did this get in here? Though these aren't really climbers, some work well when grown in hanging baskets (so long as you water them enough. The best thing about growing them in this way is that they are much less bothered by slugs and fungus disease (though birds may appreciate them).

Jiao-gu-lan (*Gynostema pentaphyllum*) Zone 7

This vigorous vine prefers well-drained, moist soil with sun or part shade. It can be propagated from seed, but root cuttings or divisions are easier. Simply detach rooted runners from the plant as they creep along the ground.

The leaves and young stems have been eaten raw or cooked. In China they are commonly used to make a pleasant tea which has powerful medicinal properties.

This important medicinal herb is said to improve circulation, strengthen the immune system and reduce blood sugar and cholesterol levels. It is also an anti-oxidant.

Chayote (S*echium edule) Zones 9-10*

In Australia this perennial vine is widely grown for its fruits which are used like Summer Squash. It also produces edible leaves, stems and tendrils in spring (harvesting them will help to keep the plant under control) as well as edible tubers in winter.

Chayote is a very enthusiastic climber and can grow 30 feet vertically if given the chance. It is often trained along fences, or used to hide eyesores by completely enveloping them in vegetation.

Chayote is easily grown by planting the whole fruit (just bury it shallowly). In the right climate it will persist for years and can become a highly productive and ornamental feature. Unfortunately it isn't very hardy and must be grown as an annual anywhere the ground freezes in winter.

Kudzu (*Pueraria lobata*) Zone 6

Kudzu ('the weed that ate the south') has become a notorious weedy pest in the Southeast, and is a textbook example of what can happen when a plant is introduced into an ideal climate without any natural controls. In its native land it is actually an important edible wild plant and an important commercial source of food starch. In the south it swallows fences, abandoned cars, sheds, trees, houses, even whole towns (well maybe not whole towns!)

Unfortunately Kudzu has been legally banned from importation and is now quite hard to obtain in this country. This is a shame because it isn't the plant from hell, it is actually a very useful food producing, ornamental, soil improving, nitrogen fixing plant.

Madeira Vine (*Anredera cordifolia*) Zone 9

This vigorous climber can grow up to 30 feet in length and has become an invasive weed in parts of Australia.

Madeira Vine is fairly frost tender and the tops are killed by frost, however the roots will often survive in the ground and send up new growth in spring (mulch to protect the roots from freezing). It prefers a well-drained fertile soil and full sun (or light shade).

This plant is a relative of Malabar Spinach (*Basella*) and the leaves can be used like that plant (they are commonly stir fried in Taiwan). All parts of the plant are somewhat mucilaginous, but especially the root (this can be reduced by baking). The leaves are of particular interest as they are said to have medicinal (adaptogenic) properties.

Madeira Vine is very easy to propagate from softwood cuttings or the fleshy tubers (in cold climates these can be dug and kept indoors for the winter).

Magnolia Vine (*Schisandra chinensis*) Zones 4-8

Another excellent edible ornamental vine from China. Magnolia Vine is not only pretty and productive, it is also very vigorous (it may grow to 20 feet or more) and hardy to about 25° F. It demands little attention and will grow in most soils (though it does best on a fertile moisture retentive one). It can be propagated from semi-ripe or ripe cuttings.

Magnolia Vine is an important medicinal plant in China, where it is considered an adaptogen and panacea (like Ginseng). The fruits are said to have five flavors (sweet, sour, bitter, salty and warm) and are very high in anti-oxidants. It is normally dioecious, though the variety Eastern Prince is self-fertile.

Grape (*Vitis* species) Zone 4-10.

Perhaps the outstanding edible vine for all around versatility and usefulness. Hardy and very productive these vigorous vines produce an abundance of foliage every year and have attractive woody trunks too. They work as climbers on buildings and fences (or wire trellis), or can be trained to grow overhead on arbors and pergolas. In Greece you commonly see them growing on rooftop arbors, having been trained up from ground level.

Grapes are very vigorous and require serious pruning to keep them in bounds and productive. They like warm weather, well drained soil and lots of sun. They are quite drought tolerant, but need moisture for best growth and food production.

American Grapes - The hardy native American species tolerate a variety of conditions and can be grown anywhere in the country. The fruit of the best varieties can be very good.

European Grape – These produce the best flavored fruit, but they are quite temperamental and not very hardy. They grow best in western areas. They are prized for wine, table grapes (including the seedless varieties) and for making raisins (an important use if you have a lot of vines and dry sunny weather).

Hybrids - These combine European flavor with American hardiness. Most are self-fertile.

Groundcover plants

The groundcovers are another important group of plants for landscaping and perform a number of essential garden functions.

- These plants enrich the soil with organic matter and improve its structure by creating root channels and feeding soil organisms. In this way they help to create new soil.
- They protect the soil from erosion. The leaves shelter the soil from falling raindrops, The whole mass of vegetation slows down the movement of water on slopes, giving it time to soak in rather than running off.
- They can be used to cover any bare ground that isn't needed for anything else, to prevent less desirable plants (weeds) from colonizing it.
- They also provide visual interest and texture for the garden floor.

Plants for covering ground

Any low-growing/plant (clumper, runner, mat former) that effectively covers the soil can be used as groundcover. It doesn't necessarily have to spread vegetatively and you don't have to confine yourself to just one species. In fact it is probably best to plant a variety of species and let them work it out. Just set the plants far enough apart so they will completely fill the area as they mature.

Groundcovers are often called upon to grow in difficult growing conditions where few plants do well; dry shade, harsh sun, sandy soil, steep slopes (if the area had better growing conditions it would be used for something more productive).

The ideal groundcover is vigorous, fast growing, able to grow in poor soil and can thrive and spread without any help (some might be considered weeds under other circumstances). In dry climates you don't want plants that require a lot of water, but you don't want it to be so dry that it is a potential fire hazard either. Ideally it should have some other use as well as covering the ground, maybe for food, tea or fruit.

Many of the species mentioned here are also described elsewhere, but I have included them here too because this is such an important garden role.

Some annuals can be used as a temporary groundcover (just scatter the seed). These can be useful when first establishing the garden. They can prevent weed growth in vacant areas, until you get around to dealing with them.

Some climbing plants will sprawl if not given support and can make good groundcovers (Ivy is often used in this way).

Don't plant groundcover close to young trees, as it will compete for nutrients and water.

In fire prone areas you might want to have a moisture loving groundcover near to the house. If you have to irrigate, you should be sure to use a plant that produces something in return (maybe Strawberry or a Creeping Raspberry).

Native plants for groundcover

It makes sense to use native species for groundcover where possible, as they are adapted to local growing conditions and don't require any attention. If you already have existing plants acting as groundcover there is little point in removing them and trying to establish something else (unless you have limited space and the replacement will be more productive).

Planting

Before you start planting you need to make sure there are no persistent weeds that will compete with your plants. You can do this by hand if you are thorough, but it is quite a lot of work. You could also use a sheet mulch, a plastic mulch or solarization.

Creating a dense stand of groundcover takes time. Normally you will space the plants in offset rows (the exact spacing depends upon the species) and put mulch (or temporary annuals) in between. Of course a closer spacing will result in a functioning groundcover more quickly, but takes more plants, time and (perhaps) money.

Care

Groundcover plants are chosen for their independence, so they don't need any attention once established (that's the whole point). You may have to water them for a while after planting, but that should be it.

In the early stages the more vigorous species can be cut periodically and their leaves used as mulch around the plants. Once they have filled in you can use the leaves as a source of mulch for elsewhere.

Control

Some creeping groundcovers don't just stop when they have covered the ground you want covered, they will keep going. They will try to spread beyond those areas and can become pests if not kept under control. You can prevent these spreading with walls, paths, driveways, ditches fences, hedges, water or other barriers. You can also control them by regularly chopping off advancing plants (or turning them back on themselves. Dense shade will act as a discreet barrier for sun loving species.

Groundcover plants

Most traditional groundcover plants are grown solely for their ground covering ability and aren't of much use for anything else. However there are some species with more to offer, mostly native species. If you use a little ingenuity quite a few plants can work out in this role. They may not necessarily be the best groundcovers, but they will actually produce something useful as well. You just have to give them a little attention occasionally.

Sun loving species

Chamomile (*Chamomilum nobile*) Zones 5-8
This low aromatic plant is tough enough to be used as a lawn plant. Its flowers are used for tea (See Herbs).

Chinese Artichoke (*Stachys Sieboldii*)
This species produces small tasty tubers and can be very productive (See Perennial vegetables). It grows like a weed in moist soils and can be used as groundcover (though you will have to disturb the soil if you want to harvest the tubers).

Gotu Kola (*Hydrocotyle asiatica*) Zones 8-10
This tender perennial is a member of the Parsley family and the flavor of the leaves hints at this connection. A low creeping species, it spreads quickly and can be a good productive groundcover for warm humid climates. It grows in most garden soils, but prefers very moist, or even wet, ones. It isn't at all hardy and just barely (usually) manages to survive the winter in my garden

Hottentot Fig (*Mesembryanthemum edule*)
Iceplant (*M. crystallinum*)
A drought resistant, salt tolerant groundcover with succulent leaves that give it potential as a fire retardant plant (though watch out for the buildup of dry dead material as this will burn). In suitable areas it spreads vigorously and can become a pest. It isn't very hardy, so is only useful in mild winter areas. It also produces edible fruit, though these aren't that good.

Nasturtium (*Trapaeolum minus*) - On the mild (never too hot or too cold) coast of California this plant forms dense colonies. It could be used as a groundcover for moist soils (the trailing varieties work best). See flowers for more on this useful plant.

Soapwort (*Saponaria officinalis*) Zones 3-9
This rugged and drought tolerant species is naturalized in many areas. It can be grown from seed, but it's easier to get a plant and divide it (I originally found my plant as an escape). It spreads vigorously and can be somewhat invasive. It gets its common (and genus) name because the leaves and flowers contain so much saponin they have been used as a soap substitute (plant some near the garden sink).

Garden Strawberries (*Fragaria X ananassa*)
Zones -10
Nearly everyone loves the large fruited Strawberries, but not many people think of them as a groundcover. They can work quite well in this role, though they need a lot more care and inputs than most groundcovers. They aren't very good at excluding weeds and can't really be walked upon, but they give back a lot more than most groundcovers.

The flavor of the berries varies according to variety, some are delicious and some are tasteless, so be selective. Seascape is my favorite modern variety.

Thyme (*Thymus* species) - The thymes are widely used as drought tolerant groundcovers and even in herbal lawns. Common Thyme is an important culinary herb, but of course you don't really need 300 square feet of it. See Herbs for more on these.

Yarrow (*Achillea millefolium*) Zones 3-10
This species is occasionally cultivated as an ornamental and a number of attractive improved cultivars are available. It can be grown from seed, cuttings or division and spreads to form dense colonies. Its strongly flavored young leaves can be added to salads (in moderation).

Shade tolerant species

Akebia Vine (*Akebia quinata*)
This climbing vine can be grown as a groundcover, as it will root where it touches the ground. See Vines for more on this.

Alpine Strawberry (*Fragaria vesca*) Zone 3-10
This species is justly famous for its delicious fruit. The young plants can't compete against weeds very well, but older plants are quite vigorous. In good growing conditions the plants ares very productive and fruit regularly for months (almost year round in my garden). The fruit needs to be fully ripe to develop good flavor Birds are less attracted to the yellow fruited types (some people prefer their taste too). It is a little more work than most groundcovers, but rewards you more than most too.

Alpine Strawberry is easily grown from seed and will produce fruit in its first year. The plants can also be divided, but seed is so easy its hardly worth it. It likes well-drained soil, but needs a regular supply of water. It will grow in light shade or full sun.

Corsican Mint (*Mentha requieni*) Zones 7-9
A very small and cute plant (1-2" tall) with a delicious Pennyroyal scent. It is a very low almost moss-like plants and can't tolerate weeds, It takes a considerable amount of effort to get it to take over an area, but may be worth a bit of extra effort. It needs moist soil and will grow in sun or part shade.

Creeping Comfrey (*Symphytum grandiflorum*) Zones 5-9
This attractive spreading cousin of Comfrey works well in sun or shade.

Ground Elder, Variegated (*Aegopodium podagraria "variegatum"*) Zone 3-10.
This species will grow in almost any soil with full sun or shade. Its wild sister ordinary green Ground Elder is notorious as an extremely vigorous weed, but this variety is much better behaved. It is deciduous however, so not of much use in winter. The leaves can be cooked like spinach.

Lungwort (*Pulmonaria*) - This attractive creeping plant has edible leaves, but is more important for its medicinal properties.

Mayapple (*Podophyllum peltatum*) Zones 3-9
The creeping Mayapple, with its large umbrella like leaves has potential as a groundcover for sun or part shade. It also produces tasty edible fruit.

Sweet Woodruff (*Galium odoratum*) Zones 4-10.
Grows well in dry shade. The flowers are added to salads and used to flavor wine.

Wintergreen (*Gaultheria procumbens*) Zones 4-9
This attractive, low-growing plant grows best in moist, acid (but well drained) soil, preferably in the shade of evergreens. It is self-fertile and often produces an abundance of berries, which remain on the plant for a long time. The berries and leaves can be used to make a wintergreen flavored tea.

Yerba Buena (*Satureja Douglasii*) Zones 7-10

This low creeping west coast native has a delicious mint-like aroma and makes a great tea.

Wild Ginger (*Asarum canadense* and *A. caudatum*) Zone 4-10

A good groundcover for shady acid woodland soil. The ginger-like roots have been used for tea and as a flavoring.

Shrubs as groundcovers

Some of the best groundcovers for tough conditions are low prostrate shrubs and many prostrate or low-growing cultivars have been developed for this purpose. Be careful when using it in dry areas though, as some species can be a fire hazard. Useful species include:

Bearberry (*Arctostaphylos uva ursi*) Zones 2-8

Used for poor dry soils with full sun. The berries are edible, though not very good. The dried leaves were commonly smoked by Native Americans and were known as Kinnick-Kinnick.

California Lilac (*Ceanothus*) Zones 7-10

A whole family of drought tolerant shrubs for dry sunny situations, including some low-growing ones. They flower early in spring and are important bee plants at this time. The flowers are very rich in saponins and can be used as soap (See Shrubs).

Creeping Raspberries (*Rubus species*) Zones 2-7

These low-growing *Rubus* species (mostly from northern or mountain areas) can be useful as fruit bearing groundcovers. They are easy to propagate because the stems root as they trail along the ground - just separate them and replant. The may need weeding occasionally as they are very low growing. Your biggest problem with these plants may be finding them.

Useful species include:
R. arcticus
R. caesius
R. nepalensis
R. pentalobus
R. tricolor

Huckleberry (*Gaylussacia baccata*)

This cold tolerant evergreen can be a productive groundcover for acid soils, with sun or part shade (though it produces more fruit when growing in the sun). The fruit closely resembles a blueberrry and is used in the same ways.

Cranberry (*Vaccinium macrocarpon*) Zones 3-9

This low-growing species grows best in a moist, acid (max pH 4.5) soil. In suitable conditions it spreads to form a dense mat and can be quite productive. It can be grown from seed or cuttings, or you can just divide the plants as they naturally layer themselves.

Cranberry is such a low-growing plant it often needs regular weeding to prevent it getting overgrown.

Grape (*Vitis* species)

I've seen these vigorous vines running along the ground and covering quite a large area (and fruiting). They are deciduous however so lose their leaves in winter. They are quite drought tolerant, but need moisture for best growth and food production. See Vines for more on this.

Lavender (*Lavandula angustifolia*) Zones 7-9

A low-growing, drought tolerant plant, it is useful for covering hot dry areas. Lavender is famous for its scent of course. See Shrubs for more on this.

Lingonberry (*Vaccinium vitis idaea*) Zones 3-8
Another low-growing, acid loving member of the Heath family. It is very hardy and makes an attractive and productive evergreen groundcover for cool climates. It is partially self-fertile, but produce more fruit with cross-pollination The berries are often compared to Cranberries but are better flavored (they are good enough to be eaten raw). It will grow in sun or part shade.

Lowbush Blueberry (*Vaccinium angustfolium*)
Zones 3-10
These are smaller, sweeter and less productive than the more commonly grown Highbush Blueberries. They are ideally suited for use as a groundcover, as they are naturally low-growing and spread to form a dense mat. They need acid soil.

Oregon Grape (*Mahonia species*)
These tough and fairly drought tolerant plants require little attention once established. They aren't great edibles as their berries are very seedy, though some varieties are better than others.

The Creeping Oregon Grape (*Mahonia repens*) is perhaps the most useful as groundcover, though a number of creeping cultivars have been produced from other species.

Rosemary (*Rosemarinus officinalis*)
The prostrate cultivars of this drought and heat tolerant evergreen shrub make a great groundcover. See Shrubs for more on Rosemary.

Salal (*Gaultheria shallon*) Zones 6-9
In sunny areas this evergreen shrubs can be used as a (fairly tall) groundcover. See Shrubs for more on this.

Other possibilities
Groundcover plants don't have to be low-growing creepers. Any plant that can grow independently and doesn't need much water or care can be used. You just have to plant them fairly closely together, so they will fill in and work like a ground cover. Potential candidates include:

Alfalfa, Cardoon, Sorrel, Good King Henry, Sweet Coltsfoot, Marjoram, Oregano. Dianthus, Pelargonium, Pennyroyal, Mint, Sedum,

Plants for erosion control and stabilizing slopes

Bare slopes are prone to erosion in wet weather and should be planted with a mix of plants of varying root depth. Trees and shrubs should be included in the mix because they have deep spreading roots that go down into the subsoil and help to hold everything in place. Native plants are often the best choice as they are more likely to adapt quickly.

Plants for erosion control should be easy to propagate, have a wide spreading dense mat of roots and be able to grow in poor soil. You can fill in the bare areas between newly planted plants with mulch.

Caution: Most species of grass aren't very effective at controlling erosion, because they are too shallow rooted. They may actually make matters worse by preventing more effective erosion control plants getting established.

Trees for erosion control

Acacia greggii / Catclaw Acacia
Aesculus californica, California Buckeye
Alnus species / Alder
Cercidium microphyllum / Yellow Paloverde
Celtis occidentalis / American Hackberry
Cercis occidentalis / Western Redbud
Cornus species / Dogwood
Juglans californica / Southern California Walnut
Pinus species
Populus species / Poplars, Aspens, Cottonwoods
Prosopis juliflora / Mesquite
Quercus species / Oaks
Robinia pseudoacacia / Black Locust
Salix species / Willow
Umbellularia californica / California Bay Laurel

Shrubs for erosion control

Adenostoma fasciculatum / Chamise
Arctostaphylos species / Manzanita
Arundinaria gigantea ssp. gigantea / Giant Cane
Calycanthus species / Spice Bush
Ceanothus species / California Lilac
Heteromeles arbutifolia / Toyon
Iva species / Marsh Elder
Lonicera species / Honeysuckles
Rhus species / Sumac
Ribes species / Currants and Gooseberries
Rosa species / Wild Roses
Rubus species / Blackberries
Shepherdia argentea / Silver Buffaloberry
Spiraea species
Sambucus species / Elderberry
Symphoricarpos species / Snowberry
Umbellularia californica / California Bay Laurel

Perennials for erosion control

Cakile edentula / Sea Rocket
Cucurbita foetidissima / Buffalo Gourd
Epilobium angustifolium / Fireweed
M. edule / Hottentot Fig (Syn *Carpobrutus edule*)
Monarda didyma / Bee Balm
Arctostaphylos uva ursi / Bearberry
Artemisia tridentata / Big Sagebrush
Arundo donax / Giant Reed
Oryzopsis species / Indian Millet
Phragmites australis / Common Reed
Pueraria lobata / Kudzu
Yucca species / Yucca
Bouteloua curtipendula / Sideoats Grama
Uniola paniculata / Sea Oats
Vicia americana / American Vetch

Grassland

Lawns

Every modern landscaping book has at least one chapter devoted to lawns. In some parts of North America lawns have long been elevated to cult status, with the idea that the more perfect the lawn (greener, weed free, bigger) the more perfect the owner. This has perhaps changed somewhat in recent years, as more and more houses are packed on to tiny lots, and because longer work hours have made leisure time more precious. At its peak the average upscale suburban house had enough lawn for its own golf course.

The suburban mega-lawn is another example of the folly of misdirected technology and energy use. They wouldn't even exist if it weren't for the riding lawn mower and cheap fossil fuel (it is said that America uses more fertilizer on its lawns than is used by India to grow food). It makes no sense to apply water, fertilizers and weedkillers to grow a crop of grass, so you can cut it and throw it in the trash. About half of the lawn chemicals applied to lawns get washed into streams and rivers. Some more ends up in the homeowner (it has been suggested that some breast and other cancers may be due to lawn chemical use).

The emerald green patch of lawn out in the desert goes beyond thoughtless ignorance and enters the realm of wilful stupidity (in many places fossil groundwater is being depleted to keep them alive). A lawn uses 2-5 gallons of water per square foot per month and give nothing productive in return, except grass clippings and some (usually unwanted) exercise.

Traditional cottage gardens didn't have large grassy areas we would call lawns, because space was too valuable to waste on unproductive plants (and because lawn mowers and pre-emergent weedkillers hadn't been invented). Nowadays lawns are used to fill in the wide open garden spaces because we don't know what else to do with all that space (or is it just conventional thinking that a garden must have a lawn?) If you have a large garden and want low-maintenance, it would make more sense to allow most of the land to return to its natural state.

Good things about lawns

Lawns aren't always an ecological horror story. In cool humid areas where grass grows naturally without any help, they can make sense as a low-maintenance groundcover. They require a lot of work to keep them as lawns, rather than meadows though. I suppose you could think of the lawn as a source of mulch or compost material.

The biggest argument in favor of a modest size lawn is if you have small children. A lawn gives them a clear, flat and relatively soft place to play that can't be beaten. There really is no playing surface quite like grass turf, which is why rich European soccer clubs all play on real live grass. One way to keep its size to a minimum is by using a push lawn mower. If you need a tractor to mow it, then it is too big.

If you have a really big garden and just can't give up the grass, you could have a wildflower meadow rather than a lawn. Simply cut it with a scythe in spring and autumn to keep down woody plants. You might have an area of closely mown grass near the house, small enough to push mow.

If you live in a humid climate where grass grows easily, you could always justify your lawn by using it as a source of mulch material for the rest of the garden. Maybe mix in lots of clover so it produces its own fertilizer.

Herbal lawns

Some wild plants can be used to create a low input / low-maintenance herbal lawn to replace grass (or as a mix with grass). The plants for a herbal lawn should be low-growing, creeping, resistant to trampling and ideally also drought tolerant.

An herbal lawns may look like a lawn, but it isn't really a lawn from a users viewpoint, in that you can't play games on it (not if you want it to remain a lawn), They are also more difficult to establish than grass. Some species can be direct sown, but most need to be transplanted (plant one plant per square foot and they will eventually fill in).

If you walk on an herbal lawn in bare feet beware of standing on bees, because some of the most suitable plants are important nectar producers (this kind of lawn could work great for beekeepers).

Some of the best plants for an herbal lawn include:
Yarrow (*Achillea millefolium*)
Clover (*Trifolium repens*)
Chamomile (*Chamomilum nobile*)
Wild Thyme (*Thymus serpyllum*)
Ajuga or Bugleweed (*Ajuga reptans*)
Bird's-foot trefoil (*Lotus corniculatus*)
Cinquefoil, dwarf (*Potentilla spp*)
Clover, white or Dutch (*Trifolium repens*)
Pennyroyal (*Mentha pulegium*)
Pineapple weed (*Matricaria matricarioides*)
Strawberry, wild (*Fragaria virginiana, F. vesca*)
Sweet vernal grass (*Anthoxanthum odoratum*)

The food lawn

A variation on the herbal lawn / weed bed idea, this would be a planting of low-growing edible weeds such as Purslane, Chickweed, Chamomile, Filaree, Clover and more. These should be harvested for greens periodically. You might also include edible bulbs such as *Alliums, Brodiaea, Fritillaria and Camassia.*

You could take this idea even further along the lines of the forest garden and create an edible prairie/meadow polyculture. See Wild ideas for semi-wild gardens.

Juice lawn

You could use your organic lawn as a solar collector to turn sunlight into a valuable nutritional supplement. Cut out the animals and turn grass directly into human food. Most grasses aren't edible to humans not because they contains toxins, but because we can't digest the cellulose they contain. By extracting the juice and drinking it, we can get the nutritional benefits of grass (vitamins, minerals, chlorophyll and various beneficial phytonutrients) without all the work of digesting it.

Grass juice is a fairly radical nutritional concept, and growing a lawn for juicing is a fairly radical gardening concept. Which species of grass would be most suitable for a juice lawn is something to be investigated further. Most grasses for juicing are annuals (Barley and Wheat) but the perennials could be even more useful. Possible candidates might include species from the *Agropyron, Echinochloa, Eleusine* and *Panicum* genera.

Mushrooms

You could grow mushrooms on your conventional (organic) lawn to make it more productive. See Mushrooms and fungi for how to do this.

Water plants

I have always had a particular fascination with water plants. They grow so exuberantly in warm weather, never hindered by lack of water or competition from land weeds. By creating a water garden you can not only create one of the most interesting elements in the garden, you can also grow some fascinating plants and produce more food.

Water loving plants are often quite specialized in their habitat requirements and a pond provides a variety of niches for them. Floating and emergent aquatics grow in the water, semi-aquatic marginal plants grow along the waters edge and moisture loving plants (including trees and shrubs) grow in the damp, humid conditions nearby.

A nice feature of water plants is that everything is so mobile. Floating plants and those in baskets can be moved any time. Even plants that are rooted in soil can be moved easily, because they are immersed in water all the time.

Growing aquatic plants in arid areas may seem somewhat irresponsible from a water conserving viewpoint (they can use a lot of water). However it can be justified if you are producing food and increasing the biodiversity of the garden (especially if you conserve water in other ways).

Sources of plants

In some places it may be possible to obtain the more common useful aquatic plants (Cattail, Watercress, Brooklime, Water Mint) from the wild. I know some people will criticize me for suggesting this, but these plants are very vigorous and often occupy all of the space available to them. Thinning them out a little will just give them room to grow more and certainly won't harm them. I got my Cattails from the side of the road where they were growing in the water from a leaking septic system .

Many domesticated plants can be obtained from local gardeners ponds. It is the nature of aquatics to run wild, so most gardeners with ponds have an over-supply of plants after a year or two. I have also found edible species in amongst the ornamental pond plants at the garden center, in the aquarium department of the pet store and even in an oriental produce market. As a last resort you can go to the internet to find those plants that are not available anywhere else.

Usually you don't need to get many individuals of a species, as even one plant will multiply rapidly under suitable conditions.

Edible water plants

A surprising number of common aquatic plants are not only edible, but are cultivated as food crops in Asia and elsewhere. These are especially useful because they are easy to propagate, grow quickly (they are never short of water) and are highly productive. Commonly cultivated plants include Watercress, Arrowhead, Lotus, Water Spinach and Taro. Of course my usual caution about choosing useful plants applies here, it has to be a plant you will use. If you don't eat it, then it is an ornamental not an edible.

Other uses of water plants

Aquatic plants grow so rapidly they can be useful as a source of biomass for fertilization and soil improvement. In fact you will often have to remove excess plants to prevent the pond from getting congested.

Care of water plants

Generally the hardy water plants require very little attention, in fact most often any work involves discouraging them rather than having to encourage them. The more tender species are a different matter, as they may need to be protected over the winter, which is a bit more work.

Useful water plants

Most of these are not very familiar as food plants, so you will have to adapt your eating habits. Remember that useful plants are only useful if you use them.

Submerged plants

Also known as oxygenators these are important for the healthy functioning of a pond as they add oxygen to the water during the day. They also absorb nutrients from the water, thus reducing algae growth and helping to keep the water clear. They also provide food, cover and spawning areas for fish.

These species are commonly sold in bunches, which you separate into smaller groups when planting. They can be very vigorous, so are usually planted in pots to make control easier.

This group of plants doesn't contain many edible species to my knowledge. Common oxygenating plants include the Pondweeds (*Elodea*), Eelgrass (*Vallisneria*) and Parrots feather (*Myriophyllum*).

Parrots Feather (*Myriophyllum aquaticum*)

Apparently the growing tips have been eaten, though I have never been tempted to try them.

Free floating plants

These species float freely and obtain their nutrients directly from the water, rather than the soil. By removing nutrients in this way they help to keep the water clean and reduce the growth of algae (which also get their nutrients from the water). They are important to pond dwelling creatures because they provide food, shade, hiding places and habitat.

By floating on the surface and shading the water beneath, these plants reduce algae growth and keep the water cooler. A healthy pond should have no more than 30% of the surface covered in plants though, so the submerged plants still receive enough light for good growth.

These free floating plants are fairly unique in the garden plant world, in that they live entirely independent of the soil, deriving their nutrients from the pond water. You can pick up a Water Hyacinth and move it to another pond and it will immediately be perfectly at home. This mobility means that these plants can spread very quickly if they find conditions to their liking. Some species have a tendency to be invasive and won't stop growing until they have taken over the entire surface of the pond. You don't want them covering more than 50% of the surface (ideally 30%), so thinning them can become a regular maintenance activity in summer. This isn't completely wasted time though, because they can be used as mulch or compost material.

Water Hyacinth (*Eichornia crassipes*)

Water Hyacinth is infamous for being an invasive weed and is banned in some areas. It propagates itself vegetatively from offsets and can grow very rapidly in the right conditions. It is a beautiful plant though and provides habitat for various pond creatures.

The plant is not edible raw, but the mucilaginous young leaves and flower buds have been cooked and eaten.

Water Hyacinth isn't at all hardy and is killed by frost. Young plants can be overwintered in a greenhouse (ideally at least 50° F) in a bowl of water and potting compost

In some tropical areas Water Hyacinth is an important fertilizer for home gardens and it is actually cultivated for this in special ponds.

Water Mimosa (*Neptunia oleracea*)

This small floating plant is attractive and easy to grow. It isn't very hardy but can be kept in the warm greenhouse for the winter. It is usually propagated by dividing the plants, or from seed.

Water Mimosa can be eaten raw or cooked and is quite good.

Duckweed (*Lemna minor*)

This tiny plant grows quickly in the right conditions and can cover the entire surface of a pond. It isn't normally eaten by humans, but is sometimes used as a high protein livestock feed (maybe as feed for chickens?) It can also be useful as green manure. In this way a problem can become a resource.

Mosquito fern (*Azolla filiculoides*)

This tiny floating fern harbors an algae (*Anabaena azollae*) that fixes nitrogen from the air. In the right circumstances it is very fast growing and can be used as a fertilizer (a related Asian species is very important as a fertilizer in rice fields in China and Vietnam). It doesn't tolerate cold weather very well and often dies back, but reappears in spring.

This species isn't eaten by humans, but ducks like it and can be used to control its spread.

Duckweed (*Wolffia arrhiza*)

This species has the distinction of being is the smallest flowering plant in the world (less than 1 millimeter in length. It can produce viable seed but usually propagates itself vegetatively. It can grow extremely rapidly in idea conditions and may completely cover the surface of a pond.

These plants are fairly high in protein and have been used as food for both humans and animals. Their rapid growth makes them potentially useful for cleaning polluted water. They have also been investigated as a possible source of biofuel.

Rooting floating plants

These species send their roots down into the soil at the bottom of the pond, but their leaves float on the surface of the water.

Water Hawthorne (*Aponogeton distachyus*)

This attractive species grows like a water Lily and is often planted as an ornamental in zones 5-11. The flower buds are eaten cooked or raw in its native South Africa. The starchy tuberous roots are also edible. It can be grown from seed or division.

Watershield (*Brasenia schreberi*)

The hardy Water Shield is rarely grown as an ornamental because its flowers are fairly inconspicuous. However the starchy roots are edible, as are the slimy young leaves.

This species is usually propagated by root division. It will grow in 6-24 inches of water.

Water Lilies (*Nymphaea* species)
Pond Lilies (*Nuphar* species)

These are the ultimate ornamental pond plants and some people develop an obsession with them. I built my first pond so I could see a frog sitting on a Lily pad (I didn't have to wait long). These have many of the same attributes as the Sacred Lotus and are grown in much the same ways. They are exquisitely beautiful plants and not at all difficult to grow. The more frost tender species can be over-wintered in the greenhouse.

There is a considerable variation in the size of these plants, from miniature Water Lilies for containers and very small ponds (in which case they are planted in baskets), to large ones suitable only for lakes.

Water Lilies are vigorous plants and need fairly rich soil. They are commonly removed from the pond annually and repotted in fresh soil. This also allows you to divide them easily, and harvest the roots for food. The leaves and seeds are also edible.

White Water Snowflake (*Nymphoides indica*)
Yellow Water Snowflake (*N. geminata*) (Syn *N. peltata*) Zones 5-11

These species resemble small Water Lilies and will grow in 6-24 inches of water. Often propagated by viviparous offsets that form on the leaves, they can also be grown from division or seed. They can be quite invasive if not confined.

The leaves, flower buds and stems have been cooked and eaten.

Water Chestnut (*Trapa natans*)

This isn't the familiar Water Chestnut of Chinese cooking. This species floats on the water surface and has attractive white flowers. Unfortunately it is banned in many areas because it has the potential to spread into natural watercourses. The edible seeds have 4 sharp spines.

Emergent plants

These species root in the mud of shallow water, but their leaves emerge from the water and grow in the air. They often spread out into open water, making the pond appear smaller (and eventually making it smaller). They vary in the depth of water they can tolerate, some prefer moist soil, others grow in water up to 6 inches deep and some may even send out runners that float on the surface. They may also grow in the moist soil along the margins of the pond (especially if the water level recedes).

The roots and stems are often brittle and root easily, so that parts often break off and get washed away to root elsewhere. This is an important means of propagation in the wild.

Some of these plants are able to spread so vigorously and produce so much biomass they can eventually turn a pond into a swamp.

Marginal plants absorb nutrients from water entering the pond and so are important for maintaining water quality.

Marginal plants can be planted in pots (set on blocks to the suitable height) in the water itself, or in a shelf at the pond edge. If you plant emergent species in the soil at the edge of the pond they can decide where they grow best. Often they will grow right out into the water. The more aggressive types should probably be planted in containers to keep them confined.

Alligatorweed (*Alternanthera philoxeroides*)

This low plant roots in moist soil or shallow water, but sprawls out from the margins to cover the surface of the water. It is an important source of food and habitat for water creatures. It is also eaten by humans, either raw or cooked (it is related to Amaranth).

Alligator Weed is a tropical plant and can't tolerate freezing, but can be over-wintered in the greenhouse. It can be propagated from cuttings or seed.

Brooklimes (*Veronica* species)

This fast growing evergreen is often used to disguise the edges of ponds. The plants are easily grown from seed, cuttings or division. The somewhat bitter leaves are a nice addition to salads.

Bulrush, Tule (*Schoenoplectus lacustris*)

Syn (*Scirpus lacustris*)

This plant is too big and too invasive for all but the biggest ponds and even then it will gradually take over. They could be planted in large shallow containers to keep them confined.

Bulrush is a very useful plant. Almost all parts are edible. It can be used to purify gray water, and it is a great source of biomass for mulch or compost.

Cattail Flag (*Typha angustifolia*)

Another big plant that is too invasive for all but the biggest ponds, unless you grow it in containers. It is not only ornamental but also very edible. Almost every part is edible: new buds, emerging shoots, unopened flowers, pollen, seed and roots. The wild food guru Euell Gibbons called Cattail the supermarket of the swamps.

Cattail can also be used to purify gray water and as a source of biomass for fertilizer. The green twisted leaves can be used as twine for tying up plants.

Cattail is most easily propagated from pieces of rhizome, dug while it is dormant in winter. In suitable conditions it can spread rapidly and get very tall..

Marsh Marigold (*Caltha palustris*)

A popular pond plant for its beautiful yellow early spring flowers. It grows naturally in wet soil near water and in bogs with very shallow water. It doesn't like very hot conditions and often goes dormant in summer. Propagate by division or fresh seed (stratify).

The newly emerged leaves were one of Euell Gibbons favorite green vegetables.

Sacred Lotus (*Nelumbo nucifera*) Zones 5-10

The Sacred Lotus has been cultivated for food and beauty for over 3000 years. It is a tropical plant, but the roots can survive quite well in cooler areas (to zone 5) if under the surface of the water. It is a large, very vigorous, even invasive plant, so is usually grown in large submerged baskets (24" diameter is good).

The tuberous roots are an important vegetable in Asian cuisines and are widely cultivated for them. The seeds and young leaves are also edible.

Lotus is normally grown from tubers (unfortunately those you buy in grocery stores won't usually sprout). The best way to plant a tuber is to float it in warm water (75-85° F) until it begins to produce shoots, then plant it in a pot and cover with warm water. The first leaves should float on the water surface.

Divide the tubers in spring by cutting into sections each with a growing tip (cut just behind a joint).

The plants will grow in water from 6" to 6 feet deep. They like fairly warm conditions with full sun. In fact they wont start growing in spring until the water has warmed up considerably. They also need fertile soil as they are hungry plants.

One way to grow Lotus is in its own bog. Just dig a hole 4 feet wide and 2 feet deep and line it with pond liner. Put in a length of soaker hose to supply water, then refill the hole with soil and plant.

American Lotus / *N. lutea*
This hardy native American is used in much the same ways as its Asian cousin.

Water Celery (*Oenanthe javanica*)
Though Water Celery is a tropical species it is surprisingly hardy and will grow from zones 5-11. The leaves and stems are widely cultivated in Asia for use in cooking, but can also be eaten raw.

It grows in moist soil or shallow water and can even float on the surface. It grows so vigorously it can form dense stands and sometimes becomes a pest.

This species can be grown from seed, but it roots so easily it is usually grown from cuttings. If you can find the greens in an Asian market you can root them easily (and may get a superior edible cultivar).

This species is also useful for purifying water, though you probably wouldn't want to eat plants used for this.

Flamingo is a commonly available variegated form. It is quite attractive, but not as tasty as the green type.

Water Chestnut (*Eleocharis dulcis*) Zones 7-10
This is the familiar Water Chestnut of Chinese cooking. It is pretty easy to grow, but isn't very hardy. It can survive in colder areas if protected from frost by being underwater (or it can be taken into the greenhouse). It will grow in moist soil or shallow water up to 6 inches deep.

Water Chestnut is propagated from the corms or by dividing the rhizomes. Plant them in a container and keep it just below the surface of the water. This makes it easy to harvest or to take indoors for the winter.
It takes about 6 months to produce new corms. Most grocery store corms don't sprout because they are too old, which is a shame as this would be an easy way to get plants (they aren't easy to obtain). However if you get them fresh (from a Chinese market that sells lots) they often will sprout. Once you get some plants you can save your own corms.

Water Parsnip (*Sium sauve*)
This species grows in moist soil or water to 6 inches deep. It is easily grown from seed or by division while dormant and can get to be quite a big plant.

The roots are good if gathered in late autumn and cooked like Parsnips. The young leaves have occasionally been eaten too.

Water Purslane (*Bacopa monnieri*) Zones 6-11
The fleshy leaves are eaten in the same ways as the unrelated Purslane and it has been sold in markets for this. It also has medicinal properties and is said to be beneficial for the brain.

This low-growing plant can be grown as a marginal plant (it can tolerate immersion under several inches of water), or as a groundcover for wet soils.

Water Purslane is easily propagated from cuttings, but seed works well too.

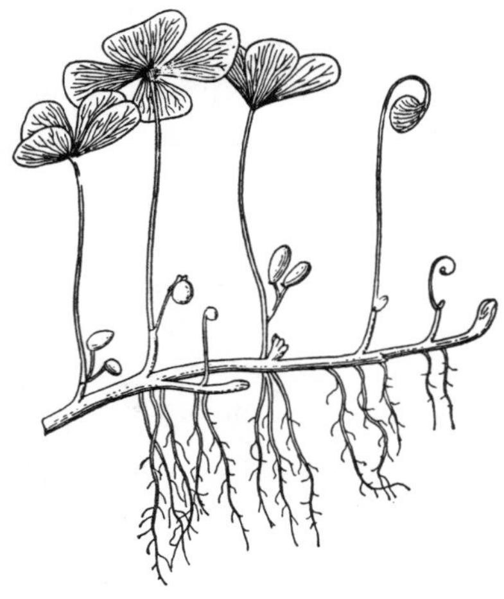

Water Clover (*Marsilea minuta*) Zone 8
This small fern can be eaten raw or cooked and is commonly sold in markets in India. This is quite a fast growing plant and produces a dense low mat of foliage. It can send out long runners that cover ground surprisingly quickly. See Herbs for more on its interesting medicinal uses.

Water Spinach (*Ipomoea aquatica*) Zone 9-11
This vigorous and fast growing plant spreads rapidly to form a dense mat of foliage. It is widely cultivated in Asia for the succulent leaf tips (these are eaten raw or cooked). However because of its invasive nature and potential to spread in waterways you can no longer buy the plant in the United States. It is still cultivated for sale in Asian communities though.

Water Spinach can be grown from seed, but you can't buy seed in the United States because it is banned. If you could grow it, then you would put it in moist soil, or water up to 18 inches deep and it could spread out over the surface of the pond, shading the water below. It would actually tolerate part shade as well.

If you can find the plants (look in a Chinese produce store), it can also be grown from easily rooted cuttings. It is not very hardy, but cuttings can be over wintered indoors in colder climates.

Watercress (*Nasturtium officinale*)
This may well be the only water vegetable here that you recognize. A nutritious and tasty plant, it is easily grown and in mild climates it can be gathered year round. It is good raw or cooked.

Watercress can be grown from seed quite easily, but stem cuttings are even easier. The fastest way to get a bed of Watercress established is to buy a bunch from the market and root it in water. Once established it will self-sow if given the chance.

In Europe Watercress was once grown in special low beds created beside streams, to take advantage of the flowing water (it doesn't do so well in stagnant water). If you were motivated enough you could devise your own bed and irrigate it with a hose.

Wild-Rice (*Zizania aquatica*)
This graceful annual plant is sometimes grown as an ornamental in large ponds. The seed ripens in stages in August and September. In warmer areas they often grow as short-lived perennials and can spread by means of creeping rhizomes (you can propagate it by division).

Wild-Rice is easily grown from fresh seed, the hard part is finding it. Store bought seed won't sprout because has been hulled and also because it has been dried (the seed must be kept moist to keep it viable).

Wild-Rice will grow in moist soil or water up to 6 feet deep and is often grown in large containers. However I'm not sure of the practicality of doing this unless you have a medium sized lake bordering your property (and can replicate its growing conditions). You won't get much of a grain harvest from a containerful of plants.

In Asia the related *Z. latifolia* is grown for the edible stem base.

Marginal plants

Marginal plants vary in the depth of water they can tolerate; some prefer merely moist soil, while others can tolerate being completely submerged for extended periods. They are useful to soften and blur the pond edge, blending the dry ground into the water.

Marginal plants commonly have a dense network of roots that binds the edges of the pond and prevents erosion. They also help to maintain water quality by absorbing nutrients from runoff before they leach into the water.

These plants are important as a source of food and habitat for wildlife such as frogs and insects. Taller marginals also help to shade the water.

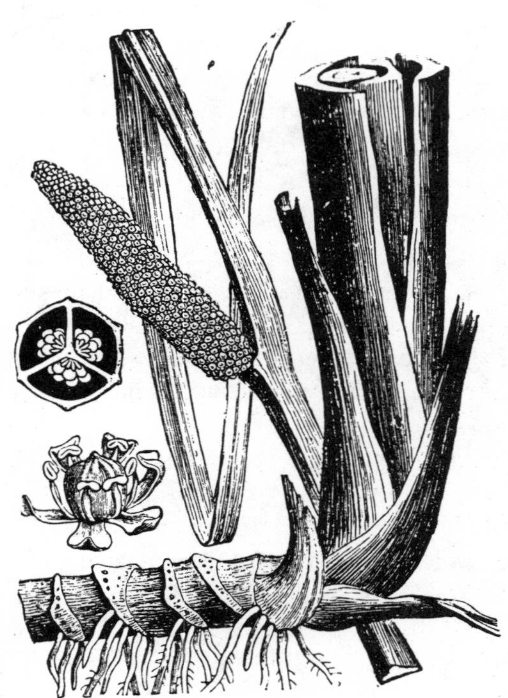

Sweet Flag (*Acorus calamus*)

Sweet Flag can be found growing wild over a large area of the northern hemisphere. It is a neat and attractive plant and is often grown purely as an ornamental. It is also edible, with an aromatic flavor somewhat reminiscent of ginger. The new spring growth is a very nice addition to salads.

I should add that some people caution against using it Sweet Flag because it contains asarone, which is banned from use as a food additive.

This slowly creeping plant (it isn't invasive) prefers moist soil rather than being submerged and will grow in full sun or part shade. Propagate by seed or root division. It is very hardy but usually dies back to the ground in winter.

Licorice Flag (*Acorus gramineus*)

This Japanese species is commonly grown as a pond plant. It is actually a better edible plant than the above.

Marshmallow (*Althaea officinalis*) Zones 3-9

The leaves and roots are edible and have soothing medicinal properties, both internally and externally. It is a perennial, but easily grown from seed. Established plants can be propagated by division. It needs constant moisture for best growth and does well alongside a pond.

Chufa (*Cyperus esculentus var sativus*)

Chufa is most familiar as a weed, yet a subspecies has been cultivated for its small tasty edible tubers since the time of the Ancient Egyptians.

Chufa prefers light marshy soil and can be grown by division, cuttings, or tubers planted in spring (best). These are soaked for 24 hours and then planted out 12 inches apart. You may have to protect the young plants from wildlife until they are well established. The first time I tried to grow them, every single tuber was eaten.

Chamaeleon Plant (*Houttuynia cordata*) Zones 5-11

The roots, seed and aromatic leaves are all used in Vietnamese cooking. This hardy species grows best in moist soil and can spread rapidly. It doesn't mind part shade.

Water Mint (*Mentha aquatica*)

This species is very similar to Spearmint and Peppermint and can be used in the same ways. Like those plants it can be invasive when growing in rich moist soil with full sun. It can be grown from seed, but it's best to propagate a superior cultivar from root cuttings.

Vegetables

If you want to grow enough food to feed your family you will have to get intense in the vegetable garden. An edible landscape or a forest garden just won't do it by itself. I am not going to go into much detail about traditional vegetable gardening here, even though it is the most important aspect of the food garden. This is because I have already written over 500 pages on the subject (in The Organic Gardeners Handbook and The Vegetable Growers Handbook). Instead I am just going to discuss a few of the more unconventional aspects of growing vegetables.

Where to grow vegetables

Vegetable crops don't have to be grown in "the vegetable garden", they can be planted almost anywhere, providing their basic needs are met. Different crops evolved in different parts of the world and have different needs. These can be grown in different ways in different parts of the garden. You just need to able to identify suitable growing conditions for each crop.

The vegetable garden

The above statement doesn't mean I don't think the vegetable garden isn't important. It still makes sense to concentrate the most demanding crops in the relatively small area of the kitchen garden, where they can receive the maximum water, fertilizers, attention and protection. I have already discussed the various types of kitchen garden (see The vegetable garden), so I won't say any more here,

Edible ornamental garden

Many vegetables are attractive enough to be grown in the ornamental garden, and give you a chance to use all of your artistic flair, You could grow them in variously shaped borders and beds, creating patchworks of color, grow different height plants interplanted with flowers. The reason they aren't used more often is that once we start harvesting from them, they start to look a lot less attractive. See The House Area for more on this.

Patio garden

The patio area is a logical place to grow some of the more demanding and specialized crops, especially those that are attractive and fairly compact. This is where you spend most of your time, so plants get more attention here. It is also close to the house (and kitchen) and its water sources.

You could have vegetable beds bordering the patio (perhaps in an ornamental potager type arrangement) and grow the most ornamental crops in them. Keep these looking good so the area becomes a visual attraction.

Path gardens

Narrow beds bordering the paths could be used as a linear vegetable garden. They are a good place to grow compact repeat harvest plants such as Kale, Chard, Tomato, Pepper and Basil. Put temperamental plants near the house, more rugged ones further away.

You might also have wider beds for the more space hungry repeat harvest crops (Cucumber, Squash, Watermelon). Put these out at the edge of the garden, where they can spread out (with a little help) into unused space

Forest garden

A number of common vegetable crops will happily grow in the sunnier parts of the wild or forest garden. All you have to do is plant them (sometimes they will even self-sow). See Forest gardening for more on this.

Drought tolerant dry garden

In areas where there isn't enough water for irrigation you can grow some crops using only the moisture held in the soil. A few crops can do very well when grown in this way, particularly Tomatoes and Watermelons (in fact if water is in short supply I suggest you don't waste it on them). This means growing crops in widely spaced rows or hills, so yields aren't as high per square foot, but they are considerably higher than nothing. The fruits are also sweeter and better flavored when grown in this way.

Dry gardening is a good way to increase the amount of food you can grow, without using any extra resources (water).

If water is in short supply every summer you should grow a lot of your staple crops in spring, when they can use the water stored in the soil from over the winter.

Growing vegetables in small patches

Wild annual plants tend to grow in colonies (known as drifts in ornamental planting) rather than as isolated individuals, because that's how the seed naturally falls. They could be looked upon as a more attractive variation on block planting. This is a good way to grow annual vegetables out in the garden, as there is safety in numbers, with the plants in the middle protected by their neighbors and having a better chance of surviving to maturity. You also get the plants in sufficient numbers to feed your family.

Drifts work best with direct sown plants, though you could also use transplants. These can played with as much as you like, until you find the best places (and the best ways) to grow them.

Before sowing a vegetable patch you need to create a fertile soil, so amend it with 3" of compost, as well as wood ashes and other nutrients.

Low/no-work vegetable beds

There are enough independent edible plants of all kinds (perennial and self sowing annuals) that you could plant beds that will almost grow themselves. The key is to find the right plants and put them together in the right way.

Listed below are a few I have found to be no work at all, either because they sow and grow themselves, or because they are perennials and just keep producing all season. The more you concentrate on this type of garden, the broader the range of plants you will find to grow. You might also encourage some wild plants to grow as crops. See Growing vegetables as wild plants.

Long season perennials include Sorrel, Vietnamese Coriander, Welsh Onions, Chives and Watercress. They can be harvested in small amounts all season long,

Short season perennials such as Good King Henry, Dandelion, Red Dock and Asparagus don't produce for very long, but come back year after year with no work at all.

Self sowing annuals: Amaranth, Orach, Lambs Quarters, Cilantro, Land Cress, Arugala, Cornsalad, Chicory, Chard, Russian Kale, Purslane can all produce tasty greens with little attention. Careful attention to harvesting can increase their productivity enormously.

Self-Sowing Crops

Some annual crops will readily self-sow if given the chance. The reason they don't do so more often is because we don't let them; they are usually cut down before they set seed. It's now November in my garden and seedlings of Cilantro, Pea, Lettuce, Chard, Cornsalad, Kale and Parsley are all starting to germinate vigorously.

Crops that self-sow readily can be allowed to grow where they appear. They help to lend an air of luxuriance and spontaneity to the garden. These will vary every year according to which plants are allowed to produce seed.

If you let lots of plants set seed (not hybrids) you will eventually get a rich seed bank in the soil and many crops will come up as volunteers. I throw all my old seed into a bag and eventually scatter it in the garden, most seeds die (if they are not already dead), but there is occasionally a surprise. Some people do this in autumn, under the theory that only the best seeds will survive the winter, so seedlings that emerge in the spring will be very strong.

Some self-sowing biennial crops can be perennialized by sowing seed two years in a row and letting them flower and set their own seed.

Locally adapted Crops

The first cottage gardeners grew a limited range of vegetables because that's all they had available. The modern gardener has a much greater number of crops to choose from, many with multiple varieties and attributes (disease and pest resistance, hardiness, heat tolerance and more).

It really pays to find the crops (and specific varieties) that do well in your particular growing conditions, as this can make growing them a lot easier. Choose 2 or 3 of the best performing varieties (a combination of vigor, productivity, low-maintenance, nutrition and flavor) for each crop category. For example for winter greens I would choose Russian Kale, Perpetual Spinach and Mustard. For summer greens I would go with Amaranth and Giant Lambs Quarters. For root vegetables I would choose Carrot, Parsnip and Potato. For salads a mix of Lettuce, Mizuna, Mustard, Radicchio, Chicory and Arugala.

Cold tolerant crops
I have often thought about trying to grow a bed of the cold tolerant edible weeds that keep growing right through the winter. Suitable plants would include Chickweed, Land Cress, Malva and Cornsalad.

Inoculating with mycorrhizal fungi
Mycorrhizal fungi aren't just for woody plants, they can also boost the growth of many vegetable crops. Commercially available preparations can be sprinkled in the planting hole before planting, or mixed with water and used as a liquid inoculant.

Annual vegetables

I'm not going to say much about the traditional annual garden crops because I have already covered them exhaustively in The Vegetable Growers Handbook. Instead I am going to list some of the food plants I have found to be particularly well suited to the low-maintenance garden. These are mostly easy to grow, as well as tasty, nutritious and productive (some are also ornamental). They can be grown in various ways to supplement the more traditional crops

Many crops produce surprising extra treats; such as Pea shoot tips, Garlic scapes, edible flowers, etc. Don't ignore these, they can add nutrition and exotic flavors to your diet.

Cooked leaf crops

Amaranth (*Amaranthus* species)
An excellent hot weather potherb when young, Amaranth is also grown as a grain crop (the seed is easy to gather in quantity and needs no processing). It also self-sows vigorously; I planted it several years ago and since then I have had as many self-sown seedlings as I can use every year.

There are some beautiful purple and golden varieties that look perfectly at home in the ornamental garden. This is also a great plant for creating a maze or kid's jungle garden. Plant it early if you want it to get really big.

The tender leaves and tops can be cooked like Spinach. The seeds can be popped like popcorn and then ground to flour for use for baking.

Chard (*Beta vulgaris*)
The colorful Ruby (red) and spectacular multi-colored Rainbow Chard (red, white, yellow) are commonly recommended as being ideal ornamental edibles. I find the thin-stemmed Perpetual Spinach (or Spinach Beet) to be one of the best varieties for eating. A good stand of this plant can keep you supplied with tasty greens for months (gather individual leaves as they get big enough).

Chard is easily grown from seed in any garden soil. I find it does best in winter, as summer plantings are commonly attacked by Leaf Miners.

Russian Kale (*Brassica napus*)
I am a big fan of Russian Kale and consider it the best winter leaf crop for my climate. These varieties are highly productive, nutritious, tender, tasty and cold tolerant enough to be harvested almost year round here in Santa Cruz. I have planted it in late spring and harvested from the same plants for almost eight months (and then obtained seed from them). The abundantly produced seed can be sprouted in the kitchen like alfalfa sprouts, or used to grow more plants.

The frilly purplish leaves are pretty enough to be used as foliage plants in the ornamental garden.

Kale is easily grown from seed in most garden soils and is so independent it can self-sow and grow completely on its own. The flowers are good in salads.

Huazontli (*Chenopodium berlanderii*)
Giant Lambs Quarters (*C. giganteum*)
These two relatives of the common weed Lambs Quarter are great warm weather green vegetables. The flowering tops are particularly good. Keep pinching these off to eat and more will be produced. Both species set seed and self-sow like weeds (because they kind of are).

Orach (*Atriplex hortensis*)
Another independent potherb that grows and seeds itself. The red variety is more ornamental than the green. Use it in a large stand for visual effect and to get a worthwhile quantity of foliage to eat.

Malabar Spinach (*Basella rubra*)
This attractive vine is somewhat slow to get growing but produces abundantly if the weather gets hot enough. See Climbing plants for more on this.

Salad growing

We should all eat more live foods, they are some of the most nutritious foods we have.

Cut and come again salad gardens

I have largely given up on rows of individual lettuces, in favor of small blocks or patches of mesclun. These are quick and east to plant, you just scatter the seed onto the prepared seedbed, so there is a seed about every ½" apart, all over the bed. You can plant a patch almost anywhere it can receive the necessary care (which mainly consists of weeding, watering and keeping them cool in summer - misters work well). They also look quite good, and you can get creative, growing sections in different patterns, colors and shapes.

You can start harvesting individual leaves when they are 2″ to 3″ tall, in about 3 to 4 weeks. You can also harvest entire plants as they get big enough and thereby thin over-crowded areas.

Sprouting seed crops

If you regularly save seed from your crops you will usually have far more than you could possibly plant. Sprouting is a good way to use some of this, while at the same time improving your health. Sprout a mix of seeds together and you have a ready made salad. The best species for this include Radish, Kale, Broccoli, Mung Bean, Chia, Clover, Sunflower and Buckwheat.

Easy salad plants

Growing your own salad plants enables you to expand your salads far beyond lettuce Here are some easily grown salad plants that require little care. Most grow best in cool weather.

Arugala (*Eruca sativa*)
You either love or hate the spicy pungent flavor of this relative of the Mustards. Easily grown from seed, it commonly self-sows.

Buckshorn plantain (*Plantago coronopus*)
This easy to grow and succulent annual is sometimes found as a weed.

Celery Leaf (*Apium graveolens*)
I have a perennial variety in my garden called Parcel (because it looks just like parsley, even though it is celery) that has been really good. It even self-sows.

Cornsalad (*Valerianella locusta*)
This very hardy cold weather salad green self-sows readily.

Cress, Garden (*Lepidium sativum*)
The tender pungent young foliage is very good in salads. It is easily grown from seed and will often self-sow.

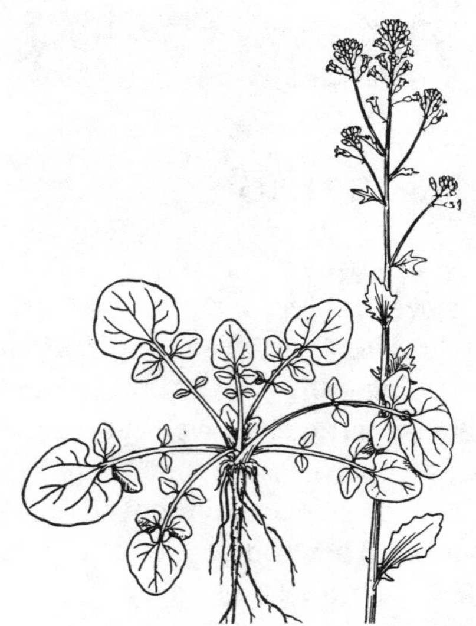

Cress, Land (*Barbarea verna*)
This very hardy biennial can be used like its aquatic cousin the watercress. It does best in cold weather and grows right through the winter in my garden.

Chicory (*Cicorium intybus*)
The beautiful deep blue flower petals can be added to salads. The bitter greens are also edible, as are the roots. It will produce an abundance of seed (it self-sows in my garden). The roots can be forced indoors to produce witloof chicory or chicons.

Endive (*Cicorium endiva*)
A close relative of Chicory and used in the same ways.

Lettuce (*Lactuca sativa*)
I generally grow Lettuce in cut and come again salad beds, or as edging. It is worth growing them as individuals as well however.

Lettuce plants make spectacular sculptural forms when they bolt (and produce seed by the bucketful). You can collect this seed and use for cut and come again salad beds, or you can scatter it around the garden. It also self-seeds readily.

Miners Lettuce (*Montia perfoliata*)
This native plant is a cool weather weed in my garden, but in Europe it is commonly grown as a salad crop. It is easily grown from seed and is a prolific self-sower.

Oriental Brassicas – *Brassica pekinensis*
B. chinensis
B. juncea
There are a lot of useful Asian Brassicas for salads and other uses. Mizuna is one of my favorites

Purslane, Golden (*Portulaca oleracea*)
A refined variety of the common weed Purslane. It is easily grown from seed and self-sows easily enough to become a weed. It is an excellent and succulent salad or potherb and has edible seeds too. There is also a large green variety. Unlike most of the plants mentioned here it likes warm weather.

Rampion (*Campanula rapunculus*)
Made famous by the fairy tale of Rapunzel, whose pregnant mother craved the roots from a witches garden (Caution: Never steal roots from a witches garden, it could get you in to trouble. Don't even take any of the tiny seeds).

Sorrel, French (*Rumex scutatus*)
This species is useful as a potherb or in salads and is particularly highly esteemed in France. Sorrel is almost invasive in its vigor, but doesn't spread very much. It is easily grown from seed and self-sows so easily it can almost become a weed. Divide plants periodically to give them more room and to get extra plants.

Spinach (*Spinacia oleracea*)
Though Spinach is most often cooked, it is also an excellent salad green. Easily grown from seed in cool weather, it is very fast growing,

Strawberry Spinach (*Chenopodium capitatum*)
This is a good minor addition to salads, but don't expect it to taste like Strawberry. It gets its name because the red fruit look vaguely like a Strawberry (well it is red at least), there is no other connection (strawberry flavored spinach would probably be a bit strange anyway). It self-sows in my garden.

Shungiku (*Chrysanthemum coronarium*)
This is on of my favorite salad greens for its aromatic flavor. It is easy to grow from seed.

Welsh Onion (*Allium fistulosum*)
This perennial Onion multiplies itself by means of offsets. It couldn't be easier to grow and provides green onions for months. Another highly recommended crop.

Edible Seed crops

These nutritious plants are usually overlooked by gardeners, but are often easy to grow and deserve to be more widely grown. Some of them produce uniquely nutritious foods and we could all benefit from eating more of them. The main drawback is that they aren't highly productive. You could perhaps gather the seeds of the various plants together and make a seed mix for baking (this is usually mixed with equal amount of wheat or other flour). You might also use it make tahini (see Sesame), though I haven't tried it yet.

Borage (*Borago officinalis*)

Sometimes considered an herb; the bright blue flowers have been used in drinks and salads (remove the hairy sepals). The seeds of Borage contain an oil that is very rich in gamma-linolenic acid (omega-6) and can be used like Evening Primrose oil. It self-sows in my garden.

Red Maids (*Calandrinia ciliata*)

This wild plant was prized by Native Americans for its tasty edible seed. The fleshy plants contain enough moisture to flower and set seed even when uprooted. In fact uprooting may actually stimulate the plant to produce seed. All you have to do is store the plants in a warm dry place until they dry up, then crush and collect the loose seed.

This attractive little annual has occasionally been planted as an ornamental. It is grown from seed in light soil.

Hemp (*Cannabis sativa*)

Hemp seed is rich in all essential amino acids and is one of the most complete plant proteins known. It is very also rich in essential fatty acids (55% linoleic acid and 25% linolenic acid. The seeds can be baked into breads and cakes, added to granola and ground into hemp butter. Of course it is mostly illegal to grow (see Magical herbs for more on this).

Jobs Tears (*Coix lacryma-jobi*)

This tropical plant grows well in warm moist conditions with full sun. The seeds are rich in starch and protein and are a very old grain crop. It was used in soups, drinks (including beer), breads and porridge. It can also be roasted and eaten like peanut. A fairly tall grass it can also be used as a source of biomass.

Pumpkin (*Cucurbita* species)

All pumpkins produce edible seeds, but the naked seeded types produce seeds that don't need shelling. These are easy to grow and also produce edible flesh.

Sunflower (*Helianthus annuus*)

The big Sunflowers are quite spectacular when in full bloom and the taller ones even add height (10 feet or more) to the garden. They can also be used as a temporary screen or hedge. The seeds can feed you, the birds and other wildlife. Sprouted Sunflower seeds are a good salad ingredient.

Limnanthes Douglasii

This species is attractive to beneficial insects and is a good companion for fruit trees. Its edible seeds contain an oil that is similar to that of Jojoba.

Evening Primrose (*Oenothera biennis*)

Though all parts are edible (leaves, flowers, seeds, roots) this species is rarely grown for food at present (though it has been). The flowers are pretty and the seed is the source of Evening Primrose oil which is very rich in gamma-linolenic acid.

Evening Primrose is easily grown from see and self-sows readily enough to be a weed in my garden.

Flax (*Linum usitatissimum*)

Flax seed oil is rich in essential fatty acids, including the omega 3 fatty acids that can help to control cholesterol in the body. They can also help the body to eliminate heavy metals and may have other health benefits.

Flax is grown from seed and likes full sun and rich fertile soil. It is an easy plant to grow, though not hugely productive.

Opium Poppy (*Papaver somniferum*)
This is the main source of the edible Poppy seed used for baked goods (the seeds don't contain significant amounts of opium alkaloids). In some places it is illegal to grow as the immature seedpods are the source of opium.

It is very easy to grow from seed and produces an abundance of seed. It has self-sown in my garden ever since I moved here, having somehow hitched a ride from my last garden (probably with another plant). It doesn't transplant well.

Purslane (*Portulaca oleracea*)
This species is most often used as a salad plant, but the seed is also edible. The fleshy plants contain enough moisture to flower and set seed after being uprooted. In fact uprooting may actually stimulate the plants to produce seed. All you have to do is gather the plant tops and leave them in a paper bag, in a warm dry place, until they dry up. You then simply crush the seed heads and collect the seed.

Mexican Chia (*Salvia hispanica*)
This annual is easy to grow from seed, and has been self-sowing in my garden for many years. The seed is rich in vitamins, calcium, potassium and other minerals, as well as omega 3

Sesame (*Sesamum indicum*)
This species produces an abundance of oily seeds that can be used to make highly nutritious (and calorific) sesame paste (tahini). This is easy, just puree 300g of sesame seeds with 2 tbsp of sesame oil in a food processor (you can also make it without the oil, but it takes a little longer). Other oily seeds might be mixed in with it.

Staple Crops

Staple foods are the nutritious crops that you eat every day to keep you alive. However the nutritional value of a plant is only one consideration in deciding its value to you. It should also be productive, require little processing and should be something you like to eat. This is why the potato is queen of the garden staples, while rice is almost unheard of.

These crops must be grown on a fairly large scale if they really are going to keep you alive. The area doesn't have to be that big however. It is possible to get 40 pounds of beans from an area 25 x 25.

To increase your chances of success the staple crops should be planted at the optimal time for the crop in your climate. Ideally they will be harvested in late summer so you don't have to store them for too long.

Most useful staple crops

Beans (*Phaseolus* species)
Beans are one of the most valuable staple crops we possess. Highly nutritious because of their high protein content, they are also easy to grow and fix their own nitrogen, so don't take it from the soil. Henry Thoreau grew a plot of beans as a source of income while at Walden Pond.

Potato (*Solanum tuberosum*)
The queen of staple food crops, the potato is unique in the ease with which it can be grown, its ability to sustain life and the ease with which it can be transformed into a variety of tasty foods. It is the only common vegetable that can keep you alive for an extended period (just add a few other vegetables). In Ireland poor people really did pretty much live on potatoes and milk at one time.

Corn (*Zea mays*)
Field Corn is an easy to grow staple, but isn't very familiar to modern Americans (at least not in its unprocessed form). If you are going to grow it you need to find tasty ways of using it. Corn is an important staple grain in Africa however. You might also try growing three staples Corn, Beans and Pumpkins together in the Native American polyculture known as the three sisters.

Other staple crops

All of these have great potential, though they may need some processing to make them useful.

Amaranth / (*Amaranthus* species)

Amaranth can be used as a potherb or as a highly nutritious grain crop (that doesn't require much processing). I grow it as a dual purpose crop. I plant it densely and harvest thin the plants for greens until I am left with a nicely spaced stand of large plants. I then leave these to produce seed.

Amaranth self-sows vigorously; I planted it several years ago and ever since then I have more self-sown seedlings than I can use every year.

Buckwheat (*Fagopyrum esculentum*)

The shortest season of any grain (though not actually a grain), Buckwheat is very easy to grow in warm weather. It does require some processing however.

Peanut (*Arachis hypogaea*)

Fairly easy to grow in a warm climate, it needs a moist, loose, well drained fertile soil to do well. Peanuts are legumes and so fix nitrogen, though probably not if you are harvesting peanuts (it goes to make their protein.

Peanut can be used as an annual groundcover, though you will have to dig it up to harvest the nuts.

Oat (*Avena sativa*)

Oat is very hardy and is grown through the winter in hotter areas. The best Oats for the gardener are the naked varieties, as they need less processing.

Quinoa (*Chenopodium quinoa*)

This species is useful as an easily grown (if it likes your climate) and productive grain crop. Like Amaranth it doesn't need much processing.

Rice

Growing rice isn't as difficult to grow as people imagine, in fact the biggest problem is not the growing, but the processing. Upland rice is the easiest to grow as it is hardier and only requires moist soil rather than shallow water. All you need is a fairly long growing season.

Soybean *Glycine max*)

Fairly easy to grow and requires no processing. It does need warm weather however.

Tepary Bean (*Phaseolus acutifolius*)

This small bean is native to the southwest and can still be found growing wild there. It has been cultivated as a drought resistant crop by native Americans for over 5000 and could be a good choice for hot dry areas.

Wheat

Not difficult to grow, but it needs some processing to remove the seed coat before it can be made into flour. Growing wheat requires quite a bit of space, but as one of our most familiar staples it may be worthwhile. The growing plants also supply a lot of organic matter to the soil, both from their roots and their stems.

In a dry climate wheat can be planted in fall, to mature in spring. In this way it can grow without irrigation. After harvest there is still time to plant a drought resistant summer crop.

Sorghum (*Sorghum bicolor*)

This easily grown grass is originally from Africa and has been used in a variety of ways.

Perhaps most importantly it was once used as a source of sweetener. The juice can be expressed from the plants and boiled down to make a tasty syrup. This was once very popular in pioneer America, but disappeared with the advent of cheap sugar.

Some varieties of Sorghum are grown for the edible seed, which can be popped like popcorn.

Others varieties are grown as a source of biomass, as they can get very tall, to 12 feet or more.

Sorghum is sometimes called Broom Corn because some varieties were used to make brooms.

Other staples

Though this section is about staple vegetables, I think I should also mention a couple of staple foods that come from trees. Both Chestnuts and Oaks provide important bulk carbohydrates and have been staple foods in their respective regions. Acorns require processing to make them edible however. See Nuts for more on these.

Perennial vegetables

Perennial vegetables deserve more attention than they normally receive. Just as fruit trees provide food year after year with relatively little work, perennial vegetables can do the same. Generally these plants need little attention once established and can be planted in any small spare space. Of course these plants are only useful if you like what they produce and actually eat them. If you don't then they are just unusual and interesting ornamentals.

Quite a few perennial vegetables exist, but only asparagus, artichoke and rhubarb are grown with any regularity. Garlic, leek, and potato are actually perennial too, though we grow them like annuals).

Perennial vegetables are not a substitute for annual crops, but provide another layer of low-maintenance crops that supplement the annual vegetable garden. Some also have other garden uses as screens, sun shades, groundcovers and more.

Long term perennial vegetables can be beneficial for the soil as they help build it up through leaf fall and root sloughing, If the soil is undisturbed its natural structure can re-establish itself (of course digging perennial roots will disturb this).

The obvious advantage of perennial crops is that you don't have to plant seed every year and they don't have to grow from tiny seeds every year. Because they start out bigger, they can grow a lot faster.

There are some disadvantages to perennial crops and in all honesty I must say they are not nearly as valuable as the fruit trees or shrubs. Annuals can put all of their energy into producing food, whereas perennials have to also put energy into growth and maintenance. Also perennials last for more than one season, thus enabling disease and insect pests to get established and spread. An example of this is the Potato, which is a perennial in mild climates, but prone to disease problems when grown in this way.

One way around the disease problem is to plant / replant, whereby you actually dig up the whole crop and then replant some part of it in a different part of the garden. This is why shallots, garlic and potatoes are normally grown in this way.

Another problem with perennials is that they take up space year round and most aren't productive enough to justify taking up space in the intensive vegetable garden. Fortunately most are also fairly independent and can be planted anywhere suitable conditions are found. You might also have some special perennial beds close to the vegetable garden. The more rugged plants work well as buffer zones to protect the more delicate annuals from insect pests and wind.

Probably one of the biggest problems of perennial vegetables really has nothing to do with their qualities or cultivation. It is simply that it can be difficult to find material (seed or vegetative) to plant. Some of the rarer crops are almost impossible to obtain.

Gophers can make it hard to grow perennial vegetables. If not protected by wire these rodents will find anything edible if given enough time. In such cases you may want to grow them in beds protected with wire mesh (you could even harvest root crops by simply pulling up the wire).

There are a surprising number of useful perennial vegetables if you start looking. Most aren't very common, but have been cultivated as crops at one time or another (sometimes frequently).

Where to grow

Where you put them depends upon the kind of plant and how it is harvested.

The root crops must be disturbed to harvest them, so they are often grown in the annual vegetable garden, where they are treated more like annuals. They are dug up every autumn and a portion of them are replanted. Often the larger roots and tubers are eaten, while the rootlets and smaller tubers are replanted to produce a crop next year. In some cases you don't have to replant part of the crop, enough will remain in the ground to regrow without your help. Such plants tend to be fairly independent and can compete well enough to go in the semi-wild garden, in their own permanent patch.

Some plants just stay in an out of the way place and you harvest their greens or bulbs for a few weeks each year. These are commonly planted in their own bed too. In some cases you might have a special bed for growing a specific perennial vegetable. Plants such as Camas, Lilies and Cannas need to increase to a critical mass of plants before they become very useful for food. Pick too early and you risk wiping them out. Other plants (Chinese Artichoke, Chufa, Oca) are almost weedy in their ability to grow and multiply. These don't need quite as much care.

Perennializing biennials and annuals

When thinking about perennial food beds don't overlook the biennials and annuals. With the right techniques some of these self-sow so readily that they can be grown in perennial beds. These include Burdock, Cilantro, Chicory, Parsnip, Carrot, Hamburg Parsley (of course you may still have pest problems when grown in this way).

Some useful perennial crops

Unfortunately a lot of the best perennial vegetables are from the tropics and can't survive the winter in northern gardens. Here are a few of the hardier types that are useful enough to be used regularly.

Artichoke, Globe (*Cynara scolymus*) Zones 9-11

The Artichoke is one of the most outstanding vegetable foods of all, a succulent almost decadent treat (canned hearts are just a pale imitation of the fresh article).

Unfortunately Artichoke isn't well suited to growing in most of the United States as it isn't very hardy and prefers mild winters and cool summers. In cold areas it can be protected with thick mulch, brought indoors or even grown as an annual. If the summer is too hot and dry (and you neglect to water) it will die back and go dormant.

This is an attractive plant in spring when it is young, but towards the end of the summer it can get a bit ragged. It is a big plant and needs quite a bit of space for the amount of food it produces, but it can be put almost anywhere (even in the ornamental garden).

Artichoke needs fertile soil and lots of moisture to be really productive, but it's worth it for those fantastic hearts.

Artichoke is also a good source of biomass and has deep penetrating roots that loosen the soil to a considerable depth.

Artichoke, Chinese (*Stachys affinis*)

The above ground parts of this plant closely resemble the related Mints, but don't have aromatic foliage. In moist fertile soil and full sun conditions it grows like a weed and produces an abundance of small tasty tubers. It is propagated by planting the tubers (or leaving some behind when harvesting).

Artichoke, Jerusalem (*Helianthus tuberosus*) Zones 2-9

This tall perennial Sunflower produces edible tuberous roots. It is hardy, easy to grow and very productive, though not particularly nutritious. It can get quite tall – to 12 feet or more, so can be useful to give temporary height to the garden and as a deciduous screen or "hedge". The small yellow Sunflowers appear in late summer and are quite pretty, but the tall plants tend to look straggly unless planted en masse. Often the lower leaves die off as the plant gets bigger, so it is sometimes planted behind other plants or a fence to hide this.

Jerusalem Artichoke is easy to grow from tubers or parts thereof. It will grow in most soils, but is most productive in a moist fertile one. Because it gets so big and spreads so easily it is best planted in a permanent bed out in the wilder part of the garden. One criticism of the plant is that it can be hard to eradicate once established, but I haven't found this. I just wait until the tubers have sent up shoots a couple of feet tall and pull them out of the ground,

Asparagus (*Asparagus officinalis*) Zones 4-9

Asparagus is a good example of what perennial vegetable can do for us. It is easy to grow, tough, salt tolerant, drought tolerant, it often self-sows and may last for 40 years. It doesn't like very mild winters where it doesn't get a long enough rest period. It must have protection from gophers too.

The main drawback with Asparagus is that it takes up quite a bit of space, which usually means planting it away from the main vegetable garden. For maximum productivity it is usually grown in its own specially fertilized and mulched bed. It can also be grown more casually, scattered around the ornamental garden, as an annual "hedge" or in the forest garden (though it needs full sun). The tall feathery plants make a good background foliage planting.

It is usually grown from seed or 1 year old roots and should be mulched regularly.

Canna (*Canna edulis*)

With a specific name like edulis you may have wondered if your ornamental Cannas were edible. They are, but they probably won't be as productive as those cultivars bred specifically for food use. The starchy roots are an important food crop in some tropical areas. They are sweet and tasty when baked like potatoes. The young leaves can also be eaten and are quite good.

Canna can be grown in temperate areas, though they may need a mulch to prevent the ground freezing (or you could bring the roots inside for the winter). They need moist soil (they are sometimes grown as pond plants) and full sun. The best varieties are propagated vegetatively, though it can also be grown from seed. Normally a stand is dug up and some are replanted, while the rest is eaten

Canna can grow into a big plant and produces a lot of biomass. It is also beautiful of course (perhaps too beautiful for you to want to eat it).

Chayote (*Sechium edule*) Zones 9-10

I already discussed this tender perennial in the section on Climbing Plants.

Chufa (*Cyperus esculentus* var *sativus*)

This species is more productive and less invasive than the wild forms. It will grow in moist soil or shallow water. It is most productive when grown in light sandy soil. See Aquatic plants for more on this.

Fuki (*Petasites japonicus*)

The leaf stalks of this large plant are commonly eaten in Japan. They can be used as groundcover in moist shady soil (it grows naturally by the side of streams), or under fruit trees. It is easily grown by dividing the rootstock to leave a bud on each piece. When my plant arrived in the mail I was immediately able to divide it into 4 plants.

This is one of those super plants, which spreads by means of creeping rhizomes and can get very big when growing in moist soil. The leaf stalks sometimes grow to 6 feet long, with leaves 3 feet wide! These large leaves require shade and a plentiful supply of moisture to support them. My potted plants wilted when in direct sunlight, even when sitting in a tray of water!

This plant is not only edible, it is also a stunning ornamental for shady moist soil, such as around the edge of a pond.

The spring leaf stalks are boiled for 10 minutes and then the skin is peeled off. They can then be eaten or added to soups and stews.

Groundnut (*Apios tuberosa*)

This species is a reliable producer of tuberous edible roots, but takes 2 years to produce them. See Vines for more on this.

Good King Henry (*Chenopodium bonus henricus*)

This European perennial is grown for its tasty spring shoots which are cooked like Asparagus. A very vigorous and independent plant, it can be propagated from seed. Once you have grown plants from seed, they can be multiplied by division.

Mashua (*Trapaeolum tuberosum*)

I already dealt with this productive, beautiful and tasty Andean tuber in the section on Climbing Plants.

Mushrooms

It is possible to cultivate some mushroom species in the garden as another crop layer. With a little knowledgeable attention some species will even naturalize and come back year after year. See Mushrooms for more on this.

Oca (*Oxalis tuberosa*) Zones 7-10

This vigorous South American tuber plant originated in the same region as the potato and like that plant it is grown for its tasty edible tubers. I have found it to be very low maintenance, in fact most of the attention it has received has been about removing if from where it wasn't wanted.

Oca is easily grown from tubers, though it is a short day plants and so doesn't produce them until late in the year.

Onion, Egyptian (*Allium cepa* var *viviparum*)
Zones 3-9
This unusual variety of Onion grows like a green Onion and then puts out a cluster of small bulbils instead of flowers. These in turn produce their own green onions and more bulbils. The weight of these bends over the stems and these bulbils then take root and send up clusters of green shoots of their own. It is sometimes called the Walking Onion because of its ability to move around in this way.

The plant can be grown from seed, but is usually propagated vegetatively by means of the bulbs or bulbils. It grows in most soils, but likes full sun. I like this plant because of its independence. It is probably the most drought tolerant and self-sufficient of all the Onion varieties and once established you can forget all about it except for harvesting.

The plants can be used as green Onions in spring, later the small bulbs and bulbils can be eaten.

Onion, Potato (Allium cepa var aggregatum)
This perennial Onion is my favorite perennial food plant and deserves to be much more widely grown. It is quite similar to the Shallot in that it is easy to grow, but produces much larger bulbs (up to 3-4" in diameter). It is also harder to find.

It can easily be grown from seed (mine grew 4" diameter bulbs in one season) and can then be propagated from the bulbs.

Onion, Welsh (*Allium fistulosum*)
This non-bulbing species is grown as a source of green onions. It is easily grown from seed and can then be multiplied from offsets.

Ostrich Fern (*Matteucia struthiopteris*)
This is one of the most widely grown ornamental ferns as well as the most useful edible species. The edible shoots (known as fiddleheads because of their resemblance to the head of a violin) are gathered and eaten in spring when they first emerge.

The newly emerging fronds are only good for 2 or 3 weeks in spring when they first begin to uncurl. They are gathered up until they get to 6 or 8 inches in height (larger fronds don't taste good) by breaking them off as low down as they snap easily. The brown fuzz is removed and they are steamed or boiled for 10 minutes (they contain toxic thiaminase so shouldn't be eaten raw).

Ostrich Fern is usually propagated by division (as a fern it doesn't produce seed). It naturally grows in shady, moist, acid, woodland soil and makes a good groundcover for such areas.

Pokeweed (*Phytolacca Americana*)
With its purple and green stems and shiny purple berries Pokeweed is a spectacular plant by any measure. It isn't very suitable for small gardens though; as it can reach ten feet in height when growing in full sun and rich moist soil. It will grow in part shade but prefers full sun.

Poke can be propagated while dormant by dividing the crown, to leave a bud on each piece. It can also be grown from seed (soak in sulfuric acid for 5 minutes to simulate the trip through a bird). It self-sows readily (bird sown seedlings spring up everywhere) and grows so vigorously that it can easily become a weed.

Pokeweed appears in every book on American poisonous plants because almost all parts are very poisonous (especially the root). However it also appears in most books on American edible plants, because the young spring shoots are very edible. They are good enough that they are sometimes cultivated and have been called the most widely used American wild green food

The shoots are eaten when up to eight inches tall, but must be properly cooked to be edible. Prepare them by peeling off the outer leaves and cooking them in boiling water for 1 minute, then drain, add new boiling water and boil for another minute. You then drain them again (to remove most of the water soluble toxins), add fresh boiling water and cook for a further 10 or 15 minutes. When they are cooked you drain them again and discard the water.

Prickly Pear Cactus (Opuntia species) Zones 6-10
These architecturally dramatic plants have beautiful flowers and colorful edible fruit (and edible pads). They go well in desert gardens, but look a bit incongruous elsewhere (there prickliness is also frowned upon in Feng Shui).

These species can be grown from seed, but this is slow. Individual pads can be separated from the plant and rooted in well drained soil. This is much faster and easier than seed.

Cacti need well-drained soil and are extremely drought tolerant (in gardens they are most often killed by over-watering). Some varieties are quite tall and make good hedge plants (the spiny varieties are best for this). Most are hardy to 20° F. and some can go much lower.

Rhubarb (*Rheum rhaponticum*) Zones 2-9

Rhubarb is a vigorous plant with a strong bold shape and makes a good ornamental. It doesn't usually self-sow, but doesn't need to because it is a long-lived perennial. Very hardy, it doesn't actually like hot weather very much (put it in part shade in hot climates). The large leaves needs plenty of moisture, especially in hot weather.

You either adore Rhubarb or don't understand why anyone would eat it. It isn't very nutritious, but nor is it very demanding and it will grow quite happily by itself in any spare corner. It can also be used as a root barrier between wild areas and tamer ones. Give it a mulch of manure annually for best production.

Rhubarb is usually propagated by root division, but some strains can be grown from seed surprisingly quickly. The not very interesting flowers may grow to 5 feet in height, though you usually cut them off to prevent seeding (and waste of energy).

Right now my whole family is asking if the rhubarb is ready.

Scorzonera (*Scorzonera hispanica*)

Scorzonera is usually grown for its edible roots, but the flower buds can also be cooked and eaten. The flowers have been added to salads, while the new spring growth has been used for salad greens.

This uncommon crop plant is grown from seed in much the same way as carrot, except that it is a perennial and is sometimes allowed to grow for 2 years to reach a larger size.

Seakale (*Crambe maritima*)

This species is a perennial relative of the Cabbage. It is a fairly easy plant to grow; the hardest part is finding seed to get started. Once you have some plants it is easily propagated by root cuttings.

The new spring shoots can be prepared like Asparagus.

Shallot (*Allium cepa* var *aggregatum*) Zones 4-9

This independent plant is the most widely used perennial Onion. It is a fairly common vegetable and easy to obtain (try the supermarket) and grow. It can produce up to 10 bulbs per plant, so can be very productive.

Skirret (*Sium sisarum*)

This member of the carrot family was once quite widely grown, but fell out of use after the introduction of the potato. It produces a cluster of fleshy edible roots that are quite good.

Skirret can be grown from seed fairly easily, but once you have some plants it's much easier to propagate them vegetatively. Select the best tasting plants and divide them annually.

Strawberries, Alpine

The berries are small but quite prolific and have a long bearing season. I have harvested Alpine Strawberries for 10 months of the year.

Taro (*Colocasia esculenta*)

Though rarely grown in this country, Taro is an important crop in tropical areas and a huge number of cultivars have been obtained. It is mostly grown for the edible tubers, but the leaves and leafstalks are also eaten. Some varieties are grown as an ornamental in cooler areas, though the tubers must be dug and stored indoors for the winter (it can survive to 32° F.). It manages to survive outdoors in my garden by going dormant.

Taro needs a moist soil and is often grown as a pond plant in shallow water. It tolerates part shade.

Taro is a member of the Arum family but the food cultivars don't have the calcium oxalate crystals commonly associated with plants of that family. The ornamental Elephant Ears is the same species but may not be edible. The Violet Stem Taro is commonly sold as a pond plant. This variety is not only attractive, but is also said to have edible stems, leaves and corms (I haven't had mine long enough to try it). If you want to grow it as a food crop I suggest you go online to find sources of suitable cultivars.

Tree Kale (*Brassica oleracea* var *ramosa*)
This perennial species can be grown from stem cuttings. It is a little tougher than the biennial Kales, so I often remove the leaf midribs, but the flavor isn't bad. It is very perennial and plants have been growing in my garden for at least 5 years with no help from me. Apparently there are some perennial Kale varieties with better flavored leaves, but I have never been able to find seed of them.

Winged Bean (*Psophocarpus tetragonobolus*)
This species is famed in the tropics as a nitrogen fixing multi-purpose wonder crop, with edible leaves, flowers, seed pods, seeds and tuberous roots. It is a vigorous plant and can grow up to 10 feet or more, but it isn't very hardy. The tops will be killed by any frost, though the roots may survive in the ground (Like a Scarlet Runner Bean) and re-sprout the following year. Then again they might not.

The seeds are harder to germinate than most beans as they have a hard seed coat. Nick or file this to allow water to penetrate.

Yacon (*Polymnia edulis*)
This species can be a very productive when grown in moist fertile soil (this shouldn't be allowed to dry out). It isn't day length sensitive like most other Andean tubers.

Yacon is usually propagated by digging up the roots in fall, removing the large tubers and replanting the rest (divide the crown to leave 2 growing buds on each piece).

The mildly sweet, crisp and succulent root resembles Jicama and can be used in the same ways. Like most members of the Sunflower family it produces a form of starch called inulin. Unfortunately this isn't very digestible for humans.

Herbs

Everyone who likes to cook and eat good food will want a selection of the familiar culinary herbs in their garden, they are truly essential. Ideally they should be grown somewhere close the kitchen door, where they will be convenient during cooking, Herbs don't just have culinary uses though, they are also used for medicines, cosmetics, teas, perfumes, potpourri, crafts, incense, dyes, insect repellents and more.

The herb garden as its own room

The history of the herb garden goes back almost as far as the cultivation of plants itself. In fact some herbs were no doubt tended in the wild before anyone had even thought of gardening. Long before gardens became places for recreation they were places for growing medicinal and culinary herbs and many gardening techniques were developed there. The herb garden of today is quite different from these old gardens, as we no longer need plants for their medicinal properties. It is still a familiar component of many conventional gardens, but it has lost a lot of its significance and become as much ornamental as useful.

I think it's time to bring back the real herb garden and expand it far beyond the familiar Parsley, Sage, Rosemary and Thyme. We may not need medicinal plants to treat serious illness, but could certainly use them to enhance our wellness. Many plants contain potent antioxidants and other valuable phytonutrients and we would be well advised to consume more of them, either as food or in tea. We can also grow flavorings, dyes, tea herbs , perfumes and more. You could have dozens or even hundreds of weird and wonderful useful plants in this garden, making it one of the most useful and horticulturally interesting parts of the garden. If you really get into this there is a real danger it could take over your whole garden (that would be an herb garden worthy of the name).

Herbs are so easy to grow that I have them all over the garden; anywhere I find their preferred growing conditions.

Companion Plants

Companion planting probably originated in the cottage garden, where aromatic herbs, flowers and vegetables are all grown in close proximity. Companion planting is a topic beloved of some fireside gardeners, but much common "lore" works better in books than it does in the garden. However even if it doesn't have semi-magical effects, it is still a good idea as it increases diversity.

Insectory plants

Plants of the carrot (*Apiaceae*), daisy (*Asteraceae*) and mint (*Lamiaceae*) families have small nectar and pollen laden flowers, that are important source of food for predatory and other beneficial insects (many of these are very small and can't get nectar from larger flowers). This is why the herb garden is always alive with bees and is another good reason for planting many of these plants.

Propagation

Most perennial herbs are propagated vegetatively (by root division, runners, cuttings or layering), as this ensures the plant is identical to its parent. It's also easy to grow most perennial herbs from seed, but their quality is often variable. Of course the annuals are usually grown from seed too.

Annual and biennial Culinary herbs

If you allow many of these annuals to set seed they will naturalize and come back every year. This means you only need to plant them once.

Anise (*Pimpinella anisum*)

This annual has a licorice-like flavor (like Fennel) and the leaves and seeds are used as flavoring. It self-sows readily and even can become a problem weed.

Basil (*Ocimum basilicum*)
Basil is easy to grow if it gets hot weather, but doesn't like cool weather at all (and can't stand frost).

This is my favorite herb (along with Garlic) and I treat it more like a vegetable than an herb. I can never have too much, because I use it by the bucketful to make pesto (and then freeze it). Basil is a great repeat harvest crop and may be cut several times in a season. It can also be multi-planted. I have never seen it volunteer, though it does produce lots of seed if allowed to flower (I save this for planting next year).

Basil is quite an attractive plant and can be grown as an ornamental for borders.

Caraway (*Carum carvi*)
The seeds are traditionally used for baked goods and in cabbage dishes. If you like the flavor the root can be eaten like carrot. It is easily grown from fresh seed and will self-sow if it likes the conditions.

Chervil (*Anthriscus cerefolium*)
This tasty herb is used for flavoring eggs, soups and salads. It is easily grown from fresh seed and prefers cool weather.

Coriander (*Coriandrum sativum*)
This important annual is a dual purpose crop providing two quite different, but equally delicious foods.

The leaves are better known by the Spanish name Cilantro or as Chinese Parsley. They have a distinctive flavor you either love or hate (I used to hate it, but through its use in Mexican food I have been converted).

The ripe seeds (pods) are known as Coriander and have an orangey spicy smell. They are used to flavor curries and other dishes. I also enjoy the green seedpods, as their flavor is a mix of Cilantro and Coriander.

This annual is grown from seed more easily than most members of the *Apiaceae*. It prefers cool weather and where I live it grows right through the winter, but disappears in summer. It self-sows so readily that I don't plant it anymore. I just make sure it sets plenty of seed.

Cumin (*Cuminum cyminum*)
The seed is used in curries, chili, soups and other dishes. It is easily grown from seed, but needs a long warm growing season to produce seed.

Dill (*Anethum graveolens*)
Dill is an essential herb if you are planning on doing any pickling. It self-sows in my garden.

Epazote (*Chenopodium ambrosioides*)
In Mexico this herb is an important flavoring for bean dishes. It is easy to grow and self-sows in my garden (it actually grows as a perennial there).

Parsley (*Petroselintum crispum*)
Invaluable for salads, sauces and flavoring. It is a biennial and grown from seed in rich moist soil. It self-sows readily, often to the point where it becomes a weed.

The tuberous rooted Hamburg Parsley has edible leaves and an edible Parsnip-like root (two crops in one).

Papaloquelite (*Porophyllum ruderale*)
This species is commonly used in its native Mexico as a warm weather substitute for Cilantro. It eventually grow up to 4 feet in height, but is best harvested when about 12″ tall.

Perennial culinary herbs

Chives (*Allium schoenoprasum*) Zones 3-8
Chives is a great edible ornamental, with a delicious mild onion flavor that is great raw or cooked. It is very easy to grow, quite drought resistant and even produces attractive purple flowers (these produce seed easily).

Chives thrive with little care and works well as an edging for paths, ornamental gardens and everywhere else. It forms dense colonies that need regular thinning, which is nice as you can just transplant the dormant clumps elsewhere in the garden.

Garlic (*Allium sativum*) Zones 3-8
This hardy perennial is one of the easiest and most rewarding crops to grow. I grow it in volume in the vegetable garden because we eat a lot of it. However if I have any small bulbs that are too much trouble to peel I plant these out around the garden for greens.

Garlic Chives (Allium tuberosum) Zones 3-8
I'm not a big fan of the flavor of Garlic Chives, but it is easy to grow and very ornamental. It can be used in much the same way as Chives.

Ginger (*Zingiber officinale*) Zones 6-10
Ginger is easily grown from a piece of root from the market, and it may grow to four feet in height. It isn't very hardy, but has survived outdoors in my garden, just dying back to the ground every winter. In colder climates it is commonly grown in pots and taken indoors for the winter. It is quite ornamental and may even produce flowers.

You can plant ginger in spring and harvest in fall, though it takes up to a year for the root to develop the best flavor. In the tropics they harvest the rhizomes and immediately replant part of it

Horseradish (*Armoracia rusticana*) Zones 3-10
Easily propagated from root cuttings and very permanent once established, it can even become a weed. Of course it is also an important (and very pungent) flavoring.

Lovage (*Levisticum officinale*) *Zones 5-8*
Not a very common culinary herb, but I've included it because it is one of my favorite no-work salad plants. The unusual flavor somewhat resembles Celery, but I like it better and crave it in salads and soups. When growing in ideal conditions it can get up to 10' tall and becomes a very spectacular edible ornamental. It is easily grown from seed, but division of dormant plants is quicker and easier.

Marjoram (*Origanum majorana*) Zones 8-10
Marjoram is great in salads, dressings, omelettes and more. It is another very independent plant, tolerant of drought but not cold. It likes well-drained sunny soil and can be grown from seed, cuttings or division.

Mexican Coriander (*Eryngium foetidum*) Zones 8-11
This species is used as a warm weather substitute for Cilantro, though I haven't had a huge amount of success with it.

Oregano (*Origanum vulgare*) Zones 5-10
Famous as the pizza herb, Oregano is hardy and drought tolerant. It has grown independently in my garden for the past 8 years.

Saffron Crocus (*Crocus sativa*) Zones 6-9
This isn't the poisonous Autumn Crocus - *Colchicum*). It is the source of the very expensive spice saffron, which is important for its color as well as its distinctive flavor. It's expensive because each plant only produces a ridiculously tiny amount (the tiny styles of the flower are the saffron), I can't imagine who first though of using the styles of a flower as food but someone did (or harvesting it for a living for that matter).

Saffron is a very independent plant, I planted some about 5 years ago and then lost it, yet it persisted with no care at all. It is propagated by means of offsets of bulb and is easy to grow.

The narrow leaves resemble long narrow blades of grass and the plant is only really obvious when in bloom in autumn.

Sage (*Salvia officinalis*) Zones 5-9
One of the most important culinary herbs, Sage can be grown from seed or cuttings in well-drained sunny soil. It is very independent and grows without any help.

There are quite a few varieties of Sage. The variegated types are more attractive, but not so hardy. There are also large leaved varieties, but according to my son (who is addicted to raw Sage) the common small leaved gray green type has the best flavor. The blue flowers can be added to salads.

Spearmint (*Mentha spicata*) Zones 4-9
This tasty mint is commonly used as culinary flavoring and for tea. It is very easy to grow and can get quite invasive. It tastes best when growing in moist soils.

Tarragon (*Artemisia dracunculus*) Zones 4-7
When buying this important culinary herb make sure you get a superior French variety. These can only be propagated from cuttings (any Tarragon seed will be of the inferior Russian Tarragon). Tarragon likes well-drained soil.

Sweet Tarragon (*Tagetes lucida*)
This species is sometimes used as a substitute for true tarragon in areas with mild winters. It can't stand frost and in colder areas can be grown in containers and brought inside for the winter. It can be grown from seed or cuttings.

Thyme (*Thymus vulgaris*) Zones 4-9
This low-growing plant is one of the most important culinary herbs in French cooking. It likes well-drained sunny soil and can be propagated from seed, cuttings or division. Some cultivars grow to a foot or more in height, others creep. Thyme is quite drought tolerant but needs occasional watering for good growth.

Vietnamese coriander (*Polygonum odoratum*) Zone 11
This species tastes similar to Cilantro and can be used in the same ways. It isn't a very common herb, but has become a staple in my garden because it likes hot weather and comes into its own in summer when Cilantro bolts and disappears. In rich moist soil it grows like a weed. It can tolerate very mild frost and usually survives the winter in my garden.

Wasabi (*Wasabia japonica*) Zone 8-10
This Japanese species is used like the related Horseradish is used in the west. It is not nearly as easy to grow however (or find the plants to grow). It grows naturally in moist soil and part shade and is propagated by seed, or by dividing the rhizomes (this is usually done when harvesting the roots). Like many other Brassicas I find it gets attacked by aphids.

Woody Herbs

Bay (*Laurus nobilis*) Zones 8-10
A tree rather than a herb, but an important culinary flavoring nevertheless. A Mediterranean plant, it is drought tolerant, but not very cold hardy but. In the right climate it can be very vigorous and one plant is usually plenty to supply the kitchen (though they work quite well in pairs as potted plants). It can be quite formal looking when clipped.

Bay is another of the key flavorings of French cooking. The tough leaves are added to dishes while cooking to impart their flavor, but they are removed when serving.

California Bay Laurel (*Umbellularia californica*)
The leaves of this native American tree can be used in the same ways as the Bay, but have a somewhat stronger flavor. Bay Laurel is commonly used on its native west coast, but is rarely seen elsewhere.

Myrtle (*Myrtus communis*) Zones 9-10
The aromatic leaves of this hardy evergreen shrub are an important flavoring in Italian cooking. They are used like Bay leaves. See Shrubs for more on Myrtle.

Rosemary (*Rosemarinus officinalis*) Zones 7-10
Rosemary is very drought tolerant, but not particularly hardy. In my garden it grows like a weed to become a large bush. There are also low-growing cultivars that make great groundcover.

Rosemary goes well with potatoes, eggs and other foods. Throw a few sprigs on the barbecue or use the slender twigs as skewers.

Tea herbs

I really enjoy growing my own tea materials rather than buying them from who knows where. If you really can't do without that morning caffeine there are even plants that contain it. You could even grow them all together in a special tea garden (maybe complete with a place to relax and prepare and drink tea).

It is easy and very rewarding to grow your own tea. Get rid of all of those boxes, go outside and grab a handful of leaves to make some real tea. Get yourself a tea pot and learn how to use it properly, or a tea ball if you normally use tea bags. Herbal tea doesn't have to be weak and watery as in many commercial tea bags. You can double or triple the amount of leaf and make real industrial strength brews. You can also mix herbs together to make your own blends. If you get good at this there may even be commercial possibilities.

Many of these herbs are vigorous spreading plants, independent enough to grow anywhere suitable conditions exist and need to be confined more than encouraged. I can use all of the Peppermint leaves I can get, so am perfectly happy with this situation.

The flavor of many of these herbs varies considerably (especially when grown from seed), so be sure to taste a plant before you buy it, to make sure it is what you expect.

The best time to harvest most herbs is just before the flowers open, as they are filled with the most essential oils at this time. I cut the whole stalks and dry them in paper grocery bags in a warm, dry, dark, place. When they are thoroughly crisp and dry, you crumble them up and store in an airtight container (it is essential that they are thoroughly dry otherwise they will mold). The whole process is easy and doesn't take much time.

The best tea plants include:

Bee Balm (*Monarda didyma*) Zones 4-10
The strongly scented flowers can be added to salads. The leaves are used for tea, either alone, with other herbs or added to black tea. It is very important to choose a good variety though as some can be quite unpleasant. Bee Balm prefers moist, rich soil and grows from seed or division. It is beautiful enough to be grown as an ornamental.

Catnip (*Nepeta cataria*) Zones 3-9
This tough plant not only survives unaided in my garden it also self-sows and spreads. You probably know that cats are attracted to the aromatic leaves. You may not know it is also makes a pleasant tea. Grow from seed or by division of established clumps.

Chamomile (*Chamomilum nobile*) Zones 5-8
Chamomile tea, made from the white daisy-like flowers, is drunk for pleasure and to aid digestion. It is also used as a skin wash and hair rinse. The more flowers you pick, the more you get, so harvest (and dry) them regularly.

Fennel (*Foeniculum vulgare*) Zones 5-11
This tough aromatic perennial is very drought tolerant. The Anise flavored seeds and flowers make great tea. The tender new spring shoots and foliage are a delicious (though strongly flavored) salad material.

Lemon Balm (*Melissa officinalis*) Zones 5-8
This perennial isn't particularly attractive, but it attracts insects and is easy to grow (it self-sows readily and can spread to become a weed). It grows in most soils, even dry ones and can be useful as a minor groundcover. Grown from seed or root cuttings, it is most often used for tea.

Lemon Verbena (*Aloysia triphylla*) Zones 8-10
This tender little plant grows into a small tree in mild winter areas. The aromatic lemon scented leaves make a nice tea. See Shrubs for more on this

Licorice (*Glycirrhiza glabra*) Zones 7-10
This hardy perennial can be used to make an outstanding tea. Unlike many delicately flavored herbal brews, licorice tea is strong and already sweet. You need to leave the root to steep for some time to get the full flavor (the same piece of root can be used for tea more than once). It is also an important medicinal herb.

Licorice can be grown from seed, but it is faster and easier to divide the plants.

Mints (*Mentha* species) Zones 4-9
Probably the most popular herbal tea plants, the mints are quite easy to grow from seed, but the resulting plants will be very variable in quality. The best varieties are usually propagated vegetatively. The Mints are very imperialistic and aggressive (which is great if you like tea), so if space is limited you might want to plant them within a barrier. Make sure you plant a high quality variety, if it is going to be invasive you may as well benefit from it.

Mints do best in rich moist soil (in dry soil their flavor is decidedly inferior). I much prefer Peppermint (*M. piperita*) for tea, though Spearmint (*M. spicata*) is nice too.

New Jersey Tea (*Ceanothus americana*) Zones 4-8
This ornamental shrub is one of the best native wild tea species. See Shrubs for information on useful western species.

Roselle (*Hibiscus sabdariffa*)
The calyx of the attractive flowers can be used to make a tart, red tea. It is a tender perennial, but has to be grown as an annual in colder areas. It can be grown from seed, but needs warm conditions to germinate. See Shrubs for more on this.

Stevia (*Stevia rebaudiana*) Zones 11+
Not a plant to drink by itself, but it is the best (the only) sweetener for any herbal tea. It can also be used as a sweetener in cooking. My children wrap a large Spearmint leaf in a small Stevia leaf for the ultimate in natural mint candies.

Stevia is a tender perennial, but has survived the last three winters in my garden (and at least 30 or more nights of freezing weather).

Tea (*Camelia sinensis*) Zones 7-11
I have been experimenting growing real tea, which is produced by an evergreen shrub. It contains caffeine of course. See Shrubs for more on this.

Yaupon (*Ilex vomitoria*)
The specific name of this evergreen shrub hardly inspires confidence, but don't let it fool you, this is one of the best native tea plants and even contains caffeine.

Wild tea herbs

There are quite a few good wild tea herbs out there and you may want to experiment with growing some. The best include:

American Pennyroyal (*Hedeoma pulegoides*)
Navajo tea (*Ephedra* species)
Navajo tea (*Thelesperma* species)
Yerba Buena (*Satureja douglasii*)
Yerba Santa (*Eriodictyon californicum*)

Flowery herbs

The following herbs are often grown purely for their ornamental qualities, but they all have other uses too.

Angelica (*Angelica archangelica*) Zones 4-9
A spectacular biennial plant up to eight feet high. It can be grown from seed, but this is only viable for a few months. It's probably best to simply allow the plants to self seed. In my garden in Connecticut I bought one plant and allowed it to set seed and the following year I had seedlings all over the place. It needs moist soil and is sometimes sold as a pond plant.

The stems are used as a flavoring for desserts.

Anise Hyssop (*Agastache foeniculum*) Zones 7-10
The sweet anise flavored leaves and flowers can be added to salads and used for tea. A vigorous perennial is self-sows in my garden (until my daughter finds and eats it). The beautiful blue flower spikes are a good source of nectar (bees love them) and can earn it a place in the ornamental garden.

Borage (*Borago officinalis*)
Annual Borage is easily grown from seed and self-sows readily (plant it once and it will usually come back). The pretty blue flowers are used in salads (remove hairy sepals) and as a decoration. This is quite a pretty and the bees like it, so I often allow it to grow itself in my garden. However I haven't found much use for it; a plant whose main product is a part of the flower doesn't strike me as very productive.

Calendula (*Calendula officinalis*)
I planted Calendula a few years ago and since then it has self-sown all around the garden and become

essentially a weed. The bright orange or yellow flowers are perhaps the most ubiquitous flower in my garden, there are some flowers in bloom pretty much year round. I recently bought seed of a new variety (Calypso Orange) that is said to contain more of the active medicinal ingredient (faradiol).

Calendula flowers are an important medicinal herb for wounds and burns. They are also used as a culinary herb, in salads and for coloring food.

Dead Nettles (*Lamium galeobdolon, L. maculatum*)
These are some of the best bee plants, as well as being edible as a salad or potherb.

Elecampane (*Inula helenium*) Zones 3-8
This spectacular yellow flowered herb is often grown as an ornamental. The root is edible and has anti-bacterial properties. The seeds are distributed on Dandelion-like parachutes and can self-sow all over the place.

Hyssop (*Hyssopus officinalis*) Zones 3-9
The young leaves and bright blue flowers are added to salads. It is usually grown from seed in a dry sunny soil.

Poppies (*Papaver* spp)
The seed of these beautiful annuals is used as flavoring for baked goods. See Magical herbs.

Milk Thistle (*Silybum marianum*)
This spectacular thistle is easily grown in most soils. The leaves have been used as a potherb and even in salads when young. It is naturalized where I live.

Soapwort (*Saponaria officinalis*) Zones 3-9
The leaves and flowering tops of this drought tolerant aggressively spreading perennial can be used as soap or shampoo (hence the name).

Sweet Cicely (*Myrrhis odorata*)
The feathery leaves have a sweet anise flavor and are a nice addition to salads. The roots and green seedpods are also very good.

Sweet Cicely is perennial and can be grown from seed, or root division. Once established it can be quite persistent.

Medicinal herbs

There is little point in growing these unless you will really use them (unless you want them as ornamentals, are a plant collector or just like them). There are a lot of medicinal herbs out there, far more than I have room to mention here. Here are some of those I have found to be most interesting.

Aloe vera (*Aloe barbadensis*) Zones 10+
Aloe is an outstanding plant for burns, cuts, insect bites and skin irritation. Just split a piece of leaf and apply the slimy interior to the injured part.

Aloe is usually propagated from offsets, which are detached from the plant and replanted. It isn't at all hardy and doesn't even survive the relatively mild winter in my garden. However it does well in containers (it is succulent enough to not need frequent watering) and can be brought indoors for the winter (it grows quite happily as an indoor plant).

Andrographis paniculata
When a plant doesn't even have a common name you can be sure it's not very well known. This relatively unknown Indian annual is said to be superior to *Echinacea* for boosting the immune system. It also has adaptogenic properties, anticancer activity and more.

Arnica (*Arnica montana*) Zones 6-9
A hardy perennial, Arnica is usually grown from seed, or by dividing established plants.

Arnica is famed as an external treatment for bruises and inflammation. It is sometimes smoked in herbal smoking mixtures.

Ashwagandha (*Withania somnifera*) Zones 11+
An easy to grow tender perennial, but usually grown as an annual (it likes the same conditions as Tomato). It is an important tonic in ayurvedic medicine and has adaptogenic properties. It is sometimes called Indian Ginseng.

Comfrey (*Symphytum x uplandicum*) Zones 4-9
This is an important medicinal herb for treating burns and skin problems. It is also used as compost material (for which it needs to be grown in bulk) and as animal feed (it is rich in protein and vitamin B12). See Soil improving plants for more on this.

Echinacea (*Echinacea purpurea*)
(*E. angustifoia*) Zones 3-9
These herbs are well known for their immune system boosting and antibacterial (and antiviral) properties. They are also attractive, easy to grow perennials and are often grown purely as ornamentals. They can be grown from seed or division.

Feverfew (*Tanacetum parthenium*) Zones 5-8
A tough, drought tolerant perennial, it self-sows in my garden as a weed. It took me several years to get rid of it and it has since come back. It has an important use in treating migraine and rheumatism.

Fo-Ti (*Polygonatum multiflorum*)
In China the root is used to promote longevity and be a general tonic. It is said that a Professor Li Chung Yun lived to be 256 (outliving 23 wives) by drinking an elixir containing this herb. You have to wonder why he never gave it to any of his wives though.

This plants is sometimes grown as a vegetable for its young spring shoots It can be grown from seed, semi-ripe cuttings or division. It likes moist woodland soil.

Gotu Kola (*Hydrocotyle asiatica*) Zones 8-10
This tender perennial is in the Parsley family and has a somewhat similar flavor. The leaves are said to promote longevity and be beneficial for the brain. It is also good for wounds and burns. This is a very important plant in Ayurvedic medicine as a blood purifier, wound herb and more. A few leaves should be eaten daily for a healthy brain (everyone needs a healthy brain).

This creeping species spreads quickly in warm humid climates and has potential as a productive groundcover. It likes very wet soil or even shallow water. It can be grown from seed, but it's quicker to buy a couple of plants and watch them spread. It likes humidity, which explains why it did so much better in my garden in Connecticut than it does in my present garden in California.

Ginseng (*Panax ginseng*) Zones 4-8
Ginseng is grown from seed and takes 3-5 years to reach maturity. Not easy to grow in the average garden, it does much better in the semi-wild or wild garden, where it finds the deciduous woodland conditions it prefers. Some people grow it successfully though and make a minor business out of it.

In Asia Ginseng is considered to be a aphrodisiac, rejuvenator, promoter of long life and a general panacea. It is also said to be an adaptogen, which helps the body to resist external stress, lowers blood pressure, increases work capacity and mental acuity and helps one keep concentration during prolonged and intense mental work.

Mimosa tree (*Albizia julibrissi*n) Zones 7-9
The bark is said to induce feelings of happiness and is used to treat depression. Some people believe this plant is an ingredient in that witches brew known as Coca Cola.

A tough and drought tolerant little tree, it is a common ornamental in gardens around Santa Cruz. It can be propagated from seed, semi-ripe cuttings or root cuttings.

Roseroot (*Rhodiola rosea*) Zones 1-7
This extremely hardy plants is one of the few native American adaptogens, it is said to improve memory and act as a tonic.

Saw Palmetto (*Serenoa repens*) Zones 9-10
Saw Palmetto berries are best known for treating prostate problems, but also have sedative and tonic properties and are said to be an aphrodisiac.

Saw Palmetto can be grown from seed or suckers and likes a moist but well-drained soil.

Magnolia Vine (*Schizandra chinensis*) Zones 4-8
The fruit of this vigorous vine have tonic and adaptogenic properties similar to those of Ginseng. See Vines for more on this.

Siberian Ginseng (*Eleutherococcus senticosus*) Zones 3-8
The roots of this hardy shrub have many of the same properties as Ginseng, but it is easier to grow. It prefers part shade and could fit well into the forest garden.

Siberian Ginseng likes a rich, well-drained soil and can be propagated form seed, root cuttings or hardwood cuttings.

St Johns Wort (*Hypericum perforatum*) Zones 4-8
Grown from seed or by dividing established plants, it is a weed in my garden and throughout much of the west (it is illegal to grow in some states). The flowering tops are used to treat depression. The whole plant may be used externally for burns, wounds and sore muscles.

Water Clover (*Marsilea minuta*) Zones 8-11
The whole green plant is said to be beneficial for the brain. It also has medicinal properties (it reduces cholesterol, is a mild sedative and even reduces epileptic seizures). See Aquatic Plants for more on this.

Valerian (*Valeriana officinalis*) Zones 4-9
Valerian root is used as a mild sedative, usually in the form of tea. It is said to smell unpleasant like smelly socks, but I find it quite nice in small doses. Valerian is usually grown by dividing plants, but seed can also be used.

Water Purslane (*Bacopa monnieri*)
This fleshy plant is believed to be beneficial for the brain, as well as a mild sedative. See Aquatic plants for more on this.

Magical herbs

Human nature being what it is, mind altering plants have been an essential part of many cultures and they were once important garden plants. I'm including them here because I find them to be fascinating plants, but I am not condoning their use, or saying that they are in any way safe to use (some are definitely not safe and should be left alone).

Hemp (*Cannabis sativa*)
The best known and probably safest of the bunch, Hemp has been loved by humans like few other plants have ever been. Absurdly illegal for many years, it is no longer as prohibited as it once was. In California you can now get a doctors prescription to grow it. I was just up in Humboldt county and saw several legal plantings. It would be nice if every user were allowed to grow it for themselves, rather than being forced to finance various forms of criminal activity.

Diviners Sage (*Salvia divinorum*) Zones 11+
The leaves were chewed (fresh) or smoked (dried) to induce visions for divination by Mexican Indians. Unlike most other sages it prefers moist soil and part shade. Quite a large plant, it can get up to 6 feet tall (or even more in ideal conditions).

Morning Glory (*Ipomoea tricolor*)
The seeds of these exquisitely beautiful plants contain their own surprise in the form of lysergic acid, which gives them hallucinogenic properties (they were

used by the Aztecs to induce visions). Maybe its no coincidence the varieties have names like Heavenly Blue, Pearly Gates and Flying Saucers.

Ololiqui (*Rivea corymbosa*) Zones 11+
This tender perennial relative of Morning Glory is used in the same ways.

San Pedro Cactus (*Trichocereus pachanoi*)
Fairly easy to grow from seed. It was used for divination.

Less benign psychoactive plants include:
Syrian Rue (*Peganum harmala*)
The seeds are said to be aphrodisiac and hallucingenic.

Opium Poppy (*Papaver somniferum*)
The seed pods are the source of opium, which is composed of a variety of potent alkaloids (including morphine). The ripe dried seed pods also contain opium and can be used to make Poppy tea, though you wouldn't want to serve it as a tea party because it is illegal. I mention it here in case you are reading this book some time in the future, after the breakdown of government as we know it, and you need a strong analgesic. It is addictive and definitely not for recreational use.

Poppy tea is made by breaking up the dried seed pods to release all of the seeds (you don't want them). The broken up pods are then put in a blender with water and lemon juice and reduced to a puree. This is then simmered for 15 minutes at 170° (any hotter and the alkaloids may break down) and then strained and allowed to cool. It is more palatable when drunk with lemon and ice.

Datura / *Datura* species
The seeds and dried leaves of a number of Datura species have been used as a hallucinogen in Central and South America. However they contain scopolamine and other fairly toxic compounds and are best avoided. The beautiful night opening flowers have a fantastic scent though.

Passion Vine / *Passiflora* species
You probably already know about the edible fruits of these species. You probably don't know that all other parts are poisonous because they contain hydrocyanic acid and a number of potent alkaloids, including harmine and harmaline (these are found in a number of hallucinogenic plants and have been used to induce visions). The leaves have been smoked like Marijuana, but I must again emphasize they are toxic and the line between intoxication and poisoning is very fine.

Tobacco / *Nicotiana tabacum*
I have grown this even though I don't smoke because I love to grow useful plants of any description. I gave some of the dried leaves to a smoker friend who said it was far superior to bought tobacco. It is a tall and attractive plant and easy to grow from (the tiny) seed. It often survives our mild winters and lives for more than one year. It produces an abundance of seed if allowed to flower (and will self-sow if given the right conditions).

Tobacco contains nicotine, one of the most addictive drugs known and unless you are already hopelessly ensnared in its ambivalent embrace I suggest you avoid it like the plague (it has probably killed more people than the plague).

Fungi

Potent Psilocybe (*Psilocybe cyanescens*)
Magic Mushroom (*P. cubensis*)
Liberty Cap (*P. semilanceata*)
These species are illegal to grow in the USA because they contain psilocybin (and related chemicals, but occur widely in nature. Most can grow in wood chip mulch in the same way as King Stropharia. In fact in the right situation you may well already have them (or related species) growing without realizing it.

Flowers

Flowers belong all over the garden, which should be as beautiful as it is productive. Flowers are challenging and fun to grow and make the garden more interesting. Many gardeners have started out growing only vegetables, but most probably start growing some flowers too at some point. How many flowers you grow depends upon which muse distracts you. When thinking about growing flowers I look to the cottage garden for inspiration.

The uses of flowers

You can't argue that flowers enhance the appearance of your garden, but you might think that by taking up space with flowers you are reducing its productivity. This isn't necessarily the case however, many cottage garden flowers were originally introduced into gardens because they served some purpose. They may have been edible, they may have had medicinal properties or they may have simply smelled good. I also tend to favor flowers that have additional uses, as well as looking pretty. They may have edible flowers, a strong scent, or be useful for tea, medicine or flavoring.

Flowers increase the diversity of the garden by attracting beneficial insects (predators, pollinators and beauties). These insect attracting properties chiefly apply to the species plants and old fashioned varieties. The highly bred cultivars often don't produce nectar or pollen and so don't attract insects.

Cutting garden

Many garden flowers are grown for use as cut flowers, to bring the garden inside the house. Some people have a special cutting garden or bed, but more often the flowers are scattered around to decorate the garden and cutting is fairly random.

If you want to grow flowers methodically and have a succession of blooms, you have to treat this area like a vegetable garden. Make succession sowings to replace the plants you are harvesting (it's not quite this simple though, because many flowers are day length sensitive). It wasn't unusual for cottage gardeners to grow cut flowers for sale and you might try this too.

Specimen plants

Particularly spectacular plants may be used singly for their ornamental effect. Such plants as Angelica, Yucca, *Allium giganteum*, Imperial Lily, Globe Artichoke and Lovage.

Wildflowers

These weren't much grown in the cottage garden because there were so common outside it. Only unusual examples such as unusual colors or double flowered types would make it into cultivation. Of course things are very different today, when many wildflowers are becoming rare and the garden gives you the perfect opportunity to grow and get to know them.

Bee and Butterfly Plants

The best insect attracting plants are those with small flowers and lots of nectar, such as the members of the Daisy, Carrot and Mint families. Native species tend to be most attractive to butterflies and other insects and might be planted (or left in place) to encourage them.

Some cultivated flowers are fairly close to their original species and these can also be valuable insectory plants. These are often the old fashioned varieties with smaller, less gaudy flowers, a shorter blooming season and more scent.

Spring flowers

You don't always spend a lot of time relaxing outside in the spring garden, so these are usually best seen from the house and on paths to and from the front door. Plant them in groups rather than singly, - a single Daffodil every 10 feet won't impress anyone.

Bulbs

These are prized by ornamental gardeners because they come in such a convenient package. Attractive species that are also edible include the *Alliums, Brodiaea, Camassia, Erythronium, Gladiolus, Lilium* and more. These can sometimes be grown under deciduous trees as they flower early and complete their yearly cycle before the trees leaf out.

Where to plant

It is important to give your flowers (and all other plants for that matter) the kind of conditions they would naturally grow in. At the same time you need plants to go in certain parts of the garden (entrance garden, around the patio). The key is to choose the right plants for each growing environment.

Flowers are most often grown in the front garden and around the outdoor living area, where they are most visible. They might also be interplanted in the vegetable beds, either in their own section or amongst the vegetables. They can also be dotted around the garden in any suitable vacant place.

Support

Tall plants sometimes fall over, especially when they get wet, or in strong winds (this is a big deal for obsessive ornamental gardeners). Obviously this doesn't show them to their best advantage so they are often given support You can buy metal plant supports, but you can make your own from brushwood. Select some woody prunings and simply sharpen the butt ends, stick them in the ground and allow plants to grow up around them. The brush will eventually be mostly hidden by the foliage.

Easy to grow flowers

Some flowers are so easy to grow they are almost weeds. You simply put the seed or transplants in the ground once and leave them to it. They then self-sow and come back year after year. Self-seeding flowers in my garden include;

Pot Marigolds (*Calendula*)
Bellflowers (*Campanulas*)
Hollyhock (*Althaea*)
Mallows (*Malva*)
Chamomile (*Anthemis*)
Honesty (*Lunaria*)
Violets (*Violas*)
Sweet Rocket (*Hesperis*)
Poppies (*Papaver*)
Love-in-a-mist (*Nigella*)
Sweet Alyssum (*Alyssum*)
Maximilian Sunflower (*Helianthus*)

Perennial flowers

Most traditional cottage garden perennials were sufficiently well adapted to the garden to thrive with little or no attention (that was the whole point). Some species get very large and you must thin them occasionally so they don't overwhelm their neighbors. A few are quite invasive (*Saponaria, Campanula, Oxalis*) and are best isolated in their own beds, or confined behind barriers (perhaps plant them in large plastic containers with holes in the bottom).

Perennials need more planning than annuals because they may remain in the same place for years. It is simpler if they are planted in their own permanent mulched beds, or sections of beds and not mixed up with annuals or vegetables.

Traditional maintenance operations for perennials include supporting, mulching, watering, weeding and dividing. If you choose your plants carefully you shouldn't have to do much of this. You will have to divide them when they get overcrowded, but this is a very productive task you won't mind doing. This is because it gives you more plants than you started with and reinvigorates them at the same time. There is always a ready market for healthy interesting plants and if you have too many of these you might have a plant sale and recoup some of your costs.

Low-work useful perennials

Here are a few of the plants I really like and that seem to like me (or at least they do well in my garden).

Hollyhock (*Althaea rosea*) Zones 2-9

This essential traditional cottage garden plant may grow up to 10 feet tall and can bloom for months. It is a short lived perennial, but in some areas it is subject to rust disease and so is often grown as a biennial. If seedlings are started early enough it will flower in its first year. It produces seed in abundance and self-sows all over the place.

Like the related mallows the flowers, young leaves and green seedpods can be eaten.

Daisy (*Bellis perennis*) Zones 6-10

A common low growing weed of lawns, it can even

survive mowing (some say a lawn isn't complete without daisies). The white ray flowers (petals) can be added to salads.

Creeping Bellflower (*Campanula rapunculoides*)
This plant is not only very beautiful, it also has edible roots, shoots, leaves and flowers. Very easy to grow, it spreads by means of creeping roots and also self-seeds. It is so easy to grow it can even become a problem and has naturalized in some areas.

Daisy, Pyrethrum (*Tanacetum coccineum*)
Also (*T. cinerarifolium*) Zones 4-9
These attractive daisies aren't edible, but the flowers are the source of the organic insecticide pyrethrum. Some cultivars are much more potent than others, so choose one carefully. Add one tablespoon of dried flowers to a quart of boiling water (and a drop of liquid soap).

Ox Eye Daisy (*Chrysanthemum leucanthemum*)
Zones 3-10
Easily grown from seed, the flowers can be added to salads, while the tasty aromatic foliage can be used as a potherb or salad (it is very good).

Chicory (*Cicorium intybus*) Zones 3-10
The beautiful deep blue flower petals can be added to salads. The bitter leaves and roots are also edible. It is naturalized in my garden.

Dahlia (*Dahlia* species)
This spectacular ornamental is not only easy to grow and low maintenance, it also produces edible tubers quite similar to those of Yacon. The tubers of all Dahlia varieties are edible, but their quality for food varies considerably so you have to experiment.

Hibiscus (*Hibiscus* species)
The beautiful flowers are edible (good for tea), as are the leaves.

Pinks (*Dianthus* species) Zones 4-8
Pinks are well adapted to hot dry conditions and do really well in my garden. The old-fashioned Pinks had a strong Clove scent and were once used to flavor wine. They can also be added to salads.

Clove Pink - *D. plumarius*
Sweet William - *D. barbatus*

Maximilan Sunflower
(*Helianthus maximillianii*)
This attractive and drought tolerant perennial is rarely bothered by deer. It also gives you edible roots and mulch material. It can be grown by dividing established plants, or from seed (and self-sows freely).

Day Lily (*Hemerocalis* species)
Few garden flowers give as much as the Day Lily and ask so little in return Every part of the plant is edible, from the green spring shoots, to the flowers to the tuberous roots. I will grow easily in any reasonable soil, in sun or part shade and is so independent it has naturalized in many areas of the country.

Lilies (*Lilium species*)
L. candidum, L. martagon, L. chalcedonicum
These species don't like disturbance. They have edible bulbs and also produce spectacular edible flowers (if you can bring yourself to eat such a beautiful plant).

Musk Mallow (*Malva moschata*)
Attractive, hardy long blooming flowers and edible foliage and flowers. They are easily grown from seed and self-sow readily.

Balloon Flower (*Platycodon grandiflorum*) Zones 4-9
This pretty blue flower produces edible shoots. It is easy to grow.

Spiderwort (*Tradescantia virginiana*)
The leaves and flowers of Spiderwort are edible. It will grow in most soil types, but prefers a moist one. It can be grown from seed or division.

Biennial flowers

These have a 2-year life span, producing leaves in their first year and flowers in their second year. They don't always follow such a strict schedule however. If growing conditions are very good they will sometimes flower in their first year. They may also live for longer than two years.

Self-seeding biennials can be naturalized by planting them in the same spot two years running. In the second year the first years plants will flower and set seed for the following years.

Honesty (*Lunaria annua*) Leaves edible

Evening Primrose (*Oenothera biennis*)

This pretty biennial is easily grown from seed and self-sows readily. It is completely edible from flower to root. See Vegetables for more on this.

Sweet Rocket (*Hesperis matronalis*)

This fragrant biennial/perennial is very independent. The young leaves and flowers have been added to salads.

Annual flowers

By definition annuals only live for one year, then flower and die. However they don't always go by this strict schedule, in mild climates they sometimes linger on for a second year. Some annuals start their lives at the end of one year, but don't flower until the spring of the following year.

Annuals are mobile and adaptable and can be used anywhere in the garden. They are the easiest plants to plan for because they can be moved around the garden at your whim. If you don't like how they turn out, you can try again next year.

You can buy a limited selection of annuals as transplants, but often the most interesting types are only available as seed, so you have to grow your own. Fortunately annuals are dependent on seed, so most germinate fairly easily.

Siting

Annual flowers can be planted anywhere there is a suitable niche for them. They work well underneath flowering shrubs (which only flower for a short while and are then quite dull). They can be used to fill in any vacant spots, or to hide the bare lower parts of taller plants.

If you allow your annuals to set seed you can collect it in abundance. You will then have lots to experiment with and can scatter it around in promising disturbed soil in various places to see what works best.

Self-sowing

Many annuals will sow themselves after their first year. These are very useful, plant them once and they re-appear in the places best suited to them. However there are self- sowers and there are self-sowers. Some annual flowers self-sow so vigorously and enthusiastically that they essentially become weeds and you spend more time weeding them out than tending to them. These include Alyssum, Poppy, Calendula, Ipomoea and Malva. Its been my experience that the variety and numbers of self-sowing plants increases as the garden matures.

My favorite annuals

These are the annuals that I have found to be the easiest to grow (almost all self-sow in my garden). Most of these produce edible flowers or have other uses as well.

Sweet Alyssum (*Lobularia maritima*)

This pretty little creeping annual is an ever-present weed in my garden. The flowers and young foliage can be used in salads. It is a good edging plant to soften paths and borders.

Love-Lies-Bleeding *(Amaranthus hybridus)*

Not only is this species a classic ornamental, but it is also an excellent potherb and even a source of edible seed. Also *A. caudatus*

Pot Marigold *(Calendula officinalis)*

This is one of the first flowers I ever learned the name of. It produces bright orange or yellow flowers almost year round in my garden. The flowers can be added to salads and also have important medicinal properties. See Herbs for more on these.

Cosmos (*Cosmos sulphureus*)

The young foliage has been used as a potherb and in salads. It is actually cultivated as a food plant in Indonesia.

Mallow (*Malva sylvestris*)

This beautiful flower has happily naturalized in my garden. The leaves can be used for greens and the flowers can be added to salads.

California Bluebell (*Phacelia tanecifolia*)

This species produces pretty blue flowers and has been grown as an ornamental. It is also often planted as a green manure and to attract insects. It is also edible.

Marigolds (*Tagetes* species)

Widely grown as ornamentals, the roots of some cultivars have nematocidal properties. A few varieties (Fantastic, Orange Gem, Lemon Gem, Lulu), have tasty edible flowers, others aren't so good.

Nasturtium (*Trapaeolum majus*)

A beautiful low work flower, some varieties grow in clumps; some climb vigorously and others trail along the ground. They are easily grown from seed and do best on poor dry sunny sites. The flowers are one of the best edible flowers for salads.

Sunflower (*Helianthus annuuus*)

I consider no garden to be complete without at least a few tall spectacular Sunflowers. The taller varieties can be staked as a windbreak and used as support for climbers (give the Sunflowers a couple of weeks head start).

Useful wildflowers

There are many wild flowers that are not only attractive, but also provide food. If you give these the right conditions they will often grow so well that you will soon have more than you can use. The main problem with many of these is that they are so beautiful you feel guilty destroying them simply to eat. As such I look upon them more as novelty foods or emergency foods. Here are a few of the most useful species:

Balsamroot (*Balsamorhiza* species)
Camas (*Camassia* species)
Dog Tooth Violet (*Erythronium* species)
Gayfeather (*Liatris* species)
Mariposa Lily (*Calochortus* species)
Milkweed (*Asclepias* species)
Shooting Star (*Dodecatheon* species)

Scented flowers

These plants come into their own in the evening and at night, when their scents become stronger and your sense of smell keener. Strongly scented plants should be sited where you can most appreciate them (especially at night), which usually means close to the house. This might be near the windows (maybe even in window boxes), in planter boxes, on trellis attached to the house and around seating areas. Ideally they should also be sheltered from wind that might dissipate the scent.

White flowered plants (and varieties) tend to have more scent than colored ones, because they often open at night and use scent to attract pollinating insects.

Citrus (Citrus species) Zones 10-11
These are some of the most exquisitely scented plants of all. Of course they also produce a variety of delectable fruits, which make them essentials in any climate where they can survive the winter. Yes I know this isn't a flower, but I felt I had to mention it (and some other shrubs). See Trees for more on this.

Lavender (*Lavandula vera*)
The strongly scented flowers are most often used in perfumes and potpourri, but they have also been added to salads and used as flavoring for cookies and cakes. It is very drought tolerant and easy to grow.

Night Scented Stock (*Mathiola incana*)
I like this inconspicuous little annual for its lovely (and very strong) night scent.

Flowering Tobacco (*Nicotiana alata*)
This pretty flower with the lovely scent is a type of tobacco.

Patchouli (*Pogostemon patchouli*) Zones 11+
Patchouli can be grown from seed or by dividing established plants, unfortunately it isn't at all hardy. The leaves are the source of the perfume ingredient Patchouli oil, once so beloved of hippie girls.

Pelargoniums Zones 10-11
These drought tolerant plants have a whole range of scented leaves (lemon, mint, orange rose), They are quite frost tender and barely survive the mild frosts in my garden (they are often killed back to the ground). They grow well in containers and so can be taken indoors for the winter. They are easily propagated by soft cuttings.

The scented leaves of Lemon and Rose scented varieties have been used to flavor cakes (lay leaves on the bottom of the pan and remove after baking), drinks, sorbet and more (they aren't eaten though). The flowers can be added to salads.

Violet (*Viola odorata*) Zones 6-8
This little plant can work as a groundcover under other plants. A very vigorous plant, it spreads vegetatively and self seeds in suitably moist and partly shady conditions. The violet scented and flavored flowers have been added to salads and even made into jam.

The flowers and leaves of other purple flowered species have been added to salads (these aren't strongly scented).

Edible Flowers

A lot of ornamental flowers are edible, though often this means simply that they can be eaten, it doesn't necessarily mean they taste good. Many are used for their decorative effect, rather than their flavor.

Edible flowers can turn an ordinary salads into a work of art and considerably enhance your reputation as a chef. They have become quite fashionable in recent years and no book about growing food and flowers would be complete without a list of the edible ones. It is possible you are already growing a lot of edible flowers without realizing it. All you have to do is start using them.

Many other plants are overlooked as a source of edible flowers, for example fruit trees, shrubs, herbs and vegetables. Also remember that plants normally grown for their flowers may also produce edible leaves, roots, even seeds.

Alliums (any flowers should be good)	Anise Hyssop	Apple
Basil	Brassicas (all)	Bee Balm
Borage (blue petal part only – remove hairy calyx)	Black Locust (flowers only – rest poisonous)	Calendula (petals give color and flavor)
Centranthus ruber	Chrysanthemum petals	Chamomile
Chicory	Cilantro (taste like Cilantro, also green seed pods)	Citrus (taste first, some don't taste good)
Day Lily (taste first- some don't taste good)	English Daisy (Bellis perennis petals)	Dandelion (use individual petals)
Dianthus caryophyllus Clove Pink best,	Dianthus plumarius Cottage Pink not bad)	Elder
Fennel (tastes strongly of Fennel)	Hollyhock	Honeysuckle (L. japonica)
Hibiscus	Lavender	Lemon Verbena
Lilac	Mallows (all)	Mullein
Nasturtium (one of best)	Oregano	Garden Pea (not Sweet Pea)
Pelargonium (taste first, scented varieties can be excellent, others not good)	Plum	Poppy (petals add color)
Sunflower (petals)	Radish (excellent)	Rocket
Red Clover (T. pratense)	Redbud	Roselle (Hibiscus sabdariffa)
Roses	Salvias (Pineapple Sage S. horminum good)	Scarlet Runner Bean (good sweet base)
Squash (Stuffed blossoms are a delicacy)	Tagetes (taste first, most are unpleasant)	Viola (V. odorata is best)
Wisteria (flowers only).		

Soil-improving plants

You shouldn't even think about planting your garden without considering those plants whose main function is to improve the garden itself. The soil-improving plants are an important component of the food garden because they help to improve the soil simply by growing, without any further effort on your part. Some of the most important soil improving plants are the nitrogen fixers, but there are others that improve soil structure, break up compaction, produce organic matter and mine the subsoil for nutrients.

Nitrogen fixing plants

The ability to fix nitrogen gives plants an advantage when growing in poor soils, which is why many nitrogen fixers are pioneer plants.

The best known nitrogen fixers are the herbaceous annuals and perennials of the Bean family (*Fabaceae*) that associate with various species of rhizobium bacteria. These include the Clovers, Alfalfa, Sweet Clovers, Peas and Beans, as well as quite a few woody shrubs and even trees.

Some species of trees and shrubs form associations with nitrogen fixing bacteria from the Frankia genus (and often with mycorrhizal fungi at the same time). These include *Alnus, Ceanothus, Eleagnus, Myrica* and more. These can be used as hedgerows and in forest gardens and harvested for their foliage for use as compost or mulch material. See Nitrogen fixing trees and Nitrogen fixing shrubs for more on these.

Nitrogen fixation requires a lot of energy, which means that most nitrogen fixing plants need full sun. In the sunny garden the best nitrogen fixers to use are the annuals. In shadier areas the trees and shrubs may work better.

Perennials

These may be planted in permanent beds or used as groundcover or living mulch. Their foliage can be harvested at regular intervals for use as mulch, green manure or compost material.

Alfalfa (*Medicago sativa*)

This hardy perennial can be grown for a single season, but is so slow to get established that it is more often used as a long- term crop for a year or more. It is a very efficient nitrogen fixer and has deep roots that enable it to search out and accumulate minerals. It dislikes wet acid soils, but is quite tolerant of drought.

Clovers (*Trifolium* species)

All Clovers are attractive to bees and other beneficial insects. A few species can become quite persistent weeds. There are species for various soil conditions and climates. Some make outstanding living mulches.

Sweet Clover *(Melilotus species)*

The biennial Sweet Clovers are outstanding nitrogen fixers.

Illinois Bundleflower (*Desmanthus brachylobus*)

This nitrogen fixing species also produces edible seed and is being studied as a possible component in a perennial grain polyculture.

Kudzu (*Pueraria lobata*)

This heat and drought resistant vine produces an abundance of nitrogen rich foliage and a dense root network that prevents soil erosion. The deeply penetrating roots loosen compacted soil, bring nutrients to the surface and fix nitrogen by means of bacteria in root nodules. The abundant organic matter is good for mulch, or as compost material.

Kudzu is notorious in the southeastern states (and banned) because neglected plantings can get our of hand and grow to cover everything in their path.

Mosquito Fern (*Azolla filiculoides*)

This tiny floating aquatic fern is unusual in that it associates with a blue green algae (*Anabaena azollae*) that fixes nitrogen from the air. In the right circumstances it is very fast growing and has been known to double in volume every 5 days. These characteristics make it potentially useful as fertilizer and a related species is very important as a fertilizer in rice fields in China and Vietnam (as well as livestock feed.)

This species doesn't tolerate cold weather very well and often dies back, but reappears in spring.

This fast growing plant also absorbs other nutrients (such as phosphorus) and so purifies the water it grows in. In ideal circumstances it grows so well it can become a weed, forming a thick mat over the surface of the water.

Other useful species

Bush Clover (*Lespedeza* species)
Crown vetch (*Securigera varia*)
Rattlebox (*Crotalaria* species)
Sesbania (*Sesbania* species)
Birds Foot Trefoil (*Lotus* species)
Common Birds Foot (*Ornithopus* species)
These species may all be grown as long- term fertility crops.

Annuals

All of the following have been used as green manures and/or cover crops. They may be interplanted between other crops as a living mulch, or grown in an entire growing area to improve the soil

Austrian Field Pea (*Pisum sativus*)
Clover Crimson (*T. incarnatum*)
Cowpea (*Vigna unguiculata*)
Kudzu (*Pueraria lobata*)
Hyacinth Bean (*Dolichos lablab*)
Pea (*Pisum sativum*)
Soybeans (*Glycine max*)
Bell (Fava) Beans (*Vicia faber*)
Fenugreek (*Trigonella foenum graecum*)
Lupin (*Lupinus angustifolius*)
Sweet Clovers (*Melilotus* species)
Winter Vetch (*Vicia sativa*)
Milk Vetch (*Astragalus*)

Nitrogen fixing trees and shrubs

These can be an important part of the garden fertility cycle and shouldn't be overlooked, especially in shady areas where most nitrogen fixing annuals and perennials don't thrive.

These plants trees supply nitrogen to neighboring plants through leaf fall, root sloughing and the mycorrhizal network. See Trees for more on these.

Non-nitrogen fixers

These species are valuable for their ability to improve soil structure, break up compaction, produce organic matter and mine the subsoil for nutrients.

Perennials

Chicory *(Cicorium intybus)*

This vigorous perennial produces a lot of biomass and has a deep taproot that break up compacted subsoil. It is usually interplanted with other crops.

Comfrey (*Symphytum officinale*)

Even though it doesn't fix nitrogen, this is one of the most important soil improving crops. It is particularly rich in potassium and nitrogen, so is sometimes used as a fertilizer or compost crop. It is easily propagated from root cuttings, but needs a year to get well established.

Once established this persistent perennial is hard to remove so should be placed in areas not needed for anything else. A good way to use Comfrey is to plant it in its' own separate bed, which can be any vacant spot (it works well as a border between wild and tame land).

Comfrey is usually cut once in its first year to prevent flowering. In following years it may be cut every 6 weeks or so and will produce an abundance of organic matter. It likes nitrogen and can be fertilized with almost anything, fresh poultry manure, kitchen scraps, composting toilet residue, urine and more. The biomass produced can be added to compost piles, used to make liquid or foliar fertilizer, used as mulch or buried in the soil as green manure. See A Comfrey fertility bed for more on this.

Giant reed (*Arundo donax*)

Giant Reed is a very adaptable plant and can grow in fairly dry soil, but prefers moist ones. It will even grow in several inches of water. This tall (sometimes to 20 feet) ornamental grass is often considered a weed in warmer climates, but is prized in cooler areas where it doesn't grow as well (such is human nature). Obviously a plant of such stature is only suitable for the large garden.

This fast growing plant is a good source of biomass for mulching or composting, though it is definitely not for small gardens. It is also a useful windbreak plant. Be aware that the abundantly produced biomass can make the plant a fire hazard in very dry conditions.

Hemp (*Cannabis sativa*)
This plant is a good producer of biomass and an accumulator of phosphorus. It is also quite an attractive plant and makes a great deciduous screen. Unfortunately it is still illegal to grow it in most countries.

Jerusalem Artichoke (*Helianthus tuberosus*)
This fast growing perennial Sunflower is a good producer of biomass for composting.

Stinging Nettle (*Urtica dioica*)
A unique accumulator plant the Stinging Nettle is a traditional companion to fruit trees. Stinging Nettle tea is a good source of quick nitrogen (it loves to grow in high nitrogen soils), but appears to stimulate the growth of plants n other ways too.

This vigorous perennial can be used as a potherb, as well as a nutrient rich compost material. They can be somewhat tricky to work around without getting stung though.

Marigold, African *(Tagetes minuta)*
The specific name *minuta* refers to the size of the flowers not the plants, as they can grow to 12 feet in height. This species produces a lot of biomass and is an excellent compost, smother crop and green manure plant (though the smell of the foliage isn't very pleasant). Root exudates have nematocidal properties and have been used to control those pests.

Sunflowers (*Helianthus annuus*)
These provide a lot of organic matter in a short time and are one of the best compost and weed suppressing mother crops. Easily grown from seed in any good garden soil, they can be harvested for composting when 3 - 5 feet high, just before they start to get woody. Older plants could be harvested for use as mulch.

Annuals
The following species are commonly used as green manures and/or cover crops.

Buckwheat (*Fagopyrum esculentum*)
Barley (*Hordeum vulgare*)
Oats (*Avena sativa*)
Wheat (*Triticum aestivum*)
Rye (*Secale cereale*)
Mustards (*Sinapis alba*)
Rape (*Brassica napus*)
Kale (*Brassica oleracea*)
California Bluebell (*Phacelia tanacetifolia*)
Radish, Fodder (*Raphanus sativus*)
Sudan Grass (*Sorghum bicolor*)

Weeds and wild plants
Weeds are nature's soil improving crops and many are perfectly adapted to growing in your garden beds. To get a free and easy green manure crop, all you have to do is prepare the seedbed and leave it. You will soon have a self-sown crop of weeds. Cut them for mulch, composting or green manure just before they start to flower (don't let them set seed). In mild climates some weeds will grow right through the winter as a cover crop.

Any fast growing wild plant can be used as a source of biomass for use as green manure, mulch or compost material. Particularly useful species include:

Bulrush
Common Reed
Cattail
Elder
Fireweed
Kudzu
Japanese Knotweed
Water Hyacinth.

Mushrooms and fungi

The fungi are some of the most important plants in the garden. The saprophytic species break down organic matter (especially the tough lignins), while the mycorrhizal fungi attach to the roots of trees and help them to gather nutrients. The true importance of fungi is only now being appreciated and they are starting to gain the recognition they deserve.

It is important to encourage the growth of these plants because they play a major role in soil fertility and healthy plant growth. Fortunately encouraging them mostly consists of doing the things you are already doing to increase soil fertility (adding organic matter, adjusting pH, reducing compaction).

Cultivating fungi is rarely mentioned in gardening books, yet they fit into the garden surprisingly well. They grow on materials we are already using (and break them down so their nutrients become available to other plants). The garden plants provide them with the shady and humid growing conditions they require.

You can "plant" a variety of food producing mushrooms into your garden, by introducing the appropriate spawn into suitable environments. Once established they improve the soil and produce edible mushrooms at the same time. This enables us to add another layer of food plants to the same area of garden.

Cultivating fungi differs from most plants in that you can find seeds and plants for sale everywhere, but finding spawn is much harder. Unless you have a specialist shop in your area you will have to go to mail order.

I haven't found growing fungi to be as easy as growing other food plants. Each species requires quite specific materials to grow on and more attention to detail than I am used to. If you really get interested in this I suggest you turn to the guru of modern mushroom cultivation: Paul Stamets and his fascinating books, particularly Mycelium Running, 10 Speed Press, 2005.

Mycorrhizal fungi

The mycorrhizal fungi are some of the least obvious, but most important, plants in the forest. The mycelial web they create exchanges nutrients with the associated tree (or trees) and acts as an extension of the plants roots. It even connects different individual plants and species. Many of the most important wild edible mushrooms are mycorrhizal, including the famously esteemed Chantarelles, Boletes, Matsutake (Tricholoma) and Truffles.

Mycorrhizal fungi are difficult to cultivate because you also have to grow their associated tree at the same time (a slow process). However these are such important (and valuable) edibles that people are working to try and solve these difficulties. The truffle is now successfully cultivated in Europe and other species will no doubt follow. The advantage of growing these species is that they stay in one place, associated with the same tree, and can fruit regularly for many years.

The traditional way to cultivate the mycorrhizal Truffles is to plant the seedlings around a tree that regularly produces a good crop of truffles. After a few years the seedling roots become infected with the mycorrhizae and they can then be transplanted elsewhere.

In some cases it may also be possible to inoculate tree roots directly by watering them with the solution of spores, sugar and salt water described below (see Spore germination). Even if a tree is successfully colonized this doesn't mean you will get an edible crop any time soon. It may grow underground for many years before it starts fruiting.

Saprophytic fungi

Saprophytic fungi are much more mobile than the mycorrhizal types, because they aren't attached to any one plant. They break down suitable plant material as they find it and when this is gone they move on to greener (or browner) pastures. This characteristic means they are much more amenable to cultivation and all of the commonly cultivated species are of this type. A number of these species are fairly easy to grow, if you provide them with the right materials.

Growing mushrooms outdoors

Growing mushrooms is a different form of gardening, requiring different tools and techniques and a different kind of garden. The simplest way to get started growing mushrooms is to buy a growing kit and follow the instructions. This will give you some experience and confidence in what they need to grow. When the kit is exhausted you can often keep the spawn alive and use it to start other beds. If you start growing a variety of species you could eventually have a succession of fruiting mushrooms crops, just as you do other vegetables.

Saprophytic fungi will only stay in one place for as long as suitable nutrients are available. Once these are used up the plants will fruit and the spores will move on. You can keep them growing happily in the same place only if you give them fresh mulch material periodically.

Habitat

Fungi need warmth, moisture (especially humidity) and a suitable substrate to grow on. Different species can be grown in different parts of the garden. Some prefer shade, others sun, some like woodland, some like lawns, mulch piles, garden beds, or old compost piles. They may be grown on cut logs, tree stumps, wood chips, grass clippings, straw or heavily composted soil. Some do well indoors, some grow on logs and some prefer to grow in garden beds.

North and east facing slopes are often used for growing fungi, as most don't like a lot of direct sunlight. They prefer dappled shade such as a woodland edge habitat, with perhaps an hour or two of sun in total daily (it shouldn't be too shady). The north side of a building, fence or hedge can work well. A few species will grow in sunny locations, including Puffballs, Shaggy Manes, Garden Giants, Morels and Meadow Mushrooms.

It may be a good idea to grow your mushrooms fairly close to the house (zone 1 or 2) as once they start fruiting it happens quickly and you need to watch them closely. Overlook them for a few days and you could miss them altogether.

> **Caution**
>
> Any time you grow a mushroom outside it is important to take the time to identify it as the right species. It is possible (if not very likely) that a poisonous wild species could out-compete your cultivated mycelium and grow in its place. Some poisonous species ones look quite similar to cultivated species and you don't want to eat them.

Hardwood logs

Some of the most easily cultivated mushrooms are the Shittake, Maitake and Oyster Mushroom. These prefer to grow on hardwood logs with thick bark (Oak, Maple, Elm, Madrone, Chestnut are all good). These are usually cut live when 4" - 8" in diameter (coppicing is a great way to get the logs), and cut up into 3 – 4 foot sections. They are then dried with the bark on (don't remove it). You can't use the wood immediately because it usually contains natural fungicides (wait a couple of months). At the same time you can't use old logs because they are usually already infected with competing fungi. It is possible to pasteurize them by boiling for 3 - 5 hours in a clean metal drum, but this is more work.

Dry wood should be moistened before inoculating, so it is thoroughly wet all the way through. The easiest way to do this is to put them in a tank of water for several days.

Spawn used for inoculating wood usually comes in the form of small impregnated wooden dowel, known as plug spawn (these are soaked before use too). Holes are drilled into the wet logs about 8 inches apart, to accept the dowel spawn. The dowels are then tapped into these holes and they are sealed with wax to protect them from predators and dehydration. The logs are stacked in a shady place and kept moist for 2 - 3 months while the mycelium grows. They produce mushrooms according to the weather and growing conditions and may continue to produce seasonally for several years.

Logs can also be inoculated with loose spawn by cutting a wedge out of the middle, packing it with spawn and then nailing the wedge back in place.

Tree stumps
Freshly cut tree stumps can also be used to grow mushrooms and this is a good way to speed up their decay. These can have a lot of mass in the ground and large ones may produce fungi for years. Old stumps can't be used because they will already be infected with mycelium. Drill and plug the stump as described above, paying particular attention to the edge of the stump (its sugar rich sapwood is the best place to establish fungi). Stumps can also be inoculated with loose spawn by the wedge method described above.

I imagine we may one day get to the point where cutting down a tree would commonly involve inoculating the stump and any unwanted logs with a suitable mycelium. This produces food and hastens decomposition at the same time.

Garden beds
Mushrooms such as the King Stropharia (*Stropharia rugoso-annulata*), Shaggy Mane (*Coprinus*) and Elm Oyster (*Hypsizygus*) can be cultivated in your mulched garden beds (straw, wood chips or sawdust may be used for mulch).

Start making your mushroom bed by clearing the soil down to mineral earth (use the topsoil elsewhere) to reduce competition from existing fungi. Lay down a layer of moist corrugated cardboard, followed by 2 inches of fresh hardwood chips and moisten thoroughly (don't use old chips as they will already contain fungi). You then spread out a layer of spawn and cover it with another 2 inches of wood chips. Finally cover it with a layer of hay. The bed should then be kept constantly moist. This kind of mulch bed closely resembles a no-dig sheet mulch garden and might be incorporated into it.

You could also incorporate the spawn into an established bed that is mulched with straw. Garden Giant is perhaps the best species to grow in vegetable beds and can actually improve the growth of some vegetables (most notably corn).

Compost piles
Some mushrooms will grow in the organic matter enriched soil around old compost piles.

Forest garden
The wood chip mulched beds of a forest garden would be a logical place to grow many species. They benefit from the shade and humidity on the woodland floor and the wood chip mulch.

You might also be able to get mycorrhizal species established on suitable host trees. Make some spore soup as described below and slop it around suitable host trees. This isn't very much work and sometimes works (especially for Chantarelles).

Mushroom propagation
Propagating fungi isn't particularly complex or difficult if you follow the right procedures and take care to avoid wild fungi. I'm don't have the space or expertise to go into much detail here, so I'm just going to mention a few of the possibilities. I suggest you read Stamets's books if you really want to get into this.

Spores
Saprophytic fungi can be grown from spores cultured on clean, moist corrugated cardboard. This doesn't have to cost anything, if you get them from wild mushrooms, or even from the fungi you get to eat from the grocery store. To avoid competition from wild fungi it is best to germinate spores in a sterile environment.

Spores can be germinated in a solution made by boiling 1 tablespoon sugar and ¼ teaspoon non iodized salt in a gallon of water. Add 1 teaspoon of spores per gallon, put in a clean covered container at 60 – 70° F. and shake twice daily. The spores should germinate within a couple of days. The germinated spores can then be placed on a cardboard substrate or burlap bags to grow. If you don't want to separate out the spores you can just put 4 or 5 mushroom caps into the solution.

You could also put a mushroom cap on wet corrugated cardboard or a sterilized burlap bag for an hour as if you were doing a spore print. Then put it in a plastic box to incubate for several weeks. When this is covered in mycelium spawn you can use it to inoculate larger pieces of cardboard.

Stem bases

One of the easiest places to obtain spawn is from the base of the stem of wild or cultivated mushrooms (these should have been plucked rather than cut, so the rhizomorphs are still attached. The cut stem base can be placed on wet corrugated cardboard in a warm place until the mycelium spreads on to the cardboard. This can then be used to inoculate more cardboard and then transferred to a suitable growth medium. Once the mycelium gets established its growth can be exponential, each piece can be used to create more and more until you have no more room for it (you could then give it away, or even sell it).

The easiest fungi to cultivate

All of these saprophytic species can work, if you give them exactly what they need.

Wood loving species

Enokitake (*Flammulina velutipes* and *F. populicola*)
This species is cultivated on stumps or logs in Japan. It is very tolerant of cold weather and fruits in winter.

Parasol Mushroom (*Macrolepiota procera*)
This large and spectacular species naturally grows at woodland edges. It can be grown in wood chip beds in the same way as the King Stropharia.

Nameko (*Pholiota nameko*)
This Asian species is very big in Japan. It is grown on hardwood logs or stumps and produces large clusters.

Shiitake (*Lentinula edodes*)
This famous Asian delicacy is the most widely cultivated species in Japan and is becoming increasingly popular in the west. It can be grown on hardwood logs as described above. It also has anti-cancer properties.

Oyster Mushroom (*Pleurotus ostreatus*)
One of the easiest species to cultivate, the versatile Oyster Mushroom will grow on a wide variety of materials, including hardwood logs, straw, paper cardboard, leaves, rice and coffee grounds.

Oyster Mushroom (*Pleurotus colombinus*)
This species differs from the above in that it grows on coniferous wood.

Hen of the woods (*Grifola frondosa*)
Often known by its Japanese name Maitake, this is very highly regarded as an edible. Growing naturally at the base of dead hardwoods trees, it is usually cultivated on partially buried logs or stumps. It also has anti-cancer activity.

Lions mane (*Hericium erinaceus*)
Prized for its Lobster like flavor and medicinal properties. It is grown on partially buried hardwood logs or stumps

Pioppino (*Agrocybe aegerita*)
This species is grown on hardwood logs or stumps. It has a very good flavor and is a favorite in Italy.

Chicken of the woods (*Laetiporus sulphureus*)
This species has an attractive orange/yellow color and is very good when young. It is grown on hardwood logs.

Chicken of the woods (*Laetiporus conifericola*)
This similar species grows on conifer logs

Reishi (*Ganoderma lucidum*)
This species is grown on logs or stumps. It is prized for its medicinal qualities as an immune system stimulant and for its anti-cancer and anti-inflammatory activity. It is too woody to eat, so is made into tea and soup

Garden loving species

King Stropharia (*Stropharia rugoso-annulata*)
This species is one of the easiest species to cultivate and is grown on wood chip or straw mulch. It produces very large burgundy colored mushrooms.

This warm weather species naturally grows on decaying straw and wood chips and can be grown anywhere you use those materials for mulch, such as vegetable beds, between fruiting shrubs, etc.

This species has recently been renamed *Psilocybe rugoso-annulata.* I find this constant name changing is a little annoying. I appreciate it keeps many taxonomists busy, but I thought the whole idea of the binomial system was to have one name for each plant, not a different one every few years.

Elm Oyster (*Hypsizygus ulmarius*)
This species is very similar to an Oyster Mushroom but even better flavored. It is naturally found on hardwood logs but is very adaptable and can be grown in wood chip mulch beds and even mulched vegetable gardens.

Shaggy Mane (*Coprinus comatus*)
This weed of the mushroom world is a pioneer of disturbed habitat and is naturally found on grassland, wood chips, old compost piles and soils with lots of organic matter (such as from heavy manuring). It can be grown in garden beds, compost piles and lawns (just put spawn underneath the turf) and fruits from late summer to winter. Its habit of rapidly dissolving itself into an inky mass precludes its use as a commercial species.

Growing Button Mushrooms and Portabellas
(*Agaricus bisporus*)

Indoors
These species are fairly easy to grow, in fact the hardest part is often obtaining the spawn and preparing the compost. They can be grown indoors year round as the outside temperature has no bearing on them. Just make sure the area is well ventilated and clean (indoor growing areas are commonly disinfected to reduce the number of wild spores). You could even grow them in an apartment because they don't even need light. Their main requirements are for moisture and an even temperature (between 50 and 80° F).

The easiest way to grow them is to buy a kit and use as directed. These kits aren't cheap but they don't have to be a one time thing. They look a lot more economical if you see them as a source of spawn. When they stop producing inside you can take the mycelium and use it to inoculate other boxes or outdoor beds.

Preparing compost
Mushroom compost is usually made from fresh horse manure and straw that has been composted so that it heats up to at least 150° F. (to kill fungal spores and other pathogens). To get this much heat a pile needs to be fairly large (4 ft. high) and moist. It should be turned several times so all of the material is thoroughly heated. This also speeds the composting process, so it should be ready for use in about a month. Sometimes moist tree leaves are added to the compost, in the proportion of 1/4 leaves to 3/4 compost.

A suitable container for growing mushrooms is 8″-10" deep and as big as is convenient. Fill the box with the prepared compost and drop it a few inches to compact it slightly). Lay a layer of spawn on the surface and cover with another layer of compost. Keep this moist and in about 10 days the mycelium should have spread over the surface. About 3 weeks after starting you cover with a casing of sterilized soil or a mix of peat and chalk. Keep this moist and the first flush of mushrooms should appear several weeks later. Harvest the mushrooms by twisting them out of the compost. Cutting leaves the stem base behind to decay.

Greenhouse growing

Some species can be grown in a greenhouse or cold frame through the winter, so long as the temperature doesn't drop below 45°.

Outdoors

You can grow mushrooms in outdoor beds any time the temperature is suitable (70° is optimal), which is mostly spring and fall. Outdoor beds are generally 8 - 18 inches high and 24 inches wide, and the compost is made in the same way as for growing indoors. They are often covered with straw to protect them from drying out and the extremes of heat and cold.

Lawns

You can also grow mushrooms in grassland. This is more hit or miss, but if you have a suitable place it's worth trying. Just peel back the turf, dig out the soil and replace it with horse manure. Lay down the spawn, cover with a layer of soil and replace the turf. If you keep it moist it may fruit in as little as a month or so. Obviously you have to prevent people walking upon it when fruiting is taking place.

Mushrooms for soil improvement

Growing saprophytic mushrooms on piles of wood chips can be a win win situation. It provides you with an edible crop, while at the same time rapidly breaking down the wood chips and releasing their nutrients into the soil. It could even be regarded as a form of composting.

The spent compost from traditional mushroom growing is one of the best soil amendments for the vegetable garden (though the commercial stuff usually contains pesticides). It may even introduce mushrooms into the beds.

Wild plants and weeds

Wild plants are those plants that grew on your land before it was a garden. Weeds are those plants that come in because it is a garden. Both kinds of plants can be useful to you because they have a variety of uses and grow without you having to do anything.

Garden weeds

A wild plant must meet two criteria to be considered for admittance into that elite group of plants known as weeds. First it must specialize in growing in soil that has been disturbed by human activity. Equally important it must cause humans some annoyance (if it doesn't then it's merely a pioneer species). This definition of weeds takes us beyond the familiar annual or perennial species, to include woody shrubs such as Blackberry and Broom, or even trees like Cottonwood, Birch and Mesquite.

Weeds are nature's first line of defense against soil degradation and have an essential role in maintaining and increasing soil fertility. When she quickly covers your newly dug planting bed with a vigorous crop of weeds, she is telling you that you should never have left the surface of the soil bare. You should always cover it with something.

The importance of weeds

Weeds are natures soil-improving crops and they should be ours too. Deep-rooted weeds are beneficial in that they mine minerals from the subsoil and bring them to the surface where they become available to other plants. Tap rooted species can break up compacted subsoil and when they die and decay these become channels for aeration and soil life. The accumulator plants have the ability to forage for scarce nutrients and concentrate them in their tissue.

A flush of weeds makes a useful self-sown cover crop to protect and enrich the soil. The hardier species can act as a cover crop, to protect the soil and store nutrients over the winter. These should be dug in or composted before they set seed in spring.

Weeds also provide cover and food for wildlife, including predatory and pollinating insects, birds, toads and more,

Fast growing weeds produce an abundance of organic matter, which feeds and stimulates soil organisms.

Weeds are useful as companions and nurse plants. They help to camouflage crop plants and hide them from insect pests and can even act as trap crops. For example many Brassica pests are more attracted to wild Brassicas (with their abundance of pungent oil) than to the rather insipid cultivated varieties.

Using weeds

Many common weeds are edible and / or have medicinal properties (maybe mother earth decided to give us some consolation for the hassle of weeding). Dandelion, Winter cress, Plantain, Lambs Quarters, Chickweed, Burdock, Amaranth, Purslane are all great food plants, if gathered at the right time and prepared properly (most have actually been cultivated at one time or another). When you start to use the edible weeds, you realize they are often fully equal in flavor to the crops you are trying to grow and a lot more nutritious. It's actually pretty silly planting and pampering your spinach and then ripping out the equally good (or better) Lambs Quarters or Pigweed.

Weeds should be looked upon as another productive layer for the garden and are especially significant because they grow without you having to do anything. In fact you would be removing them anyway, even if you didn't eat them (and eating them is better than composting them.)

Growing weeds

California summers are so dry that most herbaceous plants go dormant or die off. This is why irrigated gardens are one of the best places to find edible weeds in the summer months. You might carry this one step further and actually grow an edible wild plant/weed bed. Perhaps prepare and irrigate a bed and then let nature do the planting. Note which plants appear, in what order and in what numbers. Of course you could also do this anywhere else in the country. Given minimal care such a bed can be very productive with very little work.

California winters are mild and moist and some hardy weeds are able to thrive and produce food even in the coldest months. A winter weed bed might include Malva, Chickweed, Shepherds Purse, Wintercress, Miners lettuce and more.

I usually treat the useful weeds as a self-sown intercrop, by allowing selected individuals to grow up on the beds, in between my crop plants. I harvest thin most of them early and leave just enough plants that they won't significantly interfere with the main crop. When these are big enough I harvest those too.

Of course in the intensively cultivated beds there isn't much room for weeds and you should remove most of those that do appear. However there is plenty of room for weeds in the rest of the garden and you treat any that appear as another crop.

You can also allow woody weeds such as Blackberry or Broom to grow, but control and confine them to the areas where you want them. In my garden they seem to suppress the growth of Poison Oak.

I have transplanted some of the more useful weed seedlings into my garden, in the hope they would self-sow and stock my garden.

Edible weeds

Identification

If you want to eat a wild plant you haven't planted you need to be absolutely sure about its identity. You don't want to eat some poisonous look alike (there aren't many of these, but there are a few). I have the occasional Poison Hemlock plant in my garden (it comes in with the composted horse manure) whose leaves resemble those of carrot. Fortunately most common weeds are fairly distinctive and you probably know most of their names already. If you have young children who like to forage it is very important to teach them about such plants.

Wild grasses

Now we are getting a little extreme. Most grasses are inedible simply because we can't digest all of that cellulose, it's not that they contain anything dangerous. If we extract the juice from the plants we can get all of the benefits of the vitamins, minerals, chlorophyll and various phytonutrients (a diet of grass grows some of the biggest land animals on earth), without having to deal with all that fiber. This is the idea behind wheatgrass and barleygrass and works just as well with wilder grasses.

It is possible to harvest wild grasses and juice them at any time. Of course you need to be careful which species you use, so I'm just suggesting this as an area for further research. I can't say I enjoy drinking the juice, but I do believe it is very beneficial. Some people actually claim to enjoy it as well.

Edible annual weeds

Disturb a patch of soil and leave it for a week and annual weeds will appear. Within a month they will have completely covered the soil with a thick mat of vegetation. Of the thousands of plant species from all over the world, the annual weeds are the ones that are best adapted to life in your vegetable garden. Many of these weeds can actually be found in gardens right around the world, because gardeners everywhere strive to create the same ideal growing conditions: warm, moist, fertile, neutral pH, loose, bare soil.

Many of our commonest annual weeds are edible to some degree and some just as good as anything you could plant. Gather them at the right time and you will have some of the most nutritious and vibrant foods to be found anywhere. Some of the best species are:

Pigweed (*Amaranthus* species)
Wintercress *(Barbarea* species)
Shepherds Purse (*Capsella bursa pastoris*)
Lambs Quarters (*Chenopodium album*)
Filaree (*Erodium cicutarium*)
Mallows (*Malva neglecta, M. rotundifolia*)
Miners Lettuce (*Montia perfoliata*)
Peppergrass (*Lepidium* spp)
Purslane *(Portulaca oleracea)*
Chickweed *(Stellaria media)*
Sow Thistle (*Sonchus species*)

All of these can be used in salads or as cooked vegetables and are quite nutritious. You could even dry some of these weeds and grind them to a powder for adding to soups and stews during the winter.

Edible perennial weeds

These garden weeds aren't so common in the intensive beds because they are disturbed too frequently. They are more likely to be found growing undisturbed amongst the perennials, on pathways and elsewhere.

Ground Elder *(Aegopodium podagraria)*
Chicory *(Cicorium intybus)*
Thistles (*Cirsium species*)
Great Plantain (*Plantago major*)
Common Sorrel *(Rumex acetosa)*
Sheep's Sorrel *(R. acetosella)*
Curled Dock *(Rumex crispus)*
Patience Dock (*R. patienta*)
Red Dock (*R. sanguineus*)
Dandelion *(Taraxacum officinale)*
Stinging Nettle (*Urtica dioica*)

All of these species can be very good foods if gathered at the right time (this is even more important with these plants than it is with our cultivated crops).

Useful wild Plants

I have long had a fascination with edible and useful wild plants and weeds (which is why I wrote The Uses of Wild Plants). If you can use some of these to create the framework of your garden, you can reduce the maintenance it requires considerably. If you choose the right species (Chestnuts, Blackberries, Cattails) they will also give you extra food without you having to do anything except harvest.

Wild plants don't only produce food, drink, medicine, dyes and smoking materials. They can also contribute materials for building the garden (poles, logs, canes, wattle, thatch, brushwood, pea sticks, mulch, fertilizers). These can help you keep costs down, while making your garden more of a product of its place. It can all quite literally come from the earth.

Wild plants are also useful for attracting predatory insects and birds, and can act as trap crops to draw pests away from crop plants. Of course they also provide food for other wildlife too.

Some wild plants may be grown simply for their beauty, or simply because they belong there. I like to allow some of the more attractive plants to grow to their full potential as ornamentals. Not only do these grow without any work from you, they help to give the garden a unique regional feel.

Where to put them

You can grow these plants anywhere in the garden that the conditions suit them. One of the basic tenets of the new food garden is that you select plants to fit the site, rather than 'improving' the site to accommodate the plants. Of course no plant fit the site better than the natives that would grow there naturally.

The plants that like rich, sunny, disturbed, open sites are those we already know as garden weeds. Your challenge is to find suitable useful wild plants for the other habitats: poor soils, deep shade, dry hillsides, saturated acid soil and more. Find the right plant for such situations and they will eventually start growing independently, choosing the places they like to grow.

Care

Their independence means that wild plants require less care than more traditional crop plants. Normally they are planted and cared for until they are well established and then they are left to their own devices. If they start to get overly vigorous you may have to keep them under control. If they start to decline you will have to determine why (and then decide whether to move them or let them disappear).

Foraging

Of course there is no need to stop gathering wild plants at the boundary of your land. You can also forage for them in other places, so long as you know what to look for and can identify it correctly (not many plants are deadly, but a few are).

If we go out foraging for wild food plants we should always look out for unusually useful varieties. These might have larger leaves or bigger or better tasting fruit or roots (though of course this might be due to growing conditions not genetics). Look for those plants that are suited to the growing conditions you can provide. Or try gathering plants from different conditions.

Taking plants from the wild

I already discussed the implications of this in the section on Choosing plants.

Growing wild edible plants as crops

All of our common crops are descended from wild plants (obvious if you think about it), but only a fraction of the edible wild plants out there have been exploited to their full potential. Most of our common crop plants come from only a few regions of the earth, not because those areas are particularly special, but because they are the places where farming began. The first farmers used the plants that grew around them and these then spread around the world along with agriculture. North America was such a rich and isolated continent that agriculture was only undertaken in a few places, mostly with crops and techniques developed in central America. A few native plants were cultivated and improved (Marsh Elder, Ragweed) but they were then forgotten. This means that the wild plants of North America are largely unexplored in regard to their potential crop use.

Many wild plants are excellent food as they are (they just need to be gathered at the right time and prepared well). However many more could become useful food crops, if subjected to a little rudimentary selection for superior tasting varieties. Look at the difference between a wild Strawberry and a cultivated variety (or the difference between a wild Lettuce and a cultivated one).

You could experiment with growing particularly useful wild plants in garden beds. The rich soil will usually increase their size, productivity and palatability.

Another approach to growing wild plants is to find species that can be used as crops in less hospitable situations (shade, poor soil, dry soil).

Growing wild plants as crops opens up a whole new kind of productive gardening. There is great potential here for growing tasty, nutritious, productive, useful, low input crops for use in otherwise unused places.

Potential new crop plants

There follows a list of some species I consider to have a lot of potential. A few wild plants are already cultivated occasionally and some improved cultivars exist (though they aren't always easy to find).

Dandelion (*Taraxacum officinale*)
Burdock (*Arctium lappa*)
Good King Henry (*Chenopodium bonus henricus*)
Pokeweed (*Phytolacca americana*)
Jerusalem Artichoke (*Helianthus tuberosus*)
Evening Primrose (*Oenothera biennis*)
Miners Lettuce (*Montia perfoliata*)
Groundnut (*Apios tuberosa*)
Ramps (*Allium tricoccum*)
Tepary Bean (*Phaseolus acutifolius*)
Fritillaria (*Fritillaria* species)
Brodaiea Lily (*Brodaiea* species)
Unicorn Plant (*Proboscidea louisianica*)
Stinging Nettle (*Urtica dioica*)
Arrowhead (*Sagittaria latifolia*)
Wild Garlic (*Allium canadense*)
Wild-Rice (*Zizania aquatica*)
Milkweed (*Asclepias syriaca*)
California Soap Plant (*Chlorogalum pomeridianum*)
Camas (*Camassia* species)
Spring Beauty (*Claytonia* species)
Buffalo Gourd (*Cucurbita foetidissima*)
Toothworts (*Dentaria* species)
Wild Yams (*Dioscorea* species)
Dogtooth Violet (*Erythronium* species)
Water Parsnip (*Oenanthe sarmentosa*)
Yampa (*Perideridia* species)
Indian Turnip (*Psoralea*)
Bulrush (*Schoenoplectus* species)
Greenbriars (*Smilax* species)
Wild Potato (*Solanum jamesii*)
Woundworts (*Stachys* species)
Cattail (*Typha* species)

There are also many fruiting species with potential, some of which have already been selected for superior cultivars (I have already mentioned many of these elsewhere).

Wild Strawberry (*Fragaria virginiana*)
Elder (*Sambucus* species)
Juneberries (*Amelanchier* species)
Wild Plums (*Prunus* species)
Salal (*Gaultheria shallon*)
Huckleberries (*Gaylussacia* species)
Mayapple (*Podophyllum peltatum*)
Maypop (*Passiflora incana*)
Honeysuckles (*Lonicera* species see Gibbons)
Prickly Pear (*Opuntia* species)
Ground Cherry (*Physalis* species)

Crops for shade

Most common crop plants are adapted to growing in full sun because that's where the energy is for maximum carbohydrate production. If we want to produce food in the shady areas of our gardens we have to look elsewhere for suitable crop plants. A number of edible wild plants have potential in this regard.

Ground Elder (*Aegopodium podagraria*)
Ramps (*Allium tricoccum*)
Golden Saxifrage (*Chrysoplenium oppositifolium*)
Wintergreen (*Gaultheria procumbens*)
Miners Lettuce (*Montia perfoliata*)
Ostrich Fern (*Matteuccia struthiopteris*)
Wood Sorrel (*Oxalis* species)
Solomons Seal (*Polygonatum* species)
Stinging Nettle (*Urtica dioica*)

Garden uses of wild plants

In keeping with the philosophy of using the free resources that are available on site, we should look to the native plants for garden materials.

Free, low maintenance ornamentals

Wherever I have lived in the United States I have noticed naturalized garden plants growing on roadsides and other waste ground. These have included Daylily, Tansy, Soapwort, Calla Lilies, Centranthus, Foxglove and more. While it isn't acceptable to dig native wild plants from the wild, I don't have a problem with using these naturalized exotics, which often displace native plants. Most are so vigorous you won't harm them anyway.

Rootstocks

A number of wild plants have been used as rootstocks for grafting related cultivated crops. For example European Grape varieties have been grafted onto wild American Grape roots to increase their resistance to disease. Sand Cherry (*Prunus Besseyii*) roots have been used for grafting domesticated Cherries.

There is actually quite a lot of potential here, using the established roots of closely related wild species for grafting domesticated cultivars. If you have a suitable plant already growing in your garden, you might try grafting a scion of an improved cultivar on to it.

Soil amendments

Leaf mold from various broadleaf trees is almost pure organic matter and can be used to add humus to the soil. You can also collect tree leaves and compost them to make your own leaf mold for starting seedlings. Leaves from evergreens can be used as an acid mulch to lower the pH when growing acid loving plants such as Blueberries. Obviously you shouldn't rob your forest soil of too many leaves when doing this.

Soil life stimulants

Biodynamic gardeners (and some others) believe that some plants have a special influence on the soil and the plants around them. These special plants include Stinging Nettle (*Urtica*), Yarrow (*Achillea*), Horsetail (*Equisetum*), Valerian (*Valeriana*) and more. These can be added to compost, or made into a tea for watering the soil or as foliar fertilizers.

Soil improving crops

Some wild plants grow so quickly and exuberantly that they can be useful for improving the soil. You can plant these intentionally, allow them to grow themselves, or you can gather them from waste places outside the garden. These may be incorporated directly as green manure, put on the surface as mulch or composted.

Insecticides

A number of wild plants contain insecticidal compounds and can be used as organic dusts or sprays. The Devils Shoestring (*Tephrosia*) contains the commonly used pesticide rotenone. Other insecticidal plants include Wormwood (*Artemisia*), Ox-Eye Daisy (*Chrysanthemum*) and the Yew (*Taxus*).

Mulch materials

A dense growth of weeds isn't a problem, its a resource. Pretty much any wild plant can be used as mulch, though woody plants may need to be chipped. You might try Giant Reed (*Arundo*), Pampas Grass (*Cortaderia*), Reed (*Phragmites*), Cattail (*Typha*), Scotch Broom (*Cytisus*) and more. Some fast growing trees and shrubs may be grown and coppiced specifically for this.

Rooting hormone

A water extract of Poplar (*Populus*) or Willow (*Salix*) shoots has been used to improve the rooting of cuttings.

Subject index

T

U

V

W

Z

Plant index

Other books by Frank Tozer

When you are growing your New Food Garden you may find these books helpful.

The Vegetable Growers Handbook

The companion to The Organic Gardeners Handbook, this is a very practical guide to growing over 70 common vegetables. There are specific, step by step, instructions for each crop; soil requirements, variety selection, raising transplants, direct sowing, protection, watering, harvesting, seed saving, storage, extending the growing season and more. It forewarns you of potential problems with each crop, and explains how to deal with them. This is a book with imagination, so it doesn't stop there, but also discusses unusual crops, culinary herbs, edible flowers, enhanced nutrition foods, unusual growing ideas, additional uses for common crops, and even how to use common edible garden weeds. There is also a small selection of outstanding vegetarian recipes.

ISBN 978-0-9773489-3-0
$22.95

The Organic Gardeners Handbook

Everything you need to know to create a low cost, low input self sustaining intensive vegetable garden. A serious guide to the art and science of organic gardening, it covers the subject with a depth that is rarely seen in contemporary books. There are chapters on every aspect of organic vegetable gardening, soil dynamics, soil management, cultivation, composting, crop planning, raising seedlings, watering, harvesting, seed saving, greenhouses and much more. Whether you are a complete novice and need your hand holding through every step, or a veteran gardener with a permanent layer of soil under your fingernails this book will help you to become a better gardener. The Organic Gardeners Handbook is a companion to The Vegetable Growers Handbook.

ISBN: 978-0-9773489-1-6
$24.95

The Uses Of Wild Plants

This unique guide to the wild plants of North America describes the uses and cultivation of more than 1200 species in over 500 genera. A treasury of information on every aspect of plant use, it describes how wild plants were used for food in the past, how they can be used today and how they might one day become new crops. It also describes how plants have been used to treat sickness, and how they can help to enhance health by providing superior nutrition. It also discusses how they can be used for dyes, cosmetics, soap, paper, fuel, clothing, perfumes, glues, craft materials, and many other home, commercial and industrial uses. Looking to the future, it shows how wild plants could help us to create an ecologically sustainable society, by providing new crops for food, medicine, fuels, renewable energy, chemicals and building materials. How they could help to clean our rivers and lakes, desalinate soil, remove toxic chemicals from polluted groundwater, recover valuable nutrients from waste, and maybe even reduce global warming. A unique feature of this book for gardeners is that it also discusses the cultivation of these plants and their uses around the garden, homestead and farm.

ISBN 0-9773489-0-3
$24.95